Communication
Yearbook
27

Communication
Yearbook
27

PAMELA J. KALBFLEISCH
EDITOR

Published Annually for the
International Communication Association

LAWRENCE ERLBAUM ASSOCIATES, PUBLISHERS
2003   Mahwah, New Jersey   London

Lawrence Erlbaum Associates, Inc., Publishers
10 Industrial Avenue
Mahwah, NJ 07430

Library of Congress:
ISSN: 0147-4642
ISBN: 0-8058-4819-3 (hardcover)

Cover design by Kathryn Houghtaling-Lacey

Books published by Lawrence Erlbaum Associates are printed on acid-free paper, and their bindings are chosen for strength and durability.

Printed in the United States of America
10 9 8 7 6 5 4 3 2 1

Managing Editor: Barbara Stooksberry, ICA Headquarters
Copy & Production Editor: Scott Berkley, ICA Headquarters

CONTENTS

THE INTERNATIONAL COMMUNICATION ASSOCIATION

The International Communication Association (ICA) was formed in 1950, bringing together academics and other professionals whose interests focus on human communication. The Association maintains an active membership of more than 3,000 individuals, of whom some two thirds are teaching and conducting research in colleges, universities, and schools around the world. Other members are in government, law, medicine, and other professions. The wide professional and geographic distribution of the membership provides the basic strength of the ICA. The Association is a meeting ground for sharing research and useful dialogue about communication interests.

Through its divisions and interest groups, publications, annual conferences, and relations with other associations around the world, the ICA promotes the systemic study of communication theories, processes, and skills. In addition to *Communication Yearbook,* the Association publishes the *Journal of Communication, Human Communication Research, Communication Theory, A Guide to Publishing in Scholarly Communication Journals*, and the *ICA Newsletter.*

For additional information about the ICA and its activities, visit online at www.icahdq.org or contact Michael L. Haley, Executive Director, International Communication Association, 1730 Rhode Island NW, Suite 300, Washington, DC 20036 USA; phone (202) 530-9855; fax (202) 530-9851; email: ica@icahdq.org.

Editors of the *Communication Yearbook* series:

Volumes 1 and 2, Brent D. Ruben
Volumes 3 and 4, Dan Nimmo
Volumes 5 and 6, Michael Burgoon
Volumes 7 and 8, Robert N. Bostrom
Volumes 9 and 10, Margaret L. McLaughlin
Volumes 11, 12, 13, and 14, James A. Anderson
Volumes 15, 16, and 17, Stanley A. Deetz
Volumes 18, 19, and 20, Brant R. Burleson
Volumes 21, 22, and 23, Michael E. Roloff
Volumes 24, 25, and 26, William B. Gudykunst
Volumes 27, 28, and 29, Pamela J. Kalbfleisch

INTERNATIONAL COMMUNICATION ASSOCIATION
EXECUTIVE COMMITTEE

President and Chair
Jennings Bryant, *University of Alabama*

President-Elect
Robert T. Craig, *University of Colorado*

President-Elect Select
Wolfgang Donsbach, *University of Dresden*

Immediate Past President
Cindy Gallois, *University of Queensland*

Finance Chair
Linda L. Putnam (ex-officio), *Texas A&M University*

Executive Director
Michael L. Haley (ex-officio), *ICA Headquarters*

Associate Executive Director
Robert L. Cox (ex-officio), *ICA Headquarters*

BOARD OF DIRECTORS

Members-at-Large
Daniel Hallin, *University of California, San Diego*
Cees J. Hamelink, *University of Amsterdam*
Robyn Penman, *University of Canberra*
James Taylor, *University of Montreal*

Student Members
Katerina Tsetsura, *Purdue University*
Jody Waters, *University of Texas, Austin*

Division Chairs and Vice Presidents

Information Systems
Mark Hamilton, *University of Connecticut*

Interpersonal Communication
Laura Stafford, *Ohio State University*

Mass Communication
K. Viswanath, *National Cancer Institute*

Organizational Communication
Noshir Contractor, *University of Illinois*

Intercultural & Development Communication
Richard L. Wiseman, *California State University*

Political Communication
Christina Holtz-Bacha, *University of Mainz*

Instructional & Developmental Communication
Patti M. Valkenburg, *University of Amsterdam*

Health Communication
Michael Slater, *Colorado State University*

Philosophy of Communication
Toby Miller, *New York University*

Communication & Technology
Teresa Harrison, *State University of New York, Albany*

Feminist Scholarship
Carolyn M. Byerly, *University of Maryland*

Communication Law & Policy
Sandra Braman, *University of Wisconsin, Milwaukee*

Language & Social Interaction
Stuart Sigman, *Emerson College*

Popular Communication
Jonathan Tankel, *Indiana-Purdue University, Ft. Wayne*

Public Relations
Bonita Dostal Neff, *Valparaiso University*

Special Interest Group Chairs
Visual Communication
Catherine Preston, *University of Kansas*

Gay, Lesbian, Bisexual, & Transgender Studies
David Gleason, *MTV Networks*
Sue Lafky, *University of Iowa*

CONSULTING EDITORS

The following scholars have kindly shared their time and talents in consulting with the editor and in refereeing manuscripts for this volume of *Communication Yearbook*.

EDITOR'S INTRODUCTION

The *Communication Yearbook* series has a long and respected history of publishing state-of-the-art literature reviews across the broad discipline of communication. This volume continues this tradition, extending it to address what each reviewed area has to say about an issue of collective concern—empowerment. Within this broad discipline, researchers often engage in simultaneous endeavors totally unaware that colleagues in related areas are addressing similar concerns. As communication scholars, we draw from the rich traditions of philosophy, psychology, sociology, anthropology, behavioral research, rhetoric, cultural studies, and feminism, to name just a few; however, we seldom look across our interests to discover what we collectively have to say about an issue of appeal to the discipline in total as well as to society at large.

The theme for *Communication Yearbook 27* is "communication and empowerment." Chapters in this volume contain literature reviews featuring diverse areas of communication inquiry, and central to these reviews is the universal issue of empowerment. All of the reviews examine what each area of inquiry contributes to our collective understanding of how communication may or may not empower.

Generally, empowerment is a change from the status quo. Empowerment can lift an individual or group from the mundane, helping them to achieve excellence. Empowerment allows people to have a say in the outcomes of their existence, and communication is the mechanism through which empowerment may be accomplished. As communication scholars, it would seem that we should be in the middle of such noble efforts to empower and to seek empowerment. What does our discipline, composed of diverse knowledge and background, have to say about empowerment? How can we apply our research to understanding communication and empowerment?

The variety of perspectives on empowerment articulated in this volume is as diverse as the communication discipline itself. Empowerment is conceptualized from interpersonal, organizational, mass communication, technological, feminist, and hermeneutic perspectives. An impressive array of definitions, literature reviews, and applications are offered in this volume. In the end, it becomes clear that as a field we have something important to say about the process of empowerment and communication. The messages and mechanisms may differ but all contribute to an overarching understanding of communication and empowerment.

The first contribution, by Kirby, Golden, Medved, Jorgenson, and Buzzanell, examines communication as a catalyst for empowerment. In their chapter, "An Organizational Communication Challenge to the Discourse of Work and Family Research," they consider empowerment in situations where workers take action questioning traditional perceptions of work and family, or where they negotiate work relationships that are more amenable to personal life.

The next chapter is Luthra's "Recovering Women's Voice." In this essay, Luthra considers women living on the margins of society, who have a unique standpoint in observing equality and inequality. Luthra chronicles the resistance of these women toward inequality as well as the empowerment they stand to achieve in gaining their voice.

Rogers and Singhal describe efforts to organize disempowered individuals into groups where they can become empowered through communicating with similar others. In their chapter, "Empowerment and Communication," Rogers and Singhal describe several efforts they have been involved in that use communication to empower others.

Jacobson's chapter, "Participatory Communication for Social Change," reviews global empowerment efforts designed to improve life opportunities and describes the communication components of these efforts. Jacobson then presents a new approach to studying empowerment based on Habermas's theory of communicative action.

The relationship between communication and empowerment is explicated by Hammond, Anderson, and Cissna in their chapter, "The Problematics of Dialogue and Power." In their review of literature and theoretical perspectives on power and dialogue, Hammond, Anderson, and Cissna argue that the two concepts are completely interwoven, that is, it does not make sense to consider power without also considering dialogue.

Communication researchers can further gain perspective on communication and empowerment from Block and Lemish's review of the role that media play in empowering one culture over another. More specifically, they describe a phenomenon labeled the megaphone effect, where international renown is gained for products, ideas, and programs only after traveling through the United States. In their chapter, "The Megaphone Effect," Block and Lemish show that under the current structure only one culture has a powerful vantage point and that others can be empowered only to the degree to which they can become a part of this culture and its media.

The function of the media to empower is further scrutinized by Abrams, Eveland, and Giles in their review of the role television plays in empowering nondominant groups. In their chapter, "The Effects of Television on Group Vitality," the changes in television's portrayal of nondominant groups are chronicled and related to applications of group vitality theory.

The volume's focus then turns from the media to the communication discipline itself with Aldoory's chapter, "The Empowerment of Feminist Scholarship in Public Relations and the Building of a Feminist Paradigm." In this review, Aldoory considers the empowerment that comes to communication scholars and professionals by including feminist perspectives in the public relations literature.

Parker follows with a review of empowerment strategies for women, which are communicated differently depending on race and class. In her chapter, "Control, Resistance, and Empowerment in Raced, Gendered, and Classed Work Contexts," Parker examines particular communication practices that serve to control African American women as well as the resistance strategies that are used by these women to empower themselves.

Metzger, Flanagin, Eyal, Lemus, and McCann present a different perspective on empowerment in "Credibility for the 21st Century." In this chapter, Metzger and colleagues posit that "the ability to effectively and accurately discern credible from unreliable information is fundamentally an issue of empowerment, inasmuch as attitudes and behaviors based on accurate information are superior to those founded on less secure premises" (p. 296). These authors review the characteristics of web-based information that make credibility assessments particularly difficult and relate empowerment to the ability to determine the veracity of information in a technologically sophisticated context.

Coopman closes this volume with her chapter, "Communicating Disability." In this essay, Coopman reviews how the language we use empowers and oppresses people with disabilities. Six prominent metaphors are examined.

This volume demonstrates that as a discipline, communication has much to say about empowerment and shows myriad ways in which researchers can accomplish this social action. The literature reviews in this volume should provide a foundation for communication scholars, educators, and students to continue the examination of communication and empowerment. Further, the theoretical perspectives advanced in this volume can serve as a heuristic for communication research across the discipline.

ACKNOWLEDGMENTS

I would like to thank the Department of Communication and Journalism as well as the College of Arts and Sciences at the University of Wyoming for their support of *Communication Yearbook*. They have provided excellent resources for the *Communication Yearbook* office and have been unselfish in their backing of my editorial responsibilities.

I would also like to thank the *Communication Yearbook* editorial assistants. Valina K. Eckley has done an outstanding job copyediting manuscripts, communicating with authors, and preparing work for publication. She has a wonderful sense of humor and work ethic coupled with skill and diligence. Nathan C. MacLean has done a superb job designing *Communication Yearbook* materials for manuscript authors and referees, setting up review processes and office procedures, troubleshooting software and hardware issues, and helping solicit international manuscripts. The efforts of both assistants were vital to this publication.

I appreciate the additional assistance I received from Kelly Haigler in facilitating the set up of the *Communication Yearbook* office and hiring the editorial assistants, proofreading correspondence, and helping coordinate the office. Further, I want to thank Jan Gierman for his software program designed to manage the blind review process for the manuscripts submitted to the *Communication Yearbook*.

Finally, I would like to thank Scott Berkley and Barbara Stooksberry for their patience and direction during the production editing of this publication, as well as the International Communication Association for continuing support of the *Communication Yearbook* series.

Pamela J. Kalbfleisch
Laramie, WY

CHAPTER CONTENTS

1   An Organizational Communication Challenge to the Discourse of Work and Family Research: From Problematics to Empowerment

ERIKA L. KIRBY
Creighton University

ANNIS G. GOLDEN
University at Albany

CARYN E. MEDVED
Ohio University

JANE JORGENSON
University of South Florida

PATRICE M. BUZZANELL
Purdue University

Using a discourse perspective, we articulate four problematics, (a) boundaries, (b) identity, (c) rationality, and (d) voice that underlie work-family theory, research, and practice. We situate existing interdisciplinary research within each problematic, showing how such research examines outcomes and effects rather than the process of constructing such outcomes. We supplement these studies with emerging communication research to illustrate new ways of thinking about each problematic. We highlight the role of daily microlevel discourses as well as macrodiscourses of organizations and families in creating the current processes, structures, and relationships surrounding work and family. We link each problematic with an agenda for empowerment through (a) questioning boundaries, (b) integrating identity, (c) embracing practical knowledge and emotionality, (d) seeking diverse voices, and (e) developing a communal orientation.

D ramatic demographic, technological, and social changes are reshaping how individuals experience family and work as we begin the 21st century. As the composition of the paid workforce continues to change, men and women are rearranging what used to be a rigid distribution of wage, work, and

AUTHORS' NOTE: Although the first author created and coordinated the project, all authors contributed equally to writing the manuscript.

Correspondence: Erika L. Kirby, Department of Communication Studies, Creighton University, Omaha, NE, 68178; email: ekirby@creighton.edu

Communication Yearbook 27, pp. 1–43

family responsibilities in traditional families. Coupled with these changing demographics, technological innovations have changed the way work is accomplished. Computer technologies now enable new forms of virtual work, thus blurring the boundaries between workspaces and homespaces. Many men and women are relaxing their commitments to paid labor and increasing their commitments to family life (Galinsky, Bond, & Friedman, 1993).

Although some workers continue to struggle within organizational environments that maintain strict control over the planning of work without regard for family life, others are beginning to speak up about the difficulty of managing their conflicting commitments—often referred to as seeking "balance."[1] Employees who have challenged traditional work arrangements and achieved changes in corporate policies or benefits, illustrate the centrality of discourse as a means to empowerment in negotiating work-family relationships. As Chiles and Zorn (1995) illustrated, an empowered perception is "the symbolic construction of one's personal state as characterized by competence, or the skill and ability to act effectively, and control, or the opportunity and authority to act" (p. 2). The process of creating this state is also empowerment.

Communication can serve as a catalyst for empowerment when workers take opportunities to act by asking for family leave, pressing for flexible work schedules, and questioning traditional stereotypes surrounding who performs wage work and family labor. In other words, communication can allow workers to negotiate arrangements at work and at home to achieve "balance" or whatever ends they seek. Until recently, work and family received limited attention from communication researchers in relation to researchers situated in psychology, sociology, and organizational behavior.[2]

Across disciplines, the body of research on work-family issues is extensive, as Kingston (1989) notes, "[it] threatens to overwhelm us" (p. 55). Work-family literature examines both the impact of work on family and the effect of family characteristics on work (Loscocco & Roschelle, 1991; Voydanoff, 1989). Existing work-family research describes phenomena such as household division of labor, ways of circumventing negative career effects, methods of negotiating family-friendly benefits, factors that contribute to or lessen work-family conflicts, and ways in which productivity and motivation are impacted by work-family conflicts.

A common theme throughout work-family research is a concern with outcomes rather than a concern with the process of constructing those outcomes. Few of these studies acknowledge the central role that discourse and associated practices play in (re)constituting work-family meanings and consequences. From a meaning-centered approach, discourses of work and family are inherited and situated in historical context. These forms constrain and facilitate thought and action regarding the contextual categories of *family*, *work*, and *organization* (Barrett, Thomas, & Hocevar, 1995). Our orientation is toward destabilizing these terms by recognizing how they are communicatively constituted and by appreciating their complex connections in everyday life. In this review, our focus on communication foregrounds the contested nature of work-family discourse. We strive to document the nature of the conflict and contradictions present in negotiating work and family relationships as well as how people work with and through them. We call attention to the central role of discourse in shaping personal identities and in maintaining and transforming institutional structures.

Specifically, we articulate several problematics of work and family research that become evident through a discourse perspective.[3] Problematics operate as tensions or concerns that inform a particular area of study but often operate in the background (Mumby & Stohl, 1996). By foregrounding these problematics, we not only present communicative investigations of work-family issues in one place, but we also explore possibilities for more empowering ways of researching, as well as enacting, work and family relationships.

PROBLEMATICS IN WORK-FAMILY DISCOURSE AND PRACTICE

We see four central problematics that underlie work-family theory, research, and practice: (a) boundaries, (b) identity, (c) rationality, and (d) voice. In presenting these problematics, we begin with boundaries because the container metaphor—where the organization and the family are seen as concrete entities with discrete boundaries—is often implicit in this literature (Putnam, Phillips, & Chapman, 1996). Much work-family literature operates from this model of separation (or separation with transition), rather than treating organizations and families as overlapping realms of experience. We further illustrate work-family literature with the problematics of identity and rationality. Finally, the problematic of voice allows for an examination of who has been privileged (and marginalized) to this point in scholarship on work and family.

As an organizing framework, each problematic begins with some defining principles. We then situate current interdisciplinary research on work-family within each problematic to explore what is present in current discussions. In selecting interdisciplinary literature, we began by including well-known articles on central topics in work-family scholarship, such as Greenhaus and Beutell's (1985) definition of work-family conflict. In addition, we consulted several reviews of work-family research in other disciplines (e.g., Gonyea & Googins, 1992; Loscocco & Roschelle, 1991; Perry-Jenkins, Repetti, & Crouter, 2000; Voydanoff, 1989). We also sought articles from the Sloan Electronic Researchers Work-Family Literature Database, a collection of over 2,800 entries providing bibliographic information with selected annotations for journal articles, books, chapters, reports, papers, and dissertations that present information about work and family (Sloan Foundation, n.d.).

Following this presentation of interdisciplinary research, we examine where a discourse-centered approach can enrich our understandings of various work-family issues and present exemplars of communicative approaches that challenge the problematic. In selecting literature within the discipline of communication, we utilized many sources of scholarship—including unpublished manuscripts, unpublished dissertations, and conference papers as well as published material—because the area of work-family (work-life) communication has only recently emerged. Throughout this review, we view organizations and families as gendered institutions in U.S. society. We assume gender to be a macrodiscourse than impacts micropractices, therefore, work-family practices and processes are embedded within discourses of gender. We define gender as "a hierarchical structure that informs everyday relations in the family and the workplace" such that women and men have different expectations and demands as well as different power and control in shaping these role inequities (Milkie & Peltola, 1999, p. 476). But even amongst these different expectations, the meaning of gender is constantly negotiated within everyday family and organizational interactions.

Our analysis highlights theoretical as well as practical implications that may be relevant to women and men seeking to design more humanizing and productive spaces for living and working. Within each problematic, we conclude with suggestions for research and practice centered in communication that can empower individuals, families, organizations, and society—conceptualizing empowerment as both perception and process (Chiles & Zorn, 1995). We offer more empowering possibilities for enacting work and family in daily microlevel discourses, as well as in the macrodiscourses of organizations and families, in an attempt to reenvision the problematics.

In this chapter, we consider both the interpersonal and organizational dimensions of empowerment (Chiles & Zorn, 1995). As one example of interpersonal dimensions, we can see Albrecht's (1988) definition of empowerment, which is in terms of personal control: An individual is empowered to the extent that she or he perceives evidence of the ability to exert social influence through communication behavior. Examples of dimensions used by organizations to create empowered employees include widely distributed power, open communication, integrative problem solving, participative decision making, an environment of trust, and encouragement of high performance and self-responsibility (Burpitt & Bigoness, 1997; Pacanowsky, 1988). Such organizations are often seen as alternatives to traditional bureaucratic organizations, which typically offer a limited set of opportunities for employee empowerment (see Ashcraft, 2000).

A common orientation in organizational communication approaches to empowerment is to analyze how people behave when they are part of organizations whose characteristics facilitate personal empowerment. What often is left unexamined in this perspective is how individuals can create or seize opportunities for empowerment in organizations and situations that do not actively offer it—how people can communicatively construct empowered positions for themselves. As Trethewey (1997) illustrated, microlevel discursive acts of resistance to dominant organizational discourses (such as patriarchy) can empower individuals, influencing their identities and perhaps even transforming organizational practices.

Through emphasizing the socially constructed nature of our current array of options for managing work and family, we see many potential sites for resistance. Therefore, we reenvision discourses of work and family to move toward empowerment in theory as well as in practice. We articulate these revisions to the discourse in relation to the four problematics of empowerment through (a) questioning boundaries, (b) integrating identity, (c) embracing practical knowledge and emotionality, and (d) seeking diverse voices. We conclude with a fifth dimension by which to seek empowerment: developing a communal orientation.

BOUNDARY PROBLEMATIC: FROM COMPARTMENTALIZATION TO INTEGRATION

The problematic of "boundary" concerns the ways transitions are negotiated symbolically, emotionally, and practically between the worlds of work and family. In ordinary usage, "boundary" connotes an image of walls or barriers between distinct territories. Scholarly references to work-family boundaries often presuppose a categorical distinction between the two domains, not only in terms of their physical locations and task activities, but also in their values and psychological orientations (Hochschild, 1997; Kanter, 1977; Nippert-Eng, 1996). The problematic of boundary reflects its contradictory potential. On one hand, traditional boundary assumptions—those that sharply distinguish between home and work as separate realms—are said to place unwelcome constraints on workers' abilities to manage their conflicting commitments. On the other hand, separate spheres thinking and practices may serve a protective function for individual workers subject to the ever expanding reach of organizations into personal life.

We incorporate here several strands of work-family research that illustrate how boundary has served as an evocative and, often, theoretically problematic metaphor. We begin with the emergence of the myth of separate worlds, then explore the appearance of boundary and separate spheres imagery in research on work-family conflict. We then examine studies that show the contested nature of work-family boundaries and that challenge prevailing ideologies of separate spheres. We also consider what has been learned from studies of new technologies and alternative work arrangements with regard to boundary-setting practices and meanings.

Creating Boundaries and Separate Spheres

The notion of boundary is critical to, although often submerged within, traditional organizational discourse. Societal assumptions about the nature of appropriate work-family boundaries have varied historically as the work-home relationship has been redefined (Gonyea & Googins, 1992; Goodstein, 1994; Kanter, 1977). In the Colonial period, the family was a community of work in its own right and the home space was a site in which family members, male and female, young and old, labored together. In the move from preindustrial to industrial societies, family life was wrenched apart from the world of work (Demos, 1979). Yet, by the early 20th century, corporations exercised significant influence over the family lives of workers through the creation of company towns and lodging. However, family interests came to be seen by employers as a competing loyalty and organizational efforts shifted from incorporating and co-opting families, toward separating the spheres (Kanter, 1977).

Organizations came to perpetuate an ideology of separate worlds, which holds that work and home are bounded in space and time, carrying out autonomous functions according to distinctive rhythms. Employers act as if employees' family worlds do not exist and individuals are expected to reciprocate. According to Kanter (1977), the organizational dictates essentially stipulated to employees are that "while you are here [at work], you will *act as though* you have no other loyalties, no other life" (p. 15, italics added). The work-family relationship was not considered a legitimate area of organizational concern unless it was forced into awareness by the emergence of an employee's personal problems (Renshaw, 1976).

The boundary metaphor in organizational discourse and managerial practice has served as a subtle mechanism of organizational control. To begin with, the assumption that work and family are functionally differentiated, "bounded" systems has reinforced the taken-for-granted connection between organizational advancement and full-time work. Perlow (1995) illustrated the "cultural assumption that there is a direct relationship between one's presence at work and one's contribution to work" (p. 231). Thus, employees not conforming to organizational definitions of an effective, committed worker (i.e., maintains physical presence at work, demonstrates face time, and sustains work as a constant top priority) are at risk for negative evaluative and promotional consequences. Face time—time spent in the workplace—is taken as a prime indicator of commitment and productivity despite increasing evidence that individuals are more productive when given discretion over their work hours and locations (Bailyn, 1992, 1993; Perlow 1995, 1997, 1998; Rapoport & Bailyn, 1996).

The domain closure implied in the imagery of spheres and boundaries also supports an expectation that behavior appropriate in one sphere is not appropriate in the other. In many workplaces, informal norms persist that oblige employees to minimize or disguise their family commitments. To fail to do so—to talk openly with colleagues and supervisors about one's family—is to invite the assumption that one is not a serious organization member (Jorgenson, 2000; Kirby, 2001; Kirby & Krone, 2002; Nippert-Eng, 1996). In organizations that enforce a high degree of work-family segmentation, women employees may feel particularly compelled to edit out their family involvements. This is in large part because of the normative expectations that men's wage work will override their involvement in domestic tasks and that women will accommodate their wage work to their family responsibilities (Farley-Lucas, 2000). Recent analysis questioning accepted notions of office presence has raised awareness of the penalties extracted from women workers when their family caretaking is seen as evidence of diminished commitment to paid work (Jorgenson, 2000; Martin, 1990).

Exclusionary Borders Versus Permeable Membranes

As the imagery of boundaries and spheres has been naturalized in managerial discourse, the boundary metaphor has played a conspicuous role in work and family research based on open systems theories (Clark, 2000). Open systems are characterized by continuous interchanges within environments of energy, emotion, and information (Katz & Kahn, 1978; Lewin, 1951). From an open systems perspective, work and family are bounded by permeable membranes rather than exclusionary borders, in the sense that an individual's experiences in one domain influences or carries over to the other domain. The exact nature of the relationship has been conceptualized in a variety of ways. *Spillover* models propose that emotional reactions or coping behaviors in one domain extend to other areas. Work-family spillover is evidenced in positive correlations often found between job and family satisfaction (Barnett, 1994; Frone, Russell & Cooper, 1992; Williams & Alliger, 1994). *Compensation* models hypothesize an inverse relationship between the two, such that dissatisfaction in one realm leads to greater investment in the other.

Extensive research has centered on the nature of this relationship as work-family conflict, emphasizing the competing, rather than enhancing, role requirements of work and family as well as the strains placed on time, energy, and well-being (Greenhaus & Beutell, 1985). Work-family conflict occurs when (a) time does not allow for activities in both work and family domains, (b) emotional strain from one domain spills over and inhibits effectiveness in the other, or (c) behaviors acceptable in one area are seen as unacceptable in the other (Greenhaus & Beutell, 1985). The effects of work-family conflict on individuals include depression, burnout, and poor morale. These effects lead to organizational consequences in the form of tardiness, absenteeism, turnover, and reduced productivity (Bedeian, Burke, & Moffett, 1988; Burden & Googins, 1987; Burke, 1989; Duxbury & Higgins, 1991; Goff, Mount, & Jamison, 1990; Kelly & Voydanoff, 1985; Pleck, 1985; Ray & Miller, 1994).

Yet, although research on work-family conflicts and spillovers has served to the highlight complex interrelationships between experiential realms, it is also limited in that it tends to exclusively explore domain, role, and outcomes. Construing work and family as contextual frames rather than places or groups of people suggests new directions of inquiry focusing on how individuals in particular workplace cultures negotiate contextual shifts and reconstruct boundaries in their daily lives (Nippert-Eng, 1996; Richter, 1990). In such negotiations, there is compelling evidence that as the result of new information and communication technologies, conventional assignments of work and family in time and space are being reconstituted by workers and their employers (English-Lueck, 2002). Mobile technologies like laptops, cell phones, pagers, and personal digital assistants are blurring the temporal and spatial distinctions between domains of work and family. This blurring is reflected in and reinforced by subtle shifts in macrodiscourses of work, family, and boundaries.

At present, two contradictory strains of public discourse characterize the role of technology in negotiating work and family: exploitation and empowerment. In the discourse of exploitation, new technologies are the apparatus through which employers intrude across boundaries into their employees' personal lives to extract ever increasing amounts of time and energy. In the discourse of empowerment, new technologies are instruments that enable workers to (a) exercise increased control over when and where they do their work, (b) keep connected with loved ones, and (c) exercise increased control over the general task of managing work and family responsibilities. A communication-based, discourse-oriented approach has much to offer in understanding how technology use fits within individuals' work and home life, their attitudes toward technology, and the contexts in which technology is embraced or resisted (Geisler, Campbell, Deery, & Golden, 2001).

Boundary Management as Discursive Practice

As O'Keefe (1997) notes, work-family boundaries are not directly observable—they can only be inferred through behavioral and discursive practices such as differences in modes of dress and speech across settings. Social scientific research on the subjective reactions of individuals to work-family conflicts extensively references the idea of boundaries without questioning their empirical quality. This literature rarely attempts to situate individual reactions in the context of organizational discourse, which maintains a more or less arbitrary definition of what counts as work and what counts as family. The literature discursively constructs work as something that is performed outside the home, thereby creating the stay-at-home parent as one who does not cross into the boundary of a paid labor organization and therefore does not work.

In an emerging body of research, critically oriented and feminist scholars are now reexamining the notion of boundary embedded within the discourse of separate spheres. They argue that the notion of boundary rhetorically constructs an ideology of gender separatism, reinforcing the distinction between home as a private arena (i.e., feminine) and work as a public arena (i.e., masculine; Chow & Berheide, 1988; Gerstel & Gross, 1987; Lopata, 1993; Martin, 1990; Osmond, 1996; Thorne, 1992). The tasks of one domain continually intrude into the other, as when workers engage in telephone conversations at work with family members or manage medical emergencies via the office telephone. In a variety of ways, families are symbolically and physically present in the workplace. Workers, especially women, are always *enfamilied* (Jorgenson, Gregory, & Goodier, 1997; see also Hessing, 1992; Hochschild, 1997; Kirby, 2000a, 2000b; Nippert-Eng, 1996). Under conditions such as these, women may understandably work to disguise family involvements, thereby maintaining public-private boundaries, or they may resist organizational enforcement of separate spheres by bringing family topics and issues into the workplace. By asserting as well as subverting accepted boundaries, they attempt to arrive at a desired degree of integration (Clark, 2000).

We feel it is more appropriate to speak of boundary work as a continuous process of symbolic management, rather than to speak of boundaries in a static sense. Work and family are neither specific places nor groups of people, but social contexts, "mutually shared and ratified definitions of situation and [in] social actions persons take on the basis of those definitions" (Erickson & Shultz, 1977, p. 6). Emerging research on telecommuting, home-based work, and alternative work arrangements suggests further ramifications of boundary work for individuals who must simultaneously manage presence at home as well as absence from work (e.g., Mallia & Ferris, 2000; Russo, 1998). From a constructionist perspective, we are less concerned with the content within each of the separate domains of work-family than we are with the contextual shifts between the domains or the method by which individuals construct and enact meaning across them.

Seeking Empowerment Through Questioning Boundaries

The boundary metaphor has served indirectly to constrain work-family choices and the abilities of individuals to manage their conflicting commitments. First of all, the domain closure implied in the imagery of boundaries and spheres has tended to entrench expectations that what is appropriate in one sphere is not appropriate in the other. Kirby (2001) asked both men and women how they communicatively constructed their families to colleagues and supervisors while at work. Many simply said they rarely talked about family because they were worried about what their boss and coworkers would think (also see Kirby & Krone, 2002; Nippert-Eng, 1996).

Secondly, the boundary assumptions support the privileging of work over family. Work as a primary source of identity has come to substitute for other identifications with family, friends, and community. In a society that views happiness and success as deriving from work, we have a decreasing capacity to enjoy time away from work and have less time to explore relationships (Ciulla, 2000; see also Schor, 1991). The more we privilege work and commodify time (i.e., envision time as money), the less we protect time for those persons and activities that cannot pay for that time (e.g., elderly parents, children, volunteer work, and so on). As individuals seek to reconstruct work-family boundaries in daily life, we must also be aware of the potential for new information and communication technologies to serve as instruments for empowerment or disempowerment.

In our efforts to reprioritize these commitments, we may need to look more closely at the discursive crossovers among work and family domains. Language typically reserved for the work environment is increasingly used to help people manage their personal lives. At the same time, the language of intimacy and spirituality is being used as a way of promoting productivity and commitment at work (Caproni, 1997; Hochschild, 1997). On one hand, as Caproni (1997) noted, such crossovers reflect a breakdown of the artificial and simplistic distinctions between work and life. Yet, paradoxically, they may operate to encourage more time spent at work. In response to such pressures, some authors see their role as helping individuals engage in a process of reflective practice about how they are living their lives. By envisioning different kinds of working life in which tranquility is valued over achievement and contribution is valued over success, individuals may be helped to make more informed choices.

A fundamental tension underlying the boundary or container conceptualization of work-family is that although it perpetuates current restrictive notions of work, the dissolution of clear boundaries also entails potential costs for individuals. This tension shows up in discussions about whether to broaden current restrictive definitions of work to include activities carried out in the private sphere. Mirchandani's (1998) study of female teleworkers showed that broadening the concept of women's work to include family caregiving is not necessarily favorable to women's interests. These teleworkers were resistant to calling their domestic and childcare activities work. They preferred to maintain boundaries between different forms of work rather than place their various activities in a single conceptual category, because to do so was to increase the risk of being perceived by coworkers as always available to fulfill organizational needs. Mirchandani's research emphasized the active role these teleworkers chose to play in setting definitional boundaries. It also highlighted the inherent tensions of the metaphor of boundaries and spheres, showing how they perpetuate restrictive notions of what counts as work, yet offer interpretive resources for some workers to resist management control.

We see here how the categorical ambiguity of work and family suggests opportunities for empowerment by affording spaces for different kinds of resistance. Buzzanell (1997) talks about the ways women may sneak time for their own personal needs without their partners' knowledge. Although complicit with hegemonic processes that inform ideas about what women should be doing and that they should be doing it for others, sneaking time also empowers women to do what is of interest and value to them without expending the energy to justify and fight for this time. Similarly, using terms such as appointments or meetings for time away from work for family needs does not alter organizational members' thinking or priorities but still enables workers to blend work and family (see Jorgenson, 2000). These forms of resistance, or *hidden transcripts* (Murphy, 1998), may lessen the power of dominant discourses in individual lives on a case-by-case basis. Over time and with continuing success in experimenting with these covert processes, women and men may be able to implement more visible changes or inspire others to do so, a potential that emphasizes the importance of identity and individual agency.

IDENTITY PROBLEMATIC: FROM MULTIPLE ROLES TO HOLISTIC SELVES

The problematic of identity is both related to and distinct from the traditional construct of *role* in work-family research. In this section we overview the literature concerned with roles in work and family, demonstrating how the assumptions of communication-based discursive approaches view identity as an alternative framework to roles in order to understand how individuals define and manage different aspects of self in relation to work and family. We also consider how the central tenets of the identity problematic challenge the assumptions of a logistical approach to work and family that is implicit in recent workplace accommodation research.

Role as a Work-Family Construct

Role is a foundational construct in research on work and family. *Role strain* (Gove & Zeiss, 1987), *role conflict* (Eagle, Miles, & Icenogle, 1997; Netemeyer, Boles, & McMurrian, 1996), *role spillover* (Barnett, 1994; Grzywacz & Marks, 2000), and *role sharing* between spouses (Bardo, Shehan, & Leslie, 1987) are all dimensions of this fundamental construct that have received attention over the past 3 decades. Interdisciplinary research on work and family has refined its models for conceptualizing the relationship between family and work from separate spheres, to spillover, to a more interactive model that identifies reciprocal influences between the domains of family and work as well as the associated roles individuals occupy (Chow & Berheide, 1988). Edwards and Rothbard's (2000) model of mechanisms that link work and family exemplifies this interactive approach and the mechanisms they identify implicitly or explicitly rely on the role construct: spillover, compensation, segmentation, resource drain, congruence, and work-family conflict. Perry-Jenkins et al.'s (2000) review of the past decade of work and family research parses work-family constructs somewhat differently. However, they still feature *multiple roles* as one of four primary categories of inquiry (the others are maternal employment, work socialization, and work stress, the last two of which are also strongly role-related).

Although the trend in work-family research has been toward a more bidirectional understanding of the interaction of the two domains, with roles providing the vehicle for conceptualizing the mechanism of those interactions, it retains a fundamentally segmented orientation. Roles are conceptualized as discrete entities or aspects that must be "balanced" or constrained within boundaries in order to avoid conflict. Although nominally centered on the individual, these conceptualizations of role keep the focus more on the domains themselves, which are for many people readily identifiable as separate in terms of time and space. These conceptualizations ignore the challenge of maintaining a coherent sense of self while moving physically and mentally between the two realms. The result is a perspective that is (a) more domain oriented than person oriented, (b) more outside in than inside out, and (c) more on how circumstances and structures act on the individual than on what the individual does to positively integrate the self.

Traditional approaches to role interactions, such as Edwards and Rothbard's (2000), are mechanistic in their assumptions, implying that careful study of mechanisms linking work and family will discover an optimal set of conditions leading to maximal satisfaction and minimal conflict. Roles are treated as if they are properties of individuals that are clearly definable and unchanging rather than socially constructed. In surveying the literature, Perry-Jenkins et al. (2000) do identify a static view of roles as problematic. However, the alternative they propose emphasizes fluidity in the specific context of family life cycle, rather than the inherent fluidity of the give and take of daily life as individuals move through time, space, and social context.

Even within the ranks of traditional work-family researchers, critical voices have been raised exhorting their discourse community to conceptualize work and family more integratively, as well as to view the individual as a whole person rather than a collection of discretely defined roles (Perry-Jenkins et al., 2000). Marks and MacDermid (1996) observed the atomistic tendency of research that concerns itself with multiple roles. They urged researchers studying how individuals organize and manage multiple roles to move away from the tendency to assume roles as discrete and hierarchical, and rather to move toward a "nonatomistic, systemic view of multiple selves" in the symbolic interactionist tradition inspired by Mead (Marks & MacDermid, 1996, p. 418). This approach offers a welcome corrective, in terms of conceptualizing how different aspects of the self function in relation to one another. However, it leaves unaddressed the processes through which the individual chooses how to define different aspects of the self from among alternative self-definitions that are culturally available.

Finally, role is often discussed as though it is a neutral concept in work and family division, but roles are fundamentally gendered. Like other aspects of self, gender is typically treated as a static analytic variable rather than a component of identity that is interactively constructed according to the social contexts that frame individual interactions. Greenberger and O'Neil's (1993) study of employed parents with young children found men who had a stronger commitment to work reported greater role strain and conflict among work, parental, and marital roles. Conversely, a study of dual-income couples with preschool children found fathers experienced the least role strain when they had a low commitment to work and high commitment to parenting (O'Neil & Greenberger, 1994). These findings led the researchers to conclude that men's commitment to their family role was equal to their work role in determining psychological health, discrediting the view that men's psychological health is determined primarily by their work role (Barnett, Marshall, & Pleck, 1992). In contrast, women's patterns of commitment to work and parenting have been found to be unrelated to their role strain. Additionally, role strain was found to be less intense among women who did not hold professional or managerial jobs (O'Neil & Greenberger, 1994).

Although this research is informative, by looking primarily at strain and psychological outcomes it minimizes the meanings individuals attach to their roles. Perry-Jenkins et al. (2000) acknowledge this shortcoming when they suggest that future research should "examine the meaning that men and women assign to their roles as parents, workers, and marital partners" (p. 990) as well as the gendered differences in meaning that men and women give to costs and benefits of roles.

In summary, the way the role construct has been used to understand how individuals manage different aspects of self associated with work and family has the following problematic aspects: (a) It provides a mechanistic orientation to the ways in which different aspects of self interact; (b) it presents the self as segmented rather than integrated; (c) it takes role definitions for granted; and (d) it pays insufficient attention to the fundamentally gendered nature of roles and selves. In contrast, the construct of identity, as it will be used here (following Polkinghorne's,

1988, theory of the narrative construction of self), emphasizes *oneness* and *sameness*. In this conception, oneness is unity achieved through the self's integration of roles, whereas sameness is continuity of selfhood through time and space or, in this case, the domains of work and family.

A Communication Approach to Work, Family, and Identity

In identifying possible directions for future work-family research, Perry-Jenkins et al. (2000) suggest we should "explore the *social constructions* of work and family," "take into account how *social and historical time shapes the meaning* we give to work and family issues" (p. 993), and study "employed adults' *interpretations and constructions* of their work and family roles" (p. 994, italics added). A communication approach to work, family, and identity does precisely that, bringing a meaning-centered, discourse-oriented approach to work and family primarily informed by the construct of identity rather than role. A communication perspective, in the symbolic interactionist tradition (Blumer, 1969; McCall & Simmons, 1978), understands roles as negotiated rather than prescribed and thus emphasizes the processes through which individuals assume role identities as much as the definitions themselves. These processes include appropriating from a diverse common stock of culturally available role-identity definitions and interpersonal negotiations with role partners in the workplace and the homespace (Golden, 2002; Stamp, 1994).

Wood (1986) pointed out the potential contribution of the communication discipline in understanding how dual-career couples manage work and family through the examination of how spouses create shared meanings for their various roles. Wood's perspective on dual-career couples assumes that role definitions are constructed (and potentially problematic) rather than given because of the absence of normative role guidelines for managing work and family when both spouses engage in paid employment. Continuing work has identified the pluralistic social environment characterizing millennial America as a key construct in problematizing the definition and maintenance of self-identity as it relates to work and family (Rosenfeld, Bowen, & Richman, 1995; Sillars, 1995). Though not specifically within the context of work and family, Stephen (1994) brought the lens of modernity theory to a communication-based consideration of role-identity definition. Golden's (2001) study of working parents' accounts of their work-family arrangements examined the impact of such facets of modernity as the rise of expert authorities, the prevalence of mediated communication, and the pluralization of social life-worlds on the discursive construction of self-identity.

Work and family research has historically emphasized role interactions, with role definitions as a given, but a communication perspective emphasizes the challenge of defining any one role, especially given the diverse alternatives that are available, even in mainstream culture (Sillars, 1995). Gregory's (2001) research examined the discursive processes through which individuals constitute themselves and showed how these reveal strategies for dealing with the multiplicity of options that exist in society for defining the roles of worker, parent, child of adult parents, and relational partner. Gregory examined workers' identities in the context of a *new economy* characterized by more flexible business models and the decline of lifelong job security. Faced with a potential loss of anchorage points for personal identity construction, participants drew on dominant storylines, yet reshaped them in ways appropriate for their current situations and constraints. Their narrative identities reflected a *family first* principle, which holds family should be the first priority, even over one's career. This family first theme was combined with another guiding principle summarized as, "don't sweat the small stuff," which encourages workers to stop trying to exert total control over the details of home life and work life (Gregory, 2001).

As Golden (2001) illustrated, alternatives for constituting identity are imbued with competing truth claims advanced by expert authorities and special interest groups through traditional and new media. These conditions create potentials for both empowerment and expansion of personal identity on the one hand, and anxiety and moral uncertainty on the other (Golden, 2001). Consequently, emphasizing processes (of identity construction and maintenance) rather than outcomes (such as avoiding or minimizing conflict) shows that what individuals are trying to accomplish is not merely the avoidance of conflict but the positive accomplishment of personhood as it is defined by our "local theory of selves" (Harre, 1984, p. 257).

Yet, although a communication-based approach to work and family understands roles as aspects of self-identity that are negotiated rather than prescribed, this perspective still acknowledges the constraints of social structures and material conditions, as well as the fact that negotiators of role identity definitions may have unequal power to shape outcomes. Jorgenson (2000) examined how women engineers resist efforts by their male coworkers and supervisors to incorporate gender into professional interactions. Farley-Lucas (2000) identified communicative strategies employed by working women to subvert the suppression of motherhood in the workplace. Additionally, Kirby (2000b; Kirby & Krone, 2002) identified contradictions in supervisors' messages to employees about preferred worker role-enactments.

Gender is inextricably linked to self and is particularly important to the discussion of identity in the context of work and family. Gender has often been treated as unproblematic and bestowed rather than as constructed and variable. Many work-family processes are gendered in that they rely on gender ideologies or belief configurations about who ordinarily does what in our society (i.e., work-public-masculine and family-home-feminine orientations) as well as how these enactments are valued (see Rakow, 1992). Gilbert (1994) maintains that individuals "must still act out their private roles as spouses, parents, and homemakers within the larger world of 'gendered' occupational and institutional structures and policies" (p. 102). Gendered discourses not only frame women's experiences of work and family but also constrain men's abilities to live fully in both spheres.

Research suggests there may be societal rewards for following traditional gender role stereotypes. A study of parents with preschool-aged children found that family-oriented women with preschoolers received higher merit increases than family-oriented men with preschoolers, while career-oriented women with preschoolers received lower merit increases than career-oriented men with preschoolers (Lobel & St. Clair, 1992). Committed and involved fathers face the same conflicts and constraints as those traditionally ascribed to women (Gerson, 1993; J. Levine & Pittinsky, 1997; S. Levine, 2000; Pleck, 1993). Men employ various communicative strategies, such as, "I have another meeting," to leave work and attend to family concerns yet avoid appearing uncommitted to workplace role partners (J. Levine, 1991).

Gender has a significant and substantive influence on family leave-taking behaviors (Sandberg, 1999) with women more likely than men to take leave (Kim, 1998). Men seem to be penalized in terms of perceived commitment and reward recommendations when they take advantage of family leave (Allen & Russell, 1999). Consequently, benefits are underutilized by men, single workers, and career-oriented mothers (Bailyn, Fletcher, & Kolb, 1997). This outcome points to a process of interactive construction of role identities between parents and their role partners at work that has been documented in communication-based approaches to this phenomenon (Jorgenson, 2000; Kirby, 2000a, 2002).

A discourse approach to gender identity, work, and family has the potential to show us the consequences of the persistence of gender schematic discourse for the construction of gendered identities at home and at work. Individuals construct work to fit their gendered identities (Leidner, 1991), their workplaces to meet friendship and community needs (Lamphere, 1985), and their emotions to suit gendered role expectations (e.g., Hochschild, 1983). Yet, there is also evidence of growing convergence between women's and men's role identities at home and at work (Barnett & Rivers, 1996; Covin & Brush, 1993; Higgins, Duxbury, & Lee, 1994; Stephen, 1994). Analysis of conversational discourse suggests that as individuals discursively construct their identities as worker-parents they engage in a dialectic of gender schematicity and gender convergence (Golden, 2002). Such practices invite further study to examine how and when individuals actively resist gender schematicity or embrace it.

Seeking Empowerment by Integrating Identity

As overviewed by Gilbert (1993), work-family research has shifted from an emphasis in the 1980s on the inequitable division of domestic labor between spouses (Hochschild, 1989) to a focus in the 1990s on changing the workplace to accommodate employees with families through programs such as dependent care, alternative workplaces, and flexible scheduling. An analytical framework in which workplace accommodations are identified as the key to successful management of work and family runs the risk of privileging structure over meaning and agency. Workplace accommodations undoubtedly have value when they create a more hospitable environment for managing the work-life dialectic of self-identity. Yet, they represent a qualitatively different construct from identity because they emphasize what individuals do rather than how their interpretation of what they do constructs personal and social identity.

Consequently, the opportunities for empowerment offered by a communication approach start with the reframing of work-life management as an identity issue rather than a merely logistical issue. If work-family conflict is understood as an essential human dialectic of enterprise and relatedness (Dinnerstein, 1976), or self and other (as suggested by Golden's, 2000, analysis of working parents' discourse on work-family management), it follows that it is not possible for workplace accommodations to provide a definitive solution. Relinquishing the mechanistic, segmented approach to roles in favor of an integrated self is empowering because it releases the individual from the expectation that a static balance (and thus an elimination of conflict) between work and family is achievable or even desirable.

The focus then becomes not only what individuals do but who they are, or more precisely, the sum the meanings their own actions have for them. A discourse perspective construes individuals as self-interpreting within the context of interpersonal, organizational, and cultural discourses that relate to their concepts of selfhood within the dual contexts of work and family. We do not accept work-family "balance" as the only sensible way to talk about this complicated issue. Rather, work-life management is a process bound up with the coconstruction of meaning with role partners within the context of culturally specific public discourse on (gendered) possibilities for defining work-life relationships. Within this framework, individuals can understand themselves not as victims of conflict and stress, but as agents of selfhood. Empowerment comes in identifying opportunities to exercise agency, both interactionally and interpretively. At the same time, we acknowledge that putting such interpretive frameworks into practice may meet with resistance.

Empowerment often involves decision making in ways that benefit oneself and those aspects of life that one values, such as children or status in a community. Kinnier, Katz, and Berry (1991) illustrated that people who were more resolved about their decisions regarding work and family worried less, had higher self-esteem, and reported more satisfaction in both work and family aspects of their lives. A frequent theme among those who reported they were most resolved about work-family issues was "my family comes first." This theme was expressed equally by both husbands and wives in this most resolved group. By prioritizing family first, these people had a touchstone for decision making about what they did in their lives and when. Greater attention to the discourses and practices that ordinary individuals and families use to integrate work and family into their lives would be of heuristic and practical value.

Papa, Singhal, Ghanekar, and Papa (2000) found that the ways in which people enact their values and their gendered identities can be empowering and disempowering simultaneously. Paradoxically, as women and men achieve greater fluidity in their nonstereotypic gendered enactment, others such as family and community members or media portrayals of life in a particular culture, may sanction and pull them toward the norm (e.g., Faludi, 1991). We see this backlash occurring when career women are pressured to have children or when women ask other women to handle extra work for them so that they can meet their public obligations (e.g., Medved, 2000; Papa et al., 2000).

A discursive approach to work-family management as identity asks how the process of identity construction emerges over time and in varied contexts, how cultural prescriptions for gendered enactment of different identities paradoxically enable and constrain individuals, and how identity concerns that were once part of a particular realm (traditionally public or private) become admissible in other realms. By bringing a discursive lens to work-family research, theory, and practice, we uncover how different stakeholders have interests in maintaining or dissolving traditionally bifurcated work-family identities. By exploring work-family as a site in which meaning and enactment of these identities are contested, we open possibilities for different enactments. We can also create new possibilities for empowerment by embracing alternative forms of knowledge as a challenge to traditional forms of rationality.

RATIONALITY PROBLEMATIC: TECHNICAL OR EXPERT TO PRACTICAL RATIONALITIES

The problematic of rationalities has two sides (a) expert or technical and (b) practical. In general, expert rationality, knowledge that "privileges a concern with prediction, control, and teleological forms of behavior," is favored over practical rationality, knowledge "grounded . . . in interpreting and experiencing the world as meaningful and intersubjectively constructed" (Mumby & Stohl, 1996, p. 59; see also Deetz, 1992). Interdisciplinary and communication research on work-family issues can be situated within these two knowledge forms, exploring (a) how the privileging of expert over practical knowledges occurs; (b)what its implications are for work-family thinking, research, and practice; and (c) where research agendas can be established that empower individuals to utilize both types of knowledge in negotiating work-family issues.

Technical or Expert Rationalities

Technical knowledge usually aligns with the notion of best practices. Namely, locating optimal means of doing activities, performing services, and replicating desirable results. Expert rationalities assume researchers or managers can locate factors that enhance outcomes, including performance, and that these factors are transferable to other situations. As such, technical or expert rationalities enable researchers both to determine conditions under which individuals and organizations experience differently valenced consequences of work-family practices as well as to propose ways of changing conditions detrimental to micro- and macrolevel goals.

The privileging of technical/expert rationality is prevalent in work-family research and everyday discourse. This privileging emerges when individuals rely on experts for advice on how to manage their lives. These individuals may not explore fully their personal circumstances or develop capacities within themselves, their families, or their extended community networks (see Sotirin, Buzzanell, Turner, Sullivan, & Rosback, 2001). They may depend on others telling them that professional families manage or balance work-family conflicts by outsourcing family chores, bringing technology into the home, placing children in daycare, and scheduling time for even the most intimate acts (Hochschild, 1997; Sotirin et al., 2001). When individuals communicate in ways that are direct, rational (from corporate perspectives), and instrumentally oriented, they may not consider fully whose interests are served by decision premises or knowledge assumptions. Instead, technical/expert rationality relies on certain assumptions of traditional social science, including issues can be separated from contexts, situations can be analyzed to uncover factors contributing to certain effects, and generalizable solutions can be generated. These assumptions guide a number of work-family research areas, including (a) formulaic understandings of work-family conflict and (b) work and pay considerations in families' decision making.

As illustrated in the problematics of boundaries and identity, work-family conflict can be based on time constraints, emotional strain, or when behaviors acceptable in one area are seen as unacceptable in the other (Greenhaus & Beutell, 1985). Using this conceptualization of work-family conflict, studies have assisted individuals in "balancing" work and family roles through family-leave policies, flexible work options and dependent-care benefits (Morgan & Milliken, 1992). Family leave policies include those for maternity, paternity, adoption, eldercare, and family emergencies (Morgan & Milliken, 1992). These leaves vary widely in length and compensation as well as whether paid leave is an option (Raabe & Gessner, 1988). Different kinds of dependent care benefits also are available, including financial assistance, information and referral services, as well as childcare and eldercare services (Morgan & Milliken, 1992).

Another solution is alternative work arrangements—with alternative meaning work practices different from the norm associated with presence (time, visibility, participation, and exposure; Perlow, 1995, 1998). Flexible work options include flextime, permanent or temporary part-time work, job sharing, flexplace or telecommuting, and flexible use of vacation time or personal days (Morgan & Milliken, 1992). Flexible work policies are among the most frequently used ways of addressing work-family conflicts.

The underlying assumption in much of this research and practice is that resolving work-family conflict is both realistic and appropriate, as well as that conflict can somehow be eliminated if family and organization members just get the formula right (e.g., Edwards & Rothbard, 2000). These studies fail to illustrate how conflict is produced and reproduced in relationships, as well as how it may be productive. By not focusing on relationships and positive aspects of work-family negotiations, researchers may overlook ways in which tensions direct members to question their priorities and organizational policies. Often, once policies are in place, the problem is perceived as remedied, meaning that organizations are absolved from scrutinizing themselves to uncover how and why policies fail to be enacted. Finally, by focusing more on negative aspects of work-family conflict and roles, researchers tend not to consider the many positive outcomes and processes associated with women's and men's multiple roles (Barnett & Hyde, 2001).

Privileging of expert knowledge also surfaces in studies on work and pay considerations in family decision making. Work still is prioritized over family; men's work and careers still take precedence over women's work and careers; work time and projects still take precedence over family time and events, including births of children; and some employees report they feel more comfortable with and gain more enjoyment from work relationships than family interactions (see Aryee & Luk, 1996; Ciulla, 2000; Deetz, 1992; Hobfoll & Hobfoll, 1994; Hochschild, 1997; Martin, 1990; Perlow, 1995, 1998; Silberstein, 1992; Williams, 2000). Even in self-managing teams where coworkers have control over project management and scheduling, workers commit more to organizational product completion than to family needs (Barker, 1993, 1999).

The linear thinking within which these priorities align also plays out in family decision making. In economic discussions, the talk follows cause-effect reasoning, for example, if women earn lower wages than men, then women should stay at home and rear children (see Blau & Ferber, 1986). If women are the primary caretakers, especially because new mothers nurse babies, women intuitively know how to do household chores, and women who choose not to enact caregiving are selfish—this thinking suggests that they should be stay-at-home mothers, downscale their careers, or expect to work second shifts (Benokraitis & Feagin, 1986; Luxton, 1980; Wood, 1994). In this economic thinking, women should handle more household tasks and caregiving than men. Accordingly, women generally do—although the extent to which this occurs is dependent on class, race, gender, and marital belief systems, among other factors (Bardo et al., 1987; Barnett & Hyde, 2001; Brines, 1994; Hochschild, 1989, 1997; Rexroat & Shehan, 1987). Gender ideologies underlying these examples of so-called logical cause-effect reasoning remain unquestioned.

In short, technical or expert forms of knowledge are privileged in work-family research, theory, and practice. Although useful for developing general policies, the reliance on linear and scientific thinking cannot address the micropractices of everyday, ongoing work-family discussions that occur within particular relational contexts and organizational cultures. This privileging of technical knowledge and economic outcomes is gendered, in that it enables firms to better control people and processes by admitting mainly knowledge that is masculine in form and content.

Practical Rationalities

Practical rationalities are grounded in the daily construction of meaning through experience and discussion with others. Practical rationalities challenge the notion that experts have inherent wisdom. They encourage organization and family members to view expert or technical knowledge with suspicion. However, they also carry the burden of proof against the formidable presumption in society that certain outcomes are desirable, certain ways of achieving those outcomes are necessary, and certain ways of thinking about issues such as work-family conflict are realistic and mature. Data contrary to technical rationalities may not be believed or may be framed as isolated cases. Methods of gathering such data may be questioned as not scientific enough and findings based on specific contexts or groups of people may be considered too difficult to implement (because they may not form into easily administered general policies).

Practical knowledge is manifest in studies and practices grounded in alternative (often called women's) ways of knowing. Alternative ways of knowing are used by both men and women to develop understandings of the world that rely on personal and communal experiences (Belenky, Clinchy, Goldberger, & Tarule, 1986; Goldberger, Tarule, Clinchy, & Belenky, 1996). As people turn less toward experts for knowledge, they begin to deal with contextual complexities and their own emotional responses to situations. They critically evaluate claims by using themselves and others as knowledge bases while retaining understandings of knowledge as temporary, tentative, situated, and socially constructed.

Discourse studies of work-family discussions are consistent with practical rationalities insofar as researchers define terms and members' satisfactions from participants' own words, experiences, and feelings, even though these definitions may not coincide with prior expert interpretation. For instance, research grounded in participants' discourse finds that women workers often consider their personal and professional lives to be interrelated, so that the meanings of work and of family or personal experience are not compartmentalized (e.g., Grossman & Chester, 1990). Interpretive studies of family decision making find that participants' choices are contradictory and emotion laden. Rather than attempting to resolve contradictions or manage emotion, these studies use tensions, ironies, and feelings as sources of data to construct knowledge.

Krueger (1986) investigated whether wives in dual-career couples would exercise control and power in decision making that would correspond with their earnings or other resources. Krueger operationalized egalitarian decision-making processes as a shifting of conversational and decision-making control between partners in a fairly equal fashion. Despite varying levels of behaviors that were not equal, each couple reported high marital satisfaction suggesting that discursively constructed cooperation and perceived equity, rather than egalitarianism, may be key issues in relational satisfaction.

Studies that examine family members' talk and interactions suggest that women profess equity and satisfaction with systems that are objectively unfair. Not only is accommodation, perhaps any accommodation, to women's careers essential to their feelings of satisfaction, but women take more responsibility than men to make dual-career and family orientations work (Gilbert & Rachlin, 1987). Women may describe their relationships as egalitarian but observation reveals a relatively unequal division of household labor (Hochschild, 1989). Studies grounded in examination of talk, behavioral observations, and understanding of household situations find that thoughts and feelings about household division of labor may be influenced by gender, such that what appears as objectively unfair to an expert may be quite satisfactory to participants (Gutek, Searle, & Klepa, 1991; Hochschild, 1989).

In one investigation (Rosenbluth, Steil, & Whitcomb, 1998), when asked to define marital equality, respondents said that critical elements include reciprocity (i.e., mutual respect, commitment, and supportiveness over time) along with equal decision making and satisfaction with domestic task division. Of interest is that participants had high educational levels but half of them still reported that the husband's career was primary, and none said that the wife's career was primary. Couples who experienced satisfaction with marital equity practiced vigilance by critiquing gender injustices, enacting public acts of equality, and supporting wives' activities (Blaisure & Allen, 1995).

Rees-Edwards and Kline (2001) argued that communication is essential to the construction of egalitarian relationships. Working mothers in their study expressed distress, frustration, anger, betrayal, and stress over both work and family difficulties. These women said they handle childcare and housework on their own and have to request (or coordinate) help from their partners. This research did not indicate how partners' contradictory feelings are hidden or expressed (perhaps simultaneously) or how partners intentionally manage their feelings around other important family members. Few studies even address how nonparental family members, such as children, make sense of and manage feelings in work-family issues, thereby enabling or constraining caregivers' communicative choices (for exceptions, see Buzzanell & Turner, in press; Galinsky, 1999).

In the case of Rees-Edwards and Kline (2001), emotions figured into concerns and understandings of work-family issues. Yet, emotion is typically a secondary focus of studies, meaning that feeling expressions may be used only to support findings on other topics (Buzzanell, 1997). Feelings as sources of data to be used in intersubjectively constructing practical knowledge are downplayed or absent. Yet, the negotiation of appropriateness in public and private displays of feelings, including the context of individuals' choice and equity in family decision making, are central to understanding work-family issues for researchers and family members. Women and men may hide or trivialize childcare scheduling or other personal issues rather than engaging in discussion or expressing frustration with arrangements (see Jorgenson, 2000; Perlow, 1998).

Jorgenson (2000) found female engineers isolated themselves and their concerns in ways that inhibited dialogue. They deliberately excluded family reasons for negotiating working hours (e.g., using terms such as obligations, five o'clock, or business). Furthermore, they neither talked about nor did anything (e.g., joining the Society of Women Engineers) that could call attention to gender. By recreating a gender- and family-hostile environment, their discourse and practices maintained traditional structures and expectations but also secured their professional reputations and employability. Jorgenson focused neither on how these women felt about their need to emphasize the work aspect of their identities nor on how they could have used emotion as a basis for knowledge about themselves, their situations, or possible courses of action. Additional research focusing on emotional labor, discourse, authenticity, and construction of alternative ways of knowing would be beneficial.

This research could examine the effort that might be required in monitoring conversations to appear professional in a masculine working culture or to be nurturing and caring as mothers and fathers under stressful work situations. Medved (2000) could describe the feelings of the woman who calls her mother in to help with childcare when her workload escalates and her husband refuses to help. It would be interesting to uncover what she chooses to express, why, to whom, and under what conditions. If this woman talked to other women, studying how she expressed her anger and resentment (or elected not to do so) within different groups as well as how she gained different forms of communal support from these conversations (see Golden, 2002) would contribute to work-family understandings (see Sigel, 1996).

Underlying this discussion of work-family conflict and decision making is the idealized theme of "balance" that depicts individuals in unconstrained careers. Balance is seen as an individual family endeavor and a desirable outcome in and of itself (Fondas, 1995). By placing the burden on individuals, this view of balance mitigates against the development of diverse, personal ways of knowing that are intersubjectively constructed. In addition, the ability to create practical knowledge is curtailed. Today's boundaryless career also may inhibit development of both balance and practical knowledge. In its prototypical form, this career type necessitates geographical mobility, lack of ties to an organization or local community, and transactional exchange thinking, among other qualities (see Buzzanell, 2000). Fletcher and Bailyn (1996) illustrate how the unconstrained individual depicted in boundaryless-career materials lacks family and community involvement, making work and family adversarial rather than mutually synergistic areas of life.

Beginning research with a discursive lens allows for a communication-centered framework to explore these and other work-family issues. Rather than relying on technical rationalities that use experts and attempt to predict or control behavior, this discussion focuses on how people construct knowledge through living, examining, and discussing their own experiences. As an example of a move toward the generation of practical knowledge, Medved (2002) challenges researchers to embed balance within communication networks and discursive communities. This kind of move would foreground the contributions of communication research and thinking within work-family literature.

Seeking Empowerment Through Embracing Practical Knowledge

In order to empower research and practice through the problematic of rationality, we advocate that work-family researchers establish research agendas that incorporate knowledge created through lived experience. We also advocate that researchers dialogue with others about meanings and possibilities in this lived experience. We believe the tensions between technical/expert and practical rationalities are productive, contributing to opportunities for locating generalizable findings and policies as well as adaptations desirable for specific groups. Elaborating on the rationality problematic suggests researchers question power relations and how they developed over time in work-family models, definitions, and language.

One way of interrogating power imbalances is by critiquing current work-family models and practices as being the only sensible models. Barnett and Hyde (2001) examine assumptions that work-family conflict exists and is detrimental to individuals. Although they advocate an expansionist model based on research that displays the benefits of multiple roles for women and men, they also demonstrate where and how current and past research, derived from White, middle-class professionals and managers, may not be as positive. Communication scholars could supplement their model by presenting findings from emotion-centered and standpoint perspectives. These approaches would facilitate researchers' questioning about what is reasonable and equitable from the perspectives of diverse stakeholders.[4]

Of great importance for empowerment is the admission of data generated from different rationalities into corporate and family decision making. If researchers as well as organization and family members recognize that expert rationalities do not materialize from out of nowhere, they can expose how current work-family understandings and practices have emerged from the specific, lived, material conditions of people's lives. For instance, home management developed when scientific language and techniques became preferred over localized solutions and as industrialization limited the pool of domestic workers for upper- and middle-class White households at the turn of the 20th century (Graham, 1999). More recently, the prototypical organizational man (White, middle-class, married, professional or managerial) would have had no need for work-family policies because of separate work-family divisions of marital labor in the past. Yet, the contemporary dual-career couple has brought work-family dilemmas to the forefront (in ways that lower-class dual-earner couples could not).

Over time, locally manufactured solutions to daily work-family problems became legitimized to the point where workers often did not rethink the problem. Workers did not question the ways in which particular ways of forming knowledge (and offering solutions) secured advantages for certain groups. Advice to outsource household chores presumes that individuals have sufficient finances; similarly, advice to negotiate time and roles assumes that individuals have the ability, slack time, status, and favorable labor market conditions to raise issues or take action if their needs remain unmet. Individuals may fail to challenge corporate and media role models, which are often offered as proof that work-family balance can be achieved successfully. Additionally, individuals may not recognize the infrastructure supporting these role models' ability to balance work-family demands. If individuals buy into the idea of work-family balance and the superwoman ideal, they may blame themselves when they fall short.

There is an ongoing shifting of knowledge occurring through technical/expert and practical rationalities that should become ever more apparent when communication scholars undertake work-family research. The merging and admissibility of data across and within discourses aligned with these rationalities needs to be explored to uncover how change takes place between these rationalities and how they inform each other. The important issues in empowerment are how certain rationalities have come to exist in our lives, and how dominant meanings, terms, and outcomes are produced and reproduced. How do (and why would) individuals subscribe to constructions of themselves as nonexperts in work-family discussions? Researchers could investigate instances when presence is not assumed and how people talk to each other differently about their nonwork activities (e.g., Munck, 2001). If researchers use both types of knowledge orientation, they can locate ways within individuals' talk to reconstruct meanings of work and honor individuals' and families' rights to develop their human potential in multiple realms. In this process, we argue it is important to move from including only dominant voices to incorporating a multiplicity of diverse perspectives in issues of work and family.

VOICE PROBLEMATIC: DOMINANT INTERESTS TO MULTIPLE VOICES

The problematic of voice reflects on ways certain interests, such as those of corporations, the dominant culture, or the "generalized other" are privileged over those of family and the "concrete other" (see Haas & Deetz, 2000; Mumby & Stohl, 1996). We situate selected interdisciplinary and communication work-family research within three dominant voices: (a) the managerial or corporate voice, (b) the traditional family, and (c) the upper- or middle-class, White, professional woman. By attending to a narrow set of voices, work-family scholarship has constrained and naturalized our definitions of legitimate work-family issues for research and policy making, minimizing the potential range of ideas and ways of knowing that can contribute to a dialogue for change.

We see an opportunity to reenvision work-family research as a field where multiple concerns are identified and located as they sculpt work-family practices, policies, and outcomes through access to voice, acknowledgment of different voices, and critique of dominant voices. As hooks (2000) illustrates, the history of the second-wave feminist movement has shaped the discourse of women and work primarily through the voices of educated White women. When discourse is shaped to meet different stakeholder needs, voices may be distorted, silenced, trivialized, co-opted, or combined into a chorus that can resist disempowerment overtly and covertly (see Putnam et al., 1996). These diverse voices can be partly heard through inclusion of marginalized voices as participants in our research as well as in decision making on organizational policies.

Managerial or Corporate Voices

In work-family research and practice, the managerial or corporate voice has usurped the special qualities and interests of family in a number of different ways. The justification for organizational work-family policies is often legitimized through the discourse of technical rationality, using the language of financial contribution or bottom-line arguments (see Bailyn et al., 1997). Issues such as corporate sponsored childcare are labeled as competitive and strategic issues (Kossek, Dass, & DeMarr, 1994). Work-family practices then only become valuable as recruitment and retention tools (Honeycutt & Rosen, 1997) or as ways to reduce absenteeism and tardiness (Miranda & Murphy, 1993). Attention is primarily paid to how work-family programs impact corporate interests in terms of worker productivity related to employee stress (MacDermid, Williams, & Marks, 1994; Warren & Johnson, 1995), morale (Rapoport & Bailyn, 1996), job satisfaction (Gonyea & Googins, 1992), and organizational commitment (Grover & Crooker, 1995; Orthner & Pittman, 1986).

In allowing the corporate voice to co-opt employee family concerns, we perpetuate management's use of the generalized other in making decisions. Individuals abide by decision-making procedures that shut down or constrain the dialogue about work-family issues that could occur between management and employees (Haas & Deetz, 2000). Other justifications for the organizational implementation of work-family policies, such as family as a social good or organizations as community actors, are not seen as valid when the corporation is ultimately perceived to be the most powerful social institution.

Deetz (1992) argued that the predominance of corporate life has essentially colonized or taken precedence over family life. The structuring of work and family routines around the patterns of organizational life can be seen in our definitions of careers and career progression (Buzzanell & Goldzwig, 1991; Mumby, 1988), underlying assumptions about work (Perlow, 1995), and decisions about geographic mobility, timing of reproduction, and child-rearing practices (Deetz, 1992). Perlow (1995) explains the reproduction of assumptions about presence or face time through structuration theory (Giddens, 1984), but fails to critically question the power of the organization to sequester, counteract, and devalue employees' stories of work experiences, which contradict these assumptions. An organization's capacity to control the definition of the "ideal worker" reflects "the ability of the powerful to 'fix' meaning in ways that serve the interests of the powerful (organization)" (Mumby, 1998, p. 168). Further, Hochschild (1997) argued that work may provide a haven from family conflict for many employees overwhelmed by attempting to balance multiple sets of responsibility. Kirby (2000b) analyzed the tension between the managerial voice and the employee voice through exploring mixed messages that surround the utilization of work-family policies. She asserted that although managers profess the importance of balancing work and family, their emphasis on deadlines and role-modeling of virtual workaholics negates the emphasis on family.

The importance of industry competition reflects yet another representation of the corporate voice. Gonyea and Googins (1992) note "as corporate work-family programs have moved from the curious to the mainstream, they have also moved from the lifestyle pages to the business section of the newspapers" (p. 210). As a result, public attention to these issues has increased and work-family initiatives at one company are made known to employees and managers in other companies (Goodstein, 1994). According to institutional theory, this increased attention creates pressure for organizations to respond—thus, the adoption of childcare, eldercare, and workplace flexibility benefits is a tangible accommodation to institutional pressures; it signals to important constituents that an organization is responsive (Goodstein, 1994; Milliken, Dutton, & Beyer, 1990). The corporate voice of concern may be institutionalizing these policies and benefits to remain competitive rather than because management truly supports such initiatives (Goodstein, 1994).

Traditional Family Voices

In addition to the corporation, the dominance of supposedly traditional nuclear family structures and definitions cannot be denied in work-family research. Research within and outside the field of communication tends to rely on data sets of dual-career or single-earner, heterosexual, married couples with children, or the standard North American family (Smith, 1993). Ironically, households that consist of two biological parents and children represent less than a quarter of American families today (U.S. Census, 2001).

Coontz (1992) argues the 1950's *Ozzie and Harriet* definitions of the traditional, nuclear family are more myth than historical truth. We have a long history in the U.S. of diverse family structures that are not often reflected in the work and family equation. Current census data reveal the number of unmarried couples living together in the U.S.—nearly 5.5 million couples—has almost doubled since 1990 (U.S. Census Bureau, 2001). In addition, there were 9.8 million single mothers in 1998 and men comprised one sixth of the nation's single-parent households (U.S. Census Bureau, 1998). A variety of two-parent household arrangements (i.e., step- or blended families, nonmarried parents, and extended family relationships) are now the majority of U.S. households where children are present (U.S. Census Bureau, 2001).

In line with the traditional family voice, a number of communication researchers have explored interaction in dual-career couples. Rosenfeld et al. (1995) developed a typology of dual-career marriages, whereas Heacock and Spicer (1986) assessed communication variables across the dual-career literature. Wood (1986) questioned the role of internal structuring in the maintenance of dual-career marriages. Dual-career couples' decision-making patterns have also been explored, and it was found "that no predictable relationship exists between observed decision making egalitarianism and (marital) satisfaction" (Krueger, 1986, p. 278).

Finally, levels of self-disclosure were characterized as more equal in dual-career couples (Rosenfeld & Welsh, 1985). Although communication research from within the dual-career framework provides insight into the communicative practices of one particular segment of our population, it also serves to silence the voices of others who experience work and family from within diverse family structures. Unfortunately, such research may perpetuate myths about the primacy of parents in child rearing and the lack of need for community and governmental support (Coontz, 1992).

Parents are often privileged as the individuals worthy of concern in work-family research, however, others within the family structure are impacted as well, including children and, potentially, the parents of workers in cases of eldercare. Although most authors acknowledge the limitations of their sample, these frequent admissions of exclusion have not appeared to significantly influence researchers to do work outside the traditional family paradigm (Smith, 1993). Only a limited amount of work-family research conducted by communication scholars has not conformed to traditional notions of family. As an exception, Edley and Bihn (2001) explored the lived experiences of seven single mothers, detailing their methods of structuring work and time with their children. One finding was that although mothers with girls spoke of what "we would do," reflecting their daughters as a part of themselves, the woman who had a son spoke of how she "drags him along," reflecting a separation that may cause additional strain in terms of the parenting role.

The traditional family label not only suppresses voices of individuals in diverse heterosexual family structures but also sequesters the voices that challenge the definition of family. Using the term family often neglects large segments of the population who might classify themselves as without family in these discussions because they lack relationships with partners, do not have children (see Hall, 1996), or maintain long-term, homosexual relationships not legally recognized as families. Research on work-family challenges for homosexual couples or families are virtually, to our knowledge, nonexistent in the literature; however, dual-career challenges are certainly not confined to heterosexual relationships.

Finally, even the juxtaposition and domination of the label "work-family" versus "work-life" connotes a privileging or valuing of children as a legitimate family over alternative possibilities for a life that consists of other nonwork activities. Although the term work-life has gained some recognition over the past years, work-family policies are predominantly designed around the needs of employees with children, not interests in community volunteering, physical or spiritual health, or other life interests. In addition, the term work-life continues to perpetuate the myth of separate spheres. A modest discourse of backlash toward the privileging of children has begun to be heard (in organizations such as the Childfree Network) but remains relatively quiet (Flynn, 1996). Kirby and Krone (2002) found that single employees in an organization with family-friendly benefits complained of preferential treatment for those with more traditional families.

Middle-Class, Professional, White Women's Voices

Work-family research is also strongly overlaid with class, gender, and race or ethnicity assumptions. Much of the discussion about women's choices about work, couples' decision making, couples' sources of conflict, and men's ability to sustain manly roles (e.g., breadwinner) are based on middle- to upper-middle class, professional, White women as participants and researchers. We do not argue that this standpoint lacks value, but rather that we need to acknowledge its existence and influence as well as allow for a greater range of voices in work-family research.

First, classist assumptions are found throughout work-family literature. Discussions about women's primary responsibility for outsourcing childcare duties (Hochschild, 1997) are laden with assumptions about the financial ability to pay for childcare services. The very concept of "balance" carries the connotation of an element of choice to participate in both the paid labor market and unpaid childcare work (Johnson, 2001). Women of lower socioeconomic status have never had and do not have the option to choose whether to work for pay, indeed, they have often provided the services that free upper-class women to "balance" (hooks, 2000). Given the decline in real wages, particularly in the late decades of the 20th century, two incomes were necessary for survival—not for balance—in most poor families (Coontz, 1992). As time limits legislated by the 1996 welfare reform laws begin to run out, particularly temporary aid to needy families, lower socioeconomic women cannot choose to remain at home to care for their children. They must attain employment, regardless of the real trade-off between minimum wages and the cost of (often substandard) childcare.

In addition to classist definitions of balance, the very definition of work versus career is imbued with assumptions about socioeconomic status. Research on blue-collar career development has been limited to date (Schroedel, 1990; Thomas, 1989). Thomas (1989) argued that working-class careers are often devalued due to the constraints, limited mobility, and social perceptions of blue-collar workers—even to the point that these careers have not been sufficiently considered in research and have been referred to as merely jobs. According to Thomas, the social milieu of class, organizational arrangement of occupations, and labor market segmentation, influence the structure of blue-collar career opportunities; these same conditions would also shape the constraints within which working-class employees manage their work and family responsibilities.

Some communication research has attempted to explore classist assumptions in work-family research. Medved (2000) explored the concept of career through the lens of standpoint feminist theory and argued that classist assumptions about work-family must be revealed.[5] Johnson (2001) argued that the semantic separation of the concept of working mother privileges certain social classes. As she notes, "Working class women have been working all along, unaided by public attention to their circumstances; they are, moreover, excluded from many usages of the term (working mother) because their experiences arise from necessity and not option" (p. 25).

The inherently racist bias in work-family research must also be confronted. Work-family communication research has only been challenged from the perspective of race in a very limited way. We return to Johnson's (2001) work that delved into the linguistic construction of working mother from the perspective of race. Similar to issues of class, the historical participation of women of color in the paid labor force has often been ignored. Much work and family research for over 35 years has continued to justify itself with the claim of a "growing number of working mothers" (p. 25); this should read as a "growing number of *White, middle-class* working mothers." Johnson also connects notions of race with the dominance of the traditional family voice. For example, cultural practices of *othermothers* in the African American culture (Collins, 1990 as cited in Johnson, 2001) are not explored in the work and family research that allows only for a narrow definition of family.

In addition to the classist and racist assumptions of work and family research, the voice of men is not represented in much work-family research. As Mumby (1998) states, "men have gender too" (p. 164). By continuing to study and define work-family as only a woman's issue, we not only devalue or ignore men's experiences of conflict, stress, and challenge they face in managing work and family issues, we also continue to constrain the possibilities of change for women as we "conflate 'women' and 'gender'" (p. 164). Yet, as Kirby (2000a) discovered, such research is not always straightforward; when interviewing both men and women about their work-family experiences, men in the study often defined childcare and other responsibilities as their wife's job. Masculinity and femininity must be explored as coconstructing and constraining discourses in relation to work-family issues.

Researchers have found that a majority of men consider their family role as more important than their work role, and many men are concerned that they do not spend enough time with their children (Jacobsen & Edmonson, 1993). Employee reports indicate that work-life balance is of equal importance to both men and women (Hall, 1990). Fathers who want to be involved are choosing employment that makes it easier to balance family with workplace obligations, even at the expense of lower pay and prestige (Gerson, 1993). Nonetheless, among many researchers there is considerable skepticism that family-supportive policies are relevant for men (Pleck, 1993). Although work-family benefits and parental leave are theoretically open to both men and women, men are not expected to use them— traditional gender role conceptions of parenting responsibilities still dominate (Pleck, 1993; Raabe & Gessner, 1988; Rapoport & Bailyn, 1996; Shellenbarger, 1992). Employed fathers report that employers, supervisors, and male coworkers do not look favorably upon men taking parental leave (Haas & Hwang, 1995).

Such traditional gender role conceptions reinforce the expectation for male workers that they must subjugate their family's needs and keep quiet about balance in order to advance professionally (Hall, 1990). Research has shown men who take advantage of parental leaves or other flexible work benefits are seen as eccentrics who are not serious about their careers (Hall, 1990). Men may make work-family accommodations or adaptations, but do so in nonpublic ways that are more informal and less visible than are women's (Hall, 1990; J. Levine, 1991; Pleck, 1993; Shellenbarger, 1992). If a father with flextime changes his schedule, it may simply not occur to coworkers and supervisors that a childcare need or desire to spend more time with his family is the reason for the change (Pleck, 1993). Similar oversights result in the "invisibility of flextime as a male work-family accommodation, which further reinforces the stereotype that fathers do not adjust or limit their work role to meet family obligations" (Pleck, 1993, p. 225).

To sum up, multiple voices define and shape the experiences of work and family in everyday life, although this insight has yet to significantly reshape our research agendas. A necessity in work-family research is not just the hearing of multiple voices or the inclusion of marginalized populations, but a fundamental questioning of key assumptions and language. The powerful voices of the corporation, the traditional family, and the White, professional woman inherently bias our everyday discourses about work and nonwork domains of life. Researchers must explore how they can empower communication research agendas through multiple voices.

Seeking Empowerment Through Diverse Voices

Empowerment through hearing and honoring the multiple voices in communication research on work-family or work-life issues would open up many possibilities in scholarship and practice. Empowerment can occur through exploring the discourses previously silenced, acknowledging the differences among voices, and by challenging the dominant voices of the corporation, the traditional family, and the White, middle-class woman. Opening up this dialogue means a commitment not just to making different decisions, but also enacting different decision-making procedures in organizations (Haas & Deetz, 2000). In absence of voice, employees find strategies to undermine or resist organizational authority (Medved, 2002; Murphy, 1998).

First, we must conduct communication research into the work-family processes of people who are different from the usual respondent pool. Research on immigrant groups or migrant workers would significantly inform the literature. Additionally, studies on expatriate families' work and family struggles would provide information on the different micro- and macrolevel discursive processes involved in work-family issues across cultures. Discussions about relocation, loss of a partner's work, family members' adjustment, and related issues have also not been framed as work-family topics (one exception is Hardill & MacDonald, 1998).

Breaking down heterosexist norms in research by exploring how lesbian and gay couples manage talk about family in the workplace needs to be investigated. Heterosexual couples have the luxury of being able to explain the need for a day off because of a sick spouse or child. Yet, gay men and lesbian employees often practice distancing from coworkers to avoid exchanging personal information (Spradlin, 1998). How do these workers balance work-family when the relationship of a partner is not one socially sanctioned or accepted by a supervisor or written in an organizational policy? There may be different impression management, passing, and silencing processes involved (e.g., Spradlin, 1998). Although heterosexual couples may find it easier to talk about work-family issues during employment interviews, some gay men and lesbians may not be able to interpret cues or find ways to inquire about work-family policies (see Woods, 1993).

The voices of single parents must also be heard and explored in research and practice. These households may not have back-up plans for emergency childcare or eldercare (Edley & Bihn, 2001). There may be no one to pick up the slack if a worker needs flexibility to complete urgent work tasks. Single-parent households may not have the benefit of these kinds of flexibilities. Work-family decision making does not occur with a relational partner, but perhaps with childcare or eldercare providers, former spouses through custody agreements, or between parent and child as children get older. Differences between how single fathers and single mothers experience and interact with others in order to manage work and family are also open for exploration. The discourse of stay-at-home parents, both fathers and mothers, should be examined and situated as participation in valuable work.

Finally, we need to explicitly recognize in our research (whether it is a focus of the study or not) that a family is not limited to having children. Current research deals primarily with balancing childcare responsibilities and paid labor. But in an era of the "sandwich generation," eldercare (or both childcare and eldercare) are the salient issues. The voices of individuals, with or without children, who are experiencing work-family conflict as they care for elder parents must also be acknowledged in communication research and practice.

To hear these voices described above, we must not only include marginalized groups as participants, but more fundamentally we must begin communication inquiry from the perspectives of the marginalized (Grossman & Chester, 1990). How do we theorize about or explore the work-family discourse of single fathers? How are the work-family stories of gay and lesbian employees sequestered in everyday organizational communication? How is balance discursively constructed for employees engaged in shift work? How do children contribute to the dialogue of work-family in households?[6] These efforts at redefining long-standing concepts in work-family and work-life research could be explored through the development of different standpoints (Hartsock, 1998). Buzzanell (2001) explored the narrative of a disabled, pregnant employee to provide insight into her lived experience and into how interactions with her coworkers changed throughout this experience.

We argue that the voicing of the marginalized carries the potential for empowerment, however, the very fact of marginalization places a considerable responsibility on researchers. We must use every available research and reporting technique to ensure the representation created is as true as possible (see Cameron, Frazer, Harvey, Rampton, & Richardson, 1993). Finally, we need to address the issue of voice in the language used to define work and family. Different people and institutions (e.g., welfare) define work and families differently, but work-family research typically limits itself to predictable organizations and predictable family structures. What we want to do by empowering through voice is to articulate complex and diverse meanings so that work and family constitute multiple realities— not a homogenized picture.

To this point, our links to empowerment have largely focused on individual research agendas, or actions of empowerment that can be taken by individuals to negotiate work-family relationships. As Trethewey (1997) argued, although individual acts of resistance empower individuals, full empowerment requires understanding individual problems not just as the consequences of personal shortcomings but as manifestations of societal failures. We assert the same understanding is needed in thinking about work-family theory and practice. We need to articulate (and voice) a communal orientation as a final means to seeking empowerment.

Seeking Empowerment Through Voicing a Communal Orientation

Other nations (e.g., Sweden) show more of a communal orientation toward issues of work and family by mandating policies such as parental leave (Haas & Hwang, 1995). In the U.S., such leave is framed as a benefit rather than a necessity or right. The Family Medical Leave Act of 1993 is a start toward providing mechanisms for workers to take time for family when needed, but it still does not provide for paid leave and often requires extensive documentation. Yet, there has not been an organized push for widespread change because in an individualistic, achieving society, balance between work and personal life is not always seen as a high priority goal; instead, career and work success are often more important (Auerbach, 1988).

By defining work and family conflict as an individual, primarily psychological experience, we deny that conflict is also constructed within family, organization, and community relationships and structures. The U.S. "survival of the fittest" mentality implies that if an individual is unable to manage his or her own work-family concerns, then he or she is at fault. In other words, the privatization of work-family conflict as an individual failing serves to deny the structural and societal causes of such difficulties (Andrews & Bailyn, 1993; Rapoport & Bailyn, 1996). We fail to see how our ideology of individualism negates framing work and family issues as a communal problem. This is disempowering because such denial prohibits us from taking the "opportunity to act" (Chiles & Zorn, 1995, p. 2) toward revision of these structures.

As Clinton (1996) articulated, "It takes a village to raise a child." Everyone benefits when society raises strong and capable children, as well as when we take care of our elders. However, in the U.S., we rarely hear such a collective orientation—instead, we find work-family accommodations designed to help individual workers in their daily lives. But a potential mismatch exists between these accommodations and the ideology of individualism found in the discourse of worker-parents who are the supposed users of these programs (Golden, 2000). Individuals interested in utilizing a work-family program must consider the reactions of supervisors and coworkers. Supervisors may send mixed (or negative) messages about such policies because they make it difficult to accomplish work in traditional ways (Kirby, 2000b; Perlow, 1995; Rees-Edwards, 1997). Concomitantly, discourses of resentment and backlash may emerge from coworkers who feel they are unfairly being discriminated against in that people with families get preferential treatment (Kirby & Krone, 2002).

Because work-family programs are often merely added onto the system of employee benefits without changing the culture or daily work practices, these accommodations are often underutilized. Consequently, many employees with children—men and women—keep their family concerns separate from work in order to be seen as committed and professional. This is disempowering because it bifurcates identity, and if we could rid organizations of norms of presence such behavior would no longer be necessary. Research is beginning to emphasize the importance of culture change in organizations for true transformation to occur (Bailyn, 1993; Perlow, 1995, 1997; Rapoport & Bailyn, 1996). Schor (1991) suggested changes to organizational policy, proposing (a) shorter work weeks, (b) set hours for every job, (c) overtime paid back with time off work rather than money, and (d) collective action taken to make part-time work more feasible (also see Ciulla, 2000). We agree that organizations (and their policies) are a starting point for changes, yet we further assert that to fully realize empowerment, we also need to reenvision the cultural norms and ideologies of our society as a whole.

Although norms of presence may be attributed to organizations, cultural values that equate job with self-worth, as well as stereotypical gender roles, are attributable to broader societal ideologies. Because the meaning of gender is constantly negotiated, the ways we enact gender are open to situational and cultural changes that can create greater or lesser equity in work-family (West & Zimmerman, 1987). Ciulla (2000) argued that ongoing gendered work-family discussions and changes are critical to reframing the meaning of work. One gendered practice that warrants particular attention from a communal perspective is appreciating, as a community and a society, what caregiving actually means (Wood, 1994)—especially in the family realm.

As Seery and Crowley (2000) illustrated, women encounter additional complexities in family work, especially in doing emotion work. Women construct warmth and a social sense of family, yet this work is often not rewarded. This caregiving or concern for relationships often translates to work behaviors that are an added burden (or joy in many cases) for women that can be detrimental to careers (i.e., that take time from role obligations written into job descriptions; Kolb, 1992). Without a reprioritization of family and community in our thinking, language, and material practices, gendered work-family practices and processes cannot change in ways that can benefit both women and men.

A true step toward empowerment in practice would provide for participatory decision processes that question current priorities regarding work, family, and community. Empowerment would occur through a recognition that universal policies for work-family issues always leave someone out and that therefore, established policies do not go far enough to meet individuals' concerns. Instead, we need more innovative avenues for incorporating voices into policy formation. Empowerment may come by redefining what constitutes work-family and what constitutes a moral commitment to assisting different segments of our society. If it truly takes a village, what are family responsibilities? What are organizational responsibilities? What are governmental responsibilities? And indeed, what are global responsibilities?

To summarize, we see a means to empowerment as encouraging overt and covert resistance to the argument that women and men must balance work-family life. By prioritizing balance over informed identification with one or the other sphere, a foundation is laid for continuing conflicts. By prioritizing balance over other ways of maintaining dialectical tensions over the course of career and life phases, we tend not to envision a series of temporary and shifting solutions (see Baxter & Montgomery, 1996). We tend not to see how the ironic and contradictory juxtapositions of dominant discourses and individual or family needs provide opportunities for constructing radically different solutions on local levels that can potentially interact with and transform larger discourses of inequity. We also tend not to form alliances with others to locate collective solutions to these issues (e.g., neighborhood families coming together to discuss how they can create better solutions). Given this knowledge, communication researchers are uniquely situated to initiate dialogue concerning the micro- and macrodiscourses that sustain traditional work-family research agendas and practices.

CONCLUSION

This review illustrates four problematics that underlie work-family theory, research, and practice that become evident though a discourse perspective: (a) boundaries, (b) identity, (c) rationality, and (d) voice. By providing a foundation in interdisciplinary studies and amending such research with pieces in communication that begin to reenvision the discourse, we hope to have set an agenda for work-family and work-life research in the discipline of communication. Our attempts to ground this review in empowerment provide possibilities (in both research and practice) for (a) questioning boundaries, (b) integrating identity, (c) embracing practical knowledge and emotionality, (d) seeking diverse voices, and (e) developing a communal orientation. We challenge researchers to critically examine daily, microlevel discourses that communicatively construct work and family as a step toward enacting positive and empowering changes in the macrodiscourses of organizations and families.

NOTES

1. In much work-family literature, the term "balance" is treated as a given desired end result. Thus, much research relies on the term work-family balance, balancing work and family, and so forth. We place the word in quotes to illustrate an understanding that this language choice also sets up value judgments that such an ideal is preferable and possible.

2. Some researchers argue the term work-family both inadequately represents the workforce and unnecessarily restricts academic and popular discussion to concerns about balancing children's and employers' needs. For instance, approximately a third of the U.S. labor force consists of men and women who are not in long-term relationships and who do not have dependent children (Young, 1996). Moreover, work-family "balance" often is used to describe a desirable end in itself with families be-

coming isolated from community networks that could assist in negotiating work-life tensions (Fondas, 1995). Finally, the term work-life considers the personal needs of single workers and family members in ways that are not reflected in work-family discussions (e.g., Friedman, Christensen, & DeGroot, 1998). We choose work-family because a majority of literature to this point has used this conception. This is not to say that in our own research we do not recognize the need to conceptualize this dilemma at the broader level of work-life.

3. Our approach to the study of work-life relationships as a collection of problematics is informed by Mumby and Stohl's (1996) problematics of organizational communication. Like Mumby and Stohl, we have a dual purpose. First, we seek to identify what is problematic in the approaches of other disciplines in order to understand work-family relationships. Our problematics provide an interpretive framework that unifies existing communication based research on work-family relationships and points toward an agenda for further inquiry into this area from within the communication discipline. We found two of the specific problematics that Mumby and Stohl delineated in the context of organizational communication—voice and rationality—to be particularly helpful in identifying aspects of work-life relationships that remain underexamined. Like Mumby and Stohl, we acknowledge the divisions between the different problematics are permeable and the scheme presented here is intended to be functional rather than definitive. In fact, we assert that conflict, contradictions, and dialectics are actually present in all of the problematics.

4. Standpoint theories situate women's experiences within the unique conditions and socio-cultural-economic-historical contexts of their lives and derive understandings of how systemic forces contribute to continuing marginalization and oppression (see Harding, 1991). Our standpoints externalize women's struggles to "see beneath the appearances created by an unjust social order to illuminate how this social order is in fact constructed and maintained" (Harding, 1991, p. 127). Standpoints are political insofar as they explore the details of people's lives to raise consciousness, build theory, and encourage change (O'Brien-Hallstein, 2000).

5. Although we speak about feminist standpoint theory in reference to Medved's (2000) research, we acknowledge that multiple standpoint theories exist (Hartstock, 1998).

6. We would like to thank Kathleen Galvin for her comments at the Atlanta meeting of the National Communication Association in 2001 that inspired this line of inquiry.

REFERENCES

Albrecht, T. L. (1988). Communication and personal control in empowering organizations. In J. A. Anderson (Ed.), *Communication yearbook 11* (pp. 380–390). Thousand Oaks, CA: Sage.

Allen, T. D., & Russell, J. E. (1999). Parental leave of absence: Some not-so-family friendly implications. *Journal of Applied Social Psychology, 29*, 166–191.

Andrews, A., & Bailyn, L. (1993). Segmentation and synergy: Two models of linking work and family. In J. C. Hood (Ed.), *Men, work, and family* (pp. 262–275). Newbury Park, CA: Sage.

Aryee, S., & Luk, V. (1996). Balancing two major parts of adult life experience: Work and family identity among dual-earner couples. *Human Relations, 49*, 465–487.

Ashcraft, K. L. (2000). Empowering "professional" relationships: Organizational communication meets feminist practice. *Management Communication Quarterly, 13*, 347–392.

Auerbach, J. D. (1988). *In the business of child care: Employer initiative and working women.* New York: Praeger.

Bailyn, L. (1992). Issues of work and family in different national contexts: How the United States, Britain, and Sweden respond. *Human Resource Management, 31*, 201–208.

Bailyn, L. (1993). *Breaking the mold: Women, men, and time in the new corporate world.* New York: Free Press.

Bailyn, L., Fletcher, J. K., & Kolb, D. (1997). Unexpected connections: Considering employees' personal lives can revitalize your business. *Sloan Management Review, 38*, 11–19.

Bardo, D. H., Shehan, C. L., & Leslie, G. R. (1987). A residue of tradition: Jobs, careers, and spouses' time in housework. *Journal of Marriage and the Family, 49,* 381–390.

Barker, J. R. (1993). Tightening the iron cage: Concertive control in self-managing teams. *Administrative Science Quarterly, 38,* 408–437.

Barker, J. R. (1999). *The discipline of teamwork: Participation and concertive control.* Thousand Oaks, CA: Sage.

Barnett, R. C. (1994). Home-to-work spillover revisited: A study of full-time employed women in dual-earner couples. *Journal of Marriage and the Family, 56,* 647–656.

Barnett, R. C., & Hyde, J. S. (2001). Women, men, work, and family: An expansionist theory. *American Psychologist, 56,* 781–796.

Barnett, R. C., Marshall, N., & Pleck, J. (1992). Men's multiple roles and their relationship to men's psychological distress. *Journal of Marriage and the Family, 54,* 358–367.

Barnett, R. C., & Rivers, C. (1996). *She works/he works: How two-income families are happier, healthier, and better off.* New York: HarperCollins.

Barrett, F., Thomas, G., & Hocevar, S. (1995). The central role of discourse in large-scale change: A social construction perspective. *Journal of Applied Behavior Science, 31,* 352–372.

Baxter, L. A., & Montgomery, B. M. (1996). *Relating: Dialogues and dialectics.* New York: Guilford.

Bedeian, A. G., Burke, B. G., & Moffett, R. G. (1988). Outcomes of work-family conflict among married male and female professionals. *Journal of Management, 14,* 475–491.

Belenky, M. F., Clinchy, B., Goldberger, N. R., & Tarule, J. M. (1986). *Women's ways of knowing: The development of self, voice, and mind.* New York: Basic Books.

Benokraitis, N. V., & Feagin, J. R. (1986). *Modern sexism: Blatant, subtle, and covert discrimination.* Englewood Cliffs, NJ: Prentice-Hall.

Blaisure, K. R., & Allen, K. R. (1995). Feminists and the ideology and practice of marital equality. *Journal of Marriage and the Family, 57,* 5–19.

Blau, F. D., & Ferber, M. A. (1986). *The economics of women, men, and work.* Englewood Cliffs, NJ: Prentice-Hall.

Blumer, H. (1969). *Symbolic interactionism: Perspective and method.* Berkeley: University of California Press.

Brines, J. (1994). Economic dependency, gender, and the division of labor at home. *American Journal of Sociology, 100,* 652–688.

Burden, D. S., & Googins, B. (1987). *Balancing job and homelife study.* Boston: Boston University, School of Social Work.

Burke, R. J. (1989). Some antecedents and consequences of work-family conflict. In E. B. Goldsmith (Ed.), *Work and family: Theory, research, and applications* (pp. 287–302). Newbury Park, CA: Sage.

Burpitt, W. J., & Bigoness, W. J. (1997). Leadership and innovation among teams: The impact of empowerment. *Small Group Research, 28,* 414–423.

Buzzanell, P. M. (1997). Toward an emotion-based feminist framework for research on dual career couples. *Women and Language, 20*(2), 40–48.

Buzzanell, P. M. (2000). The promise and practice of the new career and social contract: Illusions exposed and suggestions for reform. In P. M. Buzzanell (Ed.), *Rethinking organizational and managerial communication from feminist perspectives* (pp. 209–235). Thousand Oaks, CA: Sage.

Buzzanell, P. M. (2001, November). *Maternity leave discourse: A feminist standpoint analysis of different women's experiences.* Paper presented at the annual meeting of the National Communication Association, Atlanta, GA.

Buzzanell, P. M., & Goldzwig, S. (1991). Linear and nonlinear career models: Metaphors, paradigms, and ideologies. *Management Communication Quarterly, 4,* 466–505.

Buzzanell, P. M., & Turner, L. H. (in press). Emotion work revealed by job loss discourse: Backgrounding-foregrounding of feelings, construction of normalcy, and (re)instituting of traditional masculinities. *Journal of Applied Communication Research.*

Cameron, D., Frazer, E., Harvey, P., Rampton, B., & Richardson, K. (1993). Ethics, advocacy, and empowerment: Issues of method in researching language. *Language and Communication, 13,* 81–94.

Caproni, P. (1997). Work/life balance: You can't get there from here. *Journal of Applied Behavioral Science, 33*, 46–56.

Chiles, A. M., & Zorn, T. E. (1995). Empowerment in organizations: Employees' perceptions of the influences on empowerment. *Journal of Applied Communication Research, 23*, 1–25.

Chow, E. N., & Berheide, C. W. (1988). The interdependence of family and work: A framework for family life education, policy, and practice. *Family Relations, 37*, 23–28.

Ciulla, J. (2000). *The working life: The promise and betrayal of modern work.* New York: Crown.

Clark, S. C. (2000). Work/family border theory: A new theory of work/family balance. *Human Relations, 53*, 747–770.

Clinton, H. R. (1996). *It takes a village: And other lessons children teach us.* New York: Simon & Schuster.

Coontz, S. (1992). *The way we never were: American families and the nostalgia trap.* New York: Basic Books.

Covin, T. J., & Brush, C. C. (1993). A comparison of student and human resource professional attitudes toward work and family issues. *Group & Organization Management, 18*, 29–49.

Deetz, S. A. (1992). *Democracy in the age of corporate colonization: Developments in communication and the politics of everyday life.* Albany: State University of New York Press.

Demos, J. (1979). Images of the American family, then and now. In V. Tufte & B. Myerhoff (Eds.), *Changing images of the family* (pp. 43–60). New Haven, CT: Yale University Press.

Dinnerstein, D. (1976). *The mermaid and the minotaur.* New York: HarperCollins.

Duxbury, L. E., & Higgins, C. A. (1991). Gender differences in work-family conflict. *Journal of Applied Psychology, 76*, 60–74.

Eagle, B. W., Miles, E. W., & Icenogle, M. L. (1997). Interrole conflicts and the permeability of work and family domains: Are there gender differences? *Journal of Vocational Behavior, 50*, 168–184.

Edley, P., & Bihn, G. (2001, May). *How single mothers balance work and family: Identity work and family/friends.* Paper presented at the annual meeting of the International Communication Association, Washington, DC.

Edwards, J. R., & Rothbard, N. P. (2000). Mechanisms linking work and family: Clarifying the relationship between work and family constructs. *Academy of Management Review, 25*, 178–199.

English-Lueck, J. A. (2002). *Cultures@Silicon Valley.* Stanford, CA: Stanford University Press.

Erickson, F., & Shultz, J. (1977). *The counselor as gatekeeper: Social interaction in interviews.* New York: Academic Press.

Faludi, S. (1991). *Backlash: The undeclared war against American women.* New York: Crown.

Farley-Lucas, B. (2000). Communicating the (in)visibility of motherhood: Family talk and the ties to motherhood with/in the workplace. *Electronic Journal of Communication, 10.* Available from http://www.cios.org/www/ejcrec2.htm

Fletcher, J., & Bailyn, L. (1996). In M. B. Arthur & D. M. Rousseau (Eds.), *The boundaryless career: A new employment principle for a new organizational era* (pp. 256–267). New York: Oxford University Press.

Flynn, G. (1996). No spouse, no kids, no respect: Backlash, why single employees are angry. *Personnel Journal, 75*, 59–69.

Fondas, N. (1995). The biological clock confronts complex organizations: Women's ambivalence about work and implications for feminist management research. *Journal of Management Inquiry, 4*, 57–65.

Friedman, S. D., Christensen, P., & DeGroot, J. (1998, November 1). Work and life: The end of the zero-sum game. *Harvard Business Review, 76*, 119–129.

Frone, M. R., Russell, M., & Cooper, M. L. (1992). Antecedents and outcomes of work-family conflict: Testing a model of the work-family interface. *Journal of Applied Psychology, 77*, 67–78.

Galinsky, E. (1999). *Ask the children: What America's children really think about working parents.* New York: Morrow.

Galinsky, E., Bond, J. T., & Friedman, D. E. (1993). *The changing workforce: Highlights of the national study.* New York: Families & Work Institute.

Geisler, C., Campbell, N., Deery, J., & Golden, A. (2001). *Border crossings: Representation and use of mobile technologies in work-life balance* (Unpublished report). Troy, NY: Rensselaer Polytechnic Institute.

Gerson, K. (1993). *No man's land: Men's changing commitments to family and work*. New York: Basic Books.

Gerstel, N., & Gross, H. E. (Eds.). (1987). *Families and work*. Philadelphia: Temple University Press.

Giddens, A. (1984). *The constitution of society: An outline of the theory of structuration*. Cambridge, UK: Polity Press.

Gilbert, L. A. (1993). *Two careers/one family*. Newbury Park, CA: Sage.

Gilbert, L. A. (1994). Current perspectives on dual-career families. *Current Directions in Psychological Science, 3*, 101–105.

Gilbert, L. A., & Rachlin, V. (1987). Mental health and psychological functioning of dual-career families. *Counseling Psychologist, 15*, 7–49.

Goff, S. J., Mount, M. K., & Jamison, R. L. (1990). Employer supported childcare, work/family conflict, and absenteeism: A field study. *Personnel Psychology, 43*, 793–809.

Goldberger, N., Tarule, J., Clinchy, B., & Belenky, M. (Eds.). (1996). *Knowledge, difference, and power: Essays inspired by women's ways of knowing*. New York: Basic Books.

Golden, A. G. (2000). What we talk about when we talk about work and family: A discourse analysis of parental accounts. *Electronic Journal of Communication, 10*(3). Available from http://www.cios.org/www/ejc/v10n3400.htm

Golden, A. G. (2001). Modernity and the communicative management of multiple role-identities: The case of the worker-parent. *Journal of Family Communication, 1*, 233–264.

Golden, A. G. (2002). Speaking of work and family: Spousal collaboration on defining role-identities and developing shared meanings. *Southern Communication Journal, 67*, 122–141.

Gonyea, J. G., & Googins, B. K. (1992). Linking the worlds of work and family: Beyond the productivity trap. *Human Resource Management, 31*, 209–226.

Goodstein, J. D. (1994). Institutional pressures and strategic responsiveness: Employer involvement in work-family issues. *Academy of Management Journal, 37*, 350–382.

Gove, W. R., & Zeiss, C. (1987). Multiple roles and happiness. In F. J. Crosby (Ed.), *Spouse, parent, worker* (pp. 125–137). New Haven, CT: Yale University Press.

Graham, L. D. (1999). Domesticating efficiency: Lillian Gilbreth's scientific management of homemakers, 1924–1930. *Signs: Journal of Women in Culture and Society, 24*, 633–675.

Greenberger, E., & O'Neil, R. (1993). Spouse, parent, worker: Role commitments and role-related experiences in the construction of well-being. *Developmental Psychology, 29*, 181–197.

Greenhaus, J. H., & Beutell, N. J. (1985). Sources of conflict between work and family roles. *Academy of Management Review, 10*, 76–88.

Gregory, K. W. (2001). *"Don't sweat the small stuff": Employee identity work in the new economy*. Unpublished doctoral dissertation, University of South Florida, Tampa.

Grossman, H. Y., & Chester, N. L. (Eds.). (1990). *The experience and meaning of work in women's lives*. Hillsdale, NJ: Erlbaum.

Grover, S. L., & Crooker, K. J. (1995). Who appreciates family-responsive human resource policies: The impact of family-friendly policies on the organizational attachment of parents and non-parents. *Personnel Psychology, 48*, 271–288.

Grzywacz, J. G., & Marks, N. F. (2000). Reconceptualizing the work-family interface: An ecological perspective on the correlates of positive and negative spillover between work and family. *Journal of Occupational Health Psychology, 5*, 111–126.

Gutek, B. A., Searle, S., & Klepa, L. (1991). Rational versus gender role explanations for work-family conflict. *Journal of Applied Psychology, 76*, 560–568.

Haas, L., & Hwang, P. (1995). Company culture and men's usage of family leave benefits in Sweden. *Family Relations, 44*, 28–36.

Haas, T., & Deetz, S. (2000). Between the generalized and the concrete other: Approaching organizational ethics from feminist perspectives. In P. M. Buzzanell (Ed.), *Rethinking organizational and managerial communication from feminist perspectives* (pp. 24–46). Thousand Oaks, CA: Sage.

Hall, D. T. (1990). Promoting work/family balance: An organization-change approach. *Organizational Dynamics, 18*, 4–18.

Hall, D. T. (Ed.). (1996). *The career is dead—Long live the career: A relational approach to careers.* San Francisco: Jossey-Bass.

Hardill, I., & MacDonald, S. (1998). Choosing to relocate: An examination of the impact of expatriate work on dual-career households. *Women's Studies International Forum, 21,* 21–29.

Harding, S. (1991). *Whose science whose knowledge: Thinking from women's lives.* Ithaca, NY: Cornell University Press.

Harre, R. (1984). *Personal being.* Cambridge, MA: Harvard University Press.

Hartsock, N. (1998). *The feminist standpoint revisited and other essays.* Boulder, CO: Westview Press.

Heacock, D., & Spicer, C. H. (1986). Communication and the dual career: A literature assessment. *Southern Speech Communication Journal, 51,* 260–266.

Hessing, M. (1992). Talking on the job: Office conversations and women's dual labour. In G. Creese & V. Strong-Boag (Eds.), *British Columbia reconsidered: Essays on women* (pp. 391–415). Vancouver, BC, Canada: Britims Gang.

Higgins, C., Duxbury, L., & Lee, C. (1994). Impact of life-cycle stage and gender on the ability to balance work and family responsibilities. *Family Relations, 43,* 144–150.

Hobfoll, S. E., & Hobfoll, I. H. (1994). *The dual career couple's survival guide: Work won't love you back.* New York: W. H. Freeman.

Hochschild, A. R (1983). *The managed heart: Commercialization of human feeling.* Berkeley: University of California Press.

Hochschild, A. R. (1989). *The second shift.* New York: Avon Books.

Hochschild, A. R. (1997). *The time bind: When work becomes home and home becomes work.* New York: Metropolitan Books.

Honeycutt, T. L., & Rosen, B. (1997). Family friendly human resource policies, salary levels, and salient identity as predictors of organizational attraction. *Journal of Vocational Behavior, 50,* 271–290.

hooks, b. (2000). *Feminism is for everybody.* Cambridge, MA: South End Press.

Jacobsen, L., & Edmonson, B. (1993). Father figures. *American Demographics, 15,* 22–25.

Johnson, F. L. (2001). Ideological undercurrents in the semantic notion of "working mothers." *Women & Language, 24,* 21–27.

Jorgenson, J. (2000). Interpreting the intersections of work and family: Frame conflicts in women's work. *Electronic Journal of Communication, 10.* Available from http://www.cios.org/www/ejcrec2.htm

Jorgenson, J., Gregory, K. W., & Goodier, B. C. (1997). Working the boundaries: The enfamilied self in the traditional organization. *Human Systems, 8,* 139–151.

Kanter, R. M. (1977). *Work and family in the United States: A critical review and agenda for research and policy.* New York: Russell Sage Foundation.

Katz, D., & Kahn, R. L. (1978). *The social psychology of organizations* (2nd ed.). New York: Wiley.

Kelly, R. F., & Voydanoff, P. (1985). Work/family role strain among employed parents. *Family Relations, 34,* 367–374.

Kim, S. (1998). Toward understanding family leave policy in public organizations: Family leave use and conceptual framework for the family leave implementation process. *Public Productivity and Management Review, 22,* 71–87.

Kingston, P. W. (1989). Studying the work-family connection: Atheoretical progress, ideological bias, and shaky foundations for policy. In E. B. Goldsmith (Ed.), *Work and family: Theory, research, and applications* (pp. 55–60). Newbury Park, CA: Sage.

Kinnier, R. T., Katz, E. C., & Berry, M. A. (1991). Successful resolutions to the career-versus-family conflict. *Journal of Counseling & Development, 69,* 439–444.

Kirby, E. L. (2000a). *Communicating organizational tension: Balancing work and family.* Unpublished doctoral dissertation, University of Nebraska at Lincoln.

Kirby, E. L. (2000b). Should I do as you say, or do as you do?: Mixed messages about work and family. *Electronic Journal of Communication, 10.* Available from http://www.cios.org/www/ejcrec2.htm

Kirby, E. L. (2001, May). *Blurring personal and professional boundaries: Perceptions of men and women regarding talking about family and personal life at work.* Paper presented at the annual meeting of the International Communication Association, Washington, DC.

Kirby, E. L. (2002, March). *"Gendering" careers: Discourses about work versus family at Regulators*. Paper presented at the annual meeting of the Western States Communication Association, Long Beach, CA.

Kirby, E. L., & Krone, K. J. (2002). "The policy exists but you can't really use it": Communication and the structuration of work-family policies. *Journal of Applied Communication Research, 30*, 50–77.

Kolb, D. M. (1992). Women's work: Peacemaking in organizations. In D. M. Kolb & J. M. Bartunek (Eds.), *Hidden conflict in organizations* (pp. 63–91). Newbury Park, CA: Sage.

Kossek, E. E., Dass, P., & DeMarr, B. (1994). The dominant logic of employer-sponsored work and family initiatives: Human resource managers' institutional role. *Human Relations, 47*, 1121–1149.

Krueger, D. L. (1986). Communication strategies and patterns in dual-career couples. *Southern Speech Communication Journal, 51*, 274–281.

Lamphere, L. (1985). Bringing the family to work: Women's culture on the shop floor. *Feminist Studies, 11*, 518–540.

Leidner, R. (1991). Serving hamburgers and selling insurance: Gender, work, and identity in interactive service jobs. *Gender & Society, 5*, 154–177.

Levine, J. A. (1991, June 11). *The invisible dilemma: Working fathers in corporate America* (Testimony at the hearing "Babies and briefcases: Creating a family-friendly workplace for fathers"). Washington, DC: U.S. House of Representatives, Select Committee on Children, Youth, and Families.

Levine, J. A., & Pittinsky, T. L. (1997). *Working fathers: New strategies for balancing work and family*. New York: Harcourt.

Levine, S. B. (2000). *Father courage: What happens when men put family first*. New York: Harcourt.

Lewin, K. (1951). *Field theory in social science*. New York: Harper & Row.

Lobel, S. A., & St. Clair, L. (1992). Effects of family responsibilities, gender, and career identity salience on performance outcomes. *Academy of Management Journal, 35*, 1057–1069.

Lopata, H. Z. (1993). The interweave of public and private: Women's challenge to American society. *Journal of Marriage and the Family, 55*, 176–190.

Loscocco, K. A., & Roschelle, A. R. (1991). Influences on the quality of work and nonwork life: Two decades in review. *Journal of Vocational Behavior, 39*, 182–225.

Luxton, M. (1980). *More than a labor of love: Three generations of women's work in the home*. Toronto, ON, Canada: Women's Press.

MacDermid, S. M., Williams, M., & Marks, S. (1994). Is small beautiful? Work family tension, work conditions, and organizational size. *Family Relations, 43*, 159–167.

Mallia, K. L., & Ferris, S. P. (2000). Telework: A consideration of its impact on individuals and organizations. *Electronic Journal of Communication, 10*. Available from http://www.cios.org/www/ejcrec2.htm

Marks, S. R., & MacDermid, S. M. (1996). Multiple roles and the self: A theory of role balance. *Journal of Marriage and the Family, 58*, 417–432.

Martin, J. (1990). Deconstructing organizational taboos: The suppression of gender conflict in organizations. *Organization Science, 1*, 339–357.

McCall, G., & Simmons, J. L. (1978). *Identities and interactions*. New York: Free Press.

Medved, C. E. (2000, November). *A feminist standpoint challenge to women's career development*. Paper presented at the annual meeting of the National Communication Association, Seattle, WA.

Medved, C. E. (2002). *The everyday accomplishment of work and family routines: Practical actions and commonsense rules as building blocks for theorizing about communication*. Manuscript submitted for publication.

Milkie, M. A., & Peltola, P. (1999). Playing all the roles: Gender and the work-family balancing act. *Journal of Marriage and the Family, 61*, 476–490.

Milliken, F., Dutton, J., & Beyer, J. (1990). Understanding the organizational adaptation to change: The case of work-family issues. *Human Resource Planning, 13*, 91–107.

Miranda, F. J., & Murphy, B. E. (Eds.). (1993). *Work-family: Redefining the business case*. New York: Conference Board.

Mirchandani, K. (1998). Protecting the boundary: Teleworker insights on the expansive concept of "work." *Gender and Society, 12,* 168–187.

Morgan, H., & Milliken, F. J. (1992). Keys to action: Understanding differences in organizations' responsiveness to work-and-family issues. *Human Resource Management, 31,* 227–248.

Mumby, D. K. (1988). *Communication and power in organizations: Discourse, ideology, and domination.* Norwood, NJ: Ablex.

Mumby, D. K. (1998). Organizing men: Power, discourse, and the social construction of masculinity(s) in the workplace. *Communication Theory, 8,* 164–183.

Mumby, D. K., & Stohl, C. (1996). Disciplining organizational communication studies. *Management Communication Quarterly, 10,* 50–72.

Munck, B. (2001, November 1). Changing a culture of face time. *Harvard Business Review, 79,* 125–131.

Murphy, A. G. (1998). Hidden transcripts of flight attendant resistance. *Management Communication Quarterly, 11,* 499–535.

Netemeyer, R. G., Boles, J. S., & McMurrian, R. (1996). Development and validation of work-family conflict and family-work conflict scales. *Journal of Applied Psychology, 81,* 400–410.

Nippert-Eng, C. (1996). *Home and work: Negotiating the boundaries through everyday life.* Chicago: University of Chicago Press.

O'Brien-Hallstein, D. L. (2000). Where standpoint stands now: An introduction and commentary. *Women's Studies in Communication, 23,* 1–15.

O'Keefe, B. (1997). [Review of the book *Home and work: Negotiating boundaries through everyday life*]. *Communication Theory, 7,* 186–188.

O'Neil, R., & Greenberger, E. (1994). Patterns of commitment to work and parenting: Implications for role strain. *Journal of Marriage and the Family, 56,* 101–112.

Orthner, D. K., & Pittman, J. F. (1986). Family contributions to work commitment. *Journal of Marriage and the Family, 48,* 573–581.

Osmond, M. W. (1996). Work-family linkages in early industrialization: The public-private split. In P. J. Dubeck & K. Borman (Eds.), *Women and work: A handbook* (pp. 385–391). New York: Garland.

Pacanowsky, M. (1988). Communication in the empowering organization. In J. A. Anderson (Ed.), *Communication yearbook 11* (pp. 356–379). Thousand Oaks, CA: Sage.

Papa, M. J., Singhal, A., Ghanekar, D. V., & Papa, W. H. (2000). Organizing for social change through cooperative action: The [dis]empowering dimensions of women's communication. *Communication Theory, 10,* 90–123.

Perlow, L. A. (1995). Putting the work back into work/family. *Group and Organization Management, 20,* 227–239.

Perlow, L. A. (1997). *Finding time: How corporations, individuals, and families can benefit from new work practices.* Ithaca, NY: Industrial & Labor Relations Press.

Perlow, L. A. (1998). Boundary control: The social ordering of work and family time in a high-tech corporation. *Administrative Science Quarterly, 43,* 328–357.

Perry-Jenkins, M., Repetti, R. L., & Crouter, A. C. (2000). Work and family in the 1990s. *Journal of Marriage and the Family, 62,* 981–998.

Pleck, J. H. (1985). *Working wives/working husbands.* Beverly Hills, CA: Sage.

Pleck, J. H. (1993). Are family-supportive employer policies relevant to men? In J. C. Hood (Ed.), *Men, work, and family* (pp. 217–237). Newbury Park, CA: Sage.

Polkinghorne, D. E. (1988). *Narrative knowing and the human sciences.* Albany: State University of New York Press.

Putnam, L. L., Phillips, N., & Chapman, P. (1996). Metaphors of communication and organization. In S. R. Clegg, C. Hardy, & W. Nord (Eds.), *Handbook of organization studies* (pp. 375–408). London: Sage.

Raabe, P., & Gessner, J. (1988). Employer family-supportive policies: Diverse variations on a theme. *Family Relations, 37,* 196–202.

Rakow, L. F. (1992). *Gender on the line: Women, the telephone, and community life.* Urbana: University of Illinois Press.

Rapoport, R., & Bailyn, L. (1996). *Relinking life and work: Toward a better future*. New York: Ford Foundation.

Ray, E. B., & Miller, K. I. (1994). Social support, home/work stress, and burnout: Who can help? *Journal of Applied Behavioral Science, 30*, 357–373.

Rees-Edwards, M. R. (1997, November). *The problems employed mothers face: A call for communication research*. Paper presented at the annual meeting of the National Communication Association, Chicago, Illinois.

Rees-Edwards, M. R., & Kline, S. L. (2001, May). *The problems of employed mothers and their experience of spousal support: A research summary*. Paper presented at the annual meeting of the International Communication Association, Washington, DC.

Renshaw, J. R. (1976). An exploration of the dynamics of the overlapping worlds of work and family. *Family Process, 15*, 143–165.

Rexroat, C., & Shehan, C. (1987). The family life cycle and spouses' time in housework. *Journal of Marriage and the Family, 49*, 737–750.

Richter, J. (1990). Crossing boundaries between professional and private life. In H. Grossman & N. Chester (Eds.), *The experience and meaning of work in women's lives*. Hillsdale, NJ: Erlbaum.

Rosenbluth, S. C., Steil, J. M., & Whitcomb, J. (1998). Marital equality: What does it mean? *Journal of Family Issues, 19*, 227–244.

Rosenfeld, L. B., Bowen, G. L., & Richman, J. M. (1995). Communication in three types of dual-career marriages. In M. A. Fitzpatrick & A. L. Vangelisti (Eds.), *Explaining family interactions* (pp. 257–289). Thousand Oaks, CA: Sage.

Rosenfeld, L. B., & Welsh, S. M. (1985). Differences in self-disclosure in dual-career and single-career marriages. *Communication Monographs, 52*, 253–263.

Russo, T. C. (1998, November). *Separation and integration of work and personal lives among home-based teleworkers*. Paper presented at the annual meeting of the National Communication Association, New York.

Sandberg, J. C. (1999). The effects of family obligations and workplace resources on men's and women's use of family leaves. In T. L. Parcel (Ed.), *Research in the sociology of work: Work and family*. Stamford, CT: JAI Press.

Schor, J. B. (1991). *The overworked American: The unexpected decline of leisure*. New York: Basic Books.

Schroedel, J. R. (1990). Blue-collar women: Paying the price at home and on the job. In H. Y. Grossman & N. L. Chester (Eds.), *The experience and meaning of work in women's lives* (pp. 241–260). Hillsdale, NJ: Erlbaum.

Seery, B., & Crowley, M. S. (2000). Women's emotion work in the family: Relationship management and the process of building father-child relationships. *Journal of Family Issues, 21*, 100–127.

Shellenbarger, S. (1992). Lessons from the workplace: How corporate policies and attitudes lag behind workers' changing needs. *Human Resource Management, 31*, 157–169.

Sigel, R. S. (1996). *Ambition and accommodation: How women view gender relations*. Chicago: University of Chicago Press.

Silberstein, L. R. (1992). *Dual-career marriage: A system in transition*. Hillsdale, NJ: Erlbaum.

Sillars, A. L. (1995). Communication and family culture. In M. A. Fitzpatrick & A. L. Vangelisti (Eds.), *Explaining family interactions* (pp. 375–399). Thousand Oaks, CA: Sage.

Sloan Foundation. (n.d.). Work-family researchers electronic network. Retrieved February 6, 2002, from http://www.bc.edu/bc_org/avp/wfnetwork/

Smith, D. E. (1993). The standard North American family: SNAF as an ideological code. *Journal of Family Issues, 14*, 50–65.

Sotirin, P., Buzzanell, P. M., Turner, L., Sullivan, P., & Rosback, K. (2001). *Family teams on The Oprah Winfrey Show: Resisting corporate colonization of our families and our selves*. Manuscript submitted for publication.

Spradlin, A. (1998). The price of "passing:" Lesbian perspectives on authenticity in organizations. *Management Communication Quarterly, 11*, 598–605.

Stamp, G. H. (1994). The appropriation of the parental role through communication during the transition to parenthood. *Communication Monographs, 61*, 89–112.

Stephen, T. (1994). Communication in the shifting context of intimacy: Marriage, meaning, and modernity. *Communication Theory, 4,* 191–218.

Thomas, R. J. (1989). Blue-collar careers: Interests, networks, and environments. In M. B. Arthur, D. T. Hall, & B. S. Lawrence (Eds.), *Handbook of career theory* (pp. 354–379). Cambridge, UK: Cambridge University Press.

Thorne, B. (1992). *Rethinking the family: Some feminist questions.* Boston: Northeastern University Press.

Trethewey, A. (1997). Resistance, identity, and empowerment: A postmodern feminist analysis of clients in a human service organization. *Communication Monographs, 64,* 281–301.

U.S. Census Bureau. (1998). March update, household and families characteristics. Available from http://www.census.gov/Press-Release/cb98–228.html

U.S. Census Bureau. (2001). Profiles of general demographic characteristics: 2000 Census of Population and Housing. U.S. Department of Commerce. Available from http://www.census.gov/population/www/socdemo/hh-fam.html

Voydanoff, P. (1989). Work and family: A review and expanded conceptualization. In E. B. Goldsmith (Ed.), *Work and family: Theory, research, and applications* (pp. 1–22). Newbury Park, CA: Sage.

Warren, J. A., & Johnson, P. J. (1995). The impact of workplace support on work-family role strain. *Family Relations, 44,* 163–169.

West, C., & Zimmerman, D. (1987). Doing gender. *Gender and Society, 1,* 125–151.

Williams, J. (2000). *Unbending gender: Why family and work conflict and what to do about it.* New York: Oxford University Press.

Williams, K. J., & Alliger, G. M. (1994). Role stressors, mood spillover, and perceptions of work-family conflict in employed parents. *Academy of Management Journal, 37,* 837–868.

Wood, J. T. (1986). Maintaining dual-career bonds: Communicative dimensions of internally structured relationships. *Southern Speech Communication Journal, 51,* 267–273.

Wood, J. T. (1994). *Who cares? Women, care, and culture.* Carbondale: Southern Illinois University Press.

Woods, J. D. (1993). *The corporate closet: The professional lives of gay men in America.* New York: Free Press.

Young, M. (1996). Career issues for single adults without dependent children. In D. T. Hall (Ed.), *The career is dead—Long live the career: A relational approach to careers* (pp. 196–222). San Francisco: Jossey-Bass.

CHAPTER CONTENTS

2 Recovering Women's Voice: Communicative Empowerment of Women of the South

RASHMI LUTHRA
University of Michigan-Dearborn

This chapter argues for focusing on the communicative empowerment of "women of the South" (women living in poverty and deprivation in every region of the world) in the conviction that it is by learning from these women that alternative visions for a more just and sustainable future can be created. Through a review of literature, this chapter documents the ways in which women of the South are silenced within (a) colonial discourse, (b) news and academic discourses, and (c) development discourse. The chapter then reviews literature describing a number of efforts by women to use traditional and modern communicative practice to create social change. This chapter derives insights from the literature on both the obstacles and possibilities that exist in the path to the communicative empowerment of women of the South.

Communicative empowerment of the most disenfranchised population on earth, women living at subsistence or poverty levels, is an urgent necessity if we want to move towards more sustainable and equitable futures. This population constitutes the invisible underbelly of modernization, globalization, and development. If we are serious about addressing the widening gaps between the rich and the poor, as well as coming up with alternative visions that will make possible a more just distribution of resources, we must make every effort to recover the voices of the least privileged people—women at the margins in every society. It is these women who have paid the price of progress and it is they who can see the glaring shortcomings of current systems most clearly.

As communication scholars, we can chart the discursive mechanisms by which these women have been silenced or used in the service of a variety of projects not of their own making. We can also identify ways in which these women have chal-

Correspondence: Rashmi Luthra, 37473 East Meadowhill Drive, Northville, MI 48167; email: rluthra@umich.edu

Communication Yearbook 27, pp. 45–65

lenged their subordination in the discursive sphere. In doing so, we hope to contribute to the conditions that will make it possible for disenfranchised women to articulate their visions and to project their voices in a variety of arenas. We simply cannot afford to neglect sources of knowledge and insight that could be the basis of radically new ways of organizing society.

In this chapter, I focus on the communicative empowerment of women of the South, with South used in a metaphorical sense to encompass women living in situations of poverty and deprivation, especially (but not exclusively) in postcolonial countries. This population includes indigenous women, Black women,[1] and women on welfare who head households within otherwise more prosperous nations. In the first section, I argue that it is crucial to understand the processes by which women of the South might be able to articulate and project their voices widely. As part of this endeavor, we need to understand the discursive mechanisms that have marginalized these women's voices. The standpoints and visions of women of the South can be the foundation of the most far-reaching and meaningful social change, therefore it behooves us to facilitate their entry into a variety of discourses. In the second section, I argue that a useful starting point in understanding how to empower women in the communicative sphere is to understand the many ways in which they are silenced. This can usefully be done by engaging in a deconstructive critique of the many discourses that speak of and for women of the South. I go on to describe how women are silenced, or their voices diminished, in (a) colonial discourse, (b) news and academic discourses, and (c) development discourse. In the third section, I describe how women of the South are exploiting openings to express themselves and project their voices through means such as grassroots communication, training in video technology, creation of alternative women's media, and appropriation of new communication technologies for their own purposes (when possible). In the concluding remarks I integrate some of the insights gained from the literature and suggest avenues for further research.

I have drawn from various bodies of literature for this chapter, including postcolonial feminist, women in development communication, eco-feminist, feminist media studies, women in development, and development communication. I have drawn eclectically from a variety of areas that look at the ways women of the South are silenced and also the ways that women are challenging the relegation of their voices to the margins.

WHY EMPOWER WOMEN OF THE SOUTH

Eisenstein (1998) quotes Mongella in saying, "Women's knowledge and achievements help everyone. Women are concerned with the basic needs of society, with the creation of life and the preservation of the environment," Eisenstein continues, "To improve women's lot—to eliminate illiteracy and malnutrition—is to improve the country as a whole" (p. 155). Following from this logic, women at the margins of society—those bypassed or trampled by globalization and a knowledge-based economy—are strategically placed to imagine a just, equitable, and environmentally sustainable future that would benefit everyone in the long-term. It is from the vantage point of these women that (a) the most promising alternative visions of development can be formulated (Sen & Grown, 1987) and (b) the most sustainable development can be initiated.

Taking an eco-feminist approach Mies and Shiva (1993) explain that from the perspective of the victims, the illusory character of the Enlightenment-based "White man's march" (p. 8) toward progress and development becomes clear. Development and globalization look quite different from the eyes of those in the underbelly than those riding atop. These victims are more likely to have a "subsistence perspective" (p. 8) or a "vision of freedom, happiness, the 'good life' within the limits of necessity, of nature" (p. 8) rather than a vision based on the need to transcend nature. Once again, women of the South, who are disproportionately victimized by development and globalization by definition, are in a position to envision a liberating, sustainable future for all, rather than a future benefiting and privileging a select few.

Valdivia's (2000) analysis of Rigoberta Menchu provides further insight into the value of a vision emanating from women experiencing multiple oppressions. As an indigenous woman in Guatemala fighting for land and indigenous rights, she articulates her struggle as the people's struggle. She "speaks as a social and historical subject seeking social goals" (p. 111). The experience of women at the intersection of multiple oppressions of class, race, ethnicity, and gender provides grounds for this kind of sociality, and also for the understanding of the interconnectedness between the struggles for indigenous rights, the rights to land for the landless, and women's rights. Valdivia says that because of socialized patterns connecting women to the fulfillment of basic needs, focusing on them will force us to consider "the everyday issues of power, knowledge, and transformation" (p. 123).

Reminding us that women of the South can be found in the North and speaking as a person coming from a Black, underclass community in the United States who refuses to sever her connection with her origins, hooks (1990) talks about inventing "spaces of radical openness" (p. 148). She continues, writing that "without such spaces, we would not survive" (p. 148). Creating radical alternative visions is a matter of survival for women at the margins. Additionally, hooks (1984) contends that Black women's lived experience of marginality has shaped their consciousness in such a way as to give them a special vantage point to "criticize the dominant racist, classist, sexist hegemony as well as to envision and create a counter-hegemony" (p. 15).

Therefore, it should be a concern of communication scholars to investigate the conditions and processes that would enable women of the South to fully articulate radical alternative visions for the benefit of all of humanity, and as part of that endeavor, to investigate the many ways in which women of the South are silenced.[2]

If for no other reason, the possibility of creating more sustainable futures behooves us to look in this direction. As Shiva (as cited in Mies & Shiva, 1993) points out, women at the subsistence level in many parts of the world and especially in what has been defined as the Third World, have an intimate knowledge of biodiversity, which has been the basis of their survival and the survival of their communities. Further, she argues, biodiversity in production is the basis of all diversity. In the White man's march towards progress, monocultures have become the basis of production. Through this process, the very basis of diversity and sustainability in all of their facets has been undercut. Women's indigenous knowledge will be required in order to correct the balance.

Because of their location at the intersection of multiple oppressions, their subsistence perspective, and their marginality, women of the South are strategically situated to offer radically alternative visions that hold out the possibility of creating more sustainable and equitable futures. Communication researchers must therefore focus on the communicative empowerment of the least privileged women so that their voices can be heard loudly and clearly in a variety of global discourses.

RECOVERING WOMEN'S VOICE THROUGH
DECONSTRUCTIVE CRITIQUE

Although I am advocating the recovery and unearthing of women's voices and knowledge, I am aware that such a project is fraught with contradictions and pitfalls. Spivak (1988) has pointed to the search for the voice of the subaltern woman as illusory at best, and as complicit with the current exploitative structures at worst. She suggests that to posit a unitary, pure subject, whether it be woman or subaltern woman, is disingenuous. It ignores questions of representation, ideology, and subject constitution, hiding the role of the intellectual in these processes. Spivak concludes that "The subaltern cannot speak. There is no virtue in global laundry lists with 'woman' as a pious term" (p. 308). She concludes that there is no space from which the subaltern woman can speak. Mohanty (1991b) has shown eloquently how certain Western feminist writings "discursively colonize the material and historical heterogeneities of the lives of women in the third world, thereby producing/ re-presenting a composite, singular 'third world woman'" (p. 53). Postcolonial feminist writings, such as the current essay, cannot be exempt from this logic. There is reason for caution and great reflexivity as one proceeds with any project that attempts to recover the voices of women of the South.

Yet, the project is still worth undertaking. As Lorde (1984) eloquently wrote, "Where the words of women are crying to be heard, we must each of us recognize our responsibility to seek those words out, to read them and share them and examine them in their pertinence to our lives" (p. 43). Recovery of women's standpoints and knowledges has been a central undertaking within feminist work. As Cain (1993) observed, "There are few areas where feminism has made as many inroads as in its identification and re-presentation of the subjugated knowledges of women" (p. 85). Ganguly (1992), following Spivak, urges feminist writers to engage in deconstructive critique, or "persistent self-critique, not in a disabling or paralyzing mode but, rather, as a way of marking the contingency of one's subject position as well as the truth of one's claims" (p. 66). We can neither be facile about recovering the voice of the subaltern woman in any simple, unproblematic way, nor give up the endeavor. As Mani (1992) asserts, to do the latter would be to repeat the near "erasure of women" (p. 403) we encounter in the majority of colonial and postcolonial texts of all kinds. She suggests posing Spivak's question, "Can the subaltern speak?" (p. 403) as a series of questions, among which the most pertinent here is, "How can they [the subaltern] be heard to be speaking or not speaking in a given set of materials" (p. 403)?

Perhaps the most instructive place to begin is precisely where Mohanty and Spivak have begun, that is, to "watch out for the continuing construction of the subaltern" (Spivak, 1988, p. 294). This must be done in order to deconstruct the discourses that continually absorb and incorporate the figures of the postcolonial woman, the woman of the South, and the subaltern woman, using them as the grounds for a variety of interventions and projects. Ironically, many of the projects that deploy a rhetoric of women's choice, women's empowerment, or in the older colonial guise, women's uplift, exacerbate the very conditions that restrict the exercise of power in women's real-life circumstances. These contradictions must be laid bare by feminist scholars. As Mohanty (1991b) says:

> The relationship between "Woman"—a cultural and ideological composite Other constructed through diverse representational discourses (scientific, literary, juridical, linguistic, cinematic, etc.) and "women"—real, material subjects of their collective histories—is one of the central questions the practice of feminist scholarship seeks to address. (p. 53)

We need to interrogate further the discourses that construct Third World women or women of the South and their relationship to the actual women of the South, toiling, dreaming, resisting.

Deconstructing Colonial Discourse

Feminist scholars have often engaged colonial discourse, deconstructing the ways in which it constructs *woman* and more particularly *Third World woman*. Both Spivak and Mani have deconstructed colonial discourse as it pertains to sati (widow immolation) in the Indian context.[3] Spivak (1988) shows how the voice-consciousness of the subaltern woman has been lost in history and her subjectivity ideologically suppressed. The colonial texts on sati she examines give no access to the subjectivity of the widow. Mani (1992) reads against the grain colonialist eye-witness accounts of sati to try to excavate the subjectivity of the widow. The accounts themselves oscillate between representing the widow as entirely self-determining (the voluntary sati ready to be immolated) and completely victimized. Either representation erases the widow's agency as someone "capable of evaluating the conditions of her life" (p. 398) and taking action based on this evaluation. Yet, in reading against the grain, Mani herself is able to reconstruct evidence of the widows' active suffering and their resistance. The testimonials from widows in the eyewitness accounts contradict the interpretations of the women's actions. By virtue of these contradictions, it is possible to glimpse the women's subjectivity. It sneaks through despite the colonial discourse.[4]

We can see shadows of these colonial discourses today, including the mechanism of deploying women for imperialist or neoimperialist ends. As Ganguly (1992) reminds us, the discursive agenda of colonialism "did not become defunct with the official decolonization of subject countries and peoples" (p. 71). For example, Said (1979) has shown us how orientalist approaches persist in a variety of current intellectual and political contexts.[5] I intend to show how a variety of current discourses, including news discourse, academic discourse, and development discourse, including international population discourse, utilize or absorb the figure of woman and feminist movement rhetoric in a way that undercuts the struggle against patriarchy, racism, and imperialism. Also, these discourses speak for and about women, rarely if ever allowing them to speak. The voices of women of the South are attenuated in these discourses in a variety of ways.

Deconstructing News and Academic Discourse

Rakow and Kranich (1991) showed how news in the U.S. context is a masculine narrative "in which women function not as speaking subjects but as signs" (p. 9). News discourse in its current form allows women's voices to be heard only occasionally and only in particular ways. Valdivia's (2000) analysis of news coverage of Rigoberta Menchu illustrates the many challenges that face women of the South who want to speak for their people and be heard in the global arena. It is only through the tremendous efforts of supporters that Menchu was placed on the world stage and she is fairly unique in being able to do so. Even as a Nobel Prize winner her voice was "subsumed by news frames that preclude her from speaking out in most situations" (p. 122). The news could not fully grapple with either her as a person with a "complex set of affiliations and identities" (p. 116) or her message encompassing many aspects of people's struggles. She was "reduced to one or two essentialist characteristics that would avoid or reject her complex character and would exemplify orientalism" (p. 116). Menchu can be known to Western audiences only through this kind of assimilation, mostly second hand. Menchu's own voice rarely comes through. As a result, her potentially transformative message about the struggles of indigenous peoples becomes partially muted. If this can be true of a Nobel Peace Prize-winning indigenous woman, the process of silencing is multiplied manifold when it comes to millions of women the world over. It is not only news discourse that Menchu challenges but also academic discourse. She is marginalized there as well, subjected to the oriental gaze. Valdivia makes the astute observation that even in circumstances that allow for postcolonial women to gain voice, the amplification of this voice to the global arena becomes problematic. Institutional values and practices, as well as dominant ideologies, trouble the reception of these voices. When we do encounter these voices, even within academia, it is with the will to seek "knowledge of and authority over" (p. 122) them, limiting our ability to really listen and learn from them (Valdivia, 2000). Minh-Ha (1991) sheds further light on this when she says:

> This inability and unwillingness to deal with the unfamiliar, or with a language different from one's own, is, in fact, a trait that intimately belongs to the man of coercive power. It is a reputable form of colonial discrimination, one in which difference can only be admitted once it is appropriated, that is, when it operates within the Master's sphere of having. (p. 84)

Yet, even the shadowy presence of women of the South in news and academic discourse does present the possibility of radical alterity, of an "inappropriate/d other" (Minh-ha, 1986, p. 84). Menchu manages to "sneak through the ideological fissures" (Valdivia, 2000, p. 122) at certain junctures by virtue of her presence as a multicultural being.

The ordinary, nameless woman of the South also finds her way into mainstream discourses on rare occasion, but only in particular ways and only as a sign, not as a speaking subject. In examining U.S. network news coverage of Ethiopian and Somalian famines, Fair (1996) finds that although women appear in all the stories, they appear only as exemplars of victimhood, signifying desperation and dependency. Their bodies, especially their flaccid breasts, are used to evoke pity and blame, as well as to reinforce Western notions of chaos in Africa. We almost never hear these women or encounter them as individuals. Of great pertinence here is Fair's suggestion that we as journalists and academics must turn our attention "to elucidating relations of ruling that circumscribe our abilities to embrace structures of knowledge produced by women from cultures that are 'different' from or resist the West" (p. 26). This entails turning the gaze upon ourselves to understand the factors that lead us to actively silence women of the South.

In another study by Fair (1993) of U.S. broadcast news coverage of violence among Blacks in South Africa, she once again finds strategies that actively silence African women. Women are shown either as supporters of men's actions or as victims of South Africa's violence. They are given no space as subjects capable of agency. They are confined to the domestic sphere and their actions are not imbued with political significance. Rather than recognizing women's actions in defending family, home, and community as political, powerful, active, and public, these actions and the women who engage in them are represented as powerless and nonpolitical. They are made to act "as bearers rather than as producers of meaning" (p. 288). To allow the women to speak and be heard constitutes a radical act, for it "would mean the acceptance of women's subjectivities as politically viable or powerful" (p. 288).

The colonial gaze operates not only with regard to the representation of Third World women in the postcolonial context, but also Third World women situated in the West (Narayan, 1997). Parmeswaran's (1996) analysis of *Dallas Observer* coverage of the murder of an Indian Christian woman living in Texas is instructive. Aleyamma Matthew was set ablaze by her husband after a bitter family dispute. One of the predominant news frames was that of Aleyamma being victimized by her culture. Alternative explanations of the murder such as her husband's alcoholism and history of abuse were ignored altogether. Further, the news coverage made irrelevant and unwarranted connections to sati and dowry murder, practices completely unrelated to Aleyamma's death. These tropes lead to a construction of violence against Third World women as "death by culture" (Narayan, 1997, p. 85), whereas violence against Western women is treated in a more complex fashion. As Narayan points out, whereas Western contexts are generally represented as spaces of historical change and internal complexity, Third World contexts are treated as if they were frozen in time and monolithic in their oppression of women, with no internal variation. Third World women are portrayed as being victimized primarily by traditional patriarchal cultural practices. Both Mohanty (1991b) and Narayan (1997) have shown that Western feminists also discursively colonize Third World women in these ways, assuming that they are a monolithic entity victimized by their traditions, religions, or cultures, with these terms often conflated with each other. The specificity and context of a woman's particular situation is erased to the point of misrepresenting the nature of the problem. Borrowing again from Narayan, these assumptions are problematic because they entirely elide the contribution of modernization, development, and globalization to women's oppression.

Narayan (1997) astutely points out that "colonial encounters seem to instigate a process of defining 'the Self in *contrast* to the other' on the part of both colonizer and colonized, and practices affecting women commonly seem to become central elements in this project" (p. 66). She adds that practices that involve aspects of the spectacular and the hidden are more likely to be deployed for this purpose than others, such as sati and veiling. We see this logic being played out in a variety of discourses currently using the figure of the veiled Afghani woman as a sign of oppression under the Taliban, with the unveiled or partially unveiled Afghani woman signifying liberation by Western and, more specifically, U.S. forces. Not only has the most blatantly orientalist rhetoric been used in coverage about the women of Afghanistan, but their suffering, and U.S. women's compassion for their suffering, has been actively deployed in the service of the war against terrorism (Walsh, 2002). Descriptions and visual images of the horrific conditions experienced by Afghani women under the Taliban have been "exploited by the media for purposes other than a pure interest in women's condition" (Sarikakis, 2002, p. 152). It is also ironic that although "women's human rights and voices are being constantly denied access to mainstream news, policies, and debate, these same rights become the persuasion tool for the continuation of the circle of violence" (p. 153). It is by using Afghani women as "instruments of compassion" that "the West will be able to proclaim itself as the liberator of Afghanistan and of its women from the burqas, while continuing to circulate the most racist and antifeminist discourses in Western societies" (Cere, 2002, p. 135). In this process, any notion of Afghani women's agency is eclipsed. Dunn (2002) makes the comment that she had "bought the picture of depressed, suicide-committing victims that the media had been selling" (p. 137) until she came upon the Revolutionary Association of the Women of Afghanistan (RAWA) through the Virtual International Women's University Internet Forum. The television news channel CNN aired Saira Shah's documentary *Behind the Veil* several times and although the documentary is suffused with images of Afghani women as victims, there is also heroism associated with the women of RAWA. But as Jansen says, "CNN's programming decision was probably made despite the feminist message, not because of it" (p. 140). As she astutely observes, the documentary gelled with President Bush's characterization of the Taliban as an evil enemy. The absence of the Afghani woman's voice and the relative absence of news about women's revolutionary actions, accords with Jansen's observation that women of the South are typically shown as sexualized objects or victims of male violence, whether in Bosnia, Kuwait, or Afghanistan. Further, "women's collective efforts to become agents rather than victims of history" seldom make the news (Jansen, 1996, p. 137).

Deconstructing Development Discourse

The colonial gaze is present within development discourse as well, although the language of women's empowerment and women's rights has found its way into this discourse. As a case in point, an analysis of the debate over the abortion clause in U.S. foreign population policy showed that "postcolonial women are used symbolically and physically as the grounds for foreign intervention in the international population arena" (Luthra, 1995, p. 197). Several parties speak for the postcolonial woman in this debate, but her voice is never heard. The international population establishment, neo-right economists, and the pro-life lobby all pose as "defender and protector of postcolonial women, only to enhance their own positions of power" (Luthra, 1995, p. 198).

More generally, development discourse and practice have absorbed constructs of gender and women's empowerment in ways that are deeply contradictory, throwing into question the degree to which development projects can ultimately enable the dialectical process of gaining voice and power by women of the South. Development discourse and practice are themselves historically determined, absorbing within them a colonial legacy, and working within the larger processes of globalized capitalist patriarchy (Beneria & Sen, 1981; Escobar, 1995). Beneria and Sen have drawn attention to the fallacy that women simply need to be integrated into economic development. Rather, the power relationships and structures underlying development must be challenged. An understanding of the contradictory relationship between development institutions and women's empowerment would be incomplete without attending to the historical and political situatedness of these institutions.

However, development institutions can also be viewed as sites of struggle between competing discourses and worldviews with unequal amounts of power and resources behind them. Even in this view, however, the gains made in terms of the incorporation of women in development, gender and development, and global feminist perspectives, are subsumed by the imperatives of globalization, marketing, and privatization that dominate the development process (Steeves, 1993; Wilkins, 1997; Wilkins & Mody, 2001). It should not be surprising that "Despite concerted efforts in the past two decades, development strategies have failed to improve substantially the conditions of women, as development participants or as targets" (Wilkins, 1997, p. 102).

This section has demonstrated the ways in which women of the South are silenced within colonial, news, and academic discourses, as well as development discourses. These discourses incorporate and deploy women of the South as a sign rather than allowing them to speak for themselves, and they do so in deeply contradictory ways.

WOMEN EXPLOITING OPENINGS TO CREATE CHANGE

Women's movements at varying levels, as well as other organizations involved in social change, have been able to exploit openings, fissures, and gaps in the processes of development, modernization, and globalization to create some space for the exercise of voice and power by women of the South. They have been able to do this to some extent within development institutions, grassroots groups, nongovernmental organizations, and in autonomous and semiautonomous women's organizations. Some of these experiments and efforts will be described here, always keeping in mind that these are efforts to create openings within larger power structures and within institutions that have genealogies of their own, often carrying legacies of colonialism, capitalism, and patriarchy. The global feminist movement has directly engaged the multiple bases of oppression that affect women's lives, thereby providing the greatest hope in terms of the possibility of women's empowerment in every sphere.

Empowerment has been broadly defined in development, social change organizations, and grassroots groups, encapsulating various dimensions of being or becoming empowered. It has been explored in its personal, relational, and collective aspects (Papa, Singhal, Ghanekar, & Papa, 2000; Rowlands, 1997), as well as in its economic, political, social, psychological, and spiritual aspects (Barroso & Bruschini, 1991; Newsom & Carrell, 1995; Papa, Auwal, & Singhal, 1997; Riaño, 1994; Rowlands, 1997; Steeves, 2001). Empowerment has been variously defined as "developing a sense of self and individual confidence and capacity, and undoing the effects of internalized oppression" (Rowlands, 1997, p. 15); "processes that lead people to perceive themselves as able and entitled to make decisions" (Rowlands, 1997, p. 14); the ability to resist dominant institutions and ideologies, as part of the process of being able to collectively influence the direction of social change efforts (Wilkins & Waters, 2000); and "the ability to shape the contexts within which interventions are conceived and engaged" (Wilkins, 2000, p. 389; Wilkins & Mody, 2001). Although it is important for us as feminist scholars to document the methods that have facilitated the communicative empowerment of women at an individual and group level, the most far-reaching efforts at empowerment appear to be the ones that are relatively autonomous collective engagements of women within their circumstances, using methods and idioms appropriate to the local context. Feminist intellectuals, with access to global academic, news, and other discourses, are ideally placed to research the possibilities of amplification and translation of these efforts to the global arena. Once again, we are back to the project enunciated earlier of recovering and amplifying the voices of women of the South, particularly collective revolutionary voices. In addition, we must work to forge the structural changes and new institutions that will make this possible.

Examples of feminist revolutionary moments worthy of amplification are the Chipko, or tree-hugging movement in the mountainous regions of Northern India, which has grown to encompass the salvation of living mountains and living waters; the movement to block the building of the Narmada dam in India; the Seikatsu club in Japan, a consumer-producer cooperative promoting organic farming and attempting to influence agricultural policy (Mies & Shiva, 1993); women's organized efforts on behalf of *the disappeared* in Argentina, Chile, and Guatemala; mass demonstrations of Moroccan women to protest police violence against women; the takeover of highways in northern Buenos Aires by 300 women on foot and bicycles to protest privatization of Argentine highways (Jansen, 1996); RAWA's challenge to both the corrupt regimes in Afghanistan and the war waged by the U.S. and its allies; and a revolutionary moment occurring even as I write this, the takeover by 600 Nigerian women of a Chevron Texaco oil terminal in order to force the company to give their communities something back in return for the huge oil profits made by the multinational while nearby villages do not even have electricity. These Nigerian women threatened to strip naked in front of the hundreds of workers they were holding hostage, making powerful use of a local shaming gesture (Doran, 2002).

There is a virtual news blackout of events such as these, particularly in mainstream Western media (Jansen, 1996). Not only do these stories need to be reported widely, but they need to be reported fully to convey the voices, visions, and political perspectives of the women involved. Only then will the "metaphor of women's silence" (Riaño, 1994, p. 40) be replaced with metaphors of women's activism, eloquence, and vision. In a sense, the first step in empowerment of women (despite the multiple oppressions they experience) is a recognition of the power they already harbor, power not in the sense of power over but in the sense of power from within.

Women's Media and Empowerment

Alternative media, including women's media, can help break the silence and empower women along a communicative dimension. Feminist intellectuals can document and support the efforts of these groups, doing participatory research to understand the factors that would make them most effective. Some research is already being done in this area, but it can go further. Women's networking efforts; efforts to train women in basic literacy, communicative capacities, and media technologies; use of indigenous media by women's movements; efforts to increase women's presence in mainstream media organizations; and efforts to retain and increase access to conventional and new media, all contribute to the communicative empowerment of women and further the goals of global feminism. In addition, feminist and communication scholars need to do research and intervene at the level of media ownership, management, production, and reception to ensure that women not only gain voice, but that this voice has the material backing and the communicative environment to be projected powerfully as well as to be received in a way that does not attenuate the centrality of women's concerns and women's agency, especially women of the South.

Riaño's (1994) treatment of women's grassroots communication is path breaking in bringing together in-depth articles on a variety of participatory projects that take a gender and communication perspective to the communicative empowerment of women. In addition, this work provides a rich framework for further research.

The projects in Riaño's book span both traditional and modern forms of communication. Traditional forms include dance, quilting, storytelling, and popular theater. Mlama (1994) describes the use of indigenous dance for development by women in Tanzania. Women were invited to participate in every aspect of the project, from problem definition, to performance, and to discussion of solutions emanating from the performances. Once the medium of communication shifted from conventional meetings to informal workshops and dance performances, the women's communicative capacities were easily exercised and they participated enthusiastically. Mlama concludes that the project was very successful in problem solving because dance is a familiar medium for the women and Tanzanian indigenous dance is participatory in character. The dance form allows for flexibility and improvisation, and it appeals to the emotions of the participants. Dyer-Bennem (1994) describes the use of quilting and different forms of storytelling by African American women as a means of preserving a history and sense of identity rejected by the dominant culture. These distinctive communicative practices have been part and parcel of African American women's struggle to effect social change. These practices generally emanated from their daily work lives within the slave economy. For example, slave women were required to make quilts but they transformed the mundane chore into an opportunity for historical and autobiographical representation.

Riaño (1994) says that misconceptions and assumptions about women are present not only within diffusionist and modernizing views of development but also within consciousness raising and participatory approaches. Both can and do subconsciously incorporate the ideology of "women as passive Others, as problems or issues, or as targets for integration in economic or social processes of modernization" (p. 42). This view doesn't show women as communicators and subjects capable of voice and action, oppressed by their circumstances but also acting upon them. The traditional assumptions must be challenged for the efforts at women's empowerment to be successful. Riaño encourages taking a complex view, recognizing that "the context of silence is varied and multidimensional" (p. 41), and that class, race, and sex domination all silence women, as does the internalization of oppression that manifests in a lack of confidence to write or fully develop craft and skill. Such an approach recognizes not only the many dimensions of silence, but also the many dimensions of women's communicative capacity such as their "verbal eloquence in the community realm or family" (p. 41). Riaño says that women's grassroots communication projects need to (a) take into account the multifaceted experience of subordination, (b) reclaim cultural and ethnic concerns, (c) question the private versus public dichotomy, and (d) reenvision women's silence in order to be effective.

Among modern forms of communication, video has been used by several grassroots projects as a tool for social change. Some of these experiments are described in Riaño's book (1994) as well as in other compilations describing women's use of communication for social change. Kawaja (1994) describes three process video projects involving immigrant women in the Canadian context. These projects subvert conventional media practices by placing control of the message, production, editorial decisions, and distribution with community participants rather than with centralized media institutions. Video is used by the women to initiate a process of defining their own past, present, and future history in negotiation with each other. The process helps women to recognize their capacity to communicate in multiple realms, a capacity that marginalization often negates. Rodriguez (1994) draws inferences from three participatory video production experiences in Bogota, Colombia. She finds that through the collective process of producing video stories about their own experiences, women are able to (a) empower themselves personally and collectively, (b) reverse entrenched power roles, and (c) increase their collective strength. Stuart and Bery (1996) describe experiences of participatory video with women in Bangladesh and India. They show how the camcorder has not only enhanced the individual self-confidence of the women involved but also become a potent tool for them to collectively advocate for women's human rights. For example, the Self-Employed Women's Association (SEWA) in India has used their video unit, Video SEWA, to educate the women of Gujarat state to stand up and have their work counted in the census. Their 15-minute edited program, *My Work, Myself,* reached an audience of about half a million women. In the field of electronic communication, women have also been experimenting with popular radio in Colombia (Mata, 1994) and Bolivia (Ruiz, 1994).

Women of the South have also made inroads in the area of print communication, including journalism. Lloyd (1994) describes the struggles of a women's collective in South Africa that brings out *Speak* magazine. The collective initially started with a newsletter focused on the fight for better housing conditions but evolved into a monthly magazine with a much wider scope. Yet, the magazine always remained centered around issues that are of concern to women. They have faced many challenges, including funding and distribution difficulties, but they have managed to create a high degree of trust with the women in their community. Steeves (1993) describes the work of the Manushi collective in India and its success in publishing a magazine that offers features as well as fiction confronting the oppression of women in Indian society. This magazine has managed to survive despite local resistance. She also refers to *Viva* magazine in Nairobi, Kenya, which attempted to publish stories on prostitution, birth control, female circumcision, and other issues, but was forced to close down in 1990 because of pressure from advertisers. Wadud-Muhsin (1995) documents the work of Sisters in Islam (SIS) in Malaysia, who are engaged in researching, writing, and disseminating interpretations of the Qur'an from the perspective of women's rights, leading to a broad-based reconsideration of what it means to be a Muslim. Rosario-Braid (1996), as well as Shafer and Hornig (1995), write about the central role of Filipino women journalists in the People Power Movement of 1986, and their continuing robust role in advocating for social change. Barroso and Bruschini (1991) document the experience of low-income housewives in the peripheries of Sao Paulo, Brazil, working within a Mother's Club to create booklets encapsulating their collective knowledge of sexuality as a lived experience. Women in various regions of the world are engaged in appropriating whatever spaces they can, within both the mainstream and alternative print media, to convey their unique perspectives on history, religion, sexuality, and a host of other areas.

Women have been making strides not only in the use of traditional and modern media, but also in creating news agencies that make it possible to gather and disseminate stories more widely, acting as central conduits in the news pipeline. Byerly (1995) has analyzed the work of the Women's Feature Service (WFS), the longest lived and largest women-controlled global news agency, currently headquartered in New Delhi, India. The mission of the agency when it was established was to strategically intervene to expand women's voices in international news, which in the 1970s amounted to less than 2% of overall coverage (Gallagher, 1981). Byerly notes that although the project was initiated within a liberal reformist strategy, its top priorities from the beginning were "women's informational needs, lives, views, achievements, and creative control" (Byerly, p. 112). In direct contrast with mainstream news, WFS correspondents and the stories they write take a gender perspective on development (Anand, 1992). They foreground the struggle and resistance of ordinary women of the South, and they "have been able to embed new cultural codes favorable to women" (Byerly, p. 116). Because of material and cultural constraints such as the low literacy rates and primarily oral traditions, the WFS has been less successful in disseminating its stories in Arab, African, and Caribbean regions than in Latin America, Asia, and North America. Byerly recommends renewed efforts to bring these regions into WFS activities more rigorously and for other women's news systems to emerge to carry out the enormous task. Toro (1996) has described the work of Feminist International Radio Endeavor, based in Costa Rica and heard in over 100 countries. Their 2-hour daily program, "Radio for Peace International," addresses diverse themes from a gender perspective. Like WFS, it strives not only to deliver news from a gendered perspective but also to actively project the words and views of women of the South. Werden (1996) describes the work of the Women's International News Gathering Service, a radio service that disseminates hard news about women, by women, with women speaking for themselves. Based in the United States, it has a strong international component.

New Communication Technologies and Empowerment

Recognizing the centrality and growing importance of the new communication technologies, Eisenstein (1998) points to the innovative networks being created by women on the Internet, such as Jerusalem Link, connecting Israeli and Palestinian women working for peace; the Virtual Sisterhood home page, welcoming women in nine languages and committed to enhancing their own and other women's activism; FemiNet Korea, challenging the male privilege of the information society; and *Aviva*, a feminist zine that posts bulletins about workers' rights in Bangladesh, Brazil, Cambodia, and Indonesia, and calls for the release of women prisoners in Turkey, Nigeria, Pakistan, and other countries. Kramer and Kramarae (2000) analyze both the possibilities and obstacles that exist for global feminism's use of the Internet to create an alternative public sphere. As part of their assessment, they note that since the 1980s, the Women's International Information and Communication Service, which has been housed at various times in Switzerland, Uganda, Italy, Philippines, and Chile, has promoted the use of computers in connecting more than 10,000 women's groups in 130 countries.

Much more work can be done to analyze in-depth the efforts of these groups and to explore new possibilities. This work needs to be self-reflexive, deconstructing not only mainstream media, but also the content of feminist media so that it can achieve its revolutionary potential. This work also needs to be articulated alongside that of the gendered political economy of the media, in order to understand how these particular efforts might translate into social change in global terms. Riordan (2002) makes a strong case for taking a feminist political economic approach to the study of media and communication. She says, "If communications scholars fail to elucidate the connections between the day-to-day lived experience of people and the structures of capitalism and patriarchy, then we will continue to participate uncritically in their reproduction" (p. 4). She adds, "Understanding global capitalism is imperative, and discerning how this impacts women's lives as producers and consumers is a part of the process" (p. 12). The terrain on which women negotiate and contest dominant media institutions or content, as well as create alternative institutions or content, needs to be understood fully for these efforts to have far-reaching effects.

This section has pointed to a variety of efforts that women of the South are making to challenge dominant discourses. By creating alternative avenues of expression, women help project their voices beyond their immediate and local domains into the global arenas. These efforts encompass projects experimenting with both traditional and new technologies, such as theater, radio, magazines, video, photographs, manuals, dance, and the Internet. The very act of women of the South speaking for themselves through these various means is a radical act challenging the processes by which these women are silenced.

CONCLUDING COMMENTS

This chapter made a case for focusing on the communicative empowerment of women of the South, arguing that a first step in understanding the process of empowerment is to deconstruct a variety of discourses that serve to silence these women and attenuate their voice. A review of feminist work critiquing colonial, news, and academic discourses, as well as development discourse, revealed that diverse mechanisms are used to eclipse the voices of women of the South and to relegate them to the margins of discourses where others speak for them. Not only are women's voices diminished, but they are often used as a sign in the service of a variety of projects, including imperialist projects which are not in the long-term interests of the women themselves. Even when these women manage to sneak through to the level of global discourse, as Rigoberta Menchu was able to do, the reception of their voices is deeply troubled. The institutions within which reception takes place makes it difficult, if not impossible, to actually learn from the perspectives of these least privileged women.

This chapter has also pointed to the history of the colonialist gaze within which women of the South are represented and perceived, and which continues to infect a variety of current discourses. The shadow of this gaze is present in development discourse that otherwise gestures in the direction of women in development, gender and development, and global feminism. It can even influence Western feminist discourse and women's grassroots communication projects. The metaphor of women's silence, particularly as it relates to women of the South, is pervasive.

The chapter has also reviewed literature on women's alternative media that directly challenges the metaphor of women's silence, attempting to create alternative representations and cultural codes by creating news and fiction by women of the South for women of the South. Although the review makes clear that women are using their resilience and creativity to forge alternative means and spaces of expression in every region of the world, these media struggle both to survive financially and to influence dominant discourse in a way that would translate to broader social change. They work within an overarching structure of communication industries, one of increasing economic concentration, privatization, and conglomeration that continues to erode broad access to conventional and new communication technologies. This reduces space for women's voices even as women work hard to expand these spaces. Because it is to be able to capture such contradictions, the case was made for combining participatory research and ethnographic studies of women's media with a macrolevel political economic analysis of the communicative conditions within which these media operate.

The review suggests several avenues for research in the future, in many cases extending and refining strands that are already in place. There is room for further deconstructive critiques of the dominant discourses in areas such as international diplomacy; privatization rhetoric emanating from both governments and global corporations; discourses addressing globalization of the new information technologies; and many others. It will be useful to chart the absorption of feminist critiques by the dominant discourses as an adaptive response in the process of maintaining hegemony, including the absorption of feminism of the South. A question worth asking is: Does this absorption shift the discursive terrain at all despite the incorporation of alternative voices? Further deconstruction of global feminist discourse, in the vein of Mohanty's and Narayan's work, would also be useful, in the spirit of being self-reflexive. Is there a global feminist discourse distinct from Western feminist discourse? Do these discourses allow women of the South to speak for themselves, and to what extent? Research must address contradictions within the feminist discourses as well as mainstream discourses, in an attempt to further the revolutionary potential of feminist movements.

The chapter has reviewed literature on women's alternative media geared toward women of the South and in some cases initiated by them. Some of the studies are based on extended ethnographic work but others are shorter case studies. In the case of the latter, more in-depth work can be done to look at the processes and outcomes of the projects. This work needs to include the participants' own views and assessments of the projects as well as an outside perspective on the ultimate potential of the efforts to create social change. Political, economic, ethnographic, and other methods should be combined to understand (a) factors that might contribute to the greatest success of the efforts themselves and (b) factors that would enhance their ability to create broader social change. Some of this will be done in specific studies but evaluative meta-analysis across projects would also be useful. The definition of success itself affords an avenue of research. Who defines success and what are the tensions between the definitions of success of women participants and facilitators, for example, in the participatory video projects initiated by Communication for Change (formerly Martha Stuart Communications) in India and Bangladesh? Are there differing conceptions of feminism operating in particular projects, and how are these negotiated? These are just some of the questions that might be addressed.

In the best tradition of feminist work, research on the communicative empowerment of women of the South will benefit from a sense of political engagement, a high degree of reflexivity, a recognition of multiple bases of oppression, and a spirit of eclecticism. The work needs to proceed on the micro-, meso-, and macrolevels, using a variety of approaches and methods in quilting together the pieces required to reclaim women's voice. Women of the South and sympathetic communication scholars have to work at a variety of levels to understand the total communicative situation within which women might become empowered to speak, act, and be heard. The possibility of creating more just and sustainable futures depends on our ability to listen to, and learn from, subaltern women.

NOTES

1. The term *Black* is used in a political sense and could refer variously to African American women in the U.S., Caribbean women wherever they are found, South Asian women in Great Britain, and so forth.

2. In positing the unitary identity, women of the South, I am aware of the risks of essentialism. There are enormous differences between women of the South based on race, ethnicity, class, region, nation, and so forth. For example, Mani (1992) warns against conflating people of color in the U.S. with the Third World diaspora, as this would not take into account the relationship of such diasporas to the U.S. power structure. Ideally, the analysis of conditions within which women of the South might articulate their visions, should work within a recognition of both this diversity and the "common context of struggle" (Mohanty, 1991a, p. 7).

3. Ganguly (1992) defines colonial discourse as "the tropes and strategies by means of which the material and discursive agenda of colonialism is instituted and maintained" (p. 71).

4. See also Mani (1990) for an account of how women were used as the ground for the discourse on sati in the official debate on whether to ban widow burning.

5. Interpreting Said, Ganguly (1992) defines orientalism as "the discursive apparatus by means of which the Orient is actively produced, fixed, and objectified by Western imagery and imaginations" (p. 73).

REFERENCES

Anand, A. (1992). Introduction in women's feature service. In A. Anand (Ed.), *The power to change: Women in the Third World redefine their environment* (pp. 1–21). New Delhi, India: Kali Press for Women.

Barroso, C., & Bruschini, C. (1991). Building politics from personal lives: Discussions on sexuality among poor women in Brazil. In C. T. Mohanty, A. Russo, & L. Torres (Eds.), *Third World women and the politics of feminism* (pp. 51–80). Bloomington: Indiana University Press.

Beneria, L., & Sen, G. (1981). Accumulation, reproduction, and women's role in economic development: Boserup revisited. *Signs, 7,* 279–298.

Byerly, C. M. (1995). News, consciousness, and social participation: The role of women's feature service in world news. In A. N. Valdivia (Ed.), *Feminism, multiculturalism and the media: Global diversities* (pp. 105–122). Thousand Oaks, CA: Sage.

Cain, M. (1993). Foucault, feminism and feeling: What Foucault can and cannot contribute to feminist epistemology. In C. Ramazanoglu (Ed.), *Up against Foucault: Explorations of some tensions between Foucault and feminism* (pp. 73–98). New York: Routledge.

Cere, R. (2002). "Islamophobia" and the media in Italy. *Feminist Media Studies, 2,* 133–135.

Doran, D. (2002, July 16). "Our weapon is our nakedness"—Nigerian women protesters declare. *Toronto Star,* p. A13.

Dunn, M. (2002). Where are all the women? *Feminist Media Studies, 2,* 136–137.

Dyer-Bennem, S. Y. (1994). Cultural distinctions in communication patterns of African-American women: A sampler. In P. Riaño (Ed.), *Women in grassroots communication: Furthering social change* (pp. 65–83). Thousand Oaks, CA: Sage.

Eisenstein, Z. (1998). *Global obscenities: Patriarchy, capitalism, and the lure of cyberfantasy.* New York: New York University Press.

Escobar, A. (1995). *Encountering development: The making and unmaking of the Third World*. Princeton, NJ: Princeton University Press.

Fair, J. E. (1993). The women of South Africa weep: Explorations of gender and race in U.S. television news. *Howard Journal of Communications, 4*, 283–294.

Fair, J. E. (1996). The body politic, the bodies of women, and the politics of famine in U.S. television coverage of famine in the horn of Africa. *Journalism and Mass Communication Monographs, 158*, 1–41.

Gallagher, M. (1981). *Unequal opportunities: The case of women and the media*. Paris: United Nations Educational, Scientific, and Cultural Organization.

Ganguly, K. (1992). Accounting for others: Feminism and representation. In L. Rakow (Ed.), *Women making meaning: New feminist directions in communication* (pp. 60–79). New York: Routledge.

hooks, b. (1984). *Feminist Theory from Margin to Center*. Boston, MA: South End Press.

hooks, b. (1990). *Yearning: Race, gender and cultural politics*. Boston, MA: South End Press.

Jansen, S. C. (1996). Beaches without bases: The gender order. In G. Gerbner, H. Mowlana, & H. I. Schiller (Eds.), *Invisible crises: What conglomerate control of media means for America and the world* (pp. 131–144). Boulder, CO: Westview Press.

Jansen, S. C. (2002). Media in crises: Gender and terror, September 2001. *Feminist Media Studies, 2*, 139–140.

Kawaja, J. (1994). Process video: Self-reference and social change. In P. Riaño (Ed.), *Women in grassroots communication: Furthering social change* (pp. 131–148). Thousand Oaks, CA: Sage.

Kramer, J., & Kramarae, C. (2000). Women's political webs: Global electronic networks. In A. Sreberny & L. van Zoonen (Eds.), *Gender, politics and communication* (pp. 205–222). Cresskill, NJ: Hampton Press.

Lloyd, L. (1994). Speak magazine: Breaking barriers and silences. In P. Riaño (Ed.), *Women in grassroots communication: Furthering social change* (pp. 251–259). Thousand Oaks, CA: Sage.

Lorde, A. (1984). *Sister outsider: Essays and speeches by Audre Lorde*. Freedom, CA: Crossing Press.

Luthra, R. (1995). The "abortion clause" in U.S. foreign population policy: The debate viewed through a postcolonial feminist lens. In A. N. Valdivia (Ed.), *Feminism, multiculturalism and the media: Global diversities* (pp. 197–216). Thousand Oaks, CA: Sage.

Mani, L. (1990). Contentious traditions: The debate on Sati in colonial India. In K. Sangari & S. Vaid (Eds.), *Recasting women: Essays in Indian colonial history* (pp. 88–126). New Brunswick, NJ: Rutgers University Press.

Mani, L. (1992). Cultural theory, colonial texts: Reading eyewitness accounts of widow burning. In L. Grossberg, C. Nelson, & P. Treichler (Eds.), *Cultural studies* (pp. 392–408). New York: Routledge.

Mata, M. (1994). Being women in the popular radio. In P. Riaño (Ed.), *Women in grassroots communication: Furthering social change* (pp. 192–212). Thousand Oaks, CA: Sage.

Mies, M., & Shiva, V. (1993). *Ecofeminism*. New Delhi: Kali Press for Women.

Minh-ha, T. (1986). She, the inappropriated other [Special issue]. *Discourse, 8*.

Minh-ha, T. (1991). *When the moon waxes red: Representation, gender and cultural politics*. New York: Routledge.

Mlama, P. (1994). Reinforcing existing indigenous communication skills: The use of dance in Tanzania. In P. Riaño (Ed.), *Women in grassroots communication: Furthering social change* (pp. 51–64). Thousand Oaks, CA: Sage.

Mohanty, C. T. (1991a). Cartographies of struggle: Third World women and the politics of feminism. In C. T. Mohanty, A. Russo, & L. Torres (Eds.), *Third World women and the politics of feminism* (pp. 1–50). Bloomington: Indiana University Press.

Mohanty, C. T. (1991b). Under western eyes: Feminist scholarship and colonial discourses. In C.T. Mohanty, A. Russo, & L. Torres (Eds.), *Third World women and the politics of feminism* (pp. 51–80). Bloomington: Indiana University Press.

Narayan, U. (1997). *Dislocating cultures: Identities, traditions, and Third World feminism*. New York: Routledge.

Newsom, D. A., & Carrell, B. J. (Eds.). (1995). *Silent voices*. New York: University Press of America.

Papa, M. J., Auwal, M. A., & Singhal, A. (1997). Organizing for social change within concertive control systems: Member identification, empowerment, and the masking of discipline. *Communica-

tion Monographs, 64, 219–249.

Papa, M. J., Singhal, A., Ghanekar, D. V., & Papa, W. H. (2000). Organizing for social change through cooperative action: The (dis)empowering dimensions of women's communication. *Communication Theory, 10,* 90–123.

Parmeswaran, R. (1996). Coverage of "bride burning" in the Dallas Observer: A cultural analysis of the "other." *Frontiers, 16,* 69–100.

Rakow, L. F., & Kranich, K. (1991). Woman as sign in television news. *Journal of Communication, 41*(1), 8–23.

Riaño, P. (Ed.). (1994). *Women in grassroots communication: Furthering social change.* Thousand Oaks, CA: Sage.

Riordan, E. (2002). Intersections and new directions: On feminism and political economy. In E. R. Meehan & E. Riordan (Eds.), *Sex and money: Feminism and political economy in the media* (pp. 3–15). Minneapolis: University of Minnesota Press.

Rodriguez, C. (1994). A process of identity deconstruction: Latin American women producing video stories. In P. Riaño (Ed.), *Women in grassroots communication: Furthering social change* (pp. 149–160). Thousand Oaks, CA: Sage.

Rosario-Braid, F. (1996). Filipino women in communications: Breaking new ground. In D. Allen, R. R. Rush, & S. J. Kaufman (Eds.), *Women transforming communications: Global intersections* (pp. 280–289). Thousand Oaks, CA: Sage.

Rowlands, J. (1997). *Questioning empowerment: Working with women in Honduras.* Oxford, UK: Oxfam.

Ruiz, C. (1994). Losing fear: Video and radio productions of native Aymara women in Bolivia. In P. Riaño (Ed.), *Women in grassroots communication: Furthering social change* (pp. 161–178). Thousand Oaks, CA: Sage.

Said, E. W. (1979). *Orientalism.* London: Vintage Books.

Sarikakis, K. (2002). Violence, militarism, terrorism: Faces of a masculine order and the exploitation of women. *Feminist Media Studies, 2,* 151–152.

Schafer, R., & Hornig, S. (1995). The role of women journalists in Philippine political change. In D. A. Newsom & B. J. Carrell (Eds.), *Silent voices* (pp. 177–198). New York: University Press of America.

Sen, G., & Grown, C. (1987). *Development, crises and alternative visions: Third World women's perspectives.* New York: Monthly Review Press.

Spivak, G. C. (1988). Can the subaltern speak? In C. Nelson & L. Grossberg (Eds.), *Marxism and the interpretation of culture* (pp. 271–313). Urbana: University of Illinois Press.

Steeves, H. L. (1993). Gender and mass communication in a global context. In P. J. Creedon (Ed.), *Women in mass communication* (2nd ed., pp. 32–60). Newbury Park, CA: Sage.

Steeves, H. L. (2001). Liberation, feminism, and development communication. *Communication Theory, 11,* 397–414.

Stuart, S., & Bery, R. (1996). Powerful grassroots women communicators: Participatory video in Bangladesh. In D. Allen, R. R. Rush, & S. J. Kaufman (Eds.), *Women transforming communications: Global intersections* (pp. 303–312). Thousand Oaks, CA: Sage.

Toro, M. S. (1996). Feminist international radio endeavor—FIRE. In D. Allen, R. R. Rush, & S. J. Kaufman (Eds.), *Women transforming communications: Global intersections* (pp. 226–232). Thousand Oaks, CA: Sage.

Valdivia, A. (2000). *A Latina in the land of Hollywood and other essays on media culture.* Tucson: University of Arizona Press.

Wadud-Muhsin, A. (1995). Sisters in Islam: Effective against all odds. In D. A. Newsom & B. J. Carrell (Eds.), *Silent voices* (pp. 117–138). New York: University Press of America.

Walsh, S. (2002). A blindfold of compassion? Women as pawns in the new war. *Feminist Media Studies, 2,* 153–154.

Werden, F. (1996). The founding of WINGS (women's international news gathering service): A story of feminist radio survival. In D. Allen, R. R. Rush, & S. J. Kaufman (Eds.), *Women transforming communications: Global intersections* (pp. 218–225). Thousand Oaks, CA: Sage.

Wilkins, K.G. (1997). Gender, power and development. *Journal of International Communica-*

tion, 4, 102–120.

Wilkins, K. G. (2000). Accounting for power in development communication. In K. G. Wilkins (Ed.), *Redeveloping communication for social change: Power, theory, and practice* (pp. 197–210). Boulder, CO: Rowman & Littlefield.

Wilkins, K. G., & Mody, B. (2001). Reshaping development communication: Developing communication and communicating development. *Communication Theory, 11,* 385–396.

Wilkins, K. G., & Waters, J. (2000). Current discourse on new technologies in development discourse. *Media Development, 1,* 57–60.

CHAPTER CONTENTS

3 Empowerment and Communication: Lessons Learned From Organizing for Social Change

EVERETT M. ROGERS
University of New Mexico

ARVIND SINGHAL
Ohio University

Empowerment is the process through which individuals perceive that they control situations. Such perceived agency is a fundamental behavior change, which often leads to many other behavior changes. The present chapter synthesizes research on empowerment and communication in the developing nations of Latin American, Africa, and Asia. Several investigations into the empowerment of underdogs in society are examined, including (a) women dairy farmers in India, (b) women members of the Grameen Bank in Bangladesh, (c) community-based radio listening groups in the villages of Lutsaan and Abirpur in India, and (d) people living with AIDS in Thailand. Essentially, the process of empowerment occurs in small groups at the local level when individuals organize for social change in order to accomplish goals that they cannot achieve as separate individuals. By exploring the relationship between individual and collective empowerment, we seek to draw a series of lessons learned about the empowerment process and apply them more generally to any type of system in any nation.

In 1999, the *Soul City* entertainment-education television series aired in South Africa, modeling a new collective behavior by portraying neighbors intervening in a domestic violence event (Singhal & Rogers, 2003). At that time, the prevailing cultural norm in South Africa was for neighbors not to intervene in a domestic abuse situation. Wife or partner abuse was perceived as a private matter, carried out in a private space, behind closed doors and with the curtains drawn.

AUTHOR'S NOTE: Many of the ideas expressed here are drawn from Shefner-Rogers, Rao, Rogers, & Wayangankar (1998). Various other recent publications on empowerment coauthored by one or both of the present authors (with Michael J. Papa of Michigan State University and other collaborators) are also synthesized here.

Correspondence: Everett M. Rogers, Department of Communication and Journalism, University of New Mexico, Albuquerque, NM 87131-1171, email: erogers@unm.edu

Communication Yearbook 27, pp. 67–85

In the popular *Soul City* series, however, neighbors collectively decided to break the ongoing cycle of spousal abuse in a neighborhood home. When the next wife beating occurred, they gathered around the abuser's residence, collectively banging pots and pans, censuring the abuser's actions. This prime-time entertainment-education (E-E) episode, which earned one of the highest audience ratings in South Africa in 1999, demonstrated the importance of creatively modeling collective efficacy in order to energize neighbors, who, for cultural reasons, felt previously unempowered to intervene. Evaluation research found that exposure to the *Soul City* E-E program was associated with willingness to stand outside the home of an abuser and bang pots (Soul City, 2001). After this episode was broadcast, pot banging to stop partner abuse was reported in various locations in South Africa (Singhal & Rogers, 2003). Patrons of a local pub in Thembisa Township in South Africa exhibited a variation of this practice, collectively banging bottles on the bar when a man physically abused his girlfriend (Soul City, 2001).

The *Soul City* series modeled both *self-efficacy*, an individual's perception of his or her capacity to organize and execute the actions required to manage prospective situations to produce desired attainments (Bandura, 1997), and *collective efficacy*, the degree to which the members of a system believe they have the ability to organize and execute actions required to produce desired attainments (Bandura, 1997). The pot-banging episode described how neighbors collectively displayed efficacy to intervene in a private domestic violence situation. The communication processes that raise individual and collective efficacy also contribute to individual and collective empowerment.

The objective of this review chapter is to synthesize a body of research on empowerment and communication that has been conducted by communication scholars in recent years. Much of this work has been completed in the developing nations of Latin American, Africa, and Asia. Many of the investigations studied empowerment of the underdogs in a society, particularly women in patriarchal societies. Small groups, communities, and organizations have been key components in these empowerment processes. This research, although primarily focused on individual empowerment, also gives attention to collective empowerment. We explore here the relationship between individual and collective empowerment, seeking to draw a series of lessons from the empowerment process that may apply more generally to any type of system in any nation. In doing so, we explicate the theoretical perspectives of Paulo Freire and Saul Alinsky.

EMPOWERMENT AS COMMUNICATION

Empowerment is the process through which individuals perceive that they control situations (Bandura, 1997; Bormann, 1988; Papa, Auwal, & Singhal, 1995, 1997; Papa, Singhal, Ghanekar, & Papa, 2000a; Papa et al., 2000b; Shefner-Rogers, Rao, Rogers, & Wayangankar, 1998). This concept of empowerment is the opposite of fatalism and is very similar to the self-efficacy described by Bandura (1997). The empowered person actively engages the environment instead of passively reacting to events. A collective of disempowered individuals may organize for social change so that each individual becomes more empowered. Bandura stated:

> "Empowerment" is not something bestowed through edict. It is gained through development of personal efficacy that enables people to take advantage of opportunities and to remove environmental constraints guarded by those whose interests are served by them. . . . Equipping people with a firm belief that they can produce valued effect by their collective action and providing them with the means to do so are the key ingredients in an enablement process. (p. 477)

Empowerment can be individual, or it can characterize a system or collectivity such as a group, community, or organization.

Unempowered individuals usually require external stimuli to become empowered. Often a change agent (trainer, community organizer, etc.) will become the focal point that will enable the empowerment process. In this instance, the role of the change agent is that of a facilitator, not problem solver, in order to assist and encourage the group/individual's capacity for self-empowerment. To sustain empowerment, the community (the population of empowered individuals) must establish and maintain a localized social organization. Of course, the test of any externally induced process occurs when the change agent withdraws from the system and is successful only if the empowerment process continues to function effectively (Bandura, 1997).

Although there has been notable interest in the concept of empowerment in past communication study (Albrecht, 1988; Buzzanell, 1994; Chiles & Zorn, 1995; Cooks & Hale, 1992; Craig, 1994; Deetz, 1994; Mumby, 1993; Novek, 1992; Pacanowsky, 1988), we still do not understand completely how the empowerment process occurs and how it is manifest through specific communication behaviors. When people collaborate with one another to create their own social rules, opportunities for individual and collective empowerment can emerge. Although there are different ways to conceptualize empowerment (cf. Alvesson & Willmott, 1992; Blau & Alba, 1982; Conger, 1989; Conger & Kanugo, 1988; Pacanowsky, 1988; Vogt & Murrell, 1990), we advocate the basic view of empowerment as a communication process that often results from individuals communicating in small groups.

Research in other disciplines reveals important insights into the communicative aspects of empowerment. In the community psychology literature, for example, empowerment is described as an internal process that allows people to gain mastery over issues of concern to them (Rappaport, 1987; Zimmerman, 1995). Importantly, empowerment requires an active engagement of one's system (Zimmerman, Israel, Schulz, & Checkoway, 1992).

The communication dimension of empowerment has been examined by several disciplines, including community psychology (Kroeker, 1995), feminist studies (Young, 1994), urban planning (Wilson, 1996), organizational studies (Cheney,

1995; Mumby, 1997; Papa et al., 1995, 1997), and development communication (Jacobson, 1993; Thomas, 1994; White, 1994). For example, Kroeker (1995) argued that collective action increases the potential of overcoming poverty because when people work together they can carry out communal projects, pursue resources, and overcome dependence on government assistance.

Paulo Freire and Active Participation

Empowerment as a communication process was initially defined in the theoretical works of Paulo Freire and Saul Alinsky. In *Pedagogy of the Oppressed*, Freire (1968) was critical of adult literacy classes that used a rote memory approach. To counter this, he developed problem-posing education. This approach "respond(s) to the essence of consciousness . . . rejects [one-way] communiqués and embodies communication" (p. 66). Traditionally, the instructor would show the adult students a picture of a farmer with a cow and insist that the students memorize the word "cow" (one-way communication). Freire believed that the instructor should also show a picture of a farmer with 10 cows and inquire of the adult students why it was that one farmer had 10 cows and the other only had one. This type of instruction, dialogic interaction, would then create consciousness-raising in which the students became aware of class and power contradictions. The short-term effects of both teaching methods were that all students became literate. However, the long-term effect was that many students of the one-way communication reverted to illiteracy within a few years while those taught through dialogic interaction did not because they had been empowered through a consciousness-raising process. Freire's thinking about communication and empowerment has been implemented throughout the world in adult literacy and other types of development programs.

In *Rules for Radicals,* Alinsky (1972) provides another perspective on the empowerment process—that of the change agent. Alinsky believed that the community must be involved in social change for lasting change or true empowerment to occur. Alinsky explained, "My thing, if I want to organize, is solid communication within the people in the community" (p. xix). Theorizing and research on the role of participation in development programs exists in scholarly traditions and includes intervention intended to empower (e.g., Fals Borda, 1987).

One of Alinsky's rules was to never do for someone else what they could do for themselves, that is, start with the current situation not with the desired end. Alinsky also believed that disillusionment was a necessity in order for people to take a risk on a future that they would control (Shefner-Rogers et al., 1998).

Dialogic Communication

In the Indian village of Dubbagunta, in Andhra Pradesh, the women responded as one to drunkenness and economic or physical abuse by their spouses. A fictional woman, Sithamma, inspired the women of this village. They had read about her in the adult literacy classes. Like her, they organized and destroyed the local liquor (*arrack*) shops. News of this event spread and soon the phenomenon of the antiarrack movement had spread to hundreds of villages. Because of the pressure from women, four Indian states eventually enacted prohibition laws. In many Asian nations, women have become empowered in recent years in order to combat their husband's drunkenness. In this sense, alcohol abuse by males represents one stimulus to female empowerment at the village level.

The collective action demonstrated by the women of Dubbagunta increased their potential for overcoming social inequality. When people work together, they may perceive and experience the strength of a collectivity. In reality, it is the process of organizing, talking, networking, collaboration sharing, and so forth that encourages empowerment and facilitates the new community awareness (Papa et al., 2000a).

Freire and Alinsky each believed that a communication process drives empowerment. Both Freire and Alinsky posited that through this process the relationships between two unequal entities are fundamentally altered. How empowering messages are relayed, that is, dialogic versus one-way communication, is important to this process. Also vital to empowerment is the dialogue and interaction that takes place between the subordinated group members. We see empowerment when human decision making and actions are the result of consensus.

The communication facet of empowerment is often not recognized even by communication scholars who study feminism, development, persuasion, and social change. In relating the relevant dynamics of self-efficacy, Bandura (1997) stated:

> Such beliefs influence the course of action people choose to pursue, how much effort they put forth in given endeavors, how long they will persevere in the face of obstacles and failures, their resilience to adversity, whether their thought patterns are self-hindering or self-aiding, how much stress and depression they experience in coping with taxing environmental demands, and the level of accomplishments they realize. (p. 3)

Most programs to raise levels of empowerment in various nations are essentially communication interventions, and such empowerment effects are stronger when the communication process is dialogic.

Approaching women's advancement through empowerment in the third world accepts that the use of local women's organizations is necessary to overcome the patriarchal structure of subordination. The feminist style of organizing starts with the premise that patriarchy does exist and that this dominance over women must cease (Buzzanell, 1994; Calas & Smircich, 1992). The direction one takes to empowerment will vary based upon the feminist stance taken (Buzzanell, 1994; Donovan, 1985; Jaggar, 1983; Langston, 1988; Tong, 1989).

Buzzanell (1994) argued that three primary themes characterize feminist organizing processes: (a) cooperative enactment, (b) integrative thinking, and (c) connectedness. The theme of cooperative enactment emphasizes the importance of working together to reach individual and collective goals rather than competing against one another for limited rewards. In particular, women emphasize a cooperative ethic in their talk by engaging in dialogue to coordinate their efforts to pursue common goals.

The theme of integrative thinking is centered on the importance of context in evaluating potential choices and actions. For example, although a given action, such as small business development, can bring about a specific intended effect (such as increased income), feminists think in holistic or integrative ways by considering how specific actions can produce a number of direct and indirect effects. As Buzzanell (1994) explained, when a woman thinks in an integrative manner, she considers how a given action will influence her life and the lives of her family members. She may be concerned with how a new behavior (such as assertiveness) will contribute to power imbalances in her important personal relationships. She may consider the impact of her actions (such as purchasing an additional milk buffalo for her herd) on the environment.

The feminist-organizing theme of connectedness consists of attempts to integrate the mind, body, and emotions in making sense of the surrounding world (Buzzanell, 1994). Humans are holistic beings who are not limited to displays of rationality. Rather, every individual has an emotional side. Women can thrive in environments where they have opportunities to connect with and nurture others on their pathways to collective success.

Local groups are able to facilitate change from the bottom up by raising the consciousness level of those being subordinated. Some keys to the success of female empowerment programs in the third world are (a) raising awareness of a disadvantaged societal position, (b) access to education, (c) access to employment opportunities, and (d) access to health care. In many of these nations, female empowerment was initially stimulated by the feminist movement in North America and Europe and has been encouraged by national governments, often through a ministry of women's affairs, which launches programs and promotes policies to encourage empowerment.

Community-level organizations of rural women are crucial in providing the individual with group support, collective articulation of common inequalities or problems, and as a base for bargaining. Recently, many development programs have shifted from focusing on the economic aspects of development to focusing on more cultural aspects of community relationships, such as improving the status of women. This shift has directly involved women in their own empowerment programs. This new direction closely follows the theoretical perspectives of Alinsky and Freire in that the empowered individual must desire change and must be involved in the decision that initiates and sustains the empowerment process. Freire (1968) explained that "instead of following predetermined plans, leaders and people, mutually identified, together create the guidelines of their action" (p. 183).

Studies of the female empowerment process suggest that women themselves, when organized in a women's group can best carry empowerment activities forward. As an example, take an organization of mothers in the village of Oryu Li, Korea. The group progressed to larger and larger self-development projects, each project building on previous successes. In this way, the participants gained individual empowerment and collective self-efficacy (Rogers & Kincaid, 1981). As a result, the collective group action across the village communication networks shifted the power from older males to a wider sharing of influence. Women in Oryu Li, once empowered, were able to combat problems caused by spousal alcoholism and to achieve some economic gains. Eventually, this empowerment strategy of using the interpersonal communication networks in Oryu Li positively affected the lives of 750,000 Korean women.

The early success in Korea then spread to other Asian nations like the Philippines and Bangladesh, where organizing women's clubs at the village level encouraged female empowerment. This strategy began to reveal the process of organizing for social change, a theoretical approach combining certain elements of organizational communication and development communication in order to understand the process through which a group of disempowered individuals gain control of their future.

In India, during the late 1980s, only one out of every seven tasks related to dairy farming were carried out by men; yet in 1989, as few as 16% of the women belonged to a dairy cooperative that marketed the milk. Husbands controlled income from milk and the men dominated the cooperatives, which meant that the primary workers in the dairy industry (women) were excluded from the marketing process. For the women managing the dairies, this exclusion became a form of oppression. *Oppression* exists when an individual or group systematically obtains a controlling advantage over another individual or group.

Empowerment seeks to change norms, that is, standards for expected behavior within a social system (Rogers & Steinfatt, 1999). An element in the social structure often supports and reinforces other elements in a social structure. For example, in much of the developing world, male infants are perceived as more valuable than female infants. Therefore, men are automatically afforded higher status than women. This forces women into an oppressed position. Case in point, a dowry is commonly received from the bride's family by the groom's family. Therefore, this accepted social life pattern reinforces patriarchal norms that eventually subordinated the female Indian dairy farmers.

Empowered women in India challenged previously accepted norms. For instance, in the Suburdi village of Maharashtra, one of the social life patterns was that husbands spent most of the family earnings on *hooch* (a locally made liquor). The *mahila mandal* (local women's club) that had been established as part of an empowerment program for female dairy farmers, protested the men's drinking. At a meeting, all the village women collectively formed a plan of action. They marched and demanded that the hooch brewers close their businesses. The brewers did not respond. So the women destroyed all the breweries in the village. However, hooch from nearby villages was brought into Suburdi. In response, the women organized

Suburdi as an alcohol-free zone. Here, we see empowered women becoming involved and resolving a social problem that affected their families and their financial well-being. The mahila mandal provided a structure for social change (Shefner-Rogers et al., 1998).

The importance of female empowerment in the dairy industry is exemplified in a study in a Rajasthan village. The village women received loans (through a government program) to purchase milk buffaloes (Sharma & Vanjani, 1993). They also received 12 days of technical training in dairy husbandry. However, they were not empowered nor did they have a woman's organization. They did not manage the dairy enterprise nor were they able to demand control of the payment for the sale of milk from their husbands. In fact, they now had to work harder without pay. The frustration levels understandably increased. Without female empowerment, no real progress in dairy development resulted from the government intervention.

The Cooperative Development (CD) program of the National Dairy Development Board (NDDB) realized that more was required than technical training to have lasting benefits for the female dairy farmers. They needed to be empowered to control not only a dairy enterprise but other parts of their lives. They required sustainability. *Sustainability* is the extent to which a development activity continues its effectiveness after the defining development effort ceases (Rogers & Steinfatt, 1999). Similarly, Freire (1968) found in Brazil that adult literacy training lacked sustainability unless it was accompanied by consciousness-raising and empowerment.

The NDDB saw that the females were more effective as dairy farmers and were more effective than their husbands when empowered and organized as cooperative members in mahila mandals. A positive social change had taken place. Those cooperatives with empowered female members obtained greater savings for their membership, produced more and higher quality milk, and usually did not indulge in fiscal malfeasance. The female dairy farmers as members of the cooperative used their money responsibly, purchasing food, clothing, and schooling for their children, as well as saving for the future.

TRAINING WOMEN DAIRY FARMERS IN EMPOWERMENT

In 1989 the NDDB established a female empowerment-training program. The objective was to develop more autonomous, self-reliant cooperatives. To implement this program five-person teams were trained at district-level milk unions. Minimally, two of the five team members were women, recruited from female professionals working in the villages. Veterinarians and extension workers made up most of the male component of the CD core teams. To conform to cultural norms, only female CD staff could interact directly with female dairy farmers (Shefner-Rogers et al., 1998).

When implemented in 1995 this effort became one of the largest women's empowerment programs in the world. In 1 year alone, these five-member teams typically trained approximately 250,000 women in 4,000 village-level dairy cooperatives. The CD teams were trained in dialogic and participatory processes through a 5-week CD training course that included (a) public speaking and group discussions; (b) designing and using teaching aids; (c) developing field skills by role playing; and (d) creating an environment for two-way communication. Thus, the training itself became a participatory and empowering communication process.

The first step in training a village was to educate the male members of the village dairy cooperative, because it was the male members that resisted the female empowerment program. This first step was to sensitize them to the benefits of empowering the village women.

A restricted access building was used for the women's CD training to enable the women to speak freely outside the presence of village men. Usually seated closely on the floor, the women would perform problem-solving activities and participate in group singing, led by an instructor. These group actions developed solidarity among the women. To further reinforce this bonding, the meetings were often closed by repeating slogans like "Long live cooperatives!" The empowerment process was a highly emotional experience for the women involved.

Dialogic Communication

The women CD instructors introduced empowering concepts to the women dairy farmers in a variety of ways. For example, to bring about the realization of the inferior status of Indian female dairy farmers, the instructors led them in the following dialogue.

Trainer:	Who goes to bed last in your house?
Women:	We do.
Trainer:	Who gets up first?
Women:	We do.
Trainer:	Who works hardest?
Women:	We do.
Trainer:	Who feeds and cares for the milk animals?
Women:	We do.
Trainer:	Who milks these animals?
Women:	We do.
Trainer:	Who hands over the milk to your husband to collect the payment?
Women:	We do.
Trainer:	Who are fools?
Women:	We are! (Shefner-Rogers et al., 1998, p. 329)

This dialogue emphasizes the issue of gender inequality and demonstrates one way that the CD program employed a dialogic process to raise the level of awareness among the Indian female dairy farmers to this inequality. Basically, the CD instructors created dissonance via participatory activities and through skill building, thereby enabling the women to empower themselves to gain ownership and control over their dairying operations, as well as to gain the ability to participate in decision making. Cooperation through dialogic action permitted the female dairy farmers to be empowered collectively in ways that were impossible for them as individuals.

At the conclusion of the 2-day training session, the CD team then assisted in organizing a women's club, a mahila mandal. The intent of the mahila mandal was to sustain self-empowerment by encouraging income generation, savings plans, and temperance campaigns. The sole role of the CD instructor was to instigate and catalyze the empowerment process in the villages (Shefner-Rogers et al., 1998). The empowerment process then usually continued under the complete control of the village women. Here, we see the importance of organizing for social change, a process that facilitates empowerment.

EFFECTS OF FEMALE EMPOWERMENT TRAINING

Shefner-Rogers et al. (1998) noted a number of findings directly correlated with the CD programs, including (a) greater empowerment among participants; (b) greater effectiveness of the village cooperatives; (c) increased female membership in the cooperatives and better attendance of meetings; and (d) significant increases in cattle-feed sales and milk production. Further, female dairy farmers who became members of mahila mandals were empowered to a greater extent than women who did not join the groups. Membership in the mahila mandals provided women dairy farmers with the opportunity to interact with one another, learn from each other, and to empower themselves.

Empowerment, once instigated, can also occur interactively between members of an empowering organization. For example, two women dairy framers used protein enriched cattle food to increase production (Papa et al., 2000a). One woman's cattle refused the new feed. She told her friend, who responded:

> I had problems too. Then I started mixing a little of the new cattle feed with regular green fodder. Then my cow took it. I slowly added a little more of the new feed each day until she was eating all of the recommended amount. (p. 104)

The CD empowerment program was effective in helping many women dairy farmers to increase their incomes through higher milk production and better milk quality. Women learned from one another by sharing dairying techniques that they had learned through experience.

Empowerment is not a linear process, free of barriers, paradoxes, and contradictions (Papa et al., 2000a). One woman in training to be a dairy cooperative manager was learning to test for levels of milk fat. This process required the use of acid. During the training session a glass tube exploded, spaying acid into her eyes. After being treated the woman insisted on returning immediately to continue the training, saying, my husband and the other men in this village have told all of us [women dairy cooperative members] that women can do nothing. They say that running the cooperative is their job. Women will get hurt if they try to test the milk. If I don't complete my testing today . . . the dairy cooperative will close. (Papa et al., 2000a, p. 98)

This impressed most women in the training courses; however, some became disenchanted and saw this as one more barrier to women in a male-dominated society.

In summary, a large-scale empowerment intervention for female dairy farmers in India through 2-day training meetings and the organization of village-level women's clubs led to (a) heightened empowerment, (b) increased milk production and better quality milk, and (c) stronger dairy cooperatives.

GRAMEEN BANK IN BANGLADESH: ORGANIZING FOR SOCIAL CHANGE

The Grameen (rural) Bank, founded in Bangladesh in 1983 by Professor Muhammad Yunus, exemplifies the empowerment strategy of organizing for social change, defined previously as a theoretical approach combining certain elements of organizational communication and development communication in order to understand the process through which a group of disempowered individuals can gain control of their future (Auwal, 1996; Singhal & Rogers, 2003).

Small-Group Networks as Collateral

Grameen Bank is a system of lending small amounts of money to poor women so that they can earn a living through self-employment. No collateral is needed (the poor do not have any). Instead, the women borrowers are organized in a small network of five friends. Each group member must repay their loan on time, and ensure that other group members do the same, or else their opportunity for a future loan is jeopardized. The delicate group dynamic between peer pressure and peer support among Grameen borrowers is at the heart of its widespread success (Papa et al., 1997). By 2002, the Grameen Bank in Bangladesh loaned money to about 2.5 million poor women borrowers and had an enviable loan recovery rate of 95%. The idea of microlending, based on the Grameen Bank experience, has spread throughout the world and has proven effective in gaining a high rate of repayment of the loans (Singhal, Svenkerud, & Flydal, 2002).

Borrowers from the Grameen Bank must become interdependent on the other members of their small (five-member) network of peers. If each individual fulfills their expected role by repaying her loan, all members of the five-member network are empowered. The purpose of Grameen Bank loans is to provide self-employment, which is itself empowering. By inviting individuals' participation in the Grameen Bank's local borrowers' networks, self-employment is encouraged (Fals Borda, 1987; Gumucio Dagron, 2001).

Grameen Bank has over 12,000 field workers who serve 2.5 million members in 41,000 villages in Bangladesh. The Grameen Bank exercises an empowering influence on both its field workers and its borrowers/members (Papa et al., 1995; 1997). Muhammad Sobhan, a Grameen worker from Chittagong, Bangladesh, provided insight into the empowerment of field workers.

> I could never imagine working [at] another job where I could have so much influence in helping others. Professor Yunus trusts us and respects our judgment. We decide together in the [local] branch what needs to be done to help members, and we put the plan into action. (Papa et al., 1997, p. 233)

Sobhan's comments reveal how Grameen workers experience empowerment through interaction with their peers.

Organizing for Social Change

Grameen Bank women borrowers in one village in Bangladesh organized for social change through collective action to oppose local money lenders who charged exorbitant interest rates. A village money lender threatened to break the legs of a Grameen Bank worker serving one village. In response, 30 women borrowers from the Grameen Bank went to the money lender's house and told him that he had to provide them with loans at the same interest rate as Grameen Bank, which he would not do. However, he did stop harassing the Grameen Bank worker. Here we see the power of numbers. Thirty landless women could intimidate a wealthy man when they joined forces (Shehabuddin, 1992).

Papa and associates (1995, 1997) provided another example of how Grameen Bank members experience empowerment through group interaction. Bank members in a village near Nageswari, Bangladesh, were concerned with the continuing practice of dowry in their community. They negotiated a solution among themselves by deciding not to give or take dowry in the marriage of their children. To avoid the clandestine practice of dowry, the villagers arranged marriages between their sons and daughters. On one occasion, the Grameen Bank members learned that a local bridegroom was demanding a bicycle and a radio as dowry. At the end of the wedding ceremony, the women of the village told the bridegroom that he could leave with either the bride or the dowry that he demanded, but not both. To avoid public embarrassment, the bridegroom left with the bride.

In recent years, the Grameen Bank in Bangladesh has begun making loans to village women in order for them to purchase a mobile telephone. Each borrower then provides telephone service, for a fee, to other villagers, earning enough income to support their family. Today, Grameen Bank also provides loans to village women in order to purchase laptop computers, so that borrowers can act as mobile cyber cafés and provide Internet access to fellow villagers (Rogers, 2003; Singhal et al., 2002).

Empowerment emerges among both Grameen Bank's field workers and borrowers as they meet, socialize, discuss ideas, and determine actions they can take in the face of demanding situations. These examples show how empowerment is an interactional process (Chiles & Zorn, 1995; Papa et al., 1997) in which members collectively identify specific courses of action to improve their lives socially and economically. Although the initial purpose of the Grameen Bank, and of the various microlending programs around the world today modeled after it, was economic development through job creation for poor women; one important consequence has been female empowerment achieved through organized group action.

THE LUTSAAN VILLAGE STUDY

An investigation in Lutsaan, a North Indian village, helped illuminate the process of female empowerment. In January 1997, 184 villagers in Lutsaan signed a pledge not to pay, or accept, dowry (an illegal but widespread practice in India). These villagers also refused to allow child marriages (also an illegal but common practice) and pledged to educate daughters equally with their sons (Papa et al., 2000b). The 20- by 24-inch poster-letter pledge was mailed by the villagers of Lutsaan to All India Radio, the government broadcasting network, in Delhi. The petition was inspired by an entertainment-education radio soap opera, *Tinka Tinka Sukh* (Happiness Lies in Small Pleasures), which was being broadcast in North India. In the radio program, a young women, Poonam, is continually abused by her husband and his parents for bringing an inadequate dowry, until she commits suicide.

The poster-letter stated: "Listeners of our village [to *Tinka Tinka Sukh*] now actively oppose the practice of dowry—they neither give nor receive dowry." The letter-poster was forwarded by All India Radio to the present authors, who were evaluating the effects of the entertainment-education radio soap opera. The authors conducted an in-depth case study of the empowerment process in Lutsaan over several years. At that time, research on entertainment-education had showed that this strategy could have strong effects (Singhal & Rogers, 1999), but these investigations consisted mainly of large-scale audience surveys. The Lutsaan study disaggregated this research approach, allowing us to better understand the process through which entertainment-education had its effects on knowledge, attitudes, and behavior change in regards to audience individuals.

A local group, the Shyam Club, devoted to village improvement, already existed in Lutsaan. The episodes about dowry (those dealing with the suicide of Poonam) activated members of the Shyam Club to attack the problems of dowry and gender inequality in their village. As one villager stated:

Poonam's suicide in the soap opera resounded with us because we also practice dowry. Now after listening to *Tinka Tinka Sukh*, . . . we formed a group to end dowry in this village. In this way our sisters and daughters will not suffer. (Papa et al., 2000b, p. 45)

A young tailor in the village was especially influenced by the radio program episodes about dowry and initiated the process of writing the poster-letter among the people in his tailor shop. The tailor was of lower status but he activated village leaders of the Shyam Club in the antidowry initiative.

As a result of the forces set in motion by the tailor and members of the Shyam Club, the villagers formed radio listening clubs, planted trees for reforestation, and built pit latrines for improving village sanitation. Girls' enrollment in the village's schools increased from 10% at the time of the radio broadcasts, to 38% 2 years later. Fewer dowry marriages and child marriages occurred in Lutsaan, although these practices did not disappear completely in the village (Papa et al., 2000b).

The Lutsaan case study suggests that audience members are not just passive receptors of media messages. Entertainment-education interventions have their strongest effects on audience behavior change when messages stimulate reflection, debate, and interpersonal communication about the educational topic among audience members (Papa et al., 2000b), as well as when services can be delivered locally. One means of stimulating peer conversations is to broadcast to organized listening groups (Singhal & Rogers, 2002).

THE *TARU* PROJECT

In 2002, All India Radio, in cooperation with Population Communications International, New York, broadcast an entertainment-education radio soap opera *Taru* (the name of the program's female protagonist) in four Hindi-speaking states, Bihar, Jharkhand, Madhya Pradesh, and Chhatisgarh, which together have a population of about 180 million people. The ground-based partner in these four Indian states was Janani, a nongovernmental organization that trained 20,000 rural medical practitioners (RMPs) and their spouses in reproductive health care services. Preprogram publicity about *Taru* was conducted on-air by All India Radio, encouraging people to listen and also persuading prospective audience members to organize radio listening groups. On the ground in the 20,000 villages where Janani operates, *Taru* was publicized by the rural medical practitioners through wall paintings, posters, stickers, and through folk media performances (Singhal & Rogers, 2003). Group listening was also encouraged in the villages. All India Radio provided the air cover and Janani provided the community-based ground forces to stimulate active message reception. Janani's RMPs provided local service delivery, including condoms, pills, pregnancy dipsticks, vitamins, and other medications.

One of the present authors (Singhal) is leading an investigation of *Taru* to gauge the impacts of integrating entertainment-education media broadcasts with community-based listening and service delivery. In Abirpur, a village in Bihar State, a young women's listener group is very active. It meets every Friday to listen to *Taru*, discuss the episode's contents, and to record their daily impressions in a diary. Usha Kumari, an 18-year-old listener and group member, noted:

The character of Taru has inspired me to do something with my life. Previously I lacked in self-confidence, but I have slowly gotten out of my shell. I am beginning to learn how to administer medication, including injections and saline drips from my uncle who is the rural health provider in Abirpur. (personal communication, September 2, 2002)

Another listening group member, Kumari Neha, noted:

Our discussions have given us strength and confidence. Now I am not shy of speaking in front of my parents. We have all told our parents that we will like to go to college, and we will not marry in a household which demands dowry. (personal communication, September 4, 2002)

Abirpur's experience reinforced the point that when people organize themselves around a common purpose, in this instance listening to a radio soap opera, the interactions help stimulate reflection, debate, and action, which may not occur for an individual listener. As Suneeta Kumari, a young listening group member said: "There is strength in numbers" (personal communication, September 2, 2002).

The *Taru* Project is intended to improve access to health services, provided by RMPs, in remote areas of Bihar State, as well as to empower radio listeners in the small listening groups. Here again we see the potential for social change through organizing people in small groups at the local level.

EMPOWERING PEOPLE LIVING WITH HIV/AIDS

In the past decade, the worldwide AIDS epidemic has become concentrated among poor people, especially those living in Africa and certain Asian nations. Currently, 95% of all people with AIDS (PWAs), about 40 million individuals, are in Latin America, Africa, or Asia. In certain nations like Thailand, thousands of PWAs, organized in local groups, have become empowered to make demands on their government for lower priced antiretroviral drugs, to fight the stigma of HIV/AIDS, and to provide each other with social support (Singhal & Rogers, 2003). Through the collective actions of PWA groups, individuals can accomplish objectives that are out of their reach when they act separately.

The organization of HIV-positive people was initiated in 1991 in Chiang Mai, Thailand. Individuals with HIV/AIDS were greatly stigmatized at this time and most feared to disclose their HIV status. A traditional health provider was cooking up a batch of herbal medicine for seropositive individuals and a group of PWAs gathered to await preparation of the drugs. With the encouragement of the traditional healer, the PWAs decided to form a support group.

PWA groups in Thailand grew from this first unit in Chiang Mai in 1991, to 15 in 1994, to 35 in 1995, to 78 in 1996, to 105 in 1997, to 195 in 1998, and to 224 in 1999; this just in the six northern provinces around Chiang Mai. Over 400 PWA groups existed in Thailand in 2001. These PWA groups have names that hint at their functions: New Life Friends, Doi Saket Widows, White Sky, Warmly Love, and Tapestry of Friendship. By forming these local groups, people living with HIV/AIDS gained a feeling of collective efficacy, lobbied for their civil rights, and defeated stigma (Singhal & Rogers, 2003). Several thousand members of local PWA groups in Thailand, organized nationally in the AIDS Access Foundation, massed at the Ministry of Health in Bangkok on December 1, 2001, World AIDS Day, to demonstrate for lower priced AIDS drugs. The Thai Minister of Health agreed to cover the cost of the antiretroviral drugs for PWAs enrolled in the nation-wide 30 *baht* ($1.50 U.S.) per month health scheme, at least to the extent that the Ministry budget would allow.

Here we see how local groups, in this case composed of people living with HIV/AIDS, can serve as informal schools for empowerment. PWAs, once empow-ered, became an important force in combating the worldwide AIDS epidemic.

CONCLUSIONS

What general lessons learned can be derived from the research reviewed here about the nature of empowerment and communication?

1. The empowerment process fundamentally consists of dialogic communica-tion. Individuals gain a belief in their power to achieve desired goals through talk-ing with others, particularly peers.

2. The process of empowering individuals occurs especially in small groups. These groups often must be organized by a trainer or change agent, who then withdraws from the scene, with the groups, hopefully, continuing.

3. The small groups that serve as informal schools for empowerment may be organized for a specific purpose, such as combating a particular social problem, but then the members of these groups gain a sense of empowerment and often attack other problems that are perceived as important to them.

4. The mass media can play a role in empowerment, for example, by providing role models for empowerment to an audience, but these effects are greater (a) when the media messages follow an entertainment-education strategy and (b) when au-dience members are organized in listening or viewing groups.

When vulnerable individuals organize around a common purpose, opportuni-ties for collective learning, mutual support, and group action emerge. The vulner-ability of a single individual is overcome by the strength of the many. One woman by herself has little power to confront an abusive husband or a dominating money lender. However, women organized together (i.e., in a microcredit borrowing group such as the Grameen Bank) can free themselves from financial bondage and from violent husbands.

When individuals organize in small groups to take charge of their lives, they shift community norms, which may make the social change more sustainable. For instance, when an empowered individual decides not to give or receive dowry, such action does little to change the community practice of dowry. However, when community members decide that dowry is wrong and the entire community (or most of its members) halts the practice, more lasting social change is likely.

The present review essay focused on organizing for social change, a theoretical approach that combines certain elements of organizational and development communication in order to understand the process through which a group of disempowered individuals gain control of their future. This conceptual approach to understanding the empowerment process emerged gradually through the sequential series of empowerment investigations reported here, studies that were conducted by the present authors and their colleagues over a period of 20 years. Most of these studies dealt with the empowerment of women in patriarchal Asian societies, especially India and Bangladesh.

These restricted beginnings of theorizing about organizing for social change may limit the application of this theory to other cultures and other interventions for social change, such as in organizational development in nations like the United States. Future communication research is needed to test the possible applications of organizing for social change.

REFERENCES

Albrecht, T. L. (1988). Communication and control in empowering organizations. In J. A. Anderson (Ed.), *Communication yearbook 11* (pp. 380–390). Thousand Oaks, CA: Sage.

Alinsky, S. D. (1972). *Rules for radicals: A practical primer for realistic radicals.* New York: Vintage Books.

Alvesson, M., & Willmott, H. (1992). On the idea of emancipation in management and organization studies. *Academy of Management Review, 17*, 432–464.

Auwal, M. A. (1996). Promoting microcapitalism in the service of the poor: The Grameen model and its cross-cultural adaptation. *Journal of Business Communication, 33*, 27–49.

Bandura, A. (1997). *Self-efficacy: The exercise of control.* New York: Freeman.

Blau, J. R., & Alba, R. D. (1982). Empowering nets of participation. *Administrative Science Quarterly, 27*, 363–379.

Bormann, E. G. (1988). "Empowering" as a heuristic concept in organizational communication. In J. A. Anderson (Ed.), *Communication yearbook 11* (pp. 391–404). Thousand Oaks, CA: Sage.

Buzzanell, P. M. (1994). Gaining a voice: Feminist organizational communication theorizing. *Management Communication Quarterly, 7*, 339–383.

Calas, M. B., & Smircich, L. (1992). Re-writing gender into organizational theorizing: Directions from feminist perspectives. In M. Reed & M. Hughes (Eds.), *Rethinking organization: New directions in organizational theory and analysis* (pp. 277–253). London: Sage.

Cheney, G. (1995). Democracy in the workplace: Theory and practice from the perspective of communication. *Journal of Applied Communication Research, 23*, 167–200.

Chiles, A. M., & Zorn, T. E. (1995). Empowerment in organizations: Employees' perceptions of the influences on empowerment. *Journal of Applied Communication Research, 23*, 167–200.

Conger, J. A. (1989). Leadership: The art of empowering others. *Academy of Management Review, 13*, 17–24.

Conger, J. A., & Kanugo, R. (1988). The empowerment process: Integrating theory and practice. *Academy of Management Review, 13*, 471–482.

Cooks, L. M., & Hale, C. L. (1992). A feminist approach to the empowerment of women mediators. *Discourse & Society, 3*, 277–300.

Craig, R. T. (1994, November). *What must be in a communication theory?* Paper presented at the annual meeting of the Speech Communication Association, New Orleans, LA.

Deetz, S. A. (1994). Future of the discipline: The challenges, the research, and the social contribution. In S. A. Deetz (Ed.), *Communication yearbook 17* (pp. 565–600). Thousand Oaks, CA: Sage.

Donovan, J. (1985). *Feminist theory: The intellectual traditions of American feminism.* New York: Frederick Unger.

Fals Borda, O. (1987). The application of participatory action-research in Latin America. *International Sociology, 2*, 329–347.

Freire, P. (1968). *Pedagogy of the oppressed.* New York: Herder & Herder.

Gumucio Dagron, A. (2001). *Making waves: Stories of participatory communication for social change.* New York: Rockefeller Foundation.

Jacobsen, T. J. (1993). A pragmatist account of participatory research for national development. *Communication Theory, 3*, 214–230.

Jaggar, A. (1983). Political philosophies of women's liberation. In L. Richardson & V. Taylor (Eds.), *Feminist frontiers: Rethinking sex, gender, and society* (pp. 322–329). New York: Random House.

Kroeker, C. J. (1995). Individual, organizational, and societal empowerment: A study of the processes in a Nicaraguan agricultural cooperative. *American Journal of Community Psychology, 23*, 749–764.

Langston, D. (1988). Feminist theories and the politics of difference. In J. W. Cochran, D. Langston, & C. Woodward (Eds.), *Changing our power* (pp. 10–21). Dubuque, IA: Kendall Hunt.

Mumby, D. K. (1993). Critical organizational communication studies: The next ten years. *Communication Monographs, 60*, 34–46.

Mumby, D. K. (1997). The problem of hegemony: Rereading Gramsci for organizational communication studies. *Western Journal of Communication, 61*, 343–375.

Novek, E. M. (1992). No pitiful stories: Looking at the relationship between adult literacy programs and empowerment. *Howard Journal of Communication, 3*, 267–280.

Pacanowsky, M. (1988). Communicating in the empowering organization. In J. A. Anderson (Ed.), *Communication yearbook 11* (pp. 356–379). Thousand Oaks, CA: Sage.

Papa, M. J., Auwal, M. A., & Singhal, A. (1995). Dialectic of control and emancipation in organizing for social change: A multitheoretic study of the Grameen Bank in Bangladesh. *Communication Theory, 5*, 189–223.

Papa, M. J., Auwal, M. A., & Singhal, A. (1997). Organizing for social change within concertive control systems: Member identification, empowerment, and the masking of discipline. *Communication Monographs, 64*, 219–249.

Papa, M. J., Singhal, A., Ghanekar, D. V., & Papa, W. H. (2000a). Organizing for social change through cooperative action: The [dis]empowering dimensions of women's communication. *Communication Theory, 10*, 90–123.

Papa, M. J., Singhal, A., Law, S., Pant, S., Sood, S., Rogers, E. M., et al. (2000b). Entertainment-education and social change: An analysis of parasocial interaction, social learning, collective efficacy, and paradoxical communication. *Journal of Communication, 50*(4), 31–55.

Rappaport, J. (1987). Terms of empowerment/exemplars of prevention: Toward a theory of community psychology. *American Journal of Community Psychology, 15*, 121–148.

Rogers, E. M. (2003). *Diffusion of innovations* (5th ed.). New York: Free Press.

Rogers, E. M., & Kincaid, D. L. (1981). *Communication networks: Toward a new paradigm for research.* New York: Free Press.

Rogers, E. M., & Steinfatt, T. M. (1999). *Intercultural communication.* Prospect Heights, IL: Waveland Press.

Sharma, M., & Vanjani, U. (1993). When more means less: Assessing the impact of dairy development on the lives and health of women in rural Rajasthan (India). *Social Sciences and Medicine, 37*, 1377–1389.

Shefner-Rogers, C. L., Rao, N., Rogers, E. M., & Wayangankar, A. (1998). The empowerment of women dairy farmers in India. *Journal of Applied Communication Research, 26*, 319–337.

Shehabuddin, R. (1992). *Empowering rural women: The impact of Grameen Bank in Bangladesh.* Dhaka, Bagladesh: Grameen Bank.

Singhal, A., & Rogers, E. M. (1999). *Entertainment-education: A communication strategy for social change*. Mahwah, NJ: Erlbaum.

Singhal, A., & Rogers, E. M. (2002). A theoretical agenda for entertainment-education. *Communication Theory, 14*, 117–135.

Singhal, A., & Rogers, E. M. (2003). *Combating AIDS: Communication strategies in action.* New Delhi, India: Sage.

Singhal, A., Svenkerud, P. J., & Flydal, E. (2002). Multiple bottom lines: Telenor's mobile telephony operations in Bangladesh. *Teletronikk, 98,* 153–160.

Soul City. (2001). *Series 4: Impact Evaluation—AIDS* [Television Series]. Parkstown, South Africa: Soul City Institute for Health and Development Communication.

Thomas, P. (1994). Participatory development communication: Philosophical premises. In S. A. White, K. S. Nair, & J. Ascroft (Eds.), *Participatory development communication: Working for change and development* (pp. 49–59). New Delhi, India: Sage.

Tong, R. (1989). *Feminist thought: A comprehensive introduction.* Boulder, CO: Westview.

Vogt, J. F., & Murrell, K. L. (1990). *Empowerment in organizations: How to spark exceptional performance.* San Diego, CA: University Associates.

White, S. (1994). Introduction—The concept of participation: Transforming rhetoric to reality. In S. A. White, K. S. Nair, & J. Ascroft (Eds.), *Participatory development communication: Working for change and development* (pp. 15–32). New Delhi, India: Sage.

Wilson, P. A. (1996). Empowerment: Community economic development from the inside out. *Urban Studies, 33,* 617–630.

Young, I. M. (1994). Punishment, treatment, empowerment: Three approaches to policy for pregnant addicts. *Feminist Studies, 20,* 33–57.

Zimmerman, M. A. (1995). Psychological empowerment: Issues and illustrations. *American Journal of Community Psychology, 23,* 581–598.

Zimmerman, M. A., Israel, B. A., Schulz, A., & Checkoway, B. (1992). Further explorations in empowerment theory: An empirical analysis of psychological empowerment. *American Journal of Community Psychology, 20,* 707–727.

CHAPTER CONTENTS

4 Participatory Communication for Social Change: The Relevance of the Theory of Communicative Action

THOMAS L. JACOBSON
State University of New York at Buffalo

Communication for social change refers to an approach to development communication disassociated from the tradition of modernization theory and focuses on participatory communication. However, the literature on participatory communication for social change contains a variety of definitions specifying exactly what participatory communication is. Various definitions focus on project planning, implementation, evaluation, interpersonal communication, radio, participatory communication as a means to an end, participatory communication as an end in itself, and more. There is also debate over whether social marketing and entertainment-education can be employed in a participatory manner. This chapter reviews past and current approaches, arguing that Habermas's theory of communicative action provides a useful approach to the definitional problem. It presents a scheme for differentiating among kinds of communication for social change using this theory's classification of *action types*, differentiating *communicative* from *strategic* action, as well as subtypes within these. Rather than a school of thought or program type, the theory of communicative action argues that communication behavior—in terms of action types—should be fundamental in determining participation.

T he participatory approach to communication for national development efforts arose to replace modernization's emphasis on knowledge diffusion and technology transfer. It places its highest value not on transfers of knowledge from outside developing societies, but rather on reliance upon local knowledge and local capability. Rather than encourage residents of developing societies to participate in development initiatives planned by outsiders, it encourages residents to make their own plans. Spurred by the example of Paulo Freire's (1970, 1973) pioneering work in education in Latin America, development projects began in the 1970s that keyed in on self-determination and empowerment.

Correspondence: Tom Jacobson, 147 Huntington Avenue, Buffalo, NY 14214; email: jacobson@buffalo.edu

The literature representing this approach has grown large (Servaes, Jacobson, & White, 1996). It comprises many project reports (O'Sullivan-Ryan & Kaplan, 1982). It has influenced the largest multilateral development agencies (World Bank, 1996). Theoretical studies have explored possible approaches to conceptualizing participatory communication (Jacobson & Servaes, 1999). Now participatory communication is receiving attention anew. In just the past year or two a number of useful treatments of the subject have appeared (Gumucio Dagron, 2001; Huesca, 2002; Waisbord, 2001).

Nevertheless, this literature on participatory communication should probably be considered only a beginning because the exact nature of participation is not well understood or widely agreed upon. For example, participatory communication has been defined as involvement of program beneficiaries in program implementation and evaluation. Yet, this approach has been criticized for leaving locals out of the most important program phase—that of design. Many projects employ participation as a means of obtaining beneficiary buy-in to program aims, reasoning that if locals own it they will use it. This perspective has been criticized for treating beneficiaries as tools for aims decided by others. For these critics, participation is an end in itself and ought not to be used as a means.

Much of the participatory literature focuses on small-scale programs. However, it is also recognized that large-scale problems require large-scale solutions. Is participation only local and small scale, or can it include large-scale change? The largest part of the literature focuses on interpersonal communication, but the participation literature also covers media projects, especially radio (Berrigan, 1979; Singhal & Rogers, 1988; Vargas, 1995). What makes radio participatory? Collective management? What about audiences? What kind of audience involvement characterizes participatory radio?

In addition, positions on the nature of participatory communication vary over the importance attributed to the role of culture in social change. Is culture a barrier that can be overcome? Are local cultures untouchable heritages that should be left alone? Is culture, in a more positive sense, something that can be an ally in social change? If so, how? The literature on participatory communication is replete with discussions of culture that vary greatly in practical emphasis, theoretical tradition, and normative implication.

Finally, discussions on the nature of participatory communication include a number of positions on what constitutes authentic participation, that is, what is empowering. Long-standing debate over the appropriateness of diffusion models, social marketing, and other techniques focus attention on the question of not only what is participatory, but also what is not participatory. Can diffusion processes be participatory? What about social marketing or entertainment-education? There may be good reason to ask whether a project can be considered participatory when it is used to obtain beneficiary buy-in for programs designed largely elsewhere. Is it not possible that some well-intended programs can be successful in effecting behavior change, and even normatively defensible, and yet not be participatory?

Thus, although much has been achieved in the field to develop an approach to social change that relies on local initiative and local communication, this approach is not well understood conceptually. This is perhaps the reason Gumucio Dagron (2001) stated, "participatory communication may not be defined easily because it cannot be considered a unified model of communication" (p. 8).

This chapter addresses the definitional problem by employing the theory of communicative action (Habermas, 1984, 1987). On the matter of basic definition, the concepts defining communicative action offer a compelling definition of participatory communication at the level of interpersonal communication. On questions such as those related to multiple scales of change and the potential role of mass media, communicative action is again relevant through the concept of the public sphere. Finally, the theory provides an approach to distinguishing desirable processes of cultural change from those that are not desirable. This is related in part to the theory's treatment of strategic and systematically distorted communication, and in part to its thesis on lifeworld colonization.

The chapter starts with a review of conceptualizations of participatory communication. This briefly recalls modernization theory, its conceptualization of participation, and the role it assigned communication in relation to participation. Postmodernization approaches to communication and participation are then discussed in more detail, tracking the growth in this literature and the debt it owes to the work of Paulo Freire. I discuss a number of program types and their uses of participation, highlighting a number of issues extant in this literature.

The second part of the chapter outlines aspects of the theory of communicative action that are relevant to participatory communication. It reviews the basic concepts of communicative action and the way the theory differentiates participatory from manipulative communication using the paired concepts of *communicative action* versus *strategic action*. These two kinds of action are broken down further and a list of action types is presented. I argue that this list of action types provides significant leverage on the definition problem by characterizing not only participatory, but also nonparticipatory communication, as well as subtypes of each. Part 2 also reviews the idea of the public sphere and discusses how the concepts of communicative action are related to analysis of the public sphere. This includes treatment of the concept of the cultural lifeworld and an accompanying thesis on lifeworld colonization.

Part 3 presents a classification scheme for communication programs based on action types, indicating how a number of kinds of participatory communication can be differentiated from one another. Likewise, I indicate a number of kinds of nonparticipatory communication and assign many hypothetical communication programs into the classification scheme for purposes of illustration. Finally, I explore implications of this approach for program design and evaluation.

In a summary section, this chapter discusses pros and cons of the communicative action approach to defining participatory communication for social change. It draws out implications of the theory in relation to questions of empowerment and briefly indicates directions for needed conceptual development and research.

It may be well to raise some caveats. This kind of review and conceptual analysis walks two thin lines simultaneously. One line separates the concerns of social change theorists from those of individuals who work on the front lines in efforts to improve health, education, and economic opportunities in the field. The review aims to attend to concerns of both but can attend fully to neither. The status of Habermas's work has generated a huge literature of debate. Similarly, the literature of applied social change, including various theories of behavior change with attendant methodological developments, is also large. My aim here is only to outline the relevance of the theory of communicative action for both sets of concerns.

This review also walks the line between those who are relatively comfortable with social marketing approaches and those who are not and who often take a more radical position on the question of what the priorities for social change should be. This latter position holds emancipation and political empowerment to be the highest priority, whereas the former focuses on achieving more limited but critically important solutions to quality-of-life problems. I hope it will be clear that I do not wish to treat either of these priorities as second class. There is space only to outline an approach to accomplishing this.

This is a ground-clearing exercise. If a literature review is to surpass an historical litany of viewpoints or periods, it must find a perspective that illuminates issues. This chapter attempts to illuminate some issues in the field of communication for social change by exploring a practical application of Habermas's work.

PART 1: TRENDS AND ISSUES
IN COMMUNICATION FOR SOCIAL CHANGE

Participation and Communication in Modernization Theory

Modernization theory represented a macrosociological approach to conceptualizing social change in the Third World during the post-World War II era. It envisioned a global trend of newly emancipated former colonial countries in which tradition would be abandoned in pursuit of modernity. Capital accumulation was key along with differentiation in social structure, secularization of the basis of government, the development of modern forms of personality among the citizens of new states, and more (Black, 1966; Levy, 1966; Rostow, 1960). The key role for communication was to diffuse new ideas and practices among the citizens of newly autonomous states (Rogers, 1962).

It has been some time since modernization theory was widely employed as a framework for theorizing Third World change. Nevertheless, for historical purposes it must be noted that modernization theory was not aloof from the idea of participation. To the contrary, participation was a key concept, especially in relation to the development of political institutions, and communication was important in this.

Communication played a central role in the seminal version of modernization theory developed by Lerner (1958). It was explicitly related to participation in at least two ways: through media participation and through political participation. Lerner had the insight that if economic institutions were to change and modernize, social attitudes and motivations had to change as well. Specifically, he thought that diffusion of new attitudes and motivations would further modernization. He believed psychic mobility and empathy would result from media participation. *Media participation* was defined more or less as mass media consumption. The effects of this sort of participation were thought to be the same in industrialized societies as in developing ones; the difference was the rapid pace of change faced by developing societies.

These new attitudes and motivations, which were expected to result from media participation, were supposed to be prerequisites for the second way communication would be related to participation, that is, communication as *political participation*. This directly paralleled the principal role of public communication in America's own system and its relation to political participation. Lerner had found high correlations globally between literacy and media participation on the one hand and political participation on the other. In his theory, urbanization, literacy, and media participation were the first three stages of development, which led subsequently to political participation.

Lerner was not the only theorist interested in communication and participation. Almond and Coleman's (1960) study, *The Politics of the Developing Areas,* addresses communication in relation to democratic participation. They present a functional analysis of political change with communication playing a significant role. First, their model breaks down democratic political systems into essential subsystems serving political socialization, recruitment, interest aggregation, and rule making. All of these functions "are performed by means of communication" (p. 45). Second, communication operates as a function of its own, not merely as a means for other functions to occur. This is evidenced, they argue, by the fact that in the most democratically developed societies, substantial and independent media operate largely independent of political parties. In a related study, the growth of citizen involvement, then seen as a global evolution in process, was treated as a "participation explosion" (Almond & Verba, 1963, p. 4). Pye's (1963) notable compilation, *Communications and Political Development*, presented work on communication and democracy not only by Lerner but also Frederick T. C. Yu, Ithiel de Sola Pool, Frederick Frey, and others.

Events failed to corroborate modernization theory. The disappointments have been extensively analyzed in the literature on dependency theory (Amin, 1997; Frank, 1984; Wallerstein, 1979) and related critical communication studies (Galtung, 1971; Inayatullah, 1973; McAnany, Schnitman, & Janus, 1981; Schiller, 1976). Modernization theory's basic propositions went unfulfilled, including propositions related to participation. Press systems did not engender free speech or representative political participation. Lerner (1976) noted the disappointment by observing that the "tide of rising expectations" (p. 291) he had originally predicted transpired instead as a "tide of rising frustrations" (p. 292). Schramm

(1976) noted the "end of an old paradigm" (p. 45). Rogers acknowledged in 1976 the "passing of the dominant paradigm" (p. 49) and began advocating the importance of participation.

Participatory Communication for Empowerment, Postmodernization Theory

Development priorities have changed since the passing of the modernization paradigm. Now there is less theoretical emphasis on economic growth through capital-intensive industrialization and less emphasis on the abandonment of tradition. A *basic needs* approach focuses more immediately on health and nutrition. *Sustained development* is concerned with preserving ecologies in developing nations. Improving the quality of life for rural as well as urban peoples has been given higher priority. Cultural hybridization is widely seen not only as acceptable but also as desirable. During the late 1970s, former United Nations Secretary-General Dag Hammarskjold advanced a new proposal for development under the name Another Development (Nerfin, 1977).

In the wake of this shift, communication studies have conceptualized the role of communication in development in a very different way than in modernization theory. The MacBride Commission Report discussed participation in relation to media access (MacBride,1980). Luis Ramiro Beltran held that concepts of communication embedded in modernization theory were foreign to social conditions in the Third World, and Latin America in particular. They were alien (Beltran, 1976) and oriented toward diffusion rather than emancipation. He urged more horizontal communication (Beltran, 1980). Others too numerous to mention endeavored to call attention to the importance of grassroots and local dialogue oriented toward self-reliance and emancipation (Ascroft & Masilela, 1994; Dervin & Huesca, 1999; Diaz-Bordenave, 1976; Diaz-Bordenave, 1994; Servaes, 1985).

Although participation in democratic institutions is still considered an ideal, democratic goals have generally been set to a less ambitious level. Communication is employed to achieve limited aims such as improved health and educational opportunities, and it is employed to build local capacities for collective self-reliance. A great number of communication projects have been conducted using participation as a planning keyword, and a great number of publications, both academic and applied, have documented, analyzed, and evaluated this work (Servaes et al., 1996; White, Nair, & Ascroft, 1994). Some works convey approaches to, and problems associated with, facilitating participatory communication (Dervin & Huesca, 1997; Lozare, 1994; O'Sullivan-Ryan & Kaplan, 1982; S. A. White, 1999). Others explore ways that participation can be used to impact policy (Holland & Blackburn, 1998). Participation has been recognized as an important key to effective message design for information campaigns (Mody, 1991; Thomas, 1994). A number of studies note the importance of women having a voice in participation for development (Mlama, 1991; Riano, 1994; Rodriguez, 1994; Wilkins, 1999).

Overall, the importance of participatory communication has been a major theme of development communication research in the wake of the modernization era.

The postmodernization generation of scholars producing books on communication and development in broad perspective have almost uniformly included participatory communication as a significant or a major theme (Agunga, 1997; Fraser & Restrepo-Estrada, 1998; Hedebro, 1982; Jayaweera & Amunagama, 1987; Melkote, 1991; Moemeka, 1994; Servaes, 1989; Teheranian, 1994).

Paulo Freire's Contribution

Paulo Freire has undoubtedly been the single most important contributor to what might be called a movement for participation. A Brazilian-born educator, Freire is identified with an approach to teaching that broadens education's goals from acquisition of information to personal transformation and liberation. Freire believed that humanization is a universal vocation. Teachers and students share a moral responsibility to strive to become more fully human.

Education serves this purpose. Freire characterized traditional teaching methods as a "banking" approach to education. In the banking approach, information is deposited in students to be withdrawn later for practical employment, or test taking. In its place, Freire (1970) advocated a pedagogy of the oppressed that stimulates learners to want to learn, to want to become aware of what is denied them, and to want to undertake social practices that expand life opportunities. The catchword for this pedagogical approach is *conscientization*. This refers to an ongoing process of dialogue and action that aims to expose the social contradictions of unjust power, as well as to develop a critical consciousness that can then be directed toward social change (Freire, 1973).

This dialogue involves not diffusion but rather a mutually transformative exchange of views:

> Only through communication can human life hold meaning. The teacher's thinking is authenticated only by the authenticity of the student's thinking. The teacher cannot think for his students, nor can he impose his thought on them. Authentic thinking, thinking that is concerned about reality, does not take place in ivory tower isolation, but only in communication." (Freire, 1970, pp. 63–64)

This is interaction in which the pupil's own expressions are respected and his or her own characterizations of social life are treated with dignity. Teachers themselves learn about ways of life, social conditions, and new experiences through dialogue with students and through building deep bonds of mutual trust.

Freire's work has contributed not only the philosophical idea that education and liberation should be linked together, but it involves a number of classroom techniques as well. These include codifications, or the use of pictures, photographs, and drawings representing scenes from daily life that are meaningful to students. Codifications are used as the focus of discussion aimed at identifying generative words, words that capture or illustrate key features, issues, or complexities represented in the codifications. In a related technique, the approach takes multisyllabic words and breaks them down into individual syllables. These syllables can be analyzed, both for what they teach about language and for what they teach about issues.

The influence of Freire's work has been broad as well as deep, not only in education but also in other fields, including communication. This is not to say Freire is without his critics, a great many of them sympathetic critics who admire his accomplishments and employ them but who also adopt a critical perspective on certain issues. One common criticism concerns his analysis of power. In the manner of Marxist thought, Freire's theory holds that the oppressed are powerless. However, as Foucauldian thinking tells us today, power circulates and is always available to some extent (Rahnema, 1992). In certain respects, Freire's analysis undervalues indigenous understanding of local social conditions, assuming that "lower class people do not understand their own situation, that they are in need of enlightenment on the matter, and that this service can be provided by selected higher-class individuals" (Berger, 1975, p. 113).

At the same time, the theory treats the educational interventions of outsiders as neutral or beneficial as long as the correct pedagogy is employed. However, some worry that the trust developed between teachers and students can be abused and, in some respects, controlling. Because the theory is humanistic, it largely plays down the dignity of magical ways of looking at the world and devalues spirituality as well. It is secular, and this illustrates the fact that the educator, just like other social actors, inevitably carries an ideological framework (Rahnema, 1992). Some commentators take this reasoning a step further and argue that Freirean practices can be viewed as a continuation of Western domination (Aronowitz, 1993; Bowers, 1983).

In addition, the theory is not generalizable to all development communication contexts. Social change efforts are not in all respects like teaching situations. They are not all interpersonal, but may be large scale. They are not always oriented toward individual emancipatory transformation, but may be oriented toward immediate needs (Berthoff, 1990). Similarly, one can question the adequacy of his model of dialogue itself. Not that what it portrays is wrong, but there are other kinds of dialogue. It may be useful to label as being dialogical processes that do not require deep bonds of trust (Pietrykowski, 1996).

Freire's work might not suffice for a general theory of participatory communication for social change, but it does represent a compelling account of at least some key processes of participatory communication. The theory's treatment of the dialogical requirements for democracy may be limited, but, insofar as they apply, they are exemplary. These are some of the reasons his work invigorated critique of top-down communication models during the 1960s and 1970s, as well as why his work continues to be widely read today.

Current Approaches to Participation and Communication

Freire's work may have inspired the participatory communication movement in ways that are both broad and deep, but implementations of participatory communication vary considerably. Some are interpersonal. Some are mediated. The vast majority of projects are community centered and try in one way or another to include local residents in planning, implementation, or both. Some can be questioned on the charge that they are not participatory at all. A review of some of the major approaches that have differentiated themselves within this movement suggests the nature of this variability.

One outgrowth of the participatory communication movement is a new conception of research. In modernization theory, research was conducted by First World experts from a value-neutral social science perspective and shared with beneficiary communities. In place of this perspective, a participatory communication research approach has developed that puts research activities in the hands of local individuals and groups and is aimed not at generating objective findings but at social change (Bhabha, 1994; Einsiedel, 1999; Fals Borda, 1979, 1988; Greene et al., 1995; Hall, 1975; Himmelstrand, 1982; Jacobson, 1993; Rahman, 1993). It is based on the idea that indigenous knowledge and experience are key to understanding local problems and opportunities. The participatory communication research approach might use outsiders to facilitate collective action, but it leaves the research activity itself primarily in the hands of local peoples. This is not only effective but also emancipatory: "as partisan research; it is the research of involvement; it is the research for liberation. It is not only research with the people—it is people's research" (Simbulan, 1983, p. 10).

Another development along these lines represents a refinement in one direction of participatory research. Participatory rural appraisal (PRA) is an approach to participatory community development created by development practitioners during the 1970s and 1980s (Chambers, 1994). Its initial aim was to collect data in rural areas for purposes of assessing local needs and implementing projects. Its spirit was to do this in a way that highlighted the perspectives and the indigenous understanding of local peoples. "PRA has been described as a family of approaches, methods and behaviours to enable poor people to express and analyze the realities of their lives and conditions, and themselves to plan, monitor and evaluate their actions (Holland & Blackburn, 1998, p. 4). To this end, PRA uses a number of techniques, including semistructured interviewing, focus group discussions, preference ranking, mapping, and modeling, as well as seasonal and historical diagramming. These techniques generate mostly qualitative data. They are designed to reveal an understanding of current states-of-affairs from the perspective of locals and to enhance local capacities for collective action. The mapping and diagramming techniques in particular are suited to this task even among populations where literacy skills are weak.

Social mobilization refers to a process developed at the United Nations International Children's Emergency Fund (UNICEF, 1993). One common problem in development work results from the systemic nature of social problems. Matters such as youth nutrition, health, and educational development must be simultaneously approached in multiple contexts including schools, workplaces, radical community groups, government agencies, and traditional community meetings. Actors in each of these contexts might be addressing meaningful issues, but effectiveness is blunted unless these efforts are coordinated. Social mobilization employs a comprehensive approach to planning that focuses on coalition building. It tries to get stakeholders engaged in partnerships for change (Minkler, 1990; Wallack, 1989; World Bank, 1992).

Media advocacy is another postmodernization communication approach that seeks to empower local peoples. Development communication efforts generally swim, according to media advocates, against a strong current. Attempts to improve nutrition, for example, are confronted by commercial media that barrage citizens with junk food advertisements. Attempts to encourage safer sexual practices must combat a continuous stream of television programs and Hollywood movies that glorify careless promiscuity. Attempts to promote environmental awareness must work in a communication environment in which technological quick fixes are treated like self-obvious fixes and gas guzzling SUVs are status symbols. Media advocacy tries to create a more level playing field through the strategic use of mass media to advocate social change and influence public policy. It aims to stimulate public debate over health-related behaviors (Brawley & Martinez-Brawley, 1999).

Media advocacy aims to do this not so much by influencing individuals as by influencing public agendas. On this view, smoking is not just a matter to address in antismoking campaigns. Smoking must also be addressed by holding tobacco and advertising companies responsible for the public health costs of their products. These companies must be enjoined to advertise responsibly and to honestly acknowledge health risks associated with their products. The means through which this can be accomplished are community organization and advocacy (Glanz & Rimer, 1995). News coverage can be influenced by the distribution of information packets informing reporters of relevant facts. Press conferences can be held in relation to notable events. Public service announcements can be produced and distributed to broadcast outlets (Holder & Treno, 1997).

These approaches indicate the range of communication processes undertaken today in postmodernization efforts to facilitate positive and collectively self-directed change in development contexts. Large organizations such as UNICEF and the World Bank have been experimenting in this area. There is enough evidence of this approach's effectiveness that participation is now being explored as a useful component of most kinds of social change efforts. For example, social marketing and entertainment-education programs are commonly seen as inheritors of modernization theory's diffusion practices. However, researchers and program designers employing these techniques have taken some pains to enhance participatory perspectives within these frameworks.

The concept of social marketing was proposed by Kotler & Zaltman (1971). Based on practices well developed in the private sector, social marketing aims to support prosocial change efforts through standard marketing techniques such as formative research, target audience segmentation, and systematic evaluation. The idea is that positive program outcomes are more likely when program designers understand their target population's needs and interests (Novelli, 1990). Social marketing has therefore been defined as "the design, implementation, and control of programs calculated to influence the acceptability of social ideas and involving considerations of product, planning, pricing, communication, distribution, and marketing research" (Kotler & Zaltman, 1971, p. 5).

Social marketing was initially employed in the development context with reference to products, but its application subsequently was broadened to include ideas and behavior change. As influence of the participatory communication approach has grown, efforts have also been made to seek participatory dimensions in social marketing. In this view, social marketing projects are participatory because they include target populations in formative research. Therefore, it is argued that social marketing can be seen as participatory. To this end some definitions of social marketing deliberately highlight the voluntary nature of intended behavior changes. Here, social marketing involves "the adaptation of commercial marketing technologies to programs designed to influence the voluntary behavior of target audiences to improve their personal welfare and that of the society of which they are a part" (Andreasen, 1994, p. 110).

The term entertainment-education refers to another set of practices employed for prosocial change that evolved in some respects within the diffusion tradition, but also has proponents who are interested in participation. As the rubric suggests, entertainment-education is a strategy to influence behavior by combining entertainment and educational media techniques. Information campaigns must earn audience interest before their information can be imparted. It is obvious that attractive message campaigns are more likely to gain audience interest. Thus, entertainment-education is "the process of purposely designing and implementing a media message to both entertain and educate, in order to increase audience knowledge about an educational issue, create favorable attitudes, and change overt behavior" (Singhal & Rogers, 1999, p. xii). Entertainment-education projects, for example, have employed popular singers to encourage sexual restraint in Mexico, the Philippines, and Nigeria, among other countries. Soap operas have carried messages about reproductive health in such countries as Egypt, Ghana, India, Nepal, and Zimbabwe (Singhal & Rogers, 1988). Other projects utilize cartoons, theatre, and television spots.

Conceptually, such programs are based on the intuition that positive role models are more likely to earn attention and to be persuasive than are neutral role models. Bandura's (1977) social learning theory holds that social learning takes place through modeling behavior in the presence of belief in one's ability to effect change. Like social marketing, entertainment-education programs are often conducted with the assistance of empirical research for formative needs assessment, program design, and evaluation. Like social marketing, participatory dimensions of entertainment-education programs also have been considered and advocated. Because formative research is employed, it can be argued that entertainment-education begins with a concern for audience or consumer needs and is, to this extent, participatory. In addition, entertainment-education typically employs local idiom in linguistic figures and entertainment aesthetics. For this reason, it can be argued that entertainment-education is not a cultural intrusion carrying manipulative aesthetics, but rather it is part of the local cultural scene and hence can be participatory (Storey, 1999).

Issues

Despite the considerable amount of interest in participatory communication today, and its variety, this approach is burdened by a number of issues or disputes. One such problem is relatively straightforward. That is where in the project process local residents must become involved. Because of the popularity of the approach, many projects are called participatory by their funders and planners, but they are participatory only in a limited sense. This can occur if local residents, or project beneficiaries, are involved in only evaluating a project that was designed in the ministry of a far-off national capital or, farther still, in a multilateral agency office in another country entirely. Indeed, it is not uncommon to have a straightforward diffusion project called participatory on the evidence that questionnaires were handed out to local beneficiaries during the conduct of the project. For those whose work is inspired by Freire's passionate concern for the oppressed, such uses of the term participatory reduce it to the status of a buzzword.

Another, more substantive, debate takes place with regard to the aims of participatory communication. As noted, social marketing and entertainment-education projects increasingly employ participatory communication in the conduct of formative research processes, message design, and in other ways. Often, planning documentation treats these participatory exercises as means of obtaining beneficiary buy-in to a project. It is widely understood that a sense of local ownership will result in higher rates of local involvement in project activities and can increase likelihood of project sustainability over time. Thus, participation has an instrumental value in achieving project aims (McKee, 1994).

Critics hold that this is participation only in name (Huesca, 2002). If participatory activities are employed only to achieve aims determined prior to local expression of needs, then it is in part manipulative. Participation should, on this view, be pursued only as an end in itself, not as a means to an end. Replies in defense of such practices argue that even this partial form of participation leaves enhanced participation capabilities behind, in a project's wake. They argue that this is not such a bad thing if the project's aim was to solve a highly threatening problem such as high rates of infant mortality, rapid population growth, or growth in HIV/ AIDs infections.

A related dispute concerns the kinds of models employed in social marketing and entertainment-education projects. Certain project activities may indeed involve participation, but the conceptualization fundamental to overall project design and evaluation typically employs behavioral models that are antithetical to participation. Social learning and other commonly used conceptual frameworks represent rigorous social scientific thinking. However, they predict behavior change based on variables that operate below the level of individual consciousness. Program elements are designed using such variables. Again, critics argue that participation must be deliberate and intentional. Attempts to influence behavior through unconscious appeals are not participatory.

The role of culture in social change is a subject of considerable interest and confusion. Modernization theory treated traditional culture as something to be abandoned, whereas more recent approaches see culture as something to be cherished and preserved. More practically, it is clear that culture and behavior are related in a number of ways, but the exact nature of this relationship is not at all clear.

> We have plenty of examples in which cultures did change and others in which cultures did not, but we lack solid conclusions and nuanced theoretical tools to deal with this issue. The problem remains how to attribute such changes (or lack of) to communication and program intervention. (Waisbord, 2001, p. 15)

This problem appears in relation to participatory communication. For example, message design processes today can skillfully employ cultural idiom. It is argued that use of such idiom represents a form of sharing in local cultural discourse and is therefore participatory. Critics respond with the observation that advertisers, whose aims are anything but participatory, have employed idiomatic sophistication. Social change programs may not have commercial aims, but neither can participatory communication be made of good intentions.

A related question asks whether projects should focus efforts on changing individual behavior or community and social norms. Many social change projects generally aim to encourage change in individual knowledge, attitudes, and behaviors. However, it seems clear that individual behaviors are oriented within contexts of community and social norms. It is difficult for a woman to say "no" to male sexual advances if prevailing community norms treat sexual aggression as a natural male inheritance. It is difficult to discuss HIV/AIDS risk among gay men if homosexuality is treated as a social taboo (Wilkins, 1999). It appears that communities must be addressed collectively. Proponents of a more individualist approach treat community change as an aggregate of individuals and argue that attempts to address social norms otherwise are impractical and not measurable. They cannot accurately be evaluated and are therefore unhelpful in designing and funding large-scale projects.

As noted earlier, scale itself is a matter that poses difficult questions. The participatory communication movement has been concerned primarily with very localized processes, usually at the village level. However, the problems of developing areas actually concern social processes much larger in scale. Freire talks about requirements for democracy, but his most specific techniques operate at the individual or interpersonal level. Participatory rural appraisal addresses processes primarily at a rural village or intervillage level. What though about participation on a scale that encompasses many villages across large districts or regions? Participatory radio could potentially refer to large audiences, but these tend to be fairly local, too, given the emphasis on participatory radio being participatory by virtue of collective management.

It should be recognized that in the long run opportunities for participation are limited by large-scale social, political, and economic institutions (Midgley, Hall, Hardiman, & Narine, 1986). Therefore, theories of participatory communication cannot be limited to interpersonal, village, intervillage processes, or to neighborhoods and districts in cities. They must account theoretically for the local impact of large-scale institutions within the context of the nation-state and the increasingly global economy.

One useful approach to this question argues that new social movements represent one of the few real processes that can challenge entrenched power on the large scale (R. White, 1999). At the same time, it can be hoped that projects sponsored by large organizations can be made participatory. How might this be achieved?

Evidently, the study of participatory communication is accompanied by a number of debates over both means and aims. Ultimately, they are definitional. What is participatory communication? Is it appropriately a means, or an end, or both? Large scale or small? Individualistic or collective? Mediated or interpersonal? Rational or cultural?

Extant definitions illustrate this current state of affairs. A large number of definitions of participatory communication have been advanced. Here are a few representative proposals. Participatory communication is (a) "recognition of shared interests, accountability, and facilitating decision-making processes in a shared milieu of interests, constitute true communication and participation" (Fuglesang & Chandler, 1986, p. 2); (b) "permanent dialog, the spontaneous and relevant participation, never arbitrary or conditional, generating collective decisions and the socialization of production and its fruits" (Grinberg, 1986, p. 176); (c) "the opening of dialogue, source and receiver interacting continuously, thinking constructively about the situation, identifying developmental needs and problems, deciding what is needed to improve the situation, and acting upon it" (Nair & White, 1993, p. 51); (d) "people's involvement in the decision making process, in implementing programs . . . their sharing in benefits of development and their involvement in efforts to evaluate such programs" (Cohen & Uphoff, 1980, p. 219).

There is considerable variety of emphasis in these definitions. They all emphasize the dialogical nature of participation, and they all emphasize social solidarity, but beyond these characteristics they vary. The first definition emphasizes accountability and a shared milieu of interests; the second includes the socialization of production, an economic consideration; the third emphasizes transactional dialogue; and the fourth specifies the importance of participation throughout program design, implementation, and evaluation.

All are useful, but none of them address the full range of issues reviewed above. They might seem to imply that participation should be an ends, rather than a means, but none is explicit. The problem of scale is only hinted at in the second definition's reference to the socialization of production. Culture is raised only by reference to a "share milieu" in the first one. Although these definitions serve to raise awareness of the importance of participatory communication and highlight certain key features, none of them provides theoretical guidance on the majority of pressing issues. This perhaps explains Gumucio Dagron's (2001) position on the matter of definition: "Participatory communication may not be defined easily because it cannot be considered a unified model of communication" (p. 8).

A useful synthesis of this literature can be found in Servaes (1999). He suggests that approaches are chiefly of two kinds. One of these emphasizes dialogical pedagogy and is based in Freire's work. The other emphasizes media access, participation, and self-management arising out of UNESCO meetings of the 1970s. Servaes points out a number of conflicts between these two approaches to, or treatments of, participatory communication. For example, although Freire's approach emphasizes radical change, the UNESCO work implies that gradual change may be possible. Servaes also observes the need just noted for participation to be theorized not only locally, but also in relation to large political institutions and globalization. For him, participation involves "equitable sharing of both political and economic power" (p. 85).

The model is quite comprehensive. In addition to senders, receivers, messages, and dialogue, it includes processes of national and international communication and reference to the kinds of legal or quasilegal bodies required to adjudicate rights to communicate. Still, not all issues are addressed. The question of individualism versus community emphasis is not clearly addressed. The model highlights considerations related to mediated communication over individual or interpersonal considerations, which is understandable given Servaes's emphasis on linking participatory communication to policy (1986, 1996). Servaes concludes that much needs to be done by way of fundamental definition. "There is an evident need for clarification in descriptive and normative theories of participatory media" (p. 92).

A final issue must be raised for present purposes. This is the matter of operationalizing and evaluating participatory communication projects. A theory or model can be useful for the design and evaluation of projects only to the extent that it is clear and detailed. In light of the definitional problems just reviewed, it should be no surprise that operationalizing and evaluating participatory communication have proven to be a considerable challenge. Work to date begins by trying to develop ways to evaluate participation that are commensurate with the basic aims of participation. These include involving project participants in evaluation, making the evaluation process serve the ends of capacity building and empowerment, and eschewing the traditional aim of making evaluation as objective as possible (Whitmore, 1998).

Other recent approaches aim to remain loyal to participation's goals, but hope to develop indicators from which measures can be derived. The Rockefeller Foundation's program on Communication for Social Change is dedicated to promoting an empowering approach to participatory communication, but as a funding source, it is also mindful of the benefits of effective evaluation. A recent working document identified five reasons why quantitative indicators would be useful (Rockefeller Foundation, 2001). Measures based on good indicators could help make projects accountable, identify and impact priorities, provide input for program design, provide indications of progress, and enhance credibility of participatory projects. This work, too, is still in its early stages.

Summary

Waisbord (2001) notes a number of points of convergence, assumptions that are increasingly widely held in this field. These include (a) the belief that communication for social change requires political will devoted to local empowerment, both locally and within agencies and NGOs; (b) acceptance of the idea that a wide variety of strategies and methods is required, that is, a tool-kit approach; (c) a growing consensus that both top-down and bottom-up strategies are required and can be employed in partnership with one another; (d) joint use of interpersonal and multimedia communication processes; and (e) a mix of individual and community/environmental approaches.

Nevertheless, a number of problems or tensions remain. The main need for a definition of participation is very much outstanding. Part 2 of this chapter introduces selected aspects of the theory of communicative action and argues that the theory offers leverage on a number of these problems, while focusing on three— the problems of definition, scale, and cultural change. It also addresses how the theory can be used to inform project design and evaluation.

PART 2: RELEVANT ASPECTS OF THE
THEORY OF COMMUNICATIVE ACTION

Ideal Speech, Discourse, and Action

The theory of communicative action is a form of sociological action theory that ascribes actor behavior, at least in part, to actor meanings and intentions. It attempts to account for the different kinds of action in which individuals can engage. Thus, some actions are individual whereas others are social. Social actions are employed when behavior is coordinated among individuals. Some social actions are convivial; others are aggressive or manipulative. Habermas's specific approach emphasizes the role of communication in human action. It is a modification of Weber's (1968) action theory that draws heavily on the work of Talcott Parsons, George Herbert Mead, and others (Habermas, 1984).

The broadest behavioral framework employed in Habermas's theory is action, rather than communication, but communication is a key type of action. For him, the focal issue is not whether one is communicating in the sense of exchanging information. The focal issue is what one's actions accomplish in relation to others, that is, whether it accomplishes, or attempts to accomplish, understanding. With this approach, Habermas defines *communicative action* as action oriented toward understanding. Action oriented toward manipulation, rather than understanding, is treated as noncommunicative and labeled *strategic action*. His widely read studies of reason, the public sphere, ethics, and lifeworld colonization, rely entirely on the conceptual framework elaborated in characterizing communicative action.

The theory of communicative action postulates that three reciprocal expectations underlie human communication. These are claims to the assumed validity of communicative behaviors, and called validity claims. On Habermas's view, actors implicitly claim that their messages (utterances) are true, normatively appropriate, and sincere. Messages are received with this expectation. These expectations are usually of an unconscious nature, and such unconscious expectations are what make possible the coordination of behavior among individuals. The theory recognizes that deceptive communication is common, but treats deception as a process that plays upon this deeper level of reciprocal expectations. When we lie, we play upon these expectations, by giving people to understand or feigning that we are truthful, appropriate, or sincere when in fact we are not. Thus, validity expectations are treated theoretically as a reconstruction of the necessary conditions for all communication.

Although validity expectations operate in an unconscious way as a substructure of communication, they can also be made conscious. If doubt arises as to an utterance's validity, then one or more claims can be thematized or raised for discussion. An outcome, or understanding, is determined through "yes" or "no" answers to propositions. Good faith action oriented to reaching understanding regarding a thematized claim is communicative action, strictly speaking. "I shall speak of communicative action whenever the actions of the agents involved are coordinated not through egocentric calculations of success but through acts of reaching understanding" (Habermas, 1984, pp. 285–286).

Acts of reaching understanding are analyzed at length, with particular regard for conditions that must be obtained for action to be communicative. Habermas (1990) said participants in communication must be free to "call into question any proposal" or to "introduce any proposal," as well as to "express any attitudes, wishes, or needs" (p. 89). There must be a "symmetrical distribution of opportunities to contribute" (p. 88) to discussion. There must be adequate time to arrive at agreement. Outcomes must be determined through "good reasons" or the "force of the better argument" (p. 88). This hints at the way Habermas employs the notion of communicative action in developing a discursive theory of reason.

Action oriented toward deception is a type of strategic action that is oriented toward success. Success refers to aims that are egocentric in the sense that they are pursued for self-interest. Figure 1 presents a breakdown of action types, showing the basic manner that the theory differentiates communicative from strategic action and breaks both of these down into subtypes. Strategic action has two subtypes and one of these subtypes can be further broken down to two additional subtypes.

The conditions specifying communicative action are collectively referred to, for the sake of convenience, as the *ideal speech situation*; in-process they are referred to as *discourse*. Despite appearances that may be given by the theory's formality, communicative action is not a rarified process and normal behavior only approximates it. It takes place during daily interactions among parents and children, between friends, and in workplace debates. It is institutionalized in fields such as law and the sciences. Of course, deception is practiced regularly in interpersonal interaction, but appropriateness and sincerity are seen as the necessary ingredients of ties that bind in healthy family interaction, friendships, and working relationships. Deception also occurs in law and science, but professional norms in such fields approximate communicative action. Violations of procedural embodiments of these norms carry specified forms of sanction or punishment.

If one understands communicative action as a characterization of reason, as Habermas does, then one can also understand the process of social evolution as a process of communicatively oriented social rationalization. Thus the theory includes a systematic treatment of social evolution. It analyzes the historical appearance and slow spread of institutional forms of communicative action that assumed relatively full expression initially in the Enlightenment (Habermas, 1979). Like Weber, Habermas sees social rationalization as a characteristic of social evolution. Unlike Weber, Habermas's conceptualization of reason is not instrumental or technological. It is a broader notion of reason that is discursive, and it employs different kinds of communicative action, or difference discourses, for different subjects, including normative matters.

One key site for the institutionalization of communicative action, in addition to the institutions of science and the law, is in the norms of the public sphere. Habermas's (1989) earliest treatment of this subject, *The Structural Transformation of the Public Sphere,* tracked the emergence and early historical stages of the public sphere. In this work, he analyzed the evolution of discussion among private citizens about matters of public concern, thus offering a communicative orientation to analysis of civil society. Arguments advanced in the early 1990s elaborated this analysis, treating the public sphere as a heterogeneous space comprising subspheres of different ethnic minorities, classes, gender preferences, and more, as well as the dominant media sphere (Habermas, 1996). More recently, Habermas (1998) has analyzed the public sphere as a place where viewpoints expressing cultural difference can be directed at obtaining legal protection, for example, religious freedom, ethnic holidays, and other expressions of preferred "grammars of life" (p. 392).

The public sphere, however, functions imperfectly at best. Although the theory typifies the democratic requirement of a space for public discourse, Habermas's

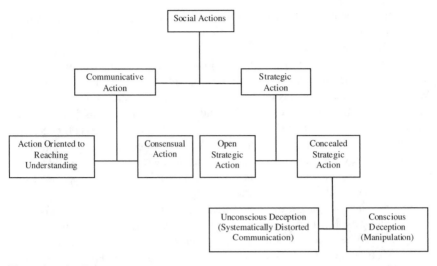

Figure 1. Action Types

analysis is critical. It holds that today's mass media do not produce the market-place of ideas Milton (1959) characterized as a "free and open encounter" (p. 561) among competing voices. Habermas shares with many critics of today's press the belief that the public interest is not well served by current ownership and operation patterns.

The important, or at least unique thing about Habermas's analysis of public discourse, is not its critical intent. Rather its critical uniqueness lies in the fact that it is universalistic. For him, free speech is not just a Western prejudice, legally characterized by private ownership of the media. Rather, speech is the historical expression of characteristically human behavior, that is, reciprocal expecta-tions. Universal law, science, and free speech are institutionalizations of this behavioral expectation.

The opus, *Theory of Communicative Action,* concerns both the fundamental defi-nition of communicative action and also the historical institutionalization of com-municative action, as a kind of reason, in modern democratic societies. This is why the idea of communicative action is relevant at multiple levels of social analysis, ranging from interpersonal, to community, to provincial, to national, and even glo-bal levels of communication. The underlying validity expectations that the theory of communicative action initially treats as necessary for the coordination of action among individuals is also necessary for the vigor of public discourse, whether small or large.

Habermas's analysis of the public sphere is probably the feature of his theory most often discussed among communication scholars, usually in reference to his early treatment of this subject in the *Structural Transformation,* which was done before the theory of communicative action was worked out. What makes his analysis of the public sphere unique is the way it is connected with this later work on communicative action.

The framework of communicative action is intended to justify the argument that there is something universally attractive about free speech. It is not merely a Western preference. Whereas the universality of the preference for free speech is assumed in the natural law doctrine that underlies most liberal political and judicial theory, Habermas's defense of universality is intended to be less ethnocentric. It aims to show that free speech is not just a Western value because it is not, in the first instance, a value, but rather a historical tendency rooted in pragmatic behavioral expectations that make human association possible, and that it appears differently in different cultural circumstances.

Second, the framework of communication is used to provide the basis for critical analysis. By no means are all social interactions supposed to be communicative. Where they are supposed to be communicative, the framework of the theory of communicative action can be used to provide a standard before which violations of communicative conditions can be criticized. Systematically distorted communication and lifeworld colonization are key to a communicatively based critical theory.

Finally, the theory of communicative action also comprises a systematic treatment of cultural change. Communicative action among individuals, as well as in its institutionalized forms, always takes place against the background of a cultural lifeworld. This lifeworld is a storehouse of historical experience and meaning that naturally varies from culture to culture. It is a set of "more or less diffuse, . . . unproblematic, background convictions" that "stores the interpretive work of preceding generations" (Habermas, 1984, p. 70). As the content of experience, tradition can no more be abandoned than can skin.

Treating the idea of a cultural lifeworld seriously provides the basis for an analysis of cultural change that values the preservation of tradition in the process of change. As new historical conditions outstrip the cognitive resources available in tradition, interpretive accomplishment is required whether in science, law, or art. The critical reflection embodied in communicative action provides a means of entertaining new behavioral options during periods of change:

> In the medium of this criticism the formerly sluggish, nature-like process of revaluation of our evaluative vocabulary, our world-disclosing and need-interpreting language in general, become more and more reflexive; the whole process becomes, as it were, discursively fluidified. (Habermas, 1992, pp. 168–169)

Social rationalization represents the integration of new communicative practices into lifeworld traditions, traditions that cannot be abandoned whole cloth, but also cannot remain forever unchanged. On one hand, a sense of modernity represents freedom from unquestioned tradition. Specific traditions can be abandoned.

On the other hand, as a cultural storehouse of historical experience, the lifeworld is also the source of social norms and much of the content of individual identity. So it must be protected. In any case, neither cultural change nor preservation can be determined from outside the culture. Only cultural participants can make such decisions. The theory of communicative action provides a model for desirable processes of cultural change, that is, in the public sphere.

At the same time, the theory provides a framework for criticism of undesirable forms of cultural change. One source of such change is market forces that can introduce products and services that are profitable, but which also violate cultural sensibilities. The application of expertise in the form of social engineering is another source of such change, where social and cultural relations are affected by policy makers often without sufficient local input. If participatory communication in the public sphere is not employed in addressing such forms of cultural change, then the cultural fabric can be rent. Rather than being embraced, such change must be endured and can result in cultural impoverishment, anomie, and the loss of motivation to abide by the law, to name just a few effects. Habermas's (1987) analysis of "lifeworld colonization" (p. 355) diagnosed postindustrial societies with just this set of problems.

There is not space here to treat the lifeworld colonization thesis at any length. Suffice it to say that any imposition of scientific, technical, or administrative rationality in place of the appropriate use of communicative action can have detrimental social effects. Lifeworld colonization can be identified at a macrosocial level with reference to policies that circumvent public input to decision making on normative and cultural matters. At micro and meso levels it can be identified wherever scientistic authority is used to justify the exclusion of local input to community change processes.

Participatory Communication as Communicative Action

This analysis is relevant to participatory communication in a number of ways reviewed in Part 1. We can give attention primarily to three, including the problems of definition, scale, and culture. First, the basic specification of communicative action closely approximates what is often discussed, even if variously defined, in the field as participatory communication. Participatory communication can therefore be treated theoretically as "action oriented towards understanding," in which participants must be free to "call into question any proposal," to "introduce any proposal," and to express any "attitudes, wishes, or needs" (Habermas, 1990, pp. 88–89). There must be a "symmetrical distribution of opportunities to contribute" (p. 88) to discussion. The basic concept of reciprocity underlying the theory reflects a concern for individual agency and dignity. The discursive negotiation of validity claims outlined in the theory makes communicative action a two-way, or multiway, process.

Second, the theory's relevance can be seen also in relation to the question of scale raised in the introduction. As noted, the concepts of communicative action are illustrated at one level in contexts resembling interpersonal communication.

However, given the manner in which the concepts of communicative action are used to underwrite the theory of the public sphere, it is clear that the theory can be used to study participatory communication at multiple levels of scale. Communicative action operates differently at different scales. For example, large-scale political discourse requires mass media, whereas interpersonal and small-group communication do not. Nevertheless, the principles of reciprocity, the equal distribution of opportunities to contribute, the freedom to raise any proposals are common to participatory communication at both levels. They are approximated in different ways and in admittedly sprawling, imperfect ways, especially at larger scales, but the basic requirements are the same.

This indicates the way that the theory links analysis of participation in interpersonal and group-level processes to its analysis in macrosocial processes. Beginning with his original work on the public sphere, Habermas's theory has always had the intent of bringing citizens back into the process of democratic governance by means of a critical analysis of illegitimate power. The theory advocates a representative form of government, but one that is as responsive and as participatory as possible given the complexity of modern societies. In the context of political theory, the approach is treated as a discursive approach to deliberative democracy. Thus, political participation for Habermas (1975) is fundamentally communicative: "participation, in my sense of taking part in discursive will-formation" (p. 137). Habermas's (1987) analysis of contemporary democracy is preoccupied with the understanding of contemporary problems facing responsive democracy: "The new problems have to do with quality of life, equal rights, individual self-realization, participation, and human rights" (p. 392).

Another related way that the theory's relevance can be seen is in its analysis of culture. Seen against the background of the cultural lifeworld, it becomes apparent that the public sphere can be used as a site for culture change. In this connection Habermas (1996) sometimes argues that the public sphere serves the "reflexive appropriation of tradition" (p. 493). This is a discursive process in which citizens decide collectively which traditions to abandon in favor of newly preferred practices and which to retain. The idea that the public sphere can and does serve in processes of cultural change is normatively desirable because it is change that is collective and participatory.

Such a participatory approach to cultural change represents an alternative to unanticipated cultural outcomes of market and administrative rationality, or lifeworld colonization. This highlights the theory's relevance for criticism of undesirable processes of cultural change. Habermas's analysis of lifeworld colonization is startling enough as an analysis of ideology-like processes in a postmodern era. What is more startling is that it applies to the global periphery as well. As globalization assumes hyper speeds, the societies of the Third and First Worlds suffer a similar burden. In the Third World, as in the First, everyday citizens ought to have more collective say in the processes of cultural change than they do, marginalized as both are by market rationality. The Third World, however, suffers a double-colonization. One is neocolonialism in the economic sphere, and the other is lifeworld colonization in the cultural sphere. Whether at the village, provincial, or national levels, cultural change processes in the Third World can take place in a legitimate manner only if handled discursively in their associated public spheres. This is denied Third World citizens even more egregiously than it is in the First World, where citizens on the whole have readier access to voluntary organizations and functioning legal systems.

The theory of communicative action is clearly relevant to participatory communication on general terms. It offers a fundamental definition, applies to multiple scales of change, and provides categories useful for the analysis of both positive and negative cultural change. Can the theory be helpful in crafting definitions of communication for social change that are useful in the context of program design and evaluation? The answer is "yes," this general theory can be useful, but to understand how this is so it is necessary to go a little deeper into action theory.

Action Theory and Communication for Social Change

The entire framework of the theory outlined above is necessary to treat the complex processes of communication for social change. However, for the purposes of differentiating kinds of communication for social change at the programmatic level, the action theory is of central importance. The analysis of communicative action leads in the direction of participation, how to understand it and identify it. The analysis of strategic action leads in the direction of understanding nonparticipatory communication. Figure 1 presented the basic action types. Definitions for these action types and their subtypes are presented below. A brief explanatory note is provided for each concept. Indents reflect hierarchical relations among the concept types.

Social action: Action that is coordinated with another or others. From this perspective, communication serves as a means for the coordination of behavior. Social action can be communicative or strategic.

> *Communicative action*: Action coordinated through the means of "yes" or "no" answers to validity claims of truth, rightness, sincerity, and so on (defined above). It takes two forms, one being consensual action and the other being action oriented to reaching understanding.

>> *Consensual action*: A form of communicative action in which "agreement about implicitly raised validity claims are *presupposed* as a background consensus by reason of common definitions of the situations" (Habermas, 1979, p. 209). Here, action oriented toward understanding is not required.

>> *Action oriented to reaching understanding*: A form of communicative action in which a "background consensus composed of common definitions of a situation is unavailable, and thus agreement about implicitly raised validity claims *must be arrived at*" (p. 209).

> *Strategic action:* Action oriented toward success, pursued regardless of the interests of another or others. This can be open and acknowledged or concealed and manipulative.

> *Openly strategic action:* A form of strategic action in which messages take the form of directive statements oriented towards motivating compliance. Being open, the motivation to gain compliance is unconcealed.
>
> *Concealed strategic action:* Action oriented toward success when motivation to obtain compliance is concealed. This occurs in two ways, conscious and unconscious deception.
>
> > *Conscious deception:* A form of strategic action in which the orientation is toward success and the sender or manipulator is aware of the intent to behave strategically, and hence is attempting to deceive or lie. It occurs when "the manipulator deceives at least one of the other participants about his own strategic attitude, in which he deliberately behaves in a pseudoconsensual manner" (p. 209).
> >
> > *Unconscious deception (systematically distorted communication)*: Concealed strategic action when the actor "deceives himself about the fact that the basis of consensual action is only apparently being maintained" (pp. 209–210). This is characteristic of unequal power relations as in much chauvinistic behavior, including sexism, racism, and class-based arrogance.

This classification of action types has been subjected to criticism and analysis within the academic specialization of common language philosophy and allied fields. It comprises a program of theory construction Habermas treats as a formal pragmatics of communication as opposed to an empirical pragmatics. The latter includes such studies as ethnolinguistics, conversation analysis, and narrative analysis.

For the present, note definitions for strategic action. Communicative action was defined above as action oriented toward understanding, and as having certain characteristics. Figure 1 and these definitions indicate Habermas's approach to analyzing noncommunicative action as well. Strategic action can be open or concealed. Concealed strategic action can be deliberate and manipulative, or can be unconscious, as in the case of systematically distorted communication.

Systematically distorted communication is key to Habermas's analysis of ideological formations that function in service of illegitimate power. As the definition implies, it is intended to address forms of action in which deception is present but not necessarily in a conscious way. It addresses power not in relation to economics, but in relation to norms and social practices involving class, gender, sexual preference, and so on.

Notably, systematically distorted communication is not a pure form of action separate from the other forms. Unconscious deception takes place in all action settings and at all scales of interaction ranging from interpersonal to large-scale public spheres. This reiterates the point that communicative action itself need not be pure. It was noted earlier that ideal speech refers to an idealized set of expectations shared by communicators unconsciously, normally only approximated in communicative action. It was also noted that deception takes place interpersonally, among family members and within the professions. To be clear, these deceptions are not all intended as such. Unacknowledged power differentials permeate social life, not perhaps uniformly but on a widespread basis, and they express themselves communicatively, as subtle but nonetheless powerful restrictions on communicative opportunities.

The critical potential of the concept of communicative action is obtained, in part, just because of this. Habermas's action theory is not aimed at cleanly distinguishing earnest participatory communications from directives or from intentional lies, though it can be employed in this manner. It is intended primarily to analyze unconscious forms of manipulation that take place in everyday, often well-intentioned, activity whether in open strategic, concealed strategic, or communicative action.

This analysis can be undertaken from the perspective of social science theory, or from the perspective of a participant in social interaction. In both cases the analysis is performed by engaging in action oriented toward understanding about how we reach understanding. The rules by which we communicate are themselves bracketed and thematized for discussion. Matters related to gender, class, and cultural bias can be foregrounded for consideration. Are all free to raise and question proposals? Has everyone had the opportunity to be heard and understood? If not, why not? What can be done by way of remedy? Action oriented to these kinds of understandings can be undertaken interpersonally or as a matter of social policy in the public sphere.

PART 3: THE THEORY OF COMMUNICATIVE ACTION AND COMMUNICATION FOR SOCIAL CHANGE

Differentiating Kinds of Communication for Social Change

This scheme of action types can be used to productively differentiate among a number of forms of communication relevant to the work of social change. Table 1 presents a preliminary cross-classification of the relationship between action types and kinds of communication for social change programs based on scale or size. The question of scale was raised in the introduction because large-scale problems of health, poverty, and education in the Third World require large-scale solutions. Table 1 differentiates small- from large-scale change heuristically in order to emphasize these differences when considering the utility of this approach.

It will be necessary in the future to explore the complementarities and differences between communicative action at different scales and in different settings. For present purposes, this analysis employs a binomial classification of participation scales, differentiating small from large. The rows of the table represent kinds of social action. The columns represent the two different program size scales. Each entry indicates whether, in the case of each row, participation is possible.

With this scheme it is possible to consider an approach to defining communication for social change. First, it can be noted that the classification acknowledges what has been commonly asserted in the literature. Participatory communication comes in a variety of kinds. The classification scheme indicates at least four, these being small- and large-scale settings for the two kinds of communicative action.

To illustrate, consensual action for small-scale participation would be seen by

TABLE 1
Prospects for Participatory Communication Based on
Action Type and Scale of Social Change

	Scale of social change	
Action types	Small scale	Large scale
Communicative action		
Consensual action	Yes	Yes
Action oriented to reaching understanding	Yes	Yes
Strategic action		
Openly strategic action	No	No
Concealed strategic action (deception)	No	No
Systematically distorted communication	Partial (relevant to all cells)	Partial (relevant to all cells)

definition as desirable—perhaps a kind of paradigmatically desirable form of participatory communication, intimate and dialogical. A hypothetical example would
be that members of a small village all agree that a well is needed to obtain additional water. The location seems self-evident. The digging method and tools are
straightforward. In the action framework this is "agreement about implicitly raised
validity claims are *presupposed* as a background consensus by reason of common
definitions of the situations" (Habermas, 1979, p. 209). Any necessary communication is task oriented.

Small-scale action oriented to reaching understanding would be widely considered desirable and participatory. This is the most common kind of action setting
designers expect to encounter or promote at the project level, where there are plenty
of unanswered questions and disagreement. It is an action situation in which "agreement about implicitly raised validity claims *must be arrived at*" (Habermas, 1979,
p. 209). A hypothetical example of small-scale action oriented toward reaching
understanding would be if members of a small village are of two minds about
whether a well is needed. Some members believe an agreement can be made with
a neighboring village for access to its irrigation system, others do not. Of those
who don't believe, there is debate over whether a single well will suffice for the
village. This would remain action toward understanding as long as the overall
process was aimed at producing functional agreement in the long run.

The theory also accounts for a number of kinds of nonparticipatory communication. These include both open and concealed strategic forms, at local and nonlocal levels. Concealed strategic action (deception or manipulation) should be deplored in all circumstances, that is, conducting a sterilization campaign with intentionally inadequate information about irreversibility. Open strategic action is different and presents a number of complexities. It may seem desirable to hold the position that participatory or responsive governments should never employ directives, but that is facile. Even responsive democratic governments must sometimes initiate unpopular programs, programs that include local directives in the operational phase (consider government-imposed quarantines and the need for associated communication programs). These should certainly be minimized, but they cannot be avoided.

Systematically distorted communication can and does take place at both small and large scales of activity. At smaller scales it can be expressed interpersonally as gender bias or the kind of silence Freire attributes to peasant consciousness. For example, a rural agricultural community experiencing declines in productivity might be approached by employees of a multilateral agency with an offer of new seeds, sowing methods, fertilizers, and instruction on how to use them. Agency employees are well intentioned but do not realize that their high status as educated outsiders enjoins local farmers to observe silence. The lack of criticism encourages the agency employees and allows them at least temporarily to consider the intervention to be successful. In fact, local interests have not been expressed. Communication has been systematically distorted.

In large-scale settings, systematically distorted communication would be embodied in content and information flow patterns in mass media. It would potentially be combated here. As proponents of media advocacy know, the circulation of meaning through mass media affects both individual behavior and institutional responses to public problems (Wallack, Dorfman, Jernigan, & Themba, 1993). Mediated expressions of class, race, and gender bias affect the ecology in which individuals make their own choices, as do mediated expressions of unhealthy lifestyles, whether intended or not.

As noted earlier, systematically distorted communication can take place in any action setting. Regardless of whether a communicator intends to act communicatively or strategically, unconscious employment of social norms expressing gender, race, or class bias can be present. This is difficult to represent graphically, but the entries for systematically distorted communication in Table 1 should represent the possibility of distortion within all possible outcomes and would be considered undesirable wherever present.

Implications for Program Design and Evaluation

If the classification scheme represented in Table 1 differentiates meaningfully among significant kinds of communication programs, then it should be possible to employ the scheme in both program design and program evaluation. The scheme could help program designers, regardless of the tradition that they work in, to be fully aware of the major kinds of action at their disposal. Opportunities to employ communicative action can be highlighted, and the likelihood of encountering strategic forms of communication, including systematically distorted communication, can be minimized wherever possible. The scheme could also be used to evaluate communication programs. Regardless of whether they are designed in the tradition of social mobilization, social marketing, or participatory communication, the scheme makes focal the actual communication processes employed in a program. Short of presenting a fully developed set of indicators here, it is possible to suggest how design and evaluation might proceed by drawing from the basic concepts of communicative action a number of relevant design and evaluation principles:

1. Participatory communication, or communicative action, can be treated as both a means and an end. As an end in itself, communicative action expresses the conditions necessary for mutual recognition and collective self-determination. As a means, it conceptualizes the communicative process of collective reason, or decision making.

2. Based as it is on participant assessment of validity claims during communication, only participants themselves can establish whether an interaction is participatory.

3. Given number 2, indicators regarding validity should be elaborated using the concepts that theoretically characterize ideal speech, focusing on the negotiation of validity claims regarding truth, appropriateness, and sincerity, the presence of symmetrical opportunities to contribute, and so on.

4. Given that communicative action takes place at multiple levels of social interaction ranging from interpersonal to small group to the public sphere, indicators will vary. Program design and evaluation will employ indicators that vary from context to context, even while focusing on the conditions required for communicative action in all contexts.

Indicators cannot be drawn directly from the principles. The possibility of using the theory of communicative action for more than a highly abstract orientation to participatory communication for social change will have to be explored empirically by using the concepts to analyze concrete cases. However, the principles do indicate the way that the concepts of communicative action point to empirical conditions related to participatory communication.

SUMMARY

This chapter addresses both the growing interest in participatory approaches to communication for social change and a number of mostly definitional problems attending this growth. The chapter addressed these problems using the theory of communicative action. It suggested that this theory offers solutions to a number of definitional problems. It finally outlined a significant avenue for theoretical and empirical development in this area.

The first problem is the lack of fundamental definition for participatory communication. The theory of communicative action provides a conceptual framework whose key terms are clearly defined, individually and in relation to one another, by reconstructing the pragmatically necessary requirements of communication. Reciprocal expectations regarding validity claims, dialogue as the redemption of validity claims, symmetrical distributions of opportunities to contribute, and the rest of the communicative action framework comprise a highly generalizable approach to participatory communication. Above all, the theory suitably characterizes participatory communication by virtue of the fact that it holds that only participants themselves can determine validity.

One of the central definitional problems concerns scale. The participatory literature tends to focus on small-scale programs, whereas large-scale problems require large-scale solutions. Can the benefits of participation be obtained in large-scale programs? The answer available from the theory of communicative action is "yes." Discourse in the public sphere is available as a support to change processes at all levels.

It is worth noting that, by providing an explanation for vigorous and healthy public spheres, the theory also bridges across the concerns of modernization theorists and postmodernization theorists. Modernization theory was much interested in communication and political participation. Modernization theory assumed a libertarian model of the press in which press vigor is guaranteed by private ownership of the press. Private ownership, it was thought, would lead to a free marketplace of ideas. As is all too apparent today, private ownership alone is not sufficient to guarantee quality news coverage, citizen confidence in being heard, or even citizen confidence they are being well informed. The theory of communicative action creates a bridge between press theory and participatory communication by shifting the justification for a free and vigorous press from the mechanism of private ownership to the direct communicative processes through which normative legitimacy is secured, that is, through discursive participation for communicative power, rather that simple media consumption (Habermas, 1996, pp. 146–168). The theory's focus on reciprocity expectations explains why this is the case and, at the same time, shows the generality of communicative conditions across levels of social interaction and change. Reciprocity expectations that are fulfilled explain legitimacy, or its equivalent, in all social interaction. These expectations fulfilled are participation in its most general sense.

Thus, it stands to reason that participatory communication is available, in principle, not only for small community change projects but also for larger scale projects. This is clear in media advocacy, social mobilization, new social movements, and a vigorous press. In addition, large-scale, well-funded behavior change programs can also be participatory to the extent that these programs solicit input and are made subject to criticism at various scales of social interaction, ranging from interpersonal, to village, to national levels (Jacobson & Storey, 2002).

Another main definitional problem concerns the role of culture in social change. Diffusion-based change efforts tended to see culture largely as a barrier to change. Postmodernization thinking abounds with the alternative view that culture should be cherished rather than abandoned. On this matter, the theory of communicative action offers a number of conceptual levers. The concept of a cultural lifeworld acknowledges the essential requirement of culture for individual identity and social reproduction. The concept of lifeworld colonization recognizes certain pressures that have begun to emaciate lifeworlds, especially in the First World but also in the Third World. The concept of systematically distorted communication can be used to analyze ways in which cultural biases can sometimes limit opportunities to contribute to dialogue, both individually and publicly. The idea of the reflexive appropriation of traditions illustrates a role that the public sphere can play in collective reflection on those traditions a public may wish to retain, and those it may wish to abandon.

Finally, the debate over using participation as a means versus its being an end in itself is another significant problem. One position holds that participation used as a means is not participation at all. The theory of communicative action casts this dichotomy in a different light. The theory implies that participation is an end in itself because communicative action is key to all social action. Furthermore, the fact that validity can be determined only by participants themselves suggests that outsiders by definition cannot use others through using communicative action. If action is manipulative then it is strategic and not communicative. Argument, through the use of good reasons, is entirely acceptable; manipulation and systematic distortion are not.

This is directly relevant to debates over whether diffusion, social marketing, and entertainment-education programs are or are not participatory. From the perspective of communicative action, whether such programs are participatory cannot be answered without knowing the communicative conditions put into play. Certainly, the diffusion models of old did not attend adequately to the agency of target populations. Social marketing and entertainment-education theories, however, have evolved considerably over early diffusion models. Serious attempts are being made to put target population agency into the models. Whether a program is designed under the banner of social marketing or entertainment-education is less relevant than are the action conditions built into the program. Programs are participatory to the extent that communicative action is present.

Further research into this subject is needed. Social marketing, entertainment-education, community radio, social mobilization, Freirean, and other kinds of programs could be reviewed to determine whether, and to what extent, communicative action takes place in each of them. Studies could explore ways to maximize the role of communicative action in such programs, essentially comprising an exploration of the toolkit approach noted by Waisbord (2001).

Thus, the theory of communicative action offers conceptual approaches to the analysis of a number of specific problems extant in the literature on participatory communication. The theory possesses some useful analytic characteristics of a more general sort as well. First, the theory is complex in comparison to other approaches to participatory communication. This might be seen as a liability, however, when considering the complexity of participatory communication, the theory is suited to the task. With a few sets of interrelated conceptual frameworks, it manages to address a remarkably wide range of social change issues, including ideal speech, validity claims, reciprocity expectations, and public discourse. These express, in a formal way, the requisite conditions for participation in a wide variety of settings.

An attendant characteristic is the theory's abstraction. The theory does not offer the thickness of Freire's treatment of dialogue, emancipation, and empowerment, but it is by virtue of this abstraction that it is able to cover the range of topics it does. Therefore, the theory of communicative action, and its abstraction, should be seen as complementary to other theories. Both the formal, in the sense of formal pragmatics, and the empirical are evidently required.

These issues aside, a number of criticisms specific to the theory's modernism require attention. A variety of critics unsympathetic to Habermas's project charge the theory with idealism, insensitivity to difference, and an aloofness from power (Escobar, 1995, p. 221). Without the space to respond here, it should be said that good faith and systematic attempts to meet these charges have been made by Habermas and others (Bernstein, 1992; Habermas, 1982; White, 1988). Much of this criticism is somewhat caricatured, as is evidenced by the common ground recently found between Habermas's theory and other approaches on many specific topics. Feminism is one example where criticism has led to useful elaboration and debate. Feminists with interests as divergent as Nancy Fraser (1992), Seyla Benhabib (1996), and Simone Chambers (1995) find productive engagement with the theory of communicative action. Generally, these engagements involve grafting to his formalistic rationalism other subjective concerns related to caring, power, and difference. As a result, "Habermas's work can be of varied use to feminists . . . as it offers a framework for analyzing the structure of modern life, its potentials for both emancipatory forms of life and forms of life issuing political repression, market manipulation, and domination" (Meehan, 1995, p. 1). Proposals have been made to show how the theory of communicative action can be used productively in relation to the work of Foucault (Bahr, 1988) and the philosophy of difference as represented by Derrida and Lyotard (White, 1991).

Returning to matters on the ground, exploring the usefulness of the approach outlined here will require both conceptual and empirical research. Can communicative action be differentiated from strategic action in the field? Can large-scale efforts feed target population viewpoints back into project design, implementation, and evaluation on a large scale, thus facilitating communicative action and participation? The need for indicators of participatory communication that would be useful in program evaluation has been noted. The concepts of validity claims and of symmetrical distributions of opportunities to contribute to discussion offer starting points from which to begin development of participatory communication indicators from an action theoretic perspective. How can these be operationalized? The theory of communicative action offers an approach to participatory communication that is both critical and modernist. It provides the basis for criticizing unjust power inflicted through systematically distorted communication and manipulation. It also provides a model for the legitimate employment of power through citizen participation at all levels of social organization. It is possible that the theory of communicative action could be used in an attempt to reorder the field of development communication as a whole. Its utility for constructive analysis and program design needs to be further elaborated. At the same time, its ability to accommodate the analysis of difference and power in Third World settings needs to be more fully explored. For the time being, the theory has much to offer, given the more limited aim of analyzing participatory communication. On this count, it offers a way to explore the ways that different facets of participation might complement one another and how distortions of communicative opportunities can be minimized in social change efforts.

REFERENCES

Agunga, R. A. (1997). *Developing the Third World: A communication approach.* Commack, NY: Nova Science.
Almond, G., & Coleman, J. (1960). *The politics of the developing areas.* Princeton, NJ: Princeton University Press.
Almond, G., & Verba, S. (1963). *The civic culture: Political attitudes and democracy in five nations.* Princeton, NJ: Princeton University Press.
Amin, S. (1997). *Capitalism in the age of globalization: The management of contemporary society.* London: Zed Books.
Andreasen, A. R. (1994). Social marketing: Its definition and domain. *Journal of Public Policy & Marketing, 13,* 108–114.
Aronowitz, S. (1993). Paulo Freire's radical democratic humanism. In P. McLaren & P. Leonard (Eds.), *Paulo Freire: A critical encounter* (pp. 1–17). New York: Routledge.
Ascroft, J., & Masilela, S. (1994). Participatory decision making in Third World development. In S. A. White, K. S. Nair, & J. Ascoft (Eds.), *Participatory communication: Working for change and development* (pp. 259–294). New Delhi, India: Sage.
Bahr, E. (1988). In defense of enlightenment: Foucault and Habermas. *German Studies Review, 11,* 97–109.
Bandura, A. (1977). *Social learning theory.* Englewood Cliffs, NJ: Prentice Hall.
Beltran, L. R. (1976). Alien premises, objects, and methods in Latin American communication research. In E. M. Rogers (Ed.), *Communication and development: Critical perspectives* (pp. 15–42). Beverly Hills, CA: Sage.
Beltran, L. R. (1980). Farewell to Aristotle: Horizontal communication. *Communication, 5,* 5–41.
Benhabib, S. (Ed.). (1996). *Democracy and difference: Contesting the boundaries of the political.* Princeton, NJ: Princeton University Press.
Berger, P. (1975). *Pyramids of sacrifice: Political ethics and social change.* New York: Basic Books.
Bernstein, R. J. (1992). *The new constellation: The ethical-political horizons of modernity/postmodernity.* Cambridge, MA: MIT Press.
Berrigan, F. (1979). *Community communications: The role of community media in development.* Paris: UNESCO.
Berthoff, A. (1990). Paulo Freire's liberation pedagogy. *Language Arts, 67,* 362–369.
Bhabha, H. K. (1994). *The location of culture.* London: Routledge.
Black, C. E. (1966). *The dynamics of modernization: A study in comparative history* (1st ed.). New York: Harper & Row.
Bowers, C. (1983). Linguistic roots of cultural invasion in Paulo Freire's pedagogy. *Teachers College Record, 84,* 935–953.

Brawley, E. A., & Martinez-Brawley, E. E. (1999). Promoting social justice in partnership with the mass media. *Journal of Sociology & Social Welfare, 26,* 63–86.

Chambers, R. (1994). Participatory Rural Appraisal (PRA): Analysis of experience. *World Development, 22,* 1253–1268.

Chambers, S. (1995). Feminist discourse/practical discourse. In J. Meehan (Ed.), *Feminists read Habermas: Gendering the subject of discourse* (pp. 163–180). New York: Routledge.

Cohen, J. M., & Uphoff, N. T. (1980). Participation's place in rural development: Seeking clarity through specificity. *World Development, 8,* 213–233.

Dervin, B., & Huesca, R. (1997). Reaching for the communicating in participatory communication. *Journal of International Communication, 4,* 46–74.

Dervin, B., & Huesca, R. (1999). The participatory communication for development narrative: An examination of meta-theoretical assumptions and their impacts. In T. L. Jacobson & J. Servaes (Eds.), *Theoretical approaches to participatory communication* (pp. 169–210). Cresskill, NJ: Hampton Press.

Diaz-Bordenave, J. (1976). Communication of agricultural innovations in Latin America: The need for new models. *Communication Research, 3,* 135–154.

Diaz-Bordenave, J. (1994). Participative communication as a part of building the participative society. In S. A. White, K. S. Nair, & J. Ascroft (Eds.), *Participatory communication: Working for change and development* (pp. 35–48). New Delhi, India: Sage.

Einsiedel, E. (1999). Action research: Theoretical and methdological considerations for development. In T. L. Jacobson & J. Servaes (Eds.), *Theoretical approaches to participatory communication* (pp. 359–379). Cresskill, NJ: Hampton Press.

Escobar, A. (1995). *Encountering development: The making and unmaking of the Third World.* Princeton, NJ: Princeton University Press.

Fals Borda, O. (1979). Investigating knowledge in order to transform it. *Dialectical Anthropology, 4,* 33–56.

Fals Borda, O. (1988). *Knowledge and people's power: Lessons with peasants in Nicaragua, Mexico, and Columbia.* New Delhi, India: Indian Social Institute.

Frank, A. G. (1984). *Critique and anti-critique: Essays on dependence and reformism.* London: Macmillan Press.

Fraser, C., & Restrepo-Estrada, S. (1998). *Communicating for development: Human change for survival.* London: I. B. Tauris.

Fraser, N. (1992). Rethinking the public sphere: A contribution to the critique of actually existing democracy. In C. Calhoun (Ed.), *Habermas and the public sphere* (pp. 109–143). Cambridge, MA: MIT Press.

Freire, P. (1970). *Pedagogy of the oppressed.* New York: Herder & Herder.

Freire, P. (1973). *Education for critical consciousness.* New York: Continuum Press.

Fuglesang, A., & Chandler, D. (1986). The open snuff-box: Communication as participation. *Media Development, 2,* 2–4.

Galtung, J. (1971). A structural theory of imperialism. *Journal of Peace Research, 2,* 81–116.

Glanz, K., & Rimer, B. K. (1995). *Theory at a Glance.* Washington, DC: National Institutes of Health.

Greene, L. W., George, M. A., Daniel, M., Frankish, C. J., Jermert, C. J., Bowie, W. R., et al. (1995). *Study of Participatory Research in Health Promotion.* Vancouver, BC: Royal Society of Canada.

Grinberg, S. M. (1986). Trends in alternative communication research in Latin America. In E. G. McAnany (Ed.), *Communication and Latin American society: Trends in critical research, 1960–1985* (pp. 165–189). Madison: University of Wisconsin Press.

Gumucio Dagron, A. (2001). *Making waves: Stories of participatory communication for social change.* New York: Rockefeller Foundation.

Habermas, J. (1975). *Legitimation crisis.* Boston: Beacon Press.

Habermas, J. (1979). *Communication and the evolution of society.* Boston: Beacon Press.

Habermas, J. (1982). Reply to my critics. In J. Thompson & D. Held (Eds.), *Habermas: Critical debates* (pp. 219–283). Cambridge, MA: MIT Press.

Habermas, J. (1984). *The theory of communicative action: Reason and the rationalization of society* (Vol. 1). Boston: Beacon Press.

Habermas, J. (1987). *The theory of communicative action: A critique of functionalist reason* (Vol. 2). Boston: Beacon Press.

Habermas, J. (1989). *The structural transformation of the public sphere: An inquiry into a category of bourgeois society*. Cambridge, MA: MIT Press.

Habermas, J. (1990). *Moral consciousness and communicative action*. Cambridge, MA: MIT Press.

Habermas, J. (1992). *Autonomy and solidarity*. London: Verso.

Habermas, J. (1996). *Between facts and norms: Contributions to a discourse theory of law and democracy*. Cambridge, MA: MIT Press.

Habermas, J. (1998). *Inclusion of the other: Studies in political theory*. Cambridge, MA: MIT Press.

Hall, B. L. (1975). Participatory research: An approach for change. *Convergence, 8*, 24–31.

Hedebro, G. A. (1982). *Communication and social change in developing nations: A critical view* (1st ed.). Ames: Iowa State University Press.

Himmelstrand, U. (1982). Innovative processes in social change: Theory, method and social practice. In T. Bottomore, S. Nowak, & M. Sokolowska (Eds.), *Sociology: State of the art* (pp. 37–66). London: Sage.

Holder, H. D., & Treno, A. J. (1997). Media advocacy in community prevention: News as a means to advance policy change. *Addiction, 92*, 189–199.

Holland, J., & Blackburn, J. (1998). *Whose voice?: Participatory research and policy change*. London: Intermediate Technology.

Huesca, R. (2002). Participatory approaches to communication for development. In W. B. Gudykunst & B. Mody (Eds.), *Handbook of international and intercultural communication* (pp. 499–518). Thousand Oaks, CA: Sage.

Inayatullah, C. (1973). Western, Asian, or global models of development: The effect of the transference of models on the development of Asian society. In W. Schramm & D. Lerner (Eds.), *Communication and change: The last ten years—and the next* (pp. 241–252). Honolulu: University Press of Hawaii.

Jacobson, T., & Storey, D. (2002, July). *Development communication and participation: Applying Habermas to a case study of population programs in Nepal*. Presented to the annual conference of the International Communication Association, Seoul, South Korea.

Jacobson, T. L. (1993). A pragmatist account of participatory communication research for national development. *Communication Theory, 3*, 214–230.

Jacobson, T. L., & Servaes, J. (Eds.). (1999). *Theoretical approaches to participatory communication*. Cresskill, NJ: Hampton Press.

Jayaweera, N., & Amunagama, S. (1987). *Rethinking development communication*. Singapore: Asian Mass Communication Research and Information Centre.

Kotler, P., & Zaltman, G. (1971). Social marketing: An approach to planned social change. *Journal of Marketing, 35*, 3–12.

Lerner, D. (1958). *The passing of traditional society: Modernizing the Middle East*. Glencoe, IL: Free Press.

Lerner, D. (1976). Technology, communication, and change. In W. Shramm & D. Lerner (Eds.), *Communication and change: The last ten years—and the next*. (pp. 287–301). Honolulu: University Press of Hawaii.

Levy, M. J. (1966). *Modernization and the structure of societies: A setting for international affairs*. Princeton, NJ: Princeton University Press.

Lozare, B. (1994). Power and conflict: Hidden dimensions of communication, participative planning, and action. In S. A. White, K. S. Nair, & J. Ascroft (Eds.), *Participatory communication: Working for change and development* (pp. 229–244). New Delhi, India: Sage.

McAnany, E. G., Schnitman, J., & Janus, N. (1981). *Communication and social structure: Critical studies in mass media research*. New York: Praeger.

MacBride, S. (Ed.). (1980). *Many voices, one world: Communication and society, today and tomorrow*. Paris: UNESCO.

McKee, N. (1994). A community-based learning approach: Beyond social marketing. In S. A. White, K. S. Nair, & J. Ascroft (Eds.), *Participatory communication: Working for change and development* (pp. 194–228). New Delhi, India: Sage.

Meehan, J. (Ed.). (1995). *Feminists read Habermas: Gendering the subject of discourse*. New York: Routledge.

Melkote, S. R. (1991). *Communication for development in the Third World: Theory and practice.* Newbury Park, CA: Sage.

Midgley, J., Hall, A., Hardiman, H., & Narine, D. (1986). *Community participation, social development, and the state*. New York: Methuen.

Milton, J. (1959). Areopagitica: A speech of Mr. John Milton for the liberty of unlicenc'd printing, to the Parliament of England. In F. Fogle & Max Patrick (Eds.), *Complete prose works of John Milton* (Vol. 2, pp. 485–570). New Haven, CT: Yale University Press.

Minkler, M. (1990). Improving health through community organization. In K. Glanz, F. M. Lewis, & B. K. Rimer (Eds.), *Health behavior and health education: Theory, research, and practice* (pp. 259–287). San Francisco: Jossey-Bass.

Mlama, P. M. (1991). Women's participation in "communication for development": The popular theater alternative in Africa. *Research in African Literatures, 22*, 41–53.

Mody, B. (1991). *Designing messages for development communication: An audience participation-based approach*. Newbury Park, CA: Sage.

Moemeka, A. A. (Ed.). (1994). *Communicating for development: A new pan-disciplinary perspective.* Albany: State University of New York Press.

Nair, K. S., & White, S. A. (1993). The development communication process: A reconceptualization. In K. S. Nair & S. A. White (Eds.), *Perspectives in development communication* (pp. 47–70). New Delhi, India: Sage.

Nerfin, M. (1977). *Another development: Approaches and strategies*. Uppsala, Sweden: Dag Hammarskjold Foundation.

Novelli, W. (1990). Applying social marketing to health promotion and disease prevention. In K. Glanz, F. M. Lewis, & B. K. Rimer (Eds.), *Health behavior and health education: Theory, research, and practice* (pp. 324–369). San Francisco: Jossey-Bass.

O'Sullivan-Ryan, J., & Kaplan, M. (1982). *Communication methods to promote grassroots participation: A summary of research findings from Latin America, and an annotated bibliography.* Paris: UNESCO.

Pietrykowski, B. (1996). Knowledge and power in adult education: Beyond Freire and Habermas. *Adult Education Quarterly, 46*, 82–97.

Pye, L. W. (Ed.). (1963). *Communications and political development*. Princeton, NJ: Princeton University Press.

Rahman, M. A. (1993). *People's self-development: Perspectives on participatory action research.* London: Zed Books.

Rahnema, M. (1992). Participation. In W. Sachs (Ed.), *Development dictionary*. London: Zed Books.

Riano, P. (Ed.). (1994). *Women in grassroots communication: Furthering social change.* London: Sage.

Rockefeller Foundation. (2001). Measuring and evaluating communication for social change. *The Communication Initiative*. Retrieved, October 30, 2002, from http://www.comminit.com/measure_eval/sld-2180.html

Rodriguez, C. (1994). A process of identity deconstruction: Latin American women producing video stories. In P. Riano (Ed.), *Women in grassroots participation* (pp. 149–160). Thousand Oaks, CA: Sage.

Rogers, E. M. (1962). *Diffusion of innovations*. Glencoe, IL: Free Press.

Rogers, E. M. (1976). Communication and development: The passing of the dominant paradigm. *Communication Research, 3*, 213–240.

Rostow, W. W. (1960). *The stages of economic growth: A non-Communist manifesto*. Cambridge, UK: Cambridge University Press.

Schiller, H. I. (1976). *Communication and cultural domination*. White Plains, NY: M. E. Sharpe.

Schramm, W. (1976). End of an old paradigm? In W. Schramm & D. Lerner (Eds.), *Communication and change: The last ten years and the next* (pp. 45–48). Honolulu: University Press of Hawaii.

Servaes, J. (1985). Towards an alternative concept of communication and development. *Media Development, 4*, 2–5.

Servaes, J. (1986). Development theory and communication policy: Power to the people! *European Journal of Communication, 1*, 203–229.

Servaes, J. (1989). *One world, multiple cultures: A new paradigm on communication for development.* Leuven, Belgium: Acco.

Servaes, J. (1996). Linking theoretical perspectives to policy. In J. Servaes, T. L. Jacobson, & S. A. White (Eds.), *Participatory communication for social change* (pp. 29–43). New Delhi, India: Sage.

Servaes, J. (1999). *Communication for development: One world, multiple cultures.* Cresskill, NJ: Hampton Press.

Servaes, J., Jacobson, T. L., & White, S. A. (Eds.). (1996). *Participatory communication and social change.* New Delhi, India: Sage.

Simbulan, R. (1983). *Participatory research: A response to Asian peope's struggles for social transformation.* Paper presented at the Second Participatory Research Conference in Asia, Manila, Philippines.

Singhal, A., & Rogers, E. M. (1988). Television soap operas for development in India. *Gazette, 41*, 109–126.

Singhal, A., & Rogers, E. M. (1999). *Entertainment-education: A communication strategy for social change.* Mahwah, NJ: Erlbaum.

Storey, D. (1999). Popular culture, discourse, and development. In T. L. Jacobson & J. Servaes (Eds.), *Theoretical approaches to participatory communication* (pp. 337–358). Cresskill, NJ: Hampton Press.

Teheranian, M. (1994). Communication and development. In D. Crowley & D. Mitchell (Eds.), *Communication theory today* (pp. 274–306). Stanford, CA: Stanford University Press.

Thomas, P. (1994). Participatory message development communication: Philosophical premises. In S. A. White, K. S. Nair, & J. Ascroft (Eds.), *Participatory communication: Working for change and development* (pp. 49–59). New Delhi, India: Sage.

UNICEF. (1993). *We will never go back: Social mobilization in the child survival and development programme in the United Republic of Tanzania.* New York: UNICEF.

Vargas, L. (1995). *Social uses & radio practices: The use of participatory radio by ethnic minorities in Mexico.* Boulder, CO: Westview.

Waisbord, S. (2001). Family tree of theories, methodologies and strategies in development communication: Convergences and differences. Retrieved October 30, 2002, from http://www.comminit.com/stsilviocomm/sld-2881.html

Wallack, L. (1989). Mass communication and health promotion: A critical perspective. In R. E. Rice & C. Atkin (Eds.), *Public communication campaigns* (2nd ed., pp. 353–368). Newbury Park, CA: Sage.

Wallack, L., Dorfman, L., Jernigan, D., & Themba, M. (1993). *Media advocacy and public health: Power for prevention.* Newbury Park, CA: Sage.

Wallerstein, I. (1979). *The capitalist world economy.* Cambridge, UK: Cambridge University Press.

Weber, M. (1968). *Economy and society.* New York: Bedminster Press.

White, R. (1999). The need for new strategies of research on the democratization of communication. In T. L. Jacobson & J. Servaes (Eds.), *Theoretical prospects for participatory communication* (pp. 229–262). Cresskill, NJ: Hampton Press.

White, S. A. (Ed.). (1999). *The art of facilitating participation: Releasing the power of grassroots communication.* New Dehli, India: Sage.

White, S. A., Nair, K. S., & Ascroft, J. (Eds.). (1994). *Participatory communication: Working for change and development.* New Delhi, India: Sage.

White, S. K. (1988). *The recent work of Jürgen Habermas: Reason, justice, and modernity*. New York: Cambridge University Press.

White, S. K. (1991). *Political theory and postmodernism*. Cambridge, UK: Cambridge University Press.

Whitmore, E. (Ed.). (1998). *Understanding and practicing participatory evaluation*. San Francisco: Jossey-Bass.

Wilkins, K. (1999). Development discourse on gender and communication in strategies for social change. *Journal of Communication, 49*(1), 46–68.

World Bank. (1992). *The determinants of reproductive change, population and health sector study*. Washington, DC: World Bank, South Asia Region, Health, Population and Nutrition Unit.

World Bank. (1996). *World Bank participation sourcebook*. Washington, DC: Author.

CHAPTER CONTENTS

5 The Problematics of Dialogue and Power

SCOTT C. HAMMOND
Utah Valley State College

ROB ANDERSON
Saint Louis University

KENNETH N. CISSNA
University of South Florida

In recent years, dialogic approaches to communication have become far more common and persuasive in interpersonal communication, organizational life, rhetoric, political communication, and media studies. Yet, the relationship between dialogue and power remains relatively unexplored. In this chapter, we clarify the distinction between convergent dialogue and emergent dialogue, offering a new synthesis of relevant sources along with personalized examples from consulting practice. After surveying definitions and research in dialogue studies, we describe the contours of dialogue by considering its characteristics as they relate to power. We then identify and explore the persistent dialogic tensions that affect power relations: identity, outcome, meaning, voice, and field. Finally, we relate the concepts of convergent and emergent dialogic styles to Foucault's descriptions of juridical and contingent power.

S ome occasions that people call dialogues are spontaneous; some are structured. Some are dyadic; some occur in small groups such as families, neighborhoods, or work teams. Others involve companies or entire communities. Some dialogue occasions are high visibility exercises where power is wielded and challenged with broad metaphorical swords, whereas others are quiet processes where power appears to creep silently and inexorably like summer crabgrass. Power infuses dialogue—dialogue empowers change.

Mailloux (1989) considered such occasions as he developed his rhetorical hermeneutics. Arguing for a conversational model of culture, he rejects our common

---

Correspondence: Rob Anderson, 2470 Kinder Place, Glen Carbon, IL 62034; email: anderro@slu.edu

Communication Yearbook 27, pp. 125–157

assumptions that conversations must be polite or enjoyable. Instead, differences and argument—elements of power—are essential aspects of conversations that matter. In fact, he writes, "In society and its conversations, power is not simply a negative force, obstructing, suppressing, canceling the energy of action. It also functions in a positive way, creating, enabling, energizing various sociopolitical activities" (p. 59). Mailloux grounds his position in the later work of Foucault, such as the philosopher's suggestion that "In human relationships, whatever they are . . . power is always present: I mean the relationships in which one wishes to direct the behavior of others" (1988, p. 11). In revealing ways, Mailloux and Foucault suggest the cultural compatibility of dialogue and power. Further, to Kogler (1999), Foucault's analysis is especially relevant for contextualizing dialogue, not only because Foucault perceived his own contribution and style as dialogic, but also because Foucault's notion of interpersonal power presumes a relationship between free agents affecting each other's behavior in a "field of possibilities" (Kogler, 1999, pp. 233–234). Paradoxically, power—which can seek to reduce freedom—can develop only within dialogic conditions of shared determination. Otherwise, under conditions of force, for example, what appears to be powerful is merely domination or oppression. Later, we will return to Foucault to cap our synthesis of the problematics of dialogue and power.

Although the powerful effects of dialogue can be obvious, the implications of power for dialogic theory have been insufficiently synthesized and clarified, especially in the communication literature. To accomplish this clearer synthesis, we develop the essay in three parts after introducing some relevant definitions and resources. First, we show how the most basic characteristics of dialogue are tinged with issues of power. Second, we explore the power implications of the central communication issues of identity, outcome, meaning, voice, and dialogic field. Finally, we bring dialogue and power together even more directly, arguing for a fuller understanding of (a) how dialogue develops differently in conditions of juridical, compared with contingent, power, and (b) how power develops differently in conditions of convergent, compared with emergent, dialogue. Because of the power factor, we cannot assume that dialogue will lead to social repair or positive emotionality. Although it could lead to calm reconciliation, it can also ignite explosive—often necessary—conflict. We begin by proposing a basic definition of dialogue, reviewing a number of possible misconceptions, and considering recent interdisciplinary scholarship on dialogue.

INTRODUCTION

Grudin's (1996) succinct and helpful definition of dialogue focuses on the essential features of reciprocity and strangeness:

By reciprocity, I mean give-and-take between two or more open minds or two or more aspects of the same mind. This give-and-take is open-ended and is not controlled or limited by any single participant. By strangeness, I mean the shock of new information—divergent opinion, unpredictable data, sudden emotion, etc.—on those to whom it is expressed. Reciprocity and strangeness carry dialogue far beyond a mere conversation between two monolithic information sources. Through reciprocity and strangeness, dialogue becomes an evolutionary process in which the parties are changed as they proceed. (p. 12)

Grudin's statement provides a clear and useful starting point. Later, our analysis will suggest that dialogue's temporal aspects are also crucial.

Conceptions and Misconceptions of Dialogue's Power

Of course, if we frame dialogue one-dimensionally—as a transcendent, calm, or loving state—then the changes to which Grudin refers in his last sentence presumably will be welcome, positive, or growthful. However, the ensuing misconceptions about the nature of everyday dialogue would hamper a clear sense of its potential, especially in its relationship to power. We have encountered a number of interesting but probably unhelpful assumptions about dialogic power in interactions with sympathetic colleagues and clients:

• *Dialogue is designed to make the strange more familiar or clarify ambiguous aspects of the world.* This is only partially true, at best. It also makes the familiar more strange. Dialogue reveals new dimensions of the things we thought we already knew, and new doubts about the supposed certainties of life. This is why much religious ecumenism is less about dialogue than about politeness or tolerance. Dialogue, especially with assertive partners, shows us unanticipated aspects of ourselves and things we take for granted, at least as much as it gives us clearer access to unique and strange others. Many sincere communicators simply do not want to be this vulnerable (Gurevitch, 1988).

• *Dialogue helps marginalized people and groups become recognized and ultimately more powerful.* Not necessarily. Dialogue may not be particularly practical or powerful for people whose concerns have been shunted off customarily to society's margins. At times, they may need prior power bases before dialogue can help provide them with attentive audiences in the public sphere (Farson, 1978). People who need resolve and solidarity may find their strength ebbing if dominant groups call for dialogue as ploys to defuse the energy of opposition, or worse, as opportunities to outvote or outwait opposition. Exploited groups may be harmed by open dialogue if participation means that deserved political rewards are diluted or delayed even further (Young, 1990, 1996).

• *Leaders should strive for more dialogic styles.* Although containing a kernel of helpful advice (those in power need not overly depend on their roles), this assumption is dangerous if taken acontextually. Effective leaders surely look for ways to implement dialogic decision making, but must recognize the exceptions, too. At times, optimal decision making could demand leadership that relies more on trusted experience or expertise than on the full reciprocity of multiple voices.

• *Dialogue resolves conflicts.* People in dialogue might resolve or manage some conflicts, but dialogue is not itself a technique that accomplishes this. In fact, dialogic conditions often unearth conflicts that groups never knew they had until they began to honestly or genuinely hear each others' stories. Sometimes things get more difficult after dialogue. Friedman (1974, 1976, 1983, 1985) often suggests that genuine dialogue means that we must hold our ground long enough and powerfully enough to ensure that others have a real person to come up against. By doing this, by not changing our minds too rapidly or too cooperatively, we do our opponents and other dialogue partners a favor: They get to test their ideas in substantial, meaningful ways—not in a crucible of soft acquiescence but in a setting where our objections are experienced deeply, in ways that really matter. Unfortunately, some will believe that a strong position signals a closed mind and will not pursue dialogue further.

• *Public forums for dialogue ensure maximum fairness to all participants.* Not necessarily. Most traditional opportunities for public dialogue, such as open classrooms or town hall meetings, privilege highly verbal or glib people, already-assertive personalities, and culturally predominant groups. Some people thrive, but others do not. Dialogue might facilitate excessive credence to well-spoken advocates with ill-considered ideas, just because they are more comfortable raising their hands.

Recent Scholarship in Dialogue

The theory and practice of dialogue has an extensive history (cf. Buber, 1965a; Christians, 1988; Habermas, 1984, 1987; Johannesen, 1971; Newcomb, 1984; Poulakos, 1974; Stewart, 1978; Wold, 1992), and a renewed relevance for communication scholars in the last decade or so (Anderson, Cissna, & Arnett, 1994; Johannesen, 2002; Stewart, 1998). Countering earlier linear transmission and efficiency models of communication (described in Carey, 1989), prominent scholars have increasingly favored more critical, nonlinear, and emergent descriptions, including discourse theorist Habermas (1984, 1990, 1992); philosophers Buber (1923/1958; 1965a, 1965b; Friedman, 1976), Levinas (1989; Murray, 2000), Gadamer (1982), and Taylor (1991); psychologists Bruner (1990), Sampson (1993), and Rogers (1959; Anderson & Cissna, 1997; Cissna & Anderson, 2002; Kirschenbaum & Henderson, 1989); social/literary theorists Bakhtin (1981; Baxter & Montgomery, 1996; Montgomery & Baxter, 1998), Friedman (1974, 1992; Czubaroff, 2000), and Ong (1982); physicist Bohm (1987, 1990, 1996; Cayer, 1997); cultural theorists Asante (1987), hooks (1994), and Tedlock (1983; Tedlock & Mannheim, 1995); educators Freire (1970; DeLima & Christians, 1979; Shor & Freire, 1987) and Noddings (1984; Johannesen, 2000); and many others.

For example, some academics have become dissatisfied with the traditional lecture-style teaching methods that follow a transmission model (Carr, 1995; Christensen, Garvin, & Sweet, 1991; Palmer, 1998). They fear students will not find their own voices in a system that fails to question the privileged views of experts (hooks, 1994). Many educators hope dialogue within the academy will broaden the range of voices represented in public discourse and enable society to deal better with issues of race and gender (Flores & McPhail, 1997). Others, going back to Follett (1924), advocate dialogue as a way to increase democracy in communities and workplaces (Barber, 1984, 1988, 1992; Bohman, 1996; Caspary, 2000; Deetz, 1992; Deetz & Kersten, 1983; Deetz & Mumby, 1990; Gutmann & Thompson, 1996; Tannen, 1998). Still others imagine dialogue enhancing the healing potential of psychotherapy (Anderson, 1997; de Mare, Piper, & Thompson, 1991; Hycner, 1991), or helping people build better relationships (Smith & Arntson, 1991; Stone, Patton, & Heen, 1999).

Organizational change practitioners such as Senge (1990) and Isaacs (1999), building on the work of Bohm (1981, 1987, 1990), claim dialogue enhances organizational learning and decision making. Ellinor and Gerard (1998) offer the Bohm model to improve workplace creativity, whereas Bristow (2000) advocates dialogue to improve performance feedback. A structured dialogue model called Future Search brings all stakeholders in a work community together to create a product, organization, or strategic plan (Weisbord et al., 1992). Saunders (1999) and Yankelovich (1999) similarly laud dialogue through evidence from their years of involvement in international and public peacemaking.

Interdisciplinary research foregrounds dialogue when it reconceptualizes communication as a more interactive and systemic phenomenon (Krippendorff, 1989). Many hope they can align their own academic inquiry with everyday life (Allen, Orbe, & Olivas, 1999; Denzin, 2002; Pearce & Littlejohn, 1997; Pearce & Pearce, 2001; Penman, 2000; Spano, 2001). Fueled by the Alta Conference on Dialogue in 1998, and the special panels that have become regular features at conferences of the International Communication Association and the National Communication Association, the *Southern Communication Journal* recently published a special double issue on dialogue (Cissna, 2000). Recent articles on dialogue have appeared in *Communication Theory* (Arnett, 2001; Barge & Little, 2002; Cissna & Anderson, 1998; Hawes, 1999; Pearce & Pearce, 2000b, 2001; Taylor, Cooren, Giroux, & Robichard, 1996), *Critical Studies in Mass Communication* (Flores & McPhail, 1997; Krippendorff, 1995; Newcomb, 1984), and many other journals (e.g., Czubaroff, 2000; Hawes, 1998; Kellett, 1999; Taylor, 1999). Recently, communication scholars have published numerous dialogically oriented books (e.g., Anderson, Cissna, & Arnett, 1994; Arnett, 1992; Arnett & Arneson, 1999; Baxter & Montgomery, 1996; Deetz, 1995; Goodall, 1996; Kellett & Dalton, 2001; McNamee & Gergen, 1999; Montgomery & Baxter, 1998). Stewart and Zediker (2000) found it significant that 92 of the 117 sources cited by Cissna and Anderson (1998) in a literature review had been published since 1990.

Such theory building informs practice. The Berkana Institute employs dialogic approaches to link African activists with resources in more developed countries. The Mondragon Cooperatives in Spain and other similar programs (Caspary, 2000) attempt dialogic democracy among workers and producers. Boston's Public Conversations Project (e.g., Roth, Chasin, Becker, & Herzig, 1992) brings opponents in the abortion controversy together in dialogue, as has the Common Ground Network for Life and Choice (Jacksteit & Kaufmann, 1995). The Public Dialogue Consortium (Pearce & Pearce, 2001; Spano, 2001) marries skill development with dialogic theory in community-building projects. The Kettering Institute's National Issues Forums (Mathews, 1994) take a structured approach to encourage dialogue among citizens about such issues of public concern as race relations, education, and local government.

This vigorous dialogue about dialogue has led to disagreements over instrumentality (Pearce & Pearce, 2000a, 2000b) and definition (Hammond, 1997), as well as to concerns about uncritical acceptance (Peters, 1999), the conflation of different types of dialogue (Hyde & Bineham, 2000; Stewart & Zediker, 2000), and the place of power in dialogic relations. We suggest that dialogue is inherently about power in virtually every conceptualization to date, although the relation is often implicit and unexamined. A well-accepted definition from sociology and cultural studies identifies power with communication (though not with dialogue). According to this definition, power is "the means by which certain individuals and groups are able to dominate others, to carry through and realize their own particular aims and interests even in the face of opposition and resistance" (O'Sullivan, Hartley, Saunders, Montgomery, & Fiske, 1994, p. 235). Despite the authors' observation that the study of this phenomenon is clearly "both indivisible from and serves as the basis for the study of communication" (p. 235), we will need later to recast the definition to include more systemic and less intentionalistic dimensions of power in order to probe its linkage with dialogue. Some see dialogue as a way to mitigate the exercise of raw power (Freire, 1970). From this view, dialogue is a process that equalizes power holdings among the powerless and the powerful, much in the manner of Habermas's (1990, 1992) *ideal speech situation*. Others see dialogue as a conduit for power, a way to create advantages for oneself, to convert, win, or win over someone else. Later, we examine linear and nonlinear conceptions of power, and show how they parallel scholars' descriptions of dialogue. First, however, we must establish the contours of dialogue itself.

DISTINGUISHING DIALOGUE FROM
OTHER FORMS OF COMMUNICATION

In this section, we extend the characteristics of dialogue synthesized by Cissna and Anderson (1994) into informal metaphorical vehicles (Richards, 1971): (a) as dialogue for Cissna and Anderson exhibits *immediacy of presence*, we will show that its process is explainable in terms of *accessing*; (b) *emergent unanticipated consequences* suggests *jamming*; (c) recognition of *strange otherness* is similar to *inviting*; (d) *collaborative orientation* is enacted as *team learning*; (e) *vulnerabil-*

ity exists as *nondefensive changing*; (f) *mutual implication* processes involve *communing*; (g) *temporal flow* suggests metaphorical aspects of *flowing*; and (h) *genuineness and authenticity* exist in terms of issues of *voicing*.

Immediacy of Presence—Dialogue as Accessing

In a world dominated by mediated communication, some critics fear the loss of conversation's immediacy (Ferrarotti, 1988). Dialogue involves participants who, as Buber (1965a) would say, "turn toward" each other to create mutual access (p. 22). They do so without a predetermined outcome in mind—which is not to say they are goal-free. Dialogue's access is not usually achieved from a podium to a crowded room, nor is it broadcast via packaged messages through privileged media with effects to be measured later. Dialogue thrives in real-time communication in which, like a tennis match, response is anticipated. In dialogue, human agency is alive and real-time choices, partially perceived by others, are assessed line upon line, layer upon layer, as meaning and mutuality are imperfectly constructed (Pearce & Pearce, 2000a).

Some dialogues are directly mediated. For example, in October of 2000, after new hostilities broke out in Israel, ABC News's *Nightline* produced a *Jerusalem Town Meeting* featuring a panel of Israeli and Palestinian leaders facing a diverse and vocal audience. Producer Sara Just (personal communication, December 10, 2000) said the intent of the meeting was to disseminate information and not to advocate peace. Still, *Nightline* was committed to broadcasting whatever happened just as it occurred. The real-time, immediate accessibility of traditional political rivals surprised the participants, host, and the audience with a momentary transcendence of the traditional barriers. Several participants reported a renewed hope in the process of peace. Although conflict in the area continues, this panel and audience showed how presence can translate to access, and in so doing modeled the kinds of dialogue that will be needed for a sustained peace.

Emergent Unanticipated Consequences—Dialogue as Jamming

The *Nightline* program and similar encounters produce unanticipated consequences that are organic and self-organizing (Hayles, 1999), much like the *jamming* of improvisational jazz groups (Eisenberg, 1990; Kao, 1997). Jamming involves the spontaneous and emergent transformation of unexpected opportunities into breakthrough insights and actions. These occurrences are not accidental, however, because improvisation is built on the bedrock of skilled discipline.

We experienced jamming in a dialogue with park planners from the National Park Service in 1993, in which participants were charged with making changes that would simplify and shorten the time it took to create a park plan. About 30 park employees were joined by another 30 stakeholders, including representatives from environmental groups, park superintendents, communities near national parks, and congressional staff. After 5 days of structured questions and open dialogue, the group suggested 56 changes in the park planning process, 22 of which they noted were completely unanticipated—they were in no one's imagination prior to the event. Dialogue's improvisation can be the key to releasing hidden resources of group creativity.

Recognition of Strange Otherness—Dialogue as Inviting

Dialogue involves recognizing *strange* (i.e., fundamentally different) *otherness* as persons connect in order to generate meaning and real solutions to social problems. Sampson (1993) sketches the monologic cultural climate in which the other is experienced only as a objective extension of self:

> When I construct a you designed to meet my needs and desires, a you that is serviceable for me, I am clearly engaging in a monologue as distinct from a dialogue. Although you and I may converse and interact together, in most respects the you with whom I am interacting has been constructed with me in mind. Your sole function has been to serve and service me. All such monologues are self-celebratory and non-dialogic. They are one-way streets that return to their point of origin. They lead from the self, back again to the same self. (p. 4)

In other words, monologic communicators do not really want the other to be Other, truly different—but merely a comfortable affirmation of self. Here, there is no invitation and no responsibility, because there is no ability to respond to another. Being open to strange otherness becomes for Levinas (1989) an indication "that the other is in no way another myself, participating with me in a common existence." Nor is our relationship with the other:

> an idyllic and harmonious relationship of communion, or a sympathy through which we put ourselves in the other's place; we recognize the other as resembling us, but exterior to us; the relationship with the other is a relationship with a Mystery. (Levinas, 1989, p. 43)

In a planning meeting for a large, community dialogue in central California, a group of academics, educators, and business leaders hoped to reduce gang violence. The facilitators insisted that gang members be included in the process. Although both planners and gang members initially resisted, three gang representatives eventually joined the planning team. In the first meetings the gang members were silent, but they later became full participants; this allowed the group to take on a multivocal perspective, which influenced plans for a community dialogue that transcended neighborhood, race, economic class, and age. Fully inviting the differences set in motion the conditions necessary for change.

Collaborative Orientation—Dialogue as Team Learning

Individuals tend not to learn without community or relational support (Palmer, 1983), and dialogic assumptions involve "caring about the future of the other, the relationship, and the joint project of sense-making" (Cissna & Anderson, 1994, p. 14). As Wheatley (1992) argues, information networks that function dialogically allow for social self-organization and create more sustainable social relationships. Thus, dialogue can lead to higher quality solutions to social problems (Tannen, 1989, 1998), more effective organizational learning (Senge, 1990), and stronger classroom relations (Palmer, 1998). Dissemination assumptions, however, presume influence, command, and control. Isaacs (1993b) condemns control-oriented management styles that prescribe a tough, independent leader/expert who practices top-down leadership, as well as the tendency for organizational conversations to turn into debates that create winners and losers. Hyde and Bineham (2000) explain the basis for unproductive debates: "Our cultural disposition is to listen for opportunities to agree and disagree, not to engage in dialogue" (p. 213).

The conflict management literature clarifies the practicality of collaborative learning. Bloomfield (1997) describes how a *settlement orientation* involves power bargaining, negotiation, compromise, and dependence on military or governmental structures for agreement and enforcement. Often, both parties become vested in the symbolic perpetuation of the conflict in order to maintain their power positions. Yet, a dialogic *resolution approach* requires ongoing, negotiated, cooperative problem solving, resulting in integrative, low-cost, low-profile, and self-sustaining solutions. Participants in such programs report stronger bonds with those once perceived as enemies. Dialogue is a form of collective team learning and that learning is itself a collaborative activity.

Vulnerability—Dialogue as Helping

Dialogue implies that people are willing to risk changing their minds and to become vulnerable to new influences. Dialogue partners do not rely on protective or territorial impulses ("I must defend my position"), nor do they operate from a position of certainty. The irony is that certainty—either when one is utterly convinced of one's own rightness, or when one is convinced that only other people have truly right positions—creates the conditions in which the person is less credible, less able to be helped, and less able to help. Vulnerable communicators enable helping because they are so open to change themselves.

Anderson (1997) describes effective therapy in terms of mutual conversational vulnerability. Although a client may request help from a therapist, that help is not a unilateral gift from the therapist. First, the client must teach the therapist, who then becomes vulnerable to the narrative of this other life. Then, help becomes a joint construction, controlled by neither party alone, from which both emerge empowered.

Anderson's dialogic therapy is similar to Palmer's (1998) subject-centered learning. Hyde and Bineham (2000) experimented with such an approach, concluding that "the dialogue groups demonstrated clearly to students the possibility of a discourse that encourages the inclusion of multiple perspectives rather than a reduction to a bipolar opposition" (p. 220; cf. Barker & Kemp, 1990; Belenky, Clinchy, Goldberger, & Tarule, 1986; Chiseri-Strater, 1991; Green, 1988).

Dialogic vulnerability, combined with a fear of excessive disclosure, can create a leverage point for psychological intervention, healing, trust, and community (Pearce & Pearce, 2000a, 2000b)—or, if exploited by dominant or unethical communicators, it can lead to control, breakdown, and abuse. In genuine dialogue, however, vulnerability provides an avenue for helping and for being helped.

Mutual Implication—Dialogue as Communing

Dialogue requires a form of transactional relationship between self and other. Thus, dialogue necessarily involves mutual implication and communion (Kaplan, 1969). The presence of one person serves to define the other's role, and vice versa. When one turns toward another, both are confronted with the problematic of dialogue. The communicative contextualizing of self and other through mutual implication provides a more complex and holistic perspective of communication events. De Mare et al.'s (1991) book about dialogue as therapy, *Koinonia*, from the Greek word for communion, proposes that dialogue creates symbolic clusters or attractors that we call communities, which reverberates with Matson and Montagu's (1967) claim that "the end of human communication is not to command but to commune" (p. 5).

Palmer (1998) describes a communal Quaker tradition called a clearness committee, where a *focus person* gathers a number of friends and family to understand an important life decision. One basic rule guides participants: "Members are forbidden to speak to the focus person in any way except to ask that person an honest, open question" (p. 153). The tradition assumes that an intense communal dialogue based on mutually interdependent roles will surface a kind of truth in the heart of an individual.

Temporal Flow—Dialogue as Flowing

Prigogine and Stengers (1984) suggest that self-organizing dialogic systems are temporally and spatially holistic. Persons in dialogue are connected not just with each other, but also with a history, a place, and a future. Although conceptual holism suggests that communication networks arise dialogically and knit society together, temporal holism suggests that all dialogue must be situated in the context of time. Moments of dialogic meeting (Cissna & Anderson, 1998, 2002) have their own histories and preview particular futures in ongoing flow. Shotter (2000) highlighted Bakhtin's reminder that "as living, embodied beings we have our being within a ceaseless unfolding flow of relational-responsive activity" (p. 120). Bakhtin (1984) effectively grounded temporal holism and spatial holism for language systems.

One contemporary example of temporal and spatially holistic dialogue—as well as mutual implication—is the public journalism movement to which we will return later. Advocates (Charity, 1995; Merritt, 1995; Rosen, 1999; Rosen & Merritt, 1994) claim journalists should not separate themselves from society by imposing artificial professional standards of objectivity. Newspapers, for example, are inseparable parts of the community and inherit a responsibility for the consequences of their words. In this way, public journalists frame media as constantly shifting forums for a wide range of voices, great and small—portraying and encouraging the repertoire of public discourse, knitting the community together, and inviting parties toward reconciliation.

Genuineness and Authenticity—Dialogue as Voicing

Buber (1957) called dialogue the "vox humana" (pp. 234–235) and knew that speaking with an authentic voice cannot be divorced from listening. He believed that the "duality of being and seeming" was the "essential problem of the sphere of the interhuman" (1965b, p. 77). Clearly, he understood that the two tendencies are often mixed, but for genuine dialogue persons need to be responsible for speaking from the actual place of their existence, their being, rather than attempting to adopt an image by which others might be impressed.

In 1994, a group of about 40 practitioners, advocates, and theorists in dialogue (including authors cited in this chapter) gathered for a 3-day dialogue about dialogue. Many in the room were dialogue facilitators and came with imposing conceptual baggage, advocating one set of dialogic practices over others. Others were well-published scholars and supposed that their own models provided superior descriptions of dialogue. Each 2-hour session became increasingly strained, as participants competed for each other's attention. What began as collaborative inquiry ended as overt competition. One possible interpretation was that we experts often voice our expertise by relying on roles rather than authentic personal experiencing. In role, each felt qualified to prescribe process and content orthodoxy without listening realistically to others. Ironically, given the announced focus, individuals seemingly sought the power of prestige, and the prestige of power. At times, teachers and trainers forget to speak in a tentative voice.

Although the characteristics and associated metaphors of dialogue more or less distinguish dialogue from such communicative forms as dissemination or debate, the separation is still problematic. Like the kids in the back of the car, communicators might be inclined to ask, "Are we there yet?" "Is this dialogue?" "Are we dialoguing yet?" For Bakhtin (1986), we are always "there": Communication is inherently dialogical because language contains the diverse voices of its own history. But for other scholars, such as Bohm, Buber, or Jaspers (Gordon, 2000), dialogue seems more similar to an ideal form that is infrequent and never fully achieved. Bakhtin (1984) thought that although all human language is dialogic at some level, a genuinely human voice can be spoken only in the context of the other: "I am conscious of myself and become myself only while revealing myself for another, through another, and with the help of another" (p. 287). Highly creative breakthrough moments, which some describe reaching in dialogue, emerge most often when we find genuine and authentic voices.

Dialogue is more a process that flashes in moments of creative meeting (Cissna & Anderson, 2002) than it is a specific destination or state. But this is not to say there is no *telos* for dialogue. It can yield different results from those possible in other kinds of communicative encounters. What are the persistent tensions of dialogic theory and how are issues of power enfolded within them?

THE PERMANENT TENSIONS IN DIALOGUE

Dialogic communication assumes many different forms and, as we have seen, theorists and practitioners approach it in different ways. In this section, we examine the different types of dialogue by describing five identifiable yet overlapping *dialogic tensions,* within which power relationships surface and are sometimes submerged. These tensions are not always obvious, but may be layered within talk and subjectively experienced as what Bakhtin called "once-occurrent events of Being" (Bakhtin, 1993, p. 13; Shotter, 2000, pp. 120–122). The previous section described distinguishing characteristics of dialogic communication; this one explores a new direction, suggesting certain experiential tensions inherent in these distinctions. The tensions can be subtle, elusive, powerful, clear, disputed, disruptive, revealing, and even transformative.

Change can be thought of as something like the vapor trail of power. In dialogue, change and power often follow traditional, rhetorical forms. However, dialogic change also allows us to glimpse power in different forms. Although the third section of this essay discusses power even more directly, here we describe how the inherent tensions in dialogue validate a socially contingent power model (rather than an individualistic or juridical model).

We intend here to suggest the persistence of these forces across relationships, times, intentions, and contexts. However, this emphasis on permanence does not imply an unchangingness of meanings. Any descriptions of the flow of dialogic meanings will be relative and incomplete. Therefore, the tensions we note as permanent are nevertheless equivocal and difficult to pin down in dialogic moments. The issue of *identity* is premised upon the tension between *self and other*; *outcome* depends on the tension between *content and process*; *meaning* becomes meaningful through the tension between *coherence and incoherence*; *voice* emerges through the tension between *monovocality and mutuality*; and the issue of *field* depends upon the tension between *convergence and emergence.*

Identity and the Tension Between Self and Other

Theories in the human sciences consistently suggest that self-knowledge and identity construction are possible only in the context of group interaction. Burke (1968) described identification as a process of not only distinguishing one's self from others, but also as a coequal process of creating relationships with others. Deleuze (1990) thought all communication begins with *I*, but Buber's (1923/1958) context is crucial for understanding such a claim: "Through the *Thou* a man becomes *I*" (p. 28). The inherent tension between self and other leads to reflexivity, self-reference, and self-implication. The negotiation of self-identity and group identity is both a motive for and a product of dialogue. In Baxter and DeGooyer's (2001) study of aesthetic perceptions of interpersonal communication, the most frequent characteristic of aesthetically pleasing conversations they found was "Completion of Self Through Other" (p. 13), a notion similar to Bakhtin's answerability and the Buber-Rogers mutuality concept that we address later. Self-implication creates dialogic possibilities of feedback, advice, and affirmation that connect persons socially and help them feel more valued and complete. Yet, our synthesis of the literature also leads us to a somewhat different point: Inherently conflicting individual and group identities function as a necessary tension in dialogue. Identity is not a static congruence with an imagined real self, but is continually negotiated between individual participants and their sense of a whole. Identity, therefore, becomes a site of power negotiation, where individuals' identities are discursively contrasted with the group, with other individuals or subgroups, and with popular or unpopular ideas.

Organizational change consultants Weisbord et al. (1992) seek participants who will ask probing identity questions as they design their Future Search dialogues. Stakeholders who are concerned with their relationship to the group lead members to question their own assumptions. Weisbord and his colleagues claim that to make progress on content issues, group members must first go through the work of seeing themselves differently. The tension between self and other identities in dialogue helps us to question and even replace old traditions and practices. Simply put, new identities create new outcomes.

Outcome and the Tension Between Process and Content

A training manager for a large software company continually used the word *downloading* in a strategic planning dialogue. At first, other participants assumed that she was referring literally to computer functions, but the group soon realized that this was her term, and model, for learning. In her metaphor, she downloaded information to trainees, ultimately making their roles increasingly power-dependent when compared with hers. This is a drastic example of a person who privileges content over process and perhaps couldn't acknowledge how the two are interdependent.

Cultures naturally define the appropriate contexts for dialogue (Kincaid, 1987). Hammond (1997) found that structured dialogues in culturally complex groups involve language that negotiates the interdependence of content and process. In some Asian cultures, process must be made explicit before issues of content can be raised, whereas in some European cultures, the content issues must be made explicit before issues of process can be discussed. Both, however, ultimately acknowledge the interdependence.

To clarify this relationship, Hyde and Bineham (2000) distinguish between two levels of dialogic focus, both of which presume participant empowerment but in differing ways. The first, dialogue$_1$, is oriented toward specific practices and is thus teachable; it presumes, for example, that participants will engage in active listening and participative decision making across their differences, while acknowledging those very differences. The success of this kind of dialogue can be determined by how well the participants address their topic(s)—rather than their identities or processes—in ways that are "rigorously collaborative" (p. 212) rather than polarized. Dialogue₁ might contain argument and rebuttal, but in the sense that these contribute to a more integrative sense of working within a shared problem area. To some extent, dialogue₁ is at least content-inflected, if not fully content-driven. Its resources and processes are marshaled in the service of content-oriented problems such as achieving consensus.

Dialogue₂, on the other hand, is less predictable and less driven by content-oriented practices. It sets in motion unpredictable processes of self-implication, communing, and flashes of self-other insight. The process of dialogue in some sense becomes its own goal. When Cissna and Anderson (1998, 2002) defined the essence of dialogue as spontaneous and transitory (yet utterly meaningful) moments of meeting, they were largely working within assumptions similar to Hyde and Bineham's dialogue₂. One way to think about this distinction is to consider what facilitators can do to help dialogue develop. In dialogue₁, facilitators teach such skills as active listening, for example, to increase the likelihood of careful consideration of content positions among presumably equal communicators. In dialogue₂, facilitators might define their task primarily as clearing a space within which moments of dialogic encounter might emerge with as few obstacles as possible. Obviously, as Hyde and Bineham (2000) observe, the differences are subtle, and to some extent the collaborative skills of the form of discourse that is dialogue₁ may serve to open the relational space that is the arena of dialogue₂.

Our earlier public journalism example might be a useful illustration of the difference between these two dialogic approaches. For more than a century, journalism in the United States has fulfilled a generalized dialogic function because it attempts to listen actively to the public drama and translate its events accurately and evenhandedly for readers who cannot experience these events firsthand. At its best, it acknowledges social and cultural differences fairly, and its content serves as the basis for public deliberation, decision making, and perhaps consensus. In this, it reflects dialogue₁ assumptions. Public journalism advocates (Charity, 1995; Rosen, 1999), though, hope to supplement traditional assumptions of objectivity with a more overt dialogue₂ approach, in which the role of journalism is also to open up dialogic spaces for the voices of everyday people who are not necessarily major political players. Citizens are not just readers of news, but potential participants in its lively conversation. Public journalism doesn't simply wait for something called news to happen, but takes the responsibility for providing the discourse space in which new processes of discourse can shape public opinion. This form of journalism does not presume that a particular consensus will emerge and its ethic of fairness remains intact. In fact, it trusts that the process of clearing the space for discourse and considering pluralistic points of view will be most consonant with democratic ideals.

Public journalists trust the conception of powerful dialogic public space advocated by political theorists Benhabib (1992) and Arendt (1959). Power, Benhabib (1992) wrote, "is not only a social resource to be distributed, say like bread or automobiles. It is also a sociocultural grid of interpretation and communication. Public dialogue is not external to but constitutive of power relations" (p. 48). Arendt (1959) observed long ago that a *polis* is not an actual geographic location but a space "in between" persons who live together through speaking and acting (pp. 177–183). This space does not automatically exist for all people, as some are unfairly excluded. Power emerges in such public presence as potentiality rather than as an object: "Power is what keeps the public realm, the potential space of appearance between acting and speaking men, in existence" (p. 179); "power is always . . . a power potential and not an unchangeable, measurable, and reliable entity like force or strength" (p. 179); "power springs up between men when they act together and vanishes the moment they disperse" (p. 179); and "only where men live so close together that the potentialities of action are always present can power remain with them" (p. 180). If it is true that, as Arendt states, "human power corresponds to the condition of plurality to begin with" (p. 180), then the central mission of public journalism (beyond reporting the news) is to ensure a pluralized public life, enabling the access of diverse citizens to each other in a *polis*.

Stewart and Zediker (2000) approach the content-process tension in dialogue differently in applying *poiesis* (action and practice with a specified product in mind) and *praxis* (action and practice with a morally worthwhile good in mind; p. 229). Although poiesis might express the hope of naïve communicators who wish for personalized power through a technique of achieving their own ends in interaction, the authors show how praxis, which entails more of what Aristotle called *practical wisdom*, is more helpful in holding the tension between content and process. Dialogic theorists such as Buber attempt to prescribe dialogue, in the sense of suggesting how to help create dialogic conditions of shared empowerment, not how to achieve one's specific content goals. To the extent that there is a prescription, it is for a *process* (that necessarily involves some forms of content), rather than for a *content* goal (that uses or employs a process of technique to guarantee its achievement).

Meaning and the Tension Between Coherence and Incoherence

Weick (1979) and Berger and associates (Berger, 1987; Berger & Bradac, 1982; Berger & Calabrese, 1975) have described communication in terms of uncertainty reduction. Weick (1995) claims that we organize in order to create environments that have a workable level of certainty. Humans hope for a coherent environment where we can predict the effects of our actions. But Weick acknowledges that this is an ongoing process that, although desired, is never fully accomplished. Uncertainty theorists rightfully argue that uncertainty reduction is often a motive for individual communicators, but we suggest that dialogue depends on the tension or interplay between coherence and incoherence. Consider Tannen's (1989) description of pleasing conversations that lead to a sense of coherence:

The experience of a perfectly tuned conversation is like an artistic experience. The satisfaction of shared rhythm, shared appreciation of nuance, [and] mutual understanding . . . surpasses the meaning of words exchanged. . . . It gives a sense of coherence to the world. (p. 152)

We desire coherence, to be sure. However, tension over meaning is inherent, coherence is affirming but temporary, and incoherence indispensably drives a need for dialogue. Smithson (1990) similarly argued for ignorance as a motive for dialogue, and Thomas (1974) described the centrality of ambiguity for meaningful communication: "Only the human mind," he observed, is "programmed to drift away in the presence of locked-on information, straying from each point in a hunt for a better, different point" (p. 95). Further, he suggests, "if it were not for the capacity for ambiguity, for the sensing of strangeness that words in all languages provide, we would have no way of recognizing the layers of counterpoint in meaning" (p. 95).

Hayles (1999) finds a similar tension in the semiotics of virtuality. She describes tensions between presence and absence, disruption and replication, and pattern and randomness in a self-organizing meaning system. In short, she is concerned with the emergence of order and chaos. For dialogue participants, each of these tensional qualities is manifest as relative coherence or incoherence. Physical or mental absence and randomness lead to incoherence, whereas presence, replication, and pattern lead to coherence. It is little wonder that the current generation's phrase for incoherence is "totally random."

One practical manifestation of the tension between coherence and incoherence plays out in the meaning of past and future. Earlier, we claimed that dialogue depends on an immediacy of presence. Yet, also present in every dialogue is the coherent voice of the subjective past and the incoherent voice of the projected future. Weisbord et al. (1992), in the Future Search dialogues, deliberately give voice to the past through timeline exercises in order to enable or empower a future orientation. They argue that if the past is not given adequate voice, then it is very difficult for the group to turn realistically toward the future. Coherence, as we achieve it, is ephemeral—and not always understood similarly or shared simultaneously with other communicators. It forms the motivation for dialogic communication, but it is a hard-won moment more often than an enduring state of clarity. What is enduring, even permanent, is the necessity of both incoherence and coherence—that is, the motivating and clarifying ends of dialogue, working in tandem to provide the impulse toward dialogue in the first place.

Voice and the Tension Between Monovocality and Mutuality

An additional tension, intimately connected with problems of power, exists between the forces of mutuality and hegemonic monovocality. Bohm's (1990, 1996) dialogue moves toward shared meaning. Isaacs (1999) believes dialogue enables collective action. But a collective can be controlling. Bakhtin (1981, 1986) understood how monologism, or privileging a single voice, may appear to clarify the human condition—but at a price. As Holquist (1990) observed, "in Bakhtin, there is no one meaning being striven for: the world is a vast congeries of contesting meanings, a heteroglossia so varied that no single term capable of unifying its diversifying energies is possible" (p. 24). Baxter and DeGooyer (2001) identified that monologic wholeness: "[the] oneness or unity achieved through the hegemony of a single fragment or voice dominant over other voices, is the wholeness of totalitarianism" (p. 3).

Such monovocality can be contrasted to a concept of mutuality that Cissna and Anderson (1998, 2002; Anderson & Cissna, 1997) credited to the 1957 Buber-Rogers dialogue. Mutuality emphasizes an awareness of the uniqueness of others. It encourages authenticity but requires neither the renunciation of roles nor the disclosure of all personal thoughts. It presumes a respect for others that includes confirmation and the willingness not to impose one's beliefs or standards, but does not presume power parity. The kind of mutuality articulated by Buber, Rogers, and others often leads to unexpected meaning.

The difference between monovocality and mutuality is that monovocal meaning can be imposed and contained by a politically hegemonic system. Buber (1965b), for example, distinguished between education, in which the subject matter is to be unfolded and the other is allowed to unfold as a person (even across asymmetrical power roles such as teacher and student), and propaganda, in which the goal is to produce predetermined action in the other. Monovocality is countered by the surprise of mutuality, where meaning emerges through relationships rather than through imposing or presuming individual will.

Not all monological messages or approaches qualify as propaganda. Dialogic facilitators might need to establish congruent interpretations of process as a starting point for dialogue. In the dialogue on gang violence described earlier, largely monovocal concerns over violence gave people reasons to commit their time and talent to talk. However, deliberations that remain monological or monovocal undercut mutuality in the long run. The presumed power of a single voice marginalizes minority perspectives. The voices of gang members, once they became validated within the dialogue, forced community leaders to relinquish their entrenched expectations. This allowed community leaders to hear about less visible forms of violence, to which they had never been attentive.

The Dialogic Field and the Tension Between Convergent and Emergent Outcomes

The final tension we describe is in the creation of the dialogic field, a concern that is crucial for community activists, organizational consultants, teachers, therapists, and journalists. Because dialogue is nonlinear, emergence and surprise are constant factors contributing to change and creativity. However, because dialogue also presumes cooperative mutuality, certain groups expect convergence on outcomes or goals. Think of dialogue as a field of meaning, much like a strange attractor such as a fractal weather pattern or an ecosystem. The vision, collective abilities, and experience of the group bind it together, but it is also open to infinite possible outcomes, some of which will be surprising to participants. The key questions regarding the dialogic field relate to intent: Is the field converging on a problem or a congruent meaning? Is it opening out, waiting for a mutual direction to emerge? Or is it doing both?

Weisbord et al. (1992) and Future Search practitioners imply that a group must converge on a question in ways that presuppose acceptable answers. Others hope for more emergent outcomes and see in dialogue a chance for new, unanticipated possibilities. Planning, presuppositions, and overt control become less desirable because they may limit dialogic possibilities.

An example of the convergent-emergent tension is found in the theory of deliberative democracy. Habermas (1990, 1992) and Cohen (1989) say people ideally enter dialogic situations ready to hear others' arguments and subject their own arguments to the same criteria of reasonableness and clarity as they do the positions they originally oppose. This kind of dialogue tends to level the power field, build common ground, and increase the chances for consensus, which appears to be the normative goal of convergent dialogue.

Young (1996) believes convergent norms of deliberation in dialogue are biased toward a competitive, agonistic model for talk—a model that is comfortable for some but not for others. Recall the misconceptions of dialogue we discussed early in this chapter. Such competitive models are, in fact, cultural—presuming, for example, that stereotypically Western and male speech and argument styles will be more appropriate than more female-oriented speech styles. Further, deliberative forums may "privilege speech that is formal and general" or "dispassionate and disembodied" (Young, 1996, p. 124). Such convergent assumptions virtually mandate that unity, in the sense of shared meaning, is *the* goal of dialogue, not merely *a* goal of dialogue. They also might inhibit the very groups (the victims, angry disenfranchised and silent marginalized) from whom we most need to hear new ideas. Unity may be less important than citizens' access to the range of different, even dissonant, voices that may emerge from dialogue. Young claims that our democratic task in dialogue is not to submerge voices if they don't reflect the right kinds of rationality, but to do what we can to bring them to the surface as contributors. The convergent-emergent tension reflects the proceduralist-pluralist tension confronting a wide range of public and governmental decision-making situations.

To this point, we have defined dialogue in relation to power, considered a number of misconceptions, and reviewed recent dialogic scholarship. We then extended our consideration of the nature of dialogue by distinguishing more explicitly between dialogue and other forms of communication. We then grounded the concept of power by considering a series of tensions, or issues, that run through all dialogic encounters and within which power relations necessarily evolve. Practitioners, though, want to ask: What should be the goal of dialogue? Is the goal managing interaction and reducing power struggles? Or, is it to diversify and pluralize who can be heard, thereby increasing the potential for power struggles? Can the goals be blended? In the next section, we address this choice point.

DIALOGUE, POWER, AND EMPOWERMENT

Although distinctions between emergent and convergent dialogue can be over-simplified, they seem to be related to what have been termed *juridical* and *contingent* approaches to power. The evocation of power in convergent dialogue is best explained by traditional juridical concepts that focus their explanatory scope on power as *product,* whereas power in emergent dialogue is best explained by more contingent postmodern perspectives that focus on power as *process.* In this final section, we (a) consider the nature of power, distinguishing between traditional juridical conceptions and more postmodern, contingent conceptions, (b) relate those conceptions of power to the notions of convergent and emergent dialogue, and (c) discuss the dialogic tensions directly in terms of power and empowerment.

From Power in Circuits to Power in Relationships

Until recently, power was widely conceived in mechanical terms. French and Raven's (1959) oft-cited description of power was based on the notion that power flows in social systems almost as it does in electrical circuits. The French and Raven model proposes five types of power—reward, coercive, referent, expert, and legitimate—described from the standpoint of an individual's ability to achieve a predecided or predictable goal relative to another person. Similarly, Pfeffer (1988, 1992) suggests that power is stored in individuals, much like in a battery. Kanter (1979) describes how empowering information comes from social networks and functions much like power grids in an electrical power system.

Research by communication scholars has extended the individualistic model of power in such areas as compliance-gaining (cf. Eisenberg & Goodall, 1997), but has also questioned such individualism by examining power in wider settings of community building and conflict management (Arnett, 1986; Brown, 1986; Goldberg, Cavanaugh, & Larson, 1983; Pearce & Littlejohn, 1997; Rosen, 1994; Zoller, 2000), ethics (Arnett, 2001; Johannesen, 2002), organizational life (Barge, 1994; Chiles & Zorn, 1995; Deetz, 1992, 1995; Deetz & Mumby, 1990), feminism (Kramerae, 1981; Kramerae, Schulz, & O'Barr, 1984; Wood, 1997), speech and language use (King, 1987; Ng & Bradac, 1993), and social constructionism (Shotter, 1993a, 1993b; Strine, 1986).

Communication scholars evidently resonate with more social and postmodern inclinations that find linear, possession-based notions of power incomplete. King's (1987) concept of autonomous empowerment rejects the notion of power as a repressive force exercised against the individual and instead conceives of power as something created in transactions between people, especially as they join together in groups. In exemplifying the more contingent postmodern positions, Clegg (1989) and Lukes (1984) offer social power analyses that account for symbolic fields and indirect networks. Havel (1985) and de Certeau (1984) highlight both the individual and institutional exercise of power, explaining also the roles of direct and indirect power. Deleuze and Guattari (1987) and Latour (1988) reconcile power gained through individual behavior with global systemic forces. Their schemas are important for communication scholars because they attempt to account for how symbols become power instruments. Deleuze and Guattari (1987) describe how signifiers take power in a line of flight, yet are still underdetermined. They argue that signifiers emerge from a point of subjectification, from which the signifier can move in many possible directions but is contained within a pattern of meaning by other forces, including the subject. In an interesting example, Latour (1988) described how dynamic material and symbolic forces in the hygienist movement in France in the 19th century led to the pasteurization of France. In this example, it is not the material reality of disease that drives power relationships, but rather the symbolic belief in the effect of disease.

In communication, Krippendorff (1995), influenced by Foucault (1970, 1980), argues that language plays on physical metaphors that evoke notions of power, concluding that all power is, in the end, symbolic. Foucault's distinction between juridical power and contingent power provides a model for explaining power in both convergent and emergent dialogic contexts. Foucault (1995b) argues that power is produced by both knowledge and practice and that it contains "instruments, techniques, procedures, levels of application and targets" (p. 215). Sawicki (1991) says Foucault's earliest writings proposed a concept of juridical power that does not significantly differ from the traditional power circuit metaphor. Juridical power, according to Foucault, is power that is possessed (by individuals in the state of nature, by a class, by the people), that flows from a centralized source from top to bottom (in the law, the economy, the state), and that is primarily repressive in its exercise (a prohibition backed by sanctions).

Juridical or traditional conceptualizations of power explain convergent dialogue because power is located in the individuals or groups that have an ability to reward. A person who has juridical power may convene a dialogue, invite certain participants, exclude others, set process restrictions, facilitate, summarize, and determine acceptable outcomes. The process of convergent dialogue is typically monitored to encourage certain desired content outcomes, such as consensus on a specific decision or a mutual clarification of workplace evaluation practices. Cohesion is assessed and declared by conveners who can certify a set of operational meanings, and this potentially leads the group toward an orthodoxy of voice.

Foucault found that juridical power was insufficient to describe all power relationships. His later writings moved toward a contingent, network-based notion of power that helps describe what can occur when dialogue is emergent. His disciplinary approach to power, according to Sawicki (1991), indicates how power is exercised rather than possessed, develops from the bottom up, and is productive rather than primarily repressive.

In his treatment of contingent power, Foucault (1995a) describes "the way in which relations of forces are deployed and given concrete expression" (p. 28) and shows how relationships function to bring about alienation, struggle, conflict, and war—or their opposites. His classic study of the penal system is not only based on how punishment developed, but also captures society's role in introducing punishment as a form of disciplinary power. He notes the elaborate systems that uphold the penal system and describes the move from traditional to contingent power (Foucault, 1995b), where power is not exercised simply as an obligation or a prohibition on those who do not have it. Rather, it invests them, is transmitted by them and through them, and exerts pressure upon them—just as they struggle to resist power. Foucault says these relations go right down into the fabric of society—that they are not localized in the relations between the state and its citizens, or on the frontier between classes. Foucault also emphasizes the bases of with/at power, created and simultaneously lived within society (1995b):

> This power had to be given the instrument of permanent, exhaustive, omnipresent surveillance, capable of making all visible, as long as it could itself remain invisible. It had to be like a faceless gaze that transformed the whole social body. (p. 214)

Kogler (1999), summarizing Foucault, claims power is a "strategic confrontation between more or less free agents who attempt to advance their own diverse interests over other agents by making use of various means within the total social situation" (p. 235). Power cannot be understood simply by looking at central authority or institutions, but must involve examining the basic relationships between different people:

> In this sense, power comes from below, not from the instances of domination mentioned here; in this respect, power is principally dispersed throughout, and implanted within, the social body and thus is not the product of a localizable subject of power. (p. 235)

Krippendorff (1995) describes dialogue as a process by which we linguistically identify, confront, control, align, coerce, embrace, and create—proposing:

> Power is felt in the being locked into a burdensome way of languaging, into a worrisome dialogical practice . . . much like being locked into a way of seeing, from which . . . there seems to be no readily apparent escape. (p. 107)

Power Within the Field of Dialogue: Convergence and Emergence

Now that we have introduced Foucault's notion of power, we can say more about the power relationships within convergent dialogue (designed to solve a particular problem or create a desired consensus) and emergent dialogue (which generates the unexpected). Traditional juridical power is technique-driven and visible through an analysis of procedures. Technique-driven convergent dialogue converges on certain problems and solves them in a certain way. We discussed previously the Future Search method, a dialogic procedure often sponsored by corporations or communities. Individuals holding power marshal resources and employ accept-able facilitators. The facilitators and the sponsors define the scope of the problem, explicitly or implicitly name an acceptable outcome, develop an acceptable timeline, and invite the appropriate participants. Participants may choose only whether to participate. Thus, consistent with Foucault, authorities predetermine outcomes or targets for their own benefit.

In these ways, convergent dialogue serves to maintain and defend a paradigm, a body of literature, a set of values, profitability, hierarchy, and other factors. Com-panies use convergent dialogue to defend their places in the market. Communities use convergent dialogue to help them defend against disruptive social forces. Thera-pists use convergent dialogue to help patients find paths to normal behavior. Teachers use convergent dialogue to cover certain material and allow students to engage that material in a useful way. In each case, the individual power of the authorities is not challenged, the social networks/power circuits are not disrupted, and paradigms, social institutions, the financial well-being of companies, and the definitions of normal behavior all remain entrenched.

Although convergent dialogue focuses on the merging of differences, emergent dialogue opens the possibility that difference should be maintained or even en-hanced (Burbules & Rice, 1992). In emergent dialogue, ideas conflict, clash, and combine until something new appears. In other words, emergent dialogue chal-lenges the processes and power bases of the status quo. Power is not exercised to generate specific outcomes or hit targets. The most profound power generated in the context of emergent dialogue is noninstrumental, based on creating relational or transactional knowledge within the social context of the interchange. Morson and Emerson (1990) describe Bakhtin's dialogic approach as involving two "voice-ideas" that interact and "produce a dialogue changing both of them and giving rise to new insights and new dialogues. The 'unity' of truth becomes the unified 'feel' of conversation, not the unity of a single proposition" (p. 237).

In emergent dialogue, those who have little formal authority may become em-powered through their participation in the process. Newly created knowledge be-comes the basis for a significant shift in power. Hayles (1999) provides a helpful description of knowledge-based change, describing a first-order emergence that is similar to convergent dialogue, in which the components of a system are negotiat-ing their relationships in ways consistent with the larger system. Hayles also ar-gues that "second-order emergence grants special privilege to those that bestow additional functionality to the system, particularly the ability to process informa-tion" (p. 243). Hayles's second-order emergence provides information that helps a system adapt based on new information, similar to emergent dialogue that subverts the status quo as it realigns relationships. Persons make decisions that are loyal to fresh and immediate knowledge rather than to institutional structures.

For example, a medical service laboratory (MSL) hired the first author to create a convergent dialogue model that would ultimately improve profitability and qual-ity. MSL quality was such a concern that some departments within its regional hospital were sending business to outside competitors. About 80 medical professionals needed to increase service and decrease costs, or face layoffs. The facilitated dialogue, which lasted for 18 months, clearly began as an effort to address and converge on problems defined by management; however, management did not fully anticipate the transformative power of dialogue. Despite the convergent design, dialogue disrupted existing hierarchical relationships as employees in isolated parts of the organization came together in new social networks. The new relationships created knowledge that empowered the group to establish new quality standards that exceeded federal standards, find new business near their testing facilities, hire new staff, create a marketing team, and win a national quality award. They also fired the facilitator. The mix of emergent dialogue and contingent power shaped a new definition of this business that became radically different from management's convergent vision, and was thus uncomfortable. Hospital leaders applauded MSL, but the manager who sponsored the original dialogue was also fired. Emergent dialogue can lead to positive change, yet some organizations value predictable structure more highly. Although managers might admit it only reluctantly, convergence and emergence may happen simultaneously in the complex, multidimensional interactions of dialogue.

The Permanent Tensions: The Vapor Trails of Power in Dialogue

Beyond the convergent-emergent distinction, the permanent tensions of identity, outcome expectation, meaning, and voice are not either/or distinctions, but rather persistent contexts that imply decisions of balance. In the case of the MSL dialogues, dialogue morphed from convergence to emergence. Similarly, dialogues at different times emphasize the identity of the self or the other, the content or the process, coherence or incoherence, and monovocality or mutuality. Although these are underdetermined positions, it is important to discuss each in its specific relationship to power.

The first inherent tension of dialogue is identity, where the convergent self encounters and negotiates space with the emergent other. In dyadic or group dialogue, the first interchanges tend to establish the roles of the participants. Generally, the portable preestablished identities or roles that individuals bring to a dialogue are based in juridical or traditional power. They include hierarchical titles (president, doctor, professor) and a base of certified knowledge (expert, specialist, scholar), or imposed ignorance (worker, patient, student). Dialogic encounters with others may lead to an entrenchment of identity roles following the juridical model or to newly established roles following the contingent power model. Participants monitor themselves to understand who they are in the context of a particular dialogue. Reflexivity and inclusion allow participants to place themselves in the context of the other, finding themselves together with others facing a common problem while recognizing the uniqueness of individual standpoints. The identities of the group and of each individual are constantly and simultaneously at play. Gadamer (1982) was aware of the inherent difficulty of the double task of negotiating self and other. Influenced by Gadamer, Kogler (1999), like Isaacs (1999), shows that imposing one's identity on the group or the group's identity on itself, is un-productive. Both recommend a partial suspension of identity that allows for new identities to emerge.

The second inherent tension in dialogue is between the convergence on content and the emergence of dialogic processes. Dialogue at MSL was born as an attempt to converge on content issues. As the participants began to see the limitations of the convergent dialogic process, they improvised their own emergent processes. These began with polite questions to the facilitator about why the group was doing certain things and ended with an equally polite but potent "we don't need you any more." Hammond (1997) noted that some cultures favor content convergence as a starting point for dialogue, whereas others favor emergence. Traditional Japanese culture appears to value a series of social encounters that clarify relationships. Such encounters entail ceremonies of social power but initially provide little con-tent convergence. Communicators in European and American cultures often ex-pect dialogue to revolve around certain content issues, and favor a more overt convergence. In both cases, implicit power negotiations establish the boundaries and process for dialogue.

The third permanent tension is between the convergence to coherence and the emergence of incoherence. For Kogler (1999), sufficient coherence is required to begin dialogue. As dialogue continues and fills in the limits of its own meaning, though, it becomes self-generating and emergence can take over, moving the group towards incoherence. Isaacs (1993a) describes this as instability and Wheatley (1992) calls it a productive localized chaos that enables participants to let go of previous assumptions. Bohm (1990) says this incoherence is an essential prerequi-site to the emergence of a new coherence.

We believe that declarations of coherence often constitute juridical power moves. When a manager calls an issue settled, when a facilitator calls a group member's comment a turning point, when a teacher calls a student speech especially mean-ingful, or when an appeals court calls a lower judge's decision just, the speech act can function as a juridical-rhetorical power play ("Well, we all could agree that . . ." or "Everyone knows . . ."). Suspending certainty and allowing new meanings to emerge invokes contingent power, as Kogler (1999) understood:

> Dialogic understanding can no longer proceed from the idea of a universal consensus . . . it must . . . make present one's own constraints through an understanding of the other, and of gaining knowledge of certain limits of the other through one's own perspective. (p. 84)

Coherence and incoherence are layered in the dialogic experience. Both are ever-present, but only one seems to surface at a time. When coherence surfaces, the dialogue is moving toward a juridical agreement on meaning tied to past under-standing. When the challenge of incoherence surfaces, dialogue participants expe-rience the shared and more kinetic power of creative change.

Finally, consider the rhetorical voice as a locus for power tensions. In some groups, the monologic voice sweeps away any opposition under the guise of guiding consensus or avoiding conflict. This was a central concern of Hawes (1999), who argued that a single, privileged voice can be oppressive, and Ellsworth (1989), who noted how populations that are raced, classed, or gendered in certain ways are so inherently unequal that real dialogue is impossible. However, the emergence of mutuality is essential, and the power tension between the monovocality and multivoiced mutuality persists in dialogue:

> Dialogue is the encounter between men, mediated by the world, in order to name the world. Hence dialogue cannot occur between those who want to name the world and those who do not wish this naming—between those who deny other men the right to speak their word and those whose right to speak has been denied them. (Freire, 1970, pp. 76–77)

According to Freire, dialogue itself is the opportunity to experience an emergent polyvocality. Hawes (1999) called this notion *radical inclusion*. Radically inclusive polyvocality creates disruptive incoherence that can lead either to progress or to breakup. Polyvocality creates incoherence around issues of identity and meaning, but—despite the potential for transcendence—some dialogue groups have a low tolerance for incoherence.

CONCLUSION

Describing convergent and emergent dialogue, and their relationships to juridical and contingent power, necessarily provides only a two-dimensional depiction of multidimensional issues. Nevertheless, we hope to stimulate new theorizing and research through our clarification of the relationships and practices of dialogue and power. After clarifying definitions, we offered a typology of the different contexts of dialogic communication. Just as Kuhn's (1970) normal science is different from a scientific revolution, convergent dialogue differs from emergent dialogue. Convergent dialogue is generally found in the discourse that uses juridical power to preserve a status quo or coalesce interpretations around a core meaning. Although open to new meanings, convergent dialogue still tends to have its own authorized goals or agreed-upon practices. Emergent dialogue is messier, as it undermines hierarchy and knowledge in order to establish creative combinations of meanings. Other scholars, we suspect, may provide finer nuances of convergent and emergent dialogue, and more cogent applications. As we mentioned in the case of MSL, it may be particularly interesting to focus on turning points or discourse thresholds that move the dialogue from convergence to emergence and vice versa, as well as how each process might be dependent on the other.

We agree with Krippendorff (1995) that power and dialogue are always about somebody. Additional research could focus on how people negotiate and manage identity at dialogic moments, as well as when and why they expand their experiential horizons from self to other. Thresholds or turning points could also be identified in the content/other, coherence/incoherence, and monovocality/ mutuality tensions.

Although power in any social setting is difficult to quantify, we note that in linear, traditional models, juridical power produces artifacts that tend to be observable and, therefore, easier to research. Ease of observation is less likely with contingent power in the context of emergent dialogue. In this setting, power is much more subtle, social/cultural, elusive, and subjective. Still, astute observation and experience may produce illustrative cases that lead to a better understanding of power in the context of dialogic creativity and learning.

In the end, dialogue is a human opportunity for discovering or creating truth and empowering action. Penman (2000) calls dialogue the truing of our symbols. She described every human's need to test the truth of personal experience in the context of the experience of others. In this view, dialogue is neither a fad nor an option, but an unavoidable requirement of the human experience. Power, we argue, is omnipresent in this human dialogue. Krippendorff (1995) helps us see that power does not exist without dialogue just as dialogue necessarily involves power: Power "is not an entity, a thing or a resource. It arises as an experience that is brought forth and clarified in dialogue" (p. 107). Far from being antithetical terms, dialogue and power are inextricably interwoven in human relationships.

REFERENCES

Allen, B. J., Orbe, M. P., & Olivas, M. R. (1999). The complexity of our tears: Dis/enchantment and (in)difference in the academy. *Communication Theory, 9*, 402–429.

Anderson, H. (1997). *Conversation, language, and possibilities: A postmodern approach to therapy.* New York: Basic Books.

Anderson, R., & Cissna, K. N. (1997). *The Martin Buber-Carl Rogers dialogue: A new transcript with commentary.* Albany: State University of New York Press.

Anderson, R., Cissna, K. N., & Arnett, R. C. (Eds.). (1994). *The reach of dialogue: Confirmation, voice, and community.* Cresskill, NJ: Hampton Press.

Arendt, H. (1959). *The human condition.* New York: Doubleday Anchor.

Arnett, R. C. (1986). *Communication and community: Implications of Martin Buber's dialogue.* Carbondale: Southern Illinois University Press.

Arnett, R. C. (1992). *Dialogic education: Conversation about ideas and between people.* Carbondale: Southern Illinois University Press.

Arnett, R. C. (2001). Dialogic civility as pragmatic ethical praxis: An interpersonal metaphor for the public domain. *Communication Theory, 11*, 315–338.

Arnett, R. C., & Arneson, P. (1999). *Dialogic civility in a cynical age: Community, hope, and interpersonal relationships.* Albany: State University of New York Press.

Asante, M. K. (1987). *The afrocentric idea.* Philadelphia: Temple University Press.

Bakhtin, M. M. (1981). *The dialogic imagination: Four essays* (M. Holquist, Ed., C. Emerson & M. Holquist, Trans.). Austin: University of Texas Press.

Bakhtin, M. M. (1984). *Problems of Dostoevsky's poetics* (C. Emerson, Ed. & Trans.). Minneapolis: University of Minnesota Press.

Bakhtin, M. M. (1986). *Speech genres and other late essays* (C. Emerson & M. Holquist, Eds., V. W. McGee, Trans.). Austin: University of Texas Press.

Bakhtin, M. M. (1993). *Toward a philosophy of the act* (V. Liapunov & M. Holquist, Eds., V. Liapunov, Trans.). Austin: University of Texas Press.

Barber, B. (1984). *Strong democracy*. Berkeley: University of California Press.

Barber, B. (1988). *The conquest of politics: Liberal philosophy in democratic times*. Princeton, NJ: Princeton University Press.

Barber, B. (1992). *An aristocracy of everyone: The politics of education and the future of America*. New York: Oxford University Press.

Barge, J. K. (1994). *Leadership: Communication skills for organizations and groups*. New York: St. Martin's Press.

Barge, J. K., & Little, M. (2002). Dialogical wisdom, communicative practice, and organizational life. *Communication Theory, 12*, 375–397.

Barker, T. T., & Kemp, F. O. (1990). Network theory: A postmodern pedagogy for the writing classroom. In C. Handa (Ed.), *Computers and community* (pp. 2–27). Portsmouth, NH: Boynton/Cook.

Baxter, L. A., & DeGooyer, D. H, Jr. (2001). Perceived aesthetic characteristics of interpersonal conversations. *Southern Communication Journal, 67*, 1–18.

Baxter, L. A., & Montgomery, B. M. (1996). *Relating: Dialogues and dialectics*. New York: Guilford Press.

Belenky, M. F., Clinchy, B. M., Goldberger, N. R., & Tarule, J. M. (1986). *Women's ways of knowing*. New York: Basic Books.

Benhabib, S. (1992). *Situating the self: Gender, community and postmodernism in contemporary ethics*. New York: Routledge.

Berger, C. R. (1987). Communicating under uncertainty. In M. Roloff & G. Miller (Eds.), *Interpersonal processes: New directions in communication research* (pp. 39–62). Newbury Park, CA: Sage.

Berger, C. R., & Bradac, J. J. (1982). *Language and social knowledge: Uncertainty in interpersonal relations*. London: Edward Arnold.

Berger, C. R., & Calabrese, R. J. (1975). Some explorations in initial interaction and beyond: Toward a developmental theory of interpersonal communication. *Human Communication Research, 1*, 99–112.

Bloomfield, D. (1997). *Peacemaking strategies in Northern Ireland: Building complementarity in conflict management theory*. New York: St. Martin's Press.

Bohm, D. (1981). *Wholeness and the implicate order*. London: Routledge & Kegan Paul.

Bohm, D. (1987). *Unfolding meaning: A weekend of dialogue with David Bohm*. London: Routledge.

Bohm, D. (1990). *On dialogue*. Ojai, CA: David Bohm Seminars.

Bohm, D. (1996). *On dialogue* (L. Nichol, Ed.). London: Routledge.

Bohman, J. (1996). *Public deliberation: Pluralism, complexity, and democracy*. Cambridge, MA: MIT Press.

Bristow, N. (2000). *Where's the gift: How to achieve phenomenal success by discovering the gift in all feedback*. Lindon, UT: Cascade Press.

Brown, W. R. (1986). Power and the rhetoric of social intervention. *Communication Monographs, 53*, 180–199.

Bruner, J. (1990). *Acts of meaning*. Cambridge, MA: Harvard University Press.

Buber, M. (1957). *Pointing the way* (M. Friedman, Ed. & Trans.). New York: Harper.

Buber, M. (1958). *I and thou* (2nd rev. ed., R. G. Smith, Trans.). New York: Scribner. (Original work published 1923)

Buber, M. (1965a). *Between man and man* (R. G. Smith, Trans.). New York: Macmillan.

Buber, M. (1965b). *The knowledge of man: A philosophy of the interhuman* (M. Friedman, Ed., M. Friedman & R. G. Smith, Trans.). New York: Harper & Row.

Burbules, N. C., & Rice, S. (1992). Dialogue across differences: Continuing the conversation. *Harvard Educational Review, 62*, 264–271.

Burke, K. (1968). *Counter-statement*. Los Angeles: University of California Press.

Carey, J. (1989). *Communication as culture: Essays on media and society*. Boston: Unwin Hyman.

Carr, W. (1995). *For education: Towards critical educational inquiry.* Buckingham, UK: Open University Press.

Caspary, W. R. (2000). *Dewey on democracy.* Ithaca, NY: Cornell University Press.

Cayer, M. (1997). Bohm's dialogue and action science: Two different approaches. *Journal of Humanistic Psychology, 37,* 41–66.

Charity, A. (1995). *Doing public journalism.* New York: Guilford Press.

Chiles, A. M., & Zorn, T. E. (1995). Empowerment in organizations: Employees' perceptions of the influences on empowerment. *Journal of Applied Communication Research, 23,* 1–25.

Chiseri-Strater, E. (1991). *Academic literacies.* Portsmouth, NH: Boynton/Cook.

Christensen, C. R., Garvin, D. A., & Sweet, A. (Eds.). (1991). *Education for judgment: The artistry of discussion leadership.* Boston: Harvard Business School Press.

Christians, C. (1988). Dialogic communication theory and cultural studies. In N. Denzin (Ed.), *Studies in symbolic interaction* (Vol. 9, pp. 3–31). Greenwich, CT: JAI Press.

Cissna, K. N. (Ed.). (2000). Studies in dialogue [Special issue]. *Southern Communication Journal, 65*(2 & 3).

Cissna, K. N., & Anderson, R. (1994). Communication and the ground of dialogue. In R. Anderson, K. N. Cissna, & R. C. Arnett (Eds.), *The reach of dialogue: Confirmation, voice, and community* (pp. 9–30). Cresskill, NJ: Hampton Press.

Cissna, K. N., & Anderson, R. (1998). Theorizing about dialogic moments: The Buber-Rogers position and postmodern themes. *Communication Theory, 8,* 63–104.

Cissna, K. N., & Anderson, R. (2002). *Moments of meeting: Buber, Rogers, and the potential for public dialogue.* Albany: State University of New York Press.

Clegg, S. (1989). *Frameworks of power.* London: Sage.

Cohen, J. (1989). Deliberation and democratic legitimacy. In A. Hamlin & P. Pettit (Eds.), *The good polity* (pp. 17–34). London: Blackwell.

Czubaroff, J. (2000). Dialogic rhetoric: An application of Martin Buber's philosophy of dialogue. *Quarterly Journal of Speech, 86,* 168–189.

de Certeau, M. (1984). *The practice of everyday life.* Berkeley: University of California Press.

Deetz, S. (1992). *Democracy in an age of corporate colonization: Developments in communication and politics of everyday life.* Albany: State University of New York Press.

Deetz, S. (1995). *Transforming communication, transforming business: Building responsive and responsible workplaces.* Cresskill, NJ: Hampton Press.

Deetz, S., & Kersten, A. (1983). Critical models of interpretive research. In L. L. Putnam & M. E. Pacanowsky (Eds.), *Communication and organizations: An interpretive approach* (pp. 147–171). Beverly Hills, CA: Sage.

Deetz, S., & Mumby, D. K. (1990). Power, discourse, and the workplace: Reclaiming the critical tradition. In J. A. Anderson (Ed.), *Communication yearbook 13* (pp. 18–47). Newbury Park, CA: Sage.

Deleuze, G. (1990). *The logic of sense* (C.V. Boundas, Ed., M. Lester, Trans.). New York: Columbia University Press.

Deleuze, G., & Guattari, F. (1987). *A thousand plateaus: Capitalism and schizophrenia.* Minneapolis: University of Minnesota Press.

DeLima, V. A., & Christians, C. G. (1979). Paulo Freire: The political dimension of dialogic communication. *Communication, 4,* 133–155.

de Mare, P., Piper, R., & Thompson, S. (1991). *Koinonia: From hate through dialogue to culture in the large group.* London: Karnac.

Denzin, N. (2002). *Interpretive interactionism* (2nd ed.). Thousand Oaks, CA: Sage.

Eisenberg, E. M. (1990). Jamming: Transcendance through organizing. *Communication Research, 17,* 139–164.

Eisenberg, E. M., & Goodall, H. L., Jr. (1997). *Organizational communication: Balancing creativity and constraint* (2nd ed.). New York: St. Martin's Press.

Ellinor, L., & Gerard, G. (1998). *Dialogue: Rediscover the transforming power of conversation.* New York: Wiley.

Ellsworth, E. (1989). Why doesn't this feel empowering: Working through the repressive myths of critical pedagogy. *Harvard Educational Review, 59,* 297–324.

Farson, R. (1978). The technology of humanism. *Journal of Humanistic Psychology, 18,* 5–35.

Ferrarotti, F. (1988). *The end of conversation: The impact of mass media on modern society.* New York: Greenwood.

Flores, L. A., & McPhail, M. L. (1997). From black and white to *Living Color:* A dialogic exposition into the social (re)construction of race, gender, and crime. *Critical Studies in Mass Communication, 14,* 106–112.

Follett, M. P. (1924). *Creative experience.* New York: Longmans, Green.

Foucault, M. (1970). *The order of things.* New York: Random House.

Foucault, M. (1980). *Power/knowledge: Selected interviews and other writings, 1972–1977* (C. Gordon, Trans.). New York: Vintage.

Foucault, M. (1984). Polemics, politics, and problemizations: An interview with Michel Foucault. In P. Rabinow (Ed.), *The Foucault Reader* (pp. 381–390). New York: Pantheon.

Foucault, M. (1988). The ethic of care for the self as a practice of freedom: An interview with Michel Foucault (J. D. Gauthier, Trans.). In J. Bernauer & D. Rasmussen (Eds.), *The final Foucault* (pp. 1–20). Cambridge, MA: MIT Press.

Foucault, M. (1995a). Critical theory/intellectual history. In M. Kelly (Ed.), *Critique and power: Recasting the Foucault/Habermas debate* (pp. 109–138). Cambridge, MA: MIT Press.

Foucault, M. (1995b). *Discipline and punish: The birth of the prison.* New York: Random House.

Freire, P. (1970). *Pedagogy of the oppressed* (M. B. Ramos, Trans.). New York: Seabury Press.

French, J. R. P., & Raven, B. (1959). The bases of social power. In D. Cartwright (Ed.), *Studies in social power* (pp. 118–149). Ann Arbor: University of Michigan Press.

Friedman, M. (1974). *Touchstones of reality: Existential trust and the community of peace.* New York: E. P. Dutton.

Friedman, M. (1976). *Martin Buber: The life of dialogue* (3rd ed.). Chicago: University of Chicago Press.

Friedman, M. (1983). *Confirmation of otherness: In family, community, and society.* New York: Pilgrim Press.

Friedman, M. (1985). *The healing dialogue in psychotherapy.* New York: Jason Aronson.

Friedman, M. (1992). *Dialogue and the human image: Beyond humanistic psychology.* Newbury Park, CA: Sage.

Gadamer, H.-G. (1982). *Truth and method* (G. Barden & J. Cumming, Trans.). New York: Crossroad.

Goldberg, A. A., Cavanaugh, M. S., & Larson, C. E. (1983). The meaning of "power." *Journal of Applied Communication Research, 11,* 89–108.

Goodall, H. L., Jr. (1996). *Divine signs: Connecting spirit to community.* Carbondale: Southern Illinois University Press.

Gordon, R. D. (2000). Karl Jaspers: Existential philosopher of dialogical communication. *Southern Communication Journal, 65,* 105–119.

Green, M. (1988). *The dialectic of freedom.* New York: Teachers College Press.

Grudin, R. (1996). *On dialogue: An essay in free thought.* Boston: Houghton Mifflin.

Gurevitch, Z. D. (1988). The other side of dialogue: On making the other strange and the experience of otherness. *American Journal of Sociology, 93,* 1179–1199.

Gutmann, A., & Thompson, D. (1996). *Democracy and disagreement.* Cambridge, MA: Harvard University Press.

Habermas, J. (1984). *The theory of communicative action: Vol. 1. Reason and the rationalization of society* (T. McCarthy, Trans.). Boston: Beacon Press.

Habermas, J. (1987). *The theory of communicative action: Vol. 2. Life world and system: A critique of functionalist reason* (T. McCarthy, Trans.). Boston: Beacon Press.

Habermas, J. (1990). *Moral consciousness and communicative action* (C. Lenhardt & W. Nicholsen, Trans.). Cambridge, MA: MIT Press.

Habermas, J. (1992). *Autonomy and solidarity: Interviews with Jurgen Habermas* (P. Dews, Ed.). London: Verso.

Hammond, S. (1997). *Communication and the new science of complexity: A paradigmatic critique.* Unpublished doctoral dissertation, University of Utah, Salt Lake City.

Havel, V. (1985). *The power of the powerless.* New York: M. E. Sharpe.

Hawes, L. C. (1998). Becoming-other-wise: Conversational performance and the politics of experience. *Text and Performance Quarterly, 18,* 273–299.

Hawes, L. C. (1999). The dialogics of conversation: Power, control, and vulnerability. *Communication Theory, 9,* 229–264.

Hayles, K. (1988). *The cosmic web.* Ithaca, NY: Cornell University Press.

Hayles, N. K. (1999). *How we became posthuman.* Chicago: University of Chicago Press.

Holquist, M. (1990). *Dialogism: Bakhtin and his world.* London: Routledge.

hooks, b. (1994). *Teaching to transgress: Education as the practice of freedom.* New York: Routledge.

Hycner, R. (1991). *Between person and person: Toward a dialogical psychotherapy.* Highland, NY: Gestalt Journal Press.

Hyde, B., & Bineham, J. L. (2000). From debate to dialogue: Toward a pedagogy of nonpolarized public discourse. *Southern Communication Journal, 65,* 208–223.

Isaacs, W. N. (1993a, April). Dialogue: The power of collective thinking. *Systems Thinker, 4*(3), 1–4.

Isaacs, W. N. (1993b). Taking flight: Dialogue, collective thinking, and organizational learning. *Organizational Dynamics, 22,* 24–39.

Isaacs, W. M. (1999). *Dialogue and the art of thinking together.* New York: Doubleday.

Jacksteit, M., & Kaufmann, A. (1995). *Finding common ground in the abortion conflict: A manual.* Washington, DC: Common Ground Network for Life and Choice.

Johannesen, R. L. (1971). The emerging concept of communication as dialogue. *Quarterly Journal of Speech, 57,* 373–382.

Johannesen, R. L. (2000). Nel Noddings's uses of Martin Buber's philosophy of dialogue. *Southern Communication Journal, 65,* 151–160.

Johannesen, R. L. (2002). *Ethics in human communication* (5th ed.). Prospect Heights, IL: Waveland Press.

Kanter, R. M. (1979, July/August). Power failure in management circuits. *Harvard Business Review, 57,* 65–75.

Kao, J. (1997). *Jamming: The art and discipline of business creativity.* New York: Harper.

Kaplan, A. (1969). The life of dialogue. In J. D. Roslansky (Ed.), *Communication: A discussion at the Nobel conference* (pp. 87–108). Amsterdam: North-Holland.

Kellett, P. M. (1999). Dialogue and dialectics in managing organizational change: The case of a mission-based transformation. *Southern Communication Journal, 64,* 211–231.

Kellett, P. M., & Dalton, D. G. (2001). *Managing conflict in a negotiated world: A narrative approach to achieving dialogue and change.* Thousand Oaks, CA: Sage.

Kincaid, D. L. (Ed.). (1987). *Communication theory: Eastern and western perspectives.* San Diego, CA: Academic Press.

King, A. (1987). *Power & communication.* Prospect Heights, IL: Waveland Press.

Kirschenbaum, H., & Henderson, V. L. (Eds.). (1989). *Carl Rogers: Dialogues—conversations with Martin Buber, Paul Tillich, B. F. Skinner, Gregory Bateson, Michael Polanyi, Rollo May, and others.* Boston: Houghton-Mifflin.

Kogler, H. (1999). *The power of dialogue: Critical hermeneutics after Gadamer and Foucault* (P. Hendrickson, Trans.). Cambridge, MA: MIT Press.

Kramerae, C. (1981). *Women and men speaking.* Rowley, MA: Newbury House.

Kramerae, C., Schulz, M., & O'Barr, W. M. (Eds.). (1984). *Language and power.* Beverly Hills, CA: Sage.

Krippendorff, K. (1989). On the ethics of constructing communication. In B. Dervin, L. Grossberg, B. J. O'Keefe, & E. Wartella (Eds.), *Rethinking communication: Paradigm issues* (Vol. 1, pp. 66–96). Newbury Park, CA: Sage.

Krippendorff, K. (1995). Undoing power. *Critical Studies in Mass Communication, 12,* 101–133.

Kuhn, T. (1970). *The structure of scientific revolutions* (2nd ed.). Chicago: University of Chicago Press.

Latour, B. (1988). *The pasteurization of France.* Cambridge, MA: Harvard University Press.

Levinas, E. (1989). *The Levinas reader* (S. Hand., Ed.). Cambridge, MA: Basil Blackwell.

Lukes, S. (1984). *Power: A radical view*. London: Macmillan.

Mailloux, S. (1989). *Rhetorical power*. Ithaca, NY: Cornell University Press.

Mathews, D. F. (1994). *Politics for people: Finding a responsible public voice*. Urbana: University of Illinois Press.

Matson, F. W., & Montagu, A. (1967). Introduction: The unfinished revolution. In F. W. Matson & A. Montagu (Eds.), *The human dialogue: Perspectives on communication* (pp. 1–11). New York: Free Press.

McNamee, S., & Gergen, K. J. (Eds.). (1999). *Relational responsibility: Resources for sustainable dialogue*. Thousand Oaks, CA: Sage.

Merritt, D. (1995). *Public journalism and public life: Why telling the news is not enough*. Hillsdale, NJ: Erlbaum.

Montgomery, B. M., & Baxter, L. A. (1998). Dialogism and relational dialectics. In B. M. Montgomery & L. A. Baxter (Eds.), *Dialectical approaches to studying personal relationships* (pp. 155–183). Mahwah, NJ: Erlbaum.

Morson, G. S., & Emerson, C. (1990). *Mikhail Bakhtin: Creation of a prosaics*. Stanford, CA: Stanford University Press.

Murray, J. W. (2000). Bakhtinian answerability and Levinasian responsibility: Forging a fuller dialogical communicative ethics. *Southern Communication Journal, 65*, 133–150.

Newcomb, H. M. (1984). On the dialogic aspects of mass communication. *Critical Studies in Mass Communication, 1*, 34–50.

Ng, S. H., & Bradac, J. J. (1993). *Power in language: Verbal communication and social influence*. Newbury Park, CA: Sage.

Noddings, N. (1984). *Caring: A feminine approach to ethics and moral education*. Berkeley: University of California Press.

Ong, W. J. (1982). *Orality and literacy: The technologizing of the word*. London: Methuen.

O'Sullivan, T., Hartley, J., Saunders, D., Montgomery, M., & Fiske, J. (1994). *Key concepts in communication and cultural studies* (2nd ed.). London: Routledge.

Palmer, P. J. (1983). *To know as we are known*. New York: HarperCollins.

Palmer, P. J. (1998). *The courage to teach*. San Francisco: Jossey-Bass.

Pearce, K. A., & Pearce, W. B. (2001). The public dialogue consortium's school-wide dialogue process: A communication approach to develop citizenship skills and enhance school climate. *Communication Theory, 11*, 105–123.

Pearce, W. B., & Littlejohn, S. W. (1997). *Moral conflict: When social worlds collide*. Thousand Oaks, CA: Sage.

Pearce, W. B., & Pearce, K. A. (2000a). Combining passions and abilities: Toward dialogic virtuosity. *Southern Communication Journal, 65*, 161–175.

Pearce, W. B., & Pearce, K. A. (2000b). Extending the theory of the coordinated management of meaning (CMM) through a community dialogue process. *Communication Theory, 10*, 405–423.

Penman, R. (2000). *Reconstructing communicating: Looking to a future*. Mahwah, NJ: Erlbaum.

Peters, J. D. (1999). *Speaking into the air: A history of the idea of communication*. Chicago: University of Chicago Press.

Pfeffer, J. (1988). *Power in organizations*. New York: Pittman.

Pfeffer, J. (1992). *Managing with power: Politics and influence in organizations*. Cambridge, MA: Harvard Business School Press.

Poulakos, J. (1974). The components of dialogue. *Western Speech, 38*, 199–212.

Prigogine, I., & Stengers, I. (1984). *Order out of chaos: Man's new dialogue with nature*. New York: Bantam.

Richards, I. A. (1971). *The philosophy of rhetoric*. London: Oxford University Press.

Rogers, C. R. (1959). A theory of therapy, personality, and interpersonal relationships, as developed in the client-centered framework. In S. Koch (Ed.), *Psychology: A study of a science: Vol. 3. Formulations of the person and social context* (pp. 184–256). New York: McGraw-Hill.

Rosen, J. (1994). Making things more public: On the political responsibility of the media intellectual. *Critical Studies in Mass Communication, 11*, 363–388.

Rosen, J. (1999). *What are journalists for?* New Haven, CT: Yale University Press.

Rosen, J., & Merritt, D., Jr. (1994). *Public journalism: Theory and practice*. Dayton, OH: Kettering Foundation.

Roth, S., Chasin, L., Chasin, R., Becker, C., & Herzig, M. (1992). From debate to dialogue: A facilitating role for family therapists in the public forum. *Dulwich Centre Newsletter*, 2, 41–48.

Sampson, E. E. (1993). *Celebrating the other: A dialogic account of human nature*. Boulder, CO: Westview Press.

Saunders, H. H. (1999). *A public peace process: Sustained dialogue to transform racial and ethnic conflicts*. New York: St. Martin's Press.

Sawicki, J. (1991). Foucault and feminism: Toward a politics of difference. In M. L. Shanley & C. Pateman (Eds.), *Feminist interpretations and political theory* (pp. 220–221). Cambridge, MA: Polity Press.

Senge, P. M. (1990). *The fifth discipline: The art and practice of the learning organization*. New York: Doubleday.

Shor, I., & Freire, P. (1987). *A pedagogy for liberation: Dialogues on transforming education*. Granby, MA: Bergin & Garvey.

Shotter, J. (1993a). *Conversational realities: Constructing life through language*. London: Sage.

Shotter, J. (1993b). *Cultural politics of everyday life*. Toronto, Canada: University of Toronto Press.

Shotter, J. (2000). Inside dialogic realities: From an abstract systematic to a participatory holistic understanding of communication. *Southern Communication Journal, 65*, 119–132.

Smith, C. R., & Arntson, P. H. (1991). Identification in interpersonal relationships: One foundation of creativity. *Southern Communication Journal, 57*, 61–72.

Smithson, M. (1990). *Ignorance and uncertainty: Emerging paradigms*. New York: Springer Verlag.

Spano, S. (2001). *Public dialogue and participatory democracy*. Cresskill, NJ: Hampton Press.

Stewart, J. (1978). Foundations of dialogic communication. *Quarterly Journal of Speech, 64*, 183–201.

Stewart, J. (1998). Social theory and dialogue. In J. S. Trent (Ed.), *Communication: Views from the helm for the 21st century* (pp. 337–344). Boston: Allyn & Bacon.

Stewart, J., & Zediker, K. (2000). Dialogue as tensional, ethical practice. *Southern Communication Journal, 65*, 224–242.

Stone, D., Patton, B., & Heen, S. (1999). *Difficult conversations: How to discuss what matters most*. New York: Viking.

Strine, M. S. (1986). Between meaning and representation: Dialogic aspects of interpretation scholarship. In T. Colson (Ed.), *Renewal and revision: The future of interpretation* (pp. 69–91). Denton, TX: NB Omega.

Tannen, D. (1989). *Talking voices: Repetition, dialogue, and imagery in conversational discourse*. Cambridge, UK: Cambridge University Press.

Tannen, D. (1998). *The argument culture: Moving from debate to dialogue*. New York: Random House.

Taylor, C. (1991). *The ethics of authenticity*. Cambridge, MA: Harvard University Press.

Taylor, J. R. (1999). What is "organizational communication"?: Communication as a dialogic of text and conversation. *Communication Review, 3*, 21–63.

Taylor, J. R., Cooren, F., Giroux, N., & Robichard, D. (1996). The communicational basis of organization: Between the conversation and the text. *Communication Theory, 6*, 1–39.

Tedlock, D. (1983). *The spoken word and the work of interpretation*. Philadelphia: University of Pennsylvania Press.

Tedlock, D., & Mannheim, B. (Eds.). (1995). *The dialogic emergence of culture*. Urbana: University of Illinois Press.

Thomas, L. (1974). *Lives of a cell*. New York: Viking.

Weick, K. (1979). *The social psychology of organizing*. New York: Random House.

Weick, K. (1995). *Sensemaking in organizations*. Newbury Park, CA: Sage.

Weisbord, M. R., Schindler-Rainman, E., Lippitt, R., Emery, F. E., Baburoglu, O. N., Garr, M. A., III, et al. (1992). *Discovering common ground*. San Francisco: Berrett-Koehler.

Wheatley, M. (1992). *Leadership and the new science: Learning about organization from an orderly universe*. San Francisco: Berrett-Koehler.

Wold, A. H. (Ed.). (1992). *The dialogical alternative: Towards a theory of language and mind*. London: Scandinavian University Press.

Wood, J. T. (1997). *Gendered lives: Communication, gender, and culture.* Belmont, CA: Wadsworth.

Yankelovich, D. (1999). *The magic of dialogue: Transforming conflict into cooperation.* New York: Simon & Schuster.

Young, I. M. (1990). *Justice and the politics of difference.* Princeton, NJ: Princeton University Press.

Young, I. M. (1996). Communication and the other: Beyond deliberative democracy. In S. Benhabib (Ed.), *Democracy and difference: Contesting the boundaries of the political* (pp. 120–135). Princeton, NJ: Princeton University Press.

Zoller, H. M. (2000). "A place you haven't visited before": Creating the conditions for community dialogue. *Southern Communication Journal, 65,* 191–207.

CHAPTER CONTENTS

6 The Megaphone Effect: The International Diffusion of Cultural Media via the USA

LINDA-RENÉE BLOCH
DAFNA LEMISH
Tel Aviv University

Within the context of globalization, this chapter shows how some cultural texts become internationally popular after traveling via the United States. Through the *megaphone effect*, items acquire a new aspect as they are diffused from America to the rest of the globe, with a new aura of success. Our analysis of television programs, news networks, children's culture, and pop music reveals that as mainstream culture spreads, the opportunity is provided for other voices, representing local cultures, to be heard around the world. The megaphone effect proposes an explanation of how successful cultural elements are processed so as to give them the aspect of a universal language.

M any cultural texts are widely adopted internationally only after having been successfully integrated into the culture of the United States. This endorsement transforms a local product into a global phenomenon. We have coined the term *megaphone effect* (Bloch & Lemish, 1999) to describe how "true acceptance of a cultural product seems to come from crossing the Atlantic and becoming a success in the United States [following which] items seem to acquire an ever-expanding sphere of appeal" (p. 285) extending across the globe. The purpose of this work is to describe what the megaphone effect is and how it functions against the background of theories of globalization and Americanization,[1] in order to provide the outline for a model of cultural diffusion. This model is intended as a heuristic guide toward empirical research for communication scholars.

Essentially, the megaphone effect shows how the local can achieve prominence

---

AUTHORS' NOTE: The authors wish to thank Dr. Gilles Wust and Dr. Peter Lemish for their assistance and for their inspiring comments.

Correspondence: Linda-Renée Bloch, 24 Shalom Asch St. #27, Tel Aviv, 69483, Israel; email: lindabw@netvision.net.il

on an international scale by joining forces with a larger power. As of 2003, the largest, most powerful megaphone is located in the United States.[2] In this initial model, rather than viewing the U.S. categorically as an *over*powering force, it is seen here as a source that can offer the potential for a certain measure of *em*power-ment. The international diffusion of cultural texts is explained by reframing and reformulating existing knowledge, showing how, despite a strong American ac-cent, local voices can also be heard worldwide, thus affording them increased lev-els of empowerment.

Our interest in how cultural texts are disseminated is inherently rooted in com-munication studies; the investigation of the megaphone effect is an attempt to de-scribe on a global scale, how a selected cultural text can be represented and how important it can become depending on who transmits it. This may be traced to Lasswell's (1948) seminal model for communication research: Who says what, in which channel, to whom, with what effect?

Our intellectual, professional, and personal backgrounds form a bridge between the American sociological-functionalists, prioritizing the effects tradition in com-munication research, and the European cultural studies approach, which places a stronger emphasis on active audiences, open texts, and neo-Marxist concepts. We see ourselves, and indeed this model, as representing an integration of both schools of thought. On one hand, we view texts as presenting opportunities for their recipi-ents to engage in "cultural *bricolage*" (Sreberny-Mohammadi, 1991, p. 134). On the other hand, we are very aware of the power and constraints of the social struc-ture behind their production, distribution, and reception (Stevenson, 1995). This duality is illustrated in Lemish's (1998) case study on the Spice Girls.

Beyond our concern with media effects, our work is also partially motivated by critical theory that focuses on the distribution of power in society and, perhaps more precisely, by a sociocultural approach, in which communication assumes a dominant role in the negotiation, construction, perpetuation, resistance, and deconstruction of meaning in society. Further inspiration comes to us from social constructionism, whereby reality is seen to be formed through communication.

We conceived the megaphone model based on the premise that it is through communication—both mass mediated and interpersonal—that these cultural texts are disseminated and made meaningful. To put it differently, the diffusion process is contingent on communication. Moreover, both mass and interpersonal commu-nication are integral parts of culture, each being strongly influenced by the other. We view the term *culture* from a predominantly semiotic perspective, in the sense of a repertoire of symbolic resources shared by a group of people that allows them to make sense of the world around them (see Geertz, 1973; LeVine, 1984). Diffu-sion, culture, and communication are all intertwined.

In this chapter, we extend the understanding of the principles involved in the diffusion of communication and how it is influenced by power. We explore how power mediates culture and the complexity of this relationship. Finally, we show the process by which domination itself can be partially exploited for the purpose of empowerment.

The literature used to support the existence of the megaphone effect is drawn from a synthesis of the dominant theories of globalization within the context of communication research, cultural exchange, and diffusion. Because our concern is limited to communication, we did not include the wealth of literature related to this topic from the fields of international marketing and political science.

This chapter reviews the literature on globalization, Americanization, and related themes as they pertain to communication and culture. Next, it presents the megaphone effect within the context of another diffusion model, as well as through an analysis of how the mechanism works, using an analogy from the physical sciences, followed by a discussion of critical elements at each stage. At this point, we draw upon a number of case studies in the realms of television, news, children's culture, and pop music to illustrate the way the megaphone effect has worked in relation to a variety of cultural texts. Finally, we discuss some of the implications of this model, notably the potential for empowerment it affords, and conclude with a research agenda for the future. In order to show the diversity of applications, we have cast a wide net. Subsequent research is needed for in-depth analysis of how the thesis presented here applies to phenomena across a variety of fields.

GLOBALIZATION

In its ideal form, globalization would be the utopian realization of a world in which resources are shared and exchanged with each party being enriched in the process. The critical approach to globalization is that it constitutes a type of Western imperialism, motivated by profit-driven calculations, that rides roughshod across local cultures with no regard for indigenous traditions, heritages, or values. This process is said to have an impact across all realms of human existence, from the civic to the cultural, the economic to the ecological, the personal to the political. Cultural products originating in the West are embedded within a particular perspective whose value system is self-serving (Meyrowitz, 1993).

Although there is much debate about how the concept of globalization should be interpreted, to the point of trivializing its meaning (Gurevitch, 1991), frequently it refers to issues relating to how the production and consumption of commodities have transcended national borders (Walters, 1995). Much of the discourse surrounding this topic in cultural studies has been concerned with the process of transculturation, the interchange of cultural elements, the implications for changing cultural identities, and the impact on the nation-state (e.g., Bird, Curtis, Putnam, Robertson, & Tickner, 1993; Featherstone, 1990).

Sreberny-Mohammadi's (1991) analysis of the global and the local in international communication uses Giddens's (1990) often-quoted definition of globalization as a starting point: Globalization is "the intensification of world-wide social relations which link distant localities in such a way that local happenings are shaped by events occurring many miles away and vice versa" (Giddens, 1990, p. 64). She

cautions that "globalization has often been applied to the spread of Western mediated products across the globe, from which few places seem immune" (p. 126),
and later emphasizes: "Global rarely means universal" (p. 134). Indeed, others
have proposed that the term *transnational* be used in order to allow for the variation in scale and distribution that global seems to imply (Hannerz, 1996).

Discussions of globalization thus often focus on the notion of the "West and the
rest." It is possible to expand on Gerbner and Gross's (1980) concept of cultivation
by generalizing the theory to claim that the Western media are responsible for
mainstreaming all cultures and local enclaves by fostering the same worldview,
values, and beliefs.

Others argue that there is a move away from the U.S., and from Western modernity and modernization, in favor of the local (Featherstone, 1991). Parallel to this
attempt at universalism, there has been a growing trend toward the revival of cultural particularism, whereby local cultures attempt to assert their own unique identities. Barber (1995) refers to the shift toward global homogeneity as "McWorld"
and to the fanaticism of preserving the local as "Jihad."

A line of argument can be traced through the globalization literature, beginning
with the concept of *cultural imperialism* in the discourse of left-wing academe in
the 1970s (e.g., Schiller, 1976), to be replaced in the 1980s by the less harsh term
globalization. The notion carries less of a connotation of intentional takeover and
has been associated with postmodern philosophies (Bhabha, 1990; Hall, 1992).
This approach would suggest that our current cultures sustain two parallel levels:
the local place-bound culture and the trans-local one, in which identity is no longer
place bound. In this manner, globalizing cultural forces, such as the media, produce heterogeneous dialogues between cultures around the world (Appadurai,
1996). Appadurai (1996) explains that texts (together with their meanings) and
contexts (as they relate to power) are dependent upon one another to the extent that
he has devised the term "intercontextuality" (p. 187) to describe their relationship. Indeed, Appadurai (1990) specifies five dimensions of influences
flowing between cultures, which obviate the possibility of cultural domination and homogeneity (ethnoscapes, technoscapes, finanscapes, mediascapes,
ideoscapes). As a result, some contend our current cultures are referred to as *hybrid cultures* (e.g., Bhabha, 1994; Gilroy, 1995), a term that has become a contested site and has elicited much controversy in its own right (Kraidy, 2002). More
specifically, Giddens (1998) has argued that communication technologies play a
significant role in the transformation of social life.

In a cross-cultural study of children and youth's leisure activities, Lemish,
Drotner, Liebes, Maigret, and Stald (1998) found that the issue is not one of oppo-
sitions anymore: It is no longer a matter of globalization versus localization, international versus national, universal versus particular, but rather, "globalization involves the linking of their own locales to the wider world. At the same time, localization already incorporates trends of globalization" (Lemish et al., 1998, p. 553).
A similar transactional mix of symbols has been found in the nonindustrialized
world as well (Sreberny-Mohammadi, 1991).

It is possible to extract at least three different strands of thought from among the relevant literature that mediate between the two extremes of the global and the local. The first discusses the consumption of global products within a local context and the process of endowing them with meanings made relevant to their own situation. Robertson (1994) calls this process *glocalization*. Ferguson (1992) lends further support to the claim that global culture does not necessarily result in cultural assimilation in spite of the apparent homogeneity of consumption. Objections by those who view the increasing spread of influence by the U.S. as having the potential to create cultural homogeneity by wiping out local culture are frequently countered by audience reception studies. For example, reception studies of television fare (e.g., Ang, 1985; Liebes & Katz, 1993; Morley, 1993) suggest that locally contextualized audiences create their own meanings to serve their own needs.

A second form of localizing the global is articulated through the concept of *domestication* (Cohen, Levy, Roeh, & Gurevitch, 1996), studied primarily with regard to the production of news. Here, reporters decode events based on their own cultural perspectives, as full-fledged members of the audience themselves, who are in constant dialogue with their own culture.

A third possible bridge between the two poles of global versus local occurs when a culture produces its own version of another culture's product, such as popular television genres broadcast around the world (e.g., Hetsroni & Bloch, 1999). The megaphone effect will be shown to amplify each of these intermediary positions. It suggests a realistic compromise between the two approaches: the utopian view and the critical perspective of a one-way process of the globalization of world culture through economic domination.

AMERICANIZATION

Fears of globalization are frequently referred to as fears of Americanization, and the two are often used interchangeably. At a lecture given at the University of Toronto in December 1997, Pulitzer Prize winner and author Thomas L. Friedman put the matter succinctly when he said, "Globalization is so much Americanization. It wears Mickey Mouse ears and it drinks Coke, and it eats Big Macs and it works on an IBM computer with Windows 95" (Stoffman, 1997, p. 1). It is American products, business practices, and the values associated with them, more than those of any other culture, that are evident around the world. As one American journalist (Zachary, 1999) has put it:

> Free market capitalism and high-tech communications have, for better or worse, turned the world on to just one culture— ours . . . U.S. power stands at a new pinnacle, only this time victory isn't measured in the defeat of an ideological foe but in the influence gained over the world's wealth, culture, and individual identity. (p. 1)

The claim that we live in a world increasingly characterized by Americanization has been put forth repeatedly (e.g., Ritzer 1998). Beyond this, Kuisel (1993)
has claimed that what is referred to as Americanization "has become increasingly
disconnected from America" (p. 4). Rather than associating this trend with any
particular nation, "It would be better described as the coming of consumer society" (p. 4). Moreover, as Campbell and Kean (1997) note, fear or delight at the
potential effects of Americanization has been widely addressed and frequently linked
to the debate on the merits of popular culture (e.g., Duignan & Gann, 1992; Gilroy,
1992; Hoggart, 1957; Williams, 1962).

Americanization typically refers to the influence of the U.S., and more specifically, of its values, ideology, economics, and culture, beyond that nation's borders.
Rebhun and Waxman (2000) speak of an act or a process of conformity. Azaryahu
(2000) claims, "It involves cultural importation and transplantation" (pp. 41–42).
Aronoff (2000) points out, "The implication is that the diffusion of influence and
values comes directly and exclusively from the United States" (p. 93).

Beyond whatever the local audience chooses to make of it, an import that has
arrived via the U.S. has the additional cachet of having become a phenomenal
success in "America." The image projected by the United States of America has
connotations of prosperity, modernity, and the way of the future. "America" is a
symbol that represents "the ideals of endless progress, self-creation, achievement,
and success—the mythicized dream" (Campbell & Kean, 1997, p. 23). This dream
is perpetuated in novels, film, television, the print media, and advertising. It is for
many, far more real than anything else. As Vasey (1993) states:

> The popular media of the United States have had such an extraordinary influence upon the
> nation's image of itself, and upon the face it has presented to the rest of the world, that it has
> become virtually meaningless to attempt to distinguish between the creations of the media and
> "reality" in contemporary America. (p. 213)

Frith (1988) claims, "America, as experienced in film and music, has itself become the object of consumption, a symbol of pleasure" (p. 46). Likewise, Campbell
and Kean (1997) discuss the impact of the mere symbol that the country has become, or the influence of "reflection on the very idea of America" (p. 265).

Admiration for things American is evident around the world—whether it is in
China, where Budweiser beer is advertised using the slogan that it is "America's fa-
vorite beer" (Lee, 2000), or in South Africa, where one reporter wrote, "South Africans of all colors love American culture" (McNeil, 1997), or in Israel where an advertising executive stated, "The [mere] implication of America is very compelling for an
Israeli" (Klein, 1996). Item after item, regardless of its actual country of origin, is
marketed by claiming that it is the most popular in the United States. For example, a
baby pacifier made in Austria is advertised as "the pacifier most sold in America"
(Yehoshua TBWA, 1999), and the British Land Rover is marketed as having been
"elected the best multi-purpose vehicle of the year in America" (Avraham & First, in press).

Certainly outside the U.S., "America" has an existence all on its own that has nothing to do with reality. When one of the authors visited the Philippines, someone asked if she had ever visited Marlboro country, a question based on cigarette ads. In her analysis of young people's reactions to Coca-Cola ads, Gillespie (1997) found that the preference for American advertisements comes from conflating the advertisement with the product.

A cross-cultural comparative study of children and youth in Europe has also highlighted the fact that, for older children and adolescents, who are the greatest consumers of cultural products that do not originate in their own nations, American products are associated with quality, innovation, and "coolness." They are perceived as being more technically advanced, more true to life, and better marketed (Lemish et al., 1998).

In a study on the perceptions of children outside the U.S., through their reception of the World Wrestling Federation (WWF) programs, Lemish (1999) found that "America" served as a metaphor for bigger, better, and richer. She found reactions of awe and admiration for the U.S., as well as perceptions of its being the strongest, most violent, and most dangerous country in the world. At the same time, the U.S. was considered to be the most creative country, with the best infrastructure for innovations, a place where the "American dream" is alive and well.

This perception of readiness for innovation and creativity may be partly attributed to the fact that the U.S. is essentially a society of immigrants. This implies a dynamic encountering of differences with a steady influx of new values, perspectives, and ideas.

American society has long been represented by the assimilationist metaphor of the melting pot, a term derived from Israel Zangwill's 1908 play about the immigration experience. The melting pot was a utopian vision of immigration, in which each individual would be entitled to realize the American dream, significantly bettering himself or herself financially, regardless of ethnic origin. More than this, it stressed decreasing differences among people while emphasizing the communal values that brought them together. Over the years, there has been increasing disillusionment with the idealistic portrayal of the mix of immigrant groups (Glazer & Moynihan, 1970) as a melting pot, or even a mosaic, or a salad bowl, or what presidential candidate Jesse Jackson referred to as a rainbow coalition (Cooper & Nothstine, 1992). King (1993) claims, "In fact it is not clear that there is—or ever has been—an American culture or national character . . . the plurality of American culture emerged with full force as an ideal after the 1960s" (p. 373). Although nationalism subsided, ethnicity arose in its place. As Ostendorf and Palmié (1993) explained: Despite the fact that, by the 1990s, everyday culture in the U.S. had become increasingly unified, the population had become more fragmented both ethnically and ideologically, and we would add, intellectually. Hughes (1975) discussed the migration of intellectual thought from Europe to the U.S.—including the philosophy of Ludwig Wittgenstein, intellectual critiques of fascism, the mass society by the Frankfurt school, and Freud's psychoanalysis—as well as the transformations and twists that unfolded in the process.

Campbell and Kean (1997) put forth the concept of *hybridity* to express the sociocultural makeup of the United States. They maintain that this term represents the ambiguity, the contrary needs, and the processive nature. Similarly, Gitlin (1998) says that today in the U.S., "One belongs by being slightly different, though in a similar way" (p. 172). Fender (1992) talks about the U.S. behaving as a sect that defines itself through difference, where the discourse of immigration and by immigrants plays a crucial role. In a later work, Fender (1993) claims that American models of national identity involve "becoming" (p. 2) in the sense of a process of renewal after a period of trial. Fender's (1993) description might be most comparable to the process that actually occurs when an individual seeks to acquire a new nationality, or what immigration officials term "naturalization." In most countries this entails a type of trial period or time of adaptation, followed by a new identity or rebirth. This rebirth as a new immigrant is played out in such popular films as *Kane and Abel, Moscow on the Hudson,* and *Green Card.* To cite Gitlin (1998), "one becomes 'American' now by taking pluralism to be the form of American commonality" (pp. 172–173). This is similar to what happens in the case of products undergoing the megaphone effect: Foreign imports become Americanized even when their foreign origins are widely known and recognized.

The Frontier and Sea Change Theses

Beyond the fact that the U.S. is an immigrant culture, an additional explanation of why the U.S. has successfully assumed the role of diffusing texts to the rest of the world, or *megaphoning*, is the American myth of the frontier. Turner's (1961, 1962) *Frontier Thesis*, which states that the ever-receding frontier has always conditioned the American character, was one of the most dominant influences on American historians (Billington, 1971). According to this, the differences between American and European civilizations might be attributed to the unique environment of the new world, whose most distinctive feature is the continuously advancing frontier of settlement. Based on this assumption, the U.S. had not become an imitation of the old world, but was radically altered by the 300 years of pioneering the frontier. Turner (1961) contended that this process resulted in the development of a unique people with the frontier as the most formative experience of the American culture. He also attributed personality traits and the characteristic of the American intellect to this: "coarseness and strength combined with acuteness and inquisitiveness," a "practical, inventive turn of mind, quick to find expedients," a "masterful grasp of material things," a "restless, nervous energy," a "dominant individualism," and a "buoyancy and exuberance which comes from freedom" (p. viii).

Although there is a certain amount of debate over Turner's theory (e.g., Ellis, 1969; Moen & Lervik, 1996) and the importance he assigns to the frontier, his thesis is worth considering with regard to the megaphone effect. Assuming that the concept of the frontier has indeed had an influence on the mindset of the American people, it could be argued that once they reached the west coast and claimed it as their own, what remained was the rest of the world, and finally outer space. In his acceptance speech for the Democratic nomination to the presidency on July 15, 1960, John F. Kennedy stated that the U.S. was "on the edge of a new frontier" (JFK Library, 2002). Following this, the notion of breaching new frontiers was often attached to his programs.

Himmelstein (1984) discusses how the great American dream and the good life come about in terms of the myth of eternal progress, or economic expansion of both the society as a whole and of personal rewards, and a desire for personal fulfillment beyond material possessions. Fender (1992) explains that the individual attains a higher level of understanding and knowledge through the act of transcending the frontiers of communal and individual culture.

If one subscribes to the idea, a frontier mentality may serve as an explanation for the American spirit that operates the megaphone. The prominence of the various American mass media and the fact that the entire communication industry is so highly evolved in the U.S. attests that the nation has both a very loud megaphone, as well as a strong tendency to proclaim messages through it. Tunstall and Machin (1999) point out that "the United States is the only genuinely global exporter across a range of media and into most countries in the world" (p. 2).

A related theory is that of the *sea change*, originally concerning the unique relationship that has existed between the United Kingdom and the U.S. for the past 400 years. Since the time of the industrial revolution, many innovations have originated in the U.K., while the U.S. supplied the technology and market to develop and spread these concepts. This is a pattern that repeats itself in the history of the relationships between the two nations (Hughes, 1975; Abegglen, 1994).

By way of illustration, Tunstall and Machin (1999) note with regard to the mass media, the U.S. is so highly intertwined with the U.K. that:

> British films do not qualify as "foreign" films at the Academy Awards. Reuters, the London news agency, is often referred to as an American news agency; nor does the BBC seem really foreign to U.S. viewers of PBS and other up-market networks. (p. 262)

To further exploit our metaphor of the megaphone, we might say that frequently the U.K. serves as the *message* bearing with it the idea, the innovation itself, the essence of object, while the U.S. is the *medium*, representing the energy and force, the technology, and the marketing by which the voice is brought forth. In McLuhan's (1964) terms, if the U.S. is the medium, it is also the message, which could crowd the contributions of the U.K. (or any other country from which a cultural text originates) out of the picture so that in the final analysis, it is primarily the U.S. that seems to count.

Summary

Rather than seeing globalization as a lost battle against the mighty American economy and its culture, we propose that the local can and does influence the global. It does so by steering a course via the U.S. itself, thereby using that country's power to its own advantage and adhering to the prescription "if you can't beat 'em join 'em". This expression encapsulates a number of issues relevant to this work. Interestingly, its origins are uncertain. Intuitively it is American, seeming to capture the spirit of a country that offers endless possibilities, for when one route is unsuccessful, another choice can always be pursued. At the same time, the notion of compromise is reflected, together with a practical assessment of the distribution of power. In addition, the expression encourages taking advantage of the forces that exist even if one's needs are different from those of another group. Resistance is not always the only way to satisfy one's goals. Beyond this, these simple words express the possibility of combining forces with a more formidable group, thereby indicating that the larger group is both able and willing to accommodate difference. Perhaps most importantly, it advocates self-empowerment: Power is achieved, neither through passive co-optation into something, nor through aggressive domination by another group, but rather through the active, voluntary choice of joining.

Tomlinson (1999) is optimistic about the cosmopolitanism of a globalized world, exemplified by the visible presence of non-Western cultures in the Anglo American world. He claims that there is more openness to cultural pluralism in what he calls the cosmopolitanism of a globalized world. We would argue that this openness is the result of the megaphone effect because one aspect of globalization is an attempt to incorporate difference. The result of this is that as each new difference becomes incorporated into the fold, it becomes part of the established, recognized mainstream.

In other words, it is commonly accepted that texts are given a local interpretation and thus domesticated. We are claiming that the reverse is also true. Other items that do not come from the U.S. are accepted in other parts of the world after they have been given an American interpretation. To put this another way, the international popularity of many cultural items occurs precisely because they come to the world via the U.S., thereby obtaining a valued seal of approval. We contend that even elements not originally from the U.S. go through a process of being accepted in that country. It is only after they have been adopted by Americans that they become widely popular internationally.

We suggest that the process of Americanization has its roots in various cultures around the world, all of which contribute to sustaining it. Our view is optimistic: Whereas most of the literature on globalization concentrates on the influences the global has on the local, we are focusing on the influences the local has on the global. The megaphone effect provides a further refinement of the globalization argument by showing that it can be perceived, not in unidirectional terms, but rather as a dynamic, transactional process, where at least the opportunity for some measure of empowerment exists for less dominant groups.

THE MEGAPHONE EFFECT

At this point we wish to propose an outline for a model that explains the process by which a product that originates in one place becomes a phenomenon after passing through the United States. We will attempt to expose the mechanism by which the process functions, after describing how it relates to another well-known model of diffusion.

Broadening the Diffusion Paradigm

Our proposal can be seen to build upon the diffusion paradigm put forth by Rogers (1983) to explain the social adoption of innovations by individuals and organizations. According to Rogers, the process takes place in the following stages: the awareness stage, which consists of learning of the innovation; the interest stage, actively seeking out more information; the evaluation stage, in which adoption is considered; the trial stage, in which small-scale application occurs; and finally, the adoption stage, involving full-scale and continuous use.

If one broadens the focus of this proposition, from the influence of an individual or individuals on a group to that of one nation on others, the impact of adoption, by the U.S. specifically, may be comparable to that of the effect that an opinion leader has on the diffusion of innovations described by Rogers (1983):

> Opinion leaders are individuals who lead in influencing others' opinions about innovations. The behavior of opinion leaders is important in determining the rate of adoption of an innovation in a social system; in fact, the diffusion curve has its usual S-shape because of the time at which the opinion leaders adopt and owing to their ability to activate diffusion networks in a social system. (p. 271)

As the leader of the free world, the U.S. is probably "involved in the largest number of network links" (p. 279) and therefore may be said to fulfill the role of opinion leader on a global scale.

One respect in which the process we are describing differs from Rogers's (1983) diffusion model is that the megaphone effect is just that: an effect in the sense of an impression produced by something. The megaphone effect frequently occurs as a by-product of the search for market expansion, with the fertile ground of the U.S. being a natural choice. The large population with its high per capita spending power can provide huge returns if a product is successfully marketed. The ethnic diversity of the population provides a foretaste of the obstacles to be overcome in international marketing, although the common use of English in the U.S. greatly simplifies the task. Once an item is successfully adopted in the U.S., the next challenge is to expand further, advancing on to the newest frontier. Thus the American dream becomes the global dream.

Although sea change theory originated in relationship to the transformation from Europe to the U.S., it is further being discussed in the transformation from Northern America to Pacific Asia (Abegglen, 1994). Abegglen argues that the "center of the world industry" (p. 1) is moving from the North Atlantic to the Pacific, explaining the matter in economic terms of investment in infrastructure, savings, recycling surplus, foreign investment, aid, export promotion, and so forth. In these terms, the U.K. might be cast as the creators of innovation, Southeast Asia as providers of industry, and the U.S. as supplying the means of marketing by virtue of access to the required technology and services. The market or audience would consist of the entire globe.

By continuing to apply Rogers's model, together with the theory of sea change, the U.S. would be cast in the role of "early adopters" (pp. 248–249) who have "the greatest degree of opinion leadership in most social systems" and whose role "is to decrease uncertainty about a new idea by adopting it, and then conveying a subjective evaluation of the innovation to near-peers" (p. 249).

The Mechanism of the Megaphone Effect

According to the megaphone effect, certain cultural texts originating somewhere in the world can be adapted to the American culture and marketed to its population. The degree of success in conquering this enormous market serves as the litmus test of its marketing potential worldwide. Subsequently, based on lessons learned from this experience, the new and improved item, having undergone a process of so-called naturalization in the U.S., can be successfully spread to the rest of the world, including back to its own country of origin where it brings positive reinforcement through international acceptance.

The megaphone is a simple instrument used to increase the volume of a voice in order for it to be heard by a large number of people. In so doing, this device alters the voice to the point that the original sound might not be recognizable. Although on the surface it might seem that amplification is the most important function of the megaphone, or at least is the portion of the process that stands out most (i.e., is most audible), it is of least concern to us because it is strongly influenced by principles of international marketing. Instead, our main interest as communication scholars is on which local cultural texts are chosen or sampled and how they are adapted or filtered before being disseminated worldwide.

The megaphone process may be summarized as occurring in three successive steps, a process that somewhat is analogous to that of signal processing in physics (G. H. Wust, personal communication, 2000):

1. Sampling: A cultural element is selected, collected, and imported to the United States.

2. Filtering: The cultural element is detached from its foreign ties, deconstructed, and reconstructed by repositioning and by adding peripheral products.

3. Amplifying: The filtered, reconstituted text is diffused to the rest of the world through intense marketing.

It should be noted that although this model may assist in clarifying how the megaphone effect functions theoretically, the situation is not always quite so clear-cut as this in real life. The different stages are frequently hard to distinguish from one another.

Sampling. In order for the megaphone effect to take place, a product first needs to be identified as being potentially attractive. This entails sampling of cultural texts from outside the United States. Certain items achieve a significant measure of popularity from the outset in their country of origin, only to have it multiplied many times over after its reception in the U.S. and the rest of the world. Other items become successful principally after they are adopted on American soil. It should be noted that sampling can also include a type of "prefiltering," whereby an item is intended for America and henceforth international distribution from the start. Some items are sampled shortly after their creation, whereas in other cases there is a certain lag until the time is considered ripe.

One of the crucial factors influencing which texts are selected for sampling is the notion of proximity. By proximity we are referring to the similarity between the context from which the item originated and that of the United States. In the case of individuals, Rogers (1983) would refer to this as "homophily." According to him "interpersonal diffusion networks are mostly homophilous" (p. 276). By analogy, this would explain why it is easier for a text originating in Western or industrialized nations to make the transition to the U.S., because these countries tend to share the worldviews of late modernity, typified primarily by commercialism, globalization, privatization, and individualization (Fornäs & Bolin, 1995). Even under such conditions, television programs that are heavily dependent on local culture are rejected by American audiences, such as the extremely popular French *Bouillon de culture* (a literary discussion about recently published books) or Britain's consistently highest rated program *Coronation Street* (a soap opera; Broadcasters Audience Research Board, 2000, January 7).

With regard to the clothing industry, the head of the phenomenally successful Benetton company was apparently shocked to realize the differences between the European and American markets when he went on a reconnoitering visit to the U.S. in 1970. It took an additional 9 years before the company felt able to adapt to the American market. Initially the company was popular only among relatively more European clientele, and it was another 4 years before the product took off in the U.S. (Mantle, 1999). It appears that, in the case of cultural diffusion, different is all very well, so long as it is not too different.

In the case of interpersonal diffusion networks, Rogers (1983, pp. 276–277) claims that when there is dissimilarity between people (what he labels "heterophily"), followers seek out leaders who are of a higher socioeconomic status, have a higher education and greater mass media exposure, are more cosmopolite, have greater change agent contact, and are more innovative. In the current context of the discussion, the leader—that is, the U.S—is perceived as possessing the above characteristics. Tunstall and Machin (1999) note:

Britain, France, Germany and Japan all have ambitious popular culture industries. All of these look up to—and import from—the United States, but they do very little pop culture importing from each other. Both the mass media and popular culture are marked by very steep international hierarchies. Each country's position in this hierarchy is established by its patterns of media and pop culture importing and exporting. Each country only imports from countries above it in the hierarchy; for virtually all countries in the world this means importing from the United States and perhaps from a larger country which speaks the same language. (p. 14)

Filtering. The next stage of the megaphone effect entails a type of filtering. As Fender (1993) notes in the case of immigrants, to "become American" (p. 2), entails cutting off ties with the past, disassociating themselves from the old world, and reconstituting themselves in the new. As he puts it, "Initiation, transformation, perhaps even reformation: These seem appropriate words to describe the psychology of emigration to America" (p. 16). It is claimed here that this cutting off of cultural ties, followed by a reformation can be extended to the case of cultural artifacts and popular culture.

In order to be a success in the huge market that is the U.S., the item is subjected to a type of deconstruction and subsequent reconstruction. In the process, the specific benefit to be derived from a particular product, or its unique selling proposition (in the argot of marketing and advertising professionals), is isolated. The message concerning the item is sharpened and simplified to its most basic level to enable it to appeal to the widest possible audience. By this process, the object is reborn in a form that is less culture dependent. Hoskins and Mirus (1988) have described how American television programs achieve their popularity abroad with the least possible "cultural discount" (p. 500), or the reduction of value because of cultural interference, by aiming at the lowest common denominator and consequently at the widest possible audience. As a result, the item is also more easily adaptable to other cultures and still other markets—and consequently more amenable to the particular interpretation that each audience might wish to make of it.

Allison (2000) argues that Japanese products succeed when cultural specificities are effaced and made to be culturally odorless. For instance, the color gray was chosen for the Sony Walkman so that would not be perceived as being Japanese. The removal of cultural markings makes products more marketable in the United States. Allison has pointed out that people are listening to Sony all over the world, but not to Japanese music. Although Tunstall and Machin (1999) would agree that Japan exports little in the way of popular media to the West, *Time* magazine (Beals, 2000) featured an article on how the West is finally listening to the music produced by Japanese techno DJs. These DJs have acquired additional prestige by virtue of having worked with major American acts, once again bringing the matter full circle.

Amplifying. Following its deconstruction and reconstruction, the item is marketed across the U.S., frequently with an entire family of peripheral accessories supporting it. After this is achieved, the new concept (complete with part or all of the supporting retinue, where appropriate) travels to the rest of the world. This stage is what we have referred to as amplifying, which includes the return to the product's origins.

Clearly, the deconstruction-reconstruction process followed by mass distribution changes the nature of the text itself. Returning to the megaphone analogy, when something is amplified, it is also distorted; certain sounds are exaggerated, some become fuzzy, and other ones are lost completely. In developing mass appeal, a specialized text becomes acceptable to the broadest possible audience. In the process of its amplification, on returning to its origins it will have lost its aura of uniqueness (in the sense intended by Benjamin, 1936/1973, in conjunction with genuineness, authenticity, and contextual meaning), but gained a new aura in the form of success emanating from massive foreign approval.

Critical Elements of Each Stage

Three elements, each corresponding to a different stage of the megaphone effect, merit special attention. The first concerns the issue of language, the second deals with the notion of localizing a product, and the third addresses the dimension of time.

Language. A central factor in determining proximity is the use of language (English in the case of the U.S.). Use of the language can occur at one of three levels. First, the cultural item originates in an English-speaking country. The popular music group the Spice Girls originated in the U.K., but their lyrics are automatically comprehensible in the United States. A second level of linguistic proximity occurs when English is the language used, but it is not an official language in the country of origin. This is precisely how prefiltering occurs at the initial sampling stage of the megaphone effect. Examples include musicians singing in English rather than in their native tongue (e.g., the Swedish group Abba, or the Danish group Aqua); authors writing in English; or product naming, such as the Japanese selection of the label Sony Walkman (du Gay, Hall, Janes, Mackay, & Negus, 1997).

Finally, texts are translated into English as part of the process of being made palatable for the American, and later on the world, consumer market. The case of the Japanese Pokémon, a children's television program, computer game, collectible card series, and a host of other accessories illustrates this well. This phenomenon, one of the most successful ever in children's culture at the turn of the millennium, was dubbed Pokémania. As part of its American naturalization, certain changes were made:

> The names of the characters and monsters were Westernized: Satoshi became Ash, Shigeru became Gary. . . . And the Pokémon were given cleverly descriptive names. For example, Hitokage, a salamander with a ball of fire on its tail became Charmander; Fushigidane, a dinosaur with a green garlic bulb on its back, became Bulbasaur; and Zenigame, a turtle who squirts water, became Squirtle . . . and once again, the Pokémon swept a nation. (McLaughlin, Sakamaki, & Tashiro, 1999, p. 58)

The role played by language in reflecting power is undeniable. Debates over linguistic issues are highly emotional. Sometimes these debates actually bring down governments and result in violent street riots, whether in Quebec, Belgium, India, or other parts of the globe. In the U.S., there continues to be a great deal of conflict over the official status of English in the country (Crystal, 1997). Giles and Coupland (1991) point to at least four reasons for the important relationship between language and ethnicity: It is often a criterion for group membership; it is a significant cue for ethnic categorization; it represents an emotional part of a person's identity; and it serves as a means of bringing together members of a group.

Increasingly, English is being regarded as a global lingua franca (e.g., Greenbaum, 1985; Kachru, 1986). Hence, it is a language that transcends national boundaries and international borders. English can be said to be spoken by more people than any other tongue on earth when combining the number of native speakers together with those for whom it is a foreign language (Crystal, 1997, pp. 4–5).

If English has become the world's lingua franca, this is particularly true of American English. The U.S. has become so dominant across a whole range of areas of modern existence, prominent among them: international relations, the media, tourism, technology, and recently the Internet (Crystal, 1997).

American English has been found among European youth to be associated with most mediated leisure time activities, dominating popular and rock music, titles of cultural products, talk on television and film (in small linguistic communities that do not dub their content), computer games, and Internet fare. Trudgill (1983) has found that many British groups affected pseudo-American accents when playing before British and other audiences. Unless specifically configured to do otherwise, most computer spell check programs correct for American usage by default. Even in the halls of academe, in many disciplines, to publish in certain American journals is of the utmost prestige, offering potential professional advancement. Consequently using American spelling in English has become the norm for many scholars internationally. Among young people and children, mastering the English language with an emphasis on standard American dialects, provides a critical advantage in both leisure-time activities as well as for scholastic success (Drotner, 2001; Lemish et al. 1998).

It could be argued that due to certain constraints, some foreign scholars will actually adapt their work to particular outside markets from the start, a further example of prefiltering. However, it is only after acceptance in foreign nations that they gain recognition back home. As the old saying goes about people not being appreciated in their own homes, those of us who work in the social sciences outside the academic capitals of the world are obliged to publish in American journals in order to acquire academic legitimacy.[3] Local issues thus receive a voice in academia, after they make the long trip to the U.S. and back. On occasion, the return voyage can seem to take an interminable amount of time.

Localizing. Perhaps the most complex part of filtering a product comes about in making its foreignness less apparent, or localizing it. Clearly the Japanese producers of a variety of products have been long oriented to the megaphone effect, employing various techniques to ensure that their merchandise should become a hit in the U.S. and from there be successfully marketed to the rest of the world. In the case of animation series, they try to eliminate unique Japanese cultural signs, create scenery that is part of a fantastic world but not a particular location, and use names for characters that are acceptable in the West.[4] The atmosphere is usually one of fun and excitement, creating intimacy with the audience. Nonsocial behaviors, such as violence, are presented in a context that makes them exciting but not threatening (Painter, 1993).

There is even a professional niche in the U.S. for a person whose function is to adapt Japanese products to the American market, a job description known as a localizer. According to Ryota Toyama (2000), assistant producer at Konami Computer Entertainment America, this role entails identifying and extracting cultural elements from texts that may be difficult for the American market to absorb. This is especially so in the case of Japanese cartoons, emanating from a tradition in which many cultural elements are present (Maret & Katsuno, 2000). Beyond issues of comprehension, in the U.S. there is serious concern over lawsuits in the toy market resulting from violence and sexuality in the original Japanese text, requiring adaptations in the American version. The result is that today, Japanese and the American versions of such animated series as Pokémon, are being produced together to minimize the need for changes—in other words, an original text is being produced specifically for American consumption and subsequent dissemination globally.

An important issue is that the process of Americanizing does not entail total adjustment but rather leaves an edge of unfamiliarity, on the assumption that this will attract curiosity, and yet it should still be interpretable within a familiar context. Pokémon achieves this because the mythological elements are from a different non-American world, but the series can still be viewed within the familiar everyday lives of children. Localizing is a sophisticated process of creating a fine balance between making a product American and yet allowing it to remain sufficiently foreign for it to retain an element of something new and attractive. This is reminiscent of the way Benetton was finally able to market its clothes in the U.S.: Although they were somewhat different, they were not intended to be too different (Mantle, 1999). Moreover, it sounds strikingly similar to Gitlin's (1998) reading of the sociocultural mix of the population in the U.S. today as "assimilation with a difference" (p. 173).

Time. The speed at which the product is diffused internationally applies to the final stage of amplifying. Thus, in addition to issues of proximity and possibilities for localizing, there might be several variables that account for the length of time it takes for the process to occur. One consideration is the nature of the product itself: an object (perishables such as food, for example, American-style pizza, Tex-Mex, or tofu; or nonperishable items, such as the Swatch watch or Benetton clothes); ideas (philosophies from postmodernism to Zen); behaviors (Eastern methods of healing including acupuncture and Reiki, or environmental consciousness, including environment-friendly sprays and recycling); or a media text (television programs, musical disc, magazine, etc.). Another consideration is that of language or accessibility, raising issues of when it is decided that a particular item will attract sufficient interest to merit translation.

In the case of children's toys, fads, and fashions, the market responds extremely quickly with products seeming to appear only so fast as they can be replaced by the next one (for example, Ninja Turtles, Power Rangers, Tamaogotchi, Pokémon). Other items seem to move more slowly and often remain longer.

Lamont (1987) analyzes how intellectual legitimacy is conferred on academic theories by radically different audiences whose norms of evaluation are highly dissimilar. She argues that this is made possible as a function of the "adaptability" of the work "to specific environmental requirements" (p. 586). She examines how philosopher Jacques Derrida's work came to be accepted both in France and in the United States. The French newspaper *Le Monde* published a series of articles in the summer of 2000 on the popularity of Freudian psychoanalysis, noting that by the time it was becoming popular in some nations of the world, it had all but ceased to exist in the country in which it had been most wholeheartedly embraced, the U.S. (D'Hombres, 2000). The question of when and how market conditions become ripe for the adoption of items is a fascinating one that remains open to further inquiry. As several scholars have noted with respect to intellectual philosophies, their spread is not a function of the inherent merit of the ideas they present, but rather of their fit into the social, historical, and cultural context (e.g., Verman, 1997).

CASE STUDIES

At this stage we wish to examine further a number of case studies to illustrate how the megaphone effect has occurred, specifically in the realms of television programs, Cable News Network (CNN), children's culture, and pop music.

Television Programs

A number of different television programs and several distinct genres have achieved major international success after gaining massive viewer ratings in the United States. The so-called realistic television genre, which has become extremely popular around the world, is a case in point. One such series, unabashedly called *Big Brother*, documented the private lives of a group of people living together in the Netherlands during the winter of 1999. Germany and Spain next created local versions of the program that March, CBS did so in the U.S. in July, followed by the U.K. in the same month. In the highly rated American version, 10 participants were brought together under one roof and isolated from the outside world. They shared their lives with 28 cameras following them about, together with 60 stationery microphones. Many spin-offs of the original *Big Brother* have been created.

Another program is called *Survivor*, about survival on a desert island. It was CBS's summer hit for 2000, with ratings so high that similar figures are usually associated only with broadcasts of the Superbowl or the Academy Awards (Carter, 2000a). This and the nature of the show caused it to receive a great deal of media coverage. In the last episode of the series (viewed by 40 million people), tension built toward the moment at which the winner was declared, and the individual became an overnight celebrity. The original concept was British, and it was rejected for 12 years by all the British broadcasters until it was finally tested in Sweden and subsequently sold to CBS. Davis, the producer, is quoted as having said:

> It is incomprehensible that the biggest thing on television today is a semi-documentary program of CBS, based on a Swedish television program which is an adaptation of a British idea, that was produced by a British parachuter, and its owner is among others, a member of the British Parliament. (Carter, 2000b)

Another genre, the television game show, is originally American, but one of the most successful programs of this type, *Who Wants to be a Millionaire?*, was adopted from the United Kingdom. The program was rejected by the British ITV for 2 years in the U.K., but when it was shown there at the end of 1998, it became a major hit (Carter, 2000a). When it was broadcast in the U.S. on the ABC network in August 1999 as a daily summer replacement during prime time, it topped the ratings charts, even though no game show had made it onto the Nielsen ratings in over 40 years (Hetsroni, 2001). The success of the American version turned this program into one of the most successful cultural exports in the past 30 years. At the time of this writing, *Who Wants to be a Millionaire?* has become a top-rated show in 30 countries and has been sold to an additional 50 nations.

Finally, another genre worth mentioning is children's programs. Specifically, the *Teletubbies* is an unusual children's television series intended for preschool audiences. It was commissioned by the BBC in the U.K., and first aired in March 1997, to become a global success. Television companies in over 60 countries have acquired the broadcasting rights (primarily in North and South America, across Europe, throughout English-speaking countries, such as South Africa, Australia, New Zealand, as well as in several Asian countries). To date, this program is the BBC's largest investment worldwide in the area of children and television. There are also approximately 300 merchandising licenses for the *Teletubbies* internationally, including videos, books, magazines, music, audiocassettes, dolls, clothing, and much more.

Outside the U.K., the series was first broadcast in the U.S. (Dow, personal communication, November 9, 2000) by the PBS network in 1998, and it became a major hit (Stipp, 1999). As the online news service of the BBC (1998) notes:

> Perhaps the biggest sign of their popularity came when the *Teletubbies* single went straight in at No. 1 in the U.K. music charts during Christmas last year. And the *Teletubbies* have had a warm welcome elsewhere in the world. *After acquiring American accents* [italics added], their debut across the Atlantic won them rave reviews from TV critics.

These examples of television programs share a history of originating outside the United States. Although each had achieved local success, it was only after being introduced to the U.S. that they were enthusiastically adopted by dozens of countries around the world. In each case, buying the rights to these and other such programs entails adhering carefully to its general format, and making minimal local content adjustments (Hetsroni & Bloch, 1999).

Cable News Network (CNN)

Another realm in which the megaphone effect is readily noticeable is international cable news, the most renowned being Cable News Network (CNN). Although it existed long before, CNN rose to prominence during the Gulf War. Aside from its reporting of American domestic news, this network constantly samples foreign items, filters them, and amplifies them.

Its technological, rather than journalistic, capacity is at the root of its power (e.g., Hess, 1996). The actual availability of the technology itself—access to the megaphone—is a source of influence. Moreover, part of the cost of employing the megaphone is the filtering and distortion that occur. CNN illustrates the tension between two poles: On one hand it has been perceived as another tool of American imperialism, presenting the world to the world from an exclusive American perspective; on the other hand it delivers news from different parts of the world (Flournoy, 1992). Specifically, the *CNN World Report* is intended as a forum in which stories from around the globe are presented. Flournoy reports that by January 1991, CNN carried some 7,000 news items from 150 television news organizations representing 120 countries. The question arises whether or not these stories would ever have made it into the world's consciousness without CNN's potential for megaphoning.

In terms of agenda setting, and the implications for public awareness of local issues, the founder and owner of CNN, Ted Turner, has said: "The news and information traveling around this planet was controlled by the West. . . . The *World Report* is the first chance to remedy that, where we allow everyone to speak their own words" (Flournoy, 1992, p. 9). Despite the fact that they might be speaking their own words, they are using an American network to do so. Yet without CNN, their words might not have been heard at all. As Featherstone (1991) notes, "the prevalence of images of 'the other,' of different nations, previously unknown or only referred to through narrow stereotypes, may effectively help to put the other, and the sense of a global circumstance, on the agenda" (p. 127). The arrangement on CNN is that local television news organizations around the world are invited to submit their own stories (following some professional guidelines) with the network's guarantee to transmit it unedited and uncensored. In exchange, contributors receive the rights to use any of the material included in the *World Report*.

For example, an event in Jordan will pass unnoticed in neighboring Israel. If it is reported on CNN, it gains news value, becomes news, and therefore multiplies the chances of it also being picked up by the Israeli local news. News from Amman typically does not travel directly to Jerusalem (an hour's ride by car) but to Atlanta (thousands of miles away), and only then fed back via satellite, or megaphoned to the rest of the world (including to Jerusalem). What we are arguing here is that CNN provides a voice to local stories in addition to turning them into news, by the mere fact of having selected them for broadcast on its network and, consequently, endowing them with additional worth so that local, regional, and other international networks become more interested in them as well. Thus, local issues—be they famine, war, or atrocities of any sort; the ecology; the economy; women's rights; or specific celebrations—can become matters of global interest provided they travel via the United States. Ted Turner himself appears to have made strong efforts to foster the notion of an international, rather than American, channel. He has claimed that he levied fines on reporters in an effort to "eliminate the use of the word *foreign* when talking about other nations and other individuals on this planet" (McKibben, 1992, p. 39). At the same time, the voice given to local stories has a strong American accent, and despite efforts to encourage diversity, CNN imposes its own guidelines on how reporting is done.

CNN and other global media such as MTV do not necessarily homogenize the globe; they may be diversifying it by dividing it into several separate global villages, with their own centers and peripheries. Volkmer (1999) suggests that her study "interprets the emerging spheres of global political communication as various types of reciprocity—defined as the effects of rebroadcasting national political issues from a global viewpoint back into the political framework where they originated" (p. 3). She conceives of the "mediation of universal and particular elements" (p. 3) as being the model of a global public sphere. For example, in the case of regional conflicts, such as the Middle East, both sides are offered a third perspective through international reporting. In this sense, the megaphone or, more precisely, those who operate it (i.e., the U.S.), serve as the mediators.

This adds a new dimension to the traditional approaches to international news flow, such as the classical work of Galtung and Ruge. In their original model, Galtung and Ruge (1965) stated that peripheral countries do not communicate with each other directly, but rather that they employ a three-step flow, from one peripheral country to a centralized country and from there, on to another peripheral country.

Children's Culture

Children's culture represents an additional field of study in which the workings of the megaphone effect can be demonstrated, whether it is through books (e.g., Harry Potter), toys (e.g., Tamagotchi), or a convergence of various media (e.g., Pokémon).

After Joanne Rowling's Harry Potter series of children's books became a big hit in the U.K., it traveled to the U.S., then to Europe, after which it swept across the rest of the world. More than 116 million copies of the four books have been sold worldwide in 200 countries and 47 languages, with the author working on the fifth volume in a seven-part series (Lyman, 2001; Reuters, 2000). This is considered one of the greatest successes in modern publishing (Associated Press, 2001).

Both the movie and the merchandising rights belong to Warner Brothers, an

American company. It should be noted that their proposal to cast an American actor in the role of the hero met with fierce opposition (msnbc.com, 2001). Apart from relatively minor alterations,[5] the written texts of the books remained almost the same in the American and the British versions. It is the mass marketing undertaken in the U.S. that has changed the very nature of the product. Through merchandising, typical of the amplification stage of the megaphone effect, every conceivable product was tied to the name of Harry Potter and to the features of the actor playing the part in the film. As a result, the role of fantasy so vital in the fictional world is overpowered by very specific, concrete objects that leave little room for the imagination. The Warner Brothers studio has apparently become concerned with this as well (Lyman, 2001).

The Tamagotchi is the case of a computer toy originating in Japan (produced by the Bandai Corporation) and traveling to the U.S. to become one of the most phenomenal commercial successes internationally (Bloch & Lemish, 1999). Sources differ as to whether 30 or 40 million units were sold worldwide. Manufacturers singled out this item for its meteoric rise one day, where supply could not meet demand, and its phenomenal crash relatively soon thereafter, when surplus could not be gotten rid of even when sold at well below cost. An almost cult-like devotion surrounded the toy, with virtual, as well as actual, burial sites for deceased Tamagotchi. It consisted of a miniaturized LCD screen and a number of controls, resulting in a computer game that mimicked the life cycle of a pet. The Tamagotchi, meaning small egg in Japanese, was an idea originally hatched by a mother to amuse her children while accommodating the limitations of spatial restrictions typical of Japanese households. In the U.S., by contrast, considerations of space are not an issue and owning a live pet is a familiar childhood experience. In its American rebirth, the Tamagotchi fulfilled more universal functions. It served as a bridge between human relationships and computer technology, as well as between masculine interests in machinery and action, and feminine interests in caregiving and interpersonal relationships. Perhaps its major appeal was that it was so portable. The American market capitalized on this feature. Many new possibilities for carrying it about were subsequently developed, such as bracelets, watches, necklaces, and key chains. In addition, it became a licensed product and was mass merchandised in other forms, such as Tamagotchi sheets, clothing, stationery, and so forth.

Pokémon is the recent and most extreme mania in children's toys. It began as a video game for Gameboy by Nintendo, turning into a popular TV series, a card game, a movie, and then the subject of massive merchandising. From Japan it traveled to the U.S. and from there to the rest of the world, becoming an instant hit. The phenomenon has been dubbed Pokémania due to its unprecedented success. In 1999, income from merchandising reached $7 billion (Chen, 2000). The movie based on the television series made $78 million in the first 2 weeks of screening in the U.S. alone (Kopfer, 2000). According to a computer search engine, All the Web (2002), by the latter part of 2002, there were almost four million web pages connected to the word Pokémon.

The international commercial success of the Pokémon (Pocket Monster) was based on the effective use of localizing. In fact, there are five Japanese episodes (officially known as the lost episodes) that were unacceptable to the American company from the start because the female character, Misty, was overtly treated as a sex object. The original Japanese product was geared to a wider audience, including adults, whereas the American product was directed at young children. It was this version that was megaphoned to the rest of the world, and further interpreted by local audiences, who were quick to credit Japan with authorship of the program (Lemish & Bloch, in press).

According to Allison (2000), the American version of the Pokémon series is made to be more dynamic, less cute, with brighter colors, the pace is faster, and the editing is sharper and more clear-cut. In addition, the second Pokémon movie was made to have fewer ambiguous messages and more clear-cut characters, which are either good or bad. In particular, a conscious effort was made in the movie to eliminate Japanese elements, so as not to interfere with fantasy for American audiences.

The above illustrations in children's culture exemplify the complexity of the globalization discourse. It is not an issue of children around the world merely being exposed to a homogenized American culture. Rather, the situation is one in which young people are part of a global audience that transcends physical and cultural boundaries in their consumption of multicultural texts. (Lemish et al., 1998; Drotner, 2001). The fact that these texts are enveloped in American packaging and that market forces clearly play a leading role in the process is undeniable. Nonetheless, a number of other forces exist that are frequently complementary but occasionally contradictory, each with its own voice. Consequently, the process of communication can be considered to be hybrid, in the sense that Kraidy (2002) perceives it as a "map of the diffuse workings of power" (p. 334). Perhaps the process we are referring to would be more precisely described as hybrid hegemony. Although it might be tempting to simply label the whole matter American cultural imperialism, no representation of power would be complete without taking into account these other voices that are an integral part of the composition. The exact note that the megaphone effect sounds in facilitating this type of hegemony requires further investigation.

Pop Music

The Beatles and, more recently, the Spice Girls are among the best examples of British music groups who achieved phenomenal success in the world after crossing the Atlantic. Initially the U.S. was the origin of most of the music forms now popular worldwide: ragtime, jazz, blues, rock 'n roll, pop, and rap (Taylor, 1997). Each of these music styles is the product of the struggle of the groups that fell into the margins of American society, outside the confines of the dominant White middle class; their evolution thus represents a type of internal cultural immigration. Horn (1993) explains that often in the U.S. the source of musical change was in the contact and dialogue between different cultural or ethnic groups.

By contrast, the universal pop-rock aesthetics is perceived to be a transcultural form of music acceptable around the globe. Its influence is so predominant that local styles of music tend to become mere variations of a single transcultural form. Regev (1997) argues that the influence of Anglo American rock on local musical cultures is manifest in three forms: (a) importing them as is (e.g., concerts of American performers, imports of discs, popularity of MTV clips of Anglo American performers, and the like); (b) imitation of the foreign forms in local cultures (e.g., Hi Five in Israel and Aqua in Denmark; Lemish et al., 1998); and (c) hybrid mixtures of different musical genres through a process of selective adaptation of rock elements into traditional or local music styles. He talks about the apparently paradoxical phenomenon by which "a cultural form, associated with American (U.S.) culture and with the powerful commercial interests of the international music industry, is being used in order to construct a sense of local difference and authenticity" (p. 126).

The emergence of the world music genre since the 1990s illustrates the megaphone effect. The concept of world music encompasses a rich and diverse sound that originated in countries outside the predominantly Anglo American axis to become highly popular, first in the U.S., and then around the world. Initially, various heterogeneous musical cultures were sampled in a number of regions of the globe. The musical elements were then brought together, blended, and rearranged, blurring the boundaries between the familiar and otherness, or between local and global. However, by generally complying to a range of American musical standards, such as the use of rock instruments or electronic and digital means of sound production, musicians provided an American shape to the local content that warranted diffusion to a worldwide audience. Taylor (1997) cites the complexity of the famous example of Paul Simon's *Graceland*, the result of collaboration with South African musicians. This success contrasts sharply with efforts by Johnny Clegg and his band, Samvuka, to promote their multiracial musical message directly out of their native South Africa. Paul Simon's recipe for importing music was so successful, he reapplied it again a few years later with Amazonian Indians creating a whole series of musical stars.

Another illustration of musical exchange can be seen in the cooperation between African American guitarist Ray Cooder and Ali Farka Toure from Mali, culminating in the album *Talking Timbuktu*, the highest selling record of 1994 (Mitchell, 1996). Mitchell elaborates on such examples and claims, "Indigenous cultures appear to be spoken for by culturally dominant Anglocentric power groups" (p. 1). He says that:

> The world music phenomenon, which has proved to be a durable one in popular music of the 1990s, both as a marketing strategy and as a musical genre, has functioned as a positive form of cultural influence in terms of providing momentum and inspiration for the indigenous often dissident musics of ethnic minorities throughout the world. It has also helped to establish a musical language of hybridity, in which traditional, authentic, and indigenous musical forms are combined with global musical idioms. (p. 7)

Some scholars go so far as to argue that "the growing ascendance of globalizing processes actually accentuates the importance of localized processes of consumption and the identification with place as represented through unique musical forms" (Mahtani & Salmon, 2001, p. 166). Lipsitz (2001) stresses that, despite its appropriation by the West, the wide hearing that is accorded certain types of music has empowered certain cultural groups by creating a diasporic intimacy and serving

> as a conduit for ideas and images articulating subaltern sensitivities. At a time when African people have less power and fewer resources than at almost any previous time in history, African culture has emerged as the single most important subtext within world popular culture. (Idowu, 1985, p. 37, as cited in Lipsitz, 2001, p. 189)

The author cites Fela Kuti, founder of Nigeria's radical Afro-beat music subculture, who gained the following insight from his stay in the U.S.: "Most Africans . . . think everything from overseas is greater, but they do not know also that everything from overseas could have gone from here to overseas and come back to us. America gave me that line of thought" (p. 192).

This is a succinct description of the potential empowerment to be derived from the megaphone effect. Similar claims may well be made of other cultural texts and the hearing they receive by virtue of the megaphone effect.

IMPLICATIONS OF THE MEGAPHONE EFFECT

The megaphone effect offers a concise way of tracking how a cultural text can be selected from one origin, filtered through another cultural system, specifically the U.S., and subsequently disseminated worldwide. The focus of the model is on the processual nature of the events, contrary to theories of globalization or Americanization, which emphasize the final outcome almost to the exclusion of all else.

The megaphone effect represents an alternative to some of the more extreme views of cultural diffusion. It espouses a position located somewhere between those who believe that multidirectional flows of cultural texts will take place and presumably lead to a situation of parity or what Sreberny-Mohammadi calls "global pluralism" (1991, p. 122). The dire prophecy of total domination is envisaged by the hegemonic model of cultural imperialism. We are not claiming that the megaphone effect produces a balance between these two poles, only that space for other voices exists, even if they are expected to conform.

A central theme that emerges from the megaphone effect is its potential for empowerment. Giddens (1990) defines power as "the ability of individuals or groups to make their own concerns or interests count, even where others resist" (p. 52). Freire's (1970; Shor & Freire, 1987) discussion of empowerment refers to the dominated group's development of an understanding of their rights, capacities, and responsibilities in effecting social change. By empowerment we intend that which affords individuals or groups the possibility to make their voices heard.

The megaphone effect does not maintain that there is a redress in the distribution of power globally. Clearly, the prerogative to disseminate texts to the rest of the world is in the hands of those who are in a position to do so, possessing both the means and the hierarchical standing among other nations (Tunstall & Machin, 1999). This prerogative is maintained and reinforced each time a text is patronized (by the U.S.), and the benefits to be derived from its dissemination are reaped in both its adopted home and its original home. In a dialogue concerning the liberation of one culture from the domination of another, Freire (1985) states: "In the process of liberation, the dominated can and must critically incorporate some of the dimensions of the dominant culture to serve as the very instruments of their own struggle" (p. 193). If a text is megaphoned, empowerment for those who generated it originally occurs by the mere fact that massive exposure worldwide is achieved and the message is spread. Although the foreignness of a text is muted after adoption—as it undergoes certain changes and becomes tinged with the flavor of its patron culture—its original provenance is credited, nonetheless.[6]

We realize (as is true with all models) that we are simplifying a highly complex process in order to better understand its functioning. Rather than supporting the theory with a single in-depth example, we have chosen to relate it to a wide variety of different fields. We believe that it can serve as a blueprint for narrower, more detailed investigations. In proposing it, we hope to stir up a discussion over what we envisage as the megaphone effect. Moreover, this work represents a sketch that we hope will be filled in and fleshed out through further study. At this stage the model does not yet adequately account for how or why items are selected, or particularly, which will be chosen for dissemination and which will not. In other words, what are the criteria that must be met for a text to be sampled and subsequently megaphoned? Knowing why something is not sampled is at least as important as knowing why it is. This might be an indicator of part of what makes up the uniqueness of a specific culture. At this initial stage of the model, another significant matter that is noticeably absent is that of parameters to determine the three stages involved in the megaphone effect. Clear-cut distinctions are needed to differentiate between sampling, filtering, and amplifying in order to rigorously analyze how a text moves from one stage to the next. Subsequently, the model must be applied to in-depth case studies. Comparisons must be drawn between them to evaluate the differences across a variety of different realms, with more examples drawn from outside the G-8 nations.[7]

The megaphone effect is a somewhat more optimistic scenario than the widely recognized debate about globalization in general because it focuses on how physical and cultural borders are transcended, empowering voices representing local cultures and identities to be heard. Moreover, in according a place to a variety of different voices, the world is shown to appear to be in a constant state of flux in quest of at least partial innovation, never satisfied to remain stagnant and presenting what some may conceive of as a postmodern perspective made up of an eclectic pastiche.

Clearly, at times certain texts bypass the megaphone effect, traveling directly to other parts of the world without going through the United States. This can be explained in at least two ways: first, due to the proximity between the culture of origin and its members in the diaspora (such as Indian movies among the Indian community in England, or Russian satellite channels received by immigrants from the former U.S.S.R. in a variety of places); second, for financial considerations, for example, television stations that fill broadcast time by purchasing cheap productions, such as the case of *telenovelas* outside the Spanish-speaking world or dated action adventure series sold to nonindustrialized nations.

We realize that this analysis might seem terribly self-serving or ethnocentric; we recognize that the scenario presented is one in which the principal parts played are those of Western-dominated values, unequal opportunities, adoption, and even of exploitation of non-Western cultures and their heritages. Yet, the megaphone effect is a description of a situation in which an opening is provided for the other, albeit on someone else's terms.

Cohen et al. (1996) make elegant use of the Tower of Babel metaphor to describe the lack of commonality in the world. As they explain it:

> Pulling in the opposite direction is that sort of human experience often summarized by the metaphor of the Tower of Babel. As the Hebrew Bible teaches us, the human race "was of one language and one speech." And they said "come let us build us a city and a tower with its top in heaven and let us make us a name" (Genesis XI). And as the Bible records, God confounded man's audacious effort by destroying the tower and the common language (and hence shared culture). Ever since, with or without the Deity as causal variable, and like it or not, the world has been culturally and politically divided. (p. 154)

The megaphone effect is a new version of the attempt to reassemble the troops of the builders of the Tower of Babel. Clearly, we are not one world with one language and one speech any longer. We have recognized that it is not possible to enforce a single culture, American or otherwise, on the rest of the world. This would be precluded by a series of forces, including resistance, domestication, and multiculturalism. However, the megaphone effect presents a possible explanation for how various successful cultural elements are processed in such a manner as to give them the aspect of a universal language.

NOTES

1. We use the terms Americanization and American to refer to the United States, for lack of acceptable alternatives, although we recognize that these labels could apply to all or part of the American continent, or specifically, to Native Americans exclusively.

2. It is possible that in time this will change, and it might already be claimed that there are other smaller megaphones emerging elsewhere, such as in Japan (e.g., Iwabuchi, 2001). It is worth noting that Tsunoyama (1995, p. 191; cited in Iwabuchi, 2001, p. 209) also employs the

world of physics to make his point, using the metaphor of Japan being a new power plant and a transformer substation whereby filtration through a Japanese prism renders American popular culture palatable to Asian audiences.

3. Publishing in American or English-language journals (much to our students' chagrin) is the only way to infiltrate the academic agenda and obtain recognition concerning issues of particular relevance to our own countries.

4. The creators of an American initiative, Teenage Mutant Ninja Turtles, with characters supposedly adhering to principles of Japanese martial arts, stated, "We had all the Japanese fighting methods, but we didn't want to make up Japanese names because we thought they'd seem too strange to American readers. We decided to go in the opposite direction and used distinctly European names" (Eastman & Laird, 2002, p. 2).

5. For example, the spelling was Americanized, and the title of a book was changed (*Harry Potter and the Philosopher's Stone* became *Harry Potter and the Sorcerer's Stone*).

6. Indeed, connecting items to their supposed origins even occurs when this is misleading. A vehicle, such as a Ford, whose parts are manufactured and assembled in many different parts of the world is still an "American" car (see Giddens, 1989, pp. 537–539). Many of the products of a multinational company, such as the Sony Corporation, are still viewed as being Japanese although the firm employs tens of thousands of people worldwide, sells its stock on the exchanges of some dozen different countries, and specifically tries to use transcultural designing principles (du Gay et al., 1997).

7. Eastern religions and philosophies, martial arts, forms of meditation, and healing methods are among other types of cultural texts that have all been megaphoned. How and why this has happened merits its own analysis, whereas the topic of how non-American music has traveled via the U.S. to the rest of the world has been touched upon only briefly here.

REFERENCES

Abegglen, J.C. (1994). *Sea change: Pacific Asia as the new world industrial center.* New York: Free Press.

Allison, A. (2000, November). *Cuteness: Portable intimacy as Japan's millennial product.* Paper presented at Nintentionality or Pikachu's Global Adventure international conference on the Pokémon phenomenon, Honolulu, Hawaii.

All the Web. (2002) Retrieved August 26, 2002, from http://www.alltheweb.com/search?cat=web&cs=iso-8859–1&l=any&q=Pokemon

Ang, I. (1985) *Watching Dallas: Soap opera and the melodramatic imagination.* London: Methuen.

Appadurai, A. (1990). Disjuncture and difference in the global cultural economy. In M. Featherstone (Ed.), *Global culture: Nationalism, globalization and modernity.* London: Sage.

Appadurai, A. (1996). *Modernity at large: Cultural dimensions of globalization.* Minneapolis: University of Minnesota Press.

Aronoff, M. J. (2000). The "Americanization" of Israeli politics: Political and cultural change. *Israel Studies, 5,* 92–127.

Associated Press. (2001). Retrieved January 4, 2001, from http://www.msnbc.com/news

Avraham, E., & First, A. (in press). "I buy American": The America image as reflected in Israeli advertising. *Journal of Communication.*

Azaryahu, M. (2000). McIsrael? On the "Americanization of Israel." *Israel Studies, 5,* 41–64.

Broadcasters Audience Research Board (2000, January 7). Weekly television listing. *Sunday Times,* section 9, p. 50.

Barber, B. R. (1995). *Jihad vs. McWorld.* New York: Times Books.

BBC. (1998). Teletubbies pad out BBC sales. Retrieved July 13, 1998, from http://www.bbc.co.uk/education/teletubbies/information/news/sales.shtml

Beals, G. (2000, December 11). Kings of cool. *Time,* 30–32, 35–36.

Benjamin, W. (1973). *The work of art in the age of mechanical reproduction: Illuminations.* London: Fontana. (Original work published 1936)

Bhabha, H. (1990). *Nation and narration.* London: Routledge.

Bhabha, H. (1994). *The location of culture.* London: Routledge.

Billington, R. A. (1971). *The genesis of the frontier thesis.* San Marino, CA: Huntington Library Press.

Bird, J., Curtis, B., Putnam, T., Robertson, G., & Tickner, L., (1993). (Eds.). *Mapping the futures.* London: Routledge.

Bloch, L-R., & Lemish, D. (1999). Disposable love: The rise and fall of a virtual pet. *New Media and Society, 1,* 283–303.

Campbell, N., & Kean, A. (1997). *American cultural studies: An introduction to American culture.* London: Routledge.

Carter, B. (2000a, July 25). Ha'shemesh lo shokaat al *"milonaire"* [The sun never sets on "Millionaire"]. *Ha'aretz,* p. D3.

Carter, B. (2000b, August 25). *Tochnit "ha'sored" shavra si'ei tzfiya be'artzot ha'brit* [The program "Survivor" broke viewing records in the United States]. *Ha'aretz,* p. D8.

Chen, S. (2000, March 13). *Milchemet ha'tza'a'tzuim* [Toy war]. *Yediot Acharonot,* p. 14.

Cohen, A. A., Levy, M. R., Roeh, I., & Gurevitch, M. (1996). *Global newsrooms, local audiences: A study of the Eurovision News Exchange.* London: John Libbey.

Cooper, M. D., & Nothstine, W. L. (1992). *Power persuasion: Moving an ancient art into the media age.* Greenwood, IN: Educational Video Group, Alistair Press.

Crystal, D. (1997). *English as a global language.* Cambridge, UK: Cambridge University Press.

D'Hombres, D. (2000, July 12). *Non, la psychanalyze n'est pas morte* [No, psychoanalysis is not dead]. *Le Monde,* p. 14.

Drotner, K. (2001). Global media through youthful eyes. In S. Livingstone & M. Bovill (Eds.), *Children and their changing media environment* (pp. 283–305). Hillsdale, NJ: Erlbaum.

du Gay, P., Hall, S., Janes, L., Mackay, H., & Negus, K. (1997). *Doing cultural studies: The story of the Sony Walkman.* London: Sage.

Duignan, P., & Gann, L. (1992). *The rebirth of the West: The Americanization of the democratic world.* London: Blackwell.

Eastman, K., & Laird, P. (2002). The official *Teenage Mutant Ninja Turtle* web site. Retrieved August 27, 2002, from http://www. Ninjaturtles.com/origin/origin.htm

Ellis, D. M. (Ed.). (1969). *The frontier in American development.* Ithaca, NY: Cornell University Press.

Featherstone, M. (1990). (Ed.), *Global culture: Nationalism, globalization and modernity.* London: Sage.

Featherstone, M. (1991). *Consumer culture and postmodernism.* London: Sage.

Fender, S. (Ed.). (1992). *Sea changes: British emigration & American literature.* Cambridge, UK: Cambridge University Press.

Fender, S. (1993). The American difference. In M. Gidley (Ed.), *Modern American culture: An introduction* (pp. 1–22). London: Longman.

Ferguson, M. (1992). The mythology about globalization. *Journal of European Communication, 7,* 69–93.

First, A., & Avraham, E. (2000, December 24). *"My heart is in the West and I am at East's end"?! The portrayal of America as mirrored in Israeli advertising.* Paper presented at the Israeli Communication Association annual conference, Tel Aviv University, Tel Aviv, Israel.

Flournoy, D. (1992). *CNN World Report: Ted Turner's international news coup.* London: John Libbey.

Fornäs, J., & Bolin, G. (Eds.). (1995). *Youth culture in late modernity.* London: Sage.

Freire, P. (1970). *Pedagogy of the oppressed.* New York: Continuum.

Freire, P. (1985). *The politics of education: Culture, power, and liberation.* South Hadley, MA: Bergin & Garvey.

Frith, S. (1988). The pleasures of the hearth. In V. Burgin, J. Donald, & C. Kaplan (Eds.), *Formations of pleasure.* London: Routledge.

Galtung, J., & Ruge, M. H. (1965). The structure of foreign news. *Journal of Peace Research, 2,* 64–91.

Geertz, C. (1973). *The interpretation of cultures.* New York: Basic Books.

Gerbner, G., & Gross, L. (1980). The "mainstreaming" of America: Violence profile No. 11. *Journal of Communication, 30*(3), 10–29.

Giddens, A. (1989). *Sociology*. Cambridge, UK: Polity Press.

Giddens, A. (1990). *The consequences of modernity*. Stanford, CA: Stanford University Press.

Giddens, A. (1998). *The third way: The renewal of social democracy*. Cambridge, UK: Polity Press.

Giles, H., & Coupland, N. (1991). *Language: Contexts and consequences*. Milton Keynes, UK: Open University Press.

Gillespie, M. (1997). You can't beat the feeling: Coca-Cola and utopia. In H. Mackay (Ed.), *Consumption and everyday life* (pp. 55–59). London: Sage.

Gilroy, P. (1992). *There ain't no black in the Union Jack*. London: Routledge.

Gilroy, P. (1995). *Modernity and double consciousness*. Cambridge, MA: Harvard University Press.

Gitlin, T. (1998). Public sphere or public sphericules? In T. Liebes & J. Curran (Eds.), *Media, ritual and identity* (pp. 168–174). London: Routledge.

Glazer, N., & Moynihan, P. (1970). *Beyond the melting pot*. Cambridge, MA: MIT Press.

Greenbaum, S. (1985). (Ed.). *The English language today*. Oxford, UK: Pergamon Press.

Gurevitch, M. (1991). The globalization of electronic journalism. In J. Curran & M. Gurevitch (Eds.), *Mass media and society* (pp. 178–193). London: Edward Arnold.

Hall, S. (1992). The question of cultural identity. In S. Hall, D. Held, & T. McGrew (Eds.), *Modernity and its futures* (pp. 273-299). Oxford, UK: Polity Press.

Hannerz, U. (1996). *Transnational connections: Culture, people, places*. London: Routledge.

Hess, S. (1996). *International news and foreign correspondents*. Washington, DC: Brookings Institute.

Hetsroni, A. (2001). Millionaires around the world: Analysis of quiz shows in America, Israel and Poland. *Communications: The European Journal of Communication Research, 26*, 247–266.

Hetsroni, A., & Bloch, L-R. (1999). Choosing the right mate when everyone is watching: Cultural and sex differences in television dating games. *Communication Quarterly, 47*, 315–332.

Himmelstein, H. (1984). *Television myth and the American mind*. New York: Praeger.

Hoggart, R. (1957). *The uses of literacy*. London: Chatto & Windus.

Horn, D. (1993). Musical America. In M. Gidley (Ed.), *Modern American culture: An introduction* (pp. 239–261). London: Longman.

Hoskins, C., & Mirus, R., (1988). Reasons for the U.S. dominance of the international trade in television programmes. *Media, Culture and Society, 10*, 499–515.

Hughes, H. S. (1975). *The sea change: The migration of social thought, 1930–1965*. New York: Harper & Row.

Idowu, K. M. (1985). *Fela: Why blackman carry shit*. Kaduna, Nigeria: Opinion Media.

Iwabuchi, K. (2001). Uses of Japanese popular culture: Trans/nationalism and postcolonial desire for "Asia." *Emergences: Journal for the Study of Media and Composite Cultures, 11*, 199–222.

JFK Library (2002). Address of Senator John F. Kennedy accepting the Democratic Party nomination for the presidency of the United States. Retrieved September 18, 2002, from http://www.cs.umb.edu/jfklibrary/j071560.htm

Kachru, B. (1986). *The alchemy of English*. Oxford, UK: Pergamon Press.

King, R. H. (1993). American cultural criticism. In M. Gidley (Ed.), *Modern American culture: An introduction* (pp. 361–380). London: Longman.

Klein, A. (1996, September 18). We are as we advertise. *Jerusalem Post*, p. 7.

Kopfer, R. (2000, March 21). Pokémania. *Ha'aretz*, p. D4.

Kraidy, M. M. (2002). Hybridity in cultural globalization. *Communication Theory, 12*, 316–339.

Kuisel, R. (1993). *Seducing the French: The dilemma of Americanization*. Berkeley: University of California Press.

Lamont, M. (1987). How to become a dominant French philosopher: The case of Jacques Derrida. *American Journal of Sociology, 93*, 584–622.

Lasswell, H. (1948). The structure and function of communication in society. In L. Bryson (Ed.), *The communication of ideas*. New York: Institute for Religious & Social Studies.

Lee, J. (2000, August 18). China's rules make a hard sell. *International Herald Tribune*, p. 13.

Lemish, D. (1998). Spice Girls' talk: A case study in the development of gendered identity. In S. A. Inness (Ed.), *Millennium girls: Today's girls and their culture* (pp. 145–167). New York: Rowman & Littlefield.

Lemish, D. (1999). "America, the beautiful:" Israeli children's perception of the U.S. through a wrestling television series. In Y. R. Kamalipour (Ed.), *Images of the U.S. around the world: A multicultural perspective* (pp. 295–308). New York: State University of New York Press.

Lemish, D., & Bloch, L-R. (in press). Pokémon: How Israeli children "catch 'em." In J. Tobin (Ed.), *Nintentionality: Pikachu's global adventure*. Durham, NC: Duke University Press.

Lemish, D., Drotner, K., Liebes, T. Maigret, E., & Stald, G. (1998). Global culture in practice: A look at children and adolescents in Denmark, France, and Israel. *European Journal of Communication, 13,* 539–556.

LeVine, R. (1984). Properties of culture: An ethnographic view. In R. Shweder & R. LeVine (Eds.), *Culture theory* (pp. 67–87). Cambridge, UK: Cambridge University Press.

Liebes, T., & Katz, E. (1993). *The export of meaning.* Cambridge, UK: Polity Press.

Lipsitz, G. (2001). Diasporic noise: History, hip hop, and the post-colonial politics of sound. In C. L. Harrington & D. D. Bielby (Eds.), *Popular culture: Production and consumption* (pp. 180–199). Malden, MA: Blackwell.

Lyman, R. (2001, November 5). Guarding Harry Potter's magic. *International Herald Tribune,* pp. 1, 6.

Mahtani, M., & Salmon, S. (2001). Site reading?: Globalization, identity, and the consumption of place in popular music. In C. L. Harrington & D. D. Bielby (Eds.), *Popular culture: Production and consumption* (pp. 165–179). Malden, MA: Blackwell.

Mantle, J. (1999). *Benetton: The family, the business and the brand.* London: Warner Books.

Maret, J., & Katsuno, H. (2000, November). *Comparing Japanese and English-language versions of Pokémon.* Paper presented at Nintentionality or Pikachu's Global Adventure international conference on the Pokémon phenomenon, Honolulu, Hawaii.

McKibben, W. (1992). *The age of missing information.* New York: Random House.

McLaughlin, L., Sakamaki, S., & Tashiro, H. (1999, November 22). Pokémania. *Time,* pp. 50–58.

McLuhan, M. (1964). *Understanding media.* New York: McGraw-Hill.

McNeil, D. G. (1997, December 7). South Africa's American romance. *Jerusalem Post,* p. 8.

Meyrowitz, J. (1993). *Myths and realities of the global village.* Durham: University of New Hampshire.

Mitchell, T. (1996). *Popular music and local identity.* London: Leicester University Press.

Moen, O. O., & Lervik, L. M. (Eds.). (1996). *Frontiers and visions: A casebook in American civilization studies.* Oslo, Norway: Scandinavian University Press.

Morley, D. (1993). Active audience theory: Pendulums and pitfalls. *Journal of Communication, 43*(4), 13–19.

msnbc.com. (2001). Retrieved January 4, 2001, from http://www.msnbc.com/news.448072.asp

Ostendorf, B., & Palmié, S. (1993). Immigration and ethnicity. In M. Gidley (Ed.), *Modern American culture: An introduction* (pp. 142–165). London: Longman.

Painter, A. A. (1993). Japanese daytime television, popular culture and ideology. *Journal of Japanese Studies, 19,* 295–316.

Rebhun, U., & Waxman, C. I. (2000). The "Americanization" of Israel: A demographic, cultural and political evaluation. *Israel Studies, 5,* 65–91.

Regev, M. (1997). Rock aesthetics and musics of the world. *Theory, Culture, & Society, 14,* 125–142.

Reuters. (2000). Retrieved November 29, 2000, from http://www.msnbc.com/news/496176.asp

Ritzer, G. (1998). *Enchanting a disenchanted world: Revolutionizing the means of consumption.* London: Pine Forge Press.

Robertson, R. (1994). Globalization or glocalization? *Journal of International Communication,* 1, 33–52.

Rogers, E. M. (1983). *Diffusion of innovations* (3rd ed.). New York: Free Press.

Schiller, H. I. (1976). *Communication and cultural domination.* Armonk, NY: Sharpe.

Shor, I., & Freire, P. (1987). *A pedagogy for liberation.* South Hadley, MA: Bergin & Garvey.

Sreberny-Mohammadi, A. (1991). The global and the local in international communications. In J. Curran & M. Gurevitch (Eds.), *Mass media and society* (pp. 118–138). London: Edward Arnold.

Stevenson, N. (1995). *Understanding media cultures: Social theory and mass communication.* London: Sage.

Stipp, H. (1999). Under fire from American programme criticism. *Televizion, 2,* 26–27.

Stoffman, N. (1997, December 9). The life and times of Thomas L. Friedman. Retrieved December 9, 1997, from http://www.campuslife.utoronto.ca/groups/varsity/archives/118/dec10/review/friedman.html

Taylor, T. D. (1997). *Global pop: World music, world markets.* New York: Routledge.

Tomlinson, J. (1999). *Globalization and culture.* Cambridge, UK: Polity Press.

Toyama, R. (2000, November). Personal account of a "localizer": Ryota Toyama, assistant producer, Konami Computer Entertainment America. Presented at Nintentionality or Pikachu's Global Adventure international conference on the Pokémon phenomenon, Honolulu, Hawaii.

Trudgill, P. (1983). *On dialect.* Oxford, UK: Blackwell.

Tsunoyama, S. (1995). *Ajia Renessansu* [Asian Renaissance]. Tokyo: PHP Kenkyuaho.

Tunstall, J., & Machin, D. (1999). *The Anglo-American media connection.* Oxford, UK: Oxford University Press.

Turner, F. J. (1961). *Frontier and section: Selected essays.* Englewood Cliffs, NJ: Prentice-Hall.

Turner, F. J. (1962). *The frontier in American history.* New York: Holt, Rinehart, & Winston.

Vasey, R. (1993). The median. In M. Gidley (Ed.), *Modern American culture: An introduction* (pp. 213–238). London: Longman.

Verman, D. (1997). *Ha'merchav ha'tziburi shel Habermas: Nisui machshavti o nisayon histori* [Habermas's public sphere: An intellectual experiment or historical experience]. *Dvarim Achadim, 1,* 34–46.

Volkmer, I. (1999). *CNN: News in the global sphere.* Luton, UK: University of Luton Press.

Walters, M. (1995). *Globalization.* London: Routledge.

Williams, F. (1962). *The American invasion.* New York: Crown.

Yehoshua TBWA. (1999, November). [Advertisement]. *Lihiot Horim,* p. D-7.

Zachary, G. P. (1999). The world gets in touch with its inner American. *Mother Jones.* Retrieved September 15, 1999, from http://www.mojones.com/mother_jones/Jan./Feb

Zangwill, I. (1908). *The melting pot.* New York: Macmillan.

CHAPTER CONTENTS

7   The Effects of Television on Group Vitality: Can Television Empower Nondominant Groups?

JESSICA R. ABRAMS
University of California, Santa Barbara

WILLIAM P. EVELAND, JR.
Ohio State University

HOWARD GILES
University of California, Santa Barbara

The concept of vitality was first introduced to account for factors affecting language use in the late 1970s. Today, vitality has developed into a broader theory addressing issues related to ethnicity, gender, age, and intergroup communication. Theorists propose that the more vitality a group has, the more likely that group will survive as an entity in an intergroup context. Intergroup researchers claim that perceptions of vitality may be influenced by mass media. This relationship has yet to be explored in detail. Based on mass media theory, we offer a number of contrasting propositions about how television might function to impact subjective group vitality and, ultimately, intergroup communication. The integration of relevant intergroup and mass communication literature reflects the extent to which television empowers minority groups as well as how levels of empowerment are manifested in nondominant groups' behaviors.

C ommunication between groups depends on the nature of the setting in which it occurs, as well as the sociostructural background in which social categories are embedded. In order to explore the latter in the interethnic sphere, Giles, Bourhis, and Taylor (1977) introduced the concept of *ethnolinguistic vitality* that articulated the main sociostructural features defining a group's relative posi-

AUTHORS' NOTE: The authors would like to thank Jake Harwood, Beth LePoire, Dolly Mullin, and Nancy Collins for their assistance on earlier versions of this manuscript.

Correspondence: Jessica Abrams, Department of Communication, University of California, Santa Barbara, CA 93106-4020; email: jessicaabrams@earthlink.net

tion to others in society. Vitality was conceptualized as "that which makes a group likely to behave as a distinctive and collective entity within the intergroup setting" (Giles et al., 1977, p. 308). They proposed that the more vitality a group has, the more likely it is that group will survive and thrive as a collective entity in an intergroup context. With survival at stake, it is in the best interest of the group to maintain vitality.

Intergroup scholars have been keenly aware that mass media have the potential to influence a group's perceptions of its own as well as other groups' vitality (e.g., Landry & Allard, 1992). For instance, Harwood, Giles, and Bourhis (1994) contend that "vitality assessment in different groups will come to be based on different sources of information (i.e., groups' respective intragroup sources—interpersonal or mass media)" (p. 182). Even so, scholars have paid little attention to examining how media can influence perceptions of group vitality.

The current analysis explicates the role of television in shaping nondominant group vitality.[1] By interfacing the intergroup and mass media literatures, the present analysis attempts to bridge a theoretical divide prevalent in the field of communication (O'Sullivan, 1999). We begin with an examination of contextual and background literature on intergroup theory and its role in the development of the vitality concept. We then summarize research comparing historical and current portrayals of nondominant groups on television. Next, we employ two mass communication theories—(a) cultivation and (b) uses and gratifications—to develop propositions about how television can shape perceptions of nondominant group vitality. Because of the different assumptions and perspectives underlying each theory, they result in contrasting propositions about the influence of television on subjective vitality. Cultivation theory's claims about television content and selection predict that television may function to decrease perceptions of nondominant group vitality. On the other hand, uses and gratifications theory's notion of social identity gratifications, whereby individuals can select television to meet their identity needs, predicts that television could increase nondominant group vitality perceptions. The degree to which nondominant group members selectively or nonselectively view television, in conjunction with the characteristics of the content available for them to view at any given point in time, will influence their perceptions of vitality.

Perceptions of vitality affect the degree to which nondominant groups feel empowered. Empowerment has been conceptualized several different ways (e.g., Albrecht, 1988; Bandura, 1997; Bormann, 1988; Pacanowsky, 1988). Broadly defined, empowerment is the process through which individuals perceive that they control their situations. In an extension of empowerment to the group level, Fawcett and colleagues (1996) define the concept as "the process of gaining influence over events and outcomes of importance to an individual, group, or community" (p. 2). More relevant to the present analysis is the fact that empowerment has been conceptualized as both a perception and a process. According to Chiles and Zorn (1995), "empowerment as a perception is the symbolic construction of one's personal state as characterized by competence, or the skill and ability to act effectively, and control, or the opportunity and authority to act" (p. 2). Although groups who perceive themselves as possessing relatively high vitality are likely to feel empowered, researchers know little about what might influence groups' perceptions of their vitality. Our purpose here is to articulate how television might function in this regard. We also address the implications of vitality perceptions by arguing that the extent to which members of nondominant groups perceive their group as vital will be manifested in the particular strategies of change they employ to challenge the status hierarchy (Tajfel & Turner, 1986). We offer not only a set of propositions regarding the influence of television on nondominant group vitality, but also how perceptions of vitality influence the strategies of change undertaken by nondominant groups. Since dominant groups are already empowered, our discussion of empowerment focuses primarily on media influence on striving nondominant groups.

INTERGROUP COMMUNICATION

According to social identity theory (e.g., Tajfel & Turner, 1986), we categorize the social world, others, and ourselves as members of various groups. The list of groups in which we claim membership are endless, including ethnicity, culture, gender, age, sexual orientation, social class, religion, occupation, and hobby groups. We define our social identity as the knowledge of our category memberships, together with the values (positive or negative) attached to them. Social identity has meaning only in comparison with other relevant outgroups. When thinking about ourselves as group members, we are likely to assess our group standing relative to others through the process of social comparison. According to Tajfel and Turner, the main motivation for social comparison is the desire for positive distinctiveness to gain self-esteem as group members. Social identity forms an important part of the self-concept, and it is assumed that we try to achieve a positive sense of social identity to make our own social group favorably distinct from other groups on important dimensions (e.g., power and economic or political resources). Achieving positive distinctiveness enables individuals to achieve a satisfactory social identity and enhance their own group's superiority.

The process by which groups engage in social comparison is purposeful. Because intergroup relations occur in context, we need to systematically analyze the relative sociostructural positions of groups. Beginning with the notion that one's sense of identity is bound up with various group memberships and individuals' desire to belong to distinct groups, numerous investigations have examined factors that influence intergroup relations. The concept of group vitality emerged out of the critical need for situating the social psychological processes underlying group communications within their proper sociostructural contexts (cf. Bourhis, 1979; Giles & Johnson, 1981).

Group Vitality: A Focus on Its Subjective Parameters

Giles et al. (1977) first introduced the concept of ethnolinguistic vitality to explore the sociostructural factors affecting ethnolinguistic behaviors, such as the degree to which in- and outgroup members accommodate each other. Over the years, vitality has grown from an ethnolinguistic concept to a theory used to address a broad range of issues related to ethnicity, age, gender, and intergroup communication and behavior (see Giles, 2001). Scholars have proposed three main factors that constitute a group's relative vitality and position in society: status, demography, and institutional support.

Status variables are those that pertain to a configuration of prestige variables for the group and consist of four factors: (a) economic status refers to the degree of control that a group has gained over its economic life, (b) social status refers to the degree of esteem a group affords itself, (c) sociohistorical status addresses the history of the group, and (d) language status refers to the prestige of a group's language and culture. The histories of some groups contain periods in which members struggled to defend, maintain, or assert their existence. Regardless of the outcome of such struggles, history can serve to empower as well as disempower groups. A group possesses high status if it has economic control over its destiny, consensually high self-esteem, and pride in its past.

Demography refers to the distribution and sheer number of group members (Giles et al., 1977). Eight demographic variables contribute to the vitality of a group. Group distribution factors refer to the numeric concentration of group members in a particular territory, country, or region; the proportion of group members relative to outgroup members; and whether the group occupies its own traditional or national homeland. Number factors refer to the absolute numbers of members belonging to a group, a group's birthrate in relation to the outgroup's, the extent to which mixed marriages between ingroups and outgroups are taking place, and whether large numbers immigrate to or emigrate from the group. Guided by the notion of strength in numbers, large groups possess more vitality.

Institutional support refers to the degree to which a group has gained formal and informal representation in the various institutions of a nation, region, or community (Giles et al., 1977). Informal support is the extent to which a group has organized itself as a pressure group to represent and safeguard its own interests in state and private activities. Formal support refers to whether members of a particular group have gained positions of control at decision-making levels in government, business, mass media, and religious and cultural domains. Groups who have both formal and informal support have considerable leverage, and hence high vitality. Findings by Sachdev and Bourhis (1985, 1991) that showed how dominant group members used their power to establish advantages over nondominant groups illustrate the importance of garnering institutional support. Because dominant groups are likely to discount nondominant groups in decision making, and even disempower them of a strong vitality if they control the agencies of the media, nondominant groups need to achieve and maintain institutional support.

The more representation members of a group have in these three areas (i.e., status, demography, and institutional support), the more vitality they are said to have (Kraemer, 1993; Landry, Allard, & Theberge, 1991). A group's strengths and weaknesses in each of the domains can be assessed so as to provide a rough classification of groups having low, medium, or high vitality. Giles et al. (1977) propose that the more vitality a group has, the more likely the group is to survive as a distinctive collectivity in intergroup settings. Groups with low vitality are not expected to thrive and may ultimately be assimilated into the dominant group (see Allard & Landry, 1986).

In their initial treatise, Giles et al. (1977) distinguish objective from subjective vitality. Objective group vitality refers to actual available data on group memberships and activities. Groups' strengths and weaknesses on the three dimensions of vitality can be measured objectively to provide an overall assessment. Subjective vitality is defined as group members' assessments of their own and other groups' vitality with regard to their relative sociostructural positions. For example, contrary to quantifiable data, a particular social group may perceive it has less demographic strength relative to an outgroup (Barker et al., 2001).

Research over the past 25 years suggests that perceptions of dominant and nondominant groups sometimes match objective estimates on vitality dimensions (e.g., Bourhis & Sachdev, 1984; Giles & Johnson, 1987) and at other times do not match objective vitality (e.g., Pierson, Giles, & Young, 1987; Sachdev, Bourhis, Phang & D'Eye, 1987). Therefore, vitality is not a static given but a malleable social construction depending on group membership and the prevailing sociopolitical climate. Because groups in contact can manifest different vitality profiles of the same intergroup setting (see Harwood et al., 1994) and because Giles et al. (1977) contended that "a groups' subjective assessment of its vitality may be as important as the objective reality" (p. 318), we thereby concluded to focus herein upon the concept of subjective vitality.

According to vitality theorists, the more vitality individuals believe their social group possesses, the more likely they will be to invest their energies in preserving the group's identity, activities, and influences (Sachdev & Bourhis, 1993). Self-appraisals of relative vitalities are engendered by the everyday experiences of group members in an array of contexts such as schools, the workplace, and via the media. Landry and Bourhis (1997) developed the concept of the linguistic landscape, an aggregate of the language of public signs, symbols, billboards, street names, mail advertising, government information, and notifications. This concept serves as information about the linguistic characteristics of the region, city, or neighborhood, and can symbolize the relative communicative vitality of competing groups. For dominant groups, the provision of signs, materials, or advertising in languages other than their own may fuel discrimination. When linguistic and symbolic markers of demographic change begin to appear in a community traditionally dominated by one social or ethnolinguistic group, uncertainty may trigger and contribute to a disempowering of members of that group. For instance, if Anglo Americans believe that the Spanish language is likely to overwhelm the linguistic landscape—even if objective evidence suggests otherwise—they may take combative steps to limit the promotion and use of Spanish (cf. Barker et al., 2001).

One ubiquitous landscape force in Western society that can shape the vitality construction process is television. This medium is an appropriate one for us to examine for several reasons. First, the portrayals of nondominant groups on television have long been a concern (e.g., Dominick & Greenberg, 1970). Second, television (at least for Americans) is the most common source of information and entertainment (Signorielli & Bacue, 1999). Television has the ability to tell us stories about people, places, and ideas that we would otherwise be unable to experience. In so doing, television instructs us on power, inequality, and fate. It is a medium that can empower as well as disempower. According to Signorielli and Bacue, "it lets us know who is good and who is bad, who wins and who loses" (1999, p. 528). With this idea in mind, the manner in which social groups are represented and treated on television is of particular importance.

REPRESENTATION OF NONDOMINANT GROUPS IN TELEVISION

How television represents groups in society is of particular interest considering that television is often used with the specific purpose of learning about different groups (see Ferguson & Perse, 2000, who extend this motive to newer media technologies; Rubin, 1983). Early content analysis studies typically concluded that the majority of characters on television were White, middle-class, and male (Blosser, 1988; Downing, 1974; Graves, 1980; Spurlock, 1982). Nondominant groups such as ethnic minorities, the poor, the aged, children, and women were traditionally underrepresented, stereotyped, or inaccurately portrayed (Gerbner & Signorielli, 1979; Kubey, 1980; McNeil, 1975; Seggar, 1975; Seggar & Wheeler, 1973; Tedesco, 1974). Signorielli (1981) noted "a basic and consistent finding of this research is that most specific minority groups—Blacks, Hispanics, Native Americans, women, the elderly, the handicapped, etc.—are underrepresented" (p. 99). Gerbner and Gross (1976) introduced the concept of symbolic annihilation to describe the absence of nondominant social groups in early media representations (cf. Tuchman, 1978).

The question remains as to whether or not much has changed in the past few decades. Recent literature does suggest some adjustment of the television landscape. In part, this is because nondominant groups have criticized television networks for lack of representation and stereotypical portrayals. Additionally, because networks realized that expanding their target audience boosts profit (Haley, 1997), producers have increased the frequency of representation as well as the nature of portrayals of various nondominant groups on television (Mastro & Greenberg, 2000). Greenberg and Collette (1997) note that "occasional shifts, where the number of women, blacks, or others appear with greater frequency, may result from network attempts to reach a targeted audience" (p. 10). Because of technological advances such as cable and digital signaling, media companies now have the capability to capture select markets or demographics. As a result of trying to capture diverse markets, nondominant groups have the opportunity to select television shows that represent and positively portray their group. For example, Brown and Campbell (1986) found that Blacks were more likely than Whites to be shown in optimistic scenarios on music videos shown on Black Entertainment Television (BET) than on Music Television Video (MTV). Conversely, on MTV, women and Blacks remained minorities. The analysis suggests that Blacks who tune into BET are likely to be presented with a different picture than Blacks who tune into MTV.

Representation of many ethnic minorities fall far below actual population estimates, however, data indicate the number of African Americans on television actually exceeds population estimations (Greenberg & Collette, 1997). For instance, African Americans are estimated to make up 12% of the population, but Mastro and Greenberg (2000) found that African Americans played 16% of the main and minor roles in prime-time television. They argue that African Americans "have achieved a representative niche in prime time" (p. 699). Concomitantly, two relatively new broadcast networks, United Paramount Network (UPN) and Warner Brothers (WB), market and program heavily to African Americans. Nielsen ratings indicate that these networks have captured a large segment of the African American audience. In African American households, 8 of the 10 highest rated prime-time television programs are on either UPN or WB (Nielsen Media Research, 2002). These networks are in addition to entire cable television stations devoted to ethnic minorities. Kubey, Shifflet, Weerakkody, and Ukeiley (1995) found that the percentage of African Americans on cable television was 6.6%; however, when they included BET in the analysis, the percentage increased to 11%. Additionally, when they included Spanish-language channels in their analysis, the proportion of Hispanics increased dramatically.

Despite increases in the number of African Americans present on television, for some ethnic minorities depictions remain inconsistent with population figures (Atkin, 1992). Latinos constitute approximately 12% of the U.S. population, but Mastro and Greenberg (2000) found that Latinos comprised only 3% of main characters in prime-time television programs. Asian Americans, who constitute 4% of the general population, accounted for only 1% of the television population. Native Americans also were unrepresented. These findings are indicative of why no study of Native Americans or Asian Americans on television provides sufficient numbers of portrayals to permit any conclusion other than that they continue to be invisible, typically falling in the 1% range.

In addition to the frequency of ethnic minorities on television, researchers continue to track role type and ethnic stereotyping. Again evidence indicates improving images of ethnic minorities. In their content analysis of prime-time television shows, Mastro and Greenberg (2000) found that Hispanic Americans had the same income, intelligence, physical bulk, and cleanliness as their White and African American counterparts. They did not find the previously dominant stereotypes of Hispanic Americans as dirty and dumb. Elasmar, Hasegawa, and Brain (1999) found in their analysis of prime time that 11% of African Americans had white-collar, professional positions compared to 10% of Whites. However, Greenberg and Collette (1997) found that although African Americans are overrepresented relative to population estimates, they are still stereotyped as lazy and unintelligent (cf. Mastro & Greenberg, 2000).

Minority presence on television might be dependent on television genre. In her content analysis of reality-based police shows, Oliver (1994) found that the number of African American police officers was underrepresented in comparison to the Department of Labor's statistics, whereas percentages of African Americans as perpetrators on reality programs was overestimated compared to the FBI's Uniform Crime Reports. Dixon and Linz (2000) found similar results on television news (cf. Entman, 1992, 1994). They found that, in comparison to crime reports, African Americans were overrepresented as perpetrators of crime on television news (according to crime reports 21% of crimes were committed by African Americans compared to 37% as represented by television news). These findings reveal that television is still perpetuating a negative ethnic stereotype of African Americans. Clearly, recent research on the frequencies and images of ethnic minorities is equivocal. Perhaps more importantly, the reviewed literature suggests images of ethnic groups vary according to genre.

Existing literature suggests the aged, a group considered to watch the most television, are underrepresented on television (Greenberg & Collette, 1997; Robinson & Skill, 1995). Bell (1992) observed a "continuing wide gap between TV demographics and the real demographics of the American population" (p. 311). Although data clearly indicate that the elderly are underrepresented on television, it is unclear whether they are represented positively or negatively. Kubey et al. (1995) found that the aged were underrepresented relative to their actual numbers in the population but were positively portrayed. Dail (1988) found that programs portrayed older people positively on family-oriented television programs (cf. Bell, 1992). Yet, Bishop and Krause (1984) found that older persons were portrayed negatively and stereotypically on Saturday morning television.

The literature continues to indicate that male characters outnumber female characters (Elasmar et al., 1999; Lauzen & Dozier, 1999), and some portrayals of women on television remain stereotypical (e.g., Eaton, 1997; Elasmar et al., 1999; Lauzen & Dozier, 1999; Steenland, 1995). Nonetheless, images of women have improved over the past 30 years (Signorielli & Bacue, 1999). Women appear more frequently on television (Greenberg & Collette, 1997) and more women are being presented outside the home and in more prestigious occupations (Elasmar et al., 1999; Signorielli & Bacue, 1999). Lauzen and Dozier (1999) found that men and women exhibited similar patterns of powerful language use (i.e., turns at talk, first word in conversation, last word in conversation, interrupting, and advice giving).

Historically, television entertainment content has reflected dominant groups in a positive light, whereas programs have portrayed nondominant groups in either a negative light or not at all. In the past, nondominant group members have been generally unable to see frequent and positive representations of their groups on television. However, during the past decade, this symbolic annihilation has declined. The frequency of appearance of nondominant group members has increased, as has the extent to which they are portrayed positively. The increasing number of specialized television channels, as well as the desire of advertisers to market directly to more targeted subgroups for various products and services, may be responsible for this change. Although content providing positive and frequent representations of nondominant group members are more accessible to the viewing audience today than in the past, room for improvement for most nondominant groups remains.

TELEVISION AND SUBJECTIVE VITALITY

Intergroup researchers have called for the investigation of how mass media influence perceptions of vitality (Harwood et al., 1994; Landry & Allard, 1994). Television can provide information that may be used to form beliefs about various groups in society, such as (a) the number and characteristics of their members, (b) public support for the groups, and (c) the type of behaviors in which group members engage. These beliefs form the foundations of subjective group vitality. Concomitantly, theory from the area of mass communication suggests that the nature of television portrayals can have important implications for the beliefs of viewers. In the early 1970s, one group of researchers began studying the potential effects of television on audience's beliefs about social reality (e.g., Gerbner, 1973). At the same time, another group of researchers were examining what audiences do with television (Katz, Blumler, & Gurevitch, 1974) instead of looking at how television affects audiences. Although both of these theoretical traditions can be used to enhance our understanding of how television can influence group subjective vitality, they lead us to potentially different conclusions about the effects of television on subjective vitality. In the following section, we discuss cultivation as well as uses and gratifications (with a focus on social identity gratifications), in the context of how television content might shape subjective vitality.

Cultivation

One of the most prominent theories in mass communication, cultivation (Gerbner, 1973), may assist in understanding how television may negatively shape perceptions of vitality for nondominant groups. Cultivation theory directly addresses how the pervasive themes contained in television content can impact beliefs about the nature of society. Cultivation analysis is one component of a larger, ongoing research program called cultural indicators (Gerbner, 1969). The cultural indicators approach has three subcomponents. The first, *institutional process analysis*, examines how media messages are selected, produced, and distributed. *Message system analysis* examines the content of television, especially the portrayal of violence, minorities, gender roles, and occupations. The third component, *cultivation analy-*

sis, explores the extent to which viewing television content contributes to audience members' conceptions about the real world. The central proposition of cultivation theory is that individuals who are exposed to greater amounts of television will exhibit perceptions and beliefs that reflect the views presented on television (Gerbner, Gross, Morgan, & Signorielli, 1980, 1994).

The psychological process behind the influence of television on social reality perceptions has been debated for over a decade. The explanation with the most empirical support is founded on theories of human information processing developed in cognitive psychology. As part of their heuristic model of cultivation effects, Shrum and O'Guinn (1993; Shrum, 1995, 1996) argued that cultivation effects can be explained by two common psychological concepts: *construct accessibility* and the *availability heuristic*.

Construct accessibility refers to the ease with which individuals are able to recall various ideas and events from memory. Two variables are thought to be the primary determinants of construct accessibility: the recency of activation of the construct and the frequency of its activation. If certain issues, images, types of people, or events occur frequently on television, heavy television viewers will have these constructs activated frequently in their memory. The more time one spends watching television, the more recent any given memorial activation of a concept occurring frequently on television will be. Constructs that are commonly viewed on television will be high in accessibility for heavy television viewers by contrast to light television viewers.

The availability heuristic pertains to how individuals make judgments about the relative commonness of various types of people or behaviors. Most individuals do not devote tremendous mental effort to making most judgments. Instead, they use judgmental heuristics to simplify judgment tasks. One such heuristic is the availability heuristic. When asked to estimate the percentage of the population that has been the victim of crime, individuals do not attempt to conduct a full memory search for relevant statistics. Nor do they engage in a systematic assessment of all the individuals with which they are familiar regarding whether or not these individuals have been victims of a crime. Instead, they simplify the task by making use only of instances that come to mind easily. If a certain instance comes easily to mind, the person infers that this instance is a common event and the overall frequency of the event is rated as relatively high. If an instance does not come to mind easily, the instance is believed to be infrequent and is thus rated relatively low.

When put together, the notion of construct accessibility and the availability heuristic explain why heavy television viewers believe that the real world is like the world they see on television. Heavy viewing makes concepts portrayed on television easily accessible in memory. These easily accessible concepts are then the ones most likely to be used in making judgments about the frequency of events. Events that come easily to mind are considered to be more frequent or common. Thus, images, ideas, and events that individuals often and recently see on television are believed to be common in the real world. Because individuals do not often separate the source of information from the message when that information is re-trieved from memory (Mares, 1996), fictional television content and the real world commingle. Given this explanation (Shrum, 1995, 1996, 2001; Shrum & O'Guinn, 1993), we propose the following axiom:[2]

> Axiom 1: Heavy viewers of television will believe that reality is consistent with the content of television that they view over the course of time.

Cultivation theory assumes that television contains various common and under-lying themes. Although cultivation is most commonly associated with studies of media influence on perceptions of violence, many scholars have examined the communication of power through television content. The theory has been used to understand better the role of television in the development of perceptions of gen-der equality (Zemach & Cohen, 1986), physicians and attorneys (Pfau, Mullen, Diedrich, & Garrow, 1995; Pfau, Mullen, & Garrow, 1995), politics (Volgy & Schwarz, 1980), American stereotypes and ethnic groups (Allen & Thornton, 1992; Tan, 1982), and attitudes or beliefs about marriage, sex, and sex roles (McGhee & Frueh, 1980; Morgan & Rothschild, 1983; Rosenwasser, Lingenfelter, & Harrington, 1989; Signorielli, 1991; Signorielli & Lears, 1992; Ward & Rivadeneyra, 1999).

According to cultivation theorists, all networks serve the same social system and depend on the same markets and programming formulas. All viewers are ex-posed to the same underlying messages, regardless of the content and genre of the program (Signorielli, 1986). Thus, the television landscape is rather homogeneous. Cultivation theory assumes that viewers are nonselective in their television view-ing; that is, they tend to view television by the clock (Signorielli & Morgan, 2001). As a result, television viewers are exposed to stable, repetitive, and pervasive pat-terns of images and ideologies. Cultivation theorists maintain that rather than chal-lenge or weaken conventional conceptions, beliefs, and behaviors, television serves to extend and maintain established order in society (Morgan & Signorielli, 1990). Morgan and Shanahan (1997) claim that television

> messages set the hidden but pervasive boundary conditions for social discourse, wherein cul-tural ground rules for what exists, what is important, what is right, and so on, are repeated (and ritualistically consumed) so often that they become invisible. The model for cultivation is "enculturation," not persuasion. (p. 5)

Cultivation theorists are interested in the aggregate patterns of images and re-peated representations of individuals over long periods of time (Shanahan, Mor-gan, & Stenbjerre, 1997) and are not concerned with the impact of any one particu-lar program, genre, or episode. Cultivation theory focuses not on the portrayal of specific characters in specific programs but rather on the common and repetitive patterns of television content and characteristics of television characters across channels, genres, and programs over time. With regard to nondominant groups, cultivation researchers have argued that they are generally less likely to appear as significant characters on television than their numbers in reality would suggest. When nondominant groups are portrayed on television, their roles are not necessarily positive roles. This observation is true, they would claim, even in a changing environment in which more frequent and positive portrayals of nondominant groups are available on television.

Axiom 2: Television contains an overarching message that presents dominant views and current norms as more frequent or more favorable than nondominant views and challenges to current norms.

Cultivation theorists would argue that, because viewers are nonselective and because the overarching theme behind television generally supports majority group dominance, time spent viewing television would produce negative perceptions of nondominant groups. Television maintains the existing power structure by communicating the negative value of nondominant group members and sometimes denying their very existence.

Along the same lines, vitality theorists argue that one way of maintaining the status hierarchy is through television, especially if the media are owned and operated by members of the dominant group. As Giles et al. (1977) argued, "It is possible for dominant groups to manipulate the information reaching nondominant groups through the mass media (if not the factors directly themselves) in such a manner as to attenuate their perception of vitality" (p. 318). Using the terms of subjective vitality, because television presents a rather homogeneous landscape of life, either underrepresenting or stereotypically representing nondominant group members, television manipulates status and demography factors, as well as institutional support of nondominant groups. As Signorielli and Morgan (2001) explain, "the world of television shows and tells us about life—people, places, striving power, fate, and family life. It presents the good and bad, the happy and sad, the powerful and the weak, and lets us know who or what is a success or a failure" (p. 335). Guided by the assumption that media stereotypes can shape audience impressions and become reality for groups' members and audiences, Tan and Tan (1979) reasoned that negative stereotypes might be an important factor in shaping negative self-images of group members. They found that Blacks who watched more fictional television were more likely to report low self-esteem than Blacks who watched less fictional television (cf. Allen & Hatchett, 1986; Stroman, 1986). High entertainment television viewing among White participants was not related to low self-esteem (Tan & Tan, 1979). These results illustrate that low self-esteem is not a characteristic of all heavy fictional television viewers.

The impact of television on self-concept is not limited to Blacks. Korzenny and Neuendorf (1980) reported similar findings for elderly people. Kiecolt and Sayles (1988) surmised that television might help to legitimate the unequal status of nondominant groups by subtly conveying messages about their status relative to that of dominant groups. Thus, they examined whether heavy exposure to television affected nondominant groups. Their findings revealed that exposure to crime dramas decreased women's and Blacks' personal efficacy. The data indicated that viewing crime dramas increased White males' tendency to endorse individualistic explanations for gender equality and poverty, as well as depressing their awareness of Black power deprivation. The data of this study indicated nondominant group members are likely to be affected by television, as are the perceptions that others have about nondominant groups. More generally, evidence suggests that television can negatively affect nondominant group members.

Cultivation is "an attempt to say something about the more broad-based ideological consequences of a commercially supported cultural industry celebrating consumption, materialism, individualism, power, and the status quo along lines of gender, race, class, and age" (Shanahan et al., 1997, p. 309). Cultivation theory attempts to explain what television does to the audience. Although the effects of television on perceptions of group vitality in particular have yet to be empirically examined, television may function to decrease perceptions of group vitality among nondominant groups. If nondominant group members infrequently appear on television, then perceptions of demographic vitality should be affected. Nondominant group members who do appear on television may be subjected to stereotypical portrayals. Because dominant groups are more likely to be shown in positions of power on television, status perceptions of nondominant groups are likely to be influenced. If television celebrates the dominant group's culture, values, rituals, and customs, nondominant groups are likely to assume they possess low institutional support. The extent to which nondominant group members are viewing negative and infrequent portrayals of their group is likely to influence their perceptions of vitality. Thus, based on cultivation theory, we advance the following proposition:

Proposition 1 (Axiom 1 + Axiom 2): Nondominant group members who are heavy television viewers (and who are largely nonselective in their viewing habits) will have lower levels of subjective vitality than those who are light viewers of television.

Uses and Gratifications

A nagging challenge to cultivation theory is the assumption that television viewing is nonselective (Hawkins & Pingree, 1981; Perse, 1986; Rubin, Perse, & Taylor, 1988). Other perspectives in mass communication question the notion of a nonselective audience. Like cultivation, the uses and gratifications (U&G) perspective also addresses the relationship between television and the audience, but from a different angle. The U&G approach asks the question: What do audience members do with media? The U&G perspective views the audience as generally (although variably) active and selective. If individuals are selective in their viewing habits, what factors might lead them to view particular television content and how might the content differ compared to nonselective viewers? The following discussion addresses how selectivity in the use of television content might function to increase perceptions of group vitality, and lead to empowerment.

The U&G approach focuses on audience involvement with mass media. This approach seeks to replace the image of the passive receiver, inferred from traditional effects research, with one of "a person who could actively bend programs, articles, films, and songs to his own purposes" (Blumler, 1979, p. 10). A U&G perspective of television viewing emerged from early work on how people use media. The perspective challenges cultivation assumptions by contending that all television does not contain the same messages and because of people's social circumstances and roles, not all viewers watch the same programs (Blumler, 1979; Perse, 1986).

The core assumption of the U&G approach is that audience members use television to satisfy their individual needs and goals. Individuals have expectations about television content and the ability of television to satisfy needs, and they construct lines of action in order to achieve gratifications (Canary & Spitzberg, 1993; Greenberg & Woods, 1999; Kim & Rubin, 1997; Perse & Rubin, 1990; Rubin, 1994; Ward & Rivadeneyra, 1999).

In his early writings about the U&G approach, Blumler (1979; cf. Conway & Rubin, 1991; Kippax & Murray, 1980; Weaver, 1980) articulated three audience orientations that drive media use: *cognitive* (surveillance and information gathering), *diversion* (boredom relief or entertainment), and *personal identity* (salience of personal experiences). Although Blumler limits his orientation to personal identity semantically, his discussion extends to *social identity*. He contends that "people's media requirements would also vary systematically according to their differing social roles and situations" (p. 21). Blumler (1985) wrote more explicitly about the relationship between media use and social identity, noting that "little attention has been paid to the social group memberships and affiliations, formal and subjective, that might feed audience concerns to maintain and strengthen their social identities through what they see, read, and hear in the media" (p. 50). Over the years, research has indirectly addressed the issue of social identity in media use (Bleise, 1986; Katz, Gurevitch, & Hass, 1973; Mundorf & Brownell, 1990). Although this work illustrates the importance of media in intergroup relations and in particular how social group membership is related to media use, these studies interpret gratifications based on an intra- or interpersonal perspective (for an exception see Lull, 1985) rather than an intergroup perspective.

Harwood (1997) observed the lacunae in the literature and asserted that the U&G perspective and social identity theory "seem ripe for some theoretical integration" (p. 204). His notion of social identity gratifications (SIG) provides an additional motivation for media choices beyond those commonly examined by U&G researchers. He argued that individuals may seek out particular media messages that support their social identities and avoid messages that do not support their identities. In an initial test of this hypothesis, Harwood investigated the relationship between media selection and age identity. He hypothesized that individuals will seek out television shows that represent the age of the viewer. Employing both a content analysis and an experiment, Harwood found that across all age groups (child, younger adult, and older adult) television viewers demonstrate a preference for viewing television characters of their own age—even when the content of the program is controlled. This study provides initial support for the theoretical suggestion that social identity is a determinant of television use (cf. Davis & Westbrook, 1985). The literature also supports the idea that some nondominant group members prefer shows that feature television characters of their group (Greenberg & Atkin, 1982; Kielwasser & Wolf, 1994). Harwood proposed that SIG might be the underlying reason why some nondominant group members prefer to view television shows featuring their own group. In subsequent research, Harwood (1999) confirmed that SIG was a reason for television viewing.

The central thesis of the U&G approach is that individuals make choices about media use to satisfy their individual needs. In addition to television meeting diversion, entertainment, information, and personal needs, television also meets social identity needs. Harwood's (1999) findings suggest that an outcome of viewing television based on social identity needs is a reinforced social identity or an increase in one's sense of belonging to a group. We extend this approach by proposing that another outcome of viewing television shows based on SIG is an increase in subjective group vitality. This effect would be related to content, for example, those selecting television based on SIG compared to those selecting television at random or based on some other motivation. Contrary to cultivation theory's claim that television messages are homogeneous and contribute to the symbolic annihilation of nondominant groups, we argue that changes in the television landscape over the years now permit members of many groups to select television based on SIG and use television to increase their perceptions of ingroup vitality.

To elaborate, for those who use media based on SIG, television content may be significantly different compared to the nonselective viewer assumed by cultivation theory. Cultivation theory suggests that all viewers are getting the same underlying message—even if they select content from different genres or programs. U&G research suggests that viewers will select content, when possible, to meet their needs. When their needs are for social identity, individuals will attempt to select content that reflects positively on their group. To the extent that such content is available, these audience members will experience a much different television landscape than the nonselective audience members assumed by cultivation.

The underlying assumption of nondominant groups selecting television based on SIG is that nondominant group members will have television shows with sufficient representations of their social group to view. The television shows that nondominant group members choose are assumed to represent their group positively. For certain groups, such as African Americans and Hispanics, selecting television shows that meet identity needs is easier than other groups. As reported above, some groups are simply ignored by the media. Given the current television landscape, the influence of television may not operate uniformly on perceptions of vitality. If a particular nondominant group has the option to select from only a handful of television shows, perceptions of institutional support may increase, but perceptions of demography are unaffected.

Although the particulars about how television might shape perceptions of reality will vary and be unique to each group, the argument that television has the potential to influence subjective vitality remains. As change continues to come from the television industry trying to attract nondominant groups who represent untapped economic blocks, many nondominant groups who seek out representation of their group via television should find shows to view. The advent of cable and digital television is making this easier for media organizations. For instance, in January of 2002, media conglomerate Viacom announced plans for a 24-hour gay and lesbian cable channel. The channel is slated to be a joint venture between Showtime and MTV—two networks that are already known for their gay and lesbian friendly programming. MTV consultant Matt Farber remarked, "The gay community probably represents something north of 10 million adults. That represents significant buying power. Whenever you connect with and give a voice to people, it's always a good business plan" (Meers, 2002, p. 56). If television continues to target specific audiences, then more and more nondominant groups may have the opportunity to view television shows that represent their group frequently and positively. As Harwood (1999) explains, "One way in which positive social comparisons are possible is through viewing media messages featuring positive portrayals of individuals we identify as 'ingroup' members" (p. 125). By comparison to those who view nonselectively, nondominant group members who choose television programs in order to meet their social identity needs are likely to be exposed to television messages that may positively affect their perceptions of group vitality. The nondominant group is likely to be presented as one with status, high numbers, and support from various institutions. Toward that end, we propose the following axiom:

Axiom 3: Members of nondominant groups for whom there are sufficiently frequent and positive portrayals on television—and who select television in order to meet their SIG—will be exposed to content that conveys positive images of their group's vitality.

Nothing in the U&G perspective would necessarily contradict the broad notion of the effects of television as described in cultivation theory. The influence of television portrayals on perceptions of social reality and in particular perceptions of various groups in society would be the same for both theories in all senses but one. Since the nature of the content is central to producing effects in cultivation, what is different from the U&G perspective is the nature of the television world. If the content is reasonably available (even if not predominant) for those using SIG to select primarily positive and frequent representations of their social groups, heavy television viewing could encourage more positive perceptions of one's nondominant group, rather than more negative perceptions as suggested by traditional cultivation theory. That is, from either perspective we can claim that perceptions of reality are cultivated by viewing television, but cultivation argues that perceptions of vitality are likely to disempower nondominant groups, whereas from the U&G perspective we can derive the expectation that selecting television according to SIG will empower members of nondominant groups. At this juncture, Axioms 1 and 3 combine to form our second proposition:

Proposition 2 (Axiom 1 + Axiom 3): Nondominant group members who are heavy television viewers (and are selective in their viewing for SIG motives) will have higher levels of subjective vitality than those who are light viewers of television.

SUBJECTIVE VITALITY AND INTERGROUP BEHAVIOR

We should not underestimate the significance of a group's perceived vitality. As Bourhis, Giles, and Rosenthal (1981) asserted, "Subjective vitality data may provide advance indication that a particular minority group is to mobilize in an ethnic revival phase not otherwise foreseeable solely on the basis of 'objective' vitality information" (p. 147). Additionally, intergroup behavior is mediated by the individual's cognitive representations of the social conditions that affect him or her (Farr & Moscovici, 1984; Moscovici, 1981). Bourhis et al. (1981) argued further that a group's subjective assessment of its own and outgroup vitality is crucial in determining patterns of intergroup behavior (see also Giles, Rosenthal, & Young, 1985; Inglis & Gudykunst, 1982). What follows is a discussion of the implications of nondominant group vitality perceptions and propositions regarding how perceptions of vitality might contribute to nondominant group behavior.

One of the first empirical examinations of the relationship between subjective vitality perceptions and intergroup behavior involved linguistic behavior. Bourhis and Sachdev (1984) found support for their hypothesis that group members who perceived that they had high vitality were more likely to use their own language more frequently (e.g., divergence) in a wider range of settings than group members who perceived they had low vitality. Subsequent literature also supports the notion that subjective vitality perceptions influence language behavior (cf. Clachar, 1997; Hogg & Rigoli, 1996; Kraemer, Olshtain, & Badier, 1994; Yagmur, De Bot, & Korzilius, 1999). Findings suggest that the higher group members' perceive their vitality, the more likely they are to use divergent language patterns. These findings agree with Harwood et al. (1994), who proposed that

group members who perceive their ingroup to have high vitality will tend to converge little towards outgroup members, whereas group members who perceive their ingroup to have low vitality will tend to converge toward the outgroup, and especially so if their identification with their own group is low. (p. 318)

In their work on social identity theory, Tajfel and Turner (1986) talked more explicitly about intergroup behavior. As discussed earlier, they contend social identity only acquires meaning by comparison with other groups. They suggest that individuals have a desire to belong to groups that give them satisfaction and pride through membership. Intergroup comparisons will induce individuals to perceive and act in such a manner as to make their own group favorable and psychologically distinct from other groups. The theory explains that change will be desired when the existing intergroup situation provides members of a group with an inadequate or negative social identity. People who are members of dominant groups, and hence already derive a positive social identity, will not be motivated to change the relationship between their group and nondominant outgroups. Members of nondominant groups whose social identity is negative will desire change in an attempt to attain a more positive social identity. Studies have shown that nondominant ethnic groups who value their ingroup membership very strongly and construe their vitalities to be unreasonably lower than they should be differentiate communicatively from outgroup members (Giles & Johnson, 1987; Giles & Viladot, 1994).

Giles et al. (1977) were careful to acknowledge that the strategies employed by nondominant groups to increase their vitality will depend on group members' awareness that cognitive alternatives to the existing status relationship are possible between them and the superior group. Without the awareness of cognitive alternatives, members of a group may accept, albeit reluctantly, a negative social identity. Turner and Brown (1978) proposed that two independent factors contributed to a group's awareness of cognitive alternatives to existing intergroup situations: the perceived *stability-instability* (the extent to which individuals believe that their group's position in the status hierarchy can be changed or even reversed) and *legitimacy-illegitimacy* (the extent to which individuals construe their group's position in the status hierarchy to be fair and just). The intergroup strategies utilized by group members will depend largely on the degree to which a group perceives cognitive alternatives. Tajfel and Turner (1986) illustrated that quite different patterns of intergroup behaviors can be expected in circumstances where status and power differentials between groups are seen as unstable, illegitimate, and likely to change (Brown, 1986; Turner & Brown, 1978). The extent and nature of the relative vitality group members perceive their group to possess is likely to be an important mediator of the kinds of intergroup strategies they will be inclined to adopt.

A group may choose the first strategy, *group assimilation* (Tajfel & Turner, 1986), when they perceive low or no cognitive alternatives. Group assimilation distances an individual from the group that is causing them comparative discomfort into a more positively valued one, usually the dominant group. Toward this end, individuals will attempt to acquire or at least aspire toward the characteristics of the dominant group (e.g., homosexuals trying to pass as heterosexual). Because this strategy does not change the status of the group, the lower the perceived group vitality, the more likely group members will engage in assimilation strategies.

Axiom 4: Nondominant group members with perceptions of low group vitality will be more likely to engage in assimilation strategies.

We can now use Axiom 4 to build upon the relationships hypothesized in Proposition 1 and Proposition 2 to discuss the role of television in intergroup behavior. We can logically derive two new propositions, one driven by cultivation theory and the other driven by SIG, from the axioms and propositions that we have discussed so far. Interestingly, these two propositions are directly contrasting and thus are particularly ripe for future research. These propositions are also consistent with Chiles and Zorn's (1995) contention of empowerment as the opportunity and authority to act, and represent the extent to which nondominant groups feel empowered. Only when nondominant groups perceive they have the power to challenge or improve their standing on the status hierarchy will they attempt social change:

Proposition 3 (Proposition 1 + Axiom 4): Nondominant group members who are heavy television viewers (and who are largely nonselective in their viewing habits) will be more likely to engage in assimilation strategies than those who are light viewers of television.

Proposition 4 (Proposition 2 + Axiom 4): Nondominant group members who are heavy television viewers (and are selective in their viewing for SIG motives) will be less likely to engage in assimilation strategies than those who are light viewers of television.

Once group members who have a negative social identity become aware of cognitive alternatives, they are more likely to adopt *social creativity* strategies to change their status. The first social creativity strategy is the change group members make in their social comparison process. In particular, nondominant group members will cease making comparisons with the dominant group, and use other nondominant groups for comparison (e.g., Latinos comparing themselves with Blacks rather than Whites). Another strategy is to redefine or change the previously negatively valued characteristics of the group in a more positive direction (e.g., Black is beautiful). Nondominant group members can also compare themselves to the dominant group on a new dimension not previously used in intergroup comparisons and one that positively distinguishes the nondominant group from the dominant group (e.g., Asians strive for academic excellence). These strategies are least likely to be used by group members with very low or very high perceptions of group vitality, suggesting a nonlinear relationship between vitality perceptions and use of this strategy. Whereas group members with lower perceived group vitality are arguably more likely to engage in assimilation strategies, and group members with higher perceived group vitality are more likely to engage in social competition, group members with moderate vitality are most likely to use creativity strategies.

Axiom 5: Nondominant group members with perceptions of moderate group vitality will be more likely to engage in social creativity strategies.

Based on Axiom 5, another proposition can be offered. In this case, cultivation theory and SIG offer the same suggestion about how television impacts perceptions of nondominant group vitality. However, they come to the prediction from different theoretical directions:

Proposition 5 (Proposition 1 + Axiom 5 or Proposition 2 + Axiom 5): Nondominant group members who are moderate television viewers will be more likely to engage in social creativity strategies than those who are either heavy or light viewers of television.

Social competition, another strategy employed by nondominant groups, is more likely when group vitality perceptions are high and nondominant group members perceive their status, relative to the outgroup, as unstable and illegitimate. Group members may seek a positive social identity through direct competition with the outgroup. Through competition, nondominant groups will attempt to raise themselves to the position of the dominant group in order to achieve a positive social identity. Nondominant groups may try to reverse the relative positions of the ingroup and outgroup on salient dimensions (e.g., bilingual education).

Axiom 6: Nondominant group members with perceptions of high group vitality will be more likely to engage in social competition strategies.

We can employ Axiom 6, in conjunction with Propositions 1 and 2, to construct additional propositions to extend our understanding of the role of television in intergroup behavior. We offer two propositions. These final two propositions suggest contrasting hypotheses that may be fruitfully tested empirically.

Proposition 6 (Proposition 1 + Axiom 6): Nondominant group members who are heavy television viewers (and who are largely nonselective in their viewing habits) will be less likely to engage in social competition strategies than those who are light viewers of television.

Proposition 7 (Proposition 2 + Axiom 6): Nondominant group members who are heavy television viewers (and are selective in their viewing for SIG motives) will be more likely to engage in social competition strategies than those who are light viewers of television.

CONCLUSION

In their discussion of vitality, Harwood et al. (1994) called for future research to examine the diversity of forces influencing vitality perceptions. Because of its pervasiveness and the public's heavy use of it, television seems an important contributor to examine. Whereas researchers have previously alluded to the importance of mass media in transmitting messages concerning group vitality, we have attempted to elucidate the intricacies of the relationship. Based on mass communication theory, we presented propositions about how television shapes perceptions of group vitality. One set of these propositions contends that television *disempowers* nondominant groups while the other claims television may function to *empower* nondominant group members. Our approach also articulates the significance of group vitality in intergroup behavior. When nondominant groups perceive their vitality as high, they will likely engage in more active intergroup strategies to change the status hierarchy. If nondominant groups perceive their vitality as low, they are not expected to utilize active intergroup strategies. The propositions regarding intergroup behavior are consistent with the definition of empowerment as an action. Based on the propositions, scholars (intergroup and media) will hopefully be motivated to empirically examine the influence of television on subjective group vitality. Such research may reveal the importance of television to nondominant groups, as well as enable researchers to understand how mass media may function to influence intergroup behavior. The influence of television may not be based solely upon the amount of television viewed (Ward & Rivadeneyra, 1999). Instead, effects may be a function of the content to which viewers are exposed and whether individuals are selectively or nonselectively viewing content.

In addition to examining the audiences' active selection of information and entertainment from television, Bauer (1963) noted many years ago that researchers should also consider the notion that audiences avoid what they do not want. This observation is consistent with Harwood's (1997) discussion of SIG in which he contends that audiences avoid messages that do not support their social identities. Nondominant group members may actively avoid certain television content (whenever they can) in an effort to diminish the potentially deleterious effects of television. This avoidance may be especially true for those individuals who consider their group membership central to their self-concept. In their investigation of racial identity and media orientation, Allen and Bielby (1979) found that those with higher Black identity reported viewing less television. Possibly, nondominant group members who actively avoid certain television programs to preserve their group identity experience different perceptions of group vitality than those group members who do not actively avoid television, again due to the content to which they are ultimately exposed.

The framework provided here should apply to many nondominant group situations. Ethnic minorities as well as gays and lesbians are groups that seem especially ready for investigation. Although this particular chapter focused on the influence of television on nondominant groups, the proposed relationships may serve as a launch pad for an extended and broader program of research investigating the role of media on intergroup relations.

NOTES

1. We have chosen the label "nondominant" to refer to groups who lack social power. Although the term "subordinate" is sometimes used in the literature, we wanted to avoid the "less than" implication.

2. We employ the term *axiom* following Reynolds (1971). Reynolds notes that theories stated in axiomatic form include basic statements (axioms) from which all other theoretical statements can be generated through simple logic. The statements derived from axioms are termed *propositions*. Reynolds argues that although some scholars assume that to be an axiom a statement must have achieved the status of a scientific law, he points out that there is not common acceptance of this assumption. Moreover, if this standard is applied, there are few if any axioms that could be offered in the social sciences. Thus, we follow Zaller (1992) in offering axioms as statements supported by existing theory and research and then derive propositions from these axioms, in some cases in conjunction with other propositions.

REFERENCES

Albrecht, T. L. (1988). Communication and personal control in empowering organizations. In J. A. Anderson (Ed.), *Communication yearbook 11* (pp. 380–390). Newbury Park, CA: Sage.

Allard, R., & Landry, R. (1986). Subjective ethnolinguistic vitality viewed as a belief system. *Journal of Multilingual and Multicultural Development, 7*, 1–12.

Allen, R. L., & Bielby, W. T. (1979). Blacks' attitudes and behaviors toward television. *Communication Research, 6*, 437–462.

Allen, R. L., & Hatchett, S. (1986). The media and social reality effects: Self and system orientations of Blacks. *Communication Research, 13*, 97–123.

Allen, R. L., & Thornton, M. C. (1992). Social structural factors, Black media and stereotypical self-categorizations among African Americans. *National Journal of Sociology, 5*, 43–75.

Atkin, D. (1992). An analysis of television series with minority-lead characters. *Critical Studies in Mass Communication, 9*, 337–349.

Bandura, A. (1997). *Self-efficacy: The exercise of control.* New York: Freeman.

Barker, V., Giles, H., Noels, K., Duck, J., Hecht, M., & Clément, R. (2001). The English-only movement: A communication perspective. *Journal of Communication, 51*, 3–37.

Bauer, R. A. (1963). The initiative of the audience. *Journal of Advertising Research, 3*, 2–7.

Bell, J. (1992). In search of a discourse on aging: The elderly on television. *Gerontologist, 32*, 305–311.

Bishop, J. M., & Krause, D. R. (1984). Depictions of aging and old age on Saturday morning television. *Gerontologist, 24*, 91–94.

Bleise, N. W. (1986). Media in the rocking chair: Media uses and functions among the elderly. In G. Gumpert & R. Cathcart (Eds.), *Intermedia: Interpersonal communication in a media world* (pp. 573–582). New York: Oxford University Press.

Blosser, B. J. (1988). Ethnic differences in children's media use. *Journal of Broadcasting and Electronic Media, 32*, 453–470.

Blumler, J. G. (1979). The role of theory in uses and gratifications studies. *Communication Research, 6*, 9–36.

Blumler, J. G. (1985). The social character of media gratifications. In K. E. Rosengren, L. A. Wenner, & P. Palmgreen (Eds.), *Media gratifications research* (pp. 41–60). Beverly Hills, CA: Sage.

Bormann, E. G. (1988). "Empowering" as a heuristic concept in organizational communication. In J. A. Anderson (Ed.), *Communication yearbook 11* (pp. 391–404). Newbury Park, CA: Sage.

Bourhis, R. Y. (1979). Language in ethnic interaction: A social psychological perspective. In H. Giles & B. Saint-Jacques (Eds.), *Language and ethnic relations* (pp. 117–142). Oxford, UK: Pergamon.

Bourhis, R. Y., Giles, H., & Rosenthal, D. (1981). Notes on the construction of a "subjective vitality questionnaire" for ethnolinguistic groups. *Journal of Multilingual and Multicultural Development, 2*, 144–155.

Bourhis, R. Y., & Sachdev, I. (1984). Cross-cultural communication in Montreal: Two field studies since Bill 101. *International Journal of the Sociology of Language, 46*, 33–48.

Brown, J. D., & Campbell, K. (1986). Race and gender in music videos: The same beat but a different drummer. *Journal of Communication, 36*(1), 94–106.

Brown, R. J. (1986). *Social psychology: The second edition*. New York: Blackwell.

Canary, D. J., & Spitzberg, B. H. (1993). Loneliness and media gratifications. *Communication Research, 20*, 800–821.

Chiles, A. M., & Zorn, T. E. (1995). Empowerment in organizations: Employees' perceptions of the influences on empowerment. *Journal of Applied Communication Research, 23*, 1–25.

Clachar, A. (1997). Ethnolinguistic identity and Spanish proficiency in a paradoxical situation: The case of Puerto Rican return immigrants. *Journal of Multilingual and Multicultural Development, 18*, 107–124.

Conway, J. C., & Rubin, A. M. (1991). Psychological predictors of television viewing motivation. *Communication Research, 18*, 443–463.

Dail, P. W. (1988). Prime-time television portrayal of older adults in the context of family life. *Gerontologist, 28*, 700–706.

Davis, R. H., & Westbrook, G. J. (1985). Television in the lives of the elderly: Attitudes and opinions. *Journal of Broadcasting and Electronic Media, 29*, 209–214.

Dixon, T. L., & Linz, D. (2000). Overrepresentation and underrepresentation of African Americans and Latinos as lawbreakers on television news. *Journal of Communication, 50*(2), 131–154.

Dominick, J., & Greenberg, B. S. (1970). Mass media functions among low-income adolescents. In B. S. Greenberg & B. Dervin (Eds.), *Use of the mass media by the urban poor* (pp. 199–220). New York: Praeger.

Downing, M. (1974). Heroine of the daytime serial. *Journal of Communication, 24*(2), 130–137.

Eaton, C. (1997). Prime-time stereotyping on the new television networks. *Journalism & Mass Communication Quarterly, 74*, 859–872.

Elasmar, M., Hasegawa, K., & Brain, M. (1999). The portrayal of women in U.S. prime time television. *Journal of Broadcasting and Electronic Media, 43*, 20–34.

Entman, R. (1992). Blacks in the news: Television, modern racism, and cultural change. *Journalism Quarterly, 69*, 341–361.

Entman, R. (1994). Representation and reality in the portrayal of Blacks on network television news. *Journalism Quarterly, 71*, 509–520.

Farr, R. M., & Moscovici, S. (1984). *Social representations*. Cambridge, UK: Cambridge University Press.

Fawcett, S. B., Paine-Andrews, A., Francisco, V. T., Schulz, J. A., Richter, K. P., Lewis, R. K., et al. (1995). Using empowerment theory in collaborative partnerships for community health and development. *American Journal of Community Psychology, 23*, 677–689.

Ferguson, D. A., & Perse, E. M. (2000). The World Wide Web as a functional alternative to television. *Journal of Broadcasting and Electronic Media, 44*, 155–174.

Gerbner, G. (1969). Toward "cultural indicators": The analysis of mass mediated message systems. *AV Communication Review, 17*, 137–148.

Gerbner, G. (1973). Cultural indicators: The third voice. In G. Gerbner, L. Gross, & W. Melody (Eds.), *Communications technology and social policy* (pp. 555–573). New York: Wiley.

Gerbner, G., & Gross, L. (1976). Living with television: The violence profile. *Journal of Communication, 26*(2), 173–199.

Gerbner, G., Gross, L., Morgan, M., & Signorielli, N. (1980). The "mainstreaming" of America: Violence profile no. 11. *Journal of Communication, 30*(3), 10–29.

Gerbner, G., Gross, L., Morgan, M., & Signorielli, N. (1994). Growing up with television: The cultivation perspective. In J. Bryant & D. Zillmann (Eds.), *Media effects: Advances in theory and research* (pp. 17–41). Hillsdale, NJ: Erlbaum.

Gerbner, G., & Signorielli, N. (1979). *Women and minorities in television drama 1969–1978*. Philadelphia: University of Pennsylvania, Annenberg School of Communication.

Giles, H. (2001). Ethnolinguistic vitality. In R. Mesthrie (Ed.), *Concise encyclopedia of sociolinguistics* (pp. 472–473). Oxford, UK: Elsevier.

Giles, H., Bourhis, R. Y., & Taylor, D. M. (1977). Towards a theory of language in ethnic group relations. In H. Giles (Ed.), *Language, ethnicity, and intergroup relations* (pp. 307–348). London: Academic Press.

Giles, H., & Johnson, P. (1981). The role of language in ethnic group relations. In J. Turner & H. Giles (Eds.), *Intergroup behavior* (pp. 199–243). Oxford, UK: Blackwell.

Giles, H., & Johnson, P. (1987). Ethnolinguistic identity theory: A social-psychological approach to language maintenance. *International Journal of the Sociology of Language, 68,* 66–99.

Giles, H., Rosenthal, D., & Young, L. (1985). Perceived ethnolinguistic vitality: The Anglo- and Greek-Australian setting. *Journal of Multilingual and Multicultural Development, 6,* 253–269.

Giles, H., & Viladot, A. (1994). Ethnolinguistic identity in Catalonia. *Multilingual: Journal of Cross-Cultural and Interlanguage Communication, 13,* 301–312.

Graves, S. B. (1980). Psychological effects of Black portrayals on television. In S. B. Withey & R. P. Abeles (Eds.), *Television and social behavior: Beyond violence and children* (pp. 259–289). Hillsdale, NJ: Erlbaum.

Greenberg, B. S., & Atkin, C. (1982). Learning about minorities from television: A research agenda. In G. Berry & C. Mitchell-Kernan (Eds.), *Television and the socialization of the minority child* (pp. 215–243). New York: Academic Press.

Greenberg, B. S., & Collette, L. (1997). The changing faces on TV: A demographic analysis of network television's new seasons, 1966–1992. *Journal of Broadcasting and Electronic Media, 41,* 1–13.

Greenberg, B. S., & Woods, M. G. (1999). The soaps: Their sex, gratifications, and outcomes. *Journal of Sex Research, 36,* 250–257.

Haley, K. (1997). Cable channels seek promise of Hispanic market. *Broadcasting and Cable, 127,* 44–45.

Harwood, J. (1997). Viewing age: Lifespan identity and television viewing choices. *Journal of Broadcasting and Electronic Media, 41,* 203–213.

Harwood, J. (1999). Age identification, social identity gratifications, and television viewing. *Journal of Broadcasting and Electronic Media, 43,* 123–136.

Harwood, J., Giles, H., & Bourhis, R. Y. (1994). The genesis of vitality theory: Historical patterns and discoursal dimensions. *International Journal of the Sociology of Language, 108,* 167–206.

Hawkins, R. P., & Pingree, S. (1981). Uniform messages and habitual viewing: Unnecessary assumptions in social reality effects. *Human Communication Research, 7,* 291–301.

Hogg, M. A., & Rigoli, N. (1996). Effects of ethnolinguistic vitality, ethnic identification, and linguistic contacts on minority language use. *Journal of Language and Social Psychology, 15,* 76–89.

Inglis, M., & Gudykunst, W. (1982). Institutional completeness and communication acculturation. *International Journal of Intercultural Relations, 6,* 251–272.

Katz, E., Blumler, J. G., & Gurevitch, M. (1974). Utilization of mass communication by the individual. In J. G. Blumler & E. Katz (Eds.), *The uses of mass communications: Current perspectives on gratifications research* (pp. 19–32). Beverly Hills, CA: Sage.

Katz, E., Gurevitch, M., & Haas, H. (1973). On the uses of the mass media for important things. *American Sociological Review, 38,* 164–181.

Kiecolt, K. J., & Sayles, M. (1988). Television and the cultivation of attitudes toward subordinate groups. *Sociological Spectrum, 8,* 19–33.

Kielwasser, A. P., & Wolf, M. A. (1994). Silence, differences, and annihilation: Understanding the impact of mediated heterosexism on high school students. *High School Journal, 77,* 58–79.

Kim, J., & Rubin, A. M. (1997). The variable influence of audience activity on media effects. *Communication Research, 24,* 107–135.

Kippax, S., & Murray, J. P. (1980). Using the mass media: Need gratification and perceived utility. *Communication Research, 7,* 335–360.

Korzenny, F., & Neuendorf, K. (1980). Television viewing and self-concept of the elderly. *Journal of Communication, 30*(1), 71–80.

Kraemer, R. (1993). Social psychological factors related to the study of Arabic among Israeli high school students: A test of Gardner's socio-educational model. *Studies in Second Language Acquisition, 15,* 83–100.

Kraemer, R., Olshtain, E., & Badier, S. (1994). Ethnolinguistic vitality, attitudes, and networks of linguistic contact: The case of the Israeli Arab minority. *International Journal of the Sociology of Language, 108,* 79–95.

Kubey, R. W. (1980). Television and aging: Past, present and future. *Gerontologist, 20,* 16–35.

Kubey, R., Shifflet, M., Weerakkody, N., & Ukeiley, S. (1995). Demographic diversity on cable—Have the new cable channels made a difference in the representation of gender, race, and age? *Journal of Broadcasting and Electronic Media, 39,* 459–471.

Landry, R., & Allard, R. (1992). Ethnolinguistic vitality and the bilingual development of minority and majority group students. In W. Fase, K. Jaespaert, & S. Kroon (Eds.), *Maintenance and loss of minority languages* (pp. 223–251). Amsterdam: Benjamins.

Landry, R., & Allard, R. (1994). Diglossia, ethnolinguistic vitality, and language behavior. *International Journal of the Sociology of Language, 108,* 15–42.

Landry, R., Allard, R., & Theberge, R. (1991). School and family French ambiance and the bilingual development of Francophone western Canadians. *Canadian Modern Language Review, 47,* 878–915.

Landry, R., & Bourhis, R. Y. (1997). Linguistic landscape and ethnolinguistic vitality: An empirical study. *Journal of Language and Social Psychology, 16,* 23–49.

Lauzen, M. M., & Dozier, D. M. (1999). Making a difference in prime time: Women on screen and behind the scenes in the 1995–96 television season. *Journal of Broadcasting and Electronic Media, 43,* 1–19.

Lull, J. (1985). On the communicative properties of music. *Communication Research, 12,* 363–372.

Mares, M. L. (1996). The role of source confusions in television's cultivation of social reality judgments. *Human Communication Research, 23,* 278–297.

Mastro, D. E., & Greenberg, B. S. (2000). The portrayals of racial minorities on prime time television. *Journal of Broadcasting and Electronic Media, 44,* 690–703.

McGhee, P. E., & Frueh, T. (1980). Television viewing and the learning of sex-role stereotypes. *Sex Roles, 6,* 179–188.

McNeil, J. C. (1975). Feminism, femininity and the television series: A content analysis. *Journal of Broadcasting, 19,* 259–271.

Meers, E. (2002, March 5). We want our gay TV. *Advocate, 858,* 56–57.

Morgan, M., & Rothschild, N. (1983). Impact of the new television technology: Cable TV, peers, and sex-role cultivation in the electronic environment. *Youth and Society, 15,* 33–50.

Morgan, M., & Shanahan, J. (1997). Two decades of cultivation research: An appraisal and meta-analysis. In B. R. Burleson (Ed.), *Communication yearbook 20* (pp. 1–45). Thousand Oaks, CA: Sage.

Morgan, M., & Signorielli, N. (1990). Cultivation analysis: Conceptualization and methodology. In N. Signorielli & M. Morgan (Eds.), *Cultivation analysis: New directions in media effects research* (pp. 13–34). Newbury Park, CA: Sage.

Moscovici, S. (1981). On social representations. In J. Forgas (Ed.), *Social cognition: Perspectives on everyday understanding* (pp. 181–209). London: Academic Press.

Mundorf, N., & Brownell, W. (1990). Media preferences of older and younger adults. *Gerontologist, 30,* 685–692.

Nielsen Media Research. (2002). *The African American television audience.* Retrieved January 17th, 2002, from http://www.nielsenmedia.com/ethnicmeasure/african-american/programAA.html

Oliver, M. B. (1994). Portrayals of crime, race, and aggression in "reality-based" police shows: A content analysis. *Journal of Broadcasting and Electronic Media, 38,* 179–192.

O'Sullivan, P. B. (1999). Bridging the mass-interpersonal divide: Synthesis scholarship in HCR. *Human Communication Research, 25,* 569–588.

Pacanowsky, M. (1988). Communicating in the empowering organization. In J. A. Anderson (Ed.), *Communication yearbook 11* (pp. 356–379). Newbury Park, CA: Sage.

Perse, E. M. (1986). Soap opera viewing patterns of college students and cultivation. *Journal of Broadcasting and Electronic Media, 30,* 175–193.

Perse, E. M., & Rubin, A. M. (1990). Chronic loneliness and television use. *Journal of Broadcasting and Electronic Media, 34,* 37–53.

Pfau, M., Mullen, L. J., Deidrich, T., & Garrow, K. (1995). Television viewing and public perceptions of attorneys. *Human Communication Research, 21*, 307–330.

Pfau, M., Mullen, L. J., & Garrow, K. (1995). The influence of television viewing on public perceptions of physicians. *Journal of Broadcasting and Electronic Media, 39*, 441–458.

Pierson, H. D., Giles, H., & Young, L. (1987). Intergroup vitality perceptions during a period of political uncertainty: The case of Hong Kong. *Journal of Multilingual and Multicultural Development, 8*, 451–460.

Reynolds, P. D. (1971). *A primer in theory construction.* New York: Macmillan.

Robinson, J. D., & Skill, T. (1995). The invisible generation: Portrayals of the elderly on prime-time television. *Communication Reports, 8*, 111–119.

Rosenwasser, S. M., Lingenfelter, M., & Harrington, A. F. (1989). Nontraditional gender role portrayals on television and children's gender role perceptions. *Journal of Applied Developmental Psychology, 10*, 97–105.

Rubin, A. M. (1983). Television uses and gratifications: The interactions of viewing patterns and motivations. *Journal of Broadcasting, 27*, 37–51.

Rubin, A. M. (1994). Media uses and effects: A uses-and-gratifications perspective. In J. Bryant & D. Zillman (Eds.), *Media effects: Advances in theory and research* (pp. 417–436). Hillsdale, NJ: Erlbaum.

Rubin, A. M., Perse, E. M., & Taylor, D. S. (1988). A methodological examination of cultivation. *Communication Research, 15*, 107–134.

Sachdev, I., & Bourhis, R. Y. (1985). Social categorization and power differentials in group relations. *European Journal of Social Psychology, 15*, 415–434.

Sachdev, I., & Bourhis, R. Y. (1991). Power and status differentials in minority and majority group relations. *European Journal of Social Psychology, 21*, 1–24.

Sachdev, I., & Bourhis, R. Y. (1993). Ethnolinguistic vitality: Some motivational and cognitive considerations. In M. Hogg & D. Abrams (Eds.), *Group motivation: Social psychological perspectives* (pp. 33–51). New York: Harvester-Wheatsheat.

Sachdev, I., Bourhis, R. Y., Phang, S. W., & D'Eye, J. (1987). Language attitudes and vitality perceptions: Intergenerational effects amongst Chinese Canadian communities. *Journal of Language and Social Psychology, 6*, 287–307.

Seggar, J. F. (1975). Imagery of women in television drama: 1974. *Journal of Broadcasting, 19*, 273–282.

Seggar, J. F., & Wheeler, P. (1973). World of work on TV: Ethnic and sex representation in drama. *Journal of Broadcasting, 17*, 201–214.

Shanahan, J., Morgan, M., & Stenbjerre, M. (1997). Green or brown? Television and the cultivation of environmental concern. *Journal of Broadcasting and Electronic Media, 41*, 305–323.

Shrum, L. J. (1995). Assessing the social influence of television: A social cognition perspective on cultivation effects. *Communication Research, 22*, 402–429.

Shrum, L. J. (1996). Psychological processes underlying cultivation effects: Further tests of construct accessibility. *Human Communication Research, 22*, 482–509.

Shrum, L. J. (2001). Processing strategy moderates the cultivation effect. *Human Communication Research, 27*, 94–120.

Shrum, L. J., & O'Guinn, T. C. (1993). Processes and effects in the construction of social reality: Construct accessibility as an explanatory variable. *Communication Research, 20*, 436–471.

Signorielli, N. (1981). Content analysis: More than just counting minorities. In *Search of diversity: Symposium on minority audience and programming research* (pp. 97–108). Washington, DC: Corporation for Public Broadcasting, Office of Communication Research.

Signorielli, N. (1986). Selective television viewing: A limited possibility. *Journal of Communication, 36*(3), 64–76.

Signorielli, N. (1991). Adolescents and ambivalence toward marriage: A cultivation analysis. *Youth and Society, 23*, 121–149.

Signorielli, N., & Bacue, A. (1999). Recognition and respect: A content analysis of prime-time television characters across three decades. *Sex Roles, 40*, 527–544.

Signorielli, N., & Lears, M. (1992). Children, television, and conceptions about chores: Attitudes and behaviors. *Sex Roles, 27*, 157–170.

Signorielli, N., & Morgan, M. (2001). Television and the family: The cultivation perspective. In J. Bryant & J. A. Bryant (Eds.), *In television and the American family* (2nd ed., pp. 333–351). Hillsdale, NJ: Erlbaum.

Spurlock, J. (1982). Television, ethnic minorities, and mental health. In G. Berry & C. Mitchell-Kernan (Eds.), *Television and the socialization of the minority child* (pp. 71–79). New York: Academic Press.

Steenland, S. (1995). Content analysis of the image of women on television. In C. M. Lont (Ed.), *Women and media: Content, careers, and criticism* (pp. 179–189). San Francisco: Wadsworth.

Stroman, C. A. (1986). Television viewing and self-concept among Black children. *Journal of Broadcasting and Electronic Media, 30*, 87–93.

Tajfel, H., & Turner, J. C. (1986). The social identity theory of intergroup behavior. In S. Worchel & W. G. Austin (Eds.), *Psychology of intergroup relations* (pp. 7–24). Chicago: Nelson.

Tan, A. S. (1982). Television use and social stereotypes. *Journalism Quarterly, 59*, 119–122.

Tan, A. S., & Tan, G. (1979). Television use and self-esteem of Blacks. *Journal of Communication, 29*(1), 129–135.

Tedesco, N. (1974). Patterns in prime time. *Journal of Communication, 24*(2), 119–124.

Tuchman, G. (1978). Introduction: The symbolic annihilation of women by the mass media. In G. Tuchman, A. K. Daniels, & J. Benet (Eds.), *Hearth and home: Images of women in the mass media* (pp. 3–38). New York: Oxford University Press.

Turner, J., & Brown, R. J. (1978). Social status, cognitive alternatives, and intergroup relations. In H. Tajfel (Ed.), *Differentiation between social groups* (pp. 201–234). London: Academic Press.

Volgy, T. J., & Schwarz, J. E. (1980). TV entertainment programming and sociopolitical attitudes. *Journalism Quarterly, 57*, 150–155.

Ward, L. M., & Rivadeneyra, R. (1999). Contributions of entertainment television to adolescents' sexual attitudes and expectations: The role of viewing amount versus viewer involvement. *Journal of Sex Research, 36*, 237–249.

Weaver, D. H. (1980). Audience need for orientation and media. *Communication Research, 7*, 361–376.

Yagmur, K., de Bot, K., & Korzilius, H. (1999). Language shift and ethnolinguistic vitality of Turkish in Australia. *Journal of Multilingual and Multicultural Development, 20*, 51–69.

Zaller, J. R. (1992). *The nature and origins of mass opinion.* New York: Cambridge University Press.

Zemach, T., & Cohen, A. A. (1986). Perception of gender equality on television and in social reality. *Journal of Broadcasting and Electronic Media, 30*, 427–444.

CHAPTER CONTENTS

8 The Empowerment of Feminist Scholarship in Public Relations and the Building of a Feminist Paradigm

LINDA ALDOORY
University of Maryland

The impact of feminist scholarship on public relations affects practitioners, scholars, and audiences alike. Since the first comprehensive gender study in public relations was published in 1986, numerous scholars have (a) described the status of women in the profession, (b) applied feminist perspectives to prevailing public relations theories, and (c) explored new feminized concepts and theories. Taken as a whole, this scholarship has led to a new feminist paradigm for the field, which has the ability to empower women. The purpose of this chapter is threefold: first, to give a comprehensive review of the published public relations scholarship on gender and feminism; second, to synthesize the scholarship into what can be defined as a feminist paradigm; and third, to illustrate the empowerment of the new paradigm. To begin, some important concepts are defined, followed by a brief discussion of the feminization of the public relations field that marked the impetus for gender studies. The body of literature on gender and feminism in public relations is then detailed and categorized by its scholarly purpose: to describe, to explain, or to critique. The chapter concludes with propositions for a feminist paradigm and opportunities for future research.

C ompared to other areas of communication scholarship, the body of knowledge in public relations is relatively small (Vasquez & Taylor, 2001). However, according to J. E. Grunig (1993), scholars from other communication disciplines could learn much from public relations, "especially about publics; symmetrical communication; the management of communication; the effect of organizational structure, environment, culture, and power on communication behaviors; and the impact of gender and diversity on the practice of professional communication" (p. 164).

Correspondence: Linda Aldoory, Department of Communication, 2130 Skinner Building, University of Maryland, College Park, MD 20742; email: la74@umail.umd.edu

Communication Yearbook 27, pp. 221–255

The impact of gender and diversity on public relations has become widespread, and today it affects practitioners, scholars, and audiences. The first comprehensive gender study in public relations was published in 1986—*The Velvet Ghetto* (Cline, Toth, Turk, Walters, Johnson, & Smith)—since then, numerous scholars have described the status of women in the profession, applied feminist perspectives to prevailing public relations theories, and explored new feminized concepts and theories (Toth, 2001). This scholarship has led to a new feminist paradigm for the field, a paradigm that has the ability to empower women.

IMPORTANT CONCEPTUALIZATIONS

Some major concepts underlie an assessment of gender and feminist literature in public relations, as well as the development of a feminist paradigm for communication research. In an attempt to reduce ambiguity, the specific conceptualizations used in this chapter—for public relations, feminism, empowerment, and paradigm—are briefly explained here.

Public Relations

Public relations has been defined as the management of communication between an organization and its publics (J. E. Grunig & Hunt, 1984). Many scholars have indicated that the purpose of public relations should be the development of mutually beneficial relationships between organizations and publics (Cutlip, Center, & Broom, 2000; J. E. Grunig, 1992a; Kendall, 1996). The focus on relationship building evolved over time. Up until the 1920s, public relations was viewed as one-way publicity and promotion directed to audiences from organizations. One-way communication is still quite common, especially in media relations, sports, and entertainment public relations. However, two-way communication has become more accepted, emphasizing research, strategy, and management (Dozier, Grunig, & Grunig, 1995; J. E. Grunig, 1992a).

An emphasis on management and relationship building has also been the focus for much of the feminist research found in the field. However, for feminists, the goals have been to describe the low status given to women in the profession, to elaborate on the prevailing theories by applying them to female audiences, or to critique prevailing theories for their patriarchal perspectives (Aldoory, 2001b; Creedon, 1991; L. A. Grunig, Toth, & Hon, 2001).

Feminism

To this day, there is no agreement as to what defines feminism. Some scholars offer a broad, general understanding, such as Devault (1996), who defined feminism as "a movement, and a set of beliefs, that problematize gender inequality. Feminists believe that women have been subordinated through men's greater power" (p. 2). Additionally, van Zoonen (1994) stated that "gender and power, although both very much in debate, form the constituents of feminist theory" (p. 4). Other feminist authors have expanded the definition to include the oppression of all people who are marginalized by a dominant culture (Foss, Foss, & Griffin, 1999). Rush and Grubb-Swetnam (1996) defined a feminist as a person "who believes in equal rights for everyone, including women, and when women are denied their rights, especially women" (p. 499).

Scholarship defined as feminist encompasses just as many complexities as the feminist perspectives that govern it. Tetreault (1985) defined feminist scholarship as "scholarly inquiry [in pursuit of] new questions, new categories, and new notions of significance which illuminate women's traditions, history, culture, values, visions, and perspectives" (p. 370). Patai and Koertge (1994) commented, "If it is to be feminist research, there has to be, at some basic, common denominator level, a belief that women have . . . been oppressed or repressed, and that we are looking for ways to emancipate" (p. 39). According to Reinharz (1992), it is feminist research if the researcher claims the study as such, if the researcher identifies her or himself to be feminist, or if the study is published in a feminist-friendly publication. Communication researchers have examined themes that define feminist research in the discipline, including: (a) explicit attention to inequitable power dimensions of gender relations; (b) discussions of gender along with other identities, such as race and class; (c) sensitivity to research participants' lives and diversity in samples; (d) critique and reconceptualization of androcentric methods and theory; (e) action-oriented findings linked to improving the status of women or women's everyday lives; and (f) collaboration with research participants in the research design and process (Cirksena, 1996; Foss & Ray, 1996).

In public relations, feminism has been generally defined dichotomously, with two main perspectives framing its scholarship: liberal feminism and radical feminism. Liberal feminists have focused on studying the public relations profession and the status of women in the profession. These scholars assert that equality of women will come through equal numbers of women and men in management positions, equal pay, and equitable treatment of women throughout the profession. According to hooks (1984), feminists interested in this type of social equality want to obtain greater power in the existing system. Radical feminists in the field believe that equality in numbers and pay will not eliminate discrimination in public relations, because the ideological and institutional systems women work in are still guided by androcentric practices (Choi & Hon, 2002). Radical feminism espouses transformation on a systemic or organizational level to improve women's lives (hooks, 1984). Although a distinction between liberal and radical feminism is too simplistic for understanding feminism as a whole, it offers some clarification for examining feminist research in public relations. The literature examined in this chapter is grouped according to three assumed purposes: (a) to describe the inequalities found in the public relations profession (liberal feminist goal); (b) to extend theory that helps explain these inequalities (both liberal and radical perspectives illustrated); or (c) to critique and transform theory (radical feminist goal).

Empowerment

Empowerment is a principle goal of feminism and feminist scholarship, and has been defined in a number of ways depending on the field of study or the cultural frame (Jensen, 2002). According to Cosgrove (2002), empowerment has to be constantly rearticulated in relation to particular contexts and specific people. For example, conventionally defined indicators of women's autonomy have been education and income, but other aspects have included decision-making, mobility, freedom from threat, and control over or access to economic resources (Jensen, 2002). Several feminist scholars have borrowed from Freire (1972) for guidelines defining empowerment. He wrote that "conscientizacao" (p. 19) occurs when people learn to perceive social, political, and economic contradictions, and take action against oppressive elements of reality.

In examining the empowerment of public relations professionals, the field of organizational communication offers some useful definitions. To be empowered means that one comes to believe one can influence people and events in the organization to achieve desired ends (Albrecht, 1988; Kanter, 1977). According to Albrecht, at the essence is the idea of control, a personal belief that actions have desirable causal effects on the environment. Chiles and Zorn (1995) argued that, in order to feel empowered in an organization, "an employee must feel capable of competently performing the tasks of the job and believe that she has the authority or freedom to make the necessary decisions for performing the tasks of the job" (p. 2).

Development communication research offers a framework to assess empowerment of public relations audiences as well as scholars and professionals. Steeves (2001) likened empowerment to "emancipation," "liberation," and "dialogue" (p. 398). Other scholars in this area have focused on the dialogic nature of empowering others. For example, Papa, Singhal, Ghanekar, & Papa (2000) asserted that empowerment for women is embedded in democratic practices, especially when women discuss issues and make decisions that improve their quality of life. These authors argued that dialogue is the route to self-reflection, self-knowledge, and liberation from disempowering beliefs: "It is also the route to mutual learning, acceptance of diversity, trust, and understanding, and therefore, a means to individual and group empowerment" (p. 94). Centrally important to women's empowerment is consciousness-raising talk, where talking together and sharing experiences generates new webs of meaning—the beginning of internal empowerment.

Different feminist authors have given examples of empowerment rather than offer specific definitions of the concept. For example, hooks (1984) argued that middle-class women during the women's movement of the 1960s attempted to eliminate women's "weakness" (p. 87) and replace it with confidence and independence. For lower- and working-class women of that era, empowerment was illustrated when they refused to accept the definitions of themselves put forward by the powerful. Another example of empowerment was offered by hooks when she described Black readers' response to her first book, which "compelled Black women to either rethink or think for the first time about the impact of sexism on our lives and the importance of [the] feminist movement" (p. vii). Evidence of empowerment may include increased awareness and knowledge, strengthened agency and self-identity, or increased voice and action. In public relations, empowerment may be reflected (a) in young scholars who make women's devalued position a central focus of their research; (b) in professionals who voice complaints about discrimination; and ultimately, (c) in audiences of communication efforts, who become agents in their own decision making and behavior change.

Paradigm

Kuhn (1970) used the term paradigm to refer to the fundamental points of view characterizing a science. According to Kuhn, paradigm "stands for the entire constellation of beliefs, values, techniques, and so on shared by the members of a given community" (p. 35). Similarly, Laudan (1977) defined paradigm as a research tradition: "a set of general assumptions about the entities and processes in a domain of study, and about the appropriate methods to be used for investigating the problems and constructing the theories in that domain" (p. 81). Paradigms provide ways of looking at life (Babbie, 1995; Denzin & Lincoln, 1998).

Many feminist scholars have argued that there exists a paradigm for feminist scholarship (Belenky, Clinchy, Goldberger, & Tarule, 1986; Harding, 1991; Reinharz, 1992). Foss and Foss (1989) indicated that researchers who identify with this feminist paradigm would exhibit a collective sense of dissatisfaction with the dominant research paradigm. They would incorporate into their approaches "assumptions and methods consistent with the qualities of women's experiences that are fundamental to the feminist perspective" (p. 69). Harding (1991) defined a feminist paradigm in her support of sciences and technologies specifically for women: "Feminists (male and female) would invent modes of thought and learn techniques and skills to enable women to get more control over the conditions of their lives" (p. 5).

A public relations paradigm has also developed over the last 20 years. It emphasizes public relations as a management function rather than a technical one; examines public relations with the goal of maintaining balance between organizations and their environments; and attempts to find new ways for building relationships with publics who are critical to an organization's success.

THE FEMINIZATION OF PUBLIC RELATIONS

Historically, males were the majority in public relations, but over the past 20 years, women have been entering the profession in droves and currently comprise 70% of the field (Toth, 2001). In 1989, Rakow stated, "The feminization of public relations should now be recognizable as nothing less than a gender crisis for the whole field, triggered by the entrance of substantial numbers of women, but fed by a long-standing conflict over [masculine and feminine] ideologies" (p. 295).

Today, feminization sparks serious debate about dramatic changes seen in the profession, its reputation, and its scholarship (Rakow, 1989; Toth, 1988, 1989). On one hand, critics have argued that feminization has negatively affected the profession and its reputation (Kucera, 1994). Its main effects have included a decline in salaries and status (Lesly, 1988), an increased likelihood of encroachment from other professional fields (Lauzen, 1992), the exclusion of public relations from primary decision-making in organizations (Lesly, 1988), and the denial of feminine characteristics as valuable to the field (Scrimger, 1989; Toth, 1989; Toth & Cline, 1991). This institutional- and ideological-level sexism has disempowered the individual women who work in public relations through lowered salaries and a lack of managerial and decision-making power.

However, feminization has opened doors to feminist scholars, feminine ideals, and a desirable transformation of the profession and scholarship (Rakow, 1989). With 70% of the field being women, the nature of the profession has changed accordingly (Hon, Grunig, & Dozier, 1992; Rakow, 1989). For example, the push for relationship building with publics is seen as a direct result of feminization— women are socialized or misperceived to be naturally inclined towards sensitivity, collaboration, and relationship building. Also, Sha (1996) asserted that feminization makes public relations more ethical, "not merely in appearance, but in practice" (p. 3). Feminization has offered alternative perspectives and has introduced more symmetrical management because women know both the dominant male reality and their own reality. With this "dual-consciousness" (p. 9), women may be more sensitive to the perspectives of different organizational publics, and therefore be more ethical in their practice of public relations.

In terms of scholarship, the feminization of public relations was the impetus for the early studies of gender in the field (Creedon, 1991, 2001; Dozier, 1988; L. A. Grunig, 1989b; Mathews, 1988; Rakow, 1989; Toth, 1988, 1989). Scholars were searching for evidence that discrimination existed and explanations as to why discrimination occurred. With so many women in the profession, scholars found support for their feminist perspectives in the form of funding and willing research participants. Today, scholars are still exploring explanations, but they are also critiquing the discipline and suggesting transformative solutions to the androcentric nature of public relations that exists even with a majority of women in the field. The research and its findings have helped to empower women, by increasing their awareness and by helping them find their voice.

DESCRIPTIVE SCHOLARSHIP: EXAMINING THE STATUS OF WOMEN

Most of the research on gender and feminism in public relations has focused on describing the status, roles, and perceptions of women as compared to men in public relations (Cline et al., 1986; L. A. Grunig, Toth, & Hon, 2001; O'Neil, 1999; Tam, Dozier, Lauzen, & Real, 1995; Weaver-Lariscy, Sallot, & Cameron, 1996; Wright, Grunig, Springston, & Toth, 1991). This is an important area of study because, for the first time since the feminization of the field, research was used to highlight the impact of the influx of women on both themselves and the profession as a whole. Additionally, the research helped to explain communication processes within organizations where female practitioners worked. It also examined factors that influenced communication management and production. Several studies were comprehensive research programs, in that they addressed numerous workplace issues at once (Aldoory & Toth, 2002; Cline & Toth, 1993; Cline et al., 1986; L. A. Grunig et al., 2001; Toth & Cline, 1989; Wright et al., 1991). Some of the more significant findings from these and other studies are detailed below.

Roles and the Glass Ceiling

One of the most prolific areas of gender and feminist scholarship in public relations assesses roles theory. Roles are considered important to the study of public relations because they affect professional success, the process of the public relations functions, and the relationship between public relations and organizations (Broom & Smith, 1979; Dozier, 1992; Ferguson, 1979). Originally, four roles were found to exist in public relations, three that defined managerial responsibilities and one that defined technical tasks (Broom & Smith, 1979). Broom (1982) later argued that the three managerial roles were likely to be performed by the same practitioner. Therefore, Broom reduced the four roles to a dichotomous typology, that of manager and technician. Technicians have been described as: "practitioners who provide the communication and journalistic skills—writing, editing, audiovisual production, graphics, and production of messages—needed to carry out public relations programs. Communication technicians do not make organizational decisions. They implement the decisions of others" (J. E. Grunig & Hunt, 1984, p. 91). Managers coordinate programs and staff, conduct systematic research, make decisions, and discuss results with executive management.

Dozens of studies have described main differences between men and women with regards to technical and managerial roles (L. A. Grunig et al., 2001; Hon et al., 1992; Wright et al., 1991). Others have examined detailed cases or characteristics of roles among men and women (Dozier, 1995; Weaver-Lariscy, Cameron, & Sweep, 1994). Broom and Dozier (1986; Broom, 1982) identified a glass ceiling in public relations by reporting that, for the two-role typology, women were more likely to be found in technical roles.

For years, the term glass ceiling has been used to describe the invisible barriers women face when attempting to be promoted. Although women comprise 70% of the jobs in public relations today, they do not comprise this percentage of higher positions in public relations. Wootton's (1997) analysis indicated that in 1995, only 35.7% of managers were women in marketing, advertising, and public relations. Dozier and Broom (1995) reported that attaining the manager role was explained more by experience than by gender. However, many studies have argued that, in addition to experience, gender discrimination also keeps women in technical positions long after men are promoted (Choi & Hon, 2002; Creedon, 1991; Dozier, 1987, 1988; L. A. Grunig, 1995; L. A. Grunig et al., 2001; Hon et al., 1992; Toth, 1988; Toth & Cline, 1991; Wright et al., 1991).

To assess perceptions of gender and promotion, the Public Relations Society of America (PRSA) funded three research teams, in 1990, 1995 (L. A. Grunig et al., 2001; Toth, Serini, Wright, & Emig, 1998; Wright et al., 1991), and most recently, 2000 (Aldoory & Toth, 2002; Toth & Aldoory, 2001). In all three studies, researchers found that women agreed more strongly that men were promoted more quickly in their organizations. Women believed this to be the case throughout public relations. Men disagreed that they were promoted more quickly in their organizations, but they were uncertain about the field itself. Also, women considered it more difficult for them to reach the top, both in their organizations and throughout public relations. Men agreed more than women that they had a fair shot at promotion in their organization (L. A. Grunig et al., 2001). L. A. Grunig et al. remarked: "One could conclude that women actually have made little gain in breaking through that glass ceiling. . . . With the added burden of juggling home and work, women find it particularly difficult to ascend to the level of highest responsibility" (p. 251).

In the studies conducted in the early 1990s, women were found to "do it all" more than men, frequently retaining technical responsibilities even after reaching manager levels (Creedon, 1991; Kucera, 1994; Toth & Grunig, 1993; Toth et al., 1998). Toth and Grunig found that female respondents conducted some managerial activities, including: implementing new programs, meeting peers, conducting or analyzing research, and implementing event planning or logistics. However, they also found technical tasks for women managers, including: making media contacts, handling correspondence, and implementing the decisions of others. The authors explained that perhaps women do it all because "women started in the technical roles at lower salaries and kept performing these technical roles while continuing to assume greater responsibilities for their organizations" (p. 171). More recently, one study indicated that technical and managerial tasks were distributed randomly across both male and female managers (Toth & Aldoory, 2001).

Salaries

Studies examining salaries have found a significant difference in the mean and median salaries between men and women, where men made more than women ("30th Survey of the Profession," 1998; Cline & Toth, 1993; Jacobson & Tortorello, 1992; Leyland, 2000; Selnow & Wilson, 1985; Toth, 1988; Toth & Cline, 1991; Wright et al., 1991). Some of these studies used regression analysis to assess the impact of different variables on the relationship between gender and salary, and found that women were still paid less when years of experience, age, job interruptions, and level of education were taken into consideration (Cline et al., 1986; Toth & Aldoory, 2001). In 1986, women were making between $6,000 and $30,000 a year less than an equally qualified man, even when controlling for age, education, and experience (Cline et al., 1986). An update 3 years later found that the gap still existed (Toth & Cline, 1989, 1991). In 1995, a report by Simmons Market Research confirmed a salary difference, which existed across age, experience, and job title. On average, men's salaries were 45% higher than women's ($59,460 vs. $41,110; "Salary Survey of Public Relations Professionals," 1995, p. 4).

Recently, Seideman and Leyland (2000) asserted that there was "distinct discrimination" (p. 29) in salary by gender. In 2000, the average salary for men ($73,700) was higher than the overall average, and the average for women ($56,000) was a little lower. When looking at median salary, for men it was $65,000 whereas for women it was $48,000 (Toth & Aldoory, 2001). Years of public relations experience accounted for much of the variance in the relationship between gender and salary, but gender also accounted for part of the salary difference.

Several of the studies reporting salary differences also measured perceptions. L. A. Grunig et al., (2001) found that men disagreed that women are paid less for doing comparable work in their organizations whereas women agreed. In another study, respondents agreed that women in management positions get paid less than men, both in their organizations and throughout public relations. Men were also significantly more satisfied with their income as a public relations practitioner (Toth & Aldoory, 2001).

Job Satisfaction

Job satisfaction has been defined as "an organizational member's perceptual response to the aspects of his or her job and organization environment considered most important to meeting his or her work needs/expectations" (Pincus & Rayfield, 1989, p. 189). The concept of job satisfaction has been dichotomized to include: (a) personal or individual satisfaction, and (b) satisfaction with the organization, due to external rewards or recognition given by the organization to an employee (Dozier et al., 1995). Feminist scholars have not studied job satisfaction as frequently as they have other workplace issues, but the research that has been done indicates little difference in overall satisfaction between men and women in public relations. When examining specific dimensions of satisfaction, however, studies revealed gender differences (L. A. Grunig et al., 2001; Selnow & Wilson, 1985; Serini, Toth, Wright, & Emig, 1996). For example, Selnow and Wilson indicated that women were less satisfied than men in several aspects, including: level of creativity required by their job, salary, and opportunities for promotion. Women also reported placing greater emphasis on the social relationships of their jobs, compared to men who emphasized job security.

The 1990, 1995, and 2000 gender studies funded by PRSA measured job satisfaction using an index of several variables (L. A. Grunig et al., 2001; Serini et al., 1996; Toth & Aldoory, 2001). Between 1990 and 1995, authors found that male respondents remained satisfied with their income but not with their jobs. Women remained satisfied with their jobs, but not with their income (L. A. Grunig et al., 2001; Serini et al., 1996). Female respondents in 2000 showed significantly greater satisfaction than they did in 1995 in regards to: prestige of working in public relations, overall knowledge of public relations, value of job to society, prospects for future in the field, and job security. Men showed an increase in satisfaction over time with: public relations as an occupation, autonomy, opportunities for advancement, and prospects for future, both in the field and with present employer (Toth & Aldoory, 2001).

Sexual Harassment

Serini, Toth, Wright, and Emig (1998) cited a study by Women Executives in Public Relations that found sexual harassment of female public relations practitioners to be widespread (Bovet, 1993). According to these authors, public relations practitioners deal with sexual harassment both as professionals who have the potential to either harass or be harassed and as counselors or liaisons to management who work with organizations to communicate internally and externally about sexual harassment policies and problems.

However, only a few published studies have examined sexual harassment (Serini et al., 1998; Toth & Aldoory, 2001). In 1995, one study showed women were more likely than men to recognize sexual harassment issues in public relations (L. A. Grunig et al., 2001; Serini et al., 1998). Men tended to believe that the incidence of sexual harassment was declining, but women were not sure. Women agreed more than men that sexual harassment limits women's opportunities for advancement, both in their organization and throughout public relations, and that people who report sexual harassment lose career opportunities. Men considered sexual harassment a minor issue relative to other problems in the workplace, whereas women disagreed with this statement. In 2000, survey respondents agreed that there was less sexual harassment in public relations today than 5 years ago. Men agreed with this statement significantly more than women.

Focus group studies have revealed important details regarding the perceptions and experiences of sexual harassment in public relations (L. A. Grunig et al., 2001). For example, in a study by L. A. Grunig et al. (2001), men believed that there was more reporting of harassment, rather than more actual instances. The men characterized the problem as one of male ego and power. The women told stories of sexual harassment, either personal ones or ones they heard from women they knew. Some female participants seemed to blame sexual harassment on the insecurities some men felt about women. As one participant put it, "They have to kind of bring [women] down a little bit" (L. A. Grunig et al., 2001, p. 283). Recent focus groups found that men did not see sexual harassment as much of a problem anymore, due to the heightened awareness and political incorrectness of it. A few men discussed what they thought was a more urgent, current problem, that of women dressing and acting inappropriately. One male participant asserted, "Women appear to use sexuality consciously or as a tool in the work place at the same time they collectively bemoan sexual harassment" (Toth & Aldoory, 2001, p. 9). The women still viewed sexual harassment as a concern, but also agreed that women are being more aggressive in responding to inappropriate comments and behavior. One woman asserted, "You have to be ever vigilant. There really are dangers in thinking the problems have been solved" (Toth & Aldoory, 2001, p. 9).

The Intersection of Gender and Race

A few scholars have focused on the intersection of race and gender in public relations (Kern-Foxworth, 1989a, 1989c; Kern-Foxworth, Gandy, Hines, & Miller, 1994; Tillery-Larkin, 2000; Zerbinos & Clanton, 1993). Kern-Foxworth found in her studies that African American males are paid more than African American females, but that overall, people of color have not attained the same status and salary level as their White counterparts. Studies of minority public relations practitioners examined the roles these practitioners played and found a gap between the role that participants assigned themselves—middle-level management—and the one they actually fulfilled—technician, not problem-solver. Kern-Foxworth (1989a, 1989c) argued that larger organizations did not allow minorities the opportunities to advance in their careers, rather the larger the organization, the lower the salaries and the less chance for people of color to become managers.

In a follow-up study 5 years later, Kern-Foxworth et al. (1994) reported that about half of the African American female public relations practitioners they surveyed spent time giving advice and counsel. According to authors, their study gained insight into "how Black females in the field view themselves" (p. 431) and not how others viewed them in the workplace. The researchers concluded:

It was assumed when this project was undertaken that the status of Black women in public relations would be somewhat dismal. Nevertheless, the results obtained are positive and show that Black women in this field perceive themselves as occupying meaningful roles within the profession and interface quite frequently with management. (p. 431)

The authors of this study stressed that the findings support the idea that it is important to segment research samples between White and Black women for gender studies, because Black women "may not share the same experiences as others who work in the profession" (Kern-Foxworth et al., 1994, p. 432). Some scholars have argued that future research should consider the possibility that practitioners of color have different experiences in the field, and therefore, might have different roles, role expectations, perceptions, and so forth (Aldoory, 2001b; Kern-Foxworth et al., 1994). As Houston (1992) stated, "The only important aspects of what black women do as communicators are considered to be those that are somehow related to what white women do" (p. 51).

Other public relations researchers have discussed the challenges of having research participants who are almost all White (Aldoory, 2001b; Hon, 1995; Toth & Cline, 1991). Hon (1995) described how her study's sample was narrow because the participants were middle class, mostly White, and American. Her study included one American Asian (participant preferred this order), one African American, and one Briton. According to Hon, "although these women's experiences spoke powerfully about gender discrimination in public relations, their stories were just part of a larger picture" (p. 41). In conclusion, Hon asserted, "The paucity of research about African Americans' contribution to public relations suggests a conspicuous void in mass communication scholarship" (p. 165).

Public Relations Education

Studies have examined gender in public relations education by: exploring discrimination issues among faculty members (L. A. Grunig, 1989a), surveying student opinions (DeRosa & Wilcox, 1989; Farmer & Waugh, 1999), and conducting content analyses of textbooks (Creedon, 1989a; Kern-Foxworth, 1989b). L. A. Grunig (1989a) conducted a case study of faculty members at a large Eastern U.S. university, where females accounted for less than 25% of a 21-person faculty. Only 1 of the department's 13 tenured professors was a woman. L. A. Grunig found that the women she interviewed spoke of a subtle pattern of bias, misunderstanding, and insensitivity that women perceived as limiting their chances for success in higher education. The participants also cited tokenism, a heavier advising load, lack of role models, and fewer opportunities for sharing resources, mentoring, and coalition building.

A couple of studies have focused on studying female students in undergraduate programs. Over 90% of Public Relations Student Society of America members (Cline & Toth, 1993) and 68% of public relations undergraduates are female (L. A. Grunig, 1989b). In addition, in 1989, female graduates took three out of four entry-level jobs in public relations (L. A. Grunig, 1989b). One early study found little difference in how serious-minded and management-oriented female students were compared to male students (DeRosa & Wilcox, 1989). There was also no difference in salary expectations for first jobs, but there were significant differences with salary expectations after 5 years in the profession, with male students expecting higher salaries than the female students. Authors also cited significant differences with confidence, where male students were more confident than female students. A more current study determined that female students expected less beginning salary and slower promotions than did male students (Farmer & Waugh, 1999). The women in this study also believed they would postpone raising a family so they could be promoted.

Two studies were found that described the representation of women in major undergraduate public relations textbooks (Creedon, 1989a; Kern-Foxworth, 1989b). Kern-Foxworth analyzed 60 textbooks (21,841 pages) published between 1979 and 1988. She found that less than one half of 1% contained information about women or women's issues (103 pages from the textbooks). Kern-Foxworth additionally argued that the information on women that was found did not offer accurate assessments of roles women played in the profession. Creedon found that there was little substantive description of women's contributions in the public relations textbooks she analyzed.

Historical Perspective

Feminists have tried to remedy the all-White, all-male evidence given in text-books and historical accounts by highlighting stories of women who have contrib-uted to public relations (Creedon, 1989a, 2001; L. A. Grunig, 1989b). One ex-ample of uncovering women's history is the work on the life of Doris Fleischman Bernays (Henry, 1988, 1996; Lamme, 1999). Bernays was the wife and partner of Edward Bernays for 58 years, and she made great contributions to public relations as well as to Edward's business. Yet, she went unnoticed until Henry (1988, 1996) brought Fleischman Bernays's stories to light. Miller (1997) profiled Jane Stewart, who served as vice president and then president of Group Attitudes Corporation, an independent consulting firm that became a subsidiary of Hill and Knowlton, New York, in 1956. Although Stewart had to compromise and adopt a certain con-servative practice of public relations to handle the masculine profession, she also developed a collaborative management style that gave her clients a different out-look on public relations problems.

A couple of scholars analyzed publications for representations of women over time to assess women's visibility in public relations history. In her analysis, Creedon (2001) listed the several women who were given little mention in public relations textbooks: Susan B. Anthony, Elizabeth Cady Stanton, Matilda Joslyn Gage, and Harriet Beecher Stowe. As Creedon explained, these women influenced public relations through their work as activists and promoters. Gower (2000) examined the images and roles of women as they were covered in the *Public Relations Jour-nal* from 1945 through 1972. The *Journal* was a well-known trade magazine for the industry published by PRSA. Gower found that during the years between 1945 and 1955, women were established and active in PRSA and were shown as such in the *Journal*. However, in the late 1950s when societal expectations of women in-cluded staying home with children, the number of women represented in the maga-zine decreased. According to Gower, this gave an overall impression that public relations was a male profession. The numbers and positive representations of women increased again in the late 1960s. This was "almost surely reflecting the influence of the women's liberation movement on the profession, at least in terms of an acknowledgment that women were in the field" (p. 16).

Summary

Most of the scholarship in public relations conducted with a feminist perspec-tive has described the status of individual women in the profession. It has focused on roles practitioners perform, salaries, job satisfaction, sexual harassment, rac-ism, education, and the historical invisibility of women's contributions. The range of methodologies used has included not only quantitative surveys and qualitative focus groups, but also historical assessment. Taken as a whole, the body of knowl-edge reflects a liberal feminist standpoint, where equality is the implicit goal. From the earliest studies conducted in the 1980s to today, findings consistently show evidence of discrimination by gender and race, as well as awareness among research participants of this discrimination.

Empowerment of Descriptive Scholarship

The descriptive studies in public relations have empowered scholars and practitioners in three main ways. First, these studies have raised consciousness and awareness. Consciousness-raising occurred following the brief deluge of gender research published in the late 1980s. The findings from several of these studies were abstracted and printed in professional magazines and newsletters. Practitioners thereby gained access to the research in lay language. The research resonated with hundreds of practitioners who had thought their gendered experiences were unique (Aldoory & Toth, 2002; Wrigley, 2002). Specifically for scholars, the published research on race increased sensitivity among feminist researchers to the impact of their whiteness and the whiteness of common research samples in public relations. The research on race helped empower some students and scholars to reconsider the use of all-White samples (Aldoory, 2001a, 2001b; Hon, 1995; Tillery-Larkin, 2000).

Second, this research created opportunities for new and different directions for feminist scholarship. For example, younger scholars and graduate students now confidently pursue gender as a valid concept of study in public relations (Choi & Hon, 2002; Kucera, 1994; Sha, 1996). Gender scholars seek out explanations for gender differences found, and they build theory in order to strengthen feminism's place in public relations scholarship. Due to the importance and rigor of the descriptive studies, research foundations and professional associations increased their financial support of research programs focusing on gender issues, which then allowed for further scholarship and theory building (Toth & Aldoory, 2001).

Finally, the descriptive studies empowered scholars and practitioners with voice, providing them the tools with which to defend against feminist backlash. The backlash was illustrated in trade publications that argued against any gender discrimination. Scholars and practitioners counterargued based on substantive research findings. According to Elizabeth Toth, "We could argue logically against myths and conclusions, showing the fallacies of the arguments. We didn't need to be emotional, hysterical, or frustrated" (personal communication, July 23, 2002). Also, the professional organizations that funded studies created opportunities for more research and action by creating task forces. PRSA for example, created a commission solely to address gender issues, which is now titled the Commission on Work, Life, and Gender.

EXPLANATORY SCHOLARSHIP: MOVING AHEAD TO THEORY

There is a growing body of scholarship that has moved beyond the description of women's status in order to focus on two general goals: (a) to elaborate on mainstream theories in public relations by using women as research participants or by including gender as an intervening variable; and (b) to take the earlier descriptive studies and suggest explanations and predictor variables for what was found. Explanatory research is important because, theoretically, it has added intervening variables to mainstream public relations theories, making them more heuristic. It has also contributed a greater understanding to how communication strategies are managed. This body of work has helped build theory toward a new feminist paradigm.

Elaborating Theory

Several scholars have examined the impact of gender on mainstream public relations theories (Aldoory, 1998, 2001b; L. A. Grunig, 1991; Slater, Chipman, Auld, Keefe, & Kendall, 1992; Wright & Haynes, 1999). One frequently tested theory is that of two-way communication and the models of public relations. The models, developed by J. E. Grunig (1984) and J. E. Grunig and Hunt (1984), categorize how public relations was developed and is practiced in the United States. First, the press agentry model of public relations consists of one-way information for purposes of propaganda. A second model is public information, where information is disseminated one-way, but it is disseminated with truth and accuracy. In the third model of public relations, two-way asymmetrical communication, research is conducted to identify opinions of audiences. It is then used to manipulate messages to be more persuasive. Finally, the fourth model of public relations is not only two-way in communication flow, but also symmetrical in purpose: two-way symmetrical communication results in the public and the organization both changing in some way in response to communication. Research is practiced by organizations using this model not for manipulative purposes, but to facilitate understanding and build relationships. Characteristics of the two-way symmetrical model include strategic management, systematic research, collaboration, negotiation, compromise, social responsibility, and ethics (Deatherage & Hazelton, 1998; Dozier et al., 1995; J. E. Grunig, 1992a; J. E. Grunig & Hunt, 1984).

Currently, the most realistic and effective model for public relations is considered to be a mixed-motive model (Conrad, 1985; Murphy, 1991; Wilson & Putnam, 1990). According to Murphy, organizations want to not only forward their own interests but also reach a solution acceptable to its publics. Murphy (1991) and others (Dozier et al., 1995; J. E. Grunig & L. A. Grunig, 1992) have argued, then, that although the original concept of a two-way symmetrical model was the most idealistic, in reality, effective organizations use a mixed-motive model. The mixed-motive model of communication combines two-way asymmetrical and two-way symmetrical public relations models (J. E. Grunig & L. A. Grunig, 1992; J. E. Grunig & White, 1992). Today, the mixed motive model is termed two-way communication and works within a symmetrical, ethical worldview of public relations.

There have been a variety of studies that have examined the impact of gender on two-way communication. For example, L. A. Grunig (1991) conducted a case study of a sex discrimination lawsuit filed by women in a public relations foreign service. Wetherell (1989) studied the effects of gender, masculine traits, and feminine traits on the practice of and preference for two-way communication as well as the other models of public relations. She found that femininity facilitates practice of the two-way symmetrical model. However, the correlation was weak. More importantly, she found that far more men than women practiced two-way communication. She explained that the two-way symmetric model is a big-picture model; it looks beyond the effects of the program on the environment in which that organization exists. Women have not been socialized to look at the big picture, whereas men have. Aldoory (1998) used two-way and one-way models of public relations to examine communication practices of women in leadership positions. In-depth interviews were conducted with female leaders in both public relations education and in the public relations profession. Findings indicated that participants illustrated a mix of two-way and one-way models when hypothetically responding to staff and employees. Educators tended to use two-way communication more than one-way models and incorporated compromise into conflict resolution. Aldoory concluded that the women in her study were "situational" (p. 97) rhetors, utilizing language and resolution strategies that they deemed most appropriate for the particular individuals they were speaking to and the particular events they were addressing.

A couple of studies helped extend the situational theory of publics. The situational theory of publics predicts communication behavior according to three independent variables: problem recognition, constraint recognition, and level of involvement (J. E. Grunig, 1978, 1983, 1987, 1989; J. E. Grunig & Hunt, 1984; J. E. Grunig & Ipes, 1983; J. E. Grunig & Stamm, 1979). Problem recognition is the extent to which individuals recognize that issues or events are problems to be concerned about. Constraint recognition is the extent to which individuals see their behaviors limited by obstacles or barriers beyond their control. Involvement has been a key concept for many communication theories and is defined as the extent to which an issue is personally relevant (Chaffee & Roser, 1986; Flora & Maibach, 1990; J. E. Grunig & Childers, 1988; J. E. Grunig & Hunt, 1984; J. E. Grunig & Repper, 1992; Hamilton, 1989; Heath & Douglas, 1990, 1991; Roser & Thompson, 1995). If someone personally connects to an issue or message, they are more likely to actively seek information, attend to it, and comprehend it (J. E. Grunig & Hunt, 1984). Studies have shown that, in general, members of a public are more likely to seek information and communicate actively when they (a) perceive an issue to be a problem, (b) perceive that the issue involves them, and (c) believe they can do something about it (Berkowitz & Turnmire, 1994; Cameron, 1992; Elliott, Mahmoud, Sothirajah, & Camphor, 1991; J. E. Grunig, 1992b; J. E. Grunig, Clifford, Richburg, & White, 1988; Heath, Liao, & Douglas, 1995; Major, 1993; Slater et al., 1992; Vasquez, 1993).

The studies that extended situational theory did so by applying the theory to the experiences of female publics. Slater et al. (1992) used situational theory to assess female consumers' reactions to public education messages describing the use of chemicals. After conducting experiments and focus groups, the authors found that three independent variables were more predictive when the participants' positive or negative cognitive responses to the message content were taken into consideration (p. 200). Participants had more positive thoughts and fewer negative thoughts about a message when they scored high in involvement. Aldoory (2001a) also tested the situational theory, exploring factors that could impact women's involvement with mass media health messages. She found that five factors consistently influenced level of involvement for her focus group and interview participants: consciousness of everyday life, source preference, self-identity, consciousness of personal health, and cognitive analyses of message content. These two studies extended the already strong theory by applying its concepts to women-only samples, offering a greater understanding of how involvement resonates for female publics.

Building Theory

One way that new theory was developed was in the wake of a backlash in public relations against feminist research. After findings from the descriptive studies were published in professional magazines and newsletters, critics argued that the studies were poorly constructed and methodologically flawed. They claimed that several explanations other than discrimination accounted for gender differences found in hiring, salaries, and promotions. Feminist scholars reacted to these arguments, which were not based on new research or evidence, by pursuing studies that would help explain gender differences, and thus created avenues to new theory (Aldoory & Toth, 2002; Creedon, 1991; L. A. Grunig et al., 2001; Hon, 1995; Wrigley, 2002).

Hon's (1995) pivotal work was one of the first studies that focused on the factors explaining general discrimination against women in public relations. She conducted 37 in-depth interviews and three focus groups with female practitioners. Several themes emerged from her data that helped explain obstacles women faced, including: the marginalization of the public relations function, faulty college curriculum, a male-dominated work environment that led to women's exclusion from men's networks, women's lack of self-esteem, too few female role models, outmoded attitudes of senior men, conflicting messages for women, gender stereotypes, sexual harassment, ageism, and women's balancing act between career and family. In conclusion, Hon mapped out characteristics of a feminist theory defined by holism, inclusiveness, and complexity. The scholarly contribution of her new theory "presupposes unifying solutions for effecting equity for women" (p. 80). According to Hon, "moving beyond women's assimilation into patriarchal systems to a genuine commitment to social restructuring launches communication theory forward by providing the opportunity for meaningful transformations" (p. 80).

Other explanatory studies have focused particularly on the glass ceiling and the management role (Choi & Hon, 2002). L. A. Grunig et al. (2001) found through focus groups that women perceived themselves as insecure and weak as decision makers, making it more difficult for them to move up to management positions. Men in the focus groups talked about different management styles that made women less attractive as managers. For example, one man apologized for sounding sexist but pointed out that the women he worked for were more thin-skinned, "more alert to perceived slights or resistance" (p. 231). However, many of the male participants acknowledged that what they considered to be a woman's managerial style was good for public relations, composed of a "people orientation" (p. 231), sensitivity, intuitiveness, ethics, social responsibility, and willingness to communicate. Some researchers found that female participants in focus groups still perceived a good-old-boy network preventing them from reaching top management positions in public relations (Aldoory & Toth, 2002; Cline & Toth, 1993; Hon, 1995).

According to Cline and Toth, "Breaking into the management circle and getting onto the fast track are secrets that most women do not learn in male-oriented, male-dominated companies" (1993, p. 191). In addition, one woman interviewed by Hon said that she missed the input of "off-the-cuff" (1995, p. 47) discussions that occurred, for example, on the basketball court. More current focus groups found that both men and women felt that women were less inclined to stay late at work due to family commitments, but that after 5 o'clock was when the networking and informal decision-making occurred (Aldoory & Toth, 2002). Lauzen (1992) reported that professional encroachment occurred more often when women were top public relations practitioners in their organizations than when men were. Companies were more likely to assign decision making to others when women were top public relations practitioners than when men were the top practitioners. Some scholars have argued that women tended to cluster in technician roles because of their interests in the creative arts (Cline et al., 1986; Creedon, 1991). Creedon claimed, however, that women were as interested in status-related careers as men were and expressed a desire not to perform technician roles. Other reasons for women's inability to reach top management positions have included: socialization, women's lack of skills and knowledge about male-defined rules for advancement, and simple discrimination based on gender alone (Aldoory & Toth, 2002; Dozier, 1988; Hon, 1995).

Salary differences have also been a focus for explanatory research. Age, experience, type of organization and public relations roles have been cited as factors in gender differences in salary (L. A. Grunig et al., 2001). In addition, many women and men in recent focus groups said that women in public relations lacked the negotiation skills and knowledge necessary to request higher salaries (Aldoory & Toth, 2002). One male participant said, "For those [men] who are willing to put on a show and press the issue, my guess is they do better" (p. 17). Participants talked about women being socialized at home and at jobs to not be aggressive or demanding. A couple of participants asserted that women were socialized to perceive only two options with salary, taking the offer or not taking the job. A woman explained the socialization process:

> Men are taught to negotiate a lot stronger and a lot harder than women . . . a mother might say to her daughter, "Are you sure? You don't want to push things, you don't want to push it too hard because don't you need the job?" Whereas men, their father, they're more judged by how much money they're making. (p. 18)

Another explanation for salary differences was actual discrimination. A male participant asserted that upper management "still hasn't gotten over the mentality that women should be at home maintaining a fifties lifestyle, then they tend to be paid lower. I have a wife who complains about that all the time" (p. 18). A related explanation was that balancing work and family limits salary level for women. Whether they worked less hours each day or went part-time, participants said that women who were still the major caregivers would have lower salaries. Another factor was that men were offered more money for recruitment and retention purposes. Finally, historical disparity was difficult to remove and, therefore, might contribute to lower salaries for women. In other words, if women started out making lower salaries in the past—when there was overt sex discrimination—then they would continue to make lower salaries as they moved jobs or moved up to management (Aldoory & Toth, 2002).

L. A. Grunig (1993) studied female faculty members and found that men perceived women to not fit in with the academic department or climate. Women had feelings of powerlessness or ineptness, and continued to accept the additional burdens of home responsibilities. In addition, women professed to an "imposter syndrome" (p. 280) that caused them to downplay or dismiss their accomplishments.

Summary

Many feminist studies have moved beyond describing women's status in public relations by expanding well-known theories and by developing new theories explaining gender discrimination. This body of knowledge has moved public relations scholarship to a new level of theoretical, institutional, and ideological understanding of women's disempowerment in public relations. Although the work here mostly illustrates liberal feminism, much of it resonates with a radical feminist perspective in its focus on systemic problems.

The mainstream public relations theories that have been extended have included two-way communication, the situational theory of publics, and public relations roles and leadership. Studies found that gender did influence whether two-way communication was practiced and that women did not necessarily engage in two-way communication more than men. In addition, research with women as participants has led to a greater understanding of the nature of involvement as a factor in information seeking.

In building feminist theory for the discipline, several feminist scholars used qualitative methods to uncover explanations for the gender differences found in previous descriptive studies. Often, female participants in these studies voiced feelings of disempowerment, particularly in regards to taking control over their salary decisions and moving to management. Some of the more common explanatory factors for this disempowerment included women's communication style, socialization, family commitments, and their perceptions of a good-old-boy network.

Empowerment of Explanatory Scholarship

Although the explanatory research revealed feelings of disempowerment by research participants, it also raised a feminist consciousness among them during the act of evidence gathering (Aldoory, 2001a; Aldoory & Toth, 2002). As part of focus group discussions, women expressed and shared fears, stories, and frustrations. For the first time, several of them became aware of gender bias, whereas others became aware that they were not the only ones experiencing it. The participants also taught each other the lessons they had learned. These examples support Papa et al.'s (2000) arguments for empowerment through dialogue. These participants expressed a desire to share what they learned with friends and colleagues after leaving the research setting.

Of particular note, this consciousness raising occurred in focus groups of women who were studied as audiences of communication efforts (Aldoory, 2001a). The explanatory scholarship included feminist studies that focused on audiences and an applied feminist approach. Issues such as health and the environment that affect women's everyday lives came to the forefront of scholarly activity (Aldoory, 2001a; Slater et al., 1992). These studies offered strategies for involving audience members in the research and design of communication messages. The findings suggested more realistic, sensitive, and diverse ways to communicate to improve everyday life. The goals included offering women ways to interpret messages with a critical eye and become agents over their own health and well-being. Therefore, empowerment as a result of feminist scholarship in public relations occurred not only within public relations, but also outside the field as well.

The findings from explanatory studies have also empowered feminist scholars by giving them fodder to use to respond to antifeminist critics. For example, last year several feminists voiced concern over a published article that stated only age and experience accounted for sex differences in salary. These feminists shared with the editor of the publication research findings indicating that gender did indeed account for variance in salary. This year, when the editor was questioned about his prospective treatment of salary and gender, he admitted that explanations over salary disparities were complicated and that he was not going to attempt a simplistic explanation of them (E. L. Toth, personal communication, July 22, 2002).

Another way this research has empowered scholars is in its development of stronger, more heuristic theory. It has opened doors to a greater diversity of research topics as well as research methodology. Feminist researchers have also illustrated confidence and skills through their move towards critique and self-assessment.

CRITICAL SCHOLARSHIP:
RADICAL FEMINISM FOR PURPOSES OF CHANGE

Though few in number, critical feminist scholars are well publicized due to the controversy of their arguments, their threat to the status quo, and their ability to empower younger scholars to follow in their scholarly pursuits. The research included here reflects a more radical feminist perspective, through which theory, the profession, education, and research are examined.

Critique of Theory

The prevailing conceptualizations of public relations roles have led feminist scholars to critique roles theory. In particular, one area of concern has been the enduring acceptance of a two-role typology applied to various types of public relations (Broom & Dozier, 1986; Dozier, 1983, 1984, 1992; Dozier & Broom, 1995; Dozier et al., 1995; Ekachai & Komolsevin, 1996; Reagan, Anderson, Sumner, & Hill, 1990; Toth & Aldoory, 2001; Toth, Serini, Wright, & Emig, 1998). Another concern has been the assertion that public relations should be a management function rather than a technical one, as some recent research has indicated that having public relations function at a management level increases the effectiveness of public relations efforts (Dozier et al., 1995; J. E. Grunig, 1992a; McElreath, 1993). Critical feminists have questioned the validity of these findings and the dichotomous nature of public relations roles (Aldoory, 2001b; Creedon, 1991, 2001; Toth, 1988, 1989, 2001). Toth (2001) claimed that, although the two-role dichotomy allowed for empirical parsimony and a clearer understanding of factors involved in excellent public relations, "it disadvantaged thinking about the complexity of public relations practices and about how we viewed women and public relations" (p. 243). Creedon (1991) asserted that the dichotomization "appears to have homogenized the meaning of work by making all technicians appear to be similar, when in fact there is ample evidence that this is not the case" (p. 78). She termed public relations roles theory "the trash compactor model we have used to condense a multiplicity of experiences into two hierarchical roles" (p. 80).

A couple of authors have indicated flaws in methodology that may have led to the dichotomous roles. For example, Toth (1989) stated that roles research does not consider such contexts as the political, legal, economic, and educational areas that also are indicative of organizational life. Toth and Grunig (1993) argued that the same role activities have been used as variables for over 10 years, although the nature of public relations, as well as the activities carried out by practitioners, has changed since then. New variables should be explored through observations of public relations work and focus groups of practitioners, and then tested for predictability through surveys.

As the managerial role was being touted as the best, women were staying in technical positions making lower salaries and men were moving into higher paying managerial positions. Therefore, by dichotomizing the field into only two roles and emphasizing the managerial role as the one that the profession should strive for, women's main role was minimalized and devalued (Creedon, 1991; Toth, 1988, 1989). According to Creedon, roles theory is an example of institutional sexism. It is the manager who has the power to make decisions and the manager is more often male. The technician role is then seen as having less value if it is deemed by the masculine status quo as "women's work" (p. 67).

A couple of scholars have critiqued systems theory and two-way communication from a feminist perspective (Creedon, 1993; Toth, 1989). Two-way communication and the other models of public relations derive from using systems theory as the paradigm for understanding managerial public relations in 20th-century organizations (Creedon, 1993; J. E. Grunig, 1992a). Systems theory describes the interactions and interrelatedness of various components that make up an organization and the environment in which it functions. It is based on a metaphor of the organization as a living organism that needs to interact with and adapt to its environment in order for it to survive and grow (Trujillo & Toth, 1987). The organizational whole is composed of interrelated subparts, and the performance of any single subsystem will affect the entire system. The public relations departments within organizations have been considered parts of the adaptive and managerial subsystems, where maintaining balance and managing change are fundamental roles (J. E. Grunig, 1992a; J. E. Grunig & Hunt, 1984). Two-way communication facilitates the public relations manager's ability to be flexible, adapt, and manage change.

Creedon (1993) questioned the pattern of privilege reflected in the ultimate motivation behind adaptation and balance, two concepts in systems theory. She quoted from Murphy (1991), who asserted that symmetry tends to discourage innovation while encouraging custom and tradition, even when both sides in a conflict would prefer to break with the status quo. Creedon explained, "From a critical feminist perspective, custom, tradition, and status quo are code words for patriarchal privilege" (p. 159). She pushed for an analysis of underlying infrasystem factors, such as gender, race, class, and sexuality, as fundamental organizing principles. She used a case study, the institution of sport, as an example of dissecting the hidden patterns of dominance embedded in systems theory. Her goal was to transform systems theory into a new paradigm that emphasized "respect for disparate ability levels and positive interpersonal relationships with self-esteem at the core" (p. 164).

Critique of the Profession

Feminist scholars have strongly critiqued the masculinist standards and ideology that have suppressed women's promotional opportunities, salaries, and status in public relations (L. A. Grunig, 1991; Hon et al., 1992; Toth, 1988, 1989). Toth (1988) assessed the devaluation of women, sexism, and discrimination that led to the subsequent devaluation of public relations as an organizational function. She took seven common rationalizations that were often used to defend gender discrimination or to ignore it, such as "the salary gap is narrowing" (p. 39) and "women perceive themselves as technicians" (p. 42). She proceeded to dissect each one to show how they are based on poor research methodology, masculinist ideology, or socialization processes of both men and women in U.S. society. In 1989, Toth examined the assumptions behind the argument for a gender balance in public relations. Due to the fear of lower status and salaries across the profession, critics had begun proposing as a solution the push for more male students in public relations and more male practitioners. Toth asserted that the devaluation of women's contributions to public relations was the impetus behind the push for more males. Toth questioned whether the call for gender balance was an argument for the maintenance of the status quo and an attempt by male public relations practitioners to maintain personal positions of power.

Hon et al. (1992) examined the power differentials between women and men in public relations. They argued that women lacked organizational power and were excluded from key information and decision-making alliances. According to the authors, "Those in power are often willing to share their special privileges only with those they perceive to be similar to themselves" (p. 427). They proposed that the most excellent organizations would have structurally adapted to help nurture women's careers, that is, implementing flextime policies, formal mentoring programs, maternity leave, and an equitable number of female practitioners in management roles.

Other scholars have assessed the feminization of the profession and have asserted that the feminine characteristics associated with feminization change public relations for the better. Rakow (1989) believed that feminized public relations might alter relations of power between organizations and individuals, provide for communal need rather than organizational greed, and create a politics of egalitarian participation. However, this would only be accomplished if, in addition to women entering the field, "the values assigned to women are embraced as well. . . . Organizations must be feminized if we are to create a non-bureaucratic collective life, anti-hierarchical and participatory" (p. 296).

For some feminist scholars, feminist and feminine values will create a more ethical public relations practice. Sha (1996), for example, explained that women are more likely to possess a symmetrical worldview, which is an overall mindset that allows for consideration of interests of both an organization and its publics. This worldview, which most often manifests itself through organizational use of two-way communication, has been shown to be the most ethical means of practicing public relations because it allows for dialogue between organizations and publics (J. E. Grunig, 1992a). Therefore, the influx of women into public relations will lead to a more ethical profession. A more current treatise by L. A. Grunig, Toth, and Hon (2000) connected the feminine values of respect, caring, reciprocity, self-determination, honesty, and sensitivity to an ethical practice of today's public relations. The authors concluded that learning feminine values began in the classroom, where future professionals could be enculturated to adhere to certain values and ethics.

Critique of Higher Education

Some feminist scholars have analyzed the gendered nature of academics in public relations (L. A. Grunig, 1988, 1989b, 1993, 2000; Rakow, 1993a, 1993b). L. A. Grunig (1989b) wrote: "Minority students, female and male, considering a career in public relations would benefit from the elimination of the ahistorical and imperialistic generalizations that have characterized too much of the body of knowledge in public relations to date" (p. 11). Other articles have focused on curriculum reform. Rakow (1993a) stated, "Reforming the curriculum would have the ultimate effect of changing our systems of communication and eventually, society" (p. 366). She and others (L. A. Grunig, 1989b, 1993) have outlined steps towards making this transformation. Rakow (1993b) argued that the curriculum of the future needs to be independent of media industry support and resources, as well as holistic, in that it integrates speech, interpersonal, organizational, and mass communication. In addition, curriculum needs to be both inclusive, where gender and race are central tenets (cf. L. A. Grunig, 1989b) and visionary, where it plans for students' long-range future.

There have also been a couple of case studies examining outcomes from undergraduate courses that increased critical thinking about feminism, feminization of public relations, and gender issues (Creedon, 1989b; L. A. Grunig, 1989b). Creedon for example, described a course she taught on feminization in public relations. Graduate students were able to voice their own opinions about what the gender switch meant and develop action steps that could be taken. Creedon concluded that her course "demonstrates that given a framework and an opportunity, students can find a solution and/or a positive outcome for the gender switch" (p. 4).

Critique of Feminist and Gender Research

L. A. Grunig (1988, 2000) has assessed the status and goals of feminist research conducted in public relations. She proposed a feminist research agenda that included three criteria: (a) research and teaching about women in public relations, (b) feminist scholarship that would show what a conceptual democracy might be like, and (c) scholarship that would serve as a laboratory for thinking through the complexities of community. Using these criteria, L. A. Grunig (1988, 2000) examined the scholarship published in *Public Relations Review, Journal of Public Relations Research* and *Public Relations Research Annual* for its usefulness in furthering a feminist research agenda. She found that most of the articles fell within a "bifocal"(p. 94) phase of feminist scholarship, where men and women were conceptualized as separate, equal sexes—neither is better, just different. Research had not advanced to the feminist phase, where women are studied on their own, or the multifocal phase, where men and women are reconceptualized as a gender continuum rather than a dichotomy. She called for a transformation of the public relations field, which may lead to more comprehensive choices for our students—the future of the field (p. 113).

Summary

The critical research conducted in public relations has used radical feminist theory as the lens through which to view roles theory, two-way communication, ethics, education, and feminists' own research efforts. Overarching goals for this body of work include uncovering masculinist ideologies guiding theory and practice, as well as transforming the institutional systems that drive discriminatory practices. Reforms have been suggested for theoreticians, organizations, higher education curricula, and for feminists themselves.

Empowerment of Critical Scholarship

This area of research is unique from the other literature on gender and feminism in public relations in that critical feminist scholars have not only challenged mainstream theories, but have also assessed how far feminist research has advanced. Through this critique, scholars have identified gaps in public relations knowledge and ways that prevailing theories have been oppressive to women. In doing so, they have empowered other scholars to see beyond the status quo, the dichotomous nature of public relations work, and a monolithic feminist theory of public relations. Hence, scholars become empowered to alter the theories, opening them up to broader applicability for more diverse audiences. By restructuring the way public relations is theorized and practiced, scholars can also empower practitioners and, ultimately, audiences of communication efforts. For example, by suggesting public relations is practiced within the domains of respect, caring, reciprocity, self-determination, honesty, and sensitivity (L. A. Grunig et al., 2000), practitioners are given tools to work with audiences to be more aware and critical of their communication environment.

A FEMINIST PARADIGM FOR PUBLIC RELATIONS RESEARCH

The research topics, units of analysis, and methods for feminist scholarship in public relations have varied, but they are interconnected in their development of a new paradigm for research and theory in public relations. In the past, some scholars have proposed characteristics for a feminist paradigm. A feminist paradigm, for example, emphasizes wholes rather than parts, process rather than structure, knowledge as a process of interconnection rather than hierarchy, approximate descriptions rather than absolute truth, and cooperation rather than competition (Foss & Foss, 1983). Cirksena (1996) offered five points that she said defined a feminist paradigm for communication studies: (a) explicit and critical attention to inequitable power dimensions of gender relations, (b) women placed at the center of research, (c) no attempts to abstract gender from other aspects of identity, (d) action orientation linked to improving the status of women, and (e) having the researched offer some input into the research design. These characteristics describe a normative paradigm for the field rather than one that has emerged from actual scholarship in communication.

Below are presuppositions for a paradigm that emerged from the actual body of feminist scholarship in public relations. This list begins the process of developing a worldview, a methodological range, and a theoretical outlook for future research.

- A feminist paradigm for public relations is multimethodological. According to Reinharz (1992), science needs to take into account the astonishing variations among women and the work they do. She argued that a new perspective requires "listening to the voices of feminist researchers at work and accepting their diversity" (p. 5). In public relations, there has been a mixing and melding of quantitative, qualitative, critical, and historical methodology to help describe and explain gender in the field.

- A feminist paradigm is multifeminist. Harding (1991) claimed that feminist analyses of science and knowledge are not monolithic. She asserted, "There is no single set of claims beyond a few generalities that could be called 'feminism' without controversy among feminists" (p. 6). Similarly, no one feminist theory or perspective has guided the gender and feminist research in public relations. Rather, liberal, radical, and other feminist perspectives have been brought to bear on the scholarship.

- A feminist paradigm is critical. Although most of the work has been descriptive in nature, there is a growing body of work that assesses status quo and norms in public relations with both suspicion and an eye towards change.

- A feminist paradigm focuses on power relations. Even with the descriptive research, feminists in public relations guide their work with an understanding of power differentials in public relations. This became even more relevant for research when the profession became predominantly female but discrimination on multiple levels endured.

- A relationship between researcher and researched is interdependent in a feminist paradigm. Researchers see themselves as intimately connected with research participants; their well-being is dependent on the participants' well-being. In public relations, this may be due to the applied and professional nature of the field. Many public relations scholars were once practitioners themselves and, therefore, may be more sensitive to research participants.

- Feminist scholarship in the paradigm is collective and collaborative. Although several studies in public relations have been single-authored, many other projects on gender and feminism have been collaborative efforts. This increases diversity in perspectives brought to bear on research findings.

- A feminist paradigm is contextual. This paradigm takes into consideration the various factors surrounding and influencing gender and communication behavior. Gender and feminist research in public relations has included factors such as historical events, organizational life, family and work balance, and the race and ethnicity of professionals and audiences.

- A feminist paradigm applies research findings to everyday communicative behavior. The gender and feminist scholars in public relations have examined very real issues that impact practitioners' lives, such as salary, job satisfaction, and education. Research has also attempted to explain barriers to communication, factors that lead publics towards information seeking, and relationships between organizations and publics. These issues show a connection between studying the public relations profession and understanding the communication processes used everyday by publics.

The above presuppositions will likely spark dialogue among scholars about the usefulness of a feminist paradigm and the value of it for research and theory. Admittedly, as a burgeoning worldview, the paradigm has weaknesses. First, the list of presuppositions is not exhaustive. Further analysis of the body of research can help set more parameters for a useful paradigm. Second, the presuppositions derive predominantly from the perspective of White U.S. women, because most of the gender and feminist research has been conducted and analyzed by this group. This may lead to a narrow, ethnocentric view for the paradigm itself. Third, there are institutional challenges that may disrupt further development of the paradigm. For example, there are still stereotypical attitudes in the discipline about the concept of feminism. These may keep scholars from seeing the value of the paradigm for public relations research in general. The backlash against gender and feminist research alluded to earlier in this chapter may also delay paradigm development. Finally, the paradigm is transformative in that it changes the way research is conducted and theory is processed. This is difficult to accomplish in a short period of time—it may take years for a new paradigm to begin to feel like a natural way of doing science.

Even with its weaknesses, however, a feminist paradigm illustrates several strengths. The development of the paradigm itself can be empowering to scholars. According to Oakley (2000), paradigms play a key role in providing covert reference points, which bind people together in a shared commitment to their discipline. Ultimately, this shared commitment may encourage scholars to discuss their work more, recruit graduate students to continue the new tradition, and voice criticism when masculinist ideals are espoused in scholarship. Also, the paradigm will continue to expand established theories by applying them to diverse issues and audiences, which in turn will increase the reliability and validity of the theories. The paradigm can also be useful to young scholars who can use its presuppositions as guidelines for designing research studies that will be more applicable to the diverse audiences of real-world communication phenomena.

Finally, the paradigm creates opportunities for future research. It helps illuminate the gaps in the body of knowledge that future research can help close. For example, additional surveys can help detail gender differences in types of jobs, types of public relations, and different organizational structures. Also, there is a dearth of research on the relationship of race and ethnicity to gender. Many more studies need to examine the relationship of race to communication processes and communication management in public relations settings. In addition, there has been limited research assessing the political economy of public relations and the impact of the profession's class status. More research needs to work on recovering the historical contributions of women. A major topic for future scholarship should be the attitudes and behaviors of female publics of public relations efforts. Additionally, a great deal of work needs to be done in the critical realm, with feminists assessing the utility and diversity of theories and principles guiding public relations.

CONCLUSION

The body of gender and feminist scholarship in public relations has continued to grow and strengthen. Although most of the research over the past several years has been descriptive in nature, these studies were essential first steps toward feminist theory building. These studies mainly focused on professional, pragmatic issues, such as roles played, salaries, job satisfaction, sexual harassment, and the status of women of color in the field. However, several scholars expanded the descriptive scholarship to further develop and elaborate established theory. In particular, public relations roles theory, two-way communication, and the situational theory of publics have been applied to gendered situations. Also, critical researchers have successfully applied a feminist perspective to public relations scholarship.

On a practical level, the feminist and gender scholarship in public relations has increased connections between academia and practice by addressing important concerns of the majority of practitioners in the profession, the women. Many studies have been funded by professional associations, and therefore, have had outlets to speak to the profession about essential issues. The studies have increased awareness about women's status in public relations and have helped change some thinking and policies about sexual discrimination, the velvet ghetto, and the glass ceiling. Ultimately, this empowerment will trickle down to audiences of communication efforts, especially if feminist scholars and practitioners continue to see women as integral participants in the design of research and communication messages. This involvement on the part of audience members will help increase their awareness, agency, and voice.

Equally important are the contributions to theory and scholarship offered by feminist research. A new feminist paradigm can greatly impact the general body of knowledge in public relations. It will open doors to alternative areas of scholarship in public relations, such as postmodernism or rhetorical and critical perspectives. Additionally, it will allow for a refocusing on the audience. Feminist research has already increased our understanding of communication production, communication management, and the effects of public relations efforts on different publics. The feminist paradigm for public relations must now force attention towards the transformation and theory building that will allow for a more ethical, effective, and empowering discipline.

REFERENCES

30th survey of the profession: Salaries, benefits, and work conditions. (1998, October 12). *PR Reporter*, 1–6.

Albrecht, T. L. (1988). Communication and personal control in empowering organizations. In J. A. Anderson (Ed.), *Communication yearbook 11* (pp. 380–390). Newbury Park, CA: Sage.

Aldoory, L. (1998). The language of leadership for female public relations professionals. *Journal of Public Relations Research, 10*, 73–101.

Aldoory, L. (2001a). Making health messages meaningful for women: Factors that influence involvement. *Journal of Public Relations Research, 13*, 163–185.

Aldoory, L. (2001b). The standard White woman in public relations. In E. L. Toth & L. Aldoory (Eds.), *The gender challenge to media: Diverse voices from the field* (pp. 105–149). Cresskill, NJ: Hampton Press.

Aldoory, L., & Toth, E. L. (2002). Gender discrepancies in a gendered profession: A developing theory for public relations. *Journal of Public Relations Research, 14*, 103–126.

Babbie, E. (1995). *The practice of social research* (7th ed.). Belmont, CA: Wadsworth.

Belenky, M. F., Clinchy, B. M., Goldberger, N. R., & Tarule, J. M. (1986). *Women's ways of knowing: The development of self, voice, and mind.* New York: BasicBooks.

Berkowitz, D., & Turnmire, K. (1994). Community relations and issues management: An issue orientation approach to segmenting publics. *Journal of Public Relations Research, 6*, 105–123.

Bovet, S. F. (1993). Sexual harassment: What's happening and how to deal with it. *Public Relations Journal, 49*, 26–29.

Broom, G. M. (1982). A comparison of sex roles in public relations. *Public Relations Review, 8*, 17–22.

Broom, G. M., & Dozier, D. M. (1986). Advancement for public relations role models. *Public Relations Review, 12*, 37–56.

Broom, G. M., & Smith, G. D. (1979). Testing practitioner's impact on clients. *Public Relations Review, 5*, 22–28.

Cameron, G. T. (1992). Memory for investor relations messages: An information-processing study of Grunig's situational theory. *Journal of Public Relations Research, 4*, 45–60.

Chaffee, S., & Roser, C. (1986). Involvement and the consistency of knowledge, attitudes, and behaviors. *Communication Research, 13*, 373–399.

Chiles, A. M., & Zorn, T. E. (1995). Empowerment in organizations: Employees' perceptions of the influences on empowerment. *Journal of Applied Communication Research, 23*, 1–25.

Choi, Y., & Hon, L. C. (2002). The influence of gender composition in powerful positions on public relations practitioners' gender-related perceptions. *Journal of Public Relations Research, 14*, 229–263.

Cirksena, K. (1996). Feminism after ferment: Ten years of gendered scholarship in communications. In D. Allen, R. R. Rush, & S. J. Kaufman (Eds.), *Women transforming communications: Global intersections* (pp. 153–160). Thousand Oaks, CA: Sage.

Cline, C. G., & Toth, E. L. (1993). Re-visioning women in public relations: Practitioner and feminist perspectives. In P. J. Creedon (Ed.), *Women in mass communication* (2nd ed., pp. 183–198). Newbury Park, CA: Sage.

Cline, C. G., Toth, E. L., Turk, J. V., Walters, L. M., Johnson, N., & Smith, H. (1986). *The velvet ghetto: The impact of the increasing percentage of women in public relations and business communication.* San Francisco: International Association of Business Communicators.

Conrad, C. (1985). *Strategic organizational communication: Cultures, situations, and adaptation.* New York: Holt, Rinehart, & Winston.

Cosgrove, S. (2002). Levels of empowerment: Marketers and microenterprise-lending NGOs in Apopa and Nejapa, El Salvador. *Latin American Perspectives, 29*(5), 48–65.

Creedon, P. J. (1989a). Public relations history misses "her story." *Journalism Educator, 44*, 26–30.

Creedon, P. J. (1989b, June). Teaching "feminization" by reframing the perspective. *Teaching Public Relations, 13*, 1–2.

Creedon, P. J. (1991). Public relations and "women's work": Toward a feminist analysis of public relations roles. *Public Relations Research Annual, 3*, 67–84.

Creedon, P. J. (1993). Acknowledging the infrasystem: A critical feminist analysis of systems theory. *Public Relations Review, 19*, 157–166.

Creedon, P. J. (2001, August). *From making PR macro to making PR feminist: The battle over values in a female-dominated field.* Paper presented at the Association for Education in Journalism and Mass Communication, Washington, DC.

Cutlip, S. M., Center, A. H., & Broom, G. M. (2000). *Effective public relations.* Upper Saddle River, NJ: Prentice-Hall

Deatherage, C. P., & Hazleton, V., Jr. (1998). Effects of organizational worldviews on the practice of public relations: A test of the theory of public relations excellence. *Journal of Public Relations Research, 10,* 57–71.

Denzin, N. K., & Lincoln, Y. S. (Eds.). (1998). *The landscape of qualitative research: Theories and issues.* Thousand Oaks, CA: Sage.

DeRosa, D., & Wilcox, D. L. (1989). Gaps are narrowing between female and male students. *Public Relations Review, 15,* 80–89.

Devault, M. L. (1996). Talking back to sociology: Distinctive contributions of feminist methodology. *Annual Review of Sociology, 22,* 29–50.

Dozier, D. M. (1983, November). *Toward a reconciliation of "role conflict" in public relations research.* Paper presented at the meeting of the Western Communication Educators Conference, Fullerton, CA.

Dozier, D. M. (1984). Program evaluation and roles of practitioners. *Public Relations Review, 10,* 13–21.

Dozier, D. M. (1987, May). *Gender, environmental scanning, and participation in management decision making.* Paper presented at the annual meeting of the International Communication Association, Montreal, Canada.

Dozier, D. M. (1988). Breaking public relations' glass ceiling. *Public Relations Review, 14,* 6–13.

Dozier, D. M. (1992). The organizational roles of communications and public relations practitioners. In J. E. Grunig (Ed.), *Excellence in public relations and communication management* (pp. 327–355). Hillsdale, NJ: Erlbaum.

Dozier, D. M. (1995). Evolution of the manager role in public relations practice. *Journal of Public Relations Research, 7,* 3–26.

Dozier, D. M., & Broom, G. M. (1995). Evolution of the manager's role in public relations practice. *Journal of Public Relations Research, 7,* 3–26.

Dozier, D. M., Grunig, L. A., & Grunig, J. E. (1995). *Manager's guide to excellence in public relations and communication management.* Mahwah, NJ: Erlbaum.

Ekachai, D., & Komolsevin, R. (1996). Public relations in Thailand: Its functions and practitioners' roles. In H. M. Culbertson & N. Chen (Eds.), *International public relations: A comparative analysis* (pp. 155–170). Mahwah, NJ: Erlbaum.

Elliott, W. R., Mahmoud, M. A., Sothirajah, J., & Camphor, T. (1991, August). *Mass media and the third AIDS epidemic: AIDS knowledge and acceptance in a rural area.* Paper presented to the Association for Education in Journalism and Mass Communication, Boston, MA.

Farmer, B., & Waugh, L. (1999). Gender differences in public relations students' career attitudes: A benchmark study. *Public Relations Review, 25,* 235–237.

Ferguson, M. A. (1979). *Role norms, implicit relationship attributions, and organizational communication: A study of public relations practitioners.* Unpublished master's thesis, University of Wisconsin, Madison.

Flora, J. A., & Maibach, E. W. (1990). Cognitive responses to AIDS information: The effects of issue involvement and message appeal. *Communication Research, 17,* 759–774.

Foss, K. A., & Foss, S. K. (1983). The status of research on women and communication. *Communication Quarterly, 31,* 195–204.

Foos, K. A., & Foss, S. K. (1989). Incorporating the feminist perspective in communication scholarship: A research commentary. In K. Carter & C. Spitzack (Eds.) Doing research on women's communication: Perspectives on theory and method (pp.65-91). Norwod, NJ: Ablex Publishing Corporation.

Foss, K. A., Foss, S. K., & Griffin, C. L. (1999). *Feminist rhetorical theories.* Thousand Oaks, CA: Sage.

Foss, S. K., & Ray, E. B. (1996). Introduction: Theorizing communication from marginalized perspectives. *Communication Studies, 47,* 253–256.

Freire, P. (1972). *Pedagogy of the oppressed.* New York: Herder & Herder.

Gower, K. (2000, October). *Rediscovering women in public relations: Public relations women in the Public Relations Journal from 1945 through 1972.* Paper presented to the American Journalism Historians Association, Pittsburg, PA.

Grunig, J. E. (1978). Defining publics in public relations: The case of a suburban hospital. *Journalism*

Quarterly, 55, 109–118.

Grunig, J. E. (1983). Communication behaviors and attitudes of environmental publics: Two studies. *Journalism Monographs, 81.*

Grunig, J. E. (1984). Organizations, environments, and models of public relations. *Public Relations Research and Education, 1,* 6–29.

Grunig, J. E. (1987, May). *When active publics become activists: Extending a situational theory of publics.* Paper presented at the annual meeting of the International Communication Association, Montreal, Canada.

Grunig, J. E. (1989). Sierra club study shows who become activists. *Public Relations Review, 15,* 3–24.

Grunig, J. E. (Ed.). (1992a). *Excellence in public relations and communication management.* Hillsdale, NJ: Erlbaum.

Grunig, J. E. (1992b, November). *Generic and specific concepts of multi-cultural public relations.* Paper presented to the Association for the Advancement of Policy, Research, and Development in the Third World, Orlando, FL.

Grunig, J. E. (1993). Implications of public relations for other domains of communication. *Journal of Communication, 43,* 164–173.

Grunig, J. E., & Childers, L. (1988, July). *Reconstruction of a situational theory of communication: Internal and external concepts as identifiers of publics for AIDS.* Paper presented to Association for Education in Journalism and Mass Communication, Portland, OR.

Grunig, J. E., Clifford, L., Richburg, S. J., & White, T. J. (1988). Communication by agricultural publics: Internal and external orientations. *Journalism Quarterly, 65,* 26–38.

Grunig, J. E., & Grunig, L. A. (1992). Models of public relations and communication. In J. E. Grunig (Ed.), *Excellence in public relations and communication management* (pp. 285–325). Hillsdale, NJ: Erlbaum.

Grunig, J. E., & Hunt, T. (1984). *Managing public relations.* New York: Holt, Rinehart, & Winston.

Grunig, J. E., & Ipes, D. A. (1983). The anatomy of a campaign against drunk driving. *Public Relations Review,* 36–52.

Grunig, J. E., & Repper, F. C. (1992). Strategic management, publics, and issues. In J. E. Grunig (Ed.), *Excellence in public relations and communication management* (pp. 117–157). Hillsdale, NJ: Erlbaum.

Grunig, J. E., & Stamm, K. R. (1979). Communication situations and cognitive strategies in resolving environmental issues: A second study. *Journalism Quarterly, 56,* 715–726.

Grunig, J. E., & White, J. (1992). The effect of worldviews on public relations theory and practice. In J. E. Grunig (Ed.), *Excellence in public relations and communication management* (pp. 31–64). Hillsdale, NJ: Erlbaum.

Grunig, L. A. (1988). A research agenda for women in public relations. *Public Relations Review, 14,* 48–57.

Grunig, L. A. (1989a). Sex discrimination in promotion and tenure in journalism education. *Journalism Quarterly, 66,* 93–100.

Grunig, L. A. (1989b, August). *Toward a feminist transformation of public relations education and practice.* Paper presented to the Public Relations Division, Association for Education in Journalism and Mass Communication, Washington, DC.

Grunig, L. A. (1991). Court-ordered relief from sex discrimination in the foreign service: Implications for women working in development communication. *Public Relations Research Annual, 3,* 85–113.

Grunig, L. A. (1993). The "glass ceiling" effect on mass communications students. In P. J. Creedon (Ed.), *Women in mass communication* (2nd ed., pp. 276–300). Newbury Park, CA: Sage.

Grunig, L. A. (1995). The consequences of culture for public relations: The case of women in the foreign service. *Journal of Public Relations Research, 7,* 139–161.

Grunig, L. A. (2000). A feminist phase analysis of research on women in postmodern public relations. In D. Moss, D. Vercic, & G. Warnaby (Eds.), *Perspectives on public relations research* (pp. 87–120). London: Routledge.

Grunig, L. A., Toth, E. L., & Hon, L. C. (2000). Feminist values in public relations. *Journal of Public Relations Research, 12,* 49–68.

Grunig, L. A., Toth, E. L., & Hon, L. C. (2001). *Women in public relations.* New York: Guilford Press.

Hamilton, P. K. (1989). Application of a generalized persuasion model to public relations research. In C. H. Botan & V. Hazleton, Jr. (Eds.), *Public relations theory* (pp. 309–321). Hillsdale, NJ: Erlbaum.

Harding, S. (1991). *Whose science? Whose knowledge? Thinking from women's lives.* Ithaca, NY: Cornell University Press.

Heath, R. L., & Douglas, W. (1990). Involvement: A key variable in people's reaction to public policy issues. In J.E. Grunig & L.A. Grunig (Eds.), *Public relations research annual* (Vol. 2, pp. 93–204). Hillsdale, NJ: Erlbaum.

Heath, R. L., & Douglas, W. (1991). Effects of involvement on reactions to sources of messages and to message clusters. In J. E. Grunig & L. A. Grunig (Eds.), *Public relations research annual* (Vol. 3, pp. 179–193). Hillsdale, NJ: Erlbaum.

Heath, R. L., Liao, S. H., & Douglas, W. (1995). Effects of perceived economic harms and benefits on issue involvement, use of information sources, and actions: A study in risk communication. *Journal of Public Relations Research, 7,* 89–109.

Henry, S. (1988, July). *In her own name? Public relations pioneer Doris Fleischman Bernays.* Paper presented to the Association for Education in Journalism and Mass Communication, Portland, OR.

Henry, S. (1996, August). *The retiring feminist: Doris E. Fleischman and Doris Fleischman Bernays.* Paper presented to the Association for Education in Journalism and Mass Communication, Anaheim, CA.

Hon, L. C. (1995). Toward a feminist theory of public relations. *Journal of Public Relations Research, 7,* 27–88.

Hon, L. C., Grunig, L. A., & Dozier, D. M. (1992). Women in public relations: Problems and opportunities. In J. E. Grunig (Ed.), *Excellence in public relations and communication management* (pp. 419–438). Hillsdale, NJ: Erlbaum.

hooks, b. (1984). *Feminist theory: From margin to center.* Boston, MA: South End Press.

Houston, M. (1992). The politics of difference: Race, class, and women's communication. In L. Rakow (Ed.), *Women making meaning* (pp. 45–59). New York: Routledge.

Jacobson, H. K., & Tortorello, N. J. (1992). PRJ's seventh annual salary survey. *Public Relations Journal, 48,* 9–21, 26–30.

Jensen, A. (2002). Women's empowerment and demographic processes: Moving beyond Cairo. *Feminist Economics, 8,* 146–148.

Kanter, R. M. (1977). *Men and women of the corporation.* New York: Basic Books.

Kendall, R. (1996). *Public relations campaign strategies* (2nd ed.). New York: Harper Collins.

Kern-Foxworth, M. (1989a). An assessment of minority female roles and status in public relations: Trying to unlock the acrylic vault and assimilate into the velvet ghetto. In E. L. Toth & C. G. Cline (Eds.), *Beyond the velvet ghetto* (pp. 241–286). San Francisco: International Association of Business Communicators.

Kern-Foxworth, M. (1989b). Public relations books fail to show women in context. *Journalism Educator, 44,* 31–36.

Kern-Foxworth, M. (1989c). Status and roles of minority public relations practitioners. *Public Relations Review, 5,* 14–22.

Kern-Foxworth, M., Gandy, O., Hines, B., & Miller, D. A. (1994). Assessing the managerial roles of Black female public relations practitioners using individual and organizational discriminants. *Journal of Black Studies, 24,* 416–434.

Kucera, M. (1994). *Doing it all: Why women public relations managers tend to fulfill both the managerial and technical roles.* Unpublished master's thesis, University of Maryland, College Park.

Kuhn, T. (1970). *The structure of scientific revolutions.* Chicago: University of Chicago Press.

Lamme, M. O. (1999, October). *Furious desires and victorious careers: Doris E. Fleischman, counsel on public relations and advocate for working women.* Paper presented to the American Journalism Historians Association, Portland, OR.

Laudan, L. (1977). *Progress and its problems: Toward a theory of scientific growth.* Berkeley: University of California Press.

Lauzen, M. (1992). Effects of gender on professional encroachment in public relations. *Journalism*

Quarterly, 69, 173–180.

Lesly, P. (1988). Public relations numbers are up but stature down. *Public Relations Review, 14,* 3–7.

Leyland, A. (2000, March 27). Competition drives PR salaries up 8% in '99. *PR Week,* p. 1.

Major, A. M. (1993). Environmental concern and situational communication theory: Implications for communicating with environmental publics. *Journal of Public Relations Research, 5,* 251–268.

Mathews, W. (1988). Women in PR: Progression or retrogression? *Public Relations Review, 14,* 24–28.

McElreath, M. (1993). *Managing systematic and ethical public relations.* Madison, WI: Brown & Benchmark.

Miller, K. S. (1997). Woman, man, lady, horse: Jane Stewart, public relations executive. *Public Relations Review, 23,* 249–269.

Murphy, P. (1991). The limits of symmetry: A game theory approach to symmetric and asymmetric public relations. In J. E. Grunig & L. A. Grunig (Eds.), *Public relations research annual* (Vol. 3, pp. 115–132). Hillsdale, NJ: Erlbaum.

Oakley, A. (2000). *Experiments in knowing: Gender and method in the social sciences.* New York: New Press.

O'Neil, J. W. (1999, August). *The strategist: Positioning women as "outsiders within" the public relations profession.* Paper presented to the Association for Education in Journalism and Mass Communication, New Orleans, LA.

Papa, M. J., Singhal, A., Ghanekar, D. V., & Papa, W. H. (2000). Organizing for social change through cooperative action: The [dis]empowering dimensions of women's communication. *Communication Theory, 10,* 90–123.

Patai, D., & Koertge, N. (1994). *Professing feminism.* New York: BasicBooks.

Pincus, J. D., & Rayfield, R. E. (1989). Organizational communication and job satisfaction: A metaresearch perspective. In B. Dervin & M. J. Voigt (Eds.), *Progress in communication sciences* (pp. 183–208). Norwood, NJ: Ablex.

Rakow, L. F. (1989). From the feminization of public relations to the promise of feminism. In E. L. Toth & C. G. Cline (Eds.), *Beyond the velvet ghetto* (pp. 287–298). San Francisco: International Association of Business Communicators.

Rakow, L. F. (1993a). A bridge to the future: How to get there from here through curriculum reform. In P. J. Creedon (Ed.), *Women in mass communication* (2nd ed., pp. 363–374). Newbury Park, CA: Sage.

Rakow, L. F. (1993b). The curriculum is the future. *Journal of Communication, 43*(4), 154–162.

Reagan, J., Anderson, R., Sumner, J., & Hill, S. (1990). A factor analysis of Broom and Smith's public relations roles scale. *Journalism Quarterly, 67,* 180.

Reinharz, S. (1992). *Feminist methods in social research.* New York: Oxford University Press.

Roser, C., & Thompson, M. (1995). Fear appeals and the formation of active publics. *Journal of Communication, 45,* 103–121.

Rush, R. R., & Grubb-Swetnam, A. (1996). Feminist approaches. In M. B. Salwen & D. W. Stacks (Eds.), *An integrated approach to communication theory and research* (pp. 497–518). Mahwah, NJ: Erlbaum.

Salary survey of public relations professionals. (1995). New York: Simmons Market Research Bureau for the Public Relations Society of America.

Scrimger, J. (1989). Women communicators in Canada: A case for optimism. In E. L. Toth & C. G. Cline (Eds.), *Beyond the velvet ghetto* (pp. 219–240). San Francisco: International Association of Business Communicators.

Seideman, T., & Leyland, A. (2000, March 27). PR Week salary survey report 2000. *PR Week,* pp. 23–25, 27, 29, 31, 33, 35.

Selnow, G. W., & Wilson, S. (1985). Sex roles and job satisfaction in public relations. *Public Relations Review, 11,* 38–47.

Serini, S. A., Toth, E., Wright, D. K., & Emig, A. (1996). Watch for falling glass . . . women, men, and job satisfaction in public relations: A preliminary analysis. *Journal of Public Relations Research, 9,* 99–118.

Serini, S. A., Toth, E., Wright, D. K., & Emig, A. (1998). Power, gender, and public relations: Sexual harassment as a threat to the practice. *Journal of Public Relations Research, 10,* 193–218.

Sha, B. L. (1996, May). *Does feminization of the field make public relations more ethical?* Paper presented at the annual meeting of the International Communication Association, Chicago, IL.

Slater, M. D., Chipman, H., Auld, G., Keefe, T., & Kendall, P. (1992). Information processing and situational theory: A cognitive response analysis. *Journal of Public Relations Research, 4,* 189–203.

Steeves, H. L. (2001). Liberation, feminism, and development communication. *Communication Theory, 11,* 397–414.

Tam, S. Y., Dozier, D. M., Lauzen, M. M., & Real, M. R. (1995). The impact of superior-subordinate gender on the career advancement of public relations practitioners. *Journal of Public Relations Research, 7,* 259–272.

Tetreault, M. K. T. (1985). Feminist phase theory. *Journal of Higher Education, 56,* 363–384.

Tillery-Larkin, R. (2000). *Surveying perceived pigeonholing among African American public relations professionals.* Unpublished doctoral dissertation, Southern Illinois University at Carbondale.

Toth, E. L. (1988). Making peace with gender issues in public relations. *Public Relations Review, 14,* 36–47.

Toth, E. L. (1989). Whose freedom and equity in public relations? The gender balance argument. *Mass Comm Review, 16,* 70–76.

Toth, E. L. (2001). How feminist theory advanced the practice of public relations. In R. L. Heath & G. Vasquez (Eds.), *Handbook of Public Relations* (pp. 237–246). Newbury Park, CA: Sage.

Toth, E. L., & Aldoory, L. (2001, April). *Year 2000 gender study: Report of the committee on work, life, and gender issues.* Presentation to the Public Relations Society of America National Board, New York.

Toth, E. L., & Cline, C. G. (Eds.). (1989). *Beyond the velvet ghetto.* San Francisco: International Association of Business Communicators.

Toth, E. L., & Cline, C. G. (1991). Public relations practitioner attitudes toward gender issues: A benchmark study. *Public Relations Review, 17,* 161–174.

Toth, E. L., & Grunig, L. A. (1993). The missing story of women in public relations. *Journal of Public Relations Research, 5,* 153–175.

Toth, E. L., Serini, S. A., Wright, D. K., & Emig, A. G. (1998). Trends in public relations roles: 1990–1995. *Public Relations Review, 24,* 145–163.

Trujillo, N., & Toth, E. L. (1987). Organizational perspectives for public relations research and practice. *Management Communication Quarterly, 1,* 199–281.

van Zoonen, L. (1994). *Feminist media studies.* Thousand Oaks, CA: Sage.

Vasquez, G. M. (1993). A *homo narrans* paradigm for public relations: Combining Bormann's symbolic convergence theory and Grunig's situational theory of publics. *Journal of Public Relations Research, 5,* 201–216.

Vasquez, G. M., & Taylor, M. (2001). Public relations: An emerging social science enters the new millennium. In W. B. Gudykunst (Ed.), *Communication yearbook 24* (pp. 319–342). Thousand Oaks, CA: Sage.

Weaver-Lariscy, R. A., Cameron, G. T., Sweep, D. D. (1994). Women in higher education PR: An inkling of change? *Journal of Public Relations Research, 6,* 125–140.

Weaver-Lariscy, R. A., Sallot, L., & Cameron, G. T. (1996). Justice and gender: An instrumental and symbolic explication. *Journal of Public Relations Research, 8,* 107–121.

Wetherell, B. L. (1989). *The effect of gender, masculinity, and femininity on the practice and preference for the models of public relations.* Unpublished master's thesis, University of Maryland, College Park.

Wilson, S. R., & Putnam, L. L. (1990). Interaction goals in negotiation. In J. A. Anderson (Ed.), *Communication yearbook 13* (pp. 374–406). Newbury Park, CA: Sage.

Wootton, B. H. (1997, April). Gender differences in occupational employment. *Monthly Labor Review, 120,* 15–24.

Wright, D. K., Grunig, L. A., Springston, J. K., & Toth, E. L. (1991). *Under the glass ceiling: An analysis of gender issues in American public relations.* New York: Public Relations Society of America.

Wright, D. K., & Haynes, J. R. (1999, August). *An innovative look at gender in public relations:*

Examining relationships between gender and source credibility in employee communication messages and media. Paper presented to the Association for Education in Journalism and Mass Communication, New Orleans, LA.

Wrigley, B. J. (2002). Glass ceiling? What glass ceiling? A qualitative study of how women view the glass ceiling in public relations and communications management. *Journal of Public Relations Research, 14,* 27–55.

Zerbinos, E., & Clanton, G. A. (1993). Minority practitioners: Career influences, job satisfaction, and discrimination. *Public Relations Review, 19,* 75–91.

CHAPTER CONTENTS

9 Control, Resistance, and Empowerment in Raced, Gendered, and Classed Work Contexts: The Case of African American Women

PATRICIA S. PARKER
University of North Carolina at Chapel Hill

This chapter uses feminist and critical organizational communication perspectives to examine control, resistance, and empowerment as revealed in the literature on African American women's work experiences. Acker's (1991) model of gendered organizations is extended to include race and class, and to frame an understanding of African American women's subordination (control) and resistance (empowerment) in work situations. This chapter presents evidence of African American women's subordination in three aspects of raced, gendered, and classed work contexts: (a) organizational divisions (e.g., divisions of labor, allowed behaviors, and work spaces), (b) symbolic constructions, and (c) workplace interactions. African American women's empowerment in these work contexts are revealed in five themes that are informed by a Black feminist perspective and that are expressed somewhat differently by working-class or working-poor women as compared to middle- and upper-class women in the professions. Implications for theory, research, and practice are discussed.

I n the past decade a number of organizational communication scholars have employed critical-feminist perspectives in their research (e.g., B. J. Allen, 1995, 1996, 1998; Bullis, 1993; Buzzanell, 1994; 2000; Marshall, 1993; Mumby & Putnam, 1992; Tretheway, 1997). Virtually excluded from this literature is one of the primary concerns of contemporary critical-feminist research—diversity and the belief that "the oppression of women through sexism is not independent from their oppression through racism and classism" (Taylor & Trujillo, 2001, p. 172).

AUTHOR'S NOTE: The author wishes to thank Dennis Mumby for his insightful coments on drafts of this chapter. The manuscript was completed with support from the Institute for the Arts and Humanities, University of North Carolina at Chapel Hill, where the author is the 2002 Burress Faculty Fellow.

Correspondence: Patricia S. Parker, Uniniversity of North Carolina at Chapel Hill, Department of Communication Studies, 115 Bingham, CB #3285, Chapel Hill, NC 27599; email: psparker@email.unc.edu

With few exceptions organizational communication scholars using feminist perspectives have not taken up issues of race, gender, and class as interdependent processes (vs. B. J. Allen, 1996, 1998; Buzzanell, 2000; Mumby & Stohl, 1998). Instead the focus has been almost exclusively on unraced constructions of gender,[1] revealing the work experiences of women who are "[W]hite, heterosexual, middle class, and corporate-managerial" (Taylor & Trujillo, 2001, p. 172).[2] That gap in the literature is addressed in this chapter by calling attention to the intersections of race, gender, and class in the work experiences of African American women.[3]

Specifically, this chapter employs feminist and critical organizational communication perspectives to explore issues of control, resistance, and empowerment as revealed in the growing literature on African American women's work experiences. Research interest in African American women and work has increased in the last decade. Scholars have called attention to the exclusion of African American women from studies on women in management and executive leadership, despite dramatic increases in their numbers in this sector (Nkomo, 1992; Parker & Ogilvie, 1996). Also, researchers from several disciplines, particularly sociology and economics, have investigated issues related to the persistence of low-wage jobs and poverty for the majority of African American women. Despite tangible gains following the civil rights and feminist movements of the 1960s and 1970s, African American women are among the most economically disadvantaged groups in the U.S. labor market (Browne, 1999a).[4] This chapter uses a critical-feminist framework to synthesize this literature, directing attention to the ways organizational communication scholars can—and should—conduct research exploring the intersections of race, gender, and class in the workplace.

There are two purposes of this essay. The first is to illuminate the ways race, gender, and class structure communicative practices in everyday organizational life—such as hiring and recruitment rituals, interaction patterns, and symbolic processes—that contribute to African American women's continued subordination and oppression in the U.S. labor market. Revealing the communicative structuring of oppressive organizational systems that marginalize groups is a crucial step toward transforming and changing those systems.

The second goal is to identify specific forms of resistance and empowerment as revealed in the literature on African American women and work. In contemporary culture, marginalized group interests and experiences are often suppressed, devalued, and muted (Orbe, 1998b). For example, in national policy debates about work and family issues, job training, and welfare-to-work programs, often the people most affected by these issues—poor and working-class women and men of color—are left out of the conversation (Fine & Weis, 1998). However, everyday acts of resistance to oppression have the potential for providing creative strategies for system transformation that can inform national work policy initiatives. One aim of this chapter is to focus on the contradictions and struggles inherent in the lives of African American women who are marginalized by oppressive practices. Most importantly, the aim is to affirm the knowledge and op-portunities for empowerment revealed in their own efforts to work through those contradictions and struggles.

USING A CRITICAL COMMUNICATION PERSPECTIVE TO STUDY CONTROL, RESISTANCE, AND EMPOWERMENT IN THE WORKPLACE

This chapter underscores the need for a critical communicative perspective to study groups that are marginalized and oppressed in work situations. Much of the research on African American women and work has used sociological or economic perspectives that lack a critical focus. These perspectives provide important infor-mation about broad-based trends in the labor market, such as economic restructur-ing and demographic changes, that structure the work experiences of African American women (cf. Woody, 1992). However, these studies do not explicate the micropractices of power that sustain systems of domination (vs. Amott & Matthaei, 1996; Browne, 1999b), nor do they emphasize the ways in which gender, race, and class are constituted communicatively in everyday work practices. A critical orga-nizational communication perspective in general, and feminist perspectives in par-ticular, direct attention to the gendered, raced, and classed communicative prac-tices that constitute organizational control and resistance. Additionally, these per-spectives compel African American women's empowerment in work situations.

A critical organizational communication perspective examines organizations as intersubjective structures of meaning in which identity and power relationships are produced, maintained, and reproduced through the ongoing communicative practices of members (Deetz, 1982; Mumby, 2001). Connections among power, ideology, and hegemony are central to this view of organizational communication. Power is viewed as a dialectical process of domination and resistance that is mani-fested in everyday organizational life. In this context, hegemonic control functions not simply as ideological domination of one group by another, but is "a dynamic conception of the lived relations of social groups and the various struggles that constantly unfold between and among these groups" (Mumby, 2001, p. 598). From this perspective, the process of control and resistance can be understood as a struggle over meaning, where "the group that is able to get a certain meaning system to 'stick' is the group with the most power" (p. 601).

Feminist perspectives provide an understanding of empowerment as resistance to control, emphasizing that the struggle over organizational meanings is gendered, raced, and classed. Drawing on both critical and postmodern views of power, femi-nist perspectives reveal empowerment as a form of resistance within systems of unequal power relations. Important to this conceptualization of empowerment is the postmodern view that power and resistance are simultaneously manifested in the everyday level of organizing. Foucault (1980) contends that "there are no rela-tions of power without resistances; the latter are all the more real and effective

because they are formed right at the point where relations of power are exercised
. . . hence, like power, resistance is multiple" (p. 142). Foucault's (1979, 1980)
perspective on power and resistance suggests two important points that advance
the model of resistance as empowerment. First, because power and resistance are
inextricably related, persons in systems of power relations have immediate access
to power through resistance at the local, contextual level. Power relations are
ongoing processes and involve "strategies and counter-strategies of power" (Pringle,
1988, p. 96). Second, there are multiple forms of resistances to power, suggesting that
there are multiple routes to empowerment in systems of power relations. For example, resistance has been manifested as (a) collective resistance and change through
coalition formation and community building; and (b) individual acts of resistance,
including self-definitions and self-determination that often occur in varied, immediate, and idiosyncratic ways.

The central premise of this chapter is that aspects of contemporary racial, gender, and class politics serve the ideological function of fostering hegemonic control in the micropractices of everyday organizational communication (Mumby,
1987), reproducing systems of meaning that contribute to African American
women's continued oppression and subordination in the workforce. It is further
argued that these same processes provide a source of resistance and empowerment
for African American women. Within the larger, societal context of race, gender,
and class politics, African American women's empowerment in work settings can
be seen as resistance to attempts to fix meanings of appropriate identity and behavior, where such meanings are interpreted as controlling, exploitative, and otherwise oppressive to African American women. This chapter examines research on
communicative practices that constitute control of African American women's
behavior and identity in contemporary work situations. Additionally, this chapter
explores theoretical and empirical research related to African American women's
empowerment as resistance to control.

The chapter is presented in four parts. First, I establish a critical-feminist framework for analyzing the literature on African American women's work experiences.
The second part is a survey of the literature using the established framework, revealing communicative practices that constitute control and resistance in African American women's work experiences. Third, I present a summary and discussion of
issues related to African American women's subordination and empowerment as
revealed in the literature. The chapter concludes with a discussion of the implications
of this analysis for theory, research, and practice in organizational communication.

EMPOWERMENT AS RESISTANCE TO ORGANIZATIONAL SYSTEMS OF CONTROL: A CRITICAL-FEMINIST FRAMEWORK

In this section, I establish a critical-feminist framework emphasizing
intersectionality to conceptualize control, resistance, and empowerment as revealed
in the literature of African American women's work experiences. Intersectionality

calls attention to the ways organizational members "do difference" in their everyday interactions (West & Fenstermaker, 1995). P. H. Collins (1998a) defines intersectionality as "an analysis claiming that systems of race, economic class, gender, sexuality, ethnicity, nation, and age form mutually constructing features of social organization" (p. 278).

Empirical and theoretical work in organizational studies has focused almost exclusively on gendered patterns of control (cf. Calas & Smircich, 1996). Acker's (1991) theory of gendered organizations is one of the most comprehensive models (cf. Kanter, 1977; Marshall, 1993). Acker's framework draws attention to the everyday social processes of "advantage and disadvantage, exploitation and control, action and emotion, meaning and identity" (p. 167) that are patterned through and in terms of gender. The sole focus on gender, however, masks the influences of race, gender, and class in women's work experiences (Amott & Matthaei, 1996; Essed, 1994; Rowe, 2000; Spelman, 1988). Essed argued that such approaches

> do not provide insight into possible contradictions, for example, in the experiences of middle class African American women who may reproduce dominance along one axis (e.g., in class terms) and resist oppression at other levels (e.g., through opposition against racism). (p. 100)

Yoder and Aniakudo (1997) point out, following Spelman, that "there is no raceless, classless, generic woman" (p. 325). Thus, the focus should be on the ways in which race, gender, and class intersect in women's lives.

In this chapter, intersectionality is used to expand aspects of Acker's model of gendered organizations by focusing on the simultaneous structuring of organizations as gendered, raced, and classed.

Organizations: Raced, Gendered, and Classed Systems of Control

Critical-feminist perspectives demonstrate that, although organizations are often seen as gender and race neutral, they should be revealed as gendered and raced (Acker, 1991; B. J. Allen, 1996; Buzzanell, 2000; Ferguson, 1984; Marshall, 1993; Martin, 1990; Nkomo, 1992; Parker, 2001). That is, control is manifested in the hidden microprocesses and micropractices that produce and reproduce unequal, and persistent, sex-, race-, and class-based patterns in work situations. From this perspective, gender and race are constitutive elements of organizing and are primary ways of signifying power in social systems, and all class relations in organizations are gendered and raced (Scott, 1986; Acker, 1991).

Acker's model of gendered organizations should be extended to focus on the simultaneous structuring of organizations as gendered, raced, and classed. Although Acker conceptualizes persisting gendered organizational structuring in a number of ways, here the focus is on raced, gendered, and classed structuring in three areas where most of the literature on African American women and work is centered. First is the construction of divisions along lines of race, gender, and class—divisions of labor, of allowed behaviors, of locations in physical space, and of power.

Second is the construction of symbols and images that explain, reinforce, or sometimes oppose race, gender, and class divisions. Third are the interactions between women and men, women and women, men and men, including all the patterns that enact dominance and submission.

This extended version of Acker's (1991) model provides a useful framework for illuminating raced, gendered, and classed organizational practices of control. Additionally, this analysis uses a communication perspective that focuses attention to the ways that these practices are constituted communicatively. Before applying Acker's extended model to the literature on African American women's work experiences, it is necessary to conceptualize how race, gender, and class intersect with empowerment as resistance to control.

Em(power)ment-as-Resistance

For the purposes of this chapter, empowerment is conceptualized as local and contextualized resistance to systems of control, manifested as collective action and individual agency. This view of empowerment is informed by critical-feminist perspectives generally and Black feminist standpoint theories specifically. Consistent with critical-feminist views, empowerment is viewed as a process that (a) breaks the boundaries between the public and private domain, (b) comes out of the personal into the social, and (c) connects the sense of the personal and the communal. As collective action, empowerment is a process by which oppressed persons gain some control over their lives by taking part with others in the development of activities and structures that allow people increased involvement in matters that affect them directly (Bystydzienski, 1992). As individual agency, empowerment can be felt momentarily, "where resistance 'crystallizes in isolated acts or gestures' in the context of on-going power relations" (Okely, 1991, p. 7, as cited in Tretheway, 1997, p. 283).

Black Feminist Perspectives on Empowerment

Black feminist perspectives on empowerment (cf. P. H. Collins, 1990; Gilkes, 1980; hooks, 1981; Hull, Scott, & Smith., 1982; King, 1988; Lorde, 1984; Rogers-Rose, 1980; Smith, 1983) emphasize a particular expression of resistance to power from African American women's location in systems of power relations. At the intersections of economic, political, and ideological systems of oppression that suppress African American women's ideas and reproduce controlling images of Black womanhood, African American women must negotiate and reconcile the contradictions separating internally defined images of self as African American women whose identities are (re)produced through patriarchal systems of domination and subordination (P. H. Collins, 1990). It is the process of negotiating and reconciling identities that has historically informed African American women's strategies for empowerment, through both collective action and individual agency (P. H. Collins, 1990, 1998a; hooks, 1981; Jones, 1985). This literature emphasizes five themes related to African American women's empowerment: (a) developing and using voice, (b) being self-defined, (d) being self-determined, (d) connecting to and building community, and (e) seeking spirituality and regeneration.

One predominant theme related to empowerment evident in the Black feminist literature is developing and using voice, a conceptualization of empowerment employed in Black feminist writing as early as the 19th century.[5] More recently, hooks (1990) described the concept of voice in terms of three strategies for empowerment and resistance: (a) breaking silence against oppression, (b) developing reflexive speech through dialogues among individual women, and (c) confronting or talking back to elite discourses. P. H. Collins (1998a) argued that the contours of African American women's voices are simultaneously confrontational (in response to different interests) and collaborative (in response to shared interests).

Being self-defined and self-determined are two interrelated forms of empowerment in the Black feminist literature. P. H. Collins (1990, 1998a) described a Black feminist standpoint perspective that conceptualizes self-definition as the power to name one's own reality and self-determination as the power to decide one's own destiny. P. H. Collins (1990) argued that a Black feminist standpoint emerges from African American women's location as outsiders within systems of domination and directs attention to African American women as self-defined, self-reliant individuals confronting race, gender, and class oppression. Lorde (1984) emphasized this theme in her essay, *The Masters Tools Will Never Dismantle the Master's House*, in which she described the process of becoming self-defined and self-determined as "learning how to take our differences and make them strengths" (p. 111).

The fourth empowerment theme in the Black feminist literature is connecting to and building community. Since the era of slavery in the United States, African American women have demonstrated a history of activism through community work (Gilkes, 1980; McCluskey, 1997). Activism through community work consists of activities to strengthen family and kinship ties, combat racism, and empower communities to survive, grow, and advance, thus reinforcing the theme, "lifting as we climb" (Gilkes, 1983; McCluskey, 1997).

A final theme suggests that African American women's empowerment through resistance is most effective when it is sustained through energies that elevate the human spirit and create new strategies for liberation from oppressive situations. Spirituality and regeneration can be defined as a reliance on a spiritual center for answers, explanations, and a focus toward the future. P. H. Collins (1998a) asserted that spirituality continues to move countless African American women to struggle in everyday life. Similarly, Omalade (1994) argued that African American women's empowerment "cannot be understood without knowing her spirit and spiritual life" (p. 112, as cited in Collins, 1998a, p. 247).

The themes of empowerment emphasized in the Black feminist literature, along with an extended version of Acker's (1991) model of organizational control, provide a useful framework for examining African American women's empowerment as resistance within raced, gendered, and classed work situations.

CONTROL, RESISTANCE, AND EMPOWERMENT IN THE LITERATURE
ON AFRICAN AMERICAN WOMEN'S WORK EXPERIENCES

The critical-feminist framework established earlier is used in this section to explore theoretical and empirical research as it relates to African American women's empowerment as resistance to control in workplace situations. Most of the research reviewed is from sociology and economics, where the majority of the work in this area has been done. Research from communication studies, African American studies, women's studies, psychology, and management and organization studies is also included. This literature is limited to books and articles published in the past 10 years. In some cases, classic research is included to emphasize a particular trend or to establish a historical perspective. The searches were limited to research focusing on African American women and work, which had relevance to communication, control, resistance, and empowerment as defined in this chapter.

Acker's (1991) extended model of organizations as raced, gendered, and classed was used here to frame an understanding of African American women's subordination (control) and resistance (empowerment) in work situations, drawing upon the empowerment themes from Black feminist literature. Evidence of African American women's subordination and empowerment in the aspects of raced, gendered, and classed work contexts is presented as: (a) organizational divisions (e.g., divisions of labor, allowed behaviors, and work spaces), (b) symbolic constructions, and (c) workplace interactions.

Raced, Gendered, and Classed Organizational Divisions

Communicative practices of control in constructing organizational divisions. From critical-feminist perspectives, persistent structuring of organizations along race, gender, and class lines occurs through ordinary, daily procedures and decisions that segregate jobs, set policies, and control work processes. For example, race-, gender-, and class-based decisions in recruiting and promoting practices contribute to job segregation. Feminist scholars argue that recruiting and promoting practices should be seen as boundary maintenance, or more specifically, as a way of keeping "outsiders" out of specific jobs, organizations, or occupations (Bullis & Stout, 2000). Research on African American women's experiences in choosing, preparing for, and entering careers provides some evidence of how organizations work to (re)produce outsider status at various occupational levels (B. J. Allen, 1996, 2000; Bell & Nkomo, 2001; S. M. Collins, 1989; Parker, 2002; Reid-Merritt, 1996).

The process begins with African American girls. Their location at the intersections of race, gender, and class oppression makes African American girls especially vulnerable to exclusionary communication practices from counselors, teachers, and others charged with guiding and preparing young people for their future. Several studies have documented anecdotal evidence of African American girls' receiving what Parker (1997) terms "negative achievement" messages from counselors, teachers, and administrators during high school and college, a time when most students are planning for their future (Bell & Nkomo, 2001; Calabrese & Underwood, 1994; Cohn, 1997; Farmer, 1997; Fordham, 1993; Parker, 1997, 2002; Pennington, 1999; Reid-Merritt, 1996).

For instance, Parker (2002) conducted in-depth interviews with 15 African American women executives in senior leadership, who completed high school during the 1960s and 1970s. Participants recounted stories from their childhood, adolescence, and early career experiences involving negative interactions with (primarily) White teachers, counselors, and work supervisors, whom they perceived as having discouraged their academic and career development. The women's high school years were particularly rife with both opportunities and challenges. Most of these women reported having aspirations of going to college, and many of them were already very clear about pursuing specific careers in professions such as medicine and law. Although they found support from their parents and other influential adults during this time, these women began to encounter discourses that marked them as outsiders, that is, as not being college material or not being considered for careers in medicine or other White, male-dominated professions.

Research on more recent school experiences of African American girls suggests that practices of exclusion in schools persist, but they are often (but not always) subtle and largely ignored, denied, and suppressed by school administrators, teachers, and counselors (Calabrese & Underwood, 1994; Cohn, 1997; Farmer, 1997; Fordham, 1993, 1996). For contemporary African American girls, practices of exclusion emerge within school environments in both rural and urban areas of the United States, in which "White [middle-class] womanhood" (Fordham, 1993, p. 4) is normalized and defined as a cultural norm of the good woman. "[B]lack womanhood" is constructed as "the antithesis of White women's lives, the 'slur' or 'the nothingness' used to perpetuate and control the White-defined image of the 'good girl' and by extension the good woman" (p. 4). In this context, when African American girls express themselves in culturally distinct ways, they experience a number of problems in their interactions with teachers and school counselors: (a) they are sometimes defined as problem students by both White and African American teachers, (b) the frequency of conflicts with their teachers may increase, (c) they may experience feelings of isolation and rejection, and (d) they are at risk of becoming disengaged from learning (Holcom-McCoy & Moore-Thomas, 2001). In some cases, African American girls may find themselves in an alternative school that may actually contribute to students' disengagement from learning (Souza, 1999).

Other research relates more generally to the racialized context of schooling in the United States. In their study of the effects of school-generated racism on students of color, including African American girls, Calabrese and Underwood (1994) found evidence that "systemic racism . . . is expressed overtly and covertly [in our schools]" (p. 269). The authors contend that because of school-generated racism, "schooling is very different for [W]hite middle and upper class adolescents than it is for [students] of color" (p. 267). Cohn's (1997) research found evidence of these differences in the stories of 22 people of color (including African American women), whom she interviewed about their high school experiences in the late 1970s and early 1980s. These participants believed they did not receive the same treatment as their White counterparts. They tell stories of "encountering uncaring teachers and school administrators, none of whom seem to consider these students an integral, important part of the student body. It was almost as if they were invisible" (p. 165).

What emerges from this literature is a picture of an environment in which African American girls and other students of color feel ignored, isolated, unsupported, and even despised (Cohn, 1997; Fordham, 1993, 1996). In this context, even communication from teachers intended to be supportive of students of color may be perceived as biased. For instance, Rosenfeld and Richman (1999) studied supportive communication and school outcomes, comparing two groups of low income high-school students: those identified as academically at-risk and those academically not-at-risk. The at-risk group was comprised of predominantly African American (both male and female) students, whereas the not-at-risk students included African American and Hispanic students. Their research showed that neither group of students identified their teachers as primary or secondary sources of support. This finding was especially surprising for the at-risk students, who were participants in a community intervention program for which teacher support measures were high. Rosenfeld and Richman concluded that "Teachers' behaviors that could, in another context, be [seen by the students as] supportive, may be dismissed by the students as 'part of class,' 'education,' 'school stuff,' or even acting out of some hidden agenda" (p. 303). However, in the raced, gendered, and classed context of urban schooling, these findings could be seen as further evidence of the feelings of alienation and exclusion experienced by students of color.

African American women's exclusion from certain occupations typically held by White men and women is one possible outcome of the raced, gendered, and classed context of schooling, especially at the college level. For example, although integrated institutions enroll larger numbers of African American students, and typically have much more funding and other resources, historically Black colleges and universities yield more African American scientists (Rosser, 1998).

After navigating the raced, gendered, and classed context of schooling, African American women face further exclusionary practices in the U.S. labor market. Job segregation is perhaps most pronounced during the time of job entry, when recruiters' enact race-, gender-, and class-based interpretations in their hiring practices. African American women workers with a high school degree or less are particularly vulnerable.

In his study of jobs requiring a high school degree or less, Holzer (1996) found that jobs entailing reading and writing, math, or computer skills are less likely to go to African American women than to White women. White women's relative advantage in hiring for these jobs could be due to negative employer biases regarding African American women, particularly those in urban areas. Some evidence suggests that employers sometimes exclude African American applicants who appear raced, such as those who exhibit speech and dress patterns of the inner city, during the recruitment phase (Kirschenman & Neckerman, 1992). This claim is reinforced by a recent study that showed that group-related physical features may directly activate related stereotypes, leading to more stereotypic inferences over and above those resulting from categorization (Blair, Judd, Sadler, & Jenkins, 2002).

These practices are especially salient under current conditions of industrial restructuring, which have produced residential segregation by race, class, and concentration of poverty. These conditions create increased competition for low-skill jobs from immigrants and other vulnerable groups (Browne, 1999a). For example, some research suggests that discrimination in hiring may operate in favor of some Latinos and Latinas who may be viewed as belonging to the nonracialized category, "Whiteness of a different color" (Guinier & Torres, 2002, p. 7). Even within the central city, there is evidence that some employers may hire Mexican immigrants before they hire native-born African Americans residing in adjacent neighborhoods (Moore & Vigil, 1993).

These race and class-based practices of exclusion are indicative of the precarious and shifting economic status of poor and working-class African American women and their families. Fine and Weis (1998) observed, "The categories 'poor' and 'working class' are fluid, with shifting boundaries. . . . [I]ndividuals travel between these class categories over their lives . . . [and] losing a job can make one 'poor' with a relatively short period of time" (p. 5). For African American working mothers raising children in poor neighborhoods, their precarious position in the labor market is further complicated by issues related to child care and child-rearing responsibilities (Browne & Kennelly, 1999; Weis, Fine, & Morton-Christmas, 1999). However, the complicating issues are not related to the logistics of managing child care and paid work, but rather that these problematic issues are constituted communicatively. That is, some research suggests that employers systematically devalue and exploit African American women workers in low-wage service and clerical jobs, based on their symbolic constructions of African American women as poor single mothers with child-care problems, regardless of the accuracy of these descriptors (Browne & Kennelly, 1999). Employers "rely on racial and gender stereotypes to sort individuals into different positions. White men are disproportionately allocated into jobs with the greatest rewards, while African American women are restricted to positions with low earnings and little authority" (p. 305).

Occupational segregation occurs also for African American women in managerial and executive-level positions (S. M. Collins, 1989; Higginbotham, 1987, 1997; Sokoloff, 1987). In the 1960s and 1970s, as they began to enter managerial and technical jobs, educated African American women faced discrimination that limited their employment in certain sectors of the labor market. For example, S. M. Collins (1989) conducted an interview study of career mobility among 76 African American executives (men and women) who worked in 37 major firms in Chicago during the 1980s. She found that the executives were marginalized into racialized positions that were created to help corporations handle Black problems and denied opportunities to work in more politically powerful or lucrative mainstream positions. S. M. Collins's observations are supported by other anecdotal research on African American managers' positioning into racialized jobs (Bascom, 1987; Fulbright, 1986).

More recently, a significant number of African American women have broken into occupations traditionally occupied by White men—as physicians, dentists, lawyers, accountants, and senior-level management. However, raced, gendered, and classed divisions persist even in these occupations. Instead of being evenly split between public and private sectors, the majority of professional and executive African American women are employed in the public sector, whereas the majority of White women in these positions are in the private sector (Higginbotham, 1997). Public sector jobs traditionally pay less than private sector positions and require considerably more emotional labor.

In summary, applying a critical-feminist lens to the research on African American women's work experiences reveals the persistent structuring of organizational divisions along race, gender, and class lines that occurs through power-based communicative practices, such as the enactment of ordinary, daily procedures and decisions. The next section explores African American women's empowerment as resistance to these practices.

Empowerment as resistance to organizational divisions. The literature in this area reveals that forms of resistance to raced, gendered, and classed organizational divisions are expressed somewhat differently by poor and working-class African American women than by middle- and upper-class women in the professions. Resistance for many poor and working-class African American women takes shape as a collective action created in the boundary spaces of managing work and family (Fine & Weis, 1998; Harley, 1997; Rollins, 1985; Weis et al., 1999). Researchers have documented that historically, African American women across class statuses have formed a community of *othermothers* and *fictive kin* to help each other with balancing work and family (Collins, 1990; Stack, 1974). However, contemporary working-class African American women create networks that must cross multiple boundaries. Weis et al. (1999) describe the experiences of poor and working-class African American mothers in Jersey City, New Jersey, and Buffalo, New York. They characterized these women's empowerment in terms of *border guards*, focusing on how managing the boundaries between work and family is often one of several borders they manage. In addition, many African American women manage the border between home and street, trying to protect their children from gangs and gang violence rooted in the illicit drug economy. In their roles as border guards, these women employed collective forms of empowerment that included shared resources among families trying to keep their children and homes safe in neighborhoods riddled with violence and drug use.[6]

In addition to collective action, the literature on working-class and working-poor women revealed evidence of individual resistance and resilience through spirituality. This was evident in Fine and Weis's (1998) ethnographic study of the "voices, politics, disappointments, and hopes of young urban adults" (p 1.), including working African American women. In the midst of their struggles, victories, and passions, the women gained personal strength "through expressions of hope . . . and a connection with God" (p. 109).

Among middle-class African American women in the workforce, the research suggests that empowerment and resistance takes shape as both individual agency and collective agency through self-definition, self-determination, and coalition building. Several case study accounts of successful, professional African American women emphasize that, despite efforts by some school counselors, college professors, and supervisors to impose negative definitions on them, these women remained confident in their own definitions of themselves as African American women (Bell & Nkomo, 2001; P. H. Collins, 1986; Parker, 2002; Pennington, 1999; Reid-Merritt, 1996). That is, in the face of race, gender, and class oppression, these women drew upon their own inner strength to define their own reality, rather than having their reality defined for them (B. J. Allen, 1998; Parker, 2002; Pennington, 1999).

Research on African American women's empowerment through self-definition is consistent with preliminary research on contemporary African American girls' identity development. Research by Fordham (1993) and Duke (2002) indicates that African American girls may use communication behavior as a way of resisting images of White womanhood. Using data obtained from an ethnographic study of academic success in a predominantly African American urban high school, Fordham argued that loudness reflects the efforts of the African American girls to subvert the consuming images of White middle-class womanhood. Duke also found evidence of African American adolescent girls' resistance to a White feminine ideal. As part of a longitudinal study of adolescent girls' interpretations of mainstream teen magazines, Duke (2002) found that White girls actively sought out the magazines' alternate, improved version of a feminine ideal (e.g., thin body type, European-American facial features, and a preference for makeup). Conversely, African American girls' compared the fictional images to their real world experience. They not only denied the veracity of the ideal, but they preferred their reality to it. This research suggests that in the context of racialized images of feminine identity, African American girls work to remain self-defined and develop a propensity for rejecting controlling images perpetuated by others. However, in the context of contemporary urban schooling, it is unclear whether, and under what circumstances, African American girls' attempts to remain self-defined can actually facilitate their academic success (Fordham, 1996).

In addition to self-definition as an empowerment strategy, African American professional women use self-determination (defining one's own destiny) as a form of empowerment. Catalyst's (1998) study revealed four areas that relate to African American women's success in career advancement: (a) seeking and gaining high visibility projects, (b) exceeding performance expectations, (c) using an acceptable communication style, and (d) obtaining an influential mentor or sponsor. Although some of these opportunities may arise serendipitously, research suggests that African American women's self-determination through the use of voice and agency may also play a role (Bell & Nkomo, 2001; Reid-Merrit, 1996; Thomas & Gabarro,1999). Based on her study of 45 African American professional women, Reid-Merrit characterizes their self-determination as "a unique combination of historical legacy, a sense of social justice, hard work, and style" (p. 5). Often, African American women find themselves confronting attempts at racial and sexual exclusion directly, through verbal confrontations (Barnes, 2000; Reid-Merrit, 1996; Pennington, 1999), or through legal action, which often is highly publicized because of the racial, sexual, and class implications (Byrd & Tharps, 2001; "Excerpts From Tapes in Discrimination Lawsuit," 1996; Gilkes, 1983).

For many African American women professionals, self-determination is interrelated with their community activism (Bell & Nkomo, 2001; Gilkes, 1980, 1983). Gilkes (1983) described a career path of upwardly mobile African American women as being organized around the goals of community work, including empowerment of the African American community, change in the quality of individual and group life, and change in the larger social structure. Similarly, Bell and Nkomo (2001) found evidence of "Black women's tempered radicalism" (p. 182) among 297 African American women managers. These women frequently cited their deep interconnectedness with their communities of origin and their nested circles of community inside and outside the corporation. Bell and Nkomo asserted that "retaining a collective identity keeps African American women connected even as they ascend the corporation with what might otherwise become an individualistic quest for success" (p. 183). Unlike the African American executives described in S. M. Collins' (1989) study who were forced into positions that serve the African American community, the model Gilkes (1983) and Bell and Nkomo describe is one based on choice born out of race and class consciousness.

Given many African American professional women's commitment to community advocacy, it is not surprising that coalition building serves as a major form of resistance for African American women professionals. Indeed, coalition building can be seen as a primary career strategy for upwardly mobile African American women in raced, gendered, and classed systems (Bell & Nkomo, 2001; Nottingham, 2001; Thomas & Gabarro, 1999). For example, Nottingham found that information seeking by first-year African American women MBA students at a predominantly White private university was focused almost exclusively on sources within the African American community, both inside and outside the university community. Similarly, studies of African American women managers reveal strategies of coalition building and networking with other African Americans as a key strategy for upward mobility (Bell & Nkomo, 2001; Thomas & Gabarro, 1999).

Organizational divisions are explained, reinforced, reproduced, and resisted through symbolic processes (Acker, 1991). The next section explores control and resistance to symbolic constructions of race, gender, and class in the workplace.

Symbolic Constructions of Race, Gender, and Class at Work

Communicative practices of control through symbolic construction. Structuring of organizations occurs through symbols, images, and ideologies that attempt to fix race, gender, and class inequalities (Acker, 1991). The projection of negative stereotypes through literature, media, and societal practices has structured African American women's experiences in work situations throughout history (P. H. Collins, 1998a; Dumas, 1980; Hine & Thompson, 1998; Lubiano, 1992; Morton, 1991). At the intersection of racist and sexist ideologies created during the era of slavery, and perpetuated throughout U.S. history, African American women have been denigrated as mammies, matriarchs, superwomen, castrators, and sapphires (Morton, 1991; Walker, 1983). Bell and Nkomo (2001) found that certain racialized images of African American women influence White women's perceptions of African American women managers. Specifically they found that the two primary stereotypical images White women had of African American women were the *Mammy* and *Sapphire*.

The Mammy image refers to "a motherly, self-sacrificing [B]lack woman who takes care of those around her" (Bell & Nkomo, 2001, p. 245). Bell and Nkomo found evidence that White women managers invoke the image of Mammy in describing their perceptions of African American women's communicative style as "having a tendency to be a little more demonstrative in style" (p. 245). Their study suggests that the White women they interviewed perceived the symbolic Mammy as a senior ranking woman or an older African American women who serves as an advocate of other African Americans in the company. She is also perceived as someone whom management looks to "when there are minority problems" (p. 245). The authors conclude, following Dumas (1980), that

> A Mammy's power is derived from her relationships in the formal [organizational] system . . . and her willingness to put her person at the disposal of those around her. And it can be maintained only as long as she is willing or able to provide what is demanded of her. (p. 246)

Another stereotypical image of African American women in the workplace is the Sapphire. The Sapphire is invoked through perceived images of "a dramatic, bossy African American woman who is full of complaints and mistrust" (Bell & Nkomo, 2001, p. 246). Based on their analysis, Bell and Nkomo (2001) contend that, "Often, when a African American woman is too outspoken and aggressively pursues privileges that are customarily given to Whites, she can find herself seen as a Sapphire, and can quickly find herself marginalized in the company" (p. 247).

Other images of African American women have been characterized in contemporary media. Images of economically poor African American women as intensely raced Welfare Queens and Bad African American Mothers (Lubiano, 1992) are created and fixed in the public eye via newspaper editorials, popular press, news coverage, documentaries, and talk show appearances (P. H. Collins, 1998a). As these images are watched by a public entranced by increasingly powerful media, these women as individuals become less visible. Poor African American women become identified as symbols of what is wrong with America and targets of social policies designed to shrink the government sector (P. H. Collins, 1998b; Lubiano, 1992). In contrast, the Black Lady Overachiever is a new image applied to the growing population of middle-class, professional African American women (Lubiano, 1992). The Black Lady Overachiever image is reinforced through high-profile cases such as those involving Anita Hill, Lani Guinier, and Bari-Ellen Roberts.[7] It is also furthered through fictional representations of this new image, such as the character Claire Huxtable on the *Cosby Show* of the 1980s. "Both sets of highly visible images . . . obscure the experiences of the majority of actual African American women, namely working-class African American women who fall into neither category" (P. H. Collins, 1998a, p. 41).

Unequal power relations in the workplace enables employers to define African American women in terms of pervasive stereotypes and use these controlling images to reinforce and legitimate the status quo (Browne & Kennelly, 1999; Collins, 1990). There is some evidence that employment supervisors are apt to focus on symbolic racialized perceptions of African American women as single mothers. Browne and Kennelly (1999) compared White employers' perceptions of African American women workers with profiles of the actual labor market participation of African American women. They found that White employers stereotyped African American women according to two raced and gendered images—the African American woman as poor worker and as a suspiciously reliable worker. Browne and Kennelly's findings indicate that White employers enacted stereotypes that were unique to African American women workers. They observed that in the study:

> Black women were not seen as "lazy" or "scary" as the Black man was (Kischenman & Neckerman, 1991), nor was she seen as the secondary earner in a nuclear family, as the White woman was. The Black woman, according to the White Atlanta employers interviewed, was a single mother in a suspicious sort of way, or the most likely person to be late, distracted, and absent because of her child care concerns. (p. 316)

Browne and Kennelly (1999) found that the White employers in the study enacted these images of employed African American women regardless of their accuracy. African American women who are not mothers of young children, or who have actually resolved conflicts between child care and paid work, are less visible to employers than are African American women who fit the common cultural stereotype of the matriarch.

Empowerment as resistance to controlling images. African American girls and women use individual and collective empowerment strategies to resist both the controlling images of White womanhood as well as the stereotypical images of African American womanhood. The primary form of resistance is through the construction of, and reliance upon, self-defined images. As demonstrated in the research by Duke (2002) and Fordham (1993, 1996) reviewed earlier, and supported by pioneering research by Ladner (1972), African American girls develop a mix of individual strategies to remain self-defined in their interactions with school counselors, teachers, and administrators. These strategies often are manifested as culturally distinct expressions of Black womanhood, juxtaposed with contradictory and normalized images of White womanhood (Fordham, 1993, 1996; Ladner, 1972). Although remaining self-defined provides a source of control and momentary empowerment for African American girls resisting the consumption of images of White womanhood, it remains unclear under what circumstances this form of resistance can actually facilitate their academic success (Fordham, 1996).

African American professional women also use self-definition as a form of resistance to controlling images (Bell, 1990; Bell & Nkomo 1992, 2001; Essed, 1994; Etter-Lewis, 1993; Parker, in press; Squire, 1994). For example, studies indicate that many African American women develop a bicultural life structure to manage their identities within predominantly White work environments and within their own African American communities (Bell, 1990; Bell & Nkomo, 2001). The risk of resisting conventions of femininity and racial position could be costly in a society that demands conformity (Taylor, 1991). Some Black feminist theorists argue, however, that the tensions of holding conventions of womanhood from two cultures produce positive effects, such as behavioral flexibility and creativity (P. H. Collins, 1986; hooks, 1984). Thus, biculturalism becomes a mechanism for some African American women's self-definition (Bell, 1990).

There is evidence of African American women's collective resistance to controlling images in work situations. This sometimes takes shape as women-centered support groups (Bell, 1990; King & Ferguson, 2001). King and Ferguson identify *centering* as a group process of self-restoration for African American professional women. The process of centering occurs within workshops and retreats where African American women examine the meaning of their experiences in the context of their individual and collective identities. The process enables them to work through psychological injury that often accompanies their marginal status. It also provides a forum for cultivating community within and across their immediate work contexts, while developing strategies for social change within their organizations and professions.

Finally, within the literature reviewed here, it is unclear how resistance to controlling images is manifested in the lives of contemporary working-class and working-poor women. Given the intensely raced work context for working-class and working-poor women (P. H. Collins, 1998a), it seems surprising that little research exists that examines their resistance to controlling images in work contexts.

Raced, Gendered, and Classed Workplace Interactions

Raced, gendered, and classed structuring is also sustained through social interactions (Acker, 1991). These patterns are evident at the organizational, group, and dyadic levels. At the organizational level, the reproduction of racial, gender, and class oppression often occurs through the social construction of monoculturalism, even as organizations emphasize multiculturalism through diversity initiatives (Prasad, Mills, Elmes, & Prasad, 1997). Prasad and associates reviewed the vast literature on workplace diversity, focusing on a number of different dimensions, such as gender, race, ethnicity, migrancy, immigration, colonialism, and globalization. They concluded that despite the proliferation of research on discrimination, the value of diversity, and multiculturalism in organizations, the literature fails to address the more serious dimensions of difference in organizations. The authors contend that a host of gender conflicts, race tensions, and cultural frictions lie hidden in the shadows of the elaborate showcasing of the diversity movement. The current literature on diversity demonstrates that past strategies have had limited effectiveness in addressing interpersonal, institutional, and cultural issues that hinder the development of organizational diversity and, indeed, may even reproduce oppression rather than eliminate it.

Thomas and Gabarro (1999) described two types of organizations that limit the opportunity structure for women and men of color, illustrating the point made by Prasad et al. (1997). First are those corporations where there is a widely shared set of unchallenged biases that have the effect of setting low targets for advancement by women and men of color. In these organizations, few people of color even make it into middle management; the executive level is inconceivable. Instead of a "glass ceiling," a phenomenon used to describe the barriers just below the top level of the organization, these organizations have "squishy floors" and "revolving doors." That is, people of color "can never gain a firm enough footing in the organization to even test whether they can penetrate the top. As a result, the best of them leave" (Thomas & Gabarro, 1999, p. 241).

In the second type of organization, there is some genuine intent to diversify the workforce; however, there is a lack of alignment between the organization's diversity strategy and its culture and values. These organizations are often pursuing diversity as a goal but are using a strategy that consists of a patchwork of disconnected programs and compliance efforts. African American women and other people of color sometimes make it to threshold positions in middle- or upper-middle management, but are not able to advance further. In other words, they hit the glass ceiling.

Processes that sustain squishy floors, revolving doors, and glass ceilings can be made visible at the group and dyadic organizational levels, where barriers to advancement are produced and reproduced through interactions among organizational members. African American women within the corporate sector face a variety of barriers that can be understood as constructed within raced, gendered, and classed power relations. Most of the work in this area is based on retrospective accounts in case studies of college and professional women (Bell & Nkomo, 2001; Feagin & Sikes, 1994; Fulbright, 1986; Higgenbotham & Weber, 1997; Parker, 1997; Rosser, 1998; St. Jean & Feagin, 1997a, 1997b; Yoder & Aniakudo, 1997). Collectively, the findings of these studies are reinforced by the results of a nationwide survey focusing on the barriers and opportunities for women of color in the corporate world (Catalyst, 1998). This study surveyed 1,700 women of color, including African American (54%), Hispanic (24%), and Asian American (21%). Approximately 60 focus groups and 80 interviews amplified the survey. The study found that the most significant barriers faced by all the women were not having an influential mentor or sponsor (48.8%), a lack of informal networking with influential colleagues (39.8%), a lack of company role models of same race or ethnic group (29.4%), and a lack of high visibility projects (27.9%). Finally, it found that African American women were the most likely to leave their current companies.

Anecdotal evidence from case studies of African American professional women in the workplace contextualize the Catalyst (1998) survey data as persistent race and gender discrimination. African American women must contend with gendered racism in their everyday interactions (Essed, 1991; St. Jean & Feagin, 1997b). Following Essed, St. Jean and Feagin use the term "subtle gendered racism" (p. 180) to characterize certain types of subtle discrimination that target African American women. Their analysis revealed that for African American women, subtle gendered racism at work takes the form of subtle devaluations that are communicated in workplace interactions. Communicative practices that constitute these subtle devaluations may take the form of White exceptionalism, in which White coworkers make statements to African American women that reflect judgments as to whether African American women are the exception to raced and gendered stereotypes. Other subtle devaluations noted in St. Jean and Feagin's research include "constant scrutiny" (p. 190), "invisibility" (p. 193), the expectation that African American women "will sooner or later fail" (p. 193), and "supportive discouragement" (p. 193).

These practices of gendered racism are consistent with P. H. Collins's (1998a) analysis of how racialized images of African American women function ideologically in the workplace. She argues that the socially constructed juxtaposed images of intensely raced working-class and working-poor African American women as compared to unraced middle- and upper-class African American women, creates standards through which the dominant White culture can judge African American women. Control of African American women operates through everyday practices of racism, sexism, and classism (such as those revealed in St. Jean & Feagin's, 1997b, research) that "keep race at bay" (Collins, 1998a, p. 39) in work settings.

St. Jean and Feagin's (1997b) findings on professional African American women's experiences with gendered racism are supported by other anecdotal research (A. Allen, 1994; B. J. Allen, 1996, 1998, 2000; Barnes, 2000; Bell & Nkomo, 1992, 2001; Benokraitis, 1997; Bhavnani & Phoenix, 1994; Collins, 1998a; Essed, 1991, 1994; Etter-Lewis, 1993; Feagin & Sikes, 1994; McDonald & Ford-Ahmed, 1999; St. Jean & Feagin, 1997a; Parker, 1997, 2002; Pennington, 1999; Porter, 1999; Yoder & Aniakudo, 1997). For example, in an extensive survey study of 24 African American women career firefighters nationwide, Yoder and Aniakudo (1997) found persistent and pervasive patterns of subordination through the exclusion of African American women. Patterns of exclusion emerged through their interactions with coworkers at the firehouse, reflected as insufficient instruction, coworker hostility, silence, close supervision, lack of support, and stereotyping. Additionally, the social interactions that made the African American women firefighters outsiders within, occurred not only with White men, but also with other subordinate groups, including African American men and White women firefighters. In this context, African American men and White women firefighters gained some acceptance by virtue of their gender and race, respectively, and thus reportedly distanced themselves from African American women firefighters.

Compared to the research on African American professional women, less research explores the raced, gendered, and classed group-level interactions of working-class and working-poor African American women (Browne & Kennelly, 1999; Byrd & Tharps, 2001; Fine & Weis, 1998; Harley, 1997; Rollins, 1985; Weis et al., 1999). However, this research provides evidence of everyday gendered racism that working-class and working-poor African American women endure, particularly among young African American women working in low-wage service jobs in restaurants, hotels, and public institutions (Barnes, 2000). Collectively, these studies provide anecdotal evidence of "racist treatment, racist stereotypes, racial slurs, failure to get earned promotions, and job punishment for excellence" (p. 87).

Current occupational data reveal that African American women are most likely to work in lower paying jobs with other African Americans, mostly women (Browne, 1999a). One consequence of labor market discrimination is a devaluation of occupations when a substantial number of African American workers take up these roles, such as African American women's high concentration in low-wage jobs (Jacobs & Blair-Loy, 2001). The raced-based devaluation of occupations is indicative of how the working-poor in the current service economy are framed and understood in U.S. society (Cheever, 2001; Ehrenreich, 2001). Cheney, Lair, and Gill (2002) observed, following Cheever and Ehrenreich, that the working-poor "may be looked upon as not wanting to advance, when in fact advancement is not an option; or they or often the objects of pity or derision, when they are looked upon at all" (p. 636). Additionally, workers and job seekers in these low-wage jobs must constantly monitor their appearance and style to look professional (Cheney et al., 2002).

For example, Byrd and Tharps (2001) reported that over a thousand African American women, mostly workers in the service or hospitality industries, were victims of "bans on cornrows" (p. 107) in the late 1980s and early 1990s. Cornrows, a braided hairstyle with roots in African culture, was deemed "not fit for the 'corporate' image" (Byrd & Tharps, 2001, pp. 107–108). African American women who worked in front line jobs, such as restaurant cashiers and airline ticket agents, were reprimanded or fired for choosing to wear braided hairstyles.

In addition to race, gender, and class structuring at the organizational and group levels, these processes also structure interaction at the dyadic level. Mentoring is an important site for illuminating race-, gender-, and classed-based interaction, because it is a crucial mechanism for facilitating career mobility. Mentoring is defined as "a communication relationship in which a senior person supports, tutors, guides, and facilitates a junior person's career development" (Hill, Bahniuk,

& Dobos, 1989, p. 15). A mentor can be distinguished from a role model in that a role model may only influence a person indirectly and not within the developmental context of a relationship.[8] Kalbfleisch (2002) postulates an enactment theory of mentoring, emphasizing the interpersonal developmental context of mentoring relationships.

Research on African American managerial women's work experiences reveals that race, gender, and class add complexity to developing mentoring relationships. For example, Kalbfleisch (2002) theorized that in developing mentoring relationships, protégés should get to know the potential mentor first and then allow the relationship to develop. With cross-race relationships, it may be challenging to initiate and develop these mentoring relationships. Thomas (1993) presents a complex picture of cross-culture interactions within raced, gendered, and classed organizations. Thomas interviewed 22 individuals in cross-race (African American and White), supportive work relationships between pairs of juniors and their seniors, to examine how strategies for dealing with the issue of race affect the kind of relationship that develops. He also examined whether the senior becomes merely a sponsor for the protégé, providing him or her with career support such as advocacy for promotions, feedback, and coaching, or a mentor, offering psychosocial support and friendship along with instrumental career support. The results showed that only when the parties preferred the same strategy—either denying or suppressing the race issue or discussing it openly—did the more supportive mentor-protege relationship develop. Additionally, the results showed that White mentors who openly discuss race with their proteges are more successful in getting them promoted than those who do not.

More specific to African American women, Blake's (1999) interview study of 11 African American professional women in a corporate setting found two themes relative to mentoring relationships. This study showed that there is a general lack of African American role models who might serve as mentors, and that these women's relationships with White women mentors are largely characterized by mistrust. Similarly, Bell and Nkomo's (1992, 2002) studies of African American and White career-oriented women within dominant culture organization revealed that race and gender may be a salient factor in career mentoring and sponsorship. The African American women in their studies reported having less positive relationships with their bosses than the White women. Bell and Nkomo interpret this finding in terms of the interactive effects of race and gender. They argue that the relationship between an African American woman and a White male boss could be affected by race and gender discrimination compounded by sexual taboos. To support this latter point, they cite Thomas's (1990) finding that African American women in an earlier study were reluctant to establish developmental relationships with White men because it conjured up images of White men and their slave concubines.

African American women's empowerment in raced, gendered, and classed interactions. Research on African American women's empowerment in raced, gendered, and classed interactions reveals resistance through individual agency as well as collective action. However, as demonstrated earlier, the context for resistance is quite different for working-class, working-poor, and middle- and upper-class African American women.

In terms of individual agency, African American women's resistance can be seen as a way of finding and asserting their voices through strategic attempts to negotiate meaning, identity, and power (Houston & Kramarae, 1991; Jackson, 1999; Orbe, 1998a; Orbe 1998b; Parker, in press). For working-poor African American women the use of voice as an empowerment strategy emerges within the intensely raced context of negotiating the borders between home, welfare, the street, and low-wage, often temporary jobs. In their extensive ethnography of working-poor African American women, Fine and Weis (1998) revealed instances of the women breaking silence about raced-based discrimination on the job, employers' insensitivity to the needs of their children, and "dealing with nasty caseworkers" (p. 181). Similarly, but within the context of somewhat more stable economic conditions, working-class African American women use voice as a strategy as they seek to survive and empower themselves and their families in the face of exploitation at work. Using a historical perspective, and focusing on the work experiences and working-class consciousness of African American women, Harley (1997) revealed multiple instances when speaking up transformed work sites and conditions.

Middle- and upper-class African American women must resist surveillance mechanisms designed to insure that they remain unraced and assimilated (P. H. Collins, 1998a, p. 38). The growing literature on professional African American women's experiences with gendered racism suggests that African American women in the professions use a range of strategies in response to gendered racism (Barnes, 2000; Bhavnani & Phoenix, 1994; Bell & Nkomo, 2001; Benokraitis, 1997; Essed, 1991, 1994; Feagin & Sikes, 1994; McDonald & Ford-Ahmed, 1999; Pennington, 1999; Porter, 1999; Slevin & Wingrove, 1998; St. Jean & Feagin, 1997a, 1997b). Common among these strategies is an emphasis on their identity as African American women. They start from the standpoint of being self-defined and confident as African American women, especially as it is related to inner strength and self-empowerment (Bell & Nkomo, 2001; P. H. Collins, 1990). However, this may be expressed in different ways among individual women, including direct confrontation in response to a perceived racist comment, or more indirect approaches, such as emphasizing aspects of Black culture, or avoidance strategies such as leaving the organization for new opportunities (Orbe, 1998a; Parker, in press; Pennington, 1999).

B. J. Allen's pioneering work on African American women's standpoints in organizational communication provides insights about African American women's empowerment in raced and gendered organizational interactions. B. J. Allen's (1996, 2000) work demonstrated that African American women's empowerment across class status is a process whereby these women become self-defined, self-determined, and regenerated through consciousness raising. B. J. Allen's view, reinforced by the perspectives of other Black feminist writers (Collins, 1998b, hooks, 1990; Hull et al., 1982), stands in more hopeful contrast to St. Jean and Feagin's (1997a) view that "Black women are under survival pressures to acquiesce in their own exploitation" (p. 161). B. J. Allen's work emphasizes that the process of becoming empowered is not determined in singular instances of choosing to confront a racist attack or to remain silent. Rather it is an ongoing process of resistance and transformation through individual agency and collective action.

Collective action as a form of empowerment is evident among African American women across age groups and economic class status. This form of empowerment is manifested through connecting to and building community. The literature on gendered racism reveals organizational and institutional environments in which African American girls and women often feel unwelcome and isolated, sometimes even when they make attempts to form cross-cultural connections (Mathis, 2002). Connecting with similar others who would potentially provide social support and affirmation seems too obvious to mention. Yet, African Americans are often questioned about forming race-based groups at work or choosing to sit together in the classroom or cafeteria on college campuses (Tatum, 1997).

Empowerment through collective action is also manifested in grassroots community organizing among African American women living in poor and working-class neighborhoods (Gittell, Ortega-Bustamante, & Steffy, 1999; Stack, 2000; Stall & Stoecker, 1998). They use the knowledge and visions gained through experiences as border guards (negotiating the boundaries of home, work, and school) to create community-based organizations that broaden the concept of community development. In their study of women-led community development organizations (CDOs), including several headed by African American women, Gitell et al. (1999) found evidence of CDOs that were holistic programs, creating social capital through leadership, community participation, and networking with other organizations, such as churches, cultural institutions, other CDOs, and state legislators.

SUMMARY

In this chapter, I used feminist and critical organizational communication perspectives to review the literature on African American women's work experiences, focusing on their empowerment as resistance to control in raced, gendered, and classed organizational contexts. This review was intended to accomplish two purposes. The first was to illuminate the ways in which race, gender, and class structure communicative practices in everyday organizational life that contribute to African American women's continued subordination and oppression in the U.S. labor market. The second was to identify specific forms of resistance and empowerment as revealed in the literature on African American women and work.

The first goal was accomplished by presenting evidence of African American women's subordination and resistance in three aspects of raced, gendered, and classed work contexts: (a) organizational divisions (e.g., divisions of labor, allowed behaviors, and work spaces), (b) symbolic constructions, and (c) workplace interactions. This review demonstrates how aspects of the larger, societal context of race, gender, and class politics inform communicative practices that constitute organizational control and contribute to the continued subordination of African American women in the U.S. labor market. Specifically, this review revealed race-, gender-, and class-based control manifested in exclusionary practices in hostile or unwelcome school environments, in occupational segregation through racial and class-based stereotyping, and in raced, gendered, and classed organizational interactions at the corporate, group, and dyadic levels, which sustain unequal power relations.

My second goal was to identify specific forms of resistance and empowerment in the literature on African American women and work. Five themes identified in the Black feminist literature frame an understanding of specific forms of resistance as empowerment. These themes are: (a) developing and using voice, (b) being self-defined, (c) being self-determined, (d) connecting to and building community, and (e) seeking spirituality and regeneration. The literature on African American women reveals these themes, but they are utilized and expressed differently by the working-class and the working-poor as compared to middle- and upper-class women in the professions. These two groups clearly occupy different locations within raced, gendered, and classed systems of power.

In the next section, I suggest a research agenda for communication scholars interested in studying race, gender, and classes organizational systems, particularly as related to African American women's resistance and empowerment in work settings.

DOING DIFFERENCE: IMPLICATIONS FOR ORGANIZATIONAL COMMUNICATION RESEARCH, THEORY, AND PRACTICE

As noted at the beginning of this chapter, organizational communication scholars using critical-feminist perspectives have rarely explored issues of race, gender, and class as interdependent processes. As demonstrated in this review, organizational communication scholarship should attempt to understand how organizational members "do difference" in their everyday interactions, focusing on the ways gender, race, and class simultaneously structure work experiences (West & Fenstermaker, 1995). This calls for research that is grounded in the experiences of people marginalized by oppressive practices in order to illuminate the ways that difference is manifested in everyday organizational communication as well as to envision possibilities for change and transformation. In the case of African American women, there is a need for research in three areas: (a) occupational segregation through race, gender, and class structuring in school environments, recruitment, and hiring practices; (b) race- and class-based stereotyping that constructs controlling images of African American women; and (c) raced, gendered, and classed organizational interactions that sustain unequal power relations. There also are implications for theory building in these areas.

Implications for Research and Practice

Related to occupational segregation processes embedded in school environments, research needs to analyze the communicative context of African American girls in terms of their access to, and opportunities for, professional careers. The empowerment of African American adolescent girls is often neglected in social policy initiatives that focus on African American youth despite a clear need to focus on this group. For contemporary African American girls across socioeconomic statuses, the potential for success occurs within a complex social, cultural, and political environment that, by many important measures, is becoming increasingly difficult for them to navigate (Holcomb-McCoy & Moore-Thomas, 2001; Twine, 2000). African American adolescent girls, particularly those living in impoverished neighborhoods with high crime rates, are at risk for low academic achievement, teen pregnancy, drug abuse, and victimization by violence (Arnold, 1994). Furthermore, they are contending with racialized images in the press and popular media of African American women as welfare queens and video divas, juxtaposed with inaccessible images of the overachieving Black lady and the good White woman (Fordham, 1993; Radford-Hill, 2002).

Research is clearly needed to document the communicative contexts of contemporary African American girls' career socialization and identity development, as well as to identify specific strategies to foster their empowerment in school and work contexts. The research reviewed here suggests that a good place to start would be to listen closely to the girls' own strategies of resistance and self-definition. These strategies should be incorporated into the design of empowerment programs targeting African American girls and in interventions aimed at creating more inclusive school environments. In other words, the research should start from the girls' standpoints.

Communication scholars should focus also on the ways persistent structuring of organizational divisions along race, gender, and class lines occurs through power-based communicative practices in recruitment, hiring, and promotion. Specifically, this review demonstrates the need for empirical evidence of how controlling images of African American women are used to reinforce and legitimate organizational divisions that exploit and subordinate African American women (Browne & Kennelly, 1999; P. H. Collins, 1990). The research reviewed in this chapter suggests that employers and coworkers routinely enact negative stereotypical images of African American women as they engage in practices such as hiring, promoting, and firing (Browne & Kennelly, 1999). Research is needed to make these practices visible. Shuter and Turner (1997), Browne and Kennelly (1999), and Bell and Nkomo (2001) demonstrated that simply asking employers and coworkers about their perceptions of African American women is itself revealing. This simple practice could provide a way of disrupting the process of othering (cf., Fine, 1994).

The second area of needed research relates to race- and class-based stereotyping that constructs controlling images of African American women. Specifically, research is needed to document working-class African American women's resistance to controlling images in raced, gendered, and classed organizational systems. Given the intensely raced work context for working-class and working-poor women, it is surprising that very little research exists that examines their resistance to controlling images at work. Historical accounts of such resistance is well documented in the literature on African American women's forced labor during the era of slavery and their labor force participation through the early part of the 20th century (cf. Harley, 1997; Hine & Thompson, 1998; Jones 1985; Mullings, 1997). Researchers should analyze the specific communicative forms of resistance that are manifested in the daily lives of contemporary working-class and working-poor African American women.

The communicative nature of raced, gendered, and classed organizational interactions is the third area where study is needed. Research should focus on unraveling the ways race, gender, and class structure interaction at the organizational, group, and dyadic levels. At the organizational level, researchers should investigate the specific communicative nature of opportunity and exclusion (cf. Fine, 1995). For example, what is the communicative nature of the types of organizations described by Thomas and Gabarro (1999) that limit the opportunity structure for women and men of color? Equally importantly, how is opportunity communicatively constituted in organizations that empower all organizational members? Communication scholars are well positioned to address these questions through research that identifies the best communication practices for advancement of traditionally excluded groups.

At the group level, researchers should focus on the communicative nature of everyday racism and gendered racism. The increasing volume of this literature is itself provocative evidence of the hostile and unwelcome organizational environments with which members of excluded groups must contend. What is missing is an in-depth analysis of the communicative character of gendered racism (cf. Hecht, 1998). For example, one fruitful area of research is a communication-based, in-depth textual analysis of the literature on gendered racism revealing practices of control, as well as evidence of resistance and empowerment.

One consequence of group-level practices of exclusion is the use of community building as a form of resistance and empowerment. This form of collective agency is particularly instructive with regard to resistance and empowerment among working-class and working-poor African American women. The studies highlighted here revealed a level of empowerment through self-determination that has not been emphasized in the economic literature. Future research should focus on ways the community empowerment and support already initiated by women, as highlighted in this review, can be supported, expanded, and sustained. Specifically, researchers should investigate the communicative nature and function of the social networks that working-class and working-poor African American women create to manage the boundary spaces between work and family, often in the context of deteriorating neighborhoods and schools with limited resources (Fine & Weis, 1998). Knowledge gained from such studies could be used to inform communication-based program initiatives designed to support poor and working-class women's efforts to attain and advance in, jobs and careers (Waldron, Lavitt, & McConnaughy, 2001).

Also, grassroots organizing among working-class and working-poor women often leads to the creation of innovative community development organizations. Critical-feminist communication scholars should study women-led community development organizations, such as those mentioned in this review headed by African American women (Gitell, et al., 1999). Not only can these organizations provide new insights about collective agency as a form of empowerment, they also can serve as models for alternative forms of organizing, often neglected in the organizational communication literature.

At the dyadic level there is clearly a need for research examining the race, gender, and class structuring of mentoring. Thomas's (1993) research provides important insights about the communicative character of cross-racial mentoring. However, further investigations are needed to understand the context for successful mentoring relationships and to tease out communication dynamics in other types of mentor or protégé relationships, such as those related to intraracial mentoring.

Implications for Theory

Finally, this review has implications for theory building in organizational communication. Theorizing in organizational communication should unmask exclusionary assumptions about race, gender, and class, as well as other systems of subordination that are reinforced, or not acknowledged, in communication theory development. Marshall (1993) observed that "theory making is essentially an ideological process, an exercise of power that can privilege certain social groups, certain points of view" (p. 139). Thus, organizational communication theory and research must make visible the taken-for-granted assumptions about race, gender, class, and other forms of exclusion that inform theory and research. The goal should be to expose the hidden logics that govern practices such as work socialization, hiring, recruitment rituals, and diversity initiatives.

Buzzanell's (2000) edited volume, *Rethinking Organizational Communication From Feminist Perspectives*, is an important step forward. The contributors to the volume reanalyze aspects of organizational and managerial communication, focusing on "the ways conventional approaches often exclude the concerns, values, and life experiences voiced by members of traditionally underrepresented groups" (p. x). They explore specific areas of organizational communication, such as chaos theory, leadership, and careers, in addition to identifying exclusionary assumptions that guide organizational communication practice.

Grimes (2002) analysis of whiteness in the diversity management literature is also instructive. She identifies three perspectives on whiteness—interrogating, recentering, and masking whiteness—and illustrates how one of these (interrogating whiteness) works to name, unmask, and decenter whiteness, bringing to light hidden assumptions about difference. Similarly, in a review of interpersonal communication research, Houston (2002) demonstrated that, by positioning African Americans in relation to White Americans, communication scholars inadvertently centered whiteness in African American communication scholarship. Parker (2002) makes a similar point her critique of the leadership literature.

CONCLUSION

In applying a critical-feminist lens to the work experiences of African American women, this review demonstrates that there is much to be learned about the ways in which everyday organizational communication is structured by race, gender, and class. Researchers should examine opportunities for resistance and transformation. My hope is that communication scholars will actively pursue research in these important areas of study, particularly as related to African American women's resistance and empowerment in work settings. Doing so is crucial for enabling researchers and organizational members to illuminate practices of exclusion and oppression as well as to visualize opportunities for social justice and change.

NOTES

1. I use the term unraced to denote the tendency in Western culture to construct "White" as a race-neutral cultural category, in which the benefits of racial privilege are taken for granted and unexamined (cf. Frankenberg, 1993; McIntosh, 1988).

2. Following Dugger (1991), I capitalize the terms Black and White to emphasize the point that race structures the experiences of both groups but in different ways. "Both racial privilege and racial oppression create categories of people with unique historical experiences that significantly shape their gender identity and attitudes" (Dugger, 1991, p. 57).

3. I use the popular term African American to refer to women of African descent that work in dominant-culture U.S. organizations. It is important to acknowledge, however, that some African American women, including myself, find special resonance in using the term Black instead of African American, for it can in some ways function as an affirmation of personal Black cultural identity (cf. Mathis, 2002, pp. 185–187). I also acknowledge that the term African American refers to a large category of people, including women in the U.S. who are of African descent, but who define themselves according to their country of origin (e.g., Jamaican American).

4. The occupational profile of African American women has changed dramatically over past decades. In 1949, 42% of African American female employees worked in domestic service. In 1990, 19% of African American women were in managerial and professional occupations, whereas 39% were in technical or administrative jobs (O'Hare, Pollard, Mann, & Kent, 1992). Reports indicate that African American women's advancements in the labor market began to stall and reverse direction near the end of the 1980s (Corcoran & Parrott, 1992; A. P. Jones, 1986; Simms & Malveaux, 1986). This reversal created especially harsh consequences, such as poverty and low wages, for the most economically vulnerable African American women—the young, unskilled, and single parents (Corcoran & Parrot, 1992). Even for African American women at higher economic levels, there is increasing economic disadvantage relative to White women and African American men. The gap between the wages of African American women compared to White women and African American men is widening (Blau & Beller, 1992; Levy & Murnane, 1992). African American women also face restricted opportunities for

upward mobility (Bell & Nkomo, 2001). More than 30 years after the passage of the Civil Rights Act of 1964, African American women continue to be among the most severely disadvantaged in the U.S. labor market (Browne, 1999a; Browne & Kennelly, 1999).

5. See Anna Julia Cooper's (1892) book of essays, *A Voice From the South.*

6. Some research suggests that in the absence of such family and community advocacy and support in the lives of economically disadvantaged African American girls who are victims of violence and sex abuse, criminality may be a form of resistance (Arnold, 1994).

7. Anita Hill, Lani Guinier, and Bari-Ellen Roberts are three African American women whose individual lives became the subject of intense media scrutiny in 1991, 1993, and 1994, respectively. Anita Hill, a Yale-trained law professor, gained international attention when she testified against U.S. Supreme Court nominee Clarence Thomas, a conservative African American Republican, accusing him of sexual harassment during a time they worked together 10 years earlier. In 1993, when President Bill Clinton nominated law professor Lani Guiner to head the Justice Department's Civil Rights Division, Guinier was vilified in the media for weeks as a "quota queen" with "strange hair, strange name, and strange writing" (cf. Williams, 1995, p. 141). Guinier's nomination was withdrawn without the opportunity to defend her ideas in the open forum of a confirmation hearing. Finally, in 1994, senior financial analyst Bari-Ellen Roberts and a coworker filed a racial discrimination lawsuit against the Texaco Corporation. While the lawsuit was in progress, someone delivered an audiotape to the press containing a transcript of a formal meeting among top-level Texaco executives discussing the lawsuit. In one segment of the transcript, Roberts's superiors refer to her as " a smart-mouthed colored girl," and to African American employees as "black jelly beans." In one segment, a Texaco executive is heard commenting, "That's funny. All the black jelly beans seem to be glued to the bottom of the bag" ("Excerpts From Tapes in Discrimination Lawsuit," 1996).

8. Although the focus here is on the complexities of the mentoring relationship, A. Allen (1994) a law professor at Georgetown University, noted that being a role model is itself quite complex for African American women. For example, one problem with the role model argument is "that while it trumpets our necessity, it whispers our inferiority. . . . The argument makes it possible to assume that Black women can be more competent than [W]hites only insofar as they are better role models" (p. 192). On the other hand, "Black women may be better able to take themselves seriously as intellectuals knowing that others like them are concerned professors, deans, provosts, and university presidents" (p. 187).

REFERENCES

Acker, J. (1991). Hierarchies, jobs, bodies: A theory of gendered organizations. In J. Lorber & S. A. Farrell (Eds.), *The social construction of gender* (pp. 162–179). Newbury Park, CA: Sage.

Allen, A. (1994). On being a role model. In D. T. Goldberg (Ed.), *Multiculturalism: A critical reader* (pp. 180–199). Cambridge, UK: Blackwell.

Allen, B. J. (1995). "Diversity" and organizational communication. *Journal of Applied Communication Research, 3,* 143–155.

Allen, B. J. (1996). Feminist standpoint theory: A Black woman's (re)view of organizational socialization. *Communication Studies, 47*(4), 257–271.

Allen, B. J. (1998). Black womanhood and feminist standpoints. *Management Communication Quarterly, 11,* 575–586.

Allen, B. J. (2000). "Learning the ropes": A Black feminist standpoint analysis. In P. M. Buzzanell (Ed.), *Rethinking organizational and managerial communication from feminist perspectives* (pp. 177–208). Thousand Oaks, CA: Sage.

Amott, T., & Matthaei, J. (Eds). (1996). *Race, gender, and work: A multicultural economic history of women in the United States* (2nd ed.). Boston: South End Press.

Arnold, R. (1994). Black women in prison: The price of resistance. In M. Baca Zinn & B. T. Dill (Eds.), *Women of color in U.S. society* (pp. 171–184). Philadelphia: Temple University Press.

Barnes, A. (2000). *Everyday racism: A book for all Americans.* Naperville, IL: Sourcebooks.

Bascom, L. (1987, April/May). Breaking through middle management barrier. *Crisis*, pp. 13–16, 61, 64.

Bell, E. L. (1990). The bicultural life experience of career-oriented Black women. *Journal of Organizational Behavior, 11*, 459–477.

Bell, E. L., & Nkomo, S. (1992). *The glass ceiling vs. the concrete wall: Career perceptions of White and African-American women managers* (Working Paper No. 3470–92). Cambridge: Massachusetts Institute of Technology.

Bell, E. L., & Nkomo, S. (2001). *Our separate ways: Black and White women and the struggle for professional identity*. Boston: Harvard Business School Press.

Benokraitis, N. V. (Ed.). (1997). *Subtle sexism: Current practice and prospects for change*. Thousand Oaks, CA: Sage.

Bhavnani, K., & Phoenix, A. (Eds.). (1994). *Shifting identities, shifting racisms: A feminism & psychology reader*. London: Sage.

Binion, V. (1990). Psychological androgyny: A Black female perspective. *Sex Roles, 22*, 487–507.

Blair, I. V., Judd, C. M., Sadler, M. S., & Jenkins, C. (2002). The role of Afrocentric features in person perception: Judging by features and categories. *Journal of Personality and Social Psychology, 83*, 5–25.

Blake, S. (1999). At the crossroads of race and gender: Lessons from the mentoring experiences of professional Black women. In A. Murrell & F. Crosby (Eds.), *Mentoring dilemmas: Developmental relationships within multicultural organizations* (pp. 83–104). Mahwah, NJ: Erlbaum.

Blau, F., & Beller, A. (1992). Black-White earnings over the 1970s and 1980s: Gender differences in trends. *Review of Economics and Statistics, 7*(2), 276–86.

Browne, I. (1999a). Introduction: Latinas and African American women in the U.S. labor market. In I. Browne (Ed.), *Latinas and African American women at work: Race, gender, and economic inequality* (pp. 1–31). New York: Russell Sage Foundation.

Browne, I. (Ed.). (1999b). *Latinas and African American women at work: Race, gender, and economic inequality*. New York: Russell Sage Foundation.

Browne, I., & Kennelly, I. (1999). Stereotypes and realities: Images of Black women in the labor market. In I. Browne (Ed.), *Latinas and African American women at work: Race, gender, and economic inequality* (pp. 302–326). New York: Russell Sage Foundation.

Bullis, C. (1993). At least it's a start. In S. Deetz (Ed.), *Communication yearbook 16* (pp. 144–154). Newbury Park, CA: Sage.

Bullis, C., & Stout, K. R. (2000). Organizational socialization: A feminist standpoint approach. In P. Buzzanell (Ed.), *Rethinking organizational & managerial communication from feminist perspectives* (pp. 47–75). Thousand Oaks, CA: Sage.

Buzzanell, P. M. (1994). Gaining a voice: Feminist perspectives in organizational communication. *Management Communication Quarterly, 7*, 339–383.

Buzzanell, P. M. (Ed.). (2000). *Rethinking organizational & managerial communication from feminist perspectives*. Thousand Oaks, CA: Sage.

Byrd, A., & Tharps, L. (2001). *Hair story: Untangling the roots of Black hair in America*. New York: St. Martin's Press.

Bystydzienski, J. M. (1992). *Women transforming politics: Worldwide strategies for empowerment*. Bloomington: Indiana University Press.

Calabrese, R. L., & Underwood, E. (1994). The effects of school-generated racism on students of color. *High School Journal, 415*, 267–273.

Calas, M. B., & Smircich, L. (1996). From the "woman's" point of view: Feminist approaches to organization studies. In S. Clegg, C. Hardy, & W. R. Nord (Eds.), *Handbook of organization studies* (pp. 218–257). London: Sage.

Catalyst (1998). *Women of color in corporate management: A statistical picture*. New York: Catalyst.

Cheever, B. (2001). *Selling Ben Cheever: Back to square one in a service economy*. New York: Bloomsbury.

Cheney, G., Lair, D., & Gill, R. (2002). Trends at work at the turn of the 21st century: Implications for organizational communication. *Management Communication Quarterly, 15*, 632–641.

Cohn, J. (1997). The effects of racial and ethnic discrimination on the career development of minority persons. In H. Farmer (Ed.), *Diversity and women's career development* (pp. 161–171). Thousand Oaks, CA: Sage.

Collins, P. H. (1986). Learning from the outsider within: The sociological significance of Black feminist thought. *Social Problems*, *33*(6), 14–32.

Collins, P. H. (1989, May). *Toward a new vision: Race, class, and gender as categories of analysis and connection*. Paper presented at Integrating Race and Gender Into the College Curriculum, a workshop conducted at the Center for Research on Women, University of Memphis, Memphis, TN.

Collins, P. H. (1990). *Black feminist thought: Knowledge, consciousness, and the politics of empowerment*. New York: Routledge.

Collins, P. H. (1998a). *Fighting words: Black women and the search for justice*. Minneapolis: University of Minnesota Press.

Collins, P. H. (1998b). It's all in the family: Intersections of gender, race, and nation. *Hypatia*, *13*, 62–82.

Collins, S. M. (1989). The marginalization of Black executives. *Social Problems*, *36*, 317–331.

Cooper, A. J. (1892). *A voice from the South*. Xenia, OH: Aldine.

Corcoran, M., & Parrott, S. (1992). *Black women's economic progress*. Unpublished manuscript, University of Michigan, Ann Arbor.

Deetz, S. (1982). Critical interpretive research in organizational communication. *Western Journal of Speech Communication*, *46*, 131–149.

Dugger, K. (1991). Social location and gender role attitudes: A comparison of Black and White women. In B. Lorber & S. Farrell (Eds.), *The social construction of gender* (pp. 38–55). Newbury Park, CA: Sage.

Duke, L. (2002). Get real!: Cultural relevance and resistance to the mediated feminine ideal. *Psychology & Marketing*, *19*(2), 211–233.

Dumas, R. G. (1980). Dilemmas of Black females in leadership. In L. Rogers-Rose (Ed.), *The Black woman* (pp. 203–215). Beverly Hills, CA: Sage.

Ehrenreich, B. (2001). *Nickel and dimed: On (not) getting by in America*. New York: Holt.

Essed, P. (1991). *Understanding everyday racism*. Newbury Park, CA: Sage.

Essed, P. (1994). Contradictory positions, ambivalent perceptions: A case study of a Black woman entrepreneur. In K. Bhavnani & A. Phoenix (Eds.), *Shifting identities, shifting racisms: A feminism & psychology reader* (pp. 99–118). London: Sage.

Etter-Lewis, G. (1993). My soul is my own: Oral narratives of African American women in the professions. New York: Routledge.

Excerpts from tapes in discrimination lawsuit. (1996, November 4). *New York Times*, p. D4.

Farmer, H. S. (Ed.). (1997). *Diversity and women's career development: From adolescence to adulthood*. Thousand Oaks, CA: Sage.

Feagin, J. R., & Sikes, M. P. (1994). *Living with racism: The Black middle-class experience*. Boston: Beacon Press.

Ferguson, K. (1984). *The feminist case against bureaucracy*. Philadelphia: Temple University Press.

Fine, M. G. (1995). *Building successful multicultural organizations*. Westport, CT: Quorum Books.

Fine, M. (1994). Working the hyphens: Reinventing self and other in qualitative research. In N. K. Denzin & Y. S. Lincoln (Eds.), *Handbook of qualitative research* (pp. 70–82). Thousand Oaks, CA: Sage.

Fine, M., & Weis, L. (1998). *The unknown city: The lives of poor and working-class young adults*. Boston: Beacon.

Fordham, S. (1993). "Those loud Black girls": Black women, silence, and gender, "passing" in the academy. *Anthropology and Education Quarterly*, *24*, 3–32.

Fordham, S. (1996). *Blacked out: Dilemmas of race, identity, and success at Capital High*. Chicago: University Press of Chicago.

Foucault, M. (1979). *Discipline and punish: Birth of the prison* (A. Sheridan, Trans.). New York: Vintage.

Foucault, M. (1980). *Power/knowledge*. New York: Pantheon.

Frankenberg, R. (1993). *White women, race matters: The social construction of whiteness*. Minneapolis: University of Minnesota.

Fulbright, K. (1986). The myth of the double-advantage: Black female managers. In M. Simms & J. Malveaux (Eds.), *Slipping through the cracks: The status of Black women* (pp. 33–46). New Brunswick, NJ: Transaction.

Gilkes, C. T. (1980). Holding back the ocean with a broom: Black women and community work. In L. Rogers-Rose (Ed.), *The Black woman*, (pp. 217–232). Beverly Hills, CA: Sage.

Gilkes, C. T. (1983). Going up for the oppressed: The career mobility of Black women community workers. *Journal of Social Issues, 39*, 115–139.

Gittell, M., Ortega-Bustamante, I., & Steffy, T. (1999). *Women creating social capital and social change: A study of women-led community development organizations.* New York: Howard Samuels State Management and Policy Center, Graduate School and University Center, City University of New York.

Grimes, D. S. (2002). Challenging the status quo? Whiteness in the diversity management literature. *Management Communication Quarterly, 15*, 381–409.

Guinier, L., & Torres, G. (2002). *The miner's canary: Enlisting race, resisting power, transforming democracy.* Cambridge, MA: Harvard University Press.

Harley, S. (1997). Speaking up: The politics of Black women's labor history. In E. Higginbotham & M. Romero (Eds.), *Women and work: Exploring race, ethnicity, and class* (pp. 28–51). Thousand Oaks, CA: Sage.

Hecht, M. L. (Ed.). (1998). *Communicating prejudice.* Thousand Oaks, CA: Sage.

Higginbotham, E. (1987). Employment for Black professional women in the twentieth century. In C. Bose & G. Spitze (Eds.), *Ingredients for women's employment policy* (73–91). Albany: State University of New York Press.

Higginbotham, E. (1997). Black professional women: Job ceilings and employment sectors. In D. Dunn (Ed.), *Workplace/women's place: An anthology* (pp. 234–246). Los Angeles: Roxbury.

Higginbotham, E., & Weber, L. (1997). Perceptions of workplace discrimination among Black and White professional-managerial women. In I. Browne (Ed.), *Latinas and African American women at work: Race, gender, and economic inequality* (pp. 327–353). New York: Russell Sage Foundation.

Hill, S. E., Bahniuk, M. H., & Dobos, J. (1989). The impact of mentoring and collegial support on faculty success: An analysis of support behavior, information adequacy, and communication apprehension. *Communication Education, 38*, 15–33.

Hine, D. C., & Thompson, K. (1998). *A shining thread of hope: The history of Black women in America.* New York: Broadway Books.

Holcomb-McCoy, C. C., & Moore-Thomas, C. (2001, October). Empowering African-American adolescent females. *Professional School Counseling, 5*, 19–27.

Holzer, H. J. (1996). *What employers want: Job prospects for less-educated workers.* New York: Russell Sage Foundation.

hooks, b. (1981). *Ain't I a woman: Black women and feminism.* Boston: South End Press.

hooks, b. (1984). *Feminist theory from margin to center.* Boston: South End Press.

hooks, b. (1990). *Yearning: Race, gender, and cultural politics.* Boston: South End.

Houston, M. (2002). Seeking difference: African Americans in interpersonal communication research, 1975–2000. *Howard Journal of Communication, 13*, 25–41.

Houston, M., & Kramarae, C. (1991). Speaking from silence: Methods of silencing and resistance. *Discourse & Society, 2*, 387–399.

Hull, G. T., Scott, P. B., & Smith, B. (Eds.). (1982). *All the women are White, all the men are Black, but some of us are brave: Black women's studies.* Old Westbury, NY: Feminist Press.

Jacobs, J. A., & Blair-Loy, M. (2001). Gender, race, local labor markets, and occupational devaluation. In E. Anderson & D. Massey (Eds), *Problem of the century: Racial stratification in the United States* (pp. 347–374). New York: Russell Sage Foundation.

Jackson, R. L., II. (1999). *The negotiation of cultural identity: Perceptions of European Americans and African Americans.* Westport, CT: Praeger.

Jones, A. P. (1986). Black women and labor force participation: An analysis of sluggish growth rates. In M. Simms & J. Malveaux (Eds.), *Slipping through the cracks: The status of Black women* (pp. 11–32). New Brunswick, NJ: Transaction.

Jones, J. (1985). *Labor of love, labor of sorrow: Black women, work and the family from slavery to the present.* New York: Basic Books.

Jorgenson, J. (2002). Engineering selves: Negotiating gender and identities in technical work. *Management Communication Quarterly, 15*, 350–380.

Kalbfleisch, P. J. (2002). Communicating in mentoring relationships: A theory for enactment. *Communication Theory, 12*, 63–69.

Kanter, R. M. (1977). *Men and women of the corporation*. New York: Basic Books.

King, D. K. (1988). Multiple jeopardy, multiple consciousness: The context of a Black feminist ideology. *Signs: Journal of Women in Culture and Society, 14*, 42–72.

King, T. C., & Ferguson, S. A. (2001). Charting ourselves: Leadership development with Black professional women. *NWSA Journal*, 13, 123–154.

Kirschenman, J., & Neckerman, K. (1992). "We'd love to hire them, but . . .": The meaning of race for employers. In C. Jencks & P. Petersen (Eds.), *The urban underclass* (pp. 203–232). Washington, DC: Brookings Institute.

Ladner, J. (1972). *Tomorrow's tomorrow: The Black woman*. New York: Anchor Books.

Levy, F., & Murnane, R. (1992). U.S. earnings levels and earnings inequality: A review of recent trends and proposed explanations. *Journal of Economic Literature, 30*, 1333–1381.

Lorde, A. (1984). *Sister outsider.* Trumansburg, NY: Crossing Press.

Lubiano, W. (1992). Black ladies, welfare queens and state minstrels: Ideological war by narrative means. In T. Morrison (Ed.), *Race-ing justice, en-gendering power* (pp. 321–361). New York: Pantheon.

Marshall, J. (1993). Viewing organizational communication from a feminist perspective: A critique and some offerings. In S. Deetz (Ed.), *Communication yearbook 16* (pp. 122–143). Newbury Park, CA: Sage.

Martin, J. (1990). Deconstructing organizational taboos: The suppression of gender conflict in organizations. *Organization Science, 1*, 339–359.

Mathis, D. (2002). *Yet a stranger: Why Black Americans still don't feel at home*. New York: Warner Books.

McCluskey, A. T. (1997). "We specialize in the wholly impossible": Black women school founders and their mission. *Signs: Journal of Women in Culture and Society, 22*, 403–426.

McDonald, T., & Ford-Ahmed, T. (1999). *Nature of a sistuh: Black women's lived experiences in contemporary culture*. Durham, NC: Carolina Academic Press.

McIntosh, P. (1988). *White privilege and male privilege: A personal account of coming to see correspondences through work in women's studies* (Working Paper No. 189). Wellesley, MA: Center for Research on Women, Wellesley College.

Moore, J., & Vigil, J. D. (1993). Barrios in transition. In J. Moore & R. Pinderhuges (Eds.), *In the barrios: Latinos and the underclass debate* (pp. 27–49). New York: Russell Sage Foundation.

Morton, P. (1991). *Disfigured images: The historical assault on Afro-American women*. Westport, CT: Greenwood Press.

Mullings, L. (1997). *On our own terms: Race, class, and gender in the lives of African American women*. New York: Routledge.

Mumby, D. K. (1987). The political function of narrative in organizations. *Communication Monographs, 54*, 113–127.

Mumby, D. K. (2001). Power and politics. In F. M. Jablin & L. L. Putnam (Eds.), *The new handbook of organizational communication: Advances in theory, research, and methods* (pp. 585–623). Newbury Park, CA: Sage.

Mumby, D. K., & Putnam, L. L. (1992). The politics of emotion: A feminist reading of bounded rationality. *Academy of Management Review, 17*, 465–486.

Mumby, D. K., & Stohl, C. (1998). Commentary: Feminist perspectives in organizational communication. *Management Communication Quarterly, 11*, 622–634.

Murphy, A. G. (1998). Hidden transcripts of flight attendant resistance. *Management Communication Quarterly, 11*, 499–535.

Nkomo, S. M. (1992). The emperor has no clothes: Rewriting race in organizations. *Academy of Management Review, 17*, 487–513.

Nottingham, D. (2001). *African American women's information seeking behavior: A study of MBA students*. Unpublished manuscript, University of North Carolina at Chapel Hill.

O'Hare, P., Pollard, K., Mann, T., & Kent, M. (1992). African Americans in the 1990s. *Population Bulletin, 46*, 1.

Okely, J. (1991). Defiant moments: Gender, resistance and individuals. *Man, 26*, 3–22.

Omolade, B. (1994). *The rising song of African American women*. New York: Routledge.

Orbe, M. P. (1998a). An outsider within perspective to organizational communication: Explicating the communicative practices of co-cultural group members. *Management Communication Quarterly, 19*, 230–279.

Orbe, M. P. (1998b). *Constructing co-cultural theory: An explication of culture, power, and communication*. Thousand Oaks, CA: Sage.

Parker, P. S. & Ogilvie, D. T. (1996). Gender, culture, and leadership: Toward a culturally distinct model of African-American women executives' leadership strategies. *Leadership Quarterly, 7*, 189–214.

Parker, P. S. (1997). *African American women executives within dominant culture organizations: An examination of leadership socialization, communication strategies, and leadership behavior*. Unpublished doctoral dissertation, University of Texas, Austin.

Parker, P. S. (2001). African American women executives within dominant culture organizations: (Re)conceptualizing notions of instrumentality and collaboration. *Management Communication Quarterly, 15*, 42–82.

Parker, P. S. (2002). *Learning leadership: Communication, resistance, and African American women's executive leadership development*. Manuscript submitted for publication.

Parker, P. S. (in press). Negotiating identity in raced and gendered workplace interactions: The use of strategic communication by African American women senior executives within dominant culture organizations. *Communication Quarterly*.

Pennington, D. L. (1999). *African American women quitting the workplace*. Lewiston, NY: Edwin Mellen Press.

Porter, J. L. (1999). There's always a line of separation: The figuring of race, gender, and class in the construction of corporate identities. In T. McDonald & T. Ford-Ahmed (Eds.), *Nature of a sistuh: Black women's lived experiences in contemporary culture* (pp. 133–142). Durham, NC: Carolina Academic Press.

Prasad, P., Mills, A. J., Elmes, M., & Prasad, A. (Eds.). (1997). *Managing the organizational melting pot: Dilemmas of workplace diversity*. Thousand Oaks, CA: Sage.

Pringle, R. (1988). *Secretaries talk*. London: Verso.

Radford-Hill, S. (2002). Keepin' it real: A generational commentary on Kimberly Springer's "Third wave Black feminism?" *Signs: A Journal of Women in Culture and Society, 27*, 1083–1090.

Reid-Merritt, P. (1996). *Sister power: How phenomenal Black women are rising to the Top*. New York: Wiley.

Reinharz, S. (1992). *Feminist methods in social research*. New York: Oxford University Press.

Rogers-Rose, L. (Ed.). (1980). *The Black woman*. Beverly Hills, CA: Sage.

Rollins, J. (1985). *Between women: Domestics and their employers*. Philadelphia: Temple University Press.

Rosenfeld, L., & Richman, J. (1999). Supportive communication and school outcomes: Academically "at-risk" low income high school students. *Communication Education, 48*, 294–307.

Rosser, S. V. (1998). Applying feminist theories to women in science programs. *Signs: Journal for Women in Culture and Society, 24*, 171–200.

Rowe, A. (2000). Locating feminism's subject: The paradox of White femininity and the struggle to forge feminist alliances. *Communication Theory, 10*, 64–80.

Scott, J. (1986). Gender: A useful category of historical analysis. *American Historical Review, 91*, 1053–1075.

Shuter, R., & Turner, L. H. (1997). African American and European American women in the workplace: Perceptions of workplace communication. *Management Communication Quarterly, 11*, 74–96.

Simms, M., & Malveaux, J. (Eds.). (1996). *Slipping through the cracks: The status of Black women* (pp. 11–32). New Brunswick, NJ: Transaction.

Slevin, K. F., & Wingrove, C. R. (1998). *From stumbling blocks to stepping stones: The life experiences of fifty professional African American women*. New York: New York University Press.

Smith, B. (1983). *Home girls: A Black feminist anthology*. New York: Kitchen Table Press.

Sokolof, N. (1987). Black and White women in the professions: A contradictory process. In C. Bose & G. Spitze (Eds.), *Ingredients for women's employment* (pp. 53–72). Albany: State University of New York Press.

Souza, T. J. (1999). Communication and alternative school socialization. *Communication Education, 48*, 91–108.

Spelman, E. (1988). *Inessential woman: Problems of exclusion in feminist thought.* Boston: Beacon Press.

Squire, C. (1994). Empowering women? *The Oprah Winfrey Show.* In K. Bhavnani & A. Phoenix (Eds.), *Shifting identities, shifting racisms: A feminism & psychology reader* (pp. 63–79). London: Sage.

Stack, C. B. (1974). *All our kin: Strategies for survival in a Black community.* New York: Harper & Row.

Stack, C. B. (2000). Different voices, different visions: Gender, culture, and moral reasoning. In M. B. Zinn, P. Hondagneu-Sotelo, & M. Messner (Eds.), *Gender through the prism of difference* (2nd ed., pp. 42–48). Boston: Allyn & Bacon.

Stall, S., & Stoecker, R. (1998). Community organizing or organizing community? Gender and the crafts of empowerment. *Gender & Society, 12*(6),729–756.

St. Jean, Y., & Feagin, J. R. (1997a). Racial masques: Black women and subtle gendered racism. In N. V. Benokraitis (Ed.), *Subtle sexism: Current practice and prospects for change* (pp. 179–199). Thousand Oaks, CA: Sage.

St. Jean, Y., & Feagin, J. R. (1997b). Black women, sexism, and racism: Experiencing double jeopardy (pp. 157–180). In C. R. Ronai, B. A. Zsembik, & J. R. Feagin (Eds.), *Everyday sexism in the third millennium.* New York: Routledge.

Tatum, B. (1997). *Why are all the Black kids sitting together in the cafeteria? And other conversations about race.* New York: Basic Books.

Taylor, J. (1991, August). *Breaking the silence: Questions about race.* Paper presented at Resisting Silence: Women Listening to Girls, a symposium conducted at the annual meeting of the American Psychological Association, San Francisco, CA.

Taylor, B. C., & Trujillo, N. (2001). Qualitative research methods. In F. M. Jablin & L. L. Putnam (Eds.), *The new handbook of organizational communication: Advances in theory, research, and methods* (pp. 161–194). Thousand Oaks, CA: Sage.

Thomas, D. A. (1990). The impact of race on managers' experiences of developmental relationships (mentoring and sponsorship): An intra-organizational study. *Journal of Organizational Behavior, 11*, 479–492.

Thomas, D. A. (1993). Racial dynamics in cross-race developmental relationships. *Administrative Science Quarterly, 38*, 169–194.

Thomas, D., & Gabarro, J. J. (1999). *Breaking through: The making of minority executives in corporate America.* Boston: Harvard Business School Press.

Tretheway, A. (1997). Resistance, identity, and empowerment: A postmodern feminist analysis of clients in a human service organization. *Communication Monographs, 64*, 281–301.

Twine, F. W. (2000). Feminist fairy tales for Black and American Indian girls: A working-class vision. *Signs: Journal of Women in Culture and Society, 25*, 1227–1230.

Waldron, V. R., Lavitt, M., & McConnaughey, M. (2001). "Welfare-to-work": An analysis of the communication competencies taught in a job training program serving an urban poverty area. *Communication Education, 50*, 15–33.

Walker, A. (1983). *In search of our mothers' gardens.* New York: Harcourt Brace Jovanovich.

Weis, L., Fine, M., & Morton-Christmas, R. (1999). "I was going up for assistant manager [at McDonalds], but I had to quit because I didn't have a babysitter and welfare wouldn't pay for one": African American women crossing borders. *Educational Foundations, 13*(2), 5–26.

West, C., & Fenstermaker, S. (1995). Doing difference. *Gender & Society, 9*, 8–37.

Williams, P. (1995). *The rooster's egg: On the persistence of prejudice.* Cambridge, MA: Harvard University Press.

Woody, B. (1992). *Black women in the workplace: Impacts of structural change in the economy.* New York: Greenwood Press.

Yoder, J. D., & Aniakudo, P. (June, 1997). "Outsider within" the firehouse: Subordination and difference in the social interactions of African American women firefighters. *Gender & Society, 11*, 324–341.

Yuval-Davis, N. (1994). Women, ethnicity and empowerment. In K. Bhavnani & A. Phoenix (Eds.), *Shifting identities, shifting racisms: A feminism & psychology reader.* (pp. 179–197) London: Sage.

CHAPTER CONTENTS

10 Credibility for the 21st Century: Integrating Perspectives on Source, Message, and Media Credibility in the Contemporary Media Environment

MIRIAM J. METZGER
ANDREW J. FLANAGIN
KEREN EYAL
DAISY R. LEMUS
ROBERT M. MCCANN
University of California, Santa Barbara

Technological capabilities and features of the Internet and World Wide Web have prompted concerns about the verity of online information, the credibility of new media, and the new responsibilities placed on media consumers. Reflecting these concerns, scholars have shown a renewed interest in the credibility of sources, their messages, and the media that carry them. Nonetheless, researchers who are currently reengaging the issue of information credibility have yet to take full advantage of the rich heritage left by credibility research conducted over the last half century. The primary aim of this chapter is to show how past research can inform present attempts to understand credibility in the new media environment, focusing particularly on Web-based information. Toward that end, this chapter reviews, synthesizes, and integrates the substantial literature on source, message, and media credibility; addresses issues of credibility conceptualization, operationalization, and measurement; suggests strategies to empower online users and information providers; and culminates with strategies for credibility research and an agenda for the study of credibility in the contemporary media environment.

N ew technologies have recathected an old area of interest in the field of communication. By connecting users in ways never before possible, technologies such as the Internet and World Wide Web have brought new attention to the issue of credibility across sources, messages, and media.[1] These technologies have changed human association by making point-to-point commu-

---

Correspondence: Miriam J. Metzger, University of California, Santa Barbara, Department of Communication, Santa Barbara, CA 93106-4020; email: metzger@comm.ucsb.edu

Communication Yearbook 27, pp. 293–335

nication increasingly feasible, resulting in greater availability of more diverse information sources and resources than at any time in the past. A consequence is that the filters and control mechanisms, which formerly served to validate and endorse a rather limited number of information outlets, may not be as effective in this new media environment. Absent such controls, information assessment and verification—core components of source, message, and medium credibility—now often become the responsibility of the media consumer.

Scholars have recognized this essential change in the information environment and have shown a renewed interest in the credibility of sources, messages, and the media that carry them (e.g., Flanagin & Metzger, 2000, 2002a; Johnson & Kaye, 1998, 2000, 2002; Kim, Weaver, & Willnat, 2001; Kiousis, 2001; Morris & Ogan, 1996; Schweiger, 2000; Sundar, 1998, 1999; Sundar & Nass, 2001). Within the field of communication few concepts have received more scholarly attention than the issue of credibility. However, researchers who are currently reengaging the issue of information credibility have not taken full advantage of the rich heritage left by credibility research conducted over the last half century. The primary aim of this chapter is to show how past research can inform present attempts to understand credibility in the new media environment, focusing particularly on Web-based information.

On a practical level, accurately assessing credibility has significant consequences for users. As the amount of information available via the Internet increases steadily, so too does the amount of fraud and misinformation online (Caruso, 1999; GomdaWeb, 1998; Null, 2000; Ward, 1997). A study by the National Consumers' League (2000) showed a 16-fold increase in Internet fraud complaints from 1996–1999. Agencies such as the Federal Trade Commission and the Securities and Exchange Commission have recently launched aggressive antifraud initiatives and public education programs to combat the growing problem of Internet-based commerce and investment scams (Chandrasekaran, 1999; Simons, 1999). Inaccurate news reports disseminated online are also a concern (GomdaWeb, 1998; Shaw, 1998; Sundar, 1998). Several heavily reported instances of unsubstantiated stories perpetuated via the Web serve to erode public confidence in the reliability of Internet-based information (Nadarajan & Ang, 1999).

Because of the danger of inaccurate or biased information available online, assessing online information quality should be a core concern of all Internet users. In addition to the issues already raised, research suggests that people are less likely to pay attention to media that they do not perceive as credible (Johnson & Kaye, 1998). Accordingly, credibility is a necessary condition for the Internet and Web to compete with other viable sources of information.

INFORMATION FEATURES OF THE CONTEMPORARY MEDIA ENVIRONMENT

Several characteristics of Web-based information prompt concerns about its credibility. One distinctive feature of the Internet is its relative lack of professional gatekeepers. Whereas newspapers, books, magazines, and television all undergo certain levels of factual verification, analysis of content, and editorial review, Web-based information is not always subject to the same level of scrutiny. Of course, Web sites that parallel their print counterparts, such as major newspapers and periodicals, invoke the same editorial processes as their print forms, but these sites constitute a small portion of the information available over the Internet. More common on the Internet is less formal information generated by special interest groups, individuals, and organizations—material for which the level of editorial review is not explicit. Johnson and Kaye (1998) point out that the lack of editorial review processes in the online environment results in less social and professional pressure to ensure the overall accuracy of Web-based information.

Another distinctive feature of the Web is its convergence of genres of information, particularly the blending of advertising and informational content (Alexander & Tate, 1999; Flanagin & Metzger, 2000). Unlike traditional print publishing, it may be harder to discern between the two forms in the online environment because material is often presented seamlessly, without clear distinctions between advertising and other information. Alexander and Tate also note that it is sometimes difficult to know if the advertising and informational content on a Web site are produced by the same source. Not knowing the source of information or its intent makes it difficult to know whether to trust it.

Although some Web sites parallel their traditional media counterparts, the lack of established reputations for many sites prevents Internet users from applying prior knowledge of the medium or content genres to assess information veracity. For instance, although differences between the *New York Times* and *New York Post* may be widely understood, there are less familiar sites where consumers are not guided by such name recognition. Furthermore, because computers have an air of authority about them (Johnson & Kaye, 1998; Witmer, 1998), people may treat information found online as more credible. This is compounded by the fact that professional-looking Web sites are fairly easy to create and can appear to be credible, regardless of authorship (Flanagin & Metzger, 2000, 2002a; Johnson & Kaye, 1998). Indeed, there have been several well-publicized instances of fraudulent Web sites successfully mimicing legitimate ones (Alexander & Tate, 1999; GomdaWeb, 1998; Johnson & Kaye, 1998; Rieh & Belkin, 1998).

Lastly, Internet-based information differs from that delivered through more traditional channels in that it is prone to digital alteration, which is difficult to detect (Alexander & Tate, 1999). Online information may be altered intentionally or unintentionally, for example, when technical problems occur during the data conversion process when information is uploaded or transferred. In sum, there are several factors of the Internet and Web to suggest that those relying on online information should scrutinize it carefully.

CREDIBILITY RESEARCH HERITAGE

Research on credibility began with interest in its role in the persuasion process, with scholars studying the impact of *source credibility* on interpersonal influence. Researchers later recognized, however, that organizations also constitute sources that strive to influence human behavior through communication. *Message credibility* was also explored as part of this early research, focusing on characteristics of messages that could make them more or less credible. Also, scholars interested in mass communication looked at *media credibility* in determining the relative believability of particular forms of communication (e.g., newspapers versus television). Although the knowledge gained from these streams of research was substantial, its application to current research could be better realized.

The application of past research on credibility to the present media environment is especially appropriate because the Internet blends forms of communication traditionally viewed as distinct (Chaffee, 2001). For example, email and chat rooms allow for interpersonal communication, and Web sites are used by both individuals and organizations to communicate with audiences on either a modest or mass scale. The result of this media convergence is that credibility on the Internet is complex. It is logical to assess credibility of the Internet as a conduit or medium, as well as to assess the credibility of an entire Web site, a Web site sponsor, or information residing on a particular Web page. In view of this diversity, new research can profitably approach Web credibility from the traditional perspectives of source, message, and medium credibility and incorporate the lessons learned from past research in each of these domains. In addition, it is important for researchers to distinguish the locus of credibility in their work, and this chapter attempts to sort out this difficult issue.

Synthesizing past research also provides a better understanding of the important issues that researchers will need to devote their energies to when examining credibility in the new media environment. Researchers can take advantage of the multilevel perspective of credibility gained from past studies in interpersonal, organizational, and mass communication literature. Perhaps most important, scholars can learn from the missteps of the work that has come before. Significant criticisms of past conceptualizations and measurements of credibility (Cronkhite & Liska, 1976; Delia, 1976) are considered in this chapter as a means to help scholars avoid them in future research on the new media environment.

INFORMATION LITERACY, CREDIBILITY, AND EMPOWERMENT

The ability to effectively and accurately discern credible from unreliable information is fundamentally an issue of empowerment, inasmuch as attitudes and behaviors based on accurate information are superior to those founded on less secure premises. Several characteristics of Web-based information mentioned earlier make assessing information credibility particularly challenging in the online environment. As a consequence, empowerment and credibility are yoked in the new media environment.

Underlying empowerment in the contemporary media environment is the development of appropriate information literacy, or the ability to critically analyze and evaluate information from media sources (Cortes, 1992; Potter, 1998). The benefits of information literacy accrue to both information consumers and information providers in the new media environment. For information consumers, accurate assessments of online credibility help to avoid the negative consequences of mistakenly being guided by poor data, and provide the benefits of using reliable information. The importance of credibility is no less crucial for information providers, for whom an understanding of information literacy may translate to the ability to capture users' attention in the vast array of online information and engender trust from Internet consumers. These perspectives are considered in this chapter, along with recommendations for Internet users and providers to empower themselves in the new media environment.

SOURCE CREDIBILITY

Empirical research on source credibility began in the 20th century with studies that considered credibility to be an important characteristic of persuasive speakers. These researchers defined source credibility as "judgments made by a perceiver concerning the believability of a communicator" (O'Keefe, 1990, pp. 130–131; Wilson & Sherrell, 1993). According to Self (1996), academic interest in the concept of source credibility was stirred in the 1940s. World War II created new incentives for scholarly research on persuasion, as the U.S. sought ways to enhance public support for the war. Carl Hovland and his colleagues at Yale University launched an ambitious program to study communication and attitude change, with the goal of developing a systematic theory of persuasion (Lowery & DeFleur, 1995). Their approach to persuasion focused on attitude change but was also concerned with source credibility and its influence on attitude formation.

The Yale group defined credibility in terms of a speaker's *expertise* and *trustworthiness*. Expertise referred to a communicator's qualifications or ability to know the truth about a topic, whereas trustworthiness was conceptualized as perceptions of the communicator's motivation to tell the truth about a topic (Hovland, Janis, & Kelley, 1953). The Yale team suggested a deductive approach in which source credibility is a receiver-based construct, determined by the audience's acceptance of the speaker and message. Building on this notion, McCroskey (1966) investigated how message recipients perceived particular communicators (Perloff, 1993). This foundation led to hundreds of empirical studies that sought to determine the dimensions of source credibility from the perspective of message recipients.

Dimensions of Source Credibility

Research on source credibility during the 1960s and 1970s consisted of several factor analytic studies of audience member's credibility perceptions (Gass & Seiter, 1999). Most researchers found evidence for two primary dimensions of source credibility, trustworthiness and expertise, but also identified several secondary dimensions of source credibility such as dynamism, composure, and sociability (Berlo, Lemert, & Mertz, 1969; Gass & Seiter, 1999; Jurma, 1981; McCroskey, 1966; Perloff, 1993; Whitehead, 1968). Thus, more qualified, reliable, animated, poised, and good-natured speakers were judged to be higher in credibility. This research also identified two variables that may influence audience perceptions of trustworthiness and expertise: liking for and similarity to the source.

O'Keefe (1990) noted that liking tends to influence source trustworthiness perceptions, although it does not influence competence perceptions. Other studies indicated that items assessing liking for a source (e.g., friendliness, pleasantness, physical attractiveness) tend to load on the same factor as items denoting trustworthiness (e.g., McCroskey, 1966; Widgery & Webster, 1969). Similarity with a speaker may also impact credibility perceptions, through its influence on liking or by affecting perceptions of the speaker's competence or expertise (Aune & Kikuchi, 1993). However, this is more true for similarity in attitudes than similarity in traits, abilities, or demographic variables such as occupation, age, and social status (Atkinson, Brady, & Casas, 1981; Byrne, 1969; Worthington & Atkinson, 1996).[2]

Following attempts to identify the various factors that might influence source credibility perceptions, researchers next turned their efforts to determining the relative effectiveness of each dimension on attitude change. In a meta-analysis of 114 articles about this topic from 1950 to 1990, Wilson and Sherrell (1993) found that source expertise is a stronger influence on persuasion than other source characteristics (cf. Leathers, 1992). They suggested that because the expertise dimension of source credibility is more objective than other dimensions, it is easier for audience members to assess. In contrast, Lui and Standing (1989) found that sources manipulated to have higher trustworthiness are perceived as more credible than sources manipulated to have more expertise. Disagreements about the relative importance of the dimensions of source credibility led to the construction of various scales to measure this concept, each reflecting the priority of dimensions identified by particular researchers.

Measurement and Validation of Source Credibility Dimensions

Several scales have been developed to measure source credibility, most notably those by McCroskey (1966; McCroskey, Holdridge, & Toomb, 1974; McCroskey & Jenson, 1975), Berlo et al. (1969), and Leathers (1992). Although each scale uses a similar semantic differential question format, they measure slightly different dimensions of source credibility. McCroskey's scales assess five dimensions of source credibility (character, competence, sociability, extroversion, and composure), whereas the other scales include only three dimensions: Berlo et al. measure safety (i.e., friendliness, trustworthiness), qualification (i.e., expertise), and dynamism; Leathers measures competence, trustworthiness, and dynamism.

The fact that different researchers found different dimensions of source credibility prompted criticism of the factor analytic approach to studying source credibility (Cronkhite & Liska, 1976; Delia, 1976; A. M. Rubin, 1994). Cronkhite and Liska demonstrated that the factors identified in each study were merely the result of which items were selected for inclusion by the researcher. Delia asserted that the study of source credibility had been driven too much by measurement considerations and too little by theoretical explications of credibility. Attempts at validating the various standard source credibility scales exacerbated these concerns. Wanzenreid and Powell (1993; Powell & Wanzenreid, 1995) found four instead of the five dimensions they expected to see from the McCroskey and Jenson scale (character was not a stable factor). They also found that the Leathers scale produced only two, rather than the expected three dimensions (competence was not found to be a separate factor). Powell and Wanzenreid's results showed considerable inconsistency in the dimensions of source credibility, thereby undermining the validity of the standard source credibility scales.

Together, these studies suggest that credibility dimensions may differ depending upon the type of source being evaluated and the context in which the evaluation occurs (Cronkhite & Liska, 1976; Delia, 1976; Gass & Seiter, 1999; Gunther, 1988, 1992; Stamm & Dube, 1994). For the most part, only one type of source and context had been examined in source credibility research: individuals giving a speech in front of a live audience. Only recently has this narrow view broadened to include organizations and Web sites as sources.

Organizations as Sources

There is increasing understanding that institutions may also generate persuasive messages and that the credibility of organizational sources can be an important factor in influencing consumers' attitudes and behaviors (Gass & Seiter, 1999). The idea of organizations as sources has been advanced in the advertising and marketing literature as corporate credibility, institutional credibility, retailer credibility, or advertiser credibility. Goldsmith, Lafferty, and Newell (2000) define corporate credibility as the degree to which consumers, investors, and others believe in the organization's trustworthiness and expertise. The notion of organizational credibility suggests that the source of the message is not an individual person but is rather a complex institutional structure with a history of experience and information, to which the public has already been exposed.

Studies have focused on the effects of organizational credibility on consumer attitudes and behaviors and on identifying the dimensions of organizational credibility. In terms of effects, Goldsmith et al. (2000; Lafferty & Goldsmith, 1999) find that organizational credibility directly influences consumers' attitudes toward a brand and their purchase intentions. Researchers have also identified several dimensions of organizational credibility that resemble the dimensions found in earlier source credibility research (cf. Bobinski, Cox, & Cox, 1996; Hammond, 1987; MacKenzie & Lutz, 1989; O'Reilly & Roberts, 1976). For example, dimensions of organizational credibility consistently include expertise, trustworthiness, and attractiveness (Haley, 1996; Ohanian, 1990, 1991), although prestige, competitiveness, and familiarity have also been identified as organizational credibility factors (Vanden Bergh, Soley, & Reid, 1981).[3]

Overall, many similarities exist between source and organizational credibility. Both constructs seem to include the dimensions of trustworthiness and expertise. As Gass and Seiter (1999) suggest, whereas the same primary dimensions of source credibility might apply to organizations, the secondary dimensions will likely vary. Interestingly, both credibility constructs seem to include the notion of attractiveness, although in organizations this seems to be more appropriately viewed as likeability. Haley (1996) suggests that this might reflect a value congruency between the values held by consumers and those perceived as being endorsed by the organization.

Migrating Source Credibility Research to the Web

In some respects, Web sites may be considered to be analogous to individuals or organizations—that is, as information sources whose characteristics engender greater or lesser credibility. Although not all interpersonal traits identified in the source credibility literature translate to a Web environment, other important communicator dimensions become interesting in this context. For example, Web site expertise may be reflected in site informativeness, displaying appropriate credentials, the sponsor's reputation, or the type of site sponsor (i.e., institutional versus individual). Trustworthiness may be communicated through explicit policy statements or a lack of advertising and commercial content. Attractiveness or dynamism may be communicated through various dimensions of the Web site's appearance (e.g., layout, graphics, color, etc.). Although still in its formative stages, research has already begun to approach Web site credibility from this perspective.

For example, low reputable banner ads have been found to reduce the perceived expertise of a Web page's content, and the existence of a formal photograph of the author has led people to rate a Web article as more believable, trustworthy, competent, and expert (Fogg et al., 2001a). In addition, expertise may be communicated through information coverage or completeness (Alexander & Tate, 1999). Web site credibility may also be enhanced by authority such as listing authors' credentials (Fogg et al., 2001b), but displaying awards won by a Web site has been shown to have no significant effect on ratings of site believability (Shon, Marshall, & Musen, 2000).

Trustworthiness also factors into Web site credibility assessments. Web site credibility is decreased for sites with commercial implications, such as sites with one or more ad on each page, or by a feeling of amateurism, such as sites with broken links (Fogg et al., 2001b), both of which seem to suggest lower consumer trust.

Moreover, Web site credibility may be enhanced by a real-world feel (e.g., when a site lists a physical address), perceived integrity (e.g., states its policy on content and information disclosure), and tailoring (e.g., site sends emails confirming transactions; Fogg et al., 2001b). Trustworthiness may also be communicated through explicit policy statements (Alexander & Tate, 1999; Culnan & Armstrong, 1999), third party endorsements (Alexander & Tate, 1999; Palmer, Bailey, & Faraj, 2000), secure servers and encryption (Alexander & Tate, 1999), listed contact information (Fogg et al., 2001b), and the use of privacy seals (Palmer et al., 2000).

Dimensions of attractiveness and dynamism have been shown to be relevant in users' Web site evaluations as well. Using a series of adjectives describing Web sites, Chen and Wells (1999) developed a measure of "attitude toward the site" with three dimensions: organization (e.g., neat, easy to navigate), informativeness (e.g., informative, useful, helpful), and entertainment (e.g., fun, exciting, flashy). Similarly, users' first impressions of Web pages have been found to align along four dimensions: beauty, overview (i.e., lucidity, clearness, ease of understanding), structure, and pages with mostly illustrations versus mostly text (Schenkman & Jönsson, 2000). Among these, beauty was an important factor in determining users' assessments of Web sites. Accordingly, Bruner and Kumar (2000) and Stevenson, Bruner, and Kumar (2000) found negative attitudes associated with Web sites that use more complex backgrounds. Finally, Eastin (2001) suggests that dynamism, as reflected in Web site layout, color, and graphics, could also influence credibility perceptions (cf. Schweiger, 2000).

Beyond specific Web site features, Flanagin and Metzger (2002a) examined differences among Web site sponsors (i.e., media organization, electronic commerce, special interest organization, and individual) as well as the influence of branding on credibility assessments. They found that sponsorship was important: for the most part, media organization sites were perceived as more credible than other types and individual sites were found to be least credible. However, branding did not influence perceptions of message or site credibility, suggesting that factors communicated through Web site design may indeed be more important in Web site credibility assessments than name recognition.

The foregoing research demonstrates that it is possible to translate several components of source and organizational credibility to the Web environment. Synthesizing the findings described above, expertise may be communicated through the comprehensiveness of a Web site's information, professionalism, and sponsor credentials. Trustworthiness is associated with a Web site's integrity as demonstrated by displaying its policy statements, use of advertising, professionalism, and sponsor reliability or reputation. Attractiveness and dynamism may be reflected in a site's use of colorful graphics, interesting content, or interactive features. Finally, the likeability of a Web site may be enhanced by its perceived beauty (Schenkman & Jönsson, 2000). Overall, Web site design, features, and sponsorship combine to suggest many elements that parallel dimensions of face-to-face and organizational credibility.

MESSAGE CREDIBILITY

Although the emphasis in credibility research has been on the characteristics of the source, characteristics of the message have also received attention. Message credibility examines how message characteristics impact perceptions of believability, either of the source or of the source's message. In this way, source and message credibility are overlapping concepts (Cronkhite & Liska, 1976; Slater & Rouner, 1997; Smith, 1978; Stamm & Dube, 1994). In some cases, message factors may be even more important than source factors in credibility judgments (Austin & Dong, 1994; Eastin, 2001; Slater & Rouner, 1997). The elaboration likelihood model of persuasion predicts that message factors become more influential than source characteristics when issue involvement, knowledge, and personal relevance are high, because they increase motivation to scrutinize message content (Benoit, 1987; Eagly & Chaiken, 1993; O'Keefe, 1990; Petty & Cacioppo, 1981). Also, in situations where little information is available about the source of a message, recipients must turn to message cues to make credibility assessments (Eagly & Chaiken, 1993; Eastin, 2001; Petty & Cacioppo, 1988).

According to Carl Hovland and colleagues' message learning approach to persuasion, attitude change depends upon receivers' attention to and comprehension of some information, as well as their willingness to yield to and retain that information. This process is affected by source, message, recipient, and channel factors (Hovland et al., 1953; Petty & Cacioppo, 1981). In terms of message factors, researchers have examined the influence of message comprehensibility, number of arguments, incentives, fear appeals, one-sided versus two-sided messages, repetition, and presentation style on recipients' attitude change. Many of these message variables not only influence persuasion, but also affect people's credibility assessments (Slater & Rouner, 1997). Research on the dimensions of message credibility finds several factors that may be categorized according to message structure, message content, and message delivery or presentation style.

Dimensions of Message Credibility

Message structure. Research on message structure has focused on the organization of the message, and has demonstrated consistent results: unorganized messages are perceived as less credible than well-organized messages (Gass & Seiter, 1999; Sharp & McClung, 1966). Message organization has been shown to affect perceptions of source expertise but not source trustworthiness (McCroskey & Mehrley, 1969), although Hamilton and Hunter (1998a, 1998b) found positive correlations for perceived message clarity and ratings of all dimensions of source credibility, including expertise, trustworthiness, and dynamism.

Message content. Several variables have been studied pertaining to the actual content of messages. Research shows that credibility judgments are influenced by such message content factors as information quality, language intensity, and message discrepancy (e.g., Bacon, 1979; Hamilton, 1998; McCroskey, 1969).

Slater and Rouner (1997) found that as perceptions of message quality increased, so did assessments of source credibility. They defined message quality as how well-written and interesting readers perceived the message to be, but other aspects of message quality have been studied as well. For example, McCroskey demonstrated that the use of evidence significantly enhanced listeners' assessments of a speaker's credibility when the speaker's initial credibility was low to moderate (1967, 1969; cf. Fleshler, Ilardo, & Demoretcky, 1974; Reinard, 1988). Others have demonstrated that the positive relationship between the use of evidence and perceptions of source credibility is contingent on the speaker's use of high-quality and relevant evidence (Hamilton, 1998). Luchok and McCroskey (1978) found that irrelevant evidence from an unqualified source resulted in attitude change in the opposite direction from that advocated even when the speaker was judged to be highly credible.

But what counts as high-quality evidence? According to the information science literature, there are five dimensions people use to assess the quality of information: accuracy, comprehensiveness, currency, reliability, and validity (Rieh & Belkin, 1998). Error-free messages are considered to enhance message quality, as are comprehensive treatments of a topic and up-to-date, consistent, and logically sound information (Hamilton, 1998).

Language intensity. The use of opinionated language has also been studied for its impact on credibility perceptions (e.g., Bradac, Bowers, & Courtright, 1980; Hamilton, 1998; Hamilton & Hunter, 1998b). This research finds that communicators who use more opinionated language in their messages are rated as less credible than those who use less intense language. A meta-analysis by Hamilton (1998) showed that although message intensity had a positive effect on a speaker's dynamism ratings, it had a small negative effect on ratings of source expertise and a moderately negative effect on ratings of source trustworthiness. It is important to note that message discrepancy plays an important moderating role in this relationship.

Message discrepancy is defined as the distance between the perceived position of the source and the premessage position of the receiver (Hamilton, 1998). Evaluations of credibility are higher when message discrepancy is low (Hovland & Weiss, 1951). Stamm and Dube (1994) suggest that messages that support our views are seen as unbiased, and therefore trustworthy. Studies of Bradac et al.'s (1980) reinforcement expectancy theory and Hamilton's (1998) information processing theory show that message discrepancy is important to understanding the relationship between language intensity and credibility. They have found interaction effects such that sources with discrepant messages that use more intense language are rated most negatively in terms of credibility (Bradac et al., 1980; Hamilton & Hunter, 1998b).

Related to message discrepancy, there is evidence that receivers are likely to believe messages that reaffirm existing knowledge (Bacon, 1979). Some researchers call this the illusory-truth effect. Begg, Anas, and Farinacci (1992) argue that the effect is based on familiarity: "People believe statements that confirm remembered information and doubt statements that contradict it" (p. 456; Boehm, 1994). Familiarity may impact credibility ratings by increasing liking for the source, and research on both message repetition and the use of humor corroborates this idea (e.g., Bacon, 1979; O'Keefe, 1990). Psychologists have long understood that familiarity with an object or person increases liking (Cialdini, 1984) and liking can influence credibility judgments.

Message delivery. The way in which the message is presented by a source may also impact recipients' credibility judgments. Studies examining nonfluencies in a speaker's language (e.g., vocalized pauses, slips of the tongue, and articulation difficulties) found that the more delivery flaws present in a message, the lower the source is rated in terms of credibility (McCroskey & Mehrley, 1969; Miller & Hewgill, 1964; Soreno & Hawkins, 1967). The use of powerful versus powerless communication style also impacts credibility perceptions. A powerless communication style is one that uses such devices as hedges and hesitations, qualifiers, polite forms, and tag questions, whereas powerful language is more assertive (Gass & Seiter, 1999). Burrell and Koper (1998) showed that powerful language enhances perceptions of source credibility (cf. Perloff, 1993).

Finally, speed of message delivery has been shown to affect credibility perceptions. Research finds a positive, but nonlinear relationship between rate of speech and credibility such that fast and moderately fast communicators are judged to be more credible than slow or extremely fast speakers (Perloff, 1993).

Measurement of Message Credibility

Because messages are rarely treated as dependent variables, there have been few attempts to measure the credibility of messages directly. Instead, researchers typically manipulate various message characteristics and then measure message recipients' credibility perceptions of the source who delivered the message. Rosenthal (1971) was among the first to point out the disparity between the study of source credibility and research on the credibility of messages. His position was that credibility assessments were a function of features of the source and of the message (cf. Cronkhite & Liska, 1976). He theorized that, absent any information about the source of the message, audiences determine the credibility of a message based on two factors: the specificity and verifiability of the message content. Thus, ambiguous information and information that was unable to be validated should be perceived as less credible. Although this was a fine starting point for a measure of message credibility, it lacked empirical traction in the research that was to follow.

Scholars seemed to be more influenced by the emerging factor analytic approaches that were being used to measure source credibility. For example, Smith's (1978) message measurement inventory (MMI) was developed to evaluate receivers' perceptions of messages, including message credibility, but instead of measuring people's reactions to various message elements, it predominantly assessed recipients' evaluations of message sources. The MMI includes items such as *confident, passive,* and *uncooperative,* which seem to apply to sources rather than to messages. Thus, the MMI confounded source and message credibility dimensions, perhaps due to an over reliance on existing source credibility literature in the early phases of its development. Few studies have used the MMI since the early 1980s, but later research on message credibility has been no more successful at avoiding confounding source factors in their measures of message credibility.

The foregoing review suggests that scholars should be cautious when incorporating past measures of message credibility in their work. Communication researchers interested in measuring message credibility may instead want to turn to the information quality literature described earlier to develop scales assessing evaluations of a message's accuracy, comprehensiveness, currency, reliability, and validity (Rieh & Belkin, 1998). As will be seen next, researchers investigating the credibility of online messages have in fact begun to take this approach.

Message Credibility and Web Information

Although little research has directly addressed message credibility online, it is likely that message components shown to be important in other research contexts—such as message structure, content, and delivery—remain important when messages are conveyed across new media. For instance, message accuracy, comprehensiveness, currency, reliability, and validity are important in people's assessments of information quality offline, and Internet users report very similar criteria in judging information online (Rieh & Belkin, 1998). Furthermore, people invoke common cognitive elements when assessing news information in both print and online forms (Sundar, 1999). It would appear that elements of research on message credibility may be profitably applied to the contemporary media environment.

Although it is somewhat difficult to separate message structure from Web site structure, elements of message structure have been shown to affect the perceived credibility of messages on Web sites. Perceived amateurism of a Web message and inconsistencies in page design across a site have been demonstrated to decrease information quality perceptions and overall site credibility (Alexander & Tate, 1999; Fogg et al., 2001b). In addition, message or site organization are facilitated by features such as a site map or index as ways to enhance site navigability and, consequently, perceptions of information quality.

Aspects of message content have also been shown to affect perceptions of message credibility online (Rieh & Belkin, 1998). Among the most important factors for enhancing trustworthiness are information accuracy, comprehensiveness, and currency (Alexander & Tate, 1999; cf. Fogg et al., 2001b). Inaccurate news stories, such as rumors perpetuated via the Internet and Web, decrease perceptions of the reliability and credibility of online information—the willingness and ability of online sources to correct errors when they occur is an important buffer against this type of credibility challenge (GomdaWeb, 1998; Hess, 1998; Nadarajan & Ang, 1999). Relatedly, the use of evidence has been shown to be an important factor in online message credibility. For example, quotations in online stories have been shown to increase users' evaluations of both the credibility and quality of news stories (Sundar, 1998). Finally, analogous to perceived interpersonal credibility, language intensity and opinion are also important dimensions of Web message credibility. Alexander and Tate (1999) discuss how the objectivity of information affects site and message evaluations of trustworthiness. Commercial aspects associated with messages can reduce their perceived credibility, apparently due to vested interests of message sources (Fogg et al., 2001b).

Presentation style also influences perceived Web message credibility. The degree to which a site looks to be professionally designed has been demonstrated to increase a Web site's credibility (Fogg et al., 2001b). Rieh and Belkin (1998) suggest that message format and presentation (i.e., how Web pages are presented and the writing style of messages) are important dimensions of perceived credibility as well. Alexander and Tate (1999) argue that Web message nonfluencies such as technical glitches may negatively impact site evaluations and Fogg et al. (2001b) showed that typographical errors (inasmuch as they represent site amateurism) and nonworking links also negatively impact credibility assessments. Finally, speed also seems to matter: a longer wait time for Web site loading can have negative effects on site evaluations (Dellaert & Kahn, 1999; Fogg et al., 2001b).

Evidence also suggests that research considering messages on the Web should explicitly consider information type in message evaluation. Flanagin and Metzger (2000) found that Web-based reference, news, and entertainment information were perceived as more credible than commercial information and that reference information was perceived to be more credible than entertainment information. This suggests the importance of expanding omnibus considerations of information in order to delve into differences across specific information types. Nonetheless, this component of messages is often neglected, particularly in cross-media comparisons of information credibility.

MEDIA CREDIBILITY

Mass communication scholars have a longstanding interest in the relative credibility of various media channels through which a source sends a message. The impetus for research on media credibility dates back to the late 1930s, when the newspaper industry became concerned that increasing numbers of people were turning to the radio for news. During the 1950s, competition from television again prompted the industry to examine the relative market position of the various news media vis à vis their credibility in the eyes of the public (Erskine, 1970; Self, 1996).

In the late 1950s, the Roper Organization began regularly asking respondents which medium they would believe if they got conflicting reports of the same news story from radio, television, magazines, and newspapers. At first, newspapers were judged to be more believable than television, but in 1961 television became the most-believed medium and has remained so ever since (see Roper, 1991, for the actual data; Jacobson, 1969; Self, 1996). The decline of newspaper credibility corresponded closely with the diffusion of television in the United States.

The Roper findings were puzzling to many, but especially to the intellectual elite who considered television a vast wasteland of lowbrow entertainment (Mulder, 1980). Many felt that newspapers should have the advantage due to more in-depth coverage and time to check facts, as well as the ability for news audiences to read and digest stories at their own pace (e.g., Williams, 1975). Consequently, the first phase of academic research consisted of replicating the Roper finding (e.g., Carter & Greenberg, 1965; Jacobson, 1969; Westley & Severin, 1964). Next, researchers explored why television was superior to newspapers (Mulder, 1980). Many arguments were advanced about how the media differed, including technological and structural differences that might contribute to news consumers' greater belief in television over newspaper news.

Factors Affecting Media Credibility

Technological features. Researchers initially thought that television's ability to bring live coverage of news events was a disadvantage compared to newspapers because it was assumed to come at the expense of accuracy. However, in studies of news accuracy, audiences viewed newspapers as less accurate and more biased (e.g., Carter & Greenberg, 1965; Wilson & Howard, 1978). People felt that live reports of breaking news stories gave television news a greater sense of importance and authority compared to newspapers (Chang & Lemert, 1968), perhaps due in part to television's ability to engage and involve viewers without requiring too much of their attention (Andreoli & Worchel, 1978; Worchel, Andreoli, & Eason, 1975). The ease of television seems to translate to higher favorability for television overall, including credibility ratings (American Society of Newspaper Editors, 1985).

The visual nature of television also contributes to its sense of authority. Unlike newspapers, television allows news consumers to see what is happening, which enhances television's trustworthiness in the minds of viewers (Carter & Greenberg, 1965; Gaziano & McGrath, 1986; Westley & Severin, 1964). Gunther (1988) argues that the visual nature of television news makes it appear more objective than newspaper news, because "with greater apparent mediation comes a greater opportunity to impute motives and intentions of the communicator" (p. 287). The idea that seeing is believing when it comes to news is apparently quite powerful: it is the most frequently cited reason for television's superior believability among television news consumers (American Society of Newspaper Editors, 1985; Carter & Greenberg, 1965; Chang & Lemert, 1968; Wilson & Howard, 1978). The visual aspect of television also makes the news seem more personal, resulting in ratings of television as more accurate, sincere, responsible, impartial, and higher in quality than newspapers (Chang & Lemert, 1968; Sargent, 1965). Newhagen and Nass (1989) demonstrate that when assessing the credibility of various media, people use different judgment criteria: people evaluate the credibility of television news by the newscasters who present the news, whereas they evaluate the credibility of the newspaper as an institution.

Structural features. Other researchers proposed that television's high perceived believability might be explained by differences in the structure of the newspaper and television industries. Until 2000, the political editorializing rule precluded broadcasters from stating editorial positions on issues or candidates, whereas newspapers were free to make their political leanings explicit. Some scholars suggested that if these leanings differed from readers' own positions, they would cause readers to feel the newspaper was biased (Carter & Greenberg, 1965; Edelstein, 1978; Westley & Severin, 1964). Research finds that when people do not hear what they want to hear from the news, it is perceived as less credible (Stamm & Dube, 1994; Zanna & Del Vecchio, 1973). However, although public perceptions of the media formed during periods of heavy government regulation may linger for some time, recent deregulatory efforts have lead television and cable to air their political views openly, making this explanation of the credibility gap less plausible today.

The economics of television have also been cited as an explanation for its greater believability over newspapers. Because television is accountable to larger and more diverse audiences and advertisers than are newspapers, it cannot afford to be biased in its news coverage (Carter & Greenberg, 1965; Chang & Lemert, 1968). Another constraint stemming from its economic structure is television's brevity of reporting due to the limited time it can devote to news. Newspapers have more space and are able to provide greater coverage of issues. Although newspapers' greater quantity of coverage would seem to favor them as the more believable medium, newspapers are apt to be judged as inaccurate more frequently than television news due to the sheer volume of reporting (Wilson & Howard, 1978). Also, Chang and Lemert found that the very meaning of the completeness of news stories can be problematic. They discovered that people judge completeness of news coverage by factors such as the ability to access a comprehensive range of topics and to the provision of greater sensory information.

In sum, structural, economic, and legal constraints acting on television combine to make users perceive it as more believable and less political than newspapers, which positively impacts perceptions of its credibility. Coupled with television's technological features (i.e., its visual nature), this may explain its advantage over newspapers in audience credibility ratings. Other explanations include audience factors and issues in the measures used to assess media credibility.

Measurement of Media Credibility

Much of the literature on media credibility has been devoted to its measurement, resulting in multiple measures of the concept, which have been blamed for inconsistent and confusing research results (Gantz, 1981; Gaziano, 1988; Greenberg & Roloff, 1974; Rimmer & Weaver, 1987). The credibility of various media has been measured by comparing perceptions of the believability, accuracy, fairness, bias, trustworthiness, ease of use, completeness, reliability, or attractiveness of the media themselves, of news reporters, or of the coverage of specific news issues. As with the source credibility literature, this intense focus on measurement has perhaps come at the cost of developing clear conceptual definitions of media credibility that could be used to form consistent operationalizations of the concept.

The origins of most media credibility measures come from source credibility and studies of newspaper accuracy (Gaziano & McGrath, 1986). In 1959, Roper began asking respondents which medium (e.g., television, newspapers, magazines, or radio) they got "most of their news" from and, second, which medium they would believe if they received conflicting reports. Although these questions have been used in many studies of media credibility, both inside and outside of academe, they were criticized on several grounds.

Carter and Greenberg (1965) and Rimmer and Weaver (1987) pointed out problems in the wording of the Roper questions that led to a bias against newspapers in people's usage and credibility responses. Carter and Greenberg demonstrated that when asking about the believability of each medium separately, rather than in comparison to one another, the difference between newspaper and television credibility ratings narrowed. They also argued that in the special case of receiving conflicting news reports, the visual nature of television gave that medium an edge in believability assessments. They suggested a better measure of credibility would be to assess the believability of each medium in isolation. Rimmer and Weaver argued that measures of media use can be *affective* (asking which medium respondents prefer to use for news, as in the Roper question) or *behavioral* (asking how often respondents actually use each medium for news). Because credibility is in part an affective judgment, they say that it is not surprising that studies found it to be correlated to affective measures of media use. However, they showed that this correlation did not hold up when behavioral measures of media use were used. Their findings imply that television news may be rated as the most credible medium over newspapers simply because it is cheaper or takes less time and effort than reading a newspaper rather than because it is truly thought to be of higher quality.[4]

A potentially devastating criticism of the Roper credibility questions came from Greenberg and Roloff (1974) who suggested that people might use different points of reference when evaluating various media. They claimed that when asked to assess the credibility of television news, people probably thought of national network news, whereas when asked to evaluate newspaper news, they likely did so on the basis of the local newspaper serving their area. Greenberg and Roloff argued that this creates a comparison that favors television as more credible overall, particularly in communities with smaller newspapers. Since their critique, a number of studies have confirmed their suspicions, by specifying both the type of news (e.g., local, national, international) and the type of issue (e.g., sports, entertainment) to be compared across media channels (Abel & Wirth, 1977; Gantz, 1981; Gaziano & McGrath, 1986; Lee, 1978; Newhagen & Nass, 1989; Reagan & Zenalty, 1979). Nonetheless, despite refinements in the measure, and after providing a consistent frame of reference, television was still rated as more believable than newspapers, although the margin of difference was smaller compared to the Roper findings.[5]

Because of problems with the Roper measures, researchers sought alternative ways to assess media credibility. This research is characterized by increasing precision in measurement over time, with two evident trends: a movement from unidimensional to multidimensional measures, and a movement from measures derived from source credibility to measures developed specifically to address media credibility.

By the late 1960s, scholars began to realize the complexity of the concept they were studying and moved away from unidimensional measures of media credibility (e.g., Jacobson, 1969; McCroskey & Jenson, 1975; Meyer, 1974). This resulted in a series of factor analytic studies of the dimensions of media credibility, parallel to those in the source credibility literature. McCroskey and Jenson relied on several existing (interpersonal) source credibility scales to generate items for their study of mass media sources. Not surprisingly, their study found that the dimensions of media credibility were very similar to those found for source credibility. Researchers employing items from other research, such as that on media image or accuracy, found different dimensions (e.g., Sargent, 1965).

The result was that the concept of media credibility became confusing, confounded, and open to criticism. Several scholars noted the inadequacy of using items derived from interpersonal settings to measure mass communication concepts, as well as the need to have separate measures of the credibility of the source originating a message and the credibility of the medium through which the message is transmitted (e.g., Edelstein, 1978). Others pointed out that scale items should be generated by media users according to their own notions of media credibility rather than relying on items used in past research on other types of credibility (e.g., Lee, 1978; Singletary, 1976).

Some clarity came in the 1980s, as researchers began to conduct more wideranging assessments of mass media credibility (American Society of Newspaper Editors, 1985; Times Mirror Company, 1986; Gannett Center for Media Studies, 1985). One particularly massive and comprehensive effort was funded by the American Society of Newspaper Editors. Out of this research, Gaziano and McGrath (1986) developed a 12-item credibility scale assessing how respectful of the public's interest and privacy a medium is, how concerned the news organization is about community well-being, the quality of the news organization's staff, and perceptions of the extent to which the medium is fair, biased, complete, trustworthy, factual, opinionated, and profiteering. Their scale was refined by Meyer (1988), who suggested including only the fair, biased, complete, accurate, and trust items. By the late 1980s, these two scales became the most widely used standard measures of media credibility. In a head-to-head comparison of the two scales, West (1994) established the Meyer scale to be more reliable and valid.

Finally, television and newspapers were not the only channels to be compared in the media credibility literature. Radio, newsmagazines, face-to-face, and other channels of communication were included in some studies, including the original Roper studies (see Cline & Engel, 1991). A few studies have explored media credibility for other types of information besides news (e.g., Flanagin & Metzger, 2000). Overwhelmingly, however, attention has been on newspapers and television, although the introduction of the Web is now causing researchers to shift their attention to this new medium. As this shift occurs, researchers must be careful in using prior findings on traditional media credibility—which are based exclusively on assessments of news information—to new media that carry a much broader array of information.

Credibility of the Web as a Medium

Past research on media credibility may help to understand the relative credibility of the Web as a conduit of information compared to more traditional channels. Indeed, cross-media comparisons have sought to assess the credibility of the Web relative to other communication channels. The majority of studies in this area focus on political (Johnson & Kaye, 1998, 2000; Mashek, 1997) or news information (Kim et al., 2001; Kiousis, 2001; Pew Research Center, 1999; Sundar, 1999; . Sundar & Nass, 2001), although a diversity of information types has also been examined (Flanagin & Metzger, 2000). The technological and structural features that have been identified as important in studies of traditional media credibility may also impact perceptions of the Web as a medium of communication. The technological features of the Internet that are likely to impact credibility ratings include the ease of publishing professionally-appearing content, the vast amount of information and information producers online, the convergence of genres, and the malleability of digital information.

Other features may be significant in influencing the credibility of the Web as well. Many Web sites use ample visual information, which may impart the same kind of "seeing is believing" effect enjoyed by television. Like television, the Web offers currency by giving audiences up-to-the-minute coverage of issues and events. However, at the same time, Web sites' heavy reliance on text and their ability to cover issues in-depth, without the time and space constraints of television, make the Web more similar to newspapers. These features imply that Web credibility ratings should be higher than either television or newspapers. However, Nadarajan and Ang (1999) point out that the chance for error in news is magnified on the Web due to unlimited capacity, high speed, and use of hyperlinking from source to source. In the Web environment there may be increased pressure to report breaking news and update stories constantly, leaving little time to verify the information either on news organizations' own Web sites or on other sites to which they are linked.

Structural features too may influence credibility judgments. The Web is more allied with newspapers than television in terms of regulation, which may detract from people's perceptions of its objectivity or trustworthiness, at least in the United States. Nadarajan and Ang (1999) argue that the free and unregulated flow of information over the Web might detract from credibility ratings "because not every piece of inaccurate information can be uncovered or even corrected" (p. 22; cf. Eastin, 2001). The economics of the Web are similar to both newspapers and television in its reliance on advertising, yet different in that many Web sites profit from using personal information collected from site visitors. These data-collection practices may negatively impact the credibility of the medium. Together, these perspectives suggest that the Web may be perceived as more, less, or equally credible to traditional media. Existing research supports all of these views.

Some studies indicate that Web information is perceived to be more credible than information obtained via other channels. In the delivery of political information, online newspapers and candidate literature have been judged to be more credible than their traditional counterparts (Johnson & Kaye, 1998). However, this finding was demonstrated among a sample of politically interested Web users only. Johnson and Kaye (2000) note that a user's general reliance on the Web predicts perceived credibility of a number of online sources of political information. However, reliance on traditional media was an even stronger predictor of credibility of online media (cf. Johnson & Kaye, 2002). It should be noted that people tend not to judge either online or traditionally delivered sources of information as particularly credible overall (Flanagin & Metzger, 2000; Johnson & Kaye, 1998; Kiousis, 2001).

Other research finds that Web-based news sources were not rated as different from traditional sources in terms of credibility (Online News Association, 2001; Pew Research Center, 1999). However, Mashek (1997) found that traditional media sources were rated by users as more fair and unbiased than their online equivalents for obtaining political information. In Germany, although the Web was viewed as a credible source of information, it was judged less credible than newspapers and television (Schweiger, 2000). Two other studies found that newspapers were rated as significantly more credible than other media, including the Internet, magazines, radio, and television (Flanagin & Metzger, 2000; Kiousis, 2001). The Flanagin and Metzger finding held across a diversity of information types, including news, reference, entertainment, and commercial information.

Overall, research indicates that although the Web may be considered an equally credible source of information as compared to most traditional venues, it is not perceived as more credible than traditional information sources, except among those who may be particularly motivated to seek out specific types of information and who may rely on the Web to a large extent. This result may be due to the fact that people use the same criteria to judge the credibility of news stories across both print and online formats. Sundar (1999) demonstrated that individuals assess both print and online news stories in terms of their representativeness, quality, liking, and credibility, suggesting that people process news information consistently regardless of the medium through which it is presented. However, it should be noted that accuracy and believability—traditionally core dimensions of credibility—are notably absent from Sundar's credibility factor, suggesting that perhaps objectivity (rather than credibility) is a common feature of news information processing across traditional and online venues.

To this point, we have considered the substantial body of literature on credibility in communication research, focusing on the three main currents in this tradition: source, message, and media credibility. We have applied relevant conceptualizations of credibility from each area to the contemporary media environment, with a particular emphasis on Web-based information. Despite the value of this application, there remain several open issues in Web credibility research. We turn to such issues next by considering the measurement of Web credibility, potential conflation among source, message, and media credibility in the new media environment, audience factors that impact these views, and finally, we propose several directions that future research must consider in order to maximize knowledge from past research and take full advantage of the considerable lessons available from existing scholarship.

FURTHER CONSIDERATIONS IN WEB CREDIBILITY

The studies reviewed thus far share an assumption that credibility resides in the source, message, or medium of transmission. However, several scholars have suggested that these concepts of credibility overlap (e.g., Chaffee, 1982; Kiousis, 2001). Chaffee argues that many receivers do not distinguish between the source of a message and the channel through which they receive it. Nowhere is this more evident than in the new media environment, specifically the Web, which offers a mind-boggling array of information from a melange of providers. Nevertheless, most contemporary studies of credibility rely on these traditional distinctions and thus conflate source, message, and channel in measuring the credibility of Web-based information. To assess the nature and severity of this issue, this section first reviews measures of Web credibility used in prior research and then argues that assessing credibility across Web sites, messages, and media can be difficult, due to overlap among these concepts, the complexity of the Web environment, and research designs that do not always enable clear distinctions among these factors.

Measurement of Web Credibility

Web site credibility. The credibility of individual Web sites has been assessed by having web page visitors rate aspects thought to contribute to the site's overall credibility or by assessing common Web site content across different site conditions, such that differences in the assessment of the content could be traced to the Web site on which it resides. Interestingly, items used to assess Web site credibility draw mainly from the interpersonal source credibility literature, but also include items from the traditional media credibility literature. Common terms include the extent to which sites or information on them are believable, trustworthy, (un)biased, competent, credible, and expert. Other dimensions include assessment of the accuracy, relevance, and the comprehensiveness or completeness of the Web site or its content. Typical single item scales measure the believability of Web sites (e.g., Pew Research Center, 1999; Shon et al., 2000) or site credibility by agreement with the item, "I know the sponsor is reliable" (Eighmey & McCord, 1998).

In order to bring some clarity to the measurement of Web site credibility, Flanagin and Metzger (2002a) had respondents rate a variety of Web sites on a series of semantic differential items derived from previous studies of Web site credibility and from interpersonal source credibility scales (R. B. Rubin, 1994) adapted for the Web environment. Analyses showed that users' Web site credibility ratings included perceptions of site trustworthiness and expertise, as well as attractiveness and dynamism. The correspondence between the dimensions found in this study and those from traditional source and media credibility speaks to the relevance of previous credibility research to the Web environment.

Web site message credibility. The few studies that have endeavored to assess the credibility of messages delivered on Web pages do so in a roughly parallel manner to earlier message credibility research, although the greatest emphasis is placed on information content, as opposed to structure or delivery. Credibility scales in this domain typically ask readers of online stories to assess the degree to which the information is accurate, biased, believable, fair, objective, and sensationalistic (Sundar, 1998, 1999; Sundar & Nass, 2001). Perceptions of the credibility of commercial information online have been assessed by individuals' ratings of information fairness, bias, completeness, accuracy, and trustworthiness (Ha, 2001). Similarly, the credibility of health-related information has been measured by asking respondents to rate its accuracy, believability, and factualness (Eastin, 2001).

In developing their measures, these approaches have relied upon media credibility literature. A better strategy is that taken by Rieh and Belkin (1998) who used the information quality literature to assess users' reactions to Web-based information and found that the credibility of online messages is indicated by perceived authority, which is increased by connection to other authorities, such as authentication by some well-regarded third party.

Internet/Web credibility. Across the research on traditional media, the most consistent dimension of media credibility is believability, but accuracy, trustworthiness, bias, and completeness of information are other dimensions commonly used by researchers (e.g., American Society of Newspaper Editors, 1985; Austin & Dong, 1994; Carter & Greenberg, 1965; Gaziano, 1988; Greenberg, 1966; Gunther, 1988; Jacobson, 1969; Meyer, 1988; Mulder, 1980; Rimmer & Weaver, 1987; Robinson & Kohut, 1988; Shaw, 1973; Wanta & Hu, 1994; West, 1994; Westley & Severin, 1964; Zanna & Del Vecchio, 1973). Comparisons of the Internet and Web to more traditional media have largely invoked these same dimensions.

For example, studies have assessed the relative credibility of multiple media, including the Internet, by asking the degree to which individuals found information on each medium to be believable, accurate, trustworthy, biased, and complete (Flanagin & Metzger, 2000). Johnson and Kaye (1998, 2000) used a similar measure of credibility for both online and traditional sources of political information (see also Sundar, 1999). Working from the source credibility literature, Tseng and Fogg (1999) define computer credibility as believability, which is made up of trustworthiness and expertise. Schweiger (2000) used the following semantic differential items to measure Web credibility in comparison to other media: contradictory-clear, nonserious-serious, unthoroughly researched-thoroughly researched, cursory-detailed, noncritical-critical, incredible-credible, partial-neutral, unbalanced-balanced, incompetent-competent, amateurish-professional, cautious-fresh. Several of these items clearly come from research on source and message credibility.

Other studies have asked respondents to rate the credibility of Internet journalists in comparison to journalists working in traditional media as well as to assess the relative credibility of online versus print information by asking which medium people trust in cases when there is conflicting coverage (Schweiger, 2000). Absolute credibility has been measured by rating media channels on an objectivity scale and by asking which among several media "report truly, and show facts the way they really are" (Schweiger, 2000, p. 43).

Conflation of Web Sites as Source, Message, and Medium

Precise measures of Web credibility are important, as research in other contexts clearly shows that that the way in which the concept is operationalized can make a difference in credibility ratings (Gaziano & McGrath, 1986; Newhagen & Nass, 1989; Rimmer & Weaver, 1987; Shaw, 1973; West, 1994). Yet, most research on new media relies rather indiscriminately on past measures of source, message, and medium credibility to measure various aspects of Web credibility. Part of the problem is that the very concept of source is problematic in the new media environment because the source of an online message may be attributed to the author of the material on a particular Web site, the operator or sponsor of the site, the medium itself, or perhaps even the site programmer (Eastin, 2001; Kiousis, 2001; Sundar, 1998; Sundar & Nass, 2000, 2001). Further, different source attributions are shown to result in different evaluations of content (Newhagen & Nass, 1989; Sundar & Nass, 2000, 2001).[6]

Source attribution research is just beginning to sort out this issue. Sundar and Nass (2001), for example, propose a typology for online news sources. They argue that there are at least three distinct sources of online news information. Visible sources are the people or entities who present the information, technological sources consist of the channel or medium through which the information is delivered, and because receivers of online news may themselves select the information they read, or because other receivers may select information for each other, receivers may be considered sources too.

Schweiger (2000) has proposed six levels of reference objects, which serve to distinguish the several potential sources or targets of credibility attributions. These levels comprise a rough hierarchy of sources, which are not necessarily mutually exclusive, and apply to many types of information, not just news. *Presenters* are the author or presenter of Web information. *Actors* of messages represent the person whose actions or statements are reported. *Editorial units* consist of such things as a specific program or Web article. *Media products* are the specific networks, newspapers, or Web sites upon which credibility attributions can be made. *Subsystems* of a media type refer to the genre of the media product (e.g., quality versus tabloid newspapers). Finally, *media types* refer to the medium or channel of communication.

Credibility attributions may occur at each of these levels independently or across multiple levels simultaneously. For example, it makes sense to consider the editorial unit of a Web article, the media product (the Web site), and the subsystem (the type of Web site) at the same time. In addition, *credibility transfer* may occur when "recipients use the credibility of a medium or media product as a (heuristic) indicator for the credibility of a single news story or programme" (Schweiger, 2000, p. 41). This type of transfer is possible both vertically (between levels) and horizontally (across different media types). As a result, Schweiger points out that research on media credibility merits criticism because cross-media comparisons may hide important within-media differences, and potentially lead to unusable results. He says, "future studies on credibility should not only examine the credibility of the Web as a whole, but also its single subsystems" (p. 56). This is but one example of the importance and difficulty of taking multiple levels into account.

For this reason, source attribution research recognizes that the source is a psychological construct (i.e., the source of Internet-based information is what or who the receiver believes it to be), and that source attributions matter in evaluating online information (Sundar & Nass, 2000, 2001). Sundar and Nass (2001) demonstrated experimentally that different levels of source attribution (visible, technological, and receiver) affect receivers' reactions to online news stories, as well as their perceptions of story quality and representativeness, although not perceptions of credibility. Thus, it is necessary to differentiate between various sources or source levels because information receivers find them to be psychologically distinct. This research also suggests that sourcing may occur at many levels simultaneously, an idea labeled source layering (Sundar & Nass, 2001), whereby combinations of source attributes may interact to influence credibility perceptions of online information. As a result, credibility assessments may vary depending upon which source attributes are salient in the receiver's mind at the time of evaluation.

Confusion among message, source, and medium credibility also occurs when research crosses definitions of concepts or measurements of variables without due regard for the phenomenon of interest. When cross-media comparisons either fail to cue respondents to the medium level, or measure message factors rather than medium factors, credibility assessments may be invalid (Newhagen & Nass, 1989). Due to conflation of source, message, and medium credibility as well as the multiple levels of reference objects for credibility attributions, the assessment of credibility in the contemporary media environment can be extremely complex. Researchers must be clear in pinpointing the psychological locus of credibility that receivers use to evaluate online information.

Audience Factors in Web Credibility

Critics of credibility research on interpersonal communication and traditional media have argued for years that credibility is highly situational and depends on the receiver's relationship to the medium, the source of the message, and the message itself (Chaffee, 1982; Cronkhite & Liska, 1976; Edelstein, 1978; Gunther, 1992). This appears to be true for new media as well, as certain audience factors such as demographics, Internet use and reliance, and issue involvement have been found to influence perceptions of the credibility of Web-based information.

Demographics. Early studies of media credibility examined demographic characteristics of audiences to see if these factors impacted receivers' relative rankings of the believability of newspapers and television. Several studies examined the demographic correlates of age, education, and sex on media credibility rankings (Abel & Wirth, 1977; Greenberg, 1966; Gunther, 1992; Mulder 1980, 1981; Reagan & Zenaty, 1979; Westley & Severin, 1964). These studies generally found that women, as well as younger and less educated people, were more likely to find television to be more credible than newspapers.

Studies of the credibility of Web-based information similarly find some differences in credibility perceptions among different types of users. There is some evidence that females assess news and political Web sites as more credible than males do (GomdaWeb, 1998; Johnson & Kaye, 1998), although more recent studies have found conflicting results (Johnson & Kaye, 2000, 2002). Flanagin and Metzger (2002b) found that male participants rated personal Web sites as more credible overall and that women found a female site to be less credible than a parallel male site. For the most part, younger Internet users rate online news to be more credible and trustworthy than older users (GomdaWeb, 1998; Johnson & Kaye, 2002; Online News Association, 2001). Age may be a proxy for media skepticism, a variable that has been empirically linked to media credibility in past research (Gunther, 1992), with older users being more skeptical of the Internet as a whole than younger users. The GomdaWeb survey found education and income to be negatively related to credibility of online news, but Johnson and Kaye (1998, 2000, 2002) found no significant relationship.

Internet use and reliance. Scholars have recently investigated reliance on the Internet/Web as a potential influence on credibility perceptions. Several studies have found a positive association between Web use and credibility ratings of online news and political information (Johnson & Kaye, 2000; Kiousis, 2001; Pew Research Center, 1999; cf. Johnson & Kaye, 2002).[7] Moreover, amount of Internet experience has been shown to be positively related to assessments of the credibility of Web-based information (Flanagin & Metzger, 2000; Ha, 2001). These results imply that credibility is a function of a person's preference for and familiarity with a medium.

Involvement. In addition to whether people rely on a medium for information, the degree to which they know and care about specific topics also influences their credibility judgments. This connection was initially made in studies of source and media credibility (Abel & Wirth, 1977; Gass & Seiter, 1999; Gunther, 1988, 1992; O'Keefe, 1990; Reagan & Zenalty, 1979). Similar results are now emerging in the new media environment (Eastin, 2001; Flanagin & Metzger, 2002a). The explanation for the link between audience members' involvement with a message (defined as personal relevance and knowledge of a topic) and their credibility perceptions has centered on the elaboration likelihood model (ELM), which says that people have greater trust for consonant messages and greater suspicion of dissonant messages when issue involvement is high.

Along these lines, Eastin (2001) examined how knowledge of AIDS impacted the perceived credibility of messages on a health-related Web site. Results showed that knowledge of the issue positively influenced message credibility ratings, regardless of the expertise of the putative site author. In another study of online information, greater issue salience was associated with greater credibility ratings of Web-based information (Flanagin & Metzger, 2002a).

In summary, conceptualizing Web credibility in terms of source, message, and media credibility research can be helpful in thinking about the various factors that may combine to impact credibility perceptions in the new media environment, although these categories are not simple to apply to this context. Measurement of the credibility of Web sites, Web-based messages, and the Web itself can be problematic. Future research can benefit from considering more carefully the nominal definitions that form the core phenomena of interest, selecting the appropriate operationalization of those concepts, and selecting measures accordingly. In addition, analyses of Web users or study participants, including their demographic characteristics, usage patterns, and attitudes toward specific messages on the Web, are important for a full understanding of credibility perceptions in the new media environment.

AN AGENDA FOR THE FUTURE OF WEB CREDIBILITY RESEARCH

Reviewing past research on credibility in traditional interpersonal and mediated contexts brings into focus several avenues for future research on perceptions of the credibility of online information. Highlighted is the need to study more variables that may be particularly influential on credibility assessments of online information, as well as more channels and types of information available over the Internet. Researchers are challenged to increase their precision in defining and measuring credibility as a dependent variable. Previous research also suggests how perceptions of credibility may change over time. Thus, this review provides researchers an agenda to pursue in theorizing about credibility in the new media environment.

Unexplored Variables in Web Credibility Research

It is clear from the review that researchers have already migrated the expertise and trustworthiness dimensions discovered in earlier credibility research to their explorations of Web credibility. Yet, other dimensions of credibility have not received adequate attention, even though findings from offline contexts suggest several variables that Internet researchers might study. For example, the dynamism of a Web site, as reflected in site design elements or degree of interactivity, may influence credibility assessments but has rarely been explored in scholarly research. Yet, it is both theoretically and empirically warranted in studies of Web credibility to date (Burgoon et al., 2000; Eastin, 2001; Flanagin & Metzger, 2002a; Schweiger, 2000). Site attractiveness and, therefore, liking may also be conveyed in the graphical interface of online information (e.g., layout, graphics, organization, navigability of a site, or other features such as downloading speed or the functionality of hyperlinks). As mentioned earlier, it seems reasonable too that the perceived trustworthiness of a Web site may hinge in part on the presence of privacy seals, trusted third party endorsements and recommendations, or specific privacy practices and policies (e.g., the use or nonuse of "cookies"). Research on these issues and how they impact perceptions of the credibility of Web-based information is only just beginning.

Expanded Considerations of Internet Technologies and Information Types

Researchers must begin to examine a broader array of Internet-based communication technologies and a greater diversity of Web sites. The versatility of the Internet suggests that rather than being viewed unidimensionally, it may properly be conceived in terms of its many communication and information functions, such as information retrieval, information giving, and its capacity to support conversational uses (Flanagin & Metzger, 2001). Most researchers have looked at the credibility of the Web only, rather than other forms of Internet-based communication, such as chat rooms, email, Usenet, or listservs, to name a few examples. The credibility of each of these channels must be evaluated independently because it is likely that they vary greatly in terms of receivers' assessments (see Newhagen & Nass, 1989). For example, perceptions of the credibility of email probably depend on personal knowledge of the communicator, whereas the credibility of chat rooms is more likely based on the content of the communication or the subject matter for the venue.

Several studies of the relative credibility of the Internet and Web compared to more traditional media are further limited by the fact that they only consider news and political Web sites. However, both the type of site (e.g., news, commercial, personal) and type of information within a Web site (i.e., news, advertising, entertainment) have been shown to impact credibility ratings (Flanagin & Metzger, 2000, 2002a). This suggests the importance of expanding omnibus considerations of sites and information in order to understand credibility in the new media environment, particularly in studies of the relative credibility of new media compared to more traditional channels.

It is also important to consider site and information type because credibility perceptions vary depending upon users' motivation and orientation toward specific media and media content. Greenberg and Roloff (1974) argued that whereas most people approach newspapers for their informational content, television is used primarily to gratify entertainment needs, and media consumers in an entertainment processing mode are likely to be less critical than those in an information-processing mode (cf. Reagan & Zenalty, 1979). Mulder (1980) found that people with a more active orientation toward news rated newspapers to be significantly more credible than passive news consumers. Thus, an avenue for research is to examine motives for using different types of online information to see if and how audience orientations impact credibility assessments.

Toward Greater Precision in Web Credibility Research

Prior research also highlights the importance of developing different measures of credibility for specific Internet-based technologies and specific sources of information within those technologies. One way to do this is for researchers to specify the type of source they are investigating, as discussed earlier (cf. Sundar & Nass, 2001). Schweiger's (2000) proposal that there are six levels of reference objects for Web credibility assessments goes a step further in explicating the notion of source in the new media environment and helping researchers to establish the locus of online users' credibility attributions.

Tseng and Fogg (1999) propose measuring several different types of credibility of Web-based information. Presumed credibility is based on general assumptions and stereotypes of the source or presenter of the information; reputed credibility is founded on reports about the source from third parties such as awards and titles; surface credibility is derived from simple inspection, such as a Web site that appears credible by virtue of its visual design; and experienced credibility is based on firsthand experience such as that gained from interacting with entities over time. These types of credibility imply a temporal dimension to credibility studies that is as yet unexplored.

Tracking Changes in Credibility Perceptions

Credibility perceptions of the Internet as a medium may change over time. As more people come to rely on the Web for news, it may increase in its relative credibility ratings. Evidence that credibility ratings are impacted by Web use is beginning to accumulate, for example, the credibility of online political information increased from the 1996 to 2000 election seasons (e.g., Johnson & Kaye, 2000, 2002). Researchers could examine changes in relative credibility perceptions as the composition of the Web audience changes over time. Although once dominated by middle-class White males, the demographics of Internet users have recently changed to include people of all backgrounds as well as nearly equal numbers of both sexes (e.g., Pew Research Center, 1999; U.S. Department of Commerce, 2000). Based on past research, demographics and experience with the Web could contribute to changes over time in users' judgments of the credibility of online information or of the Web relative to other media.

Changes in Web content could also result in changes in the relative credibility of the medium. As the economic potential of the Web forces it to lose its roots as an unregulated bastion for individual expression in favor of its use as a tool for corporate communication, ratings of the credibility of the medium may shift. Flanagin and Metzger (2000) found commercial information to be the lowest in credibility of several types of information. If Internet users begin to associate the Web with primarily commercial information, then overall ratings of credibility may decline. Future research might also consider the notion of credibility transfer, the process whereby the reputation of an established media outlet crosses over to the Web environment (Schweiger, 2000), which may, for example, occur when the Web sites of well-regarded print newspapers are also considered credible (Saul, 1999; Schweiger, 2000) or when the branding of well-known media and commercial organizations translates across channels (Flanagin & Metzger, 2002a). Early evidence suggests that the credibility of online news outlets is a function of users' reliance on the traditional form of that medium (Johnson & Kaye, 2002).

Synthesizing past work on source, message, and media credibility in traditional contexts places research on credibility in the new media environment in proper perspective and suggests several important new variables and issues for this research to explore. Prior credibility research also alerts researchers to the fact that variations in the variables studied, media examined, motivations for using each medium, measures used, and audience members studied can make a difference in credibility results. Specifically, research is needed to explore other Internet-based communication technologies besides Web sites because prior studies have found that people use different technologies for different ends and apply different criteria to evaluate the credibility of different media. Reviewing the credibility literature also makes clear that further development of credibility scales and items is needed to reduce confusion surrounding the measurement of Web sites, particular messages on those sites, and the medium that carries both. Finally, past research highlights that credibility perceptions of the Internet and Web relative to other media may change over time, as users become more experienced with, or more reliant on, the new media and as these media continue to evolve.

Theoretical Development

Historically, source and message credibility were examined primarily as independent variables in theories of persuasion. In media research, credibility was used to explain the public's use of various news media outlets. Thus, applied concerns have been stressed over more theoretical development on credibility, although there has been some work in this respect as well (e.g., Gunther, 1992). With regard to Internet and Web credibility, only recently have researchers begun to propose theoretical mechanisms to explain the evidence that necessarily must precede theory development (Flanagin & Metzger, 2002a; Johnson & Kaye, 2002). Given the novelty of credibility research in the new media environment, this development is still in its very early stages. Nonetheless, some directions toward theory construction are developing, as evidence and explanations mutually evolve. Many of these directions stem from the rich heritage of credibility research that has come before, while also drawing on current research in the contemporary media environment.

Any theory of online credibility must consider the appropriate level of emphasis (source, message, or medium) in order to arrive at a clear definition of the core concept. Research is inching toward consistent definitions of Internet and Web credibility, although conflation across levels makes this extremely challenging. Credibility in the online environment appears to be consistent in key ways with credibility in other contexts. Specifically, source credibility on the Web can be conceptualized by the main dimensions of expertise, trustworthiness, and dynamism. For messages on the Web, expertise and trustworthiness appear to constitute the main dimensions of credibility. Internet (medium) credibility seems largely to encompass believability of the medium itself, as evidenced through its technical features and capabilities.

To facilitate theory development, the locus of credibility assessment must be identified as well: Is credibility a relational, situational, or dispositional response on the part of audience members (Chaffee, 1982; Gunther, 1992), or is it an attribute of the medium? Most likely, Web credibility consists of assessments made at several levels. Audience factors are extremely important, as discussed earlier in the chapter. In addition, credibility can be intentionally communicated by online information providers both through their offline reputation and in the messages that those sources create (e.g., through the use of accurate and current information). Further, characteristics of the medium can trickle down to affect perceptions of Web sites and of online messages when the Internet's relative novelty or lack of gatekeepers influences people's trust of the medium as a whole and information or sources within the medium.

The few studies that have examined predictors of credibility may be a starting point for theory construction. Gunther (1992) considered various explanations for the perceived credibility of newspaper and television news coverage of social groups, including media attributes (e.g., ownership structure), audience involvement with social issues, and audience demographics and disposition (e.g., skepticism). He found that audience involvement with particular groups explained the most variance in perceptions of credibility (defined as the fairness of news coverage of specific social groups) and that age and skepticism were significant but much less important predictors. This research suggests that in the Web environment, involvement or salience of information content are important components of ratings of Web site and message credibility.

Johnson and Kaye (2002) examined consumers' credibility judgments of online news sources. Based on prior research, they expected to find reliance on the Web for political information to predict Web credibility ratings. Interestingly, reliance on traditional news media and perceived convenience of the Web as a source of political information predicted judgments regarding the credibility of online versions of traditional media outlets, but Web reliance did not, contradicting results of a 1996 study that found Web reliance to be an important predictor of Web credibility (Johnson & Kaye, 2000). This is perhaps due to shifts in the character-istics of users as diffusion of the Web spreads. These studies suggest that reliance on and convenience of using traditional and new media may emerge as important predictors of credibility assessments but need further study as the Internet and its users change over time.

Whereas Gunther (1992) and Johnson and Kaye (2002) sought to discover theo-retical mechanisms driving news credibility perceptions, Flanagin and Metzger (2002a) considered the role of Internet experience, information salience, and de-mographics in perceived credibility across a variety of online sources, including news, commercial, personal, and public interest advocacy Web sites. They found differences across sources and evidence that site credibility depends to a degree on design features. In addition, salience was positively related to site, message, and sponsor credibility. Coupled with Gunther's (1992) findings for audience involve-ment described earlier, this suggests that audience factors such as personal rel-evance, source identification, and site design features may all play key roles in future theories of Internet and Web credibility.

Although recent research provides some helpful starting points, there remains much to be done toward building a theoretical model of Internet and Web credibility. Along the way, the applied concerns that have served as the traditional focus of credibility research will continue to warrant researchers' attention. Among par-ticularly timely concerns, given the current development of the Internet and Web, is the issue of empowering users of this global communication and information tool.

COMMUNICATION, EMPOWERMENT, AND THE CONTEMPORARY MEDIA ENVIRONMENT

The idea that information is a resource, leading to knowledge that results in increased power has a long history in communication research (e.g., Tichenor, Donohue, & Olien, 1970). However, the role that contemporary communication technologies play in this aphorism and their function in the empowerment process remains relatively unexplored. There is no doubt that the Internet and Web have the potential to inform users. But Gilster (1997) cautions that although contempo-rary media technologies offer access to an unprecedented amount of information, that information is only as valuable as it is credible. For users of these technolo-gies, this suggests that learning to discern credible from unreliable information is a requisite skill for harnessing the power of new media.[8]

Several challenges exist, however, for Internet users attempting to determine the quality of online information. The relatively low cost of disseminating digital information has resulted in a plethora of information providers on the Internet, many of whom operate without much oversight. Moreover, the Internet may create a psychological leveling effect whereby the technology places all information on the same level of accessibility, which in turn puts all authors on the same level of credibility (Burbules, 1998). For this reason, Eastin (2001) and others have argued that the Internet makes information evaluation more important than ever before, and that "perceptions of information found online should be framed within the digital literacy literature" (p. 10).

As more people have ventured into cyberspace, the meaning of digital or Internet literacy has evolved from the acquisition of basic connection and search skills to the ability to critically analyze and evaluate online information (Hobbs, 1998; Snyder, 1998). This new conception of Internet literacy involves higher-level processing of information and implies being selective about information, making informed judgments about content, and evaluating the impact of that information (Gurak, 2001; Hobbs, 1998; Kubey, 1997; Snyder, 1998). Several guidelines have been developed to help Internet users judge the quality of online information (Alexander & Tate, 1999; Jadad & Gagliardi, 1998; Silberg, Lundberg, & Musacchio, 1997; Smith, 1997). Additionally, consumer groups are being formed to evaluate Web sites' credibility on this basis. Despite these strides, questions remain about the extent to which these efforts have been successful and to what degree users exercise this critical aspect of Internet literacy. Moreover, there remain questions about what else can be done to instill media literacy competencies in users and online information providers.

Empowering Online Information Consumers

Methods for judging the quality of information obtained through newspapers, magazines, and television are well established, relatively clear, and socially derived and spread. Validation of information in these contexts is often achieved by referring to sources with credible reputations, seeking the advice of trusted others, and by relying on personal experiences to determine the characteristics of trustworthy sources. However, with information obtained from the Internet and Web, these strategies are not always effective or available, although they may be more necessary (e.g., Gilster, 1997). Recommendations for evaluating online information have appeared from such agencies as the American Library Association (Kapoun, 1998), the National Institute for Literacy (Rosen, 1998), and many colleges and universities around the world (Smith, 1997).

These recommendations generally suggest that Internet users should take steps to verify the accuracy, authority, objectivity, currency, and coverage of online information (Alexander & Tate, 1999; Brandt, 1996; Gilster, 1997; Harris, 1996; Jones, 1998; Kapoun, 1998; Smith, 1997). Steps include such efforts as verifying online information offline, noting who authored the site, whether contact information is provided, whether the Web site is recommended by a trusted source, and whether the information is up-to-date. These recommendations require a range of activities on the part of users, from simple visual inspection of a Web site to more laborious information verification and triangulation efforts.

In the first study of online verification behavior, Flanagin and Metzger (2000) found that respondents verified the information they obtained via the Internet only rarely to occasionally. People scored highest on the actions that were easiest to perform and that required their opinion. Lowest scores were recorded on the recommendations that were difficult to perform and that required action. This suggests that few users are rigorously verifying the quality of the information they obtain via the Internet. Interestingly, this study also found a negative relation between user experience with the Internet and reported verification behaviors, indicating that users who might benefit the most from verifying online information (because they may lack experience that helps to discern valid from bogus material) are doing so the least. As new users discover the Internet as a source of information, they may not invoke the tools that will help them become appropriately cyberliterate.

These findings reinforce the call for Internet literacy as a means by which to empower media consumers. Toward that end, specific recommendations should include refocusing efforts on teaching the verification strategies already outlined. Other simple verification techniques, such as noting if a Web site has a .org or .edu domain name (Lubans, 1999), are easily adopted as well. Periodic assessments of the frequency with which people verify online information will help in this effort by providing direction for literacy educators who hope to encourage people to assess the value of the information they find on the Internet and Web.

Empowering Online Information Providers

In addition to empowering Web site users, there is a need to empower those who create and sponsor online information so that they can better communicate with target audiences. The need for information producers to establish credibility among audiences is certainly not new. However, due to differences between traditional and new media, establishing credibility in the Internet environment might not be as simple as in the past.[9] Many companies are starting to recognize this fact: a survey of 150 company executives found that over 75% believed that digital literacy was important in order to keep up with businesses that are using the Web to target diverse audiences (Frazee, 1996). Furthermore, learning how to communicate credibly is a necessity for anyone trying to command attention in the increasingly competitive new media environment.

Attention has recently focused on identifying strategies to enhance the perceived credibility of Web-based information. The notion of empowering Web site sponsors and the importance of establishing trust has been addressed in commercial, educational, and health applications (Chadwick, 2001). Trust may be even more important for electronic commerce than for face-to-face business transactions because the impersonal nature of computer-mediated communication magnifies consumers' perceived risk of engaging in commercial transactions online (Kasper-Fuehrer & Ashkanasy, 2001). Browne, Freeman, and Williamson (2000) note the increasing use of the Internet by students for academic purposes and the resulting need for reliable online information. Christensen and Griffiths (2000) argue that the accessibility, attractiveness, and wide range of information available online have made the Internet a growing source of medical information, although the quality of online health information is often dubious.

Cutting across these domains, researchers have recently offered several recommendations for Web site sponsors interested in enhancing the credibility of the information they provide (e.g., Fogg et al., 2001b). Chadwick (2001) suggests that site sponsors focus on two aspects: Web site design, including several technical aspects, and trust building behaviors, which include the use of both technical and interpersonal mechanisms.

Technical design elements that may enhance Web site operators' credibility include: (a) logical organization of information that is functional for users and takes advantage of the hypertextual nature of the Web (Agency for Health Care Policy and Research [AHCPR], 1999; December & Randall, 1994; Fogg et al., 2001b), (b) inclusion of navigation tools such as internal search capabilities and interface consistency from page-to-page (AHCPR, 1999; Alexander & Tate, 1999), (c) use of cool color tones and a balanced layout (Chadwick, 2001; Fogg et al., 2001b), (d) inclusion of simple tools to verify the currency and accuracy of the information, such as a date stamp or links to authoritative external sites (Flanagin & Metzger, 2000); and (e) maintaining links and other site features so that they are both functional and current (Alexander & Tate, 1999; Fogg et al., 2001b).

Regarding trust-building behaviors, strategies for online information providers include: (a) clearly identifying information sponsors and sources, providing options for verifying identities through real-world contact information or affiliations, and offering suggestions for audience feedback (Alexander & Tate, 1999; AHCPR, 1999; Fogg et al., 2001b); (b) disclosing sponsor intent or bias (e.g., commercial interests; AHCPR, 1999); (c) displaying credentials and third party recommendations (Fogg et al., 2001b; Palmer et al., 2000); (d) demonstrating concern for audiences' interests through explicit privacy protection policies, opt-in provisions, participation in privacy seal programs, and use of encryption and other security measures (Alexander & Tate, 1999; AHCPR, 1999; Chadwick, 2001; Fogg et al., 2001b); and (e) partaking in professional editorial board or review processes (Griffiths & Christensen, 2000; Huang & Alessi, 1996).

Credibility is also established when online information providers demonstrate their expertise. According to Fogg et al. (2001b), expertise may be communicated by listing authors' credentials and including citations or references for information provided on Web sites. The use of strong evidence from highly credible sources will increase perceptions of site expertise more when those sources are cited, as well as when they are linked to by other credible sources (Neilsen, 1999; Sundar, 1998). Offering comprehensive, current, and accurate product selection or content is also likely to increase Internet users' perceptions of a site's expertise (Neilsen, 1999).

In sum, several avenues exist for Web site operators to enhance their credibility in the new media environment. Recommendations cover (a) appearance and graphical design issues, (b) disclosure and security measures, (c) functionality and connectedness, and (d) accuracy and comprehensiveness of content. These strategies, together with online user awareness of information quality on the Web, would enhance Internet literacy programs and would serve to empower online information consumers and sponsors alike.

Credibility and the Future of New Media

Several characteristics of Web-based information stimulate concerns about its credibility. Given the newness and complexity of these concerns, information assessment and verification have now become largely the responsibility of the media consumer. Lessons from a rich research legacy provide some guidance by suggesting that crucial elements of credibility include aspects of the source, the message, and the medium of transmission. By applying knowledge from each of these domains, scholars are moving toward a clearer understanding of the factors that influence individuals' perceptions of credibility in the online environment. By recognizing connections between existing credibility scholarship and the new media environment, researchers stand to make important contributions in this pursuit. This knowledge is likely to have considerable practical consequence. Indeed, the long-term viability of the Internet/Web as a consequential information resource may hinge on individual perceptions of the credibility of the sources and messages carried by this communication medium.

NOTES

1. Terminology to describe the Internet, Web, and related technologies has often been used inaccurately or inconsistently. Internet refers to the physical infrastructure of interconnected computers, cables, and other devices that serve as the infrastructure for global communication. Web refers to a system of computers, utilizing graphical user interfaces and accessed via the Internet, that provides access to documents, multimedia files, and Web sites, that are connected by hyperlinks to other documents, multimedia files, and Web sites. Research often groups the Internet and Web together, particularly when addressing media credibility, because many users and respondents tend not to make the distinction noted above. In addition, although the Internet does encompass the Web and other resources (such as chat rooms), the Web typically refers only to hypertext linked sites and their content. In this chapter we strive to use the terms appropriately, although at times we do refer to the Internet and Web together, when the overlap is informative and relevant.

2. O'Keefe (1990) and others also note that similarities must be relevant to the topic being advocated by a speaker in order to influence audience's competence ratings (e.g., Miller & Hoppe, 1973). However, dissimilarity can also influence competence or expertise ratings when the source is seen to be more knowledgeable on a topic than the receiver.

3. Another characteristic of organizational credibility is the nature of the organization: that is, whether the organization is for profit or nonprofit. It seems that nonprofit and government organizations are perceived as more credible sources than commercial, for profit, organizations (e.g., Hammond, 1987; Lynn, Wyatt, Gaines, Pearce, & Vanden Bergh, 1978).

4. Shaw (1973) found problems not with the wording of the Roper measures but with the order in which the questions were posed to respondents. He suggested that asking respondents what medium

they rely on for news before asking which medium they find most believable sets up demand characteristics that favor television over newspapers because most people rely on television rather than newspapers for news.

5. This is not to say that Greenberg and Roloff's criticism is invalid. Newhagen and Nass (1989) found that people do indeed evaluate television and newspaper news according to different criteria.

6. For example, eBay might receive higher credibility ratings compared to other online auction sites, but is eBay a source, message, or medium? One could argue that the person who is putting an object up for auction is the source, that the content of his or her descriptions of the object constitutes the message, and that the Web is the medium. Others might say that eBay is also a source in this situation, although a different kind of source (cf. Sundar & Nass, 2001).

7. Unfortunately, these studies leave the question of causality unanswered. That is, does usage of a medium affect credibility assessments or do credibility assessments drive usage? For traditional media, there is some evidence for both. Shaw (1973) shows how reliance influences credibility assessments, whereas Wanta and Hu (1994) find evidence that the perceived credibility of a channel leads to reliance on and exposure to that medium. This suggests that credibility perceptions and media reliance may be mutually reinforcing.

8. Because our focus is on the credibility of the Internet and Web-based information, and thus on current users of these tools, we do not consider issues of empowerment that implicate nonusers. Consequently, we do not address the important issues of the digital divide or the knowledge gap, both of which consider discrepancies between those with access and those without access to new media.

9. Of course, Web sites of entities with established, positive reputations outside of the Internet environment enjoy substantial benefits in this regard. Web sites of well-regarded publications such as the *New York Times* might naturally be highly regarded as well, across both site and message credibility. Such distinctions are crucial to take into account in Web credibility research.

REFERENCES

Abel, J. D., & Wirth, M. O. (1977). Newspapers vs. TV credibility for local news. *Journalism Quarterly, 54*, 371–375.

Agency for Health Care Policy and Research. (1999). *Criteria for assessing the quality of health information on the Internet—policy paper*. Retrieved April 24, 2002 from www.ahcpr.gov/data/infoqual.htm

Alexander, J. E., & Tate, M. A. (1999). *Web wisdom: How to evaluate and create information quality on the Web*. Hillsdale, NJ: Erlbaum.

American Society of Newspaper Editors. (1985). *Newspaper credibility: Building reader trust*. Washington DC: Author.

Andreoli, V., & Worchel, S. (1978). Effects of media, communicator, and message position on attitude change. *Public Opinion Quarterly, 42*, 59–70.

Atkinson, D. R., Brady, S., & Casas, J. M. (1981). Sexual preference similarity, attitude similarity, and perceived counselor credibility and attractiveness. *Journal of Counseling Psychology, 28*, 504–509.

Aune, R. K., & Kikuchi, T. (1993). Effects of language intensity similarity on perceptions of credibility, relational attributions, and persuasion. *Journal of Language and Social Psychology, 12*, 224–237.

Austin, E. W., & Dong, Q. (1994). Source v. content effects on judgments of news believability. *Journalism Quarterly, 71*, 973–983.

Bacon, F. T. (1979). Credibility of repeated statements: Memory for trivia. *Journal of Experimental Psychology: Human Learning and Memory, 5*, 241–252.

Begg, I. M., Anas, A., & Farinacci, S. (1992). Dissociation of processes in belief: Source recollection, statement familiarity, and the illusion of truth. *Journal of Experimental Psychology: General, 121*, 446–458.

Benoit, W. L. (1987). Argumentation and credibility appeals in persuasion. *Southern Speech Communication Journal, 52*, 181–197.

Berlo, D. K., Lemert, J. B., & Mertz, R. J. (1969). Dimensions for evaluating the acceptability of message sources. *Public Opinion Quarterly, 33*, 563–576.

Bobinski, G. S., Jr., Cox, D., & Cox, A. (1996). Retail "sale" advertising, perceived retailer credibility, and price rationale. *Journal of Retailing, 72*, 291–306.

Boehm, L. E. (1994). The validity effect: A search for mediating variables. *Personality and Social Psychology Bulletin, 20*, 285–293.

Bradac, J. J., Bowers, J. W., & Courtright, J. A. (1980). Lexical variations in intensity, immediacy, and diversity: An axiomatic theory and causal model. In R. N. St. Clair & H. Giles (Eds.), *The social and psychological contexts of language* (pp. 193–223). Hillsdale, NJ: Erlbaum.

Brandt, D. S. (1996). Evaluating information on the Internet. *Computers in Libraries, 16*, 44–46.

Browne, M. N., Freeman, K. E., & Williamson, C. L. (2000). The importance of critical thinking for student use of the Internet. *College Student Journal, 34*, 391–398.

Bruner, G. C., & Kumar, A. (2000). Webpage background and viewer attitudes. *Journal of Advertising Research, 40*, 35–42.

Burbules, N. C. (1998). Rhetorics of the Web: Hyperreading and critical literacy. In I. Snyder (Ed.), *Page to screen: Taking literacy into the electronic era* (pp. 102–122). London: Routledge.

Burgoon, J. K., Bonito, J. A., Bengtsson, B., Cederberg, C., Lundeberg, M., & Allspach, L. (2000). Interactivity in human-computer interaction: A study of credibility, understanding, and influence. *Computers in Human Behavior, 16*, 553–574.

Burrell, N. A., & Koper, R. J. (1998). The efficacy of powerful/powerless language on attitudes and source credibility. In M. Allen & R. W. Preiss (Eds.), *Persuasion: Advances through meta-analysis* (pp. 203–215). Cresskill, NJ: Hampton Press.

Byrne, D. (1969). Attitudes and attraction. In L. Berkowitz (Ed.), *Advances in experimental social psychology* (Vol. 4, pp. 34–89). New York: Academic Press.

Carter, R. F., & Greenberg, B. S. (1965). Newspapers or television: Which do you believe? *Journalism Quarterly, 42*, 29–34.

Caruso, D. (1999, November 22). Digital commerce: After a year on the credibility trail, a columnist finds that the Internet industry is still dangerously self-indulgent. *The New York Times*, p. C5.

Chadwick, S. A. (2001). Communicating trust in e-commerce interactions. *Management Communication Quarterly, 14*, 653–658.

Chaffee, S. H. (1982). Mass media and interpersonal channels: Competitive, convergent, or complementary? In G. Gumpert & R. Cathcart (Eds.), *Inter/Media: Interpersonal communication in a media world* (pp. 57–77). New York: Oxford University Press.

Chaffee, S. H. (2001). Studying the new communication of politics. *Political Communication, 18*, 237–244.

Chandrasekaran, R. (1999, May 13). SEC targets more online investment scams. *Washington Post*, p. E1.

Chang, L. K. H., & Lemert, J. B. (1968). The invisible newsman and other factors in media competition. *Journalism Quarterly, 45*, 436–444.

Chen, Q., & Wells, W. D. (1999). Attitude toward the site. *Journal of Advertising Research, 39*(5), 27–37.

Christensen, H., & Griffiths, K. M. (2000). The Internet and mental health literacy. *Australian & New Zealand Journal of Psychiatry, 34*, 975–979.

Cialdini, R. B. (1984). *Influence: The new psychology of modern persuasion.* New York: Quill.

Cline, R. W., & Engel, J. L. (1991). College students' perceptions of sources of information about AIDS. *Journal of American College Health, 40*(2), 55–63.

Cortes, C. E. (1992). Media literacy: An educational basic for the information age. *Education and Urban Society, 24*, 489–497.

Cronkhite, G., & Liska, J. (1976). A critique of factor analytic approaches to the study of credibility. *Speech Monographs, 43*, 91–107.

Culnan, M. J., & Armstrong, P. K. (1999). Information privacy concerns, procedural fairness, and impersonal trust: An empirical investigation. *Organization Science, 10*(1), 104–115.

December, J., & Randall, N. (1994). *The World Wide Web: Unleashed.* Indianapolis, IN: Sams Publishing.

Delia, J. G. (1976). A constructivist analysis of the concept of credibility. *Quarterly Journal of Speech, 62*, 361–375.

Dellaert, B., & Kahn, B. E. (1999). How tolerable is delay? Consumers' evaluations of Internet Web sites after waiting. *Journal of Interactive Marketing, 13*, 41–54.

Eagly, A., & Chaiken, S. (1993). *The psychology of attitudes*. Orlando, FL: Harcourt Brace.

Eastin, M. S. (2001). Credibility assessments of online health information: The effects of source expertise and knowledge of content. *Journal of Computer-Mediated Communication, 6*(4). Retrieved January 12, 2002, from http://www.ascusc.org/jcmc/vol6/issue4/eastin.html.

Edelstein, A. S. (1978). An alternative approach to the study of source effects in mass communication. *Communications, 4*, 71–90.

Eighmey, J., & McCord, L. (1998). Adding value in the information age: Uses and gratifications of sites on the World Wide Web. *Journal of Business Research, 41*, 187–194.

Erskine, H. (1970). The polls: Opinion of the news media. *Public Opinion Quarterly, 34*, 630–643.

Flanagin, A. J., & Metzger, M. J. (2000). Perceptions of Internet information credibility. *Journalism & Mass Communication Quarterly, 77*, 515–540.

Flanagin, A. J., & Metzger, M. J. (2001). Internet use in the contemporary media environment. *Human Communication Research, 27*, 153–181.

Flanagin, A. J., & Metzger, M. J. (2002a). *The role of site features, user attributes, and information verification behaviors on the perceived credibility of Web-based information*. Manuscript submitted for publication.

Flanagin, A. J., & Metzger, M. J. (2002b). *The perceived credibility of personal Web page information as influenced by the sex of the source*. Manuscript submitted for publication.

Fleshler, H., Ilardo, J., & Demoretcky, J. (1974). The influence of field dependence, speaker credibility set, and message documentation on evaluations of speaker and message credibility. *The Southern Speech Communication Journal, 39*, 389–402.

Fogg, B. J., Marshall, J., Kameda, T., Solomon, J., Rangnekar, A., Boyd, J., et al. (2001a). *Web credibility research: A method for online experiments and early study results*. Unpublished manuscript.

Fogg, B. J., Marshall, J., Laraki, O., Osipovich, A., Varma, C., Fang, N., et al. (2001b). What makes Web sites credible? A report on a large quantitative study. CHI 2001, ACM Conference on Human Factors in Computing Systems, *CHI Letters, 3*(1), 61–68.

Frazee, V. (1996). Internet literacy is the key to career success. *Personnel Journal, 75*, 24.

Gannett Center for Media Studies. (1985). *The media and the people: Soundings from two communities*. New York: Author.

Gantz, W. (1981). The influence of researcher methods on television and newspaper news credibility evaluations. *Journal of Broadcasting, 25*, 155–169.

Gass, R. H., & Seiter, J. S. (1999). *Persuasion, social influence, and compliance gaining*. Boston, MA: Allyn & Bacon.

Gaziano, C. (1988). How credible is the credibility crisis? *Journalism Quarterly, 65*, 267–278.

Gaziano, C., & McGrath, K. (1986). Measuring the concept of credibility. *Journalism Quarterly, 63*, 451–462.

Gilster, P. (1997). *Digital literacy*. New York: John Wiley & Sons.

Goldsmith, R. E., Lafferty, B. A., & Newell, S. J. (2000). The impact of corporate credibility and celebrity credibility on consumer reaction to advertisements and brands. *Journal of Advertising, 29*, 43–54.

GomdaWeb. (1998). *Perceptions of reliability*. Retrieved July 24, 2001, from http://www.stanford.edu/class/comm217/reliability/perceptions

Greenberg, B. S. (1966). Media use and believability: Some multiple correlates. *Journalism Quarterly, 43*, 665–671.

Greenberg, B. S., & Roloff, M. E. (1974, November). Mass media credibility: Research results and critical issues. *News Research Bulletin of the American Newspaper Publishers Association, 6*, 1–48.

Griffiths, K. M., & Christensen, H. (2000). Quality of web based information on treatment of depression: Cross sectional survey. *British Medical Journal, 321*, 1511–1515.

Gunther, A. C. (1988). Attitude extremity and trust in media. *Journalism Quarterly, 65*, 279–287.

Gunther, A. C. (1992). Biased press or biased public? Attitudes toward media coverage of social groups. *Public Opinion Quarterly, 56*, 147–167.

Gurak, L. J. (2001). *Cyberliteracy: Navigating the Internet with awareness.* New Haven, CT: Yale University Press.

Ha, J. (2001, May). *Questioning Internet credibility: A test on the cyber marketplace.* Paper presented at the annual conference of the International Communication Association, Washington, DC.

Haley, E. (1996). Exploring the construct of organization as source: Consumers' understanding of organizational sponsorship of advocacy advertising. *Journal of Advertising, 25,* 19–35.

Hamilton, M. A. (1998). Message variables that mediate and moderate the effect of equivocal language on source credibility. *Journal of Language and Social Psychology, 17,* 109–143.

Hamilton, M. A., & Hunter, J. E. (1998a). A framework for understanding: Meta-analysis of the persuasion literature. In M. Allen & R. W. Preiss (Eds.), *Persuasion: Advances through meta-analysis* (pp. 1–28). Cresskill, NJ: Hampton Press.

Hamilton, M. A., & Hunter, J. E. (1998b). The effect of language intensity on receiver evaluations of message, source, and topic. In M. Allen & R. W. Preiss (Eds.), *Persuasion: Advances through meta-analysis* (pp. 99–138). Cresskill, NJ: Hampton Press.

Hammond, S. (1987). Health advertising: The credibility of organizational sources. In M. L. McLaughlin (Ed.), *Communication yearbook 10* (pp. 613–628). Newbury Park, CA: Sage.

Harris, C. (1996). *An Internet education: A guide to doing research on the Internet.* Belmont, CA: Wadsworth.

Hess, S. (1998). *Credibility: Does it drive the bottom line?* Retrieved July 24, 2001, from http://www.nas.org

Hobbs, R. (1998). Literacy in the information age. In J. Flood, D. Lapp, & S. B. Heath (Eds.), *Handbook of research on teaching literacy through the communicative and visual arts* (pp. 7–14). New York: Macmillan.

Hovland, C. I., Janis, I. L., & Kelley, J. J. (1953). *Communication and persuasion.* New Haven, CT: Yale University Press.

Hovland, C. I., & Weiss, W. (1951). The influence of source credibility on communication effectiveness. *Public Opinion Quarterly, 15,* 635–650.

Huang, M. P., & Alessi, N. E. (1996). The Internet and the future of psychiatry. *American Journal of Psychiatry, 153,* 861–869.

Jacobson, H. K. (1969). Mass media believability: A study of receiver judgments. *Journalism Quarterly, 46,* 20–28.

Jadad, A. R., & Gagliardi, A. (1998). Rating health information on the Internet: Navigating to knowledge or to Babel? *Journal of the American Medical Association, 279,* 611–614.

Johnson, T. J., & Kaye, B. K. (1998). Cruising is believing?: Comparing Internet and traditional sources on media credibility measures. *Journalism & Mass Communication Quarterly, 75,* 325–340.

Johnson, T. J., & Kaye, B. K. (2000). Using is believing: The influence of reliance on the credibility of online political information among politically interested Internet users. *Journalism & Mass Communication Quarterly, 77,* 865–879.

Johnson, T. J., & Kaye, B. K. (2002). Webelievability: A path model examining how convenience and reliance predict online credibility. *Journalism & Mass Communication Quarterly, 79,* 619–642.

Jones, D. (1998). *Exploring the Internet: Using critical thinking skills.* New York: Neal-Schuman.

Jurma, W. E. (1981). Evaluations of credibility of the source of a message. *Psychological Reports, 49,* 778.

Kapoun, J. (1998). *Teaching undergrads WEB evaluation: A guide for library instruction.* Retrieved June 25, 2001, from http://www.ala.org/acrl/undwebev.htm

Kasper-Fuehrer, E. C., & Ashkanasy, N. M. (2001). Communicating trustworthiness and building trust in interorganizational virtual organizations. *Journal of Management, 27,* 235–254.

Kim, S. T, Weaver, D., & Willnat, L. (2001). Media reporting and perceived credibility of online polls. *Journalism & Mass Communication Quarterly, 77,* 846–864.

Kiousis, S. (2001). Public trust or mistrust? Perceptions of media credibility in the Information Age. *Mass Communication & Society, 4,* 381–403.

Kubey, R. (Ed.). (1997). *Media literacy in the information age: Current perspectives.* New Brunswick, NJ: Transaction.

Lafferty, B. A., & Goldsmith, R. E. (1999). Corporate credibility role in consumers' attitudes and purchase intentions when a high versus low credibility endorser is used in the ad. *Journal of Business Research, 44,* 109–116.

Leathers, D. G. (1992). *Successful nonverbal communication: Principles and applications*. New York: Macmillian.

Lee, R. S. (1978). Credibility of newspaper and TV news. *Journalism Quarterly, 55*, 282–287.

Lowery, S. A., & DeFleur, M. L. (1995). *Milestones in mass communication research: Media effects* (3rd ed.). White Plains, NY: Longman.

Lubans, J. (1999). *Students and the Internet*. Retrieved July 23, 2001, from http://www.lib.duke.edu/staff/orgnztn/lubans/docs/study3.htm

Luchok, J. A., & McCroskey, J. C. (1978). The effect of quality of evidence on attitude change and source credibility. *Southern Speech Communication Journal, 43*, 371–383.

Lui, L., & Standing, L. (1989). Communicator credibility: Trustworthiness defeats expertness. *Social Behavior and Personality, 17*, 219–221.

Lynn, J., Wyatt, R., Gaines, J., Pearce, R., & Vanden Bergh, B. (1978). How source affects responses to public service announcements. *Journalism Quarterly, 55*, 716–720.

MacKenzie, S. B., & Lutz, R. J. (1989). An empirical examination of the structural antecedents of attitude toward the ad in an advertising pretesting context. *Journal of Marketing, 53*, 48–65.

Mashek, J. W. (1997). *Lethargy '96: How the media covered a listless campaign*. Arlington, VA: The Freedom Forum.

McCroskey, J. C. (1966). Scales for the measurement of ethos. *Speech Monographs, 33*, 65–72.

McCroskey, J. C. (1967, December). *Studies of the effects of evidence in persuasive communication* (SCRL 4–67). East Lansing, MI: Michigan State University, Speech Communication Research Library.

McCroskey, J. C. (1969). A summary of experimental research on the effects of evidence in persuasive communication. *Quarterly Journal of Speech, 55*, 169–176.

McCroskey, J. C., Holdridge, W., & Toomb, J. K. (1974). An instrument for measuring the source credibility of basic speech communication instructors. *Speech Teacher, 23*, 26–33.

McCroskey, J. C., & Jenson, T. A. (1975). Image of mass media news sources. *Journal of Broadcasting, 19*, 169–181.

McCroskey, J. C., & Mehrley, R. S. (1969). The effects of disorganization and nonfluency on attitude change and source credibility. *Speech Monographs, 36*, 13–21.

Meyer, P. (1988). Defining and measuring credibility of newspapers: Developing an index. *Journalism Quarterly, 65*, 567–574.

Meyer, T. J. (1974). Media credibility: The state of the research. *Public Telecommunications Review, 2*, 48–56.

Miller, D. T., & Hoppe, R. A. (1973). The effect of regional similarity-dissimilarity on communicator credibility. *Language and Speech, 16*, 211–217.

Miller, G. R., & Hewgill, M. A. (1964). The effect of variations in nonfluency on audience ratings of source credibility. *Quarterly Journal of Speech, 50*, 36–44.

Morris, M., & Ogan, C. (1996). The Internet as mass medium. *Journal of Communication, 46*(1), 39–49.

Mulder, R. (1980). Media credibility: A use-gratifications approach. *Journalism Quarterly, 57*, 474–477.

Mulder, R. (1981). A log-linear analysis of media credibility. *Journalism Quarterly, 58*, 635–638.

Nadarajan, B., & Ang, P. (1999, August). *Credibility and journalism on the Internet: How online newspapers handle errors and corrections*. Paper presented at the annual meeting of the Association for Education in Journalism and Mass Communication, New Orleans, LA.

National Consumers' League. (2000). *National Consumers League warns consumers millions are lost to Internet fraud*. Retrieved June 15, 2001, from http://www.fraud.org/internet/99final.htm

Newhagen, J., & Nass, C. (1989). Differential criteria for evaluating credibility of newspapers and TV news. *Journalism Quarterly, 66*, 277–284.

Nielsen, J. (1999). *Trust or bust: Communicating trustworthiness in Web design*. Retrieved June 23, 2001, from http://www.useit.com/alertbox/990307.html

Null, C. (January 2000). Web of lies: Your online credibility faces an uphill battle. *PC/Computing, 13*, 6.

Ohanian, R. (1990). Construction and validation of a scale to measure celebrity endorsers' perceived expertise, trustworthiness, and attractiveness. *Journal of Advertising, 19*, 39–52.

Ohanian, R. (1991). The impact of celebrity spokespersons' perceived image on consumers' intention to purchase. *Journal of Advertising Research, 31*, 46–54.

O'Keefe, D. J. (1990). *Persuasion: Theory and research*. Newbury Park, CA: Sage.

Online News Association. (2001). *Digital journalism credibility survey*. Retrieved June 25, 2001, from http://www.journalists.org/Programs/ResearchText.htm

O'Reilly, C. A., III, & Roberts, K. H. (1976). Relationships among components of credibility and communication behaviors in work units. *Journal of Applied Psychology, 61*, 99–102.

Palmer, J. W., Bailey, J. P., & Faraj, S. (2000). The role of intermediaries in the development of trust on the WWW: The use and prominence of third-parties and privacy statements. *Journal of Computer Mediated Communication, 5(3)*, 1–26.

Perloff, R. M. (1993). *The dynamics of persuasion*. Hillsdale, NJ: Erlbaum.

Petty, R. E., & Cacioppo, J. T. (1981). *Attitudes and persuasion: Classic and contemporary approaches*. Dubuque, IA: William C. Brown.

Petty, R. E., & Cacioppo, J. T. (1988). The elaboration likelihood model of persuasion. *Advances in Experimental Social Psychology, 19*, 123–203.

Pew Research Center for the People and the Press. (1999). *The Internet news audience goes ordinary*. Retrieved June 24, 2001, from http://people-press.org/reports/display.php3?ReportID=72

Potter, W. J. (1998). *Media literacy*. Thousand Oaks, CA: Sage.

Powell, F. C., & Wanzenried, J. W. (1995). Do current measures of dimensions of source credibility produce stable outcomes in replicated tests? *Perceptual & Motor Skills, 81*, 675–687.

Reagan, J., & Zenalty, J. (1979). Local news credibility: Newspapers vs. TV news revisited. *Journalism Quarterly, 56*, 168–172.

Reinard, J. C. (1988). The empirical study of the persuasive effects of evidence: The status after fifty years of research. *Human Communication Research, 15*, 3–59.

Rieh, S. Y., & Belkin, N. J. (1998). Understanding judgment of information quality and cognitive authority in the WWW. *Journal of the American Society for Information Sciences, 35*, 279–289.

Rimmer, T., & Weaver, D. (1987). Different questions, different answers? Media use and media credibility. *Journalism Quarterly, 64*, 28–36.

Robinson, M. J., & Kohut, A. (1988). Believability and the press. *Public Opinion Quarterly, 52*, 174–189.

Roper Organization. (1991). *America's watching: Public attitudes toward television*. New York: Author.

Rosen, D. J. (1998). *Driver education for the information superhighway: How adult learners and practitioners use the Internet*. Washington, DC: National Institute for Literacy.

Rosenthal, P. I. (1971). Specificity, verifiability, and message credibility. *Quarterly Journal of Speech, 57*, 393–401.

Rubin, A. M. (1994). Source credibility scale—Berlo. In R. B. Rubin, P. Palmgreen, & H. E. Sypher (Eds.), *Communication research measures: A sourcebook* (pp. 327–331). New York: Guilford Press.

Rubin R. B. (1994). Source credibility scale—McCroskey. In R. B. Rubin, P. Palmgreen, & H. E. Sypher (Eds.), *Communication research measures: A sourcebook* (pp. 332–337). New York: Guilford Press.

Sargent, L. W. (1965). Communicator image and news reception. *Journalism Quarterly, 42*, 35–42.

Saul, A. (1999). *Newspapers' brand strength gives online information credibility*. Retrieved April 23, 2001, from http://www.gannett.com/go/newswatch/99/july/nw0702–1/htm

Schenkman, B. N., & Jönsson, F. U. (2000). Aesthetics and preferences of Web pages. *Behaviour and Information Technology, 19(5)*, 367–377.

Schweiger, W. (2000). Media credibility—Experience or image? A survey on the credibility of the World Wide Web in Germany in comparison to other media. *European Journal of Communication, 15*, 37–59.

Self, C. C. (1996). Credibility. In M. B. Salwen & D. W. Stacks (Eds.), *An integrated approach to communication theory and research* (pp. 421–441). Mahwah, NJ: Erlbaum.

Sharp, H., & McClung, T. (1966). Effects of organization on the speaker's ethos. *Speech Monographs, 33*, 182–183.

Shaw, D. (1998, August 6). New media playing field opens ways to more errors. *Los Angeles Times*, p. A1.

Shaw, E. F. (1973). Media credibility: Taking the measure of a measure. *Journalism Quarterly, 50*, 306–311.

Shon, J., Marshall, J., & Musen, M. A. (2000). The impact of displayed awards on the credibility retention of Web site information. In *Proceedings of the 2000 American Medical Informatics Association Symposium* (pp. 794–798). Bethesda, MD: American Medical Informatics Association.

Silberg, W. M., Lundberg, G. D., & Musacchio, R. A. (1997). Assessing, controlling, and assuring the quality of medical information on the Internet: Caveant lector et viewor—let the reader and viewer beware. *Journal of the American Medical Association, 277*, 1244–1246.

Simons, J. (1999, July 30). FTC enforcer aggressively targets online fraud. *Wall Street Journal*, p. A20.

Singletary, M. W. (1976). Components of credibility of a favorable news source. *Journalism Quarterly, 53*, 316–319.

Slater, M. D., & Rouner, D. (1997). How message evaluation and source attributes may influence credibility assessment and belief change. *Journalism and Mass Communication Quarterly, 73*, 974–991.

Smith, A. G. (1997). Testing the surf: Criteria for evaluating Internet information resources. *The Public-Access Computer Systems Review, 8*. Retrieved April 25, 2001, from http://www.aut.ac.nz/depts/commstud/theory/smith.htm

Smith, R. G. (1978). *The message measurement inventory: A profile for communication analysis.* Bloomington: Indiana University Press.

Snyder, I. (1998). Page to screen. In I. Snyder (Ed.), *Page to screen: Taking literacy into the electronic era* (pp. xx-xxxvi). London: Routledge.

Soreno, K. K., & Hawkins, G. J. (1967). The effects of variations in speakers' nonfluency upon audience ratings of attitude toward the speech topic and speakers' credibility. *Speech Monographs, 34*, 58–64.

Stamm, K., & Dube, R. (1994). The relationship of attitudinal components to trust in media. *Communication Research, 21*, 105–123.

Stevenson, J. S., Bruner, G. C., & Kumar, A. (2000). Webpage background and viewer attitudes. *Journal of Advertising Research, 40*, 29–34.

Sundar, S. S. (1998). Effect of source attribution on perceptions of online news stories. *Journalism and Mass Communication Quarterly, 75*, 55–68.

Sundar, S. S. (1999). Exploring receivers' criteria for perception of print and online news. *Journalism and Mass Communication Quarterly, 76*, 373–386.

Sundar, S. S., & Nass, C. (2000). Source orientation in human-computer interaction: Programmer, networker, or independent social actor? *Communication Research, 27*, 683–703.

Sundar, S. S., & Nass, C. (2001). Conceptualizing sources in online news. *Journal of Communication, 51*, 52–72.

Tichenor, P., Donohue, G., & Olien, C. (1970). Mass media flow and differential growth in knowledge. *Public Opinion Quarterly, 34*, 159–170.

Times Mirror Company. (1986). *The people and the press: A Times Mirror investigation of public attitudes toward the news media.* Los Angeles, CA: Author.

Tseng, S., & Fogg, B. J. (1999). Credibility and computing technology. *Communications of the ACM, 42*, 39–44.

U.S. Department of Commerce. (October, 2000). *Falling through the net: Toward digital inclusion, a report on Americans' access to technology.* Available from National Telecommunications and Information Administration Web site, http://digitaldivide.gov/reports.htm

Vanden Bergh, B. G., Soley, L. C., & Reid, L. N. (1981). Factor study of dimensions of advertiser credibility. *Journalism Quarterly, 58*, 629–632.

Wanta, W., & Hu, Y.W. (1994). The effects of credibility, reliance, and exposure on media agenda-setting: A path analysis model. *Journalism Quarterly, 71*, 90–98.

Wanzenried, J. W., & Powell, F. C. (1993). Source credibility and dimensional stability: A test of the Leathers personal credibility scale using perceptions of three presidential candidates. *Perceptual & Motor Skills, 77*, 403–406.

Ward, M. (1997). Surfing for the suckers. *New Scientist, 156*, 29.

West, M. D. (1994). Validating a scale for the measurement of credibility: A covariance structure modeling approach. *Journalism Quarterly, 71*, 159–168.

Westley, B. H., & Severin, W. J. (1964). Some correlates of media credibility. *Journalism Quarterly, 41*, 325–335.

Whitehead, J. L. (1968). Factors of source credibility. *Quarterly Journal of Speech, 54*, 59–63.

Widgery, R. N., & Webster, B. (1969). The effects of physical attractiveness upon perceived initial credibility. *Michigan Speech Association Journal, 4*, 9–15.

Williams, R. (1975). *Television: Technology and cultural form*. New York: Schoken.

Wilson, C. E., & Howard, D. M. (1978). Public perception of media accuracy. *Journalism Quarterly, 55*, 73–76.

Wilson, E. J., & Sherrell, D. L. (1993). Source effects in communication and persuasion research: A meta-analysis of effect size. *Journal of Academy of Marketing Science, 21*, 101–112.

Witmer, D. (1998). Introduction to computer-mediated communication: A master syllabus for teaching communication technology. *Communication Education, 47*, 162–173.

Worchel, S., Andreoli, V., & Eason, J. (1975). Is the medium the message? A study of the effects of media, communicator, and message characteristics on attitude change. *Journal of Applied Social Psychology, 5*, 157–172.

Worthington, R. L., & Atkinson, D. R. (1996). Effects of perceived etiology attribution similarity on client ratings of counselor credibility. *Journal of Counseling Psychology, 43*, 423–429.

Zanna, M. P., & Del Vecchio, S. M. (1973). Perceived credibility of television news: A matter of viewers' attitudes and the position taken by the media. *European Journal of Social Psychology, 3*, 213–216.

CHAPTER CONTENTS

11 Communicating Disability: Metaphors of Oppression, Metaphors of Empowerment

STEPHANIE J. COOPMAN
San José State University

This chapter frames the literature on communication and disability within six metaphors, identifying how those metaphors oppress or empower persons with disabilities. *Disability as a medical problem* suggests persons with disabilities must be repaired. This metaphor disempowers persons with disabilities, although more recent conceptualizations may provide useful tools for empowerment. *Disability as cognition* focuses on the influence of attitudes toward disability or individual differences in personality traits that influence disabled-nondisabled interaction, moving away from objective notions of disability to subjective ones. *Disability in culture* examines the influence of culture on what constitutes disability, highlighting the ways that cultural definitions oppress and disempower persons with disabilities. *Disability as culture* views persons with disabilities as forming distinct cultures or cocultures, underscoring the empowering potential of disability as a cultural identity. *Disability as politics* recognizes the importance of empowering relationships in public and private discourse. Finally, *disability as community* incorporates several perspectives to provide a more complex view of disability and communication. This metaphor of disability, particularly with its focus on new communication technologies, most clearly demonstrates empowerment strategies that provide an avenue for persons with disabilities to participate fully in the social construction of their life experiences.

A s governments and institutions implement new laws and policies, a transformation in how we construct and talk about disability continues. What we label as disabilities often do have organic, physical, and chemical origins, yet communication mediates the disability experience. That is, definitions of disability frame how we identify what constitutes disability. Language about dis-

AUTHOR'S NOTE: I thank Lance Dawson for starting me on this research path and Marty Shulter and J. W. Smith for keeping me on it. Their insights into communicating disability proved invaluable in clarifying my own thoughts on this complex subject.

Correspondence: Stephanie J. Coopman, Department of Communication Studies, San José State University, San José, CA 95192-0112; email: sjcoopman@yahoo.com

ability leads us to understand and act on disability in different ways. For example, if we define disability as a medical problem, then we see persons with disabilities as broken and in need of fixing. Viewing disability from a medical perspective makes it difficult to understand why someone with a severe hearing impairment chooses not to have cochlear implants (an electronic device providing sound information for persons who are deaf because of extensive nerve damage).[1] In contrast, if we define disability as culture, we regard persons with disabilities as developing shared beliefs and values. From this perspective, we can understand how someone embedded in the Deaf culture would find cochlear implants in opposition to her or his beliefs and values. Our language and meanings for disability constrain our interactions with persons with disabilities and how we conceptualize experiencing disability.

In the first section of this chapter, I describe the scope of this literature review and define key terms, including disability, empowerment, and oppression. Second, I review the literature on disability and communication within six metaphors of disability and their implications for disability oppression or empowerment: disability as medical problem, disability as cognition, disability in culture, disability as culture, disability as politics, and disability as community (summarized in Table 1). The chapter ends with future research suggestions for continuing the examination of oppression, empowerment, and communicating disability.

SCOPE AND DEFINITIONS

Determining what research to include and what research to omit when surveying the disability and communication studies literature presented dilemmas similar to reviewing any topic in communication studies. In this section, I discuss the parameters for including or excluding literature and offer definitions to clarify the primary concepts framing this literature review.

Scope of the Review

Disability research, much like communication research, crosses disciplinary boundaries and interests. As Zorn (2002) argued in his discussion of disciplinary fragmentation within organizational studies, "Our research can be enriched and make a broader contribution if we are informed of relevant theory and research outside our narrow subdisciplines" (p. 50). Pfeiffer's (2000) annotated bibliography highlights the interdisciplinary nature of disability research, citing articles published in journals such as the *Annals of the American Academy of Political and Social Science*, *Physiotherapy Canada*, *Nurse Education Today*, *Disability & Society*, and the *Berkeley Journal of Employment and Labor Law*. Disability researchers in communication studies publish in traditional communication journals such as *Communication Monographs*, *Journal of Applied Communication Research*, *Journal of Broadcasting and Electronic Media*, and *Southern Communication Journal*,

TABLE 1
Summary of Disability Metaphors

Disability metaphor	Communication metaphor	Central assumptions	How metaphor oppresses	How metaphor empowers
Medical problem	Conduit	disability as problem within the individual to be fixed or overcome; disabled means abnormal	individual defined as disability; dependent on others; dehumanized; objectified	suggests choices for living and individual agency; removes determinism and fate
Cognition	Lens	disability grounded in attitudes and personality traits that act as filters in communication process	persons with disabilities as Other, persons without disabilities as norm	identifies stereotypes and prejudice; indicates areas of improvement in personality traits
In culture	Performance	culture defines disability; communicators influence cultural definitions of disability	barriers restrict access to public discourses and institutions; ignores pragmatics of disability	highlights importance of participation in cultural discourses concerning disability
As culture	Symbol	language, practices, artifacts signal unique disability culture and co-cultures; communication between groups is intercultural	suggests a uniform disability culture; disability subculture(s) exists separate from and subordinate to the dominant culture	embraces cultural diversity across social contexts; legitimizes disability as a positive attribute in individual and group identity
Politics	Voice	power central to the social construction of disability and the body; enactment of identity through naming, self-definition	emphasis on body ignores some groups, such as those with learning disabilities or disabilities not readily visible	disability defined as independent, accepted, normal; encourages participation in public discourse
Community	Discourse	social and political nature of disability form the basis of a common identity across a diverse group	persons with disabilities isolated from other social groups; marginalizes some while privileging others	promotes inclusion, self-determination, empowering relationships; full engagement in all aspects of society and culture

and less traditional venues such as *Discourse Studies, International Journal of Intercultural Relations, Journal of Health Psychology,* and *Media, Culture & Society. Communication Abstracts* references studies focusing on disability and communication in a wide range of journals, including *American Annals of the Deaf, Journalism History, Journal of Leisure,* and *Journal of Special Education.*

Strictly confining this literature review to communication scholars publishing in communication journals, presenting papers at communication conventions and conferences, and authoring book chapters on disability would severely limit this review's scope and usefulness. *Communication Abstracts* generally lists just a handful of studies on disability and communication each year, beginning with only one in 1978 listed under the key term *handicapped.*[2] *Disabled* first appeared in the *Communication Abstracts* index in 1987, just 16 years ago. Although the number of disability-related studies included in *Communication Abstracts* has increased in recent years, with a high of 10 in 1999, this area still receives little attention from communication scholars—only five such studies are indexed in 2000 and just two in 2001.

Conversely, reviewing all literature in disability studies would move well beyond the concerns of communication researchers. Thus, this review includes research clearly within the boundaries of disability and communication (e.g., how students with disabilities interact with their instructors), as well as research with obvious implications for empowerment or oppression and communicating disability (e.g., health and cultural beliefs). In addition, the literature search traversed outside traditional scholarly sources to include a greater multiplicity of voices in discourse on disability issues, particularly those writing on the experience of disability (e.g., Russell, 1998; Stone, 1997; Woodward, 1994). This review excludes research focusing on technical discussions of medical procedures (e.g., recent innovations in dispensing medications), adaptive technology (e.g., screen readers for the visually impaired), and therapies for specific disabilities (e.g., speech therapy).

The review divides the literature on disability and communication into six metaphors or categories: disability as medical problem, disability as cognition, disability in culture, disability as culture, disability as politics, and disability as community.[3] Metaphors provide a way for individuals to understand the unknown in terms of the known (Lakoff & Johnson, 1980). Putnam, Phillips, and Chapman (1996) identify seven metaphors of communication: conduit, lens, linkage, performance, symbol, voice, and discourse. Each metaphor highlights certain aspects of communication while hiding others. For example, research grounded in the linkage metaphor examines network roles, patterns, and structures. In contrast, research stemming from the symbol metaphor focuses on narratives, practices, and rituals. Identifying metaphors within which studies of disability and communication are developed provides insight into the research process and outcomes. Moreover, "metaphor has the power to create a reality rather than simply providing a means of conceptualizing a preexisting reality" (McCoy, Miles, & Metsch, 1999, p. 46).

Storytelling provides a useful site for comparing metaphors of disability. From a disability as medical problem perspective, persons with disabilities or illness tell their stories to health care professionals for the purpose of diagnosis, a diagnosis that tellers may not understand or may not be told (Frank, 1998). From a disability as politics perspective, storytelling provides an avenue for persons with disabilities to articulate their experiences, which often have been silenced or ignored. The disability as community metaphor suggests that storytelling requires communicators' collective action in the process and production of narrative.

In a critique of Booth-Butterfield and Booth-Butterfield's (1994) study of deaf students, Rose (1995) persuasively argued that interpreting the results from a disability as culture perspective, rather than a medical or pathological one, leads to different conclusions. Moreover, Rose (1995) identified "substantive problems in the construction and execution" (p. 158) of the study due to the researchers' conceptualization of deafness as a medical problem. In their response, Booth-Butterfield and Booth-Butterfield (1995) stressed their care in operationalizing terms and asserted that science is neither politically nor culturally bound. Like physicians, who "see their work as based on scientific understandings of the body as opposed to heuristic approaches to, or interpretations of, the body" (Marks, 1999, p. 52), Booth-Butterfield and Booth-Butterfield ground their arguments in objective social science that focuses on behaviors and norms. Thus, the metaphors of disability influence the questions researchers ask, how they design and conduct their studies, interpretations of the results, and the conclusions drawn based on the findings. Most important for this review, each of the six metaphors of disability has different implications for the oppression and empowerment of persons with disabilities.

Definitions of Terms

In this section, I define key terms employed in this review. I begin by discussing disability as a socially constructed, contested concept. I then define oppression and empowerment, applying these terms to communicating disability.

Disability. Enacted on July 26, 1990, U.S. Public Law 336–101, also known as the Americans with Disabilities Act, defined disability as "(a) a physical or mental impairment that substantially limits one or more of the major life activities of such individual; (b) a record of such an impairment; or (c) being regarded as having such an impairment" (Americans with Disabilities Act, 1990). The inclusion of "being regarded as having such an impairment" recognizes the cultural and societal bases of disability. Turnbull, Bateman, and Turnbull (1993) observed that the ADA "reflects the social construct or transactional nature of disability—a 'disability' may be an unchangeable trait of the person, but a 'handicap' is that which the world creates by failing to accommodate to that difference" (p. 172). In their analysis of the ADA's passage, Jeon and Haider-Markel (2001) found that acceptance of the policy reframed disability as socially and politically defined, rather than as a medical issue leading to vocational problems. Haller (1999) noted that the ADA definition of disability addresses the stigma associated with invisible disabilities, such as HIV/AIDS. As Nye (2001) argued, persons living with HIV/AIDS "live with a physical and emotional stigma because of their 'impairment'" (p. 229).

Drawing a distinction between disability and impairment, Oliver (1996) observed, "the social model [of disability] does not deny that impairment is closely related to the physical body. Impairment is, in fact, nothing less than a description of the physical body" (p. 35). With the ADA, Congress recognized that defining disability as simply having or not having a physical or mental impairment neglects the social and political foundations of disability. Bérubé (1998) explained, "The definition of disability, like the definition of illness, is inevitably a matter of social debate and social construction" (p. x, emphasis omitted). In their discussion of rheumatoid arthritis as a disability, Reisine and Fifield (1992) asserted: "Political influences and societal beliefs shape the way in which disability is defined and measured in the United States" (p. 493). Moreover, Wilson and Lewiecki-Wilson (2001) argued "both for the broadest possible definition of disability and for the right of the disability community to debate, contest, and change their preferred definitions of disability" (p. 10).

How we define disability as a society and the values implicit in those definitions have real and often tragic consequences for people with disabilities. As Liachowitz's (1988) historical analysis revealed, "The philosophies and practices of nineteenth-century philanthropy reinforced negative beliefs about handicapped people. In turn, these beliefs informed later government action" (p. 10). Further, Oliver (1990) observed: "Disabled people . . . have realized that dominant definitions of disability pose problems for individual and group identity and have begun to challenge the use of disablist language" (p. 3). More recently, Pfeiffer (1999) argued that definitions of disability have important implications for research, policy, and the political clout of the disability movement. In conducting social science research, Oliver (1987) suggested that researchers examine the ways in which organizations and institutions define or create disability through their common practices. Finally, Oliver (1986) questioned the attention to defining disability without an equal, or even any, attention to defining able-bodied, abled, or nondisabled. Much like racial assumptions of whiteness (e.g., Nakayama & Martin, 1999), persons are assumed to be abled or nondisabled unless identified as disabled.

Historically, the disabled have been demonized, abused, ignored, harassed, vilified, and treated as less than human.[4] In his civil rights perspective on the history of disability, Funk (1987) noted that "People who are disabled have historically been treated as objects of pity and fear—individuals who are incapable and neither expected nor willing to participate in or contribute to organized society" (p. 9). Although persons with disabilities are not always defined in negative, condescending, or unrealistic terms, construing persons with disabilities as fully functioning human beings is rare. Definitions of persons with disabilities most often reflect their position in a nondisabled world—dehumanized, disempowered, and oppressed.

Oppression. Dominant definitions of disability entail the oppression of persons with disabilities (Oliver, 1987, 1990). As Stubbins (1988) asserted, "To be disabled is to belong to an oppressed minority" (p. 24). The roots of oppression can be traced to dehumanizing a group of people (Freire, 1970). When individuals are objectified and viewed as less than human, when persons with disabilities are simply their disability, disempowering us/them seems just and natural. Moreover, Freire observed that dehumanizing others results in negative consequences for the oppressed and the oppressor. In defining persons with disabilities as abnormal and not fully human, persons without disabilities lose their humanity as well.

More than just a static state of existence, oppression carries with it violence against the oppressed and, in turn, the oppressed fighting against their oppressors (Freire, 1970). For persons with disabilities, this violence involves lack of medical care, institutionalization under inhumane conditions, and denial of fundamental rights (e.g., due process, equal protection, education, marriage). As Barton (1996) succinctly described, "Being disabled involves experiencing discrimination, vulnerability and abusive assaults upon your self-identity and esteem. Disability is thus a form of oppression which entails social restrictions" (p. 8). Barnes (1996) identified "a consistent cultural bias against people with impairments throughout recorded history" (p. 56). The experience of disability in an environment created by and for those who are nondisabled, constitutes oppression (Imrie, 1998).

Giddens (1991) defined oppression as "differential power, applied by one group to limit the life chances of another" (p. 212). Corker (1998a) linked oppression and culture, arguing that oppression is "the process by which power imbalances are created and maintained in society and culture which disadvantage some groups when compared to others" (p. 147). Hardaway (1991) referred to this oppression in the U.S. as imposed inequality, arguing: "The history of American society's treatment of persons with impairment conditions can be summed up in two words: *segregation* and *inequality*" (p. 140). For persons with disabilities, oppression manifests itself in the denial of self-definition, restricted access to public spaces and discourse, and dehumanizing treatment across cultures and societies.

Empowerment. Empowerment forms a key foundation for the disability movement; even those in the medical community have begun to recognize the fundamental importance of empowerment for persons with disabilities (Oliver, 1996). As with oppression, empowerment finds its basis in marginalized groups. Orbe (1998) argued that disenfranchised individuals inhabit a unique position and potential for the exercise of power in that they "typically have a working knowledge of both dominant and co-cultural group structures" (p. 131). Communication provides the tool for implementing empowerment: "Empowerment occurs through a communication process in which the relationships between the oppressed and the oppressor undergo a fundamental change" (Shefner-Rogers, Rao, Rogers, & Wayangankar, 1998, p. 322). In one of the few studies on how communication facilitates empowerment, Papa, Auwal, and Singhal (1997) concluded that empowerment is "an interactional process of people working together to produce solutions to commonly experienced problems" (p. 244).

Empowerment programs often stress dominant groups giving or granting empowerment to the powerless. For example, Itzhaky and Schwartz (1998) described the empowerment process thus: "The social worker's intervention guides the disabled through a process in which they develop the abilities and skills to increase control over their own lives, fate and surroundings" (p. 307). Such a view portrays empowerment as an object rather than a process (Oliver, 1996). For true empowerment to occur, disenfranchised groups must seize opportunities to exercise power (Charlton, 1998; Oliver, 1996; Stone, 1996). Thus, Oliver (1996) defined empowerment as "a collective process on which the powerless embark as part of the struggle to resist the oppression of others, as part of their demands to be included, and/or to articulate their own views of the world" (p. 147). According to Oliver, this collective process forms the basis of individual empowerment. That is, without collective empowerment, there is no individual empowerment. Similarly, in her analysis of the Deaf social movement, Jankowski (1997) defined empowerment as "a process through which a marginalized group alters the distribution of power between itself and the dominant culture" (p. 6).

Drake's (1996) analysis of norms and power underscored the critical role of collective empowerment for persons with disabilities. Because persons with disabilities often lack individual power to change discriminatory norms, they typically respond "either by acquiescence within a subordinate role or by the rejection of the prevailing norms altogether" (p. 148). Exercising power at the individual level requires changes in power dynamics at the societal level. Thus, Corker (1998a) argued that the collective must develop strategies to empower all persons with disabilities, while facilitating the movement's empowerment via the interpersonal relationships among members of the disability community. In addition, individuals may be empowered in some contexts, such as the workplace, but not in others, such as when attending public events (Fawcett at al., 1994). The empowerment process involves multiple levels, including individuals, groups, organizations, and communities (Fawcett at al., 1995; Itzhaky & Schwartz, 1998), as well as multiple contexts.

Empowerment requires a cultural and political shift in definitions and representations of disability. Thus, for persons with disabilities, empowerment means "they have joined a liberation movement to free people with disabilities from political, economic, and cultural oppression" (Charlton, 1998, p. 115). This view of empowerment centers on four key issues: independence, inclusion, self-help, and self-determination (e.g., Charlton, 1998; Corker, 1998a; Oliver, 1996). Independence stems from making one's own decisions and having control over one's life (Fawcett et al., 1994). Inclusion involves opportunities to fully participate in public life, including travel, education, social events, and cultural and political discourse. Self-help resists the efforts of the nondisabled to define and determine courses of action for persons with disabilities. Additionally, it moves persons with disabilities out of the sick or victim role (Crossley & Crossley, 1998). Self-determination "provocatively and intuitively attacks the ideology of paternalism . . . and the political, economic, and social dependency people have been forced into" (Charlton, 1998,

p. 128). Addressing these issues, and achieving empowerment, requires transforming the discourse associated with disability (Westhaver, 2000) and the metaphors underlying that discourse.

DISABILITY AS A MEDICAL PROBLEM

Research within the disability as medical problem metaphor implicitly or explicitly addresses fixing or mediating disabilities in some way. This metaphor parallels the conduit metaphor for communication (e.g., Axley, 1984; Reddy, 1979), which "treats communication as an object that flows from a source to a receiver" (Putnam et al., 1996, p. 380). From this perspective, communication breaks down when the listener or reader does not receive the intended message. Senders fix communication problems by increasing clarity and accuracy. The disability as medical problem and conduit metaphors share a mechanistic perspective entailing the repair of broken parts. For example, Bonstetter's (1986) content analysis of 1950s and 1970s magazines found that articles from the earlier decade were concerned with the application of science to mental retardation causes and cures. Articles from the later decade, though more humantistic in tone, still focused on ways to mitigate mental retardation through technology. In his ethnomethodological examination of his own experience with amyotrophic lateral sclerosis (ALS, or Lou Gehrig's disease), Robillard (1999) pointed to "the widespread belief in technological progress and the belief that almost any problem has a technological fix" (p. 123). Consistent with the medical approach to disability, Robillard found himself inundated with assistive devices that he could not operate and disapproving health care providers when he expressed any reservations about using the technology.

Defining disability as a medical problem typically directs attention to improving or correcting health problems. Johnson and Wolinsky (1993) defined disability as physical limitations leading to restrictions on daily living activities. The researchers found that for elderly persons, disabilities negatively influenced individuals' perceptions of health and social functioning. Similarly, Verbrugge, Reoma, and Gruber-Baldini's (1994) study identified persons with disabilities as having a chronic disease, such as diabetes, or an injury, such as a broken hip. These researchers found that individuals' reported increased numbers of social contacts improved health status.

Viewing disability as a medical problem emphasizes the dichotomy between the abnormal (persons with disabilities) and the normal (persons without disabilities). Wilson and Lewiecki-Wilson (2001) traced this dichotomy back to Aristotle's writings, in which "ab/normal marks the irreducibility of otherness, the necessary gap or interval producing . . . 'humanness' (free men) and deviant Others" (p. 14). Sendelbaugh (1978), Austin (1984), and Austin and Myers (1984) applied medical definitions of hearing impairment in their studies, identifying significant differences between hearing (normal) and hearing-impaired (abnormal) persons in television viewing. Moreover, persons with disabilities must strive to mitigate their disabilities to achieve at least some degree of normalcy. For example, Cogswell (1968) suggested that paraplegics must "practice the physical skills necessary to function in the normal world" (p. 11). In their discussion of college students with learning disabilities, Brinckerhoff, Shaw, and McGuire (1992) warned that accommodations must be compatible with the workplace so the students "will be better prepared to compete with their nondisabled peers" (p. 422). Byrd (1989), Byrd and Elliott (1985), and Hyler (1988) applied medical definitions of disabilities to analyze movie characters depicted as disabled. In his discussion of using silent movies in educating deaf persons, Schuchman (1984) concluded, "There is no disagreement among educators of deaf children that the handicap of deafness is primarily a communication disorder which results in low language achievement" (p. 74).

Research examining interaction differences between persons with disabilities and persons without disabilities further draws the distinction between normal (no disability) and abnormal (disability). Erickson and Omark (1980) observed five children with disabilities and four children without disabilities in their interactions with each other and the teacher. The authors concluded that the normal children (nondisabled) served as role models for the children with disabilities. Similarly, Thompson (1981a, 1982a, 1982b) examined listener-adaptation abilities in physically handicapped and normal children (author's terms) who shared the same classroom. She identified listener-adaptation deficiencies in the children with disabilities and suggested that association with nondisabled children produced improved results for the children with disabilities. However, children without disabilities were not able to adapt to their classmates with disabilities, and interaction between the two groups seemed to have no effect on the former group (Thompson, 1981a, 1982b, 1983).

Researchers taking a medical approach to disability typically treat disability as a variable in social interactions. For example, Thompson (1981b) explored the differences in sharing and autonomy between married couples in which the husband was disabled, and couples in which the husband was not disabled. Overall, her study found only minor differences between the two groups, although the author argued that negative relationship effects can result from having a disabled husband if the wife is not fully aware of the disability's implications.

Summary and Critique

Traditional applications of disability as a medical problem leave little room for empowering persons with disabilities. Goffman (1963) suggested that we have expectations for particular social settings, including the characteristics of individuals associated with those settings. These expectations constitute what we take for granted as normal. When individuals appear to possess a characteristic that others perceive as undesirable and not meeting the expectations of the situation, stigma comes into play. Russell (1998) argued that "the social tendency is to . . . view disability as a personal tragedy, a matter for medicine to 'correct'" (p. 14).

Edwards (1997) agreed, noting that a medical approach to disability "assumes that disability is a medical condition that is inherent in the individual and that the disabled person's functional ability deviates from that of the normal human body" (p. 35). Robillard (1999) argued that we develop social categories for individuals based on their bodies. Strangers asked him so often about what kind of work he *used* to do, that he "began to think there is some bodily state that connotes being able to work" (p. 145). Although his attendants, wife, and graduate students insisted that he was still working, Robillard found that he "did not have the look of one who could work" (p. 146). From the medical perspective, disabled persons can never achieve normalcy, even through medical corrections, and endure the stigma of abnormality.

The medical metaphor of disability results in the oppression of persons with disabilities through physicalism, handicapism, and ableism (Hillyer, 1993; Russell, 1998). Like sexism and racism, these -isms define people in terms of what they are not. For women, they are not men; for persons of color, they are not White; for persons with disabilities, they are not abled. Disability becomes something to overcome, typically through the individual's extraordinary efforts (Biklen, 1986; Wendell, 1997; Woodward, 1994). Yet, because the disability is a medical problem, it can never be completely repaired, only conquered or defeated. The medical model infuses disability with "military metaphors—fighting against disability and disease (e.g., the war on cancer)—which essentially envisages those with disabilities as the enemy; an afflicted and alien other which must be stamped out" (Peters, 1996, p. 217).

The medicalization of disability (Oliver, 1996) defines persons with disabilities as *not* abled and identified *as* their disabilities. Further, from a medical perspective, the problem of disability originates with the individual; an individual dependent on others for everyday functioning. The terms *dependent* and *disability* become fused together, constructing those with disabilities as unable to live independently (e.g., Gardner & Radel, 1978). Oliver (1990) argued that "the idea of dependency has been used to socially construct, or perhaps, more accurately, socially reconstruct the problem of disability" (p. 81). The result in the medical context is that persons with disabilities are not granted the same respect and treatment as nondisabled persons (Blumberg, 1994; Brisenden, 1986).

The disability as medical problem metaphor entails symbolic, cultural, and political oppression of persons with disabilities. Yet, Stineman (2000) argued for *empowerment medicine* that elaborates on the medical model to include individual agency and the individual's physical, political, societal, and economic environment. In applying empowerment medicine, "Medical knowledge is returned to the patient in a way that enhances freedom, maximizes potential for achievement, and expands life choices" (p. 11). Condit and Williams's (1997) research on the discourse of medical genetics also suggested that this approach may provide a source of empowerment for persons with disabilities. Based on their findings, the authors proposed that "Medicalization removes genetic illness and disability from the realm of 'fate,' a realm that has carried its own negative moralistic connotations" (p.

230). Similarly, McCoy et al. (1999) argued that in the medical metaphor, "People are not blamed for the origins of their problems, nor are they held responsible for solutions to their problems" (p. 47). Yet, Longmore (1997) asserted that the medical model of disability empowers persons *without* disabilities, rather than persons with disabilities, in that the model "reassures [nondisabled] Americans that they can still transcend the human condition. Thus, fixing disabled people has become a cultural imperative" (p. 156).

Research indicates there are signs that the medical community recognizes the limitations of traditional health models. For example, in their study of health documentaries, Hodgetts and Chamberlain (1999) found that a new representation of health "does encompass the experiences and social circumstances of patients" (p. 331). Thus, Stineman's (2000) notion of empowerment medicine holds out hope for transforming the medical metaphor from one of oppression to one of empowerment. As Condit and Williams (1997) argued, "Instead of assuming that medicalization inherently disempowers, oppresses, and dehumanizes because it employs information, training, and technology, critical approaches might best be directed to asking under what kinds of conditions medicalization empowers" (p. 232). Finally, Llewellyn and Hogan (1999) observed that although the medical model provides an incomplete perspective on disability, previous research grounded in this approach should not be ignored.

DISABILITY AS COGNITION

Our communicative experiences both are influenced by and influence our internal cognitions (Hewes, 1995). Further, these mental processes act as filters in our encounters with our world in that "the individual never confronts reality directly, but always through the use of interpretive schemes" (O'Keefe, Delia, & O'Keefe, 1980, p. 26) or classification devices the individual employs in sense making. These classification devices may be attitudes, social schemas, attributions, constructs, thoughts, or other mental structures that have developed as we go about our day-to-day lives (Sypher & Higgins, 1989).

Disability as cognition shares the lens metaphor of communication in which "communication is equated with a *filtering process*: searching, retrieving, and routing information" (Putnam et al., 1996, p. 380). The vast majority of research on disability and communication from a cognitive approach focuses on interactants' attitudes that serve as internal filters in the communication process. Other research examines individual trait differences, such as communication apprehension and communicators' behaviors or interpretations.

Attitudes

Attitudes are evaluations or judgments about people, events, objects, conditions, and the like. All attitudes have some target or referent that a particular attitude is assigned (Augoustinos & Walker, 1995). Attitudes provide cognitive mechanisms for categorizing the people, events, objects, and other referents in our environment. Attitudes often act as mental shortcuts, as when one identifies a referent (such as a professor) and evaluates that referent (for example, eccentric) based on previous information associated with the referent's category. We typically assign these attitudes to particular referents so rapidly that we are completely unaware of the process (Augoustinos & Walker, 1995). However, as with cognitive structures in general, early encounters with particular referents are more mindful when we have less experience with them. With greater experience, and therefore a broader knowledge base, we tend to have more automatic responses.

We develop attitudes in our interactions with others, express our attitudes with other communicators, and modify our attitudes based on new information (Augoustinos & Walker, 1995). In addition, attitudes influence how we interact with others, what we say, and how we respond. As with all cognitive structures, attitudes are in part unique to the individual and in part socially shared. Some attitudes are held strongly and are easy for us to access. Others are weaker and less accessible. Stronger attitudes are more likely to influence our behaviors.

Nondisabled persons' attitudes toward persons with disabilities. Several studies have examined attitudes and communication between the nondisabled and the disabled in the higher educational context. The majority of these studies have focused on faculty member attitudes toward students with disabilities. For example, Fichten, Amsel, Bourdon, and Creti (1988) found a high degree of uncertainty for professors when interacting with physically disabled students, particularly when the professor had little or no experience in such interactions. Professors who had taught students with disabilities were more interested in teaching and more comfortable with such students. Interestingly, the researchers suggested that students with disabilities often take the initiative in interacting with faculty. Similarly, Fonosch and Schwab (1981) found that college faculty who had little or no contact with students with disabilities had less positive attitudes toward those students than faculty who had more experience with disabled students.

The communication situation becomes more complex when the student has a disability not readily visible, such as learning disabilities and other invisible disabilities including epilepsy, psychiatric conditions, and acquired brain injuries. Houck, Asselin, Troutman, and Arrington (1992) found that, although faculty were willing to make accommodations for students with learning disabilities, they were often unsure how to accomplish this fairly. However, faculty did express some concern about students with learning disabilities completing a program of study and selecting certain majors. The researchers believe that "such views may be inadvertently communicated to students with learning disabilities" (Houck et al., 1992, p. 683). Thus, faculty members' lack of knowledge concerning learning disabilities, and other disabilities as well, influences attitudes, which then impact their communication with disabled students. Worley's (2000) review of the literature on interaction between nondisabled teachers and disabled students suggested that teachers' attitudes are infused with ambiguity, linked in part to type and perceived severity of the disability.

Persons with disabilities who are also African American may face bias from others on two counts: their disability and their ethnic background (Alston & Mngadi, 1992). Both African Americans and persons with disabilities are often marginalized by the negative attitudes of others. Alston and Mngadi (1992) argued that rehabilitation counselors need to examine their own attitudes toward African Americans with disabilities and the ways that those attitudes might negatively impact encounters with clients. The authors acknowledged that client attitudes, capabilities, and education influence the client's vocational and social success. Still, "counselor variables such as cultural biases and prejudices are equally important in influencing rehabilitation outcome" (Alston & Mngadi, 1992, p.15).

Negative attitudes toward persons with specific disabilities may have real and long-term health consequences. Yedidia, Barr, and Berry (1993) found that physicians at different career stages were more willing to treat patients with meningococcal meningitis, hemophilia, metastatic colon cancer, epilepsy, gonorrhea, hepatitis B, and Alzheimer's disease than patients with AIDS. Indeed, the only conditions physicians were less willing to treat than AIDS were alcoholism and drug dependency. Yedidia et al. (1993) suggested that perceptions of patients' communicative styles (e.g., patients' lack of expressed appreciation and unwillingness to cooperate) provide one reason why physicians hold negative attitudes toward persons with AIDS, as well as those with Alzheimer's disease, alcoholism, and drug dependency.

Attitudes of persons with disabilities. Although much attention has focused on media portrayals of persons with disabilities (e.g., Haller, 2000a, 2000b; Hyler, Gabbard, & Schneider, 1991; Keller, Hallahan, McShane, Crowley, & Blandford, 1990; Norden, 1990; Signorielli, 1989; Wright, 1999), few researchers have examined disabled viewers' perspectives toward such portrayals. Using focus groups and a questionnaire, Ross (1997, 1998, 2001) found persons with disabilities maintained overwhelmingly negative attitudes toward media representations of persons with disabilities in mainstream fictional, factual, and news programming. Study participants identified negative stereotypes, reliance on experts who had little experience with disability, and depicting persons with disabilities primarily by their disability (i.e., only secondarily as human), as contributing to their pessimistic attitudes toward mainstream media programming.

Through an analysis of three data sources concerning the attitudes of persons with disabilities—face-to-face interviews, published autobiographies, and published essays and interviews—Weinberg (1988) identified three distinctly different groups of individuals with physical disabilities. The first group, on one end of the continuum, was "forever bitter and unhappy"(p.149) and used language that revealed an attitude defining "their disability as a tragedy" (p.149). Resignation and adaptation characterized the second, or middle group, who defined their disabilities as inconvenient and something to get used to or accommodate. The last group, at the other end of the continuum, embraced the disability, expressing satisfaction "with who they are and able to reach their life goals despite or even because of their disabilities" (p. 152). Not surprisingly, the researcher concluded that the attitudes of persons with disabilities impact their approach to life and interactions with others.

Royse and Edwards (1989) attempted to make a more direct link between attitudes and communication. Nearly 175 participants completed a brief questionnaire designed to assess the attitudes of persons with physical disabilities toward questions about their disabilities and the subsequent responses to those questions. The researchers found that most participants had fairly open attitudes to such inquiries, but were more open with their physicians, other disabled persons, and their social workers than with neighbors, potential employers, children, and strangers. Interestingly, questionnaire respondents felt that disclosing information about their disability would not make them more at ease in interactions with acquaintances or strangers. However, participants felt that such disclosure would likely make others more comfortable.

In reviewing literature on disabled students' attitudes, Fichten et al. (1988) concluded that, although overall such students are comfortable with nondisabled students, the students with disabilities did feel that the nondisabled students viewed the them in negative ways. Students with disabilities also felt that professors generally hold negative attitudes toward students with disabilities. Yet, Fichten et al. (1988) found that "disabled students rated most student initiated behaviors [in disabled student and faculty interactions] . . . as less appropriate than the professors believed them to be" (p. 17). Thus, students with disabilities underestimate the effectiveness of their communication strategies. Warnath and Dunnington (1981), primarily focusing on blind university students but generalizing to all students with disabilities, argued that disabled students' oversensitivity concerning possible misinterpretations, as well as a suspicion that they are not observing all interaction cues, hinders such students' abilities to interact comfortably with others.

A study of patients with chronic obstructive pulmonary disease (COPD) took a different approach to the attitudes of persons with disabilities. Eakin and Glasgow (1997) were interested in the relationships among COPD patient self-care (e.g., regular exercise, smoking cessation), patients' attitudes toward self-care, and the advice patients received from their health care providers. Controlling for demographic variables (age, sex, educational level), patients who viewed a particular self-care activity as more important and recalled receiving advice from a health care provider on that topic were far more likely to engage in a self-care activity than those who viewed the activity as not important and had not gotten relevant information from a health care provider. Cognitive models of communication suggest that COPD patients' attitudes stem from their previous experiences with health issues. These attitudes in turn influence interpretations of information from health care providers, as well as a willingness to seek such information. Finally, information from health care providers may influence COPD attitudes, depending on the credibility of the source and the degree to what that information is salient to the patient.

Attitudes of persons with and without disabilities. Most cognitive studies of disability and communication focus on the attitudes of persons without disabilities toward persons with disabilities *or* the reverse. Makas (1988) bridged the two by examining both the attitudes of persons with and without disabilities. In this study, Makas (1988) was interested in what constituted positive behaviors and attitudes toward persons with physical disabilities. The researcher included three groups of participants in her study: professionals with disabilities, students without disabilities, and "good-attitudes" individuals without disabilities who were recruited by respondents with disabilities. Makas (1988) found that persons with disabilities defined positive attitudes as supporting disability rights, whereas persons without disabilities defined positive attitudes as being helpful and nice. Attitudes that place persons with disabilities in a helpless or needful position will likely lead to communication strategies that victimize the target. Attitudes that promote the civil rights of persons with disabilities will likely lead to communication strategies that recognize the target as a unique individual.

Like Makas (1988), Coleman and DePaulo (1991) discussed the ways that persons with and without disabilities contribute to miscommunication in disabled-nondisabled interactions. This miscommunication stems in part from communicators' attitudes and expectations related to disability. Persons without disabilities tend to share attitudes and expectations of persons with disabilities that are (a) negative and pessimistic, (b) their own projections of what disabled persons think of nondisabled persons, or (c) so extremely positive that they are offensive to persons with disabilities. These attitudes and expectations generally lead to problems when communicating with disabled persons. Also, persons with disabilities may (a) have negative feelings about their disability and themselves, (b) expect others to view them in a negative light, or (c) resent those who are nondisabled. Coleman and DePaulo concluded that changes at the societal level in prejudice toward disabilities, along with sensitizing persons with disabilities to their contributions to miscommunication, are necessary to improving disabled-nondisabled interactions.

In their review of the literature on stuttering, Whaley and Golden (2000) found that fluent individuals' perceptions of persons who stutter "reflect a global negative and stereotypical" (p. 425) view, with an almost complete absence of any favorable qualities. Moreover, persons who stutter also evaluated stutters in negative terms. For example, Whaley and Parker (2000) found that the top three metaphors persons who stutter used to describe stuttering were incompetent/malfunction/impairment, affective pain, and lack of control/predictability. Whaley and Golden (2000) noted that research on interacting with persons who stutter is scarce due to the emphasis on identifying the underlying causes of stuttering and how to manage, cure, or fix the problem—the disability as medical problem metaphor. Thus, the researchers offer pragmatic strategies for interacting with persons who stutter that fluent individuals should employ regardless of their attitudes toward persons who stutter.

Changing persons without disabilities' attitudes. The negative attitudes of nondisabled persons toward persons with disabilities appear to be deeply engrained. Livneh (1991) suggested that multiple sources contribute to the strength of these attitudes. Social and cultural norms, early childhood experiences, unfamiliarity and anxiety, and perceived threat to body image are all possible roots of nondisabled persons' attitudes towards persons with disabilities. The origins of these attitudes are complex; accessing and applying these attitudes becomes so automatic that nondisabled individuals form their evaluations of persons with disabilities without thought and awareness. This mindlessness makes such attitudes particularly difficult to change in that nondisabled individuals are not fully cognizant of these cognitive processes. Despite Livneh's pessimism, several authors have suggested that dysfunctional and negative attitudes toward persons with disabilities can be changed. Focusing on the organizational context, Stone and Colella (1996) suggested that altering organizational norms, practices, and values to reflect more positive views of disability would modify nondisabled organization members' attitudes toward persons with disabilities. Arguing for a "sociology of acceptance" (p. 36), Schwartz (1988) observed that several studies support the position that nondisabled persons' attitudes toward persons with disabilities are becoming more positive. Similarly, Taylor and Bogdan (1991) suggested that by promoting a sociology of acceptance toward persons with mental disabilities, rather than a sociology of deviance, persons without disabilities will develop more positive attitudes towards persons with disabilities.

Several authors have noted the media's role in attitude reinforcement and attitude change. In her study of prime-time television, Donaldson (1981) found that persons with disabilities were nearly invisible. Those few disabled television characters appearing on shows during prime time were more likely to be cast in negative than positive roles. Further, even those in positive roles were portrayed strictly in terms of their disabilities; that is, the disability was central to the show's plot. Similarly, Ross's (2001) study of radio programs in Great Britain found that persons with disabilities were essentially absent from the airwaves. Keller et al. (1990) found that although U.S. newspapers frequently mentioned persons with disabilities, nearly one half of the articles portrayed the disability as negatively impacting the individual. Signorielli (1989) concluded, based on her study of U.S. television's portrayal of mental illness, that "television does little to reduce negative imagery of mental illness" (p. 330). And in their study of British television's influence on attitudes toward mental illness, Philo and Secker (1999) found "40 per cent of the people who took part in the study believed mental illness is associated with violence and gave the media as the source of the belief" (p. 141).

The ability to influence attitudes also suggests an ability to change attitudes through more positive media portrayals of persons with disabilities (Donaldson, 1981). Thomas and Wolfensberger (1982) argued that social service organizations must promote a more positive image of persons with disabilities, and act as advocates for the disabled. Of particular concern is the negative, or most often absent, image of persons with disabilities in advertisements. The authors asked:

But suppose business and industry presented their products in the same negative fashion in which persons with disabilities are so often portrayed by human services. What would have been the effect on Chevrolet sales in 1977 if, instead of "Baseball, hot dogs, apple pie, and Chevrolet," the ad had said, "High prices, poor roads, traffic accidents, and Chevrolet?" (p. 357)

Although Thomas and Wolfensberger conceded that positive images of persons with disabilities in the media do not guarantee attitude change in persons without disabilities, negative depictions certainly promote stereotypic views of and prejudice toward persons with disabilities. Byrd (1989) asserted, "If the assumption that the root of an attitude could well be in a media presentation, then there is a need to understand how that occurs and how it can be altered" (p. 37). Elliott and Byrd (1984) found that an informative film about blindness did positively affect study participants' attitudes toward persons with disabilities. Elliott and Byrd (1982) argued that negative portrayals of disability in the media reinforce negative attitudes toward persons with disabilities, which in turn leads to communication barriers between the persons with and without disabilities. The authors suggested the use of media in the classroom to promote positive attitudes toward the disabled, citing several studies in which movies, television shows, and other media were used in classroom activities and discussions to modify attitudes toward disability. However, a recent study of media influences on nondisabled persons' attitudes toward persons with disabilities produced mixed results (Farnall & Smith, 1999). After viewing films that featured persons with disabilities as strong and positive central characters, respondents reported greater sensitivity to discrimination against, and more positive emotional responses to, persons with disabilities. Viewing such films led to increased discomfort in interacting with persons with disabilities. Further, Brolley and Anderson (1988) found that exposure to positive and negative advertisements related to persons with disabilities had no effect on nondisabled persons' attitudes toward disabled persons.

The fairly one-dimensional conceptualization of attitudes limits the utility of research on attitudes toward persons with disabilities. Hahn (1988a) suggested that in the case of persons without disabilities' attitudes toward persons with disabilities, aesthetic and existential anxiety form the basis for specific attitudes. Aesthetic anxiety stems from an aversion to bodies considered culturally unattractive. Existential anxiety flows from the fears of persons without disabilities that they might become disabled; persons with disabilities present reminders of nondisablement's tentative state. Hahn argued that identifying the influence of these two different types of fears on attitudes toward persons with disabilities provides greater insight into how to change those attitudes.

Some are skeptical of the possibility of true attitude change of the nondisabled toward persons with disabilities and other stigmatized groups. Coleman (1997) argued that attitudes toward the stigmatized result from fear: fear of the unknown, the unfamiliar, the uncontrollable. This fear explains why the attitudes underlying stigma persist in the face of overwhelming evidence that runs counter to those attitudes. Often developed in childhood, fear associated with stigma provides a driving force in maintaining negative attitudes toward persons with disabilities. In a study of stigma associated with tuberculosis, Jaramillo (1999) explored the relationship between people's beliefs about the disease's transmission and prejudice toward persons with tuberculosis. Based on interviews with nearly 400 people in Cali, Columbia, Jaramillo found that deeply engrained unscientific beliefs about tuberculosis transmission and fear of persons with the disease were the primary sources of prejudice against those with tuberculosis. This held true regardless of the participant's source of information about tuberculosis. Similarly, a longitudinal study of physicians' attitudes toward persons with AIDS found that three general attitudes, homophobia, phobia of IV drug users, and cynicism, led to a decreased willingness to treat AIDS patients regardless of any positive aspects of the socialization process during the residency program (Yedidia, Berry, & Barr, 1996). However, having a positive role model in the residency program was linked to an increased willingness to treat AIDS patients in physicians who were more optimistic and had more favorable attitudes toward homosexuality and IV drug use. Still, the results of these studies suggest that firmly entrenched attitudes remain difficult to change and negatively affect interactions between persons with disabilities and those without.

Summary. As expected, research concerned with nondisabled persons' attitudes toward persons with disabilities suggests that those attitudes influence communication between the two groups. Prejudice and negative attitudes are particularly harmful and present barriers to productive communication. The attitudes of persons with disabilities also impact their communication with persons without disabilities. Further, research suggests that disabled and nondisabled persons have differing conceptualizations of what constitutes positive attitudes toward the disabled. Although some researchers argue that attitudes can change, others express skepticism. Many hold the media to blame for reinforcing negative attitudes toward persons with disabilities; some suggest the media hold the key to creating more positive attitudes toward persons with disabilities. However, these attitudinal studies must be interpreted with caution, as they rely on self-reports and paper-and-pencil measures. For example, MacLean and Gannon (1995) identified methodological problems with the scale generally used to measure attitudes toward persons with disabilities.

Traits

Unlike attitudes, which are open to change in varying degrees, personality traits are viewed as relatively static cognitive structures that influence how we communicate with others and our interpretations of our social environment. Traits may influence communicators' behaviors in broad ways across many contexts, or they may be more situation specific, activated only under particular circumstances. Personality traits influence communication in that they "are typically seen as affecting behavior by motivating (or inhibiting) the performance of certain acts" (Burleson & Caplan, 1998, p. 238). For example, research in trait aggressiveness suggests that traits (a) are to some extent grounded in our interactions with others (Infante, Myers, & Buerkel, 1994), (b) influence the messages we produce and the framing devices we use for those messages (Infante & Wigley, 1986), (c) influence how we interpret what others say and do (Sutter & Martin, 1998), and (d) may be modified through specific training strategies (e.g., Anderson & Martin, 1999; Infante, 1995). Below I discuss research in personality traits, disability, and communication.

Traits of nondisabled persons and communication with persons with disabilities. Unlike attitude research, the majority of trait research examines the traits of persons with disabilities and communication. One exception is Hart and Williams (1995), who observed classroom interactions between nondisabled instructors and disabled students. These researchers identified four roles instructors adopted when communicating with students with disabilities: avoider, guardian, rejecter, and nurturer. Avoiders distanced themselves physically and conversationally from students with disabilities. Guardians tried to protect students with disabilities, often separating them from the rest of the class and lowering performance standards. Rejecters suggested that students with disabilities were unable to meet the demands of a class. Nurturers developed a communication climate in the classroom that facilitated participation by disabled and nondisabled students alike. Hart and Williams (1995) posited that different personality traits underlie the different roles. Rejecters exhibit trait verbal aggressiveness, belittling and disconfirming students with disabilities. For example, one instructor refused to answer a disabled student's question, saying "she was not a 'baby-sitter' and told [the student] to ask someone else" (Hart & Williams, 1995, pp. 147–148), yet she later answered a nondisabled student's question. Communication apprehension, a personality trait associated with fear or anxiety toward communicating with others (Cragan & Shields, 1998), may result in avoiding and not interacting with students with disabilities.

Traits of persons with disabilities and communication with others. In a study of students in grades 7–12 attending a residential school for the deaf, Booth-Butterfield, Heare, and Booth-Butterfield (1991) examined the link between communication apprehension and signing. Teachers evaluated the students' signing competence along six dimensions: clarity, intensity, speed, size, gestures and facial expressions, and completeness. Higher levels of trait communication apprehension were related to lack of clarity in signing, the use of smaller signs, less intense signing, slower signing, and incomplete answers or sentences. A later study of 89 students attending three different residential high schools for the deaf provided similar results (Booth-Butterfield & Booth-Butterfield, 1994). Again, the researchers found that trait communication anxiety was inversely related to signing effectiveness. In addition, the results revealed that study participants in all three schools reported less trait anxiety than nondeaf high school students. When a subsample of the original study participants completed the measure for trait anxiety a year after the initial data gathering, their scores were similar to the first scores, indicating the stability of the trait for study participants. The researchers argued that trait communication anxiety not only influences signing competence for deaf students, but interpretations of students' motivations as well. That is, teachers may associate ineffective signing with attitude problems, rather than communication anxiety.

Structure building framework, a model of cognitive mapping, posits a direct link between disordered discourse associated with some forms of schizophrenia and irregularities in cognitive structuring processes (Gernsbacher, Tallent, & Bolliger, 1999). Positive disordered discourse is an overflow of talk that includes abrupt topic shifts, tangential information, and seemingly unrelated statements. Negative disordered discourse lacks both quality and quantity of information. Gernsbacher et al. argued that these observed problems in language behavior stem from impairments in the basic building blocks of cognitive structures. In addition, the authors proposed that persons diagnosed with schizophrenia who exhibit disordered discourse experience difficulty in cognitive shifting when presented with concurrent or serial multiple tasks and encounter problems when mapping new information onto existing cognitive structures. The authors concluded that programs to modify disordered discourse in persons diagnosed with schizophrenia may be less than successful because the discourse stems from a fairly stable cognitive trait.

Lumley, Kelley, and Leisen (1997) examined the relationships among (a) rheumatoid arthritis health status (pain, physical impairment, impact on mood), (b) tendency to think and talk with others about stressful events, (c) emotional expressiveness, (d) ambivalence about emotional expression, and (e) willingness to share personal information with others. Study participants who talked with others about life stress, and did not dwell on their own thoughts about that stress, reported lower levels of arthritis-related health problems. Further, ambivalence over expressing emotions and an unwillingness to share personal information had negative impacts on patients' moods. The results suggest that it is not so much stressful events that worsen rheumatoid arthritis, but how individuals with rheumatoid arthritis talk about and interpret those experiences.

Green, Platt, Eley, and Green's (1996) comparison study of persons living with HIV and those who were not found that the HIV-positive diagnosis had little influence on most personality traits. Only hopelessness was associated with the HIV-positive diagnosis. However, persons who were HIV positive, depressed, and had low self-esteem were more pessimistic about the future. Social support was not a factor in hopelessness, anxiety, depression, or self-esteem for persons living with HIV. Thus, the impact of the HIV-positive diagnosis is short-lived for most traits but significant for pessimism. However, crisis or turning points for those who are HIV positive may cause instability in personality traits such as anxiety and depression. Finally, lower levels of anxiety and depression, coupled with higher levels of self-esteem, may provide coping mechanisms for HIV-positive individuals. Similarly, Woods, Antoni, Ironson, and Kling (1999) found that women who actively employed religious coping strategies (e.g., prayed more than usual, tried to find comfort in religion) were less depressed and anxious than those who did not. Interestingly, public religious behavior, including attending religious services and having spiritual discussions with others, was not related to lower levels of depression and anxiety. As with Green et al. (1996), this suggests that personality traits such as depression and anxiety remain fairly stable in the face of dramatic life changes. In addition, interacting with others, in the form of social support (Green et al., 1996) or in a religious context (Woods et al., 1999), seems to have little impact on those traits. Finally, Brashers et al. (2000) examined uncertainty as a motivation for particular communicative strategies employed by persons living with AIDS/HIV. Drawing on responses in six focus groups, the authors found that individual internal appraisals of uncertainty (e.g., uncertainty about AIDS represents danger or opportunity) influenced how participants managed that uncertainty. For example, active information seeking was a common strategy used to manage uncertainty associated with danger. The authors concluded that uncertainty reduction involves a complex interplay of individuals' cognitions associated with uncertainty, emotional responses, and evaluations of uncertainty management efforts.

Heijmans and De Ridder (1998) were interested in the relationship between illness representations and personality traits in persons with Addison's disease (AD) and chronic fatigue syndrome (CFS). Illness representations include an individual's beliefs, emotions, knowledge, and experiences with a disease. Addison's disease and chronic fatigue syndrome have similar symptoms, but the former is better understood than the latter. The greater ambiguity associated with CFS seems to influence how individuals conceptualize their illness. Persons with AD who were more optimistic tended not to view the disease as part of their identity and felt they had control over the disease. Persons with CFS who were more optimistic tended to view the time-line for the disease as temporary, felt they had a measure of control over the disease, and did not view CFS as greatly impacting their lives. Greater pessimism in persons with AD was associated only with viewing the disease as a long-term, chronic problem. In contrast, pessimism in persons with CFS was associated with incorporating the disease into the person's identity, viewing the disease as a long-term problem, and having little control over the disease. Thus, personality traits influenced how persons with AD and CFS conceptualized and described their diseases.

Summary. Personality traits such as aggression, anxiety, and depression play an important role in disability and communication. Research in this area has focused primarily on persons with disabilities, examining the relationship between various personality traits and other factors, such as communication abilities, coping skills, and health. These studies demonstrate that traits are fairly stable across time, even in light of significant life stress, such as an HIV-positive diagnosis. Personality traits influence how we interpret and act on events, as well as our communication strategies with others. Research suggests that our interpretations of events and how we talk about them have a greater impact on our health than the actual events themselves.

Summary and Critique

Research in cognition, communication, and disability turns our attention to the cognitive filters underlying our interactions with others. As with the lens metaphor for communication, individuals' attitudes associated with disability or nondisability and personality traits identify, sort, categorize, and distort perceptions of others. These cognitive processes then influence message production and interpretation in interaction. In cognitive approaches, we begin to develop an understanding of why persons with and without disabilities communicate the way they do. Disability as cognition provides some avenues for empowerment in recognizing attitudes of prejudice and stereotyping that contribute to the oppression of persons with disabilities. Identifying these barriers to effective communication can prove an initial step in changing those attitudes and providing opportunities for persons with disabilities to exert their independence and participate more fully across communication contexts. Examining persons with disabilities' personality traits or states invests agency in disabled persons if such traits or states are viewed as dynamic rather than static.

However, this line of research disempowers persons with disabilities in two primary ways. First, cognitive approaches take a microscopic orientation, using individuals as the unit of analysis, thereby ignoring larger institutional, societal, and cultural issues that contribute to the oppression of persons with disabilities. Second, the disability as cognition metaphor casts persons with disabilities as Other in interactions with nondisabled persons; ableists and how they communicate become the norm. Still, we gain some glimpses into how individuals conceptualize and constitute aspects of disability. However, this view provides more of an instant snapshot than a streaming video.

DISABILITY IN CULTURE

Examining disability in culture focuses on the cultural influences that shape definitions, experiences, and constructions of disability in a particular culture (Whyte, 1995). Attempting to develop a definition of disability for the collection of comparable data at the international level has proved difficult due to cultural and societal interpretations and constructions of disability (Brown, 1991). Robillard (1999) observed that cultural constructions of disability, and more specifically paralysis, "limit and distort what the paralyzed person can do" (p. 183).

Cultural definitions of illness and health underscore the evaluative dimensions of disability. Williams (1998) argued that in Western cultures, illness is associated with deviance and health is associated with conformity. Although Williams's arguments focus primarily on the recalcitrant nature of bodies in terms of emotions and sensuality, the application to disability in culture is evident. More than a condition of the body, health emerges in an individual's interactions with others. What counts as health or illness stems from cultural beliefs and values manifested in everyday conversation and mediated communication. The body and culture share a reflexive relationship in that the body must be viewed "as *both* shaped by and active shaper of society and social relations" (Williams, 1998, p. 453). Thus, although definitions of disability are culturally bound, persons with disabilities participate in and influence those definitions of disability. However, the degree to which persons with disabilities participate in their identity definitions remains contested.

The disability in culture metaphor parallels the performance metaphor of communication, which emphasizes enactment, co-constructing, and folklore (Putnam et al., 1996). The performance metaphor signals a shift away from more mechanistic views of communication, such as communication as conduit or lens, to interactional and social conceptualizations of communication. Communication occurs between people working together or coordinating their actions, rather than within something. In addition, "meaning surfaces through retrospective sensemaking, co-constructing interpretations, and collaborative storytelling" (Putnam et al., 1996, p. 386). Researchers who view disability in culture examine literature, language, art, stories, and other aspects of culture that suggest definitions of disability and behavior expected from persons with disabilities.

Zola (1991) recounts the difficulties in telling and hearing stories of disability in Western culture. Particularly in the United States, with its can-do orientation to life, individuals learn at an early age to ignore those things that cannot be fixed, such as persons with disabilities. What constitutes success and failure in Western culture makes the telling of stories of disability difficult. Success stories entail those who live in a world of nondisableds and for whom disability is not a part of their self-definition. Successful individuals overcome their disability against tremendous odds. In contrast, "if we fail, it's *our* problem, *our* personality, *our* weakness" (Zola, 1991, p. 161). The pleasant success stories are the ones persons without disabilities want to hear. Cultural norms influence the stories told by persons with disabilities as well as the stories that others are willing to listen to. In turn, these stories influence cultural norms, as with what is considered success and failure for persons with disabilities. In her study of oral accounts of a mentally retarded man living in a small New England town, Groce (1992) found that townspeople's beliefs about mental retardation framed their interpretations of his behaviors and their interactions with him. However, the fundamental values of independence and self-sufficiency overshadowed most inclinations toward giving the man assistance.

Life stories of persons with disabilities can provide insight into the construction of disability in the larger culture. Monks and Frankenberg (1995) examined published accounts of eight people with multiple sclerosis (MS). The stories began with the diagnosis not as a single event, but as a series of events that combined to disrupt the writers' assumptions and meanings about everyday life. In this beginning period, activities included telling others of the diagnosis, searching for information about the disease and treatment, and attended to the body's demands. The middle stories focused on the process of MS as writers balanced their work and play with the progression of the disease. For most of this time, MS was in the background, secondary to work and other activities. However, the writers expressed a similar theme of symptoms flaring up and directly impinging on daily routines. The story endings were marked by greater differences than the beginnings and middles. All writers resolved the self and body tensions, but in three distinct ways. For some, self-oriented activities were related to the disease in some way and seen as therapeutic for the body. For others, there was a general temporal ordering of their stories: acceptance, adjustment, and coping. The final group was the least time bound, centering their stories in the present, identifying qualitative differences in the phases of their lives. Monks and Frankenberg (1995) noted the uniqueness of the Western autobiography in its construction of self, as well as differences between Western and Eastern cultures in experiencing chronic illness. Thus, these stories are products of Western culture as well as influences on cultural representations of persons with disabilities.

Focusing on representations of rehabilitation in public discourses, Ingstad (1995) compared the meaning of disability in Norway and Botswana. Prior to the 1800s in Norway, persons with disabilities participated in home and social life as much they were able to. It was not until the late 1800s and early 1900s that persons with disabilities were segregated from society in specialized schools and living institutions. An emphasis on integration and normalization occurred in Botswana not long after its independence in 1966. With the help of other countries, particularly Norway, Botswana established community-based rehabilitation (CBR) with the Ministry of Health. Although promising in theory, CBR has never taken hold in Botswana. Ingstad (1995) argued that transferring Norwegian constructions of disability and rehabilitation to Botswana ignored the cultural values and history of the latter country, as well as the time frame needed for change.

Observing that most research concerned with disability and communication focuses on Western cultures, Iwakuma and Nussbaum (2000) discussed constructions of disability in Asia and Africa. Definitions of disability, the role of persons with disabilities in society, and responses to disability vary greatly across cultures. For example, disability leads to embarrassment in China; newborns with disabilities are often abandoned and public places are rarely wheelchair accessible. In contrast, the Maasai (Kenya) recognize persons with disabilities as different, but not inferior members of society. Persons with disabilities in Japan are linked with *kagare*, meaning "death, pollution, out of order, and/or decay" (Iwakuma & Nussbaum, 2000, p. 249). Because kagare contaminates by association, family members and others connected with persons with disabilities fall within this circle of stigma. Thus, families hide kin with disabilities, often discouraging their attendance at social functions. Interestingly, Valentine's (2001) analysis of recent Japanese films and television shows demonstrated an increased attention to deaf characters. However, the portrayals generally evoked stereotypes that represent deafness as a pathology and deaf persons as other, with hearing persons as the norm. Although Valentine (2001) deplored the simplistic characterizations deaf persons, he concluded that raising deaf persons' visibility brings deaf issues and Deaf culture into the public discourse.

An interest in disability representation in postcolonial countries led Uprety (1997) to "examine the images of disability/deformity in some postcolonial cultural texts, with a primary emphasis on Salman Rushdie's *Midnight's Children* and Ben Okri's *Famished Road* and *Songs of Enchantment*" (p. 367). Uprety (1997) argued that when Western and third world cultures intersect, those who find themselves at that intersection are in an in-between space of hybridity. Identities in these spaces transcend and occupy multiple cultures simultaneously. However, in the texts the researcher analyzed, individuals given gifts in these hybrid spaces, such as telepathy, are also stigmatized, deformed, alien, insane, disabled. The books' authors constructed these images of disability in opposition to the normal. Although these writers described a new kind of normality, it is nonetheless mythical and grounded in an unattainable wholeness. Persons with disabilities are repressed psychologically and politically, marginalized to the very outer reaches of society.

Contrasting disability in the modern era with the postmodern era demonstrates cultural changes in definitions of disability and the body. Mitchell (1997) analyzed two representative novels, Sherwood Anderson's *Winesburg, Ohio* (modern) and Katherine Dunn's *Geek Love* (postmodern). Anderson's book reflected the social and cultural upheavals of the time, responses to the repression associated with the Romantic era. In the novel, the main character creates a grotesque world in his dreams that develops from unchanging identities and selves, and disability remains to a large extent internalized and hidden. Not so in *Geek Love*: "With bodily aberration on display in *Geek Love*, the most intimate details of a life lived under the auspices of disability come into full view" (Mitchell, 1997, p. 352). The distance between the narrator and his grotesque vision is carefully crafted in Anderson's book, but completely erased in Dunn's. In *Geek Love*, the reader's perspective is from the first- rather than third-person and moves from the objective experience in *Winesburg, Ohio* to the subjective experience of an individual with multiple disabilities. By making this shift, Dunn forces readers to reexamine their taken-for-granted cultural assumptions associated with physical disabilities and recognize the ways that those assumptions isolate those with physical differences.

Mirzoeff (1997) traced images of blindness in well-known paintings and photographs from the 1600s to the 1980s. In France in the late 17th century, "the simple binary opposition between the able-bodied and the disabled did not exist. . . . The artists of the period were quick to figure blindness and deafness as complex metaphors in their work" (Mirzoeff, 1997, p. 384). In the 20th century, blindness was used as a tool to produce art, with the artist controlling process and product. Blindness was also gendered, used to represent insight, creativity and courage in men, and lack of sight in women. Mirzoeff (1997) concluded that in art as in language, the imperfect body implicates a perfect body that exists in the artistic, linguistic, and physical worlds.

In addition to defining health, illness, and disability, culture and society demarcate what we should know and not know about these phenomena. O'Neill (1990) argued that in the case of AIDS, "A structure of ignorance . . . generates the fear of

AIDS upon which so much public energy is expended" (p. 331). Misinformation and ignorance, like definitions, frame individuals' understandings of disability and their interactions with persons with disabilities. A content analysis of popular African American magazines identified four main themes in HIV/AIDS articles: terminology and definitions, prevention, trends, and education (Krishnan, Durrah, & Winkler, 1997). The researchers found that the magazines provided little new information and ignored important issues, such as new treatments, discriminatory practices, and the political policy. In their study of women living with HIV/AIDS in Australia, Bennett and Travers (1999) found that for women, the stigmatism and isolation associated with AIDS "are likely to be compounded by the expectations of gender-defined behaviors and by the special needs arising from social roles" (p. 240). A study of sexual practices along the Trans-Africa Highway in Kenya revealed the influence of cultural beliefs on behavior and attitudes toward AIDS (Cameron, Witte, & Nzyuko, 1999). Skepticism toward foreign involvement in HIV/AIDS campaigns, belief in fatalism, and stereotypes associated with AIDS constrained the kinds of information study participants both would and could obtain.

Gender also plays a role in the cultural construction of AIDS. Bird (1996) examined the 1991 AIDS hoax that began with a letter to the editor of *Ebony* magazine. The author of the letter, CJ, claimed to have AIDS and purposefully was infecting men with the disease. A television news magazine picked up the story, and the tale spread rapidly. Bird (1996) argued that, like folklore, news is grounded in cultural beliefs, values, and attitudes. However, for a story to capture the attention of the media and their audiences, it must resonate with the members of the culture. As with earlier depictions of persons with disabilities as villains, the person with AIDS takes revenge on others for her disability. The researcher suggested that the narrative played on straight men's fear of AIDS, women, and gays, and women's fantasies of revenge. The hoax's success rested on cultural constructions of AIDS and African American women's sexuality.

In a similar vein, Pittam and Gallois (1997) observed first-year Australian university students discussing HIV and AIDS. The researchers found that although participants blamed outgroups for HIV and AIDS, blame was distributed across a variety of others and not confined to gays and intravenous drug users. However, nonnatives were most frequently the targets of blame, with discourse about HIV/AIDS linked to expressions of racism. Of greatest concern was discussants' acceptance of derogatory statements about nonnatives living in Australia. Because participants were strangers, the authors theorize that politeness norms superceded any impetus to rebuke speakers for racist statements. However, in a later study, Pittam and Gallois (2000) found that in discussions of personal responsibility for HIV transmission, Australian undergraduates would use racist language when talking about cultural groups perceived as most unlike themselves.

Cultural constructions of identity influence definitions of specific disabilities. Jones's (1998) examination of two AIDS celebrities in Hong Kong revealed cultural differences between Eastern and Western responses to celebrities who disclosed their HIV/AIDS status. In the U.S., positive media coverage of AIDS celebrities tends to ignore the effects of the disease on disenfranchised groups, such as the poor. Comparing two AIDS celebrities in Hong Kong, Jones's (1998) analysis suggested that the social construction of AIDS involves a complex negotiation process that includes, in this case, the Hong Kong government, the media, the public, and the person living with AIDS. Different cultures will bring different participants to the mix, resulting in different constructions of AIDS and the role of the AIDS celebrity in cultural perceptions of AIDS. Similarly, in their study of Earvin "Magic" Johnson's role as an AIDS celebrity in HIV prevention messages, Flora, Schooler, Mays, and Cochran (1996) concluded that receivers' beliefs, sociocultural identity, and cultural groups influenced definitions of AIDS and persons living with AIDS.

Arguing that the "media are important mirrors of society, and in the case of disability issues, media are crucial in framing issues for the general public" (p. 229), Haller and Ralph (2001a) compared news coverage of disability in the U.S. and Great Britain. In a quantitative content analysis of major U.S. newspapers, hard news (rather than feature or specialty columns) comprised the largest number of disability-related stories, although most were in the local or metro section. In addition, over one third of the stories were features that tended toward an inspirational focus. Most important, journalists infrequently cited persons with disabilities as sources in news stories. A qualitative analysis of a popular British soccer coach's disparaging comments about persons with disabilities found that the press generally rejected the comments as inappropriate and politically incorrect. However, the media presented little information associated with disability issues, focusing on the coach and soccer. In another study examining U.S. and British journalism, Haller and Ralph (2001b) found few differences between the two countries in coverage of disability issues associated with physician-assisted suicide. The authors identified six news frames that highlight the degree that the media in both countries ignored the concerns of persons with disabilities on this contentious topic.

More than simply framing disability issues, Longmore's (1997) analysis of telethons in the U.S. suggested that this type of media event acts as a cleansing ritual for persons without disabilities, to the detriment of persons with disabilities. Often emphasizing patriotic themes, telethons for charity organizations blend the unique and conflicting American values of individualism, altruism, competition, and community. These media productions typically cast persons without disabilities as independent givers, implying that persons with disabilities are dependent takers. Longmore (1997) argued that as cultural rites, telethons reflect and reinforce social class differences in the U.S. by promoting big contributors (wealthy persons without disabilities) and middle-class persons with disabilities while ignoring the poor. Making the contribution process public gives persons without disabilities a false sense of power over their own destinies, validating their identities, while at the same time invalidating the identities of persons with disabilities. An analysis of the United Way's founding and subsequent campaigns revealed similar patterns (Barton, 2001). The result of using fear, pity, admiration, and efficiency appeals in soliciting donations from persons without disabilities "regularly diminishes the experience of people with disabilities and ultimately diminishes the understanding of disability by society at large" (Barton, 2001, p. 195).

Summary and Critique

Culture strongly influences the meanings of disability and the role of persons with disabilities in society. As Iwakuma and Nussbaum (2000) argued, "religious systems of the cosmology in a culture have a great impact on how people view sickness, health, and/or the disability" (p. 246). How individuals talk and write about disability is culturally bound, yet communication also influences cultural constructions of disability. Peters (1996) reminded us: "Cross-culturally and throughout recorded history, people with disabilities have been differentially ac-corded special status—whether as blind shamans with spiritual powers, as martyrs under Islamic law, or as entertainers and spectacles in early European travelling shows" (p. 218). The disability in culture metaphor highlights the performative nature of culture and the ways in which individuals collectively enact definitions of disability. Individuals participate in culture's development, maintenance, and change. As persons with disabilities participate in public discourse, they exercise a greater influence over definitions of disability. Haller and Ralph (2001a) suggested that "accurate and empowering media content could lead to societies becoming more accepting of people with disabilities as equal members" (p. 250). Still, the impact of negative media portrayals of persons with disabilities on cultural beliefs cannot be underestimated (Hahn, 1987). Further, although the media may have the power to alter cultural depictions of persons with disabilities, without access to media organizations and messages, persons with disabilities face a difficult task in bringing about change.

Examining disability in culture underscores both the potential to oppress and the potential to empower persons with disabilities. As Robillard (1999) observed, "If the assaults do not come from the actual disease, they come from the cultural typifications of individuals afflicted by it. The cultural notions of competence are not forgiving" (p. 183). Often these cultural typifications disenfranchise persons with disabilities: "A silence overshadows the experience of disability when it is construed with notions of stigma and shame. This silence skips over the difficulty of surviving a marginalizing process" (Hogan, 1998a, p. 78). To the extent that persons with disabilities participate in cultural discourses concerning disability, disabled persons influence those discourses in empowering ways. To the extent that persons with disabilities remain excluded from those discussions and defined as "as not quite human" (Peters, 1996, p. 218), then disabled persons will face continued oppression. Moreover, Corker (1998a) argued that this cultural model, by focusing only on the social construction of disability to the neglect of impair-ment, ignores the pragmatic aspects of disability. Although the disability in culture metaphor brings to the foreground the crucial role of belief and value systems in the communication of disability, the metaphor backgrounds the practical day-to-day living with disability.

DISABILITY AS CULTURE

Research within the disability as culture metaphor pursues two paths: (a) intercultural communication between disabled and nondisabled persons; and (b) distinct disability cultures, as with Deaf culture. Research in the first perspective focuses on communication problems in disabled-nondisabled interactions, whereas research in the second perspective examines cultural artifacts, practices, and identity issues. Both lines of research share the symbol metaphor of communication, in which "communication is *interpretation* through the production of symbols that make the world meaningful" (Putnam et al., 1996, p. 386). In this review, discussion of this metaphor centers on earlier and more traditional conceptualizations of culture as it has been applied to disability. Later critical research, discussed in the chapter's next section, addresses the political nature of disability and disability culture more directly.

Intercultural Communication

From the intercultural perspective, "many of the problems experienced by disabled persons result from social stereotypes and conflicting norms in the environment of society rather than from the functional limitations created by persons' disabilities" (Emry & Wiseman, 1987, p. 22). For example, Braithwaite (1990) conducted in-depth interviews with individuals who acquired physical disabilities after birth. Study participants' experiences followed a three-stage cultural assimilation premised on Goffman's (1963) concept of stigma: isolation, recognition of differentness, and incorporating disability into their identity. This last step clearly moved participants into the disability culture. In a related study, Braithwaite (1991) explored how persons with visible physical disabilities maintained privacy boundaries in interactions with others. In-depth interviews with 24 participants revealed four strategies: responding to direct questions, delaying disclosure, handling inappropriate questions, and initiating disclosure. The findings suggest that persons with visible physical disabilities do not enjoy the same privacy as those without such disabilities and must use different strategies to control those boundaries. Braithwaite's (1993) later study further identified the intercultural nature of communication between persons with disabilities and persons without, finding distinct differences in conceptualizations of helping situations, as well as the risks and benefits involved for both groups of participants. Based on this and similar research, Braithwaite and Labrecque (1994) suggested that, "Future efforts of communication and rehabilitation specialists should help persons with disabilities gain awareness of, and skills in, communicating in a predominantly ablebodied culture" (p. 291). Questioning the broad application of stigma to persons with disabilities, Cahill and Eggleston (1995) examined the public kindness of walkers (persons who do not use wheelchairs) toward persons who use wheelchairs. In documenting instances of intended kindness, the researchers argued that linking stigma and deviance to persons with disabilities glosses complex issues in social interactions. Both walkers and wheelchair users must confront issues of face (identity) and place (status) in helping situations. When asking for uncommon assistance, wheelchair users may lose face as well as place in acknowledging their dependence on walkers. In turn, walkers may lose face when offering unsolicited help and lose place if their assistance attempt fails. Cahill and Eggleston (1995) concluded, "in public life at least, the issue is not so much whether wheelchair users are stigmatized, liminal, or normal but under what conditions and how" (p. 696).

Extending on the often stigmatized role of persons with disabilities in society, Agne, Thompson, and Cusella (2000) explored the intersection of face, stigma, and self-disclosure in HIV/AIDS patient-provider interactions. The decision to reveal one's HIV-positive status poses a threat to face, yet not disclosing may negatively impact treatment. Respondents reported that health reasons and feelings of responsibility toward the health care provider influenced their decision to reveal their HIV-positive status. The researchers found that health care providers' management of patients' face needs mediated feelings of stigma associated with HIV/AIDS.

In a study of over 100 U.S. college students with disabilities, Zimmermann and Spano (1995) found that nearly 60% of the students encountered discrimination by faculty members at some point in their college experience. Students with learning disabilities reported significantly more instances of discrimination by faculty than students with other disabilities. These perceptions of discrimination negatively influenced students' confidence in their communication skills with instructors and positive feelings about those interactions. Participants reported "instructor hostility, disbelief, rudeness, insensitivity, lack of cooperation, and inflexibility" in response to the disability (Zimmermann & Spano, 1995, p. 12). These study results suggest that, from the perspective of students with disabilities, faculty view them as strangers, distinctly different from nondisabled students.

Smith and Kandath (2000) suggested that conceptualizing communication between persons who are blind or visually impaired and persons who are sighted is best understood as an intercultural context. This view highlights issues associated with turn-taking in conversations, which often relies on visual cues. The authors stress the importance of vocal turn-taking cues in interactions with persons who are blind or visually impaired. In the workplace, efforts to increase cultural diversity have largely ignored persons who are blind or visually impaired. Cultural diversity discourse rarely includes persons with disabilities, with references to persons who are blind or visually impaired even more scarce.

Disability Culture

Research from the second perspective on disability as culture examines cultural artifacts, practices, and identity issues. These researchers are less concerned with improving communication between persons with and without disabilities and more concerned with detecting unique disability cultures and cocultures. Frey, Adelman, and Query (1996) argued that a cultural perspective "sheds light on the reciprocal connections among the physical, psychological and societal worlds of health by linking the body, mind and collective" (p. 386). These researchers identified metaphors, myths, and rituals associated with death, dying, and depression in the everyday communicative practices of persons with AIDS living in a residential facility. The authors concluded that the development of cultural practices sustained the community and provided coping mechanisms for study participants as they grappled with repeated loss. Further elaborating on this line of research, Frey, Adelman, Flint, and Query (2000) found that, in addition to the importance of everyday activities and special rituals in the construction of community, communicative practices associated with governing the facility and social support also proved fundamental to the group's culture.

Deaf culture has received particular attention in research on persons with disabilities. Several researchers differentiate between deafness as the physical inability to hear sounds and deafness as membership in a cultural community (e.g., Corker, 1998a, 1998b; Luey, Glass, & Elliott, 1995; Rose, 1992, 1994, 1995; Rose & Smith, 2000). Focusing on Deaf culture moves deafness out of the medical model and a pathological definition to a concern with deaf persons' experiences and interpretations of their social worlds. Rose (1994) argued that "being deaf . . . means far more than an inability to hear. The capitalized *Deaf* signifies membership in a rich, complex culture, a culture equivalent to any ethnic group because its people are connected by a specific language, American Sign Language" (p. 144). Similarly, Henderson and Hendershott (1991) identified American Sign Language (ASL) as a significant cultural indicator in the deaf community. Yet, hearing parents with deaf children may avoid using ASL because they fear the stigma associated with it in the hearing world. As Rose observed, "until they attend a deaf residential school, most deaf children of hearing parents have little grasp of any language or of Deaf culture" (p. 148).

ASL and other sign languages constitute just one part of Deaf culture. Wilson (1997) stresses the importance of Deaf arts, including theater, dance, songs, and poetry, in the creation and maintenance of Deaf culture. In a semiotic analysis of a student's poetry performance in ASL, Rose (1992) identified the ways in which the nonmanual aspects of signing (such as facial expressions and modulations of the hands and arms) provided essential elements in representing the poem, the performer's identity, and Deaf culture. The researcher stressed, "artistic ASL is . . . a *language of the body,* capable of communicating any idea, abstract or concrete" (p. 157). Although hearing persons may think of ASL as translating English words into signs, Rose (1994) demonstrated the performative and stylistic features of ASL literature. The researcher noted the increased movement among Deaf persons to develop art distinct from the hearing community. For example, changing the sign for *poetry* to link it with the heart "now represents Deaf poetry created in

ASL, not a concept borrowed from the hearing world" (p. 145). Analyzing ASL literature revealed the use of bodily rhythm and repetition, modification of ASL signs, visual metaphor, and body as camera as key stylistic features. Rose (1994) concluded, "we can define ASL literature as the union of language and gesture that results in linguistically structured aesthetic movement" (p. 153) that blends dance, film, and performance art.

Summary and Critique

Viewing disability as culture marks a critical shift in the social construction of disability. Consistent with the symbol metaphor of communication, the disability as culture metaphor identifies the language, narratives, rituals, and other symbols that persons with disabilities enact in the production and interpretation of disability culture and cocultures. Recognizing disabled-nondisabled interactions as intercultural communication underscores the ways in which persons without disabilities stereotype, discriminate against, and disempower persons with disabilities (Fox, Giles, Orbe, & Bourhis, 2000). The metaphor potentially empowers if "society would accept my experience as 'disability culture,' which would in turn be accepted as part of 'human diversity'" (Gill, 1994, p. 45). Thus, the possibility of empowerment for persons with disabilities exists in embracing cultural diversity across social contexts and recognizing individuals' embeddedness in multiple cultures (Kreps, 2000). For example, Parasnis (1996) argued that deaf persons are typically bilingual (ASL and English) and bicultural (Deaf and Hearing cultures). Identifying disability cultures or cocultures legitimizes disability as a positive aspect of identity, providing a tool for empowerment.

In spite of this optimistic view of the disability as culture metaphor, oppression may manifest itself in the subordination and rejection of disability culture and coculture. Moreover, identification with multiple disenfranchised cocultures (e.g., disabled, lesbian, Latina) results in increased levels of discrimination and dehumanizing treatment (Barile, 2000; Vernon, 1998). Vernon maintained that, "disabled people, because of the stigma of being impaired, are also excluded from the movements of 'race,' gender and sexuality" (p. 209). Further, Sprague and Hayes (2000) argued, "for people with disabilities, as diverse as they are, to be empowered requires that members of all marginalized groups are empowered" (p. 680). Moreover, conceptualizing interactions between persons with and without disabilities as intercultural communication may cast persons with disabilities as Other and persons without disabilities as the norm or dominant culture. Persons with disabilities are then expected to adapt to a nondisabled world.

An emphasis on disability culture and cocultures may also pose conflicts for persons with disabilities. For example, controversy exists within the Deaf culture concerning the extent to which deafness constitutes a disability (Dolnick, 1993; McIntosh, 2000; Rose & Smith, 2000). Dolnick (1993) observed that for many in the deaf community, "deafness is not a disability" (p. 37). Thus, "talk of cures and breakthroughs and technological wizardry is both inappropriate and offensive" (p.

43). However, Tucker (1997) detected a dilemma in this argument, asserting, "Deaf people cannot claim to be disabled for purposes of demanding accommodations under laws such as the ADA, yet claim that deafness is not a disability and thus efforts to cure deafness should cease" (Tucker, 1997, p. 36). Shultz (2000) critiqued Tucker's analysis as simplistic and one-sided, ignoring the financial, cultural, and identity implications of cochlear implants and other corrective surgery. Still, Shultz (2000) asked: "As technological fixes for deafness such as the cochlear implant and closed-captioning devices advance, can Deaf people continue to maintain their culture and identity?" (p. 268). In this respect, the disability as culture metaphor may oppress those it seeks to empower by eschewing new technology that will likely bring about cultural change.

DISABILITY AS POLITICS

Disability as politics recognizes issues of power inherent in the social construction of disability and disability cultures or cocultures (Hogan, 1998a; Oliver, 1996; Scotch, 2000; Stubbins, 1988). From this perspective, culture takes on the added dimension of power (Wade, 1994). Lull (2000) stressed the importance of symbolic power and cultural influence: "Cultural uses of symbolic power reflect how, in the situated realms of everyday life, groups and individuals construct, declare, and enact their cultural identities and activities, and how those expressions and behaviors influence others" (p. 174). The disability as politics metaphor entails the metaphor of voice for communication, which emphasizes the *"expression or suppression"* (Putnam et al., 1996, p. 389) of individuals' and groups' voices. This communication metaphor draws attention to the power of dominant groups to control access to and exclude less powerful others from participating in the social milieu. The metaphor also emphasizes the possibilities for multiple voices to participate in the construction of social and cultural institutions and identities.

Yet persons with disabilities historically have been denied access to public forums that allow the enactment of their cultural identity. As Scotch (2000) observed, "People with disabilities face a variety of barriers to social participation, including limited human capital, social isolation, and cultural stereotypes" (p. 221). In his critique of art and culture, Hevey (1997) argued that "disabled people have not an input, let alone a controlling interest, in culture and representation done in our name" (p. 209). The result, Peters (1996) argued, is this: "People with disabilities have largely assimilated these tarnished images in society and the academy" (p. 219). Defining people as disabled has real consequences: "This labelling process leads to us being excluded from all spheres of social life, and allows people to treat us either as morons or as creatures from another planet" (Brisenden, 1986, p. 175).

The disability rights movement rejects restrictive and derogatory definitions of disability (Marks, 1999; Oliver, 1996). Defining herself as crippled, yet "hardly disabled at all," Mairs (1996) underscored the politics of naming: "Whoever gets to define ability puts everyone else in place which . . . then becomes other, outside: a cheerless and chilly spot" (pp. 13–14). The power to name, define, and label is crucial in constructing identity (Eiesland, 1994; Peters, 1996). Marks (1999) referred to this linguistic move as "defiant self-naming" (p. 146). Moreover, "open display of difference is thus a political act which challenges the 'normals' who may well feel uncomfortable with such language" (Marks, 1999, p. 147).

Empowering persons with disabilities provides the central focus of the disability as politics metaphor. Corker (1998a) refers to this political view of disability as "a materialist framework which is focused on the social and economic structures which create disability oppression" (p. 5, emphasis omitted). For example, Eiesland (1994) provided a provocative analysis of Christian theology's failure to recognize contributions by persons with disabilities to the church. Indeed, Eiesland argued, the Christian church continues to stigmatize and discriminate against disabled persons. To truly include persons with disabilities in Christian theology, Eiesland proposed a disabled God, the resurrected Jesus Christ, who "is not only the one from heaven but the revelation of true personhood, underscoring the reality that full personhood is fully compatible with the experience of disability" (p. 100). Recognizing a disabled God empowers persons with disabilities to embrace Christianity as a complete member of the church, rather than as an outsider in a nondisabled religious world.

In their analysis of John Callahan's cartoons, Shultz and Germeroth (1998) deconstructed the humorist's cartoons to demonstrate the ways that the author presents disability as a normal part of human existence. The researchers identified three antithemes in which "Callahan reveals his purpose in the opposite" (Shultz & Germeroth, 1998, p. 238). The cartoons reject stereotypes of persons with disabilities through exaggeration, caricature, satire, and embellishment. For readers to understand the gag, they must face their own prejudices associated with disability. Like Eiesland's (1994) disabled God, Callahan's cartoons disassemble the disabled-nondisabled dichotomy and openly confront oppressive and disempowering social constructions of persons with disabilities.

Individuals who become deaf because of illness, disease, or an accident, often find themselves divided between the oral/hearing world of the past and the visual/ deaf world of the present. As Hogan (1998a) observed, "The onset of hearing loss sets up a paradoxical process: one is different yet one stays the same" (p. 78). When people lose their ability to hear, they typically undergo multiple rehabilitation attempts to restore their hearing or, at a minimum, help them adapt to a hearing world. This rehabilitation process embodies a site of intense power struggles, as deafened people assert self-determination and independence in their interactions with health care providers, who strive to assimilate deafened people into the hearing world. Yet, even as persons with acquired deafness move into the Deaf culture, they retain their roots in "the commonsense world of Oralism" (p. 86). Hogan found that personal associations provided important resources for the development of a new identity that incorporated deafness in positive and multifaceted ways.

Powerful-powerless relationships become particularly apparent in interactions between deaf and hearing people. Rose and Smith (2000) argue that in such interactions, hearing persons expect deaf persons to accommodate to the communication situation, thus consciously or unconsciously asserting the hearing culture's higher status. The authors describe the interactions as involving symbolic violence that privileges spoken language over signed language. Focusing on the embodied and visual aspects of communication, both in signing and in speaking, suggests a way to shift the power imbalance in deaf-hearing interactions to one of greater equality.

The disability as politics metaphor draws attention to "the human body [as] a powerful symbol conveying messages that have massive, social, economic, and political implications" (Hahn, 1988b, p. 29). Focusing on the body brings to the forefront fundamental cultural notions of health and fitness. Gillespie (2001) interviewed 16 individuals with asthma about their encounters with the U.S. Medicaid system. If inadequately treated, often the case for those who rely on Medicaid, asthma leads to disability and sometimes death. The interviews revealed disciplining the body as central to an understanding of power issues associated with disability: Health care organizations seek to manage individuals' health care practices and those individuals seek to exert control over their bodies. For example, study participants developed strategies to work the system to achieve their health care goals, gaining access to medications, appointment slots, and providers routinely denied Medicaid patients. Thus, in the face of oppression, these asthma patients found ways to fight back and take at least some control over their own health care decisions. In addition, what health care providers interpret as noncompliance or defiance typically stems from patients' living conditions and economic situations.

Although researchers typically associate discourse of the body with physical disabilities, Warin (2000) argued that defining schizophrenia as solely a disability of the mind reflects a false mind-body dichotomy. The researcher examined how persons diagnosed with schizophrenia talked about their bodies in their everyday lives. Study participants reported that outsiders watched them bathe and go about other daily routines. The participants went to great lengths to assure their personal and spatial privacy, such as wearing clothes in the shower and fortifying their homes against intruders. This sense of exposure has profound implications: "People feel vulnerable, powerless and embarrassed with the constant lack of private space" (p. 128). These findings emphasize the importance of embodied experiences in mental as well as physical disabilities. In addition, the study legitimized the discourse of persons with mental disabilities. As Prendergast (2001) observed, "To be mentally disabled is to be disabled rhetorically. . . . The mentally ill are treated as devoid of rhetoric" (p. 57).

The controversy over cochlear implants also centers on disciplining the bodies of deaf people. Hogan (1998b) analyzed this debate, arguing that the use of cochlear implants goes beyond a conflict between oralists (hearing and speaking persons) and the deaf community. The root of the issue lies in an understanding of power as not something possessed by an individual or group, but a process that legitimizes social relationships. In this latter sense, the practice of cochlear implant surgery in deaf and deafened persons arises from privileging hearing over sign language. Hogan's analysis revealed that national and state governments, professions associated with cochlear implant programs, cochlear implant manufacturers, and the media form a powerful coalition in promoting an oralist or hearing view of deafness and deaf persons. Although part of these programs, deaf and deafened persons' "acting may result as a *consequence* of these more powerful groups" (p. 493). Just as Medicaid patients must attain fit and healthy bodies to function in the breathing world (Gillespie, 2001), institutions discipline the bodies of deaf people to conform with a hearing world.

Several researchers have documented the absence of persons with disabilities in the production of media messages (e.g., Hahn, 1987; Haller & Ralph, 2001a; Ross, 1997, 1998). However, circumstances may converge to propel disability voices into mainstream media. In her analysis of newspaper coverage of the Deaf President Now movement at Gallaudet University in 1988, Kensicki (2001) found that the media depicted the movement in positive ways. A confluence of factors, including elite sources' slow response to the protest, corporate sponsorship, and protesters' personal connections with journalists, produced these positive frames. The researcher argued that the protest's success occurred in spite of a hegemonic political environment, because internal and external forces allowed for a temporary renegotiation of the status quo. Nonetheless, aside from securing a deaf president for the university, the movement failed to produce a permanent move toward empowerment. Kensicki (2001) concluded that defining persons with disabilities as Other or separate allowed persons without disabilities to support the movement, yet keep their own lives unchanged.

In contrast to Kensicki's (2001) findings, a recent study of policy changes in the U.S. suggested that redefining disability in civil rights terms directly influenced public policy, leading to the passage of the Americans with Disabilities Act in 1990. Content analyzing newspapers and Congressional hearing records, Jeon and Haider-Markel (2001) charted the change in the media's portrayal of disability as a medical issue to disability as a social and political issue. The researchers linked this change to Congress's increasingly positive stance toward the protection of persons with disabilities' civil rights. Most importantly, disability activists successfully set the agenda and tone of the policy discussions.

Personal narratives of disability reflect larger issues of cultural empowerment and oppression, as Crossley (1999) found in three case studies of persons living with HIV. Analysis of the narratives revealed three themes in interpreting the HIV-positive diagnosis: the person's continued normality in everyday life, a conversion to an improved life, and the loss of the person's previous life. The researcher argued that these narratives demonstrate the ways that the personal becomes political. Life-as-normal narratives represent a politics of refusal to accept HIV infection as a disability. The better-life narratives represent a politics of self focusing on awareness and personal growth. The loss narratives represent a politics of rejection in which the individual will not "appropriate the predominant forms of sense making available within contemporary culture" (p. 117). Ultimately, the narratives reflect the "personal and cultural fight for patients to be treated as something more than a biological entity infected by disease" (p. 117).

Interviewing persons with disabilities, particularly those with a highly stigmatized disability such as HIV/AIDS, inherently problematizes individual morality (Crossley & Crossley, 1998). In-depth interviews with 38 persons living with HIV revealed the moral accounts interviewees employed in balancing the tension between empowerment discourse and the sick or disabled role. The researchers concluded that although strategies differed, all interviewees followed the same pattern of making empowering statements, then reframing those statements within cultural norms associated with the sick role. Thus, on the one hand, the interviewees emphasized their independence, self-determination, and inclusion in public life, yet, on the other hand, they provided accounts to explain their sick-role behaviors, such as not working or not being involved in a sexual relationship. This inherent tension between empowerment and sick-role discourses stems from the larger problem that "HIV-positive individuals occupy an ill-defined social space" (p. 172).

This empowerment-dependent duality surfaces in the larger disability community as well. In an ethnography of a self-advocacy organization for people labeled developmentally disabled, Epp (2000) examined discourse associated with disability. Organization members drew a dichotomy between the disabled body as passive, requiring assistive technologies, and the disabled mind, which could be educated and improved. Definitions of identity incorporated empowering language, such as "goodness, mobility, high-functioning, self-control, verbal communication and an able mind," whereas expressions of disabled other included disempowering terms such as "bad, low functioning, needing supervision or control by others, non-verbal and rooted-in/confined-to the body" (Epp, 2000, p. 143). This dichotomized identity reflects discursive practices in the larger culture that associate health and normality with empowerment and disability and illness with dependence.

Feminist theory plays an important role in the empowerment process, particularly for women with disabilities (e.g., Hillyer, 1993; Marston, 1999; Meekosha, 1997; Wendell, 1996, 1997; Westhaver, 2000). Historically, our identities have been tied to our bodies. Although we socially construct the self, our bodies are part of the package (e.g., Do & Geist, 2000; Mitchell & Snyder, 1997; Shilling, 1997; Thomson, 1997; Wendell, 1996, 1997). Feminist theories problematize the oppression of persons with disabilities as societal, relational, and personal. The intersection of feminist theory with disability "provides us with a recognition and reminder of how a false normate standard of ability is socially constructed for human bodies—an unrealistic and damaging standard" (Marston, 1999, p. 269). Wendell (1997) argued that feminist theories foreground the ways that "disabled people can participate in marginalizing ourselves. We can wish for bodies we do not have, with frustration, shame, and self-hatred" (p. 268). Westhaver's (2000) description of a feminist phenomenological approach to women and disability illustrated how talk about their bodies by women with disabilities centered on five themes: not different, different, rejection, acceptance, and skepticism. Analysis of these themes identified body discourses as sites of resistance to societal and cultural norms that devalue the differentiated body. Women developed empowered individual perspectives on their bodies, ignoring negative societal definitions. Yet, body talk also provided sites of acquiescence or disempowerment in which participants incorporated negative views of disability into their own identities.

Critiquing the production of knowledge, Sprague and Hayes (2000) argued that research on disability stems from an inherently male bias, objectifying and decontextualizing knowledge. In addition, researchers individualize and dichotomize phenomena, such as disabled-nondisabled and body-mind, ignoring the possible linkages between two seemingly disparate elements. To understand self-determination and empowerment for persons with developmental disabilities, the authors suggested moving away from a privileged and individual standpoint, to one that focuses on relationships and connections. In their analysis of the literature on self-determination, the researchers "find what feminists see when they look at other aspects of mainstream knowledge: an objectified individual that appears detached from a context and separate from, perhaps even the dichotomous opposite of, 'us'" (p. 678). Empowerment discourse follows similar themes, suggesting that power is something given to persons with disabilities or requires exercising power or control over people and objects. In contrast, Sprague and Hayes advocated viewing empowerment as the ability to accomplish everyday tasks, manage relationships, and define one's own identity. Such a perspective emphasizes empowering relationships that connect clients and providers, the cared for and caretakers, and immediate kinships and friendships to larger social networks. From feminist standpoint theory, self-determination and empowerment become intertwined, erasing the artificial dichotomy between disabled-nondisabled and foregrounding the interdependence of social actors.

Integrating feminist and cultural theories, Marston (1999) critiqued the use of "disability as a metaphor for embodiment in cyberspace" (p. 271), arguing that occupational injuries stem from unrealistic cultural expectations concerning the physical aspects of work and the role of technology in extending the boundaries of the body. Thus, repetitive strain injury (RSI) in a college newsroom becomes more than a work-related disability; RSI represents the results of socialization into a profession that discourages activism and encourages long work hours, a larger culture that embraces only the advantages of new communication technology and ignores the disadvantages, and an inattention to the concerns of working youth. Workers, whether disabled or nondisabled, are expected to adapt to workplace structures and requirements. Marston maintained that, "this inability to integrate the complex, physical realities of work and our bodies had helped foster the current epidemic of disability from work itself" (p. 277). Feminist theories, emphasizing the embodied experience of disability, bring to the forefront the ways that societal and cultural institutions create disability.

Summary and Critique

Disability as politics directly addresses issues of oppression and empowerment for persons with disabilities. The transformation of disability identity from dependent, stigmatized, and abnormal to independent, accepted, and normal constitutes the central tenet of this approach. Recognizing disability as a political and social label provides a critique of the dominant "ableist" perspective on what defines humanness and personhood. Thus, disability as politics strikes at the core of disability oppression and the power to construct one's identity. Feminist standpoint theory offers an alternative perspective on empowerment, focusing on connections among individuals and groups that identify commonalities as well as differences. For example, Sprague and Hayes (2000) described how cut curbs benefit several groups, such as parents pushing strollers, young children, and persons who use wheelchairs for mobility.

Still, the emphasis on the link between the body and identity may not resonate with some persons with disabilities, particularly those without visible disabilities. Frank (1998) warned that we "need to remember how any practice of freedom readily becomes commodified, institutionalized, and routinized into techniques of the self through which power operates" (p. 344). Moreover, Frank (1998) cautioned against co-optation and participating in alternative conceptualizations of normal that marginalize others. Barile (2000) found evidence of this marginalization based on type of disability, as well as gender and sexual orientation. The researcher reported, "a hierarchy among disability groups" (p. 124) with some disabilities enjoying a privileged status over others. Finally, Kearney (1992) and Stone (1997) remind us of the pragmatics of disability, such as accessible housing, affordable health care, reliable transportation, willing mentors, and basic economics. Although these issues intertwine with identity, identity entails one part of the process, not the endpoint.

DISABILITY AS COMMUNITY

Community derives from the Middle English word *communite*, meaning citizenry, the Old French and Latin word *commnits*, meaning fellowship, and the Latin word *commnis*, meaning common (*American Heritage Dictionary*, 2000). We typically associate *community* with those who share a common geographical location or particular beliefs or values. Although politicians and the popular press often lament the loss of community due to the Internet and increasingly fragmented social institutions, others observe that community has simply taken new forms.

Machin and Carrithers (1996) argued that traditional conceptualizations freeze community into a static, rigid form not found in everyday life. These authors asserted that communities arise from improvised conversations among individuals "extended over time and space" (p. 350). Participants may enter, stay, or leave, yet the conversation and community still exist. Consistent with a feminist standpoint theory of disability (Sprague & Hayes, 2000), community centers on connections and relationships (Whitt & Slack, 1994). As with the metaphor of discourse, in which "communication is a *conversation* . . . that focuses on both process and structure" (Putnam et al., 1996, p. 391), community moves from simply a product of interaction and organizing to a dynamic process of achieving a dynamic product. Although Oliver (1996) prefers *empowered collective* to community, Linton (1998) observed that the experience of disability provides a link or tie that goes beyond the notion of a collectivity. Moreover, the social and political nature of disability, rather than its medical indicators, form the basis of a common identity. As Linton (1998) noted, disability as community stems in part from the cultural metaphor of disability in that empowering persons with disabilities to control their own cultural narratives forms the core of community.

In a study of AIDS patients' self-advocacy and patient-physician communication, Brashers, Haas, Klingle, and Neidig (2000) posited a link between self-advocacy and collective activism. The researchers found that three factors contributed to individual self-advocacy and collective activism: education about the disease and treatment, assertiveness toward health care, and mindful nonadherence. All three were enacted at the individual and collective levels. For example, mindful nonadherence at the collective level involves civil disobedience and disruptive actions. At the individual level, mindful nonadherence involves making informed decisions about treatment that may or may not comply with the health provider's plan. The findings underscored the interplay between the individual and community, as well as the essential nature of both in effective health care.

The process of community involves a multiplicity of conversations, as Nye (2001) underscored in her analysis of the AIDS rhetoric. Nye identified four discourse communities: AIDS the Divider, AIDS the Reformer, AIDS the Empowerer, and AIDS the Educator. AIDS the Divider reflects rhetoric associated with alienation and social isolation, as well as recognition of being cast as other. AIDS the Reformer incorporates language about change and action, especially within the gay community. When promoted by those outside the community, reforms may be viewed as oppressive and restrictive. AIDS the Empowerer primarily focuses on individuals gaining control over their bodies and treatment. AIDS the Educator involves persons with AIDS educating others. Nye argued that these different discourses both compete with and complement each other. Understanding the experience of AIDS requires understanding the different discourses associated with AIDS.

Nowhere is the disability as community metaphor more evident than in Internet communication. The great equalizer for persons with disabilities, the Internet provides accessibility to public and private discourse often not possible in face-to-face communication (Borchert, 1998; Coopman, 2001; Fox, 2000; Nelson, 2000). The Internet makes practical resources readily available for persons with disabilities, such as information on travel accommodations and various health care services (Borchert, 1998). Grimaldi and Goette (1999) found that for persons with physical disabilities, the Internet greatly increases their perceived independence in the areas of employment and education. The researchers noted that how individuals use the Internet is more important than frequency of use in increasing levels of

independence. Interestingly, support from family members proved a key component in perceptions of independence and use of the Internet. Braithwaite, Waldron,
and Finn (1999) found that persons with disabilities used computer-mediated groups
for emotional and informational support.

Nelson (2000) charted four stages in the development of a sense of community
among people with disabilities. The first stage, the Dark Ages of Disability, was
characterized by the invisibility of persons with disabilities in the media and the
larger culture. Stage 2, the Awareness of Rights, grew out of a response to soldiers
returning from World War II. The third stage, Mobilization to Action, culminated
in the passage of the Americans with Disabilities Act of 1990. Finally, Stage 4, the
Revolution of Technological Community, developed in step with the Internet and
other new communication technologies. Computer-mediated communication
(CMC) provided the foundation for persons with disabilities to connect, organize,
and mobilize. Nelson (2000) maintained that "experientially, community within
cyberspace emphasizes a community of interests, usually bounded by the topic
under discussion, that can lead to a communal spirit and apparent social bonding"
(p. 189). These communities serve as sites for communication that focuses on social and pragmatic goals, as well as communication designed to engender political
action. Nelson (2000) pointed to the growing number of Web zines develop by and
for persons with disabilities as further evidence of community building, networking, and activism on the Web.

Like Machin and Carrithers's (1996) improvisation communities, cybercommuni-
ties are unbounded by place and space (Fernback, 1999). These virtual communities
are *real* in the sense that "social practices are embedded in virtual interactions;
virtual community has a felt nature for its inhabitants" (Fernback, 1999, p. 217).
Further, these communities provide spaces for the exercise of political power. As
Koerber (2001) argued, "online interaction can be politically meaningful in itself,
and . . . can supplement, rather than replace, participation in offline political arenas" (p. 232). Online communities are both local and global, or "glocalized . . . as
worldwide connectivity and domestic matters intersect" (Wellman & Gulia, 1999,
p. 187). Thus, persons with disabilities may live in disparate locations around the
world, but common experiences suggest more local conversations. Further, Mele
(1999) argued that, for disadvantaged communities, the Internet can prove a powerful tool in facilitating collective action on local and global levels. In addition, online
interaction blurs the line between public and private, bringing to the surface in
public, online interactions, issues that might have remained private, unexamined,
and unchallenged (Koerber, 2001).

Summary and Critique

Disability as community presents the most encompassing perspective, evoking
the other five metaphors. Putnam et al. (1996) warned, "Studies that mix metaphors . . . run the risk of confounding the assumptive ground" of communication
(p. 395). Yet, McCoy et al. (1999) argued, "Contrary to what may be taught in

English class, 'mixing metaphors' is very valuable because the more different views we have of a subject, the greater the probability of understanding what a thing is really like" (p. 46). Although disability as community identifies disability based on cultural indicators, rather than medical symptoms, the metaphor nonetheless includes health issues associated with disability. Stone (1997) argued that persons with disabilities must especially attend to preventive health care practices. At the same time, she noted that as a group, persons with disabilities must work for improved health care coverage; adequate health care is essential to independent living and empowerment.

Disability as community suggests new ways for pursuing research from a disability as cognition metaphor. Research in communicating disability must consider more complex relationships between cognition and communication, as well as a more complex view of disability. Disability as community implicates both commonalities and differences among persons with disabilities. In addition, community turns our attention to the social bases of cognition and the ways that communication influences cognition. The metaphor also removes the static notion of a uniform disability culture and proposes multiple cocultures found among diverse group members who share some things in common and in other ways are distinctly different.

However, Sontag (1997) warned in her discussion of persons with AIDS that community may be a double-edged sword. The community arising from those with AIDS comprises "a community of pariahs" that both brings people together and isolates them from other social groups (p. 232). This isolation leads to further oppression, discrimination, and harassment. In addition, the use of the community metaphor may gloss important differences among persons with disabilities. Based on her analysis of differing interests and power inequities, Harney (1999) argued that the relationship between gays and lesbians can be more accurately described as a coalition than a community. Moreover, Corker (1998a) cautioned against the simplistic view of a disability community, noting "social and political tension arising from the diversity which exists in our communities and which has resulted in the marginalization of particular groups" (p. 5), such as those with learning disabilities and African Americans with disabilities. Further, communities, whether online or face-to-face, may marginalize some as they seek to include others (Koerber, 2001). Finally, the disability as community metaphor may place too great an emphasis on new communication technologies in the empowerment process. For example, Roulstone (1998) found that although technology improved job capabilities of persons with disabilities, study participants were still marginalized and disenfranchised from the larger workplace culture.

SUGGESTIONS FOR FUTURE RESEARCH: THE COMMUNITY METAPHOR AND THE DIALECTICS OF DISABILITY

As with the discourse metaphor for communication, disability as community suggests new points of intersection for disability and communication research by leading us to consider the dialectics of disability and their implications for empowerment. Just as traditional communities include individuals and groups who share both differences and similarities (Whitt & Slack, 1994), the experience of disability entails this difference-unity dialectic. Wendell (1996) explained:

> Part of asserting our similarities to people without disabilities is demanding that we not be set apart by disparaging and/or unnecessary labels, and that the words used to describe or refer to us be as respectful as the words used to describe or refer to nondisabled people. Part of asserting the value of our differences is taking control of language to describe ourselves, adopting realistic and positive descriptions. (p. 77)

Like Braithwaite and Harter's (2000) autonomy-connection dialectic in persons with disabilities' interpersonal relationships, one aspect of empowerment for persons with disabilities is articulating an identity that is at once different from (autonomous) and similar to (connected) persons without disabilities. In addition, the unity-difference dialectic recognizes that persons within a community share connections and, at the same time, bring unique concerns, beliefs, and experiences to the group. Thus, future research should explore the ways that empowering relationships simultaneously engender unity and difference for persons with disabilities, as well as how individuals enact, interpret, and manage that dialectic.

The private-public dialectic is a second tension evident in the disability as community metaphor. Paralleling Braithwaite and Harter's (2000) openness-closedness dialectic, the private-public dialectic highlights the tensions between disability as a private (closedness), subjective experience (Mitchell & Snyder, 1997) and a social or public (openness) one as well (Oliver, 1996). Westhaver (2000) suggested a variant on this dialectic, with the disabled body secluded in the private world and the abled body displayed in the public world. Researching empowerment strategies must both address ways to empower individuals in their personal experiences with disability and critique larger social practices that facilitate the oppression of persons with disabilities. As Charlton (1998) observed, "oppression is experienced both individually and collectively" (p. 154). In addition, such future research must address the hidden and private, such as the sequestered histories of persons with disabilities, to make such experiences publicly available.

Third, the disability as community metaphor suggests a permanence-temporary dialectic, similar to the stability-change dialectic Braithwaite and Harter (2000) identified in interpersonal relationships. Stone (1997) and others have pointed out that persons without disabilities are only temporarily able-bodied. In addition, the experience of disability changes over time, as Stone documented in her transitions from home, to extended care facility, and back to home. The permanence-temporary dialectic also suggests the flux and transformation of oppression/empowerment. Charlton (1998) argued that the oppression of persons with disabilities enjoys a permanence in social structures and institutions. However, that permanence leads to resistance and, ultimately, empowerment and liberation. Hahn (1988b) also suggested that beauty and attractiveness share an illusory stability and gestalt;

cultural norms for beauty incorporate both attractive and unattractive features. Moreover, "early records concerning the role of disabled people in many societies indicate that . . . the physical differences represented by disabilities . . . have been perceived as socially and sexually desirable" (p. 28). Thus, future research on communicating disability should focus on longitudinal studies of the disability experience and changes over time in empowering relationships.

Particularly when applied to Internet communication, the disability as community metaphor highlights an isolation-inclusion tension, in that persons with disabilities may interact with others online, yet remain isolated from day-to-day interactions. For example, Robillard (1999) reported frequent communication with faculty on his own campus via email, yet only rare visits to his office by colleagues wanting to chat. Email facilitates Robillard's communication with friends and peers in near and distant places. Additionally, email provides him with a steady stream of information that keeps him up-to-date on personal and professional news. At the same time, email allows his coworkers to avoid interacting with him face-to-face. More systematic research on the ways in which CMC isolates or includes persons with disabilities will increase our understandings of CMC's possibilities as a tool of empowerment and a tool of oppression.

Finally, the Internet reminds us of a local-global tension in all our interactions. For persons with disabilities, this local-global dialectic presents itself most clearly in online communication that connects the local with the global. Research on empowerment strategies must address local concerns, such as reinvisioning immediate environments as accessible to all persons (Michalko & Titchkosky, 2001). At the same time, global issues affecting persons with disabilities cannot be ignored.

CONCLUSION

This literature review examined research grouped within six metaphors of disability: disability as medical problem, disability as cognition, disability in culture, disability as culture, disability as politics, and disability as community. Each metaphor suggests different research questions, methods, and interpretations of findings, and each contributes in some way to the empowerment of persons with disabilities, although those contributions vary widely. Historically, disability as a medical problem has led to stigmatizing and dehumanizing persons with disabilities. Like the conduit metaphor for communication, the medical model of disability still exerts considerable influence on research on disability and communication. Disability as cognition defines persons with disabilities as Other and, in that respect, presents a more oppressive than empowerment model. However, identifying attitudes, personality traits, and cognitive structures that impinge on the communication process suggests avenues for change.

Disability in culture provides the first, clearest step toward disability empowerment. Demonstrating differences across cultures in disability definitions underscores the social roots of disability and the oppressive nature of those definitions. This metaphor also suggests that those definitions present an opportunity for persons with disabilities to participate in the social construction of disability. Disability as culture recognizes persons with disabilities as a legitimate social group, with particular values, beliefs, and symbolic indicators. Identifying disability culture and cocultures serves to place persons with disabilities in empowering roles as producers and consumers of culture.

Disability as politics takes disability as culture to the next level of empowerment, calling for a radical shift in how we consider identity, personhood, and the body. This metaphor highlights the power in naming and defining disability, and demands a rejection of ableist definitions of disability. In addition, work within this metaphor seeks to uncover past and present hegemonic practices that have made persons with disabilities invisible. Disability as community holds great promise for empowering persons with disabilities. The metaphor embraces the diversity of disability experiences, yet emphasizes the inclusion of persons with disabilities in political, economic, and cultural discourses. The community metaphor also embraces multiple disability identities and multiple trajectories for disability activism. Finally, disability as community recognizes sources of oppression for persons with disabilities, and points to a variety of ways in which persons with disabilities enact empowerment.

Metaphors provide powerful tools for understanding the unknown or unfamiliar. Yet, in their power to illuminate and enlighten, metaphors simultaneously obscure and conceal. For example, disability as culture legitimizes disability as a positive attribute of individual and group identities, at the same time, the metaphor implies a uniform culture that ignores differences among persons with disabilities. In addition, metaphors often function outside our consciousness, structuring our interpretations and actions without critical examination. Analysis of the metaphors guiding our theory and research reveals the ways that our scholarship both oppresses and empowers persons with disabilities. The questions we ask, the assumptions we make, the methods we use, and the interpretations of our results may reinforce or challenge the status quo. Scholarship that applies empowering metaphors to communicating disability recognizes independence, inclusion, self-help, and self-determination as central to persons with disabilities, as well as to the temporarily not disabled.

NOTES

1. Many researchers do categorize deaf persons and those with hearing impairments as disabled. In the literature review, I discuss the opposing view that deaf individuals should not be considered disabled. Still, Rose and Smith (2000) argue that the debate distracts from the more fundamental devaluing of deaf communication, particularly sign language.

2. Between 1978 and 1996 studies associated with disability and communication can also be found under the key terms, *deaf*, *deaf persons*, *mental health*, *mental illness*, and *mentally disabled*.

3. Any category scheme is imperfect; some studies may fit within more than one metaphor. For example, Rose (1995) argues that the medical metaphor of disability frames Booth-Butterfield and Booth-Butterfield's (1994) research on communication apprehension in deaf persons. However, with its emphasis on the link between traits and communication, I included the study within the disability as cognition metaphor. In addition, other researchers have proposed alternative metaphors of disability. McCoy et al. (1999) posited four models or metaphors that provide additional insight into AIDS discourse and human behavior more generally: reciprocal, rational, cost-benefit analysis, puzzle models. Haller (2000a) discussed eight models evident in media narratives of disability: medical, social pathology, supercrip, business, minority/civil rights, legal, cultural pluralism, and consumer.

4. Several researchers have examined historical accounts to identify definitions of disability in practice during various time periods. In her essay on the societal foundations of disability, Winzer (1997) traced disability definitions from prehistoric times through the 1600s. In premodern history, persons with disabilities "formed a . . . minority always exposed to the prejudices of the majority, not only because they could not partake of normal life, but also because they represented evil or were seen as public threats" (pp. 77, 80). Definitions of disability were often used for legal or religious purposes to punish those who did not conform to dominant norms. Mental illnesses in particular were associated with Satan and evil. The witch hunts that began in the 1400s and lasted for 300 years resulted in the deaths of thousands of persons with disabilities. Even before those times, people generally thought the devil or some other supernatural force constituted the root of disability (Mairs, 1996). Religious and spiritual beliefs heavily influenced definitions of disability in early human history and actions taken toward persons with disabilities (Wilson & Lewiecki-Wilson, 2001).

Evidence suggests that the ancient Greeks experienced various levels of hearing loss for many of same reasons found today. Interestingly, Edwards (1997) found that "the degree of one's hearing loss never appears to be an important issue; what mattered to the Greeks was one's ability to speak" (p. 33). Those with hearing impairments who could speak were viewed much more favorably than whose who could not, because for the Greeks "language was the hallmark of human achievement, so muteness went beyond a physical condition. An inability to speak went hand-in-hand with an inability to reason, hand-in-hand with stupidity" (p. 35). Writings from early modern England indicate that deafness was defined as a physical problem that must be fixed, because being human meant being able to hear (Nelson & Berens, 1997).

The relationship between defining disability and the humanity of persons with disabilities becomes especially evident in intelligence testing, and more specifically the term Educable Mental Retardation (EMR). In the early 1980s, a National Academy of Science panel report noted that EMR was most often associated with poor, disadvantaged students. Gelb (1989) argued that accounts detailing the origins of EMR focus attention on the term's scientific roots and ignore its social purposes and uses. Yet in 1786, Benjamin Rush, a physician and signer of the Declaration of Independence, proposed a link between intelligence and morality. Rush posited that those of lesser intelligence or mental deficiencies were also subject to poorer moral reasoning. Later, in the mid-1800s, religious and moral education was viewed as crucial in the progress of the mentally deficient, which was viewed as the result of sinful behavior. Gelb argued, "The idea that [Henry H.] Goddard discovered Educable Mental Retardation [in the early 1900s] supports the modern fiction that the task of diagnosis is a technical and morally neutral one" (p. 379).

In his review of 19th century writings on disability, Davis (1997) maintained that definitions of disability must be understood within definitions of normalcy. Foucault (1973) charted a shift in medicine from the 18th to the 19th centuries. In the former, medicine focused on health and restoring functions that were lost in illness, such as strength, flexibility, and vitality. In the latter, health was replaced by normality; illness was replaced by the pathological. This parallels Linton's (1998) argument that normal implicates its opposite, abnormal, and in so doing assigns value to both terms. Although we take norms and normalcy for granted, these terms did not make their way into the English language until the mid-1800s. Davis (1997) traces the increased emphasis on normalcy and the use of statistics to measure what is within the norm and what is outside the norm. Mixing statistics, normalcy, and eugenics moved persons with disabilities outside what was considered the perfect human being and left them subject to expulsion from society. Davis reminded us: "We have largely forgotten that what Hitler did in developing a hideous policy of eugenics was just to implement the theories of the British and American eugenicists" (p. 19). Associating normal with nondisabled and abnormal with disabled affects relationships and positions in our social worlds (Linton, 1998).

REFERENCES

Agne, R., Thompson, T., & Cusella, L. (2000). Stigma in the line of face: Self-disclosure of patients' HIV status to health care providers. *Journal of Applied Communication Research, 28*, 235–261.

Alston, R., & Mngadi, S. (1992). The interaction between disability status and the African American experience: Implications for rehabilitation counseling. *Journal of Applied Rehabilitation Counseling, 23*(2), 12–16.

American Heritage Dictionary of the English Language. (2000). Boston, MA: Houghton Mifflin. Retrieved June 15, 2002, from http://www.bartleby.com/61/

Americans with Disabilities Act. (1990). Public law 336 of the 101st Congress. Retrieved June 16, 2002, from http://www.usdoj.gov/crt/ada

Anderson, C., & Martin, M. (1999). The relationship of argumentativeness and verbal aggressiveness to cohesion, consensus, and satisfaction in small groups. *Communication Reports, 12*, 21–31.

Augoustinos, M., & Walker, I. (1995). *Social cognition: An integrated introduction.* London: Sage.

Austin, B. (1984). Motivations for television viewing among deaf and hearing students. *American Annals of the Deaf, 129*, 17–22.

Austin, B., & Myers, J. (1984). Hearing-impaired viewers of prime-time television. *Journal of Communication, 34*(4), 60–71.

Axley, S. (1984). Mangerial and organizational communication in terms of the conduit metaphor. *Academy of Management Review, 9*, 428–437.

Barile, M. (2000). Understanding the personal and political role of multiple minority status. *Disability Studies Quarterly, 20*, 123–128.

Barnes, C. (1996). Theories of disability and the origins of the oppression of disabled people in western society. In L. Barton (Ed.), *Disability & society: Emerging issues and insights* (pp. 34–60). London: Longman.

Barton, E. (2001). Textual practices of erasure: Representations of disability and the founding of the United Way. In J. Wilson & C. Lewiecki-Wilson (Eds.), *Embodied rhetorics: Disability in language and culture* (pp. 169–199). Carbondale: Southern Illinois University Press.

Barton, L. (1996). Sociology and disability: Some emerging issues. In L. Barton (Ed.), *Disability & society: Emerging issues and insights* (pp. 3–17). London: Longman.

Bennett, L., & Travers, M. (1999). Stigma, secrecy, and isolation: The impact of HIV/AIDS on women in an Australian study. In W. Elwood (Ed.), *Power in the blood: A handbook on AIDS, politics, and communication* (pp. 231–241). Mahwah, NJ: Erlbaum.

Bérubé, M. (1998). Foreword: Pressing the claim. In S. Linton (Ed.), *Claiming disability: Knowledge and identity* (pp. vii-xi). New York: New York University Press.

Biklen, D. (1986). Framed: Journalism's treatment of disability. *Social Policy, 16*, 45–51.

Bird, S. E. (1996). CJ's revenge: Media, folklore, and the cultural construction of AIDS. *Critical Studies in Mass Communication, 13*, 44–58.

Blumberg, L. (1994). Public stripping. In B. Shaw (Ed.), *The ragged edge: The disability experience from the pages of the first fifteen years of the disability rag* (pp. 74–77). Louisville, KY: Avocado Press.

Bonstetter, C. (1986). Magazine coverage of mentally handicapped. *Journalism Quarterly, 63*, 623–626.

Booth-Butterfield, M., Heare, D., & Booth-Butterfield, S. (1991). The effect of communication anxiety upon signing effectiveness among the profoundly hearing-impaired. *Communication Quarterly, 39*, 241–250.

Booth-Butterfield, M., & Booth-Butterfield, S.(1994). Communication anxiety and signing effectiveness: Testing an interference model among deaf communicators. *Journal of Applied Communication Research, 22,* 273–286.

Booth-Butterfield, M., & Booth-Butterfield, S. (1995). The study of anxiety and signing as social science. *Journal of Applied Communication Research, 23,* 163–166.

Borchert, M. (1998). The challenge of cyberspace: Internet access and persons with disabilities. In E. Bosah (Ed.), *Cyberghetto or cybertopia: Race, class and gender on the Internet* (pp. 49–63). Westport, CT: Praeger.

Braithwaite, D. (1990). From majority to minority: An analysis of cultural change from ablebodied to diabled. *International Journal of Intercultural Relations, 14,* 465–483.

Braithwaite, D. (1991). "Just how much did that wheelchair cost?": Management of privacy boundaries by persons with disabilities. *Western Journal of Speech Communication, 55,* 254–274.

Braithwaite, D. (1993, February). *Interpretive analyses of how persons with disabilities communicate to manage helping situations.* Paper presented at the annual meeting of the Western States Communication Association, Albuquerque, New Mexico.

Braithwaite, D., & Harter, L. (2000). Communication and the management of dialectical tensions in the personal relationships of people with disabilities. In D. Braithwaite & T. Thompson (Eds.), *Handbook of communication and people with disabilities* (pp. 17–36). Mahwah, NJ: Erlbaum.

Braithwaite, D., & Labrecque, D. (1994). Responding to the Americans with Disabilities Act: Contributions of interpersonal research and training. *Journal of Applied Communication Research, 22,* 287–294.

Braithwaite, D., Waldron, V., & Finn, J. (1999). Communication of social support in computer-mediated groups for people with disabilities. *Health Communication, 11,* 123–151.

Brashers, D., Haas, S., Klingle, R., & Neidig, J. (2000). Collective AIDS activism and individuals' perceived self-advocacy in physician-patient interaction. *Human Communication Research, 26,* 372–402.

Brashers, D., Neidig, J., Haas, S., Dobbs, L., Cardillo, L., & Russell, J. (2000). Communication in the management of uncertainty: The case of persons living with HIV or AIDS. *Communication Monographs, 67,* 63–84.

Brinckerhoff, L., Shaw, S., & McGuire, J. (1992). Promoting access, accommodations, and independence for college students with learning disabilities. *Journal of Learning Disabilities, 25,* 417–429.

Brisenden, S. (1986). Independent living and the medical model of disability. *Disability, Handicap & Society, 1,* 173–178.

Brolley, D., & Anderson, S. (1988). Advertising and attitudes. *Journal of Leisure, 15*(3), 23–27.

Brown, S. (1991). Conceptualizing and defining disability. In S. Thompson-Hoffman & I. Storck (Eds.), *Disability in the United States: A portrait from national data* (pp. 1–14). New York: Springer.

Burleson, B., & Caplan, S. (1998). Cognitive complexity. In J. McCroskey, J. Daly, M. Martin, & M. Beatty (Eds.), *Communication and personality: Trait perspectives* (pp. 233–286). Cresskill, NJ: Hampton Press.

Byrd, E., & Elliott, T. (1985). Feature films and disability: A descriptive study. *Rehabilitation Psychology, 30,* 47–51.

Byrd, K. (1989). Theory regarding attitudes and how they may relate to media portrayals of disability. *Journal of Applied Rehabilitation Counseling, 20*(4), 36–38.

Cahill, S., & Eggleston, R. (1995). Reconsidering the stigma of physical disability: Wheelchair use and public kindness. *Sociological Quarterly, 36,* 681–698.

Cameron, K., Witte, K., & Nzyuko, S. (1999). Perceptions of condoms and barriers to condom use among the trans-Africa highway in Kenya. In W. Elwood (Ed.), *Power in the blood: A handbook on AIDS, politics, and communication* (pp. 149–163). Mahwah, NJ: Erlbaum.

Charlton, J. (1998). *Nothing about us without us: Disability, oppression and empowerment.* Berkeley: University of California Press.

Cogswell, B. (1968). Self-socialization: Readjustment of paraplegics in the community. *Journal of Rehabilitation, 34*(3), 11–13.

Coleman, L. (1997). Stigma: An enigma demystified. In L. Davis (Ed.), *The disability studies reader* (pp. 216–231). New York: Routledge.

Coleman, L., & DePaulo, B. (1991). Uncovering the human spirit: Moving beyond disability and "missed" communications. In N. Coupland, H. Giles, & J. Wiemann (Eds.), *"Miscommunication" and problematic talk* (pp. 61–84). Newbury Park, CA: Sage.

Coopman, S. (2001, October). *Independence, identity, and credibility: Persons with disabilities commandeer the Net.* Paper presented at the Association of Internet Researchers conference, Minneapolis, MN.

Condit, C., & Williams, M. (1997). Audience responses to the discourse of medical genetics: Evidence against the critique of medicalization. *Health Communication, 9,* 219–235.

Corker, M. (1998a). *Deaf and disabled or deafness disabled?* Buckingham, UK: Open University Press.

Corker, M. (1998b). Disability in a postmodern world. In T. Shakespeare (Ed.), *The disability reader: Social science perspectives* (pp. 221–233). London: Cassell.

Cragan, J., & Shields, D. (1998). *Understanding communication theory: The communicative forces for human action.* Boston: Allyn & Bacon.

Crossley, M. (1999). Making sense of HIV infection: Discourse and adaptation to life with a long-term HIV diagnosis. *Health, 3,* 95–119.

Crossley, N., & Crossley, M. (1998). HIV, empowerment and the sick role: An investigation of a contemporary moral maze. *Health, 2,* 157–174.

Davis, L. (1997). Constructing normalcy: The bell curve, the novel, and the invention of the disabled body in the nineteenth century. In L. Davis (Ed.), *The disability studies reader* (pp. 9–28). New York: Routledge.

Do, T., & Geist, P. (2000). Embodiment and dis-embodiment: Identity trans-formation of persons with physical disabilities. In D. Braithwaite & T. Thompson (Eds.), *Handbook of communication and people with disabilities: Research and application* (pp. 49–65). Mahwah, NJ: Erbaum.

Dolnick, E, (1993, September). Deafness as culture. *The Atlantic, 272,* 37–53.

Donaldson, J. (1981). The visibility and image of handicapped people on television. *Exceptional Children, 47,* 413–416.

Drake, R. (1996). A critique of the role of traditional charities. In L. Barton (Ed.), *Disability & society: Emerging issues and insights* (pp. 147–166). London: Longman.

Eakin, E., & Glasgow, R. (1997). The patients' perspective on the self-management of chronic obstructive pulmonary disease. *Journal of Health Psychology, 2,* 245–253.

Edwards, M. (1997). Constructions of physical disability in the ancient Greek world: The community concept. In D. Mitchell & S. Snyder (Eds.), *The body and physical difference: Discourses of disability* (pp. 29–51). Ann Arbor: University of Michigan Press.

Eiesland, N. (1994). *The disabled God: Toward a liberatory theology of disability.* Nashville, TN: Abingdon.

Elliott, T. R., & Byrd, E. K. (1982). Media and disability. *Rehabilitation Literature, 43,* 348–355.

Elliott, T. R., & Byrd, E. K. (1984). Attitude change toward disability through television: Portrayal with male college students. *International Journal of Rehabilitation Research, 7,* 320–322.

Emry, R., & Wiseman, R. (1987). An intercultural understanding of ablebodied and disabled persons' communication. *International Journal of Intercultural Relations, 11,* 7–27.

Epp, T. (2000). Disability: Discourse, experience and identity. *Disability Studies Quarterly, 20,* 134–144.

Erickson, J., & Omark, D. (1980). Social perceptions and communicative interactions of handicapped and normal children in a preschool classroom. *Instructional Science, 9,* 253–268.

Farnall, O., & Smith, K. (1999). Reactions to people with disabilities: Personal contact versus viewing of specific media portrayals. *Journalism & Mass Communication Quarterly, 76,* 659–672.

Fawcett, S., Paine-Andrews, A., Francisco, V., Schultz, J. Richter, K., Lewis, R., Williams, E., Harris, K., Berkley, J., Fisher, J., & Lopez, C. (1995). Using empowerment theory in collaborative partnerships for community health and development. *American Journal of Community Psychology, 23,* 677–697.

Fawcett, S., White, G., Balcazar, F., Suarez-Balcazar, Y., Matthews, R., Paine-Andrews, A., Seekins, T., & Smith, J. (1994). A contextual-behavioral model of empowerment: Case studies involving people with physical disabilities. *American Journal of Community Psychology, 22,* 471–496.

Fernback, J. (1999). There is a there there: Notes toward a definition of cybercommunity. In S. Jones (Ed.), *Doing Internet research: Critical issues and methods for examining the Net* (pp. 203–220). Thousand Oaks, CA: Sage.

Fichten, C., Amsel, R., Bourdon, C., & Creti, L. (1988). Interaction between college students with physical disabilities and their professors. *Journal of Applied Rehabilitation Counseling, 1*, 13–20.

Flora, J., Schooler, C., Mays, V., & Cochran, S. (1996). Exploring a model of symbolic social communication: The case of "Magic" Johnson. *Journal of Health Psychology, 1*, 353–366.

Fonosch, G., & Schwab, L. (1981). Attitudes of selected university faculty members toward disabled students. *Journal of College Student Personnel, 22*, 229–235.

Foucault, M. (1973). *The birth of the clinic: An archaeology of medical perception.* New York: Pantheon.

Fox, S. (2000).The uses and abuses of computer-mediated communication for people with disabilities. In D. Braithwaite & T. Thompson (Eds.), *Handbook of communication and people with disabilities* (pp. 319–336). Mahwah, NJ: Erlbaum.

Fox, S., Giles, H., Orbe, M., & Bourhis, R. (2000). Interability communication: Theoretical perspectives. In D. Braithwaite & T. Thompson (Eds.), *Handbook of communication and people with disabilities* (pp. 193–222). Mahwah, NJ: Erlbaum.

Frank, A. (1998). Stories of illness as care of the self: A Foucauldian dialogue. *Health, 2*, 329–348.

Freire, P. (1970). *Pedagogy of the oppressed* (M. B. Ramos, Trans.). New York: Seabury.

Frey, L., Adelman, M., Flint, L., & Query, J. (2000). Weaving meaning together in an AIDS residence: Communicative practices, perceived health outcomes, and the symbolic construction of community. *Health Communication, 5*, 53–72.

Frey, L., Adelman, M., & Query, J. (1996). Communication practices in the social construction of health in an AIDS residence. *Journal of Health Psychology, 1*, 383–397.

Funk, R. (1987). Disability rights: From caste to class in the context of civil rights. In A. Gartner & T. Joe (Eds.), *Images of the disabled, disabling images* (pp. 7–30). New York: Praeger.

Gardner, J., & Radel, M. (1978). Portrait of the disabled in the media. *Journal of Community Psychology, 6*, 269–274.

Gelb, S. (1989). "Not simply bad and incorrigible": Science, morality, and intellectual deficiency. *History of Education Quarterly, 29*, 359–379.

Gernsbacher, M., Tallent, K., & Bolliger, C. (1999). Disordered discourse in schizophrenia described by the structure building framework. *Discourse Studies, 1*, 355–372.

Giddens, A. (1991). *Modernity and self identity: Self and society in the late modern age.* Stanford, CA: Stanford University Press.

Gill, C. (1994). Questioning continuum. In B. Shaw (Ed.), *The ragged edge: The disability experience from the pages of the first fifteen years of the disability rag* (pp. 42–49). Louisville, KY: Avocado Press.

Gillespie, R. (2001). The politics of breathing: Asthmatic Medicaid patients under managed care. *Journal of Applied Communication Research, 29*, 97–116.

Goffman, E. (1963). *Stigma: Notes on the management of spoiled identity.* Englewood Cliffs, NJ: Prentice Hall.

Green, G., Platt, S., Eley, S., & Green S. (1996). "Now and again it really hits me": The impact of an HIV-positive diagnosis upon psychosocial well-being. *Journal of Health Psychology, 1*, 125–141.

Grimaldi, C., & Goette, T. (1999). The Internet and the independence of individuals with disabilities. *The Internet: Electronic Networking Applications and Policy, 9*, 272–280.

Groce, N. (1992) "The town fool": An oral history of a mentally retarded individual in small town society. In P. Ferguson, D. Ferguson, & S. Taylor (Eds.), *Interpreting disability: A qualitative reader* (pp. 175–196). New York: Teachers College Press.

Hahn, H. (1987). Advertising the acceptably employable image: Disability and capitalism. *Policy Studies Journal, 15*, 551–570.

Hahn, H. (1988a). The politics of physical differences: Disability and discrimination. *Journal of Social Issues, 44*, 39–47.

Hahn, H. (1988b). Can disability be beautiful? *Social Policy, 18*, 26–32.

Haller, B. (1999). AIDS as a legally defined disability: Implications from news media coverage. In W. Elwood (Ed.), *Power in the blood: A handbook on AIDS, politics, and communication* (pp. 267–280). Mahwah, NJ: Erlbaum.

Haller, B. (2000a). How the news frames disability: Print media coverage of the Americans with Disabilities Act. In B. Altman & S. Barnartt (Eds.), *Expanding the scope of social science research on disability* (Vol. 1, pp. 55–83). Stamford, CT: JAI Press.

Haller, B. (2000b). If they limp they lead? News representations and the hierarchy of disability images. In D. Braithwaite & T. Thompson (Eds.), *Handbook of communication and people with disabilities* (pp. 273–288). Mahwah, NJ: Erlbaum.

Haller, B., & Ralph, S. (2001a). Content analysis methodology for studying news and disability: Case studies from the United States and England. In S. Barnartt & B. Altman (Eds.), *Exploring theories and expanding methodologies: Where we are and where we need to go* (pp. 229–253). New York: JAI Press.

Haller, B., & Ralph, S. (2001b). Not worth keeping alive? News framing of physician-assisted suicide in the United States and Great Britain. *Journalism Studies, 2,* 407–421.

Hardaway, B. (1991). Imposed inequality and miscommunication between physically impaired and physically nonimpaired interactants in American society. *Howard Journal of Communications, 3,* 139–148.

Harney, D. (1999). Lesbians on the frontline: Battling AIDS, gays, and the myth of community. In W. Elwood (Ed.), *Power in the blood: A handbook on AIDS, politics, and communication* (pp. 167–179). Mahwah, NJ: Erlbaum.

Hart, R., & Williams, D. (1995). Able-bodied instructors and students with physical disabilities: A relationship handicapped by communication. *Communication Education, 44,* 140–154.

Heijmans, M., & De Ridder, D. (1998). Structure and determinants of illness representations in chronic disease: A comparison of Addison's disease and chronic fatigue syndrome. *Journal of Health Psychology, 3,* 523–537.

Henderson, D., & Hendershott, A. (1991). ASL and the family system. *American Annals of the Deaf, 136,* 325–329.

Hevey, D. (1997). Controlling interests. In A. Pointon & C. Davies (Eds.), *Framed: Interrogating disability in the media* (pp. 209–213). London: British Film Institute.

Hewes, D. (1995). Introduction. In D. Hewes (Ed.), *The cognitive bases of interpersonal communication* (pp. 1–4). Hillsdale, NJ: Erlbaum.

Hillyer, B. (1993). *Feminism and disability.* Norman: University of Oklahoma Press.

Hodgetts, D., & Chamberlain, K. (1999). Medicalization and the depiction of lay people in television health documentary. *Health, 3,* 317–333.

Hogan, A. (1998a). Carving out a space to act: Acquired impairment and contested identity. *Health, 2,* 75–90.

Hogan, A. (1998b). The business of hearing. *Health, 2,* 485–501.

Houck, C., Asselin, S., Troutman, G., & Arrington, J. (1992). Students with learning disabilities: A study of faculty and student perceptions. *Journal of Learning Disabilities, 25,* 678–684.

Hyler, S. (1988). DSM-III at the cinema: Madness in the movies. *Comprehensive Psychiatry, 29,* 195–206.

Hyler, S., Gabbard, G., & Schneider, I. (1991). Homicidal maniacs and narcissistic parasites: Stigmatization of mentally ill persons in the movies. *Hospital and Community Psychiatry, 42,* 1044–1048.

Imrie, R. (1998). Oppression, disability and access in the built environment. In T. Shakespeare (Ed.), *The disability reader: Social science perspectives* (pp. 129–146). London: Cassell.

Infante, D. (1995). Teaching students to understand and control verbal aggression. *Communication Education, 44,* 51–63.

Infante, D., Myers, S., & Buerkel, R. (1994). Argument and verbal aggression in constructive and destructive family and organizational disagreements. *Western Journal of Communication, 58,* 73–84.

Infante, D., & Wigley, C. (1986). Verbal aggressiveness: An interpersonal model and measure. *Communication Monographs, 53,* 61–69.

Ingstad, B. (1995). Mpho ya modimo—a gift from God: Perspectives on "attitudes" toward disabled persons. In B. Ingstad & S. Whyte (Eds.), *Disability and culture* (pp. 246–263). Berkeley: University of California Press.

Itzhaky, H., & Schwartz, C. (1998). Empowering the disabled: A multidimensional approach. *International Journal of Rehabilitation Research, 21,* 301–310.

Iwakuma, M., & Nussbaum, J. (2000). Intercultural views of people with disabilities in Asia and Africa. In D. Braithwaite & T. Thompson (Eds.), *Handbook of communication and people with disabilities* (pp. 239–255). Mahwah, NJ: Erlbaum.

Jankowski, K. (1997). *Deaf empowerment*. Washington, DC: Gallaudet University Press.

Jaramillo, E. (1999). Tuberculosis and stigma: Predictors of prejudice against persons with tuberculosis. *Journal of Health Psychology, 4,* 71–79.

Jeon, Y., & Haider-Markel, D. (2001). Tracing issue definition and policy change: An analysis of disability issue images and policy response. *Policy Studies Journal, 29,* 215–231.

Johnson, R., & Wolinsky, F. (1993). The structure of health status among older adults: Disease, disability, functional limitation, and perceived health. *Journal of Health and Social Behavior, 34*(2), 105–121.

Jones, R. (1998). Two faces of AIDS in Hong Kong: Culture and the construction of the "AIDS celebrity." *Discourse & Society, 9,* 309–338.

Kearney, D. (1992). *The new ADA: Compliance and costs*. Kingston, MA: RSMeans.

Keller, C., Hallahan, D., McShane, E., Crowley, E., & Blandford, B. (1990). The coverage of persons with disabilities in American newspapers. *Journal of Special Education, 24,* 271–282.

Kensicki, L. (2001). Deaf president now! Positive media framing of a social movement within a hegemonic political environment. *Journal of Communication Inquiry, 25,* 147–166.

Koerber, A. (2001). Postmodernism, resistance, and cyberspace: Making rhetorical spaces for feminist mothers on the Web. *Women's Studies in Communication, 24,* 218–240.

Kreps, G. (2000). Disability and culture: Effects on multicultural relations in modern organizations. In D. Braithwaite & T. Thompson (Eds.), *Handbook of communication and people with disabilities* (pp. 177–190). Mahwah, NJ: Erlbaum.

Krishnan, S., Durrah, T., & Winkler, K. (1997). Coverage of AIDS in popular African American magazines. *Health Communication, 9,* 273–288.

Lakoff, G., & Johnson, M. (1980). *Metaphors we live by*. Chicago: University of Chicago Press.

Liachowitz, C. (1988). *Disability as a social construct*. Philadelphia: University of Pennsylvania Press.

Linton, S. (1998). *Claiming disability: Knowledge and identity*. New York: New York University Press.

Livneh, H. (1991). On the origins of negative attitudes toward people with disabilities. In R. Marinelli & A. Dell Orto (Eds.), *The psychological and social impact of disability* (3rd ed., pp. 181–196). New York: Springer.

Llewellyn, A., & Hogan, K. (1999). The use and abuse of models of disability. *Disability & Society, 15,* 157–165.

Longmore, P. (1997). Conspicuous contribution and American cultural dilemmas: Telethon rituals of cleansing and renewal. In D. Mitchell & S. Snyder (Eds.), *The body and physical difference: Discourses of disability* (pp. 134–158). Ann Arbor: University of Michigan Press.

Luey, H., Glass, L., & Elliott, H. (1995). Hard-of-hearing or deaf: Issues of ears, language, culture, and identity. *Social Work, 40,* 177–182.

Lull, J. (2000). *Media, communication, culture: A global approach* (2nd ed.). New York: Columbia University Press.

Lumley, M., Kelley, J., & Leisen, J. (1997). Predicting pain and adjustment in rheumatoid arthritis. *Journal of Health Psychology, 2,* 255–264.

Machin, D., & Carrithers, M. (1996). From "interpretative communities" to "communities of improvisation." *Media, Culture & Society, 18,* 343–352.

MacLean, D., & Gannon, P. (1995). Measuring attitudes toward disability: The Interaction with Disabled Persons Scale revisited. *Journal of Social Behavior and Personality, 10,* 791–806.

Mairs, N. (1996). *Waist-high in the world: A life among the nondisabled*. Boston: Beacon Press.

Makas, E. (1988). Positive attitudes toward disabled people: Disabled and nondisabled persons' perspectives. *Journal of Social Issues, 44,* 49–61.

Marks, D. (1999). *Disability: Controversial debates and psychosocial perspectives*. London: Routledge.

Marston, C. (1999). Learning to be a journalist: A feminist disability critique of cyborgs, college newsworkers, and RSI work culture. *Journal of Communication Inquiry, 23,* 266–287.

McCoy, C., Miles, C., & Metsch, L. (1999). The medicalization of discourse within an AIDS research setting. In W. Elwood (Ed.), *Power in the blood: A handbook on AIDS, politics, and communication* (pp. 39–50). Mahwah, NJ: Erlbaum.

McIntosh, A. (2000). When the deaf and the hearing interact: Communication features, relationships, and disability issues. In D. Braithwaite & T. Thompson (Eds.), *Handbook of communication and people with disabilities* (pp. 353–368). Mahwah, NJ: Erlbaum.

Meekosha, H. (1997). Body battles: Bodies, gender and disability. In T. Shakespeare (Ed.), *The disability reader: Social science perspectives* (pp. 163–180). London: Cassell.

Mele, C. (1999). Cyberspace and disadvantaged communities: The Internet as a tool for collective action. In M. Smith & P. Kollack (Eds.), *Communities in cyberspace* (pp. 290–310). London: Routledge.

Michalko, R., & Titchkosky, T. (2001). Putting disability in its place: It's not a joking matter. In J. Wilson & C. Lewiecki-Wilson (Eds.), *Embodied rhetorics: Disability in language and culture* (pp. 200–228). Carbondale: Southern Illinois University Press.

Mirzoeff, N. (1997). Blindness and art. In L. Davis (Ed.), *The disability studies reader* (pp. 382–398). New York: Routledge.

Mitchell, D. (1997). Modernist freaks and postmodernist geeks. In L. Davis (Ed.), *The disability studies reader* (pp. 348–365). New York: Routledge.

Mitchell, D., & Snyder, S. (1997). Introduction: Disability studies and the double bind of representation. In D. Mitchell & S. Snyder (Eds.), *The body and physical difference: Discourses of disability* (pp. 1–31). Ann Arbor: University of Michigan Press.

Monks, J., & Frankenberg, R. (1995). Being ill and being me: Self, body, and time in multiple sclerosis narratives. In B. Ingstad & S. Whyte (Eds.), *Disability and culture* (pp. 107–134). Berkeley: University of California Press.

Nakayama, T., & Martin, J. (Eds.). (1999). *Whiteness: The communication of social identity.* Thousand Oaks, CA: Sage.

Nelson, J. (2000). The media role in building the disability community. *Journal of Mass Media Ethics, 15,* 180–193.

Nelson, J., & Berens, B. (1997). Spoken daggers, deaf ears, and silent mouths: Fantasies of deafness in early modern England. In L. Davis (Ed.), *The disability studies reader* (pp. 52–74). New York: Routledge.

Norden, M. (1990). Victims, villains, saints, and heroes: Movie portrayals of people with physical disabilities. In P. Loukides & K. Fuller (Eds.), *Beyond the stars: Stock characters in American popular films* (pp. 222–233). Bowling Green, OH: Bowling Green State University Popular Press.

Nye, E. (2001). The rhetoric of AIDS: A new taxonomy. In J. Wilson & C. Lewiecki-Wilson (Eds.), *Embodied rhetorics: Disability in language and culture* (pp. 229–243). Carbondale: Southern Illinois University Press.

O'Keefe, B., Delia, J., & O'Keefe, D. (1980). Interaction analysis and the organization of interaction. In N. Denzin (Ed.), *Studies in symbolic interaction* (Vol. 3, pp. 25–57). Greenwich, CT: JAI Press.

Oliver, M. (1986). Social policy and disability: Some theoretical issues. *Disability, Handicap & Society, 1,* 5–17.

Oliver, M. (1987). Re-defining disability: A challenge to research. *Research Policy and Planning, 5,* 5–17.

Oliver, M. (1990). *The politics of disablement.* New York: St. Martin's Press.

Oliver, M. (1996). *Understanding disability: From theory to practice.* New York: St. Martin's Press.

O'Neill, J. (1990). AIDS as a globalizing panic. In M. Featherstone (Ed.), *Global culture: Nationalism, globalization and modernity* (pp. 329–342). London: Sage.

Orbe, N. (1998). *Constructing co-cultural theory: An explication of culture, power, and communication.* Thousand Oaks, CA: Sage.

Papa, M., Auwal, M., & Singhal, A. (1997). Organizing for social change with concertive control systems: Member identification, empowerment, and the masking of discipline. *Communication Monographs, 64,* 219–249.

Parasnis, I. (1996). On interpreting the deaf experience within the context of cultural and language diversity. In I. Parasnis (Ed.), *Cultural and language diversity and the deaf experience* (pp. 3–19). Cambridge, UK: Cambridge University Press.

Peters, S. (1996). The politics of disability identity. In L. Barton (Ed.), *Disability and society: Emerging issues and insights* (pp. 215–234). New York: Longman.

Pfeiffer, D. (1999). The problem of disability definition: again. *Disability and Rehabilitation, 21,* 392–395.

Pfeiffer, D. (2000). An annotated bibliography of recent works in disability studies, 1995–2000. *Disability Studies, 20,* 442–446.

Philo, G., & Secker, J. (1999). Media and mental health. In Bob Franklin (Ed.), *Social policy, the media, and misrepresentation* (pp. 135–145). London: Routledge.

Pittam, J., & Gallois, C. (1997). Language strategies in the attribution of blame for HIV and AIDS. *Communication Monographs, 64*, 201–218.

Pittam, J., & Gallois, C. (2000). Malevolence, stigma, and social distance: Maximizing intergroup differences in HIV/AIDS discourse. *Journal of Applied Communication Research, 28*, 24–43.

Prendergast, C. (2001). On the rhetorics of mental disability. In J. Wilson & C. Lewiecki-Wilson (Eds.), *Embodied rhetorics: Disability in language and culture* (pp. 45–60). Carbondale: Southern Illinois University Press.

Putnam, L., Phillips, N., & Chapman, P. (1996). Metaphors of communication and organization. In S. Clegg, C. Hardy, & W. Nord (Eds.), *Handbook of organization studies* (pp. 375–408). London: Sage.

Reddy, M. (1979). The conduit metaphor—A case of frame conflict in our language about language. In A. Ortony (Ed.), *Metaphor and thought* (pp. 284–324). Cambridge, UK: Cambridge University Press.

Reisine, S., & Fifield, J. (1992). Expanding the definition of disability: Implications for planning, policy, and research. *Millbank Quarterly, 70*, 491–508.

Robillard, A. (1999). *Meaning of a disability: The lived experience of paralysis.* Philadelphia: Temple University Press.

Rose, H. (1992). A semiotic analysis of artistic American Sign Language and a performance of poetry. *Text and Performance Quarterly, 12*, 146–159.

Rose, H. (1994). Stylistic features in American Sign Language literature. *Text and Performance Quarterly, 14*, 144–157.

Rose, H. (1995). Apprehending deaf culture. *Journal of Applied Communication Research, 23*, 156–162.

Rose, H., & Smith, A. (2000). Sighting sound/sounding sight: The "violence" of deaf-hearing communication. In D. Braithwaite & T. Thompson (Eds.), *Handbook of communication and people with disabilities* (pp. 369–388). Mahwah, NJ: Erlbaum.

Ross, K. (1997). But where's me in it? Disability, broadcasting, and the audience. *Media, Culture & Society, 19*, 669–677.

Ross, K. (1998). Disability and the media: A suitable case for treatment? *Media Development, 45*(2), 14–20.

Ross, K. (2001). All ears: Radio, reception and discourses of disability. *Media, Culture & Society, 23*, 419–437.

Roulstone, A. (1998). Researching a disabling society: The case of employment and new technology. In T. Shakespeare (Ed.), *The disability reader: Social science perspectives* (pp. 110–128). London: Cassell.

Royse, D., & Edwards, T. (1989). Communicating about disability: Attitudes and preferences of persons with physical handicaps. *Rehabilitation Counseling Bulletin, 32*, 203–209.

Russell, M. (1998). *Beyond ramps: Disability at the end of the social contract.* Monroe, ME: Common Courage Press.

Schwartz, H. (1988). Further thoughts on a "sociology of acceptance" for disabled people. *Social Policy, 27*, 36–39.

Sendelbaugh, J. (1978). Television viewing habits of hearing-impaired teenagers in the Chicago metropolitan area. *American Annals of the Deaf, 123*, 536–541.

Shefner-Rogers, C., Rao, N., Rogers, E., & Wayangankar, A. (1998). The empowerment of women dairy farmers in India. *Journal of Applied Communication Research, 26*, 319–337.

Schuchman, J. (1984). Silent movies and the deaf community. *Journal of Popular Culture, 17*(4), 58–78.

Scotch, R. (2000). Models of disability and the Americans with Disabilities Act. *Berkeley Journal of Employment and Labor Law, 21*, 213–222.

Shilling, C. (1997). The body and difference. In K. Woodward (Ed.), *Identity and difference* (pp. 63–107). London: Sage.

Shultz, K. (2000). Deaf activists in the rhetorical transformation of the construct of disability. In D. Braithwaite & T. Thompson (Eds.), *Handbook of communication and people with disabilities* (pp. 257–270). Mahwah, NJ: Erlbaum.

Shultz, K., & Germeroth, D. (1998). Should we laugh or should we cry? John Callahan's humor as a tool to change societal attitudes toward disability. *Howard Journal of Communications, 9*, 229–244.

Signorielli, N. (1989). The stigma of mental illness on television. *Journal of Broadcasting & Electronic Media, 33*, 325–331.

Smith, J., & Kandath, K. (2000). Communication and the blind or visually impaired. In D. Braithwaite & T. Thompson (Eds.), *Handbook of communication and people with disabilities* (pp. 389–403). Mahwah, NJ: Erlbaum.

Sontag, S. (1997). AIDS and its metaphors. In L. Davis (Ed.), *The disability studies reader* (pp. 232–238). New York: Routledge.

Sprague, J., & Hayes, J. (2000). Self-determination and empowerment: A feminist standpoint analysis of talk about disability. *American Journal of Community Psychology, 28*, 671–695.

Stineman, M. (2000). Medical humanism and empowerment medicine. *Disability Studies, 20*(1), 11–16.

Stone, D., & Colella, A. (1996). A model of factors affecting the treatment of disabled individuals in organizations. *Academy of Management Review, 21*, 352–401.

Stone, J. (1996). Minority empowerment and the education of deaf people. In I. Parasnis (Ed.), *Cultural language diversity and the deaf experience* (pp. 171–180). Cambridge, UK: Cambridge University Press.

Stone, K. (1997). *Awakening to disability: Nothing about us without us.* Volcano, CA: Volcano Press.

Stubbins, J. (1988). The politics of disability. In H. Yuker (Ed.), *Attitudes toward persons with disabilities* (pp. 22–32). New York: Springer.

Sutter, D., & Martin, M. (1998). Verbal aggression during disengagement of dating relationships. *Communication Research Reports, 15*, 318–326.

Sypher, H., & Higgins, E. (1989). Social cognition and communication: An overview. *Communication Research, 16*, 309–313.

Taylor, S., & Bogdan, R. (1991). On accepting relationships between people with mental retardation and nondisabled people: Towards an understanding of acceptance. In R. Marinelli & A. Dell Orto (Eds.), *The psychological and social impact of disability* (3rd ed., pp. 165–180). New York: Springer.

Thomas, S., & Wolfensberger, W. (1982). The importance of social imagery in interpreting societally devalued people to the public. *Rehabilitation Literature, 43*, 356–358.

Thompson, T. (1981a). The development of communication skills in physically handicapped children. *Human Communication Research, 7*, 312–324.

Thompson, T. (1981b). The impact of a physical handicap on communicative characteristics of a marital dyad. *Western Journal of Speech Communication, 45*, 227–240.

Thompson, T. (1982a). The development of listener-adapted communication in physically handicapped children: A cross-sectional study. *Western Journal of Speech Communication, 46*, 32–44.

Thompson, T. (1982b). "You can't play marbles—you have a wooden": Communication with the handicapped. *Communication Quarterly, 30*, 108–115.

Thompson, T. (1983). Communication with the handicapped: A three year study of the effectiveness of mainstreaming. *Communication Education, 32*, 185–195.

Thomson, R. (1997). Feminist theory, the body, and the disabled figure. In L. Davis (Ed.), *The disability studies reader* (pp. 279–292). New York: Routledge.

Tucker, B. (1997). The ADA and Deaf culture: Contrasting precepts, conflicting results. *Annals of the American Academy of Political Science, 549*, 24–36.

Turnbull, H., Bateman, D., & Turnbull, A. (1993). Family empowerment. In P. Wehman (Ed.), *The ADA mandate for social change* (pp. 157–173). Baltimore: Brookes.

Uprety, S. (1997). Disability and postcoloniality in Salman Rushdie's *Midnight's Children* and third-world novels. In L. Davis (Ed.), *The disability studies reader* (pp. 366–381). New York: Routledge.

Valentine, J. (2001). Disabled discourse: Hearing accounts of deafness constructed through Japanese television and film. *Discourse & Society, 16*, 707–721.

Verbrugge, L., Reoma, J., Gruber-Baldini, A. (1994). Short-term dynamics of disability and well-being. *Journal of Health and Social Behavior, 35*(2), 97–117.

Vernon, A. (1998). Multiple oppression and the disabled people's movement. In T. Shakespeare (Ed.), *The disability reader: Social science perspectives* (pp. 201–210). London: Cassell.

Wade, C. (1994). Disability culture rap. In B. Shaw (Ed.), *The ragged edge: The disability experience from the pages of the first fifteen years of the disability rag* (pp. 15–18). Louisville, KY: Avocado Press.

Warin, M. (2000). The glass cage: An ethnography of exposure in schizophrenia. *Health, 4*, 115–133.

Warnath, C., & Dunnington, L. (1981). Disabled students on the campus. *Journal of College Student Personnel, 22*, 236–241.

Weinberg, N. (1988). Another perspective: Attitudes of people with disabilities. In H. Yuker (Ed.), *Attitudes toward persons with disabilities* (pp. 141–153). New York: Springer.

Wellman, B., & Gulia, M. (1999). Virtual communities as communities: Net surfers don't ride alone. In M. Smith & P. Kollack (Eds.), *Communities in cyberspace* (pp. 167–194). London: Routledge.

Wendell, S. (1996). *The rejected body: Feminist philosophical reflections on disability.* New York: Routledge.

Wendell, S. (1997). Toward a feminist theory of disability. In L. Davis (Ed.), *The disability studies reader* (pp. 260–278). New York: Routledge.

Westhaver, S. (2000). Opening up spaces for difference via a feminist phenomenological approach to disability. In D. Braithwaite & T. Thompson (Eds.), *Handbook of communication and people with disabilities* (pp. 85–100). Mahwah, NJ: Erlbaum.

Whaley, B., & Golden, M. (2000). Communicating with persons who stutter: Perceptions and strategies. In D. Braithwaite & T. Thompson (Eds.), *Handbook of communication and people with disabilities* (pp. 423–438). Mahwah, NJ: Erlbaum.

Whaley, B., & Parker, R. (2000). Expressing the experience of communicative disability: Metaphors of persons who stutter. *Communication Reports, 13*, 115–125.

Whitt, L., & Slack, J. (1994). Communities, environments, and cultural studies. *Cultural Studies, 8*, 5–31.

Whyte, S. (1995). Disability between discourse and experience. In B. Ingstad & S. Whyte (Eds.), *Disability and culture* (pp. 267–291). Berkeley: University of California Press.

Williams, S. (1998). Health as moral performance: Ritual, transgression and taboo. *Health, 2*, 435–457.

Wilson, J. (1997). Signs of definitions. In A. Pointon & C. Davies (Eds.), *Framed: Interrogating disability in the media* (pp. 179–181). London: British Film Institute.

Wilson, J., & Lewiecki-Wilson, C. (2001). Disability, rhetoric, and the body. In J. Wilson & C. Lewiecki-Wilson (Eds.), *Embodied rhetorics: Disability in language and culture* (pp. 1–24). Carbondale: Southern Illinois University Press.

Winzer, M. (1997). Disability and society before the eighteenth century. In L. Davis (Ed.), *The disability studies reader* (pp. 75–109). New York: Routledge.

Woods, T., Antoni, M., Ironson, G., & Kling, D. (1999). Religiosity is associated with affective status in symptomatic HIV-infected African-American women. *Journal of Health Psychology, 4*, 317–326.

Woodward, J. (1994). Boutonnieres. In B. Shawn (Ed.), *The ragged edge: The disability experience from the pages of the first fifteen years of the disability rag* (pp. 25–27). Louisville, KY: Advocado Press.

Worley, D. (2000). Communication and students with disabilities on college campuses. In D. Braithwaite & T. Thompson (Eds.), *Handbook of communication and people with disabilities* (pp. 125–139). Mahwah, NJ: Erlbaum.

Wright, K. (1999). AIDS, the status quo, and the elite media: An analysis of the guest lists of "The MacNeil/Lehrer News Hour" and "Nightline." In W. Elwood (Ed.), *Power in the blood: A handbook on AIDS, politics, and communication* (pp. 281–292). Mahwah, NJ: Erlbaum.

Yedidia, M., Barr, J., & Berry, C. (1993). Physicians' attitudes toward AIDS at different career stages: A comparison of internists and surgeons. *Journal of Health and Social Behavior, 34*, 272–284.

Yedidia, M., Berry, C., & Barr, J. (1996). Changes in physicians' attitudes toward AIDS during residency training: A longitudinal study of medical school graduates. *Journal of Health and Social Behavior, 37*, 179–191.

Zimmermann, S., & Spano, S. (1995, February). *Do faculty weave students' diverse abilities into the classroom?: Disabled students speak out.* Paper presented at the annual meeting of the Western States Communication Association, Portland, Oregon.

Zola, I. K. (1991). Communication barriers between "the able-bodied" and "the handicapped." In R. Marinelli & E. Dell Orto (Eds.), *The psychological and social impact of disability* (3rd ed., pp. 157–164). New York: Springer.

Zorn, T. (2002). Converging with divergence: Overcoming the disciplinary fragmentation in business communication, organizational communication, and public relations. *Business Communication Quarterly, 65*(2), 44–53.

AUTHOR INDEX

SUBJECT INDEX

ABOUT THE EDITOR

PAMELA J. KALBFLEISCH (Ph.D., Michigan State University, 1985) is a professor of communication and journalism at the University of Wyoming. Her research reflects an active interest in interpersonal communication and communication in close relationships, covering such topics as social support, mentoring relationships, deceptive communication, and gender issues. Her published research is found in International Communication Association publications, *Communication Theory*, *Human Communication Research,* and the *Journal of Communication*, as well as in publications such as *Health Communication, Communication Education, Journal of Applied Communication Research, Howard Journal of Communication*, and the *Journal of Language and Social Psychology*. She edited *Interpersonal Communication: Evolving Interpersonal Relationships* and, with Michael J. Cody, coedited *Gender, Power, and Communication in Human Relationships,* both books published by Lawrence Erlbaum Associates. She authored the *Persuasion Handbook* published by Kendall Hunt, and she has authored or coauthored numerous book chapters and monographs. She has also guest-edited a special issue of *Communication Theory, 12*(1) on "Building Theories in Interpersonal Communication." She currently serves as associate editor and review board member for nine scholarly publications. She rides quarter horses and competitively paddles outrigger canoes whenever horses or the ocean are available.

ABOUT THE CONTRIBUTORS

JESSICA R. ABRAMS (M.A. in Communication, California State University, Long Beach, 1997) is currently a doctoral candidate at the University of California, Santa Barbara. Her interests include the relationship between communication and identity, the influence of mass media in shaping perceptions of social group membership, and intergenerational communication. She recently published an article on identity and intergroup communication that appeared in the *Handbook of International and Intercultural Communication* (Sage, 2002).

LINDA ALDOORY, Ph.D., received her doctorate at the S. I. Newhouse School of Public Communications at Syracuse University in 1998. She is currently an assistant professor of communication at the University of Maryland, College Park. Her research focuses on women, feminism, public relations, and health. She is coeditor of the book, *The Gender Challenge to Media: Diverse Voices from the Field* (2001) and has several published articles, including "Gender Discrepancies in a Gendered Profession: A Developing Theory for Public Relations" (with E. L. Toth) in *Journal of Public Relations Research* (2002) and "Making Health Communications Meaningful for Women: Factors That Influence Involvement and the Situational Theory of Publics" in *Journal of Public Relations Research* (2001).

ROB ANDERSON (Ph.D., University of Missouri, 1971) is a professor of communication and international studies at Saint Louis University. He has authored, coauthored, or coedited 10 books in interpersonal and public dialogue, media studies, communication theory, and contemporary cultural criticism, including *Moments of Meeting* and *The Martin Buber-Carl Rogers Dialogue: A New Transcript With Commentary* (with Kenneth N. Cissna), *The Reach of Dialogue* (with Kenneth N. Cissna and Ronald C. Arnett), and *The Conversation of Journalism* (with Robert Dardenne and George Killenberg). His communication theory text, *Questions of Communication* (with Veronica Ross), is now in its third edition. A new collection of original scholarly essays on dialogue, edited with Leslie Baxter and Kenneth N. Cissna, is forthcoming. His articles on dialogue, interviewing, and educational practices have appeared in a variety of journals related to communication studies, journalism, education, psychology, English, and education.

LINDA-RENÉE BLOCH (Ph.D., University of Texas at Austin, 1990) has taught in the Department of Communication, Tel-Aviv University, for the past several years. Her research interests are intercultural communication, language in society, and the study of culture and communication. Recent publications include "Rhetoric on the Roads of Israel: The Assassination and Political Bumper Stickers," in *The Assassination of Yitzhak Rabin* (2000); "Mobile Discourse: Political Bumper Stickers as a Communication Event in Israel," *Journal of Communication* (2000);

"Setting the Public Sphere in Motion: The Rhetoric of Political Bumper Stickers in Israel," *Political Communication* (2000); and "Pokémon: How Israeli Children 'catch 'em'" (with D. Lemish) in *Pikachu's Global Adventure: Making Sense of the Rise and Fall of Pokémon* (in press).

PATRICE M. BUZZANELL (Ph.D., Purdue University, 1987) is an associate professor in the Department of Communication at Purdue University. Her research interests center on feminist organizational communication theorizing as well as the construction of gendered workplace identities, interactions, and structures, particularly as they relate to career processes and outcomes. Her edited book, *Rethinking Organizational and Managerial Communication From Feminist Perspectives,* was published by Sage (2000). Other recent publications include coauthored articles with Lynn Turner in the *Journal of Applied Communication Research* (2003) and Venessa Bowers in *Women & Language* (2002). She also has created a case study on both communication in and paradoxes of multidisciplinary teams in an engineering team with Ed Coyle, Leah Jamieson, and Bill Oakes in Shockley-Zalabak and Keyton's *Case Studies for Organizational Communication: Understanding Communication Processes* (in press).

KENNETH N. CISSNA (Ph.D., University of Denver, 1975) is a professor of communication at the University of South Florida. His research interests include the theory and practice of dialogue, as well as related topics in communication theory, interpersonal communication, and applied communication. He has served as editor of the *Journal of Applied Communication Research* and the *Southern Communication Journal.* His most recent book is *Moments of Meeting: Buber, Rogers, and the Potential for Public Dialogue* (with Rob Anderson), published by State University of New York Press in 2002. His *Applied Communication in the 21st Century* won the "Outstanding Book" award from the Applied Communication Division of the National Communication Association. With Leslie Baxter and Rob Anderson, he is completing an edited collection, *Dialogic Approaches to Communication,* for Sage Publications. He has published scholarly articles in *Communication Theory, Health Communication, Journal of Applied Communication Research, Communication Monographs, Human Studies, Journal of Humanistic Psychology, Western Journal of Speech Communication, Southern Communication Journal, Small Group Behavior,* and *Communication Education,* among other journals.

STEPHANIE J. COOPMAN (Ph.D., University of Kentucky, 1989) is professor of communication studies at San José State University, where she primarily teaches online classes in interpersonal, organizational, persuasive, and small-group communication. Her current research interests include disability and internet communication, health care teams, and new communication technologies in organizations. She edits the *American Communication Journal,* www.acjournal.org, a premier online scholarly refereed journal dedicated to the study of communication and is past president of the American Communication Association. Her recent publications include "Democracy, Performance and Outcomes in Interdisciplinary Health Care Teams" in the *Journal of Business Communication* and "Power, Hierarchy and Change: The Stories of a Catholic Parish Staff" in *Management Communication Quarterly* (with Katherine Meidlinger). Her multimedia textbook, *Public Speaking for the Digital Age* (with James Lull), will be published by Houghton Mifflin in the fall of 2003.

WILLIAM P. EVELAND, JR. (Ph.D. in Mass Communication, University of Wisconsin-Madison, 1997) is an assistant professor in the School of Journalism and Communication at Ohio State University. His research focuses on how individuals process information and learn from mass-mediated sources, in particular, the news media. This learning can be categorized into factual or verifiable information, the structure or organization of knowledge, and perceptions or beliefs. Of particular concern in this research is how learning varies based on individual background characteristics, motivations, and information processing, as well as how learning varies across media. His recent work has appeared in journals such as *Communication Research, Journal of Communication, Media Psychology, Political Psychology, Journal of Broadcasting & Electronic Media, Journal of Applied Social Psychology, Political Communication,* and *Journalism & Mass Communication Quarterly*. A recent chapter in *The Persuasion Handbook: Developments in Theory and Practice* (2002, Sage) focuses on media and perceptions of social reality.

KEREN EYAL (M.A., Kent State University, 2000) is a doctoral candidate in the Department of Communication at the University of California, Santa Barbara. Her research interests focus on media and new technology effects, especially socialization effects on children and adolescents. Her work has appeared in *Mass Communication & Society* and *Communication Technology and Society: Audience Adoption and Use*.

ANDREW J. FLANAGIN (Ph.D., Annenberg School for Communication, University of Southern California, 1996) is an associate professor in the Department of Communication at the University of California, Santa Barbara. His research focuses on the ways in which communication and information technologies structure human interaction, with emphases on the contemporary media environment, collaborative technologies, collective action among organizational members, and organizational theory. Recent articles of his have been published in *Human Communication Research, Management Communication Quarterly, Communication Research, Journalism and Mass Communication Quarterly, Organization Science, New Media and Society, Communication Theory,* and *Critical Studies in Media Communication*.

HOWARD GILES (DSc., University of Bristol) is a professor of communication at the University of California, Santa Barbara. He has long-standing research and theoretical interests in many areas of intergroup communication, including intercultural and intergenerational. As director of the new Center on Police Practices and Community, his recent intergroup foci have been in areas of law enforcement-citizen communications.

ANNIS G. GOLDEN (Ph.D., Rensselaer Polytechnic Institute, 1998) is a visiting assistant professor in the Department of Communication at the University of Albany. Her research focuses on various aspects of communication and work-life relationships. In 2000, she edited a special issue of *The Electronic Journal of Communication* on communication approaches to work-life issues and contributed a discourse analysis of parental accounts of managing work and family. She has also published articles on communicative processes in defining role identities associated with work and family in *The Journal of Family Communication* (2001) and the *Southern Communication Journal* (2002). Golden's current research is concerned with the impact of new information and communication technologies on work-life relationships. Her analysis of interviews with users of personal digital assistants examines the interplay of workplace culture, technology use, and personal discourse in managing work-life boundaries.

SCOTT C. HAMMOND (Ph.D., University of Utah, 1997) is an associate professor of management and organizational communication at Utah Valley State College and president of Hammond Associates, Inc. He has advised national and international business and government organizations in the areas of conflict resolution, cross-cultural issues, and complex problem-solving techniques. His research interests include dialogue, problem solving, community building, and peace communication. His most recent publications include "Pan Gu's Paradigm: Chinese Education's Return to Holistic Communication in Learning" (with Hongmei Gao) in *Chinese Communication Studies: Context and Comparisons* (2002); "Transcending Linear Concepts of Power: Comments on Havel's Power of the Powerless," in *100 Years of European Social Theory* (forthcoming); "Dialogic Problem Solving in Culturally Complex Groups" (with Yeo Kee Meng) in *SIETAR International Journal* (1999); and "An Auto Mechanic's Guide to News Writing NOT!: An Essay for Dialogic Pedagogy" in *Journalism and Mass Communication Educator* (2001).

TOM JACOBSON was awarded his Ph.D. at the University of Washington in 1986. He is currently an associate professor at the University at Buffalo, State University of New York. He research interests include international communication, development communication, political communication, and new technologies. Recent publications include: "War, Peace, Media and Global Civil Society" (with W. Y. Jang) in *Handbook on International and Intercultural Communication* (2001); "Dewey,

Habermas and Pragmatism" in *Pragmatism and Communication Research* (2000, 2001). "Rights, Culture, and Global Democracy" (with W. Wang) in *Communication Theory* (2001); and, coedited with J. Servaes, *Theoretical Approaches to Participatory Communication* (1999).

JANE JORGENSON (Ph.D., University of Pennsylvania, 1986) is an associate professor in the Department of Communication, University of South Florida. Her research has focused on women's work identities and work-family practices within diverse occupational cultures. She has studied female home-based workers as well as professional engineers in terms of their distinctive approaches to managing work-family conflict. She is currently involved in a study of the place of computer technology in the lives of low-income, rural families. Her work has been published in *Management Communication Quarterly*, the *Journal of Applied Communication Research*, and *The Electronic Journal of Communication*.

ERIKA L. KIRBY (Ph.D., University of Nebraska-Lincoln, 2000) is an assistant professor in the Department of Communication Studies at Creighton University. Her research interests include organizational communication, applied communication, work-family (work-life) communication, and gender. In particular, she examines how discourse between organizational members ultimately impacts organizational structures, policies, and practices. She is currently involved in a study deconstructing the discourse of "stay-at-home" parents. She has published articles in the *Journal of Applied Communication Research* (2002), *Management Communication Quarterly* (2001), the *Electronic Journal of Communication* (2000), and *Communication Teacher* (2002). She also has published a case on negotiating paternity leave in Shockley-Zalabak and Keyton's *Case Studies for Organizational Communication: Understanding Communication Processes* (in press).

DAFNA LEMISH (Ph.D., Ohio State University, 1982) is senior lecturer and chair of the Department of Communication, Tel-Aviv University. Her research interests include children and media, gender representations and identities, and the study of media literacy. Recent publications include "Always His Wife: First Ladies in Israel" (with G. Drub) in *Parliamentary Affairs* (2002); "Gender at the Forefront: Feminist Perspectives on Action Theoretical Perspectives in Communication Research" in *Communication: The European Journal of Communication Research* (2002); "The Making of Television: Young Viewers' Developing Perceptions" (with C. Tidhar), *Journal of Broadcasting and Electronic Media* (forthcoming); and, coedited with B. Tufte and T. Lavender, *Media Education: Policies and Practices* (forthcoming).

DAISY R. LEMUS (M.A., University of California, Santa Barbara, 2002) is a doctoral student in the Department of Communication at the University of California, Santa Barbara. Her current research interests focus on group communication in both face-to-face and computer-mediated environments, specifically investigating the role of linguistic argument in group decision-making processes. She has recently published in *Human Communication Research*.

RASHMI LUTHRA received her Ph.D. from the University of Wisconsin-Madison in 1988. She teaches at the University of Michigan-Dearborn. Her research interests include women in gender and development communication; media and women's movements; feminist pedagogies in communication; and communication and women in the South Asian diaspora. Recent publications include "Journalism and Mass Communication: The Making of Meaning" in *The Encyclopedia of Life Support Systems*; "Negotiating the Minefield: Practicing Transformative Pedagogy as a Teacher of Color in a Classroom Climate of Suspicion" in *Women Faculty of Color in the White Classroom*; "The Formation of Interpretive Communities in the Hindu Diaspora" in *Religion and Popular Culture: Studies on the Interaction of World Views*; and "The Women's Movement and the Press in India: The Construction of Female Foeticide as a Social Issue" in *Women's Studies in Communication*.

ROBERT M. MCCANN (M.A., University of California, Los Angeles, 1992) is a doctoral candidate in the Department of Communication at the University of California, Santa Barbara. For the past 8 years, he has also served as a visiting instructor of communication at the Thai Chamber of Commerce University in Bangkok, Thailand. His research focuses on intergroup communication in the intergenerational and organizational spheres, cross-cultural differences in language use, and Web site credibility. He is currently investigating aging and cross-cultural organizational communication in several countries across the Pacific Rim. He has recently published in the *Journal of Asia Pacific Communication*, *Journal of Cross-Cultural Gerontology*, *Journal of Sociolinguistics*, *Communication Reports*, and *Communication Studies* and has contributed chapters to several books in the field of ageism.

CARYN E. MEDVED (Ph.D., University of Kansas, 1998) is an assistant professor in the Department of Communication Studies at Ohio University. Her primary area of research focuses on the intersections between organizational and family communication, with specific interests in feminist scholarship. Her work has been published in the *Journal of Applied Communication* (2000), *Communication Education* (2001), and *Management Communication Quarterly* (1999), along with a case study in Shockley-Zalabak and Keyton's *Case Studies for Organizational Communication: Understanding Communication Processes* (in press) on work-family role conflict. She is currently writing to challenge the discourse of work and family-life balance from a feminist perspectives standpoint, as well as conducting research that explores Third Wave Feminists' constructions of motherhood and work.

MIRIAM J. METZGER (Ph.D., Annenberg School for Communication, University of Southern California, 1997) is an assistant professor in the Department of Communication at the University of California, Santa Barbara. Her research interests include the social usage and impacts of new and traditional communication technologies, political communication, and communication law and policy. She has recently published articles in *Journalism & Mass Communication Quarterly*, *Human Communication Research*, *Mass Communication & Society*, *Communication Research Reports*, and *Critical Studies in Media Communication*.

PATRICIA PARKER is an assistant professor of communication studies at the University of North Carolina at Chapel Hill. She completed her Ph.D. in Speech Communication at the University of Texas at Austin in 1997. Her research centers on the intersections of race, gender, and class in organizational communication processes, with a current focus on leadership socialization and career development among African American teenage girls. Her work is published in *Management Communication Quarterly*, *Leadership Quarterly*, and *Communication Quarterly* (in press).

EVERETT M. ROGERS (Ph.D., Iowa State University, 1957) is Regents' Professor, Department of Communication and Journalism, University of New Mexico. He has been engaged in various research projects on empowerment since the early 1970s. Rogers is best known for his book, *Diffusion of Innovations* (5th ed., 2003). He is currently involved in research projects on bridging the digital divide for disadvantaged populations in the Southwestern United States, and with Arvind Singhal, on the meanings given to health episodes in Hollywood soap operas by people in India.

ARVIND SINGHAL (Ph.D., University of Southern California, 1990) is a professor and Presidential Research Scholar in the School of Interpersonal Communication at Ohio University. He is the coauthor, with Everett M. Rogers, of *Combating AIDS: Communication Strategies in Action* (Sage, 2003). Singhal's current research includes investigating the effects of *Taru*, an entertainment-education radio soap opera in the State of Bihar, India, where the program's reception is orchestrated to listening groups in 20,000 villages.

2158